Shifting Shale: 2006 A Race Odyssey

Jeff Scott

methanol
press

First published in Great Britain by
Methanol Press
2 Tidy Street Brighton East Sussex BN1 4EL

For a complete catalogue of current and forthcoming publications please write to the address above, or visit our website at www.methanolpress.com

ISBN 978-0-9553103-3-1

A catalogue for this book is available from the British Library

(Hardly suffering) Editor: Michael Payne
Word Wrangler: Graham Russel
Technical Advisor: Billy Jenkins
Proof Readers: Caroline Tidmarsh and Vy Shepherd
Book and Cover Design: Rachael Adams <www.scrutineer.co.uk>
Cover Photographs: Jeff Scott

UK Distributor:
Central Books
99 Wallis Road London E9 5LN
United Kingdom
020 8986 4854
www.centralbooks.com

Printed and bound in Great Britain by the Cromwell Press

Contents

"Who only by moving can balance,
Only by balancing move."
Michael Donaghy

To Sue Young

Introduction

The book you have in your hand continues my examination of the question 'what is speedway?' that I embarked on when I travelled to every track in the country in 2005 and resulted in the publication of my book *Showered in Shale*. So this is really more of the same but also something different. *Shifting Shale* is also not a club history nor the (auto) biography of a rider but a snapshot and my personal journey round every stadium that staged the sport in Britain – this time during 2006, usually as I tried to sell my book. Again, it was a pleasure to be able to have a reason to visit every track in the country, often more than once. Though I could only write about what I encountered, I have again tried to capture some of the characters that make up some parts of the speedway world as well as vaguely attempt to delve beneath the surface of what I've seen. All of life was there at speedway in our nation and many people went out of their way to be kind, tell me their thoughts on speedway or comment on my books. Overwhelmingly, the feedback was positive and, to my face, I got called all sorts of things from eccentric to self-absorbed. I was most complimented by a comparison of my work to the filmmaker Nick Broomfield (flattery indeed) and, rather provokingly, that I'd set out to "chronicle the decline of a sport and its community".

Anyway, when writing this book I have tried to adhere to the lessons I was given previously by my editor, mentor, advisor and writing coach Michael Payne. He identified many concerns, particularly:

"Because you are a smart man, you can understand the connections between several different things at one time, in short, that the world is a complex place, and so your writing should and does reflect this (although at another time I could argue that simplicity is a virtue), but be aware that it leads to very long and overly complex sentences, where clauses can proliferate and multiply, and where your reader, no matter how hard he may try, and I assure you, he truly does do his best, can get lost in a swarm as I say, of these clauses, and so in this case your reader (who is also your editor) begins to feel he must start to insert commas and periods wherever it makes sense to render the sentence more manageable, as it were."

Sadly, I think that this stylistic fault still remains one of the problems with my writing. Anyone familiar with my blog or my books will know that I'm not adverse to some pointless navel-gazing and pretentiousness or facetiousness. Nonetheless, I hope that you can forgive these faults and mostly enjoy the chance to travel to the tracks again in my company as much as I relished the visits.

There you have it. I hope that you enjoy your journey.

Brighton
6 June 2007

"[Danny Bird] was able to tell me what it would take to get him to Armadale – at that stage, I was immediately able to tell him that our interest was at an end... everyone at Edinburgh equally accepts that rivals Glasgow have every right to go for any rider they like, though the signing looks somewhat ironic beside the winter demands for essential cost cutting that were coming from the west [of Scotland]. If anyone was listening then, they are unlikely to heed any future calls of that nature."
John Campbell

"The continual jibes and snipings, particularly from our friends in the east [of Scotland], are beginning to get on my nerves... the good thing for our fans, though, is they now have two Glasgow columns to read in the *Speedway Star* because there seems to be more about the Tigers in the Edinburgh column than there is about the Monarchs these days."
Stewart Dickson lashes back to deny parsimony rumours

"I can't afford for us to get caught with our trousers down."
Ronnie Russell

"Danny's a nice lad, it's just when he puts his helmet on"
Rob Godfrey baffled by Danny Norton

A trip down memory lane before the New Year Classic
9th January

When I arrive near to the pits gate of Newport Speedway for the only outdoor meeting of the entire British speedway close season period – the annual Newport *New Year Classic* organised and run by the ebullient Newport promoter Tim Stone – I'm immediately confronted by an array of riders' vans. Many of the competitors for this afternoon's meeting have already unloaded their equipment or are in the process of doing so under dark skies and heavy cloud. Riders wheel their bikes and mechanics carry the toolboxes to what is usually either the 'home' or 'away' side of the pits pass compound. Since this is an individual competition and it's every man for himself today there are no such distinctions, but I'm sure that the allocations aren't completely random given the large number of riders in the assembled field with Newport connections. Having built up his club with a dedicated band of loyal volunteers against the odds and prevailing opinion about the dubious commercial logic of running a stadium that makes all its monies only from speedway revenues, decisions here aren't made by chance but are arrived at through a mixture of hard work, dedication and skill. After years of staging this event, Tim the helpers and the riders have all had their chance to iron out any teething problems, complications or other wrinkles. With that very much in mind, the size of the field is restricted to 12 riders who all race five times each in order then to qualify for a winner-takes-all final.

This event has achieved sufficient longevity to become an essential part of the speedway fans' calendar and attendance levels will reflect its popularity. The revenues earnt today are important factors in the long-term financial health, survival and viability of the club. With a strong belief in the development of young rider talent for the future, during the season the club

Men in anoraks gather in the Newport pits. © Jeff Scott

Riders head for parade. © Jeff Scott

'Mr Newport' – Tim Stone. © Jeff Scott

runs a team in both the Premier and Conference Leagues. Apart from two meetings held during the summer that sandwich the Cardiff Grand Prix weekend, this will be the biggest attendance seen at Hayley Stadium in Queensway Meadows, so it's crucial that, irrespective of weather conditions, this event gets completed. It's a cold crisp day and the forecast of rain later that the dark clouds attest to would appear accurate. Not that the rain (or snow!) will prevent the event from actually taking place but the threat of a soaking during the *Classic* will have an effect because it will put a damper on the volume of spectators passing through the turnstiles that Tim could expect to make their way over to Newport. Not that he has time to worry as he dashes about the pits, wanders on the track and then shuttles along in front of the home straight towards the speedway office, disappearing inside the darkened bowels of the grandstand, where the bar is housed, to conduct last minute checks before the gates open in sixty or so minutes at 11.30 a.m.

It's no secret that Tim Stone prepares that track for many weeks before the event specifically in mind to ensure the event will be able to go ahead no matter what the elements throw at him. He tire packs the track for weeks to give it a hard solid track base then often if snow looks a threat, adds a good dressing of road rock salt to melt any possible snow flurries. One unnamed rider found this out to his cost, as after riding in a previous *New Year Classic* he just threw his bike in the garage and then only went to look at it at the beginning of March with the season about to start. To his horror he found his bike frame and wheels were completely pitted and virtually eaten away such was the aggressive nature of the salted shale coating he had idly failed to clean off directly after the meeting.

It's not a day to have a casual chat but Tim just about manages to say "hello" and ask when my book is actually going to come out. I previously told him that in an ideal world, this would be the event where I hoped it would on sale for the first time since he had spoken highly of the opportunity provided by the post-Christmas interest shown in the variety of stalls at the speedway trade fair. The quality of the field of riders attracted to ride in this year's *Classic* should prove to be quite a draw for fans, as Tim has again assembled a competitive field. The *Speedway Star* noted, "like others who promote at this time of year, Stone has a nucleus of riders that he feels he can rely on." (and will generally ride in all conditions without a moan!) These include previous winners like Brent Werner, Robbie Kessler and, arguably the biggest draw on the card, diminutive Cornishman Chris 'Bomber' Harris who'll today aim to make it a hat-trick of wins (in successive years). Old stagers like Michael Coles also ride, as does the admired Hayley stadium specialist Neil Collins and Sean Wilson, the surprise omission from the 2006 Sheffield Tigers' team. His omission was a shock decision by Neil Machin, which he saw as essential to the team but other aggrieved Sheffield loyalists viewed as, in the immortal words of Sir Humphrey in *Yes, Prime Minister!* , "brave". It gives the squad he assembles without Sean a somewhat unbalanced look – a bit like gin without the tonic or chips without the fish. So Sean was here to enjoy himself and also ostensibly to put himself in the metaphorical speedway shop window. Other riders like Chris Neath and

Mads Korneliussen have strong Newport connections. There is also an appearance by Niels Kristen Iversen (or "Puck" as they call him), one of the personal favourites of Janet and Jayne, the ladies who organise the SWARM fundraising to pay for the Newport riders' tyres, oil or fuel. Another of my favourite riders, Paul Clews, has already changed into his kevlars and smiles broadly at all and sundry as is his cheerful wont. Over the far side of the pits is the tallest rider here today, Richard Hall who'll have the additional pressure of his new boss, the Peterborough promoter Colin Horton, watching him closely from the pits. The only previous winner absent, injured Phil Morris, is ironically the rider who actually lives closest to the track.

Also here is Leigh Lanham who's no stranger to the rostrum at the *Classic* and who commented on the weather and track conditions beforehand, "they work hard on the track and I'll bet it's as good for this meeting as it is for most of the meetings in the summer." Like at every club in the country, speedway meetings wouldn't get staged without their volunteers and at Newport all the familiar faces of the dedicated staff they have at the Hayley Stadium are very much in evidence. Bustling about in his muddy boots or seated on his tractor is friendly track curator, Andy Dean, and never far away is his son, David. They've industriously prepared the track all morning after overnight frost left it solid when they arrived first thing to carry on with their lengthy ministrations. Emerging from the pits lane cubbyhole is the avuncular Peter Brookes wearing a black beanie hat as a vague concession to the low temperatures. He is officially in charge of Race Day Maintenance but still finds a few minutes to question the whereabouts and progress of my book in a curious, friendly manner. Pits Marshal Ray Evans also dresses to take account of the 'fresh' temperatures and probable rain later, sporting a thick scarf and a large black hat that veers much more towards the Cossack than any of the other cold/wet weather headgear on display in the pits. The helmet is *de rigueur* among the riders and the baseball cap among their mechanics and helpers, though everyone except me appears insouciantly oblivious to how really cold it feels.

As I cannot be of assistance, I decide to wander round to the trade fair and have a look at the merchandise on display. I watch the stallholders prepare and lay out their wares; it's an area crowded with stalls, though some of them don't even sell anything that is even remotely speedway connected. You can bet your bottom dollar though that anyone prepared to pay to display at this event must know it pays or hope that it does. The largest stall selling speedway memorabilia occupies a substantial area but features a tired display of merchandise that really doesn't arouse any enthusiasm in me. A stall of novelty gifts completely unrelated to speedway excites me even less except to make me curious as to who on earth in their right mind would think of doing such a thing unless – I guess they already were true speedway fanatics. I'm just about to think no more of it when I realise that the stall is actually run by my good speedway friend Kevin and his partner Mandy. We used to stand together at Eastbourne every week (along with his good friend Stuart, a militantly passionate Scotsman) until they decided to move to the wilds of the Herefordshire countryside and we lost touch. His absence took something away from my enjoyment of evenings at Arlington as I missed Kevin's banter and insight. I'm delighted that chance and the speedway gods have thrown us back in touch; though, for the next little while, after I've excitedly explained the idea, research and travel behind my book *Showered in Shale* I barely get a word in edgeways.

"I understand your fears regarding your book Jeff, but don't worry come the season it will fly, especially if you travel back round to all the tracks. An eye opener for us has been doing markets, we do four or five a week, sometimes the public reaction is pure apathy and it's soul destroying it has happened to us often – you just got to get up, smile at the public and know your product is good. Jeff, I'm sure your book will go well it may be a slow burner but its a good idea a book for the speedway fan by one of us, hehehe, but an articulate one! I know you must be feeling apprehensive but your book will certainly be interesting and knowing you a stimulating read."

"We went quite often to Rye House the season before last I don't know your impressions when you visited Hoddesdon nor your impressions of Len Silver as a promoter but I grew up going to Hackney Wick so perhaps I'm biased but the atmosphere was excellent. I know the season before when we went a lot I thought the Rye crowd were really down on their riders. Brent Werner was often booed by them and Chris Neath, who seems to try so hard to entertain, still gets booed. Some fans think they've got a right to slag off the riders whereas others, I think of Poole fans, you would think they are royalty the way they behave. I must say when I last visited Eastbourne there was no atmosphere at all and when I went to the pits the riders didn't show any form of team spirit: they weren't even talking. What a far cry from when the Dugard, Norris, Barker etc were about!"

Children watch eagerly. © Jeff Scott

"Isn't it wild about Reading going Elite League? I bet the urinal in the loo is still broken but it won't be for long. I hope John Postlethwaite does well because the league does need fresh blood and it would be nice to see the famous Racers' body colour back where it belongs!"

"Jeff, I know you're telling it as it is in your book but you must remember that promoters have a lot of power and most of the floating support don't really look much deeper than the programme. I mean we can see things about to happen with riders coming and going etc. and some of the politics, others just buy the air horns, scarves etc. and may not believe the negativity that is just under the surface. Look at the amount of Scottish-based riders that are suffering with machinery probs and, lo and behold, three weeks later the *Speedway Star* reports they have had their van and bikes and gear all stolen. Surprise, surprise another claim and the van is always found; the riders get the insurance and the stuff's still probably stashed. When I used to go to Hackney as a youth, I was so into it; I used to watch the training sessions on a Saturday. I was so sad; I would get there really early to catch the coach to away meetings just for a glimpse of one of my heroes through the big metal gates. In retrospect, I think most of the riders felt supporters were a bit of a pain, just by what I know now to be body language. That said, look back years and years and they had more time for the fans. Nowadays when I read *Speedway Star* and in an interview they say, "yeah, I entertain the fans" by doing a freaking wheelie they think they have done enough. It's funny when they are begging for fans to sponsor them how soon they forget. I know there are exceptions and a few really friendly riders, genuine people, but really the smarter and richer ones just use *Sky Sports* as a marketing tool; they don't give a stuff about fans. I think that what I'm trying to say, in my very inept way, is that parts of the sport we love is corrupt and – if your book covers that – the promoters will probably not like their supporters knowing what they are really like and may think its bad for business! Surely, everyone must see the changes! Even if they don't acknowledge the faded glamour that speedway hasn't quite lost or ever shaken off."

"I remember one great day with Eastbourne – it was away to Bradford at Odsal – I had heard so much about it and drove up to meet a girlfriend from Bradford in a battered old Mini. When we got inside, it was like going back in time to the early seventies; John Perrin was counting the takings from his burger van. It was like a slow dream: the announcer did war cries, early eighties music, and mushy peas and gravy. The riders on parade looked bored – though Barker did wave to us – and they looked like they were thinking 'look at them idiots travelling all this way to watch this'. All a far cry from when I first went. Also the crowds are terrible. No one comments on the small crowds in the *Star*, though I'm just as bad as I don't go so much. I mostly watch on *Sky* as much as I can now, but don't get to see that much speedway as there's not many tracks near Hereford. We were winning quite well on *SkyBet*, it's easy – unless Greg Hancock's team rides his reserve partner home, hehehe – but last year there were some crazy results."

"Jeff, I really hope you succeed in showing both sides of our sport – to balance the glory but also the shabby tiger thing. This is never touched on! But from my earliest rides down to Waterden Road on my pushbike, when sadly I had all the names of the 1976 Hawks team on my pink drainpipe jeans together with Keith White's sponsors (Supreme Motorcycles down the legs) and me and my then mates lived for Friday night at 8. I earned £12 to £14 per week; we all worked in a pipe factory and a half of that would be blown wistfully on that very same night. Looking back on it, our obsession for speedway in general and Hackney in particular was almost sectionable – our all-consuming love was to become speedway riders. So it meant we clung onto every little thing we could find to imitate them. I remember dyeing my hair dark ginger – copying Keith White and trying to perfect an East Midlands accent – it's terrible in retrospect, but it seemed so important at the time. I would hunt for even the smallest snippet of news. However, when my eyes began to open and you saw terrible accidents and deaths, Vic Harding and that stuff, it kind of sickened us in the cold light of day."

"However, what me and those young men were feeling at 8 p.m. on Friday night made you forget or not realise. So when the track lights would come on Keith White, Barry Thomas and Zenon Plech would be fighting on track for OUR honour. I spray painted Plech's name on a disused weir in Walthamstow Marshes. Last year I took Mandy for a walk where me and those lost mates spent our time. There was also, believe it or not, a disused cycle speedway circuit complete with banking and centre green. Jeff, I kid you not. It also had shale on it and we went around it four times a week on our cow-horned pushbikes to race each other and bait any other groups into a match with us. Anyway, there we were walking along the river and I told her 'oh, down there we painted Plech and White in yellow spray'; so we walked towards the weir and I said 'no, they will have repainted this several times'. It was 29 years ago and, lo and behold, they had indeed painted it but you could clearly see Plechy's name. It seemed magical that the rest of the weir had black sticky stuff all over it – to prevent silly young men from risking drowning I guess."

"One last thing about that little track on Walthamstow Marshes/Stonebridge Lock there were another group of youths we would often see over there. They were from Reading but one had a cousin (I think from Tottenham); they were into speedway and loved the Racers. One of them said he was going to be a speedway rider and his name was Tim Hunt. Jeff, I have never seen Tim Hunt (the few years later Reading and Ipswich/Canterbury/Swindon rider) ride because a few years after I hit the crumpet barrier and regretfully stopped going to Hackney. My heart hopes it was him because, if so, at least he lived his dream; but truthfully, although much of it seems coincidence, in my heart I don't know for sure. One thing I do know was that group of kids were as obsessed as we were and were not the casual fan type. Tim Hunt was unknown (to me) at the time. Strangely I looked on the net last night hoping to see a pic to prove yay or nay was it him. It was great racing the Reading youths on the cycle speedway track as we were Hackney and they were the Racers. We also raced the Irish tinkers but they were more interested in stealing your jackets than race points!"

After we've returned from this incredibly evocative trip down memory lane, Kevin starts to cover the seamier and more salacious side of the sport to illustrate that speedway stars of the track often have nerves of steel but all too human feet of clay. This ranges from his personal bad experience with a contemporary Danish rider who he and Mandy helped gain support and sponsorship (when he was an unknown), to the colourful shenanigans of some famous riders who regularly enjoy three-in-a-bed sex sessions with some keen Midlands-based fans. Or even another happily married ex-World Champion rider who literally plays away in Sweden. Sadly, while this fascinates, it was all too predictable and libellous to report in detail. Luckily, the rattle of the turnstiles interrupts us as they opened and the necessary call of commercial need cut short our conversation. The afternoon is to be a disappointment for Kevin and Mandy at their stall even before the rain and sleet started to fall (as it did throughout the rest of the Classic). This is the risk you take as a stallholder and a promoter – the weather will be seasonal – and the rain or snow will arrive to accompany the cold. Rain makes the shelter of the main grandstand popular though many fans still stand without cover round the first bend and pressed close to the fence on the back straight. Since I've signed in, I have access to the pits area and should have been able to watch comfortably on the mini-grandstand-cum-steps that they have for riders and other followers, except for the sheer number of other people who've decided to do exactly the same thing. I can watch the riders get loaded onto the partially covered flat truck they use for the initial parade without difficulty but by the time the racing starts, my view is badly restricted and the sleet means that the covered grandstand is already pretty well full. Not that the rain bothers hatless Colin Horton who stands there throughout, oblivious to the downpour, casually chatting to all and sundry, including renowned SCB official and international referee Tony Steele. Colin's definitely come along with a young woman, whom I assume to be his daughter (and

Peterborough start marshal), for a good look at his new loaned recruit Richard Hall who this season will make the often difficult step up from the Premier League to the Elite League. His afternoon is a curate's egg of a performance since he follows the disappointment of a last place with a couple of firsts before he then tails off in the sleety conditions, though even so a win in his last ride would still have enabled him to possibly qualify for the final. However, a last place did not. Every time he's on track, Colin shouts words of advice and encouragement that I'd best summarise along the lines of 'open the throttle' or adopt a positive mental attitude that ignores the slippery conditions and the fearful tentative approach adopted by some of the other riders as they almost gingerly pick their way round the circuit.

It's definitely a case of who dares wins or, to be more exact, who rises above the slightly treacherous conditions to gate well and then negotiate the track without undue difficulty. It's surprising how fast some riders still manage to race, though others take an altogether wary approach, not so much in speed terms but by continually checking the surface for sudden obstacles or ostentatiously watching for mishaps that involve their fellow riders. Every rider dropped points in his race and, like all individual meetings where the points total then qualifies you for some additional knockout races to determine the ultimate victor, consistency in these conditions would prove to be the decisive success factor. Michael Coles started well on the consistency front with a couple of seconds before his star then subsequently waned and Neil Collins, arguably the most experienced rider round this track, suffered from an afternoon held back by assorted mechanical problems and difficulties. Sean Wilson won heat 2 impressively but then had a couple of scoreless rides before a couple of seconds gave his overall score some respectability. The riders selected (beforehand and afterwards Tim Stone speaks of "fantastic cooperation") and the actual format of the *Classic* are deliberately chosen so that the 12-man field can complete their races in a swift fashion – even when you allow for the additional entertainment of the quad bikes and the additional interspersed Mavericks Conference level races – should weather conditions be or become adverse. Every rider got stuck in, especially the Chris's – Neath and Harris – as well as Brent Werner and Leigh Lanham, though Niels Kristian Iversen was also the model of consistency until a last ride third place (his lowest placing of the day) cost him a place in the four-man final. Like many races during the season at any speedway track in the country, performance at the first and second bends mostly determines the ultimate victor in each race and passing remains at a premium all afternoon. In the final, it was Werner who found himself ahead as the second bend became the back straight and this was a lead that he reasonably effortlessly converted into victory. Behind him Leigh Lanham briefly pressured Chris 'Bomber' Harris on the first lap but an aggressive manoeuvre to close the apparent gap on the third bend ensured that he was placed second on the rostrum. Though the weather still isn't pleasant the crowd remains to get their money's worth and watch the presentation ceremony. The chance to spray your fellow riders with some sticky liquid is also hard to resist and the Cava soon adds to the general atmosphere of dampness that the riders have laboured under all afternoon. That said, the meeting shot by in double-quick time under the watchful eye (and even quicker finger on the control panel) of the retiring 'pensioner' referee Barrie Richardson helped in no small part by the willingness of the riders to put on a show. This was also helped by the quality of the track preparation along with an efficiently run pits and a no-nonsense display from Craig Wright, reputedly the youngest Start Marshal in British Speedway. I imagine that Tim Stone is happy with the crowd, the revenues generated and the show that was put on though I don't check this with him since he remains incredibly busy and rushes hither and thither.

Kevin hasn't enjoyed a lucrative day though he does have some words about the stallholder next to him all day when I catch up with him for a few brief words. "Do you know the bloke on the Devon shirts stand? You know the one – the frustrated speedway rider. God, what a poser! I don't know if you saw or heard his antics but all day it was 'yeah. I'll see you at the first GP, and he was talking in a really loud voice, especially when he thought people were listening. When we got here Devon shirts told us there was no room for us and I think what irked the knob was that Tim Stone came and said 'I told you to go over there!' to them, hehehe. His mate looked sheepishly at Tim and Tim said to us 'do you want to move where you should be?' We graciously declined 'cause it would have meant ten minutes longer setting up but had I known what a prime knob-end the boss was, I would have. Then they would have had to move. Tim came over just a moment ago at the end and asked how we had done and apologised about the weather. We made 70 quid but the stall was 60 quid and petrol 10 so we lost 10 quid's worth of stock in real terms. It was like that all last year – I hope it picks up though I doubt we'll be back next year. I couldn't see as much of the racing as I'd have liked but, from what I did see, they seem to go for it in the first corner and after that it gets a bit of a procession with no passing to speak of other than the initial jockeying for position. So really more of a non-classic than a Classic. Gets a good crowd though and they're friendly enough. Nice to see ya – let me know when the book finally comes out!"

In hindsight Tim Stone says he's delighted that the meeting went ahead so successfully despite the overnight frost beforehand and the sleet during the meeting. "I know some people complain that I go with some old favourites but they're tried and tested and all want to race without any grumbles. Lots of work and thinking goes into making the day a success, particularly at a time in the winter when, if you think about it, we really should never be able to do it! You have to be a bit sensible and I was pleased with being able to use the quad bikes flexibly as they 'clean' the track for the speedway boys. Their bikes don't rip the track like the speedway bikes so I switched them around throughout the course of the meeting – and they understand that's what they're there for and don't mind – to clear away the slush and smooth out the track again making it very evenly clear again. That's how we've got these meetings on every winter for years now – by picking the right riders who'll give it a go plus you have to be a bit sensible and think of stuff that you don't usually have to!" And after years of success you can't disagree with that or doubt Tim's thoughtful expertise, though perhaps with global warming we can hope for warmer, drier weather in future years.

9th January 2006 *New Year Classic*, Newport Winner: Brent Werner

"Each year one club is allowed to ignore the regulations that all the other clubs are working to and can track whatever team they like. It could be done on an annual ballot or on a rotating system. That way everyone would get an unfair advantage eventually."
Coventry fan Alan Allcott in letter to *Speedway Star*

"The management team believe this move will help us to achieve our ultimate goal of attracting more fans to the Reading area... I understand the resistance to change from some of the fans about the name... fans need to trust me that we are trying to do it for the benefit of them, as well as us, the promoters of the club. Not only have we brought a very strong team together, but we are installing new air fences, new lamps, a new pits area and bringing in four new offices."
John Postlethwaite discusses the "hundreds of thousands of pounds" BSI invests in Reading

"I answered the fans' questions as best and truthfully as I could but simply you can't please every one all the time."
Jim Lynch

"We have put forward a written proposal to the football club to build a speedway track at their stadium. They will consider the proposal in early February and if they agree we will then put in a planning application. We cannot say any more until they make a decision. If we get approval in principle from the football club, then we will be asking the Minister of Sport Richard Caborn for his backing and also that of the Mayor of Merton Councillor Judy Saunders."
Ian Perkin jumps the shark

"There's been the usual spate of rumours where it might be, but the club [Wimbledon plc] seems to be keeping it quiet at the moment. Probably they will have had to reveal its location at this week's CL chairman's meeting – I don't know. But from what I have heard – and there's nothing positive – the football club concerned is said to be in the Leatherhead area."
Matt Wright

"The reason why we were not among the eight listed starters [of the 2006 Conference League] was because I did not attend last week's Conference League chairman's meeting in Rugby. That was because at the time I was unable to put anything specific on the table regarding what we will be doing. That doesn't mean that we will not be running this season. I understand that the draft list of clubs was only provisional and that there is still time for us to enter – if we can find somewhere to race."
Ian Perkin

"They discussed this at a committee meeting last week, and we are due to meet them again to have more talks. But they have requested that we do not reveal their location for the time being and we will respect their wishes. If the project gets the club's approval, then we could be operational quite quickly. But, of course, the whole venture will face possible delays when it comes to seeking planning permission."
Ian Perkin on the 'mystery' football club

"I am really upset with Waggy because he has been so unprofessional about the way he has dealt with the issue. He has not answered one of my calls, emails or text messages...Waggy promised us before those matches that we would get our money but I guess that says everything about a guy who I used to have a lot of respect for."
Greg Hancock on Nigel Wagstaff

"Carl [Stonehewer] agrees with the theory that no one rider is bigger than the club and he has always said he understands that whatever decisions I have made have to be for the good of Workington Speedway."
Graham Drury

"Nobody could suggest that 2005 was a good season for the Islanders, but it wasn't a bad one either."
Dave Croucher

"Riders from all over Europe are realising that if they want to come to Britain, there's only one place they can go to – us."
Ronnie Russell

"I'm not a speedway killjoy but the noise level is a major problem – it's unnecessary and intolerable for local residents."
Dennis Westacott, member of the Weymouth 'Defence Against Nuisance Noise' campaign

"I've written this season off as a result and I fear my career in speedway may be over."
Weymouth captain, David Mason

"It costs us £20,000-£30,000 a year to run Conference League racing at West Row."
Mick Horton

News that the Redin fans have been "won over" appears premature if judged from a letter sent into the *Speedway Star* from the Kempshott estate in Basingstoke, in which Roger Osborne advises John Postlethwaite, "do not act like a Messiah and ride roughshod over tradition and a proud name just for marketing purposes." Apart from the decision being "crass", "wrong", "insensitive", built on "flimsy principles" he also includes an invitation that you just know will be ignored by any business visionary worth their salt ("be a man Postlethwaite and reverse your decision"). Meanwhile Jim Lynch is wowed with the new kevlars ("spectacular to say the least") and news that each Redin rider will have four different coloured helmets, just like "Grand Prix riders."

"Poles tend to be open-mouthed when they first see our track"
Ronnie Russell

March 2006

"I made a fatal comment of saying I was going to make Arena a fortress. Well, it's a good job I wasn't around a few hundred years ago when we were making forts. If I had been, there probably wouldn't be an England now."
Ronnie Russell

"I had a sandwich on the table, but now someone has put a steak there so I'm having steak instead... I was a bit embarrassed about the situation at the weekend, but then my wife pointed out that it was the number seven, not number one. I'm doing it in the best interests of the club, so I'm not embarrassed any more."
Ronnie Russell explains how Arena Essex signed three different Number 7 riders in 10 days

"[He's] rated as one of the new youngsters in Poland last year, then had a crash and swallowed his tongue, which took a while to get over."
Ronnie Russell on "better rider" Lucasz Romanek

"One of two teams we race against have a stunning likeness between their shirts and ours, for instance Oxford."
An upbeat Jon Cook discusses the innovation of 'away' shirts for Eastbourne

"I am really angry that Peter is implying that I was too expensive and that is why I was not included in 2001... for a man who does not seem to work or own a business and seems to rely on speedway for an income, it puzzles me how he seems to plead poverty and yet can take himself off to Brazil and other countries for several weeks at a time."
Alan Mogridge reacts badly to comments by Peter Waite

"I needed a break somewhere warm, and being all-inclusive there was little or nothing to worry about except enjoying ourselves... I think in the past some of my frustrations were born out of naivety, I've made the odd error here and there tactically, which I think I have learned from."
Alun Rossiter looks ahead calmly to the 2006 campaign

"Seeing Toni lying on an intensive care unit bed was so awful that I cried against racing and didn't want to see anybody who had anything to do with it. But then most of the riders and promoters came to see Toni, including Armando Castagna who is in Argentina, and I soon realised that whatever happens from now on, I shall always be grateful for the kind of life we were leading next to racing."
Adriana Svab on the darkest hours of her beside vigil beside her husband Antonin

"Some people are saying we look weak on paper. What they fail to realise is that we don't ride on paper and it is on the track where we will prove our worth."
Magnus Zetterstrom

"As for last weekend, all I will say is that we had a very weak referee that night, the wrong man in that situation without doubt. I couldn't believe what I was seeing."
Graham Drury on referee Stuart Wilson

"We are still negotiating with the football club, where it would appear there is an even-split on their management about our proposal. We should know one way or the other over the next two weeks. We cannot keep delaying like this – it isn't fair to our fans. Our director Perry Atwood is going to look at Layham's Farm and report back on whether it is worth pursuing. But I don't believe the football club venture is dead in the water yet."
Ian Perkin druthers

"At a time when everyone at Wimbledon needs to be pulling together, I find it very disheartening to read comments from Ian Perkin in the previous few issues. For him to say that the Supporters' Club events are not part of the 'Save Wimbledon Fund' is disrespectful of the efforts made in keeping the club's supporters together."
A frustrated Neil Thompson writes to the *Speedway Star*

"Winning is not everything and if I don't win the title but we get great crowds and everyone is enjoying it I will be happy."
Colin Horton

"I know that Shaun won't let it affect him and we'll be able to see just what he can do. He'll definitely turn the corner."
Mildenhall promoter Mick Horton gives Shaun Tacey the dreaded vote of confidence

"Occasionally I get people come up to me and say, 'are you Krzys Kasprzak?' It's very nice... ten years ago foreign riders used to make fun of the Polish riders, a bit like cat and mouse play, because they had superior equipment and were faster than we were."
The modest Krzysztof Kasprzak reflects on his speedway life

"My background is F1. Teamwork is vital, everyone has a job to do. We have told all the riders that we are open to suggestions, we want to make this work."
John Postlethwaite

"I'm seriously so far from happy no one could know how bad it is, and there will be major ructions about to break."
Peter Waite

"John Postlethwaite is a far, far shrewder businessman than I am so he must have a very good reason to change the club's name to the Bulldogs. He won't have just woken up one morning and done it on a whim."
Peter Oakes

"I give Jonathan Chapman full marks for the contribution he's made and while I don't agree with everything he's done and don't always agree with his attitude sometimes, I take my hat off to him."
Len Silver

"Hey Aaron [Lanney], he thinks I'm crap because I finished fourth in the World Championship two years on the trot."
Tony Rickardsson displays his legendary Swedish sense of humour when he recalls the 1996 and 1997 World Championship with Brian Burford

"It hurts me, we made it England and yet now we're Great Britain when, actually, we're still England... there are so many youngsters who get stop-start careers. They get a team place, and then the following year they don't get one, they don't ride or they get pushed around, and they've no home base to latch on to, they just drift around until somebody says 'oh, you're such a number, we'll have you'... they're on a downward spiral. These days, with the system we have, riders are not names or personalities, they're just a number, cannon fodder. The number fits the jigsaw puzzle, and that's the only reason they're there."

Peter Collins highlights that only 19 English riders will compete in the 2006 Elite League and decries the preference among modern promoters for "Mr Jetski"

Forecast of rain
24th March

The speedway season in 2006 started unfeasibly early according to some accounts when the roar of the engines was heard at tracks around the country as early as the first week of March. The BSPA had brought the opening date of the season back to March 1st, but in 2007 have decided themselves it was too early and reverted back to March 15th. I had almost nearly completed the second draft of the manuscript for my book *Showered in Shale*. It had been incredibly slow going. Apart from the fact that this was a huge task, another thing that had become clear was the lack of photos from my trip to Scotland and the Borders. I had an enviable array to choose from for practically every track except Glasgow, Edinburgh and Berwick. Still there was nothing for it but to plan an early season trip to Scotland and the Borders to try to rectify the lack of photos situation. What a sacrifice! I'd chosen so shrewdly and planned my trip so well that I'll be able to see three speedway meetings and probably another home defeat for Sunderland (this time against Blackburn) or, at least, given the season so far, another guileless execrable performance where they play like injured speedway riders in a kick about. I've decided to base myself in the Edinburgh University halls of residence near the historic centre of the city for the duration. This will allow me to travel to all of the speedway fixtures on the Edinburgh supporters coach organised by the indomitable Ella MacDonald since all the meetings feature the Monarchs as they race against the auld enemy Glasgow and also travel to Berwick.

The weather on the way up from the South looks poor throughout and the forecast looked even less wonderful on Metcheck with rain forecast throughout the weekend in both Glasgow and Edinburgh. Still hope springs eternal and I was determined that I would get some more photos to break up the densely worded text of my book and to ensure that inside its pages the book pictorially didn't look fatally unbalanced. No speedway promoter ever claims that any fixture they happen to run at any point during the season is ever "meaningless". Even the start of season pre-season friendlies are always talked of in terms of allowing the riders to "blow off their cobwebs" or as an invaluable opportunity to "try out some new set-ups on their bike for the important [always forthcoming] fixture against XX". There's always a reason or a story as to why, as a fan, you should definitely come along to see the fixture in question. After a winter deprived of the spectacle at this early stage of the season, well any time in the season, I'd really go and watch any speedway meeting anywhere of any standard. Sadly the Spring Trophy (is their actually such a trophy to be awarded?) clash at Armadale was abandoned at 5 p.m. before my train had even arrived at Waverley station. I had been deprived of my chance to see my second speedway meeting of the season (the other was at Eastbourne) without the bikes even having the chance to warm up and I'm just going to have to accept that there won't be photos of the Armadale stadium in my book. I found absolutely no consolation in the news that this was the first heavy rain after weeks of dry weather nor was I excited by the prompt rearrangement of this fixture to the next Friday night. Though given how eagerly the locals relish each and every local derby clash I'm sure that this would have offered some consolation of sorts. That said I was impressed that I'd graduated sufficiently during my travels for Ella to take the time to text me with the bad news and try to save me unnecessary disappointment and a wet but fruitless walk down to the supporters coach stop. Still, with an absolute mountain of revisions and writing still to be completed, I was definitely in the right country to feel that the task of writing *Showered in Shale* was completely akin to the travails of painting the Forth Bridge.

New Black Shale Arrives
25th March

After an intensive burst of writing and refreshed by a hall-of-residence breakfast, hope springs eternal in my breast. Well it has to if you're a Sunderland fan, generally this is true but particularly so this season. Though I've already arranged a lift back with Ella on the Edinburgh supporters' bus after the meeting from Berwick, I also hedge my bets and also purchase a cheap day return on the train from Edinburgh to Newcastle. In the madness that is post-privatisation railway tickets price matrices, this is much much cheaper than a single to Newcastle and a single from there back to Berwick. With the ticket I've bought, I can (unofficially) get off at Berwick if the weather is fine tonight and, if it's not, stay on the train back to Waverley Station. This looks the likeliest option as the forecast is for more rain. Though, that said, at this time of year Berwick promoter, Peter Waite, will need all the gate receipts he can get to cover his expenditures over the winter [1] as well as the shipment of new black shale that he's had delivered in order to improve the quality of the track surface at Shielfield Park. With different shale under their wheels it might encourage more overtaking manoeuvres on a regular basis from the home riders. The lack of said overtaking was a complaint last season but wasn't something that held true when I visited as I saw many entertaining passes on both straights and spectacular use of the steeply banked track by the home riders on the third and fourth bend. Tonight, should the weather hold, the spectacle promises to be even better because of the additional grip afforded by the arrival of this fabled new shale.

Whether the meeting is actually going to be on seems completely unlikely if judged by the torrential downpour that hits Newcastle with great severity at around 5.30 p.m. Though the Tyne and Tweed are some distance apart from each other along the North East coastline, the train journey scenically hugs the line of the coast almost throughout the entire journey. For the first 30 minutes of what is always a magnificent train ride the windows are lashed with heavy rain with menacing low black clouds overhead. From my arrival at Newcastle Railway station and for most of the train journey I keep in touch with Ella as the Monarchs white mini-bus edges its way along the roads to Berwick-upon-Tweed. Not only is there no rain in the vicinity but the skies look lovely and clear according to Ella, who is happy to patiently repeat this information many times as I call from the rainstorm that I can see through the smeared windows of the train. I'm no metrological expert but although the rain stops and the clouds brighten some 10 or so minutes before we arrive into Berwick station, even I can tell that the wind is northerly and will sweep the clouds towards the town and the general vicinity of the speedway track in Tweedmouth. As ever, the town looks fantastic from the panoramic view you get from the train from the railway bridge that crosses the Tweed. It allows you to marvel at the beautiful spectacle of the town set out below along with magnificent views of the river mouth as it tumbles towards the sea. A brief taxi ride across yet another less exciting bridge ensures I arrive with sufficient time before the 7 p.m. start to linger in quite a long queue of fans keen to get their third taste of the speedway season so far at Shielfield.

[1] Though its hard to imagine that there are too many of these as Peter Waite kept the loyal Berwick speedway fans on tenterhooks all winter in his own personal teasing dance of the seven veils. Namely the "will-he, won't-he run speedway at Berwick in 2006?" He kept mum for long enough to get everyone really worked up and to give the prophets of doom that lurked on the Internet the full chance to vent their prognostications of scorn, anger and betrayal. Eventually, the long-awaited white smoke was seen to rise from Waite Towers and news filtered out that systems were once again go at Shielfield. According to critics the inordinate delay handicapped the club since the chance to sign key riders had vanished and other more confident promoters would have already snapped them all up during Peter's many months of prevarication. According to Peter – cut from the school of the glass is half full outlook on life and someone who is unafraid to make changes but always make a virtue of necessity – this actually widened the pool of talent to choose from as it was now completely clear which riders had failed to yet secure a team berth for the 2006 season. Legendarily parsimonious, Peter's insouciant optimism was no doubt helped by the fact that riders left on the shelf and desperate to secure regular rides would be less likely to be able to command inflated points money and other fringe benefits. Not that anyone who'd been around in speedway for a while seriously thought for a moment that Peter would succumb to anything like the rumoured Postlethwaite-esque levels of rider remuneration that are the hallmark error of many new promoters.

Under floodlights – ideal viewing conditions. © Jeff Scott

Rider parade and introductions. © Jeff Scott

The all-important coin toss for gate positions. © Jeff Scott

Davina Johnston sells the programmes at Berwick Speedway from a booth just a few yards inside the turnstiles as you head towards the home-straight grandstand. She takes pride in her work and is proud to sell programmes at the club. You only have to speak with her for a few minutes to realise she has a motherlode of information and observations about the club, riders, staff and fans. Not that she shares anything that's at all contentious or controversial with a stranger like me but I quickly gather that the Johnston family have multiple links with the Berwick club. She's in charge of the programme booth; her (slightly reticent when you meet him) husband Bob helps with track preparation, evident by his almost fluorescent bright yellow anorak; and their son David is one of the Start Marshals. Only a few weeks later in the season he will rise to national prominence when he's involved in an altercation with a Newcastle Speedway rider during the meeting when Jamie Robertson attempted to head-butt him and was banned and heavily fined for the incident (though the BSPA accepted that there had been some provocation by David and all referees were subsequently told to closely watch start gate enforcement through the season). As the majority of the crowd have already arrived and bought programmes, Davina fills out the exercise book that she's used for years to record the date, meeting details, assorted information about the number of copies sold and the monies generated. It's an incredible meeting-by-meeting record, laid out in neat handwriting in a variety of ink colours or pencil on the lined pages, and in its own way exactly documents the relative fortunes and popularity of the club. It also provides an insight into the varied fortunes of speedway in general as you can easily see the changes over the years as well as the key months of the year or the teams that attract enough interest to stimulate the greatest programme sales. I gather tonight that the threat of unsettled but most likely wet weather has metaphorically (and later literally) dampened the crowd. It's not a secret that the club manages to survive on small (but loyal) attendances on a Saturday night and that this necessarily leads to a tight budget for all aspects of speedway operations that are masterminded by the always welcoming and cheerful Peter Waite.

Once through the turnstiles at this stadium you're confronted with the track almost immediately that tonight looks dark, rich and inviting. Maybe it's because it's so early in the season and I've not quite grown accustomed to visually assess the track surfaces I encounter throughout the country but the dark shale looks immaculately groomed. This is because Berwick speedway club have invested in a new "top surface" for the track and, to my untutored eye, it really looks magnificent. Later though I hear grumbles from more experienced and knowledgeable Monarchs' fans that it was "questionable whether it had been packed down correctly." Whatever the technical details and considerations, to a lay punter like me under the floodlights the reddish (?) coloured shale glints invitingly and the curve of the narrow straights to and from the sloped, banked, final bend look beautifully manicured – the ideal setting to stage the theatre of an encounter against the Monarchs in the Premier Trophy North qualifiers. Since the main grandstand by the start line appears to hardly have an empty seat in its many prime viewing positions.

It's an atmospheric night and the echo from the tannoy as the riders are introduced in turn on the parade vibrates loudly inside its interior but not half as loudly as the sound of the bike engines when they eventually roar into life for some practice and warm-up laps. Not that this happens immediately as oblivious to the threat of rain or, perhaps, in the full knowledge of the deluge that is about to arrive, the rider introductions on parade go on for an inordinate time. This would have given me the chance to take a huge number of photographs but for the extremely officious steward who is instantly over to my side to reprimand me for "using flash photography – it's completely banned". I try to pacify him with a promise that as soon as the action starts or the bikes roar into life then I will respect this essential rule of speedway life (that I'm already well aware of) but until that moment flash photography is actually permitted. These instructions are reiterated, only this time with slightly more force in the manner of a schoolteacher whose patience has been exhausted by a particularly troublesome child, with the addition of the caveat that "you should find somewhere to sit down or leave as you're blocking people's views standing there!" This is a moot point but even though no one other than the steward has complained I quickly move to the other smaller grandstand with standing terraces instead of seats at the other side of the stadium. It's a chilly night. Ella and a small conclave of other cheery Monarchs supporters stand on the raised second bend on the open-air terraces overlooking the track. This is next to the infamous "Ducket" the small corrugated covered stand on the back straight, from which Berwick FC take their nickname "The Duckets". The legendary fanaticism of the Monarchs hard core of support hasn't been sufficiently enthused to contemplate this comparatively close early season trip south for this Premier Trophy North encounter. I'm sure that it'll be different later in the season when the weather improves and league points (and local pride) are up for grabs. Ella responds to my anxiety about meeting up afterwards in the car park ("how will I know which is your coach?") with "it's the only one there so you can't miss it!" I admire her confidence but the last thing I want to happen is get stranded especially as I hold a return train ticket to Edinburgh that I've now invalidated.

Unable to take anything but blurry photos of the track and parade or only able to get close-up shots of the crowd where every item of fluorescent clothing reflects the flash back brightly, I reluctantly decide not to incur the further wrath of the slightly overly officious stewards who also lurk on this side of the stadium. Not that the racing has started yet as the aforementioned interminable introductions were followed by some pretty ropey practice starts and warm-up laps before all the riders again retreat back to the pits. This gives me the chance to study the programme in the half-light and notice that on its front cover the club appears to have been renamed the "(North) Berwick Bandits" in honour of their sponsorship by "The Andersons Quality Butchers". Great play of this new sponsorship has been made locally, even in the pages of the *Speedway Star*, which featured pictures of happily smiling butchers in aprons posed with a speedway bike outside their shop (the one opposite Chest, Heart & Stroke Scotland) along with a contently smiling Peter Waite with his supportive hand on their shoulders. The benefit that this will have on sales for this chain of butchers is hard to exactly estimate but my hopes are high that it is going to prove their shrewdest business decision ever. Still a boom (or lack of it) in sausage, mince or (haggis) kidney sales is their concern and in the meantime their sponsorship helps ensure the survival of the club and boosts its notorious shoestring budget. Even though I'm not from this neck of the woods, I know that North Berwick (the home of the Quality Butchers that are the Andersons – how refreshing it is to know that the inexorable rise of the supermarkets chains throughout Britain has yet to swamp them) is located nearly 40 miles away from Berwick-upon-Tweed. Most peculiar, but then they do do things differently up here as a casual glance inside the programme confirms, "Berwick Speedway Ltd" list all the usual job positions you'd associate with any other club along with a "historian" (Gavin Renton) and a club "cartoonist" (Jeff Baker). Even the Press Officer Lawrence Heppell has more than one string to his bow as he's also in charge of the hotline and is officially the club "DJ". Not that we'll hear any music over the tannoy tonight, in fact we don't hear much of anything until eventually the silence is broken by the arrival of the riders at the tapes.

Apparently the new reddy coloured shale surface is very much to the liking of Adrian Rymel who streaks to an easy victory over Theo Pijper of the Monarchs – the translation of whose surname from Dutch still remains a widely kept secret in speedway circles. It's not exactly an exciting race at the front since the action is all over bar the shouting after the first bend, though at the rear there's quite a tussle for the honour conferred by the third place point between David 'Victor' Meldrum and Henrik Moller. The honour eventually goes to the Berwick man giving the Bandits a 4-2 start although this looks unlikely to be decisive as the first drops of rain start to spit with increasing rapidity and soon has soaked the track enough to change the colour to a much darker hue that more easily coincides with the colour you'd expect of a speedway track. The next race has the Berwick pair of Craig Branney and Danny Warwick zoom confidently from the gate in a manner that, if it's repeated *ad infinitum* throughout the season, could make them a potent reserve partnership to be really reckoned with.

The shy Bob Johnston. © Jeff Scott

Equally if Sean Stoddart and Derek Sneddon lumber from the tapes like this every week then it's going to be a very long season for the Monarchs team management and supporters. Sadly for the Bandits, already seemingly assured of a 5-1, with field strung out like a line of washing, just when he looks the most comfortable rider so far tonight the white-dreadlocked Danny Warwick falls on the steep banking of the last bend of the penultimate lap. The Monarchs pair are sufficiently far enough behind to easily be able to take evasive action to negotiate the fallen rider and follow a considerable distance behind Craig Branney for a drawn heat, though they look far from 'smooth' in their riding techniques on the increasingly slippery surface.

With the rain now falling heavily, though the riders did come out and attempt to line up at the tapes, they were sent back to the pits by the referee, Stuart Wilson. Shortly afterwards, an announcement over the loudspeakers informed us that there would be a (hopefully) short delay while we all wait around to see if the rain will pass. The size and speed of the lengthy black clouds that followed my train up from Newcastle leads me to think that this statement is a triumph of optimism over common sense but, as there is nothing else to do and as speedway fans are wont, we all settle in to wait patiently. Soon though it's not long before even the hardiest fans retreat from the open, raised grass bank areas to shelter under the roof of the by now cosily packed back-straight grandstand. The steady rain shows no sign of subsiding though we are treated to an entertainment of sorts when a water truck slowly makes its way round the circuit; not to provide additional water but in an attempt to further pack down the newly laid shale surface. Many speedway tracks round the country are subject to the attention of various supervisory and regulatory bodies from the BSPA, the SCB, Health and Safety and their local councils. Berwick are no exception and, for noise reasons, have totally banned the use of that chosen weapon of aural destruction at speedway – the air horn – and are also subject to a strict early evening curfew time of 9.30 p.m. So the longer we wait for the rain to stop, in the unlikely event that it will, the closer we get to the dreaded witching hour of the compulsory close down of racing here.

Any chance I have to fulfil the original purpose of my trip North – obtaining some worthwhile photos for my book – has more or less completely disappeared in the rain and gloom. Two ladies who are far from gloomy are smartly wrapped up against the elements and shelter inside the darkened turnstiles where they've just spent the evening on duty are the friendly welcoming Lacey Louden and Muriel Ennis. They're speedway fanatics and die-hard fans of all things Berwick speedway where they tell me they've both worked for "years" without going into exact chronological specifics. Obviously, the size of the crowds and the fact that they work every week on the turnstiles not only means that they practically know everyone who attends (by sight if not in person), they're also strongly of the opinion that Berwick fans are some of the

[2] Though this claim is made by the fans of practically every speedway team in the country on their own behalf, in this part of the speedway world I would say that it's made pretty insistently to me by fans from Berwick, Edinburgh and Glasgow.

friendliest and most dedicated fans in the country. [2]They're enthusiastic and curious about my book, feel that it's a good idea and wish me every success when it's published. As we stand and talk, it's announced that the meeting has been abandoned, after around 30 minutes or so of our collective study of the rain as it continues to fall without any sign that it will abate. In fact the meeting has been postponed due to concerns held by the referee about the restricted visibility that the riders would have on an apparently still serviceable track, even if they tried to race in the rain (due to rain drops obscuring safe vision through the tear offs, which is made worse at Berwick with the patchy intermittent lighting across the track surface). We're also informed that our tickets will be valid for readmission at the rearranged fixture or for other meetings over the next few weeks. This isn't exactly helpful to me as I live in Brighton not Berwick (though I do have a Berwick near Eastbourne), the North East or Scotland. Lacey and Muriel immediately direct me to the speedway office located in the main home-straight grandstand, suggesting I explain my situation and try to get a refund. This strikes me as unlikely, since notoriously many speedway promoters are reluctant to countenance the possibility of a refund if (a usually narrow window) alternative dates are offered at which the ticket will subsequently be valid. I'm sure that this helps their cash flow but isn't good customer service. When I arrive in the small but very cosy speedway office located up the steep steps of the first gangway, they're already ensconced there absorbed in their work in full 'the King is in his Counting House' mode with all that night's admissions takings. I explain myself and, without any hesitation, the attractive Carol immediately refunds my entrance money in a charmingly friendly fashion, wishes me well with the book and tells me to rush back to Berwick speedway in the summer when the weather should be much better. This prompt refund surprises me and it reflects extremely well on the club, the friendly staff of the speedway office and indicates to me that Peter Waite runs a professional operation that has a clear idea of how to offer good customer service and make people want to come back to his club.

Outside in the pitch black but extremely busy car park, I eventually find the mini-bus after a plaintive call on my mobile to Ella. I was on the lookout for a coach belonging to the Monarchs supporters, when I should have been seeking a much more modestly sized mini-bus. Only the truly fanatical but now pretty wet die-hard Monarchs fans (and weather optimists) have made the trip down to the Borders tonight. Already on board are a number of familiar faces from my occasional travels with the Monarchs supporters club including Edinburgh speedway director and institution at the club – the modestly knowledgeable speedway doyen, Mike Hunter. The mood on board is as subdued as the windows are steamy until only minutes after we pull out of the Berwick speedway car park we stop for essential refreshments at Robert Smiths the local chippie, where the chips are served in sturdy cardboard boxes ("want sauce and shake with that, sir?"). This is just not any old chippie but one that is renowned locally for the quality of its fare – the food is cooked to order and there's never any cause for complaint about the taste, quantity or satisfaction levels from the Monarchs fans. Within minutes the mood has brightened considerably as they return clutching their cooked-to-order teas. While the rain continues to batter on the roof, the warmth of the van, the smell of the chips and the casual camaraderie and easy familiarity of everyone on board is a delightful atmosphere to be a small part of. I happily sit back and savour the freemasonry of speedway fans everywhere and quietly listen to all the well-informed speedway gossip, conjecture and banter that surrounds me.

25th March Berwick v Edinburgh (Premier Trophy North) 7-5 Abandoned: rain

26th March

As promised, Ella texts as soon as she knows what the situation is with this afternoon's planned meeting at Ashfield Stadium in Glasgow. The meeting is postponed in mid-morning without a wheel being turned after a track inspection revealed that the heavy overnight rain had waterlogged the track. It was an extremely prompt decision that kindly saved all the local fans the disappointment of another wasted journey. I get the chance to spend a whole day cooped up in my student hall of residence to further revise my manuscript with a dedication and application that I struggled to achieve when I was a student. The net result of my trip has been three nights away in Scotland – spent in student style near the tourist trap of the old historic part of the City of Edinburgh. I've failed in my intention to get some really useable photographs for the Glasgow, Edinburgh and Berwick chapters of my book and I only managed to see two speedway races (and have seen

Sunderland lose again). The friendliness of the people aside, hopefully this isn't a sign of how my speedway season and book tour will continue throughout 2006.

26th March Glasgow v Edinburgh (Spring Trophy Challenge) – postponed: waterlogged track

April 2006

"He made me look a bit daft at the time and I got some flak from some quarters about not knowing the rules which I didn't enjoy very much. But I give Stuart ten out of ten for having the courage to ring up and apologise. I admire him for that."
Ian Thomas on referee Stuart Wilson

"[He] is one of the most dedicated and loyal people, both as chairman and lifelong fan. I would also like to point out to those who make uninformed, disparaging remarks that, to date, Ian has lost nearly £20,000 of his own money."
Perry Attwood writes to the *Speedway Star*

"Following my eviction from the Wessex Stadium, I agreed to sell the licence to Phil Bartlett and that situation remains. The deal struck with Phil was £30,000, £5,000 of which he has paid as deposit. The rest is payable once planning permission is granted for racing to continue at the Wessex Stadium and until that time the club is owned by myself."
Brian White

"I did say at the time of signing Tony that it was never going to be perfect having a rider for such a short amount of time, so there is no surprise there. It was a gamble I was prepared to take for a new era of Oxford Speedway and I hope our fans can see that I tried very hard to make it work."
Aaron Lanney

"By his standards, he hasn't had a particularly great start to the season [but] he's Tony Rickardsson, he's going to come back."
Neil Middleditch

"I don't argue with referees and I always respect them because they have a hard job."
Neil Machin on Stuart Wilson before branding his decision at Glasgow as "laughable" and "the craziest decision I've ever seen"

"It should be an honour to ride for your country and you should feel proud. People still ask me 'did you ride for England?' and I can say, 'yes I did'."
Neil Middleditch

"We have been in talks with them since before Christmas but they have continually delayed on making a decision. They promised me they would decide on our offer last Thursday [March 30] but I have had no phone contact from them. That now indicates to me there is no chance of us going there. I know there are people on the football club's committee who are opposed to a speedway track being laid in their grounds. This subsequent lack of communication from them indicates to me that they have won the day. Probably I will get a formal rejection letter from Mole Valley later in the week."
Ian Perkin

"I don't want to slag off Peterborough Speedway as it's a fellow club, but that sort of track does nothing for the sport. The track was responsible for Paul's crash and injury. When a rider of the

class of our guest Scott Nicholls says he's wondering whether he can turn into the corners, something is wrong with the track... I have to wonder whether their track is prepared by farmers."
Ronnie Russell

"Even if I'd not known what it said, if I'd got the body colours with something on I'd not asked for, I'd have gaffer-taped it over. I certainly wouldn't have let the riders go out unless I knew what it meant."
Phil Bartlett after the Weymouth Wizards rode in a second half wearing race tabards doctored with a disguised "Dingbats phrase" that "cast a damaging slur on former club owner Brian White." The *Speedway Star* reported that the "offending phrase – was of a sexual nature and highly damaging to White's reputation and unrepeatable in a family publication." All I can say is '▶✳︎◼ ✳︎❑ ◼❑◆ ▼✳︎◼◼ ☆✳︎✳︎● ✝◉❑▼◉✳︎▼▼→▲ ✳︎◼▲✳︎✳︎✳︎▼ ✳︎▲ ▲❑ ❑❑❑❑✝'

"There was a hush on the terraces and anxiety in the pits where Mick Horton 'had words' with his men... something of a Hammer horror production – plenty of scary moments before their heroes emerged triumphant."
Reporter Randall Butt on another eventful meeting at Mildenhall

"It's time some riders realised that they have a commitment to the people on the terraces who actually pay their wages. We have got to stop ripping them off. What we saw at Swindon last week was a disgrace and then we have the fiasco at Poole. That would not have happened if either had been a Grand Prix meeting. Speaking from a Premier League perspective, I feel that this is damaging my business and others across our league because it sends out a signal to supporters that if there's any poor weather, then meetings will be off... rain-offs should be the last resort, but unfortunately we have some riders who are paid extremely well to do what they do but don't want to race unless conditions are perfect."
Neil Machin rails against 'rider power'

"We are both big men and have always resolved matters immediately after meetings. I respect Tony totally and I think he has respect for me for what I am trying to do for Oxford. Tony is quite the individual and is certainly not being used as a scapegoat in any way, shape or form... I just felt he could have helped his team-mates out when they needed it instead of being critical of them."
Aaron Lanney sort of kisses and makes up with Tony Rickardsson

"I think speedway has to look at itself in the years ahead and decide where it is going. At the moment it is a circus that mainly runs between three different countries and this is the second time in three seasons that Adam has been injured riding abroad. You can kind of accept injuries when they happen racing for your own club because that is the nature of the beast...our riders are such valuable commodities to us and they are all loved by the fans, yet every Tuesday night and every Sunday evening we sit by the phone waiting for that dreaded call. Unfortunately there isn't enough money in the sport that they only ride for us and nobody else. I only wish there was... it makes me laugh when I hear people saying the contract system in speedway needs looking at. The riders have free movement around Europe and we have no control over what a rider does."
Jon Cook

"I'll be having a talk with Shaun, something obviously isn't right with him. His body language was all wrong in the Somerset meeting. It didn't look as though he wanted to ride. And although conditions weren't the best at the start of the meeting, they were the kind he used to revel in." Mick Horton

The Corduroy Revolution
3rd April

The early start to the season still hasn't enabled me to get to visit my beloved Smallmead now that the BSI organisation has taken over, promoted the club to the Elite League and sacrilegiously changed the club nickname from the Racers to the Bulldogs. This is a decision that can only really be regarded a nonsensical folly in both marketing and historical teams. Given the nature of speedway as a sport, what better nickname could there be than the Racers? While other less fortunate clubs struggled with less apposite nomenclature (and some share the same nickname), Reading had a really distinctive but apposite name to match its tradition and the sport it competes in. Not that in the eyes of the true fan, the club can ever really lose its historic identity of the Reading Racers. Like many throughout the winter and over the coming season, I'll reserve the right to constantly whinge on about this barmy change.

The organisation that owns and runs Reading is now known as BSI Reading and is one of the sister companies under the overall BSI umbrella. The Chief Executive of the club is John Postlethwaite and he inspires strong feelings in the speedway world. Judged by his public pronouncements, he's not a modest man but then a will for self-promotion goes with the territory in many businesses and given that he has a product to promote to the general public, this is completely understandable from a commercial perspective. However, there's a fine line between self-promotion and arrogance. The presumption that he appears to hold that he best knows how to promote the speedway product based on the altogether different proposition of his success with the World Championship Grand Prix series is something he apparently expects to easily transfer to the team competition that is the Elite League.

Long time and long suffering promoters of many years' experience have frequently seen (and seen off) new arrivals into the promotional world who talk the talk and dismiss the leaden ambitions of their rivals, only to subsequently not walk the walk when they find that the task in hand is altogether more complicated and expensive than they initially predicted. It's widely expected that John Postlethwaite's reign at (what, in respect of the authentic tradition of the club, will henceforth be known to me as) the Racerdogs will take grandiose ambition to new heights and many people will keep a close watch in the full expectation that pride comes before a fall. One thing is for sure, money will initially be no object as the Racerdogs have set out to spend money like a lottery winner with no self-control and little taste. If you look at the squad (and management team!) that the club have assembled for the 2006 season you have to say that they are deservedly one of the pre-season favourites to lift the title. The club does not propose to achieve success in the time-honoured and slow manner by nurturing young rider talent to ultimate fruition. If this were cooking your evening tea, then the Racerdogs preferred to buy the most expensive ready meal in the shop rather than compose their own ultimately more rewarding fare from individual ingredients. Not that the formation of this team has been without hitches as, despite investments throughout the club and its infrastructure, it seems that the management hadn't invested in a decent calculator and didn't properly understand the rules when it came to points limits and averages or possibly both. Whatever the reasons for this oversight, it nearly had ruinous implications for Danny Bird, one of the recent crowd favourites at Smallmead. Danny fought his way back from injury in 2005 only to find that his promotion to the 'highest' echelon of British speedway was granted for only a day or so before it was withdrawn again in a fiasco of fractions of a percentage point. Apparently, Jim Lynch misunderstood which of Bird's averages took precedence – he used the converted PL CMA – when in fact Bird's previous EL CMA from when he doubled up with Ipswich was the one that counted. Ironic when you think it's the promoters that make these rules then claim they don't understand them – so what chance do the fans have? No doubt sincere public statements were issued that like Arnie he'd be back (next season) but until then his place in the team would be filled by the experienced and evergreen Andy Smith. If anyone is guaranteed to get among the opposition on a regular basis, it's the always-combative eternal journeyman 'Smudger' though it might take him a few weeks to master the Smallmead circuit after so many recent years spent at Kirkmanshulme Lane in Manchester. Both circuits are similar to the extent that they lack an excess of shale.

However, the majority of the team that's been assembled over the winter have raced at Smallmead in years gone by and the most exciting rider in many years to grace the track at Smallmead, Matej Zagar, has fulfilled his stated career ambition to race in Elite League and still remain at Reading. In fact the composition of the team appears to have been put together by someone with shrewd speedway intelligence, which you have to assume is the experienced speedway promoter Jim Lynch rather than John Postlethwaite. Equally another important source of advice could have been Sam Ermolenko who

Prices rise but 2 free children with every adult.© Jeff Scott

Derelict stands gets makeover. © Jeff Scott

Smallmead in the shadow of its posher industrial neighbours.
© Jeff Scott

has the most unique job position and incongruous title in British Speedway, "Sporting Director" as well as Ole Olsen's son, Torben, who was also brought in as marketing manager. It's a sobriquet that reflects an burgeoning trend within the modern business world – namely, if someone has a dull or demanding job that you pay them very little for then the least you can do is give them an inflated sounding job title in lieu of better pay. In Sam's case, this isn't true as he has an inflated job title and, it's strongly rumoured, pay levels to match. While there's a perception in the wider speedway world that the reason every club doesn't have a Sporting Director is not only that it's expensive but might also be as useful as an agoraphobic free-range chicken. This is an unfair comment with regards to Sam's experience and expertise, which will probably confound the naysayers as the season progresses since his avowed intention is to pay attention to the essential minutiae of speedway life.

All the important aspects – equipment preparation, bike transport and logistical planning as well as the psychology involved in race preparation for the team – will fall within his remit. Since these often remain down the list of the contemporary frequent flier rider's priorities in the ongoing treadmill that is the haste to just get to the next meeting in one piece. Sam has stressed the utility, efficacy and path-breaking nature of his new position at every opportunity – both in the speedway press and his additional public forum through the *Sky Sports* microphone when he's doing commentary work. As Christine Keeler so perceptively noted in a different context "well, he would say that, wouldn't he?" That said, while I'm sure he will add value and provide something other competitor teams don't possess, it will arguably come at a considerable financial cost.

If John Postlethwaite is about one thing it's cost inflation, particularly this season when it comes to Elite League rider payments and, as a result of the SGP series – where he still pays a relative pittance and placing payments have hardly changed since the series started (and are available for all to see in the FMI handbook) – possibly some increased travel costs for UK promoters to ferry their so-called "superstar" riders back and forth. The fact that the majority of these riders have as much chance of winning the Grand Prix series as I do to marry into royalty is obscured by the trapping and razzmatazz of the GP travelling circus and the relentless hype of this competition on *Sky Sports*. If these riders are just fodder and grist to the BSI mill, then at least a sense of lustre attaches to them that, hopefully, translates into additional sponsorship payments (in three countries minimum – Sweden, Poland and England) and increased costs for many UK promoters that doesn't ever show on the BSI profit and loss account. This is before you factor in that throughout the season on many summer Saturdays in this country, UK promoters can't use their own riders to excite the crowds and generate revenues because they are occupied elsewhere. We haven't even spoken about injuries sustained in the Grand Prix (or exacerbated when they return too early to compete in a GP or curiously remain injured for the week leading up to a GP) to riders who have signed UK contracts – the owners of which have to stand by and watch while their 'property' moonlights for another employer elsewhere leaving them to pay the consequences. It is claimed that John Postlethwaite is also on a one-man mission to transplant the professionalism and commercialism that he learnt during his time in Formula 1 into speedway (or kill the patient in the process). I have no knowledge of F1 (and find it tedious) nor JP's time and experiences within the sport, though I'm happy to take at face-value assertions made by Nicola Sands, the BSI Press Officer on this matter. You do have to wonder when there's so much money sloshing about in the world of high performance cars, why anyone would ever want to leave for the lure of speedway? The cache is higher, the coverage greater, the people and locations superficially more glamorous. Still, we all understand that once speedway gets under your skin, then it's highly unlikely that you'll ever permanently fall for any rival suitors. Very few true lovers of any sport would try to express their love and respect by attempting to make root and branch reform based on a model from elsewhere that you claim applies to the chosen object of your desire. The transfer of the skills, attitudes and techniques learnt in the world of F1 might have some limited place in speedway – for example, like it would in any sports where television rights sales assume a primary role – but in many areas this claim to expertise with regard to the general benefit of the sport remains a dog that hasn't barked. All this is a long hand way of saying, this season at Smallmead we'll all very publicly get to see – rather than platitudinously read about it in BSI press releases that invariably always talk such a good game or have this "success story" relentlessly parroted in almost NLP fashion by commercial outlets (like *Sky*) with a huge vested interest in this perspective taking hold or gaining credibility – what John Postlethwaite and BSI are really made of when it comes to delivery on their heady mix of promises and prognostications.

As I drive along the arterial road for the first time this season to the roundabout just before a slope that takes you down to the rough hewn waste land that is the Smallmead car park, I'm excited and keen to find fault all at the same time. Reading is the club that I grew up with and formed my love of speedway. Just to walk through the gates always creates a sense of arrival and of the comfort of home. It is my first love and you're always going to be fiercely protective when interlopers arrive with the best intentions but are likely to mistreat what you've always somehow considered your own and yours to keep and reverence as you choose. The dilapidated nature of Smallmead Stadium – particularly in the face of exponential changes in the look and feel of the industrial and business landscape that surrounds its walls – highlights that, while everyone else has wholeheartedly embraced the contemporary ethos and design culture of the 21st century, it has steadfastly stayed the same. This adds to its appeal in my eyes rather than detracts.

The Racerdogs are likely to be at Smallmead for a couple of seasons despite their avowed keenness to relocate to the oft-promised (by the club and council) state-of-the-art new stadium facility within the city limits. I'm not sure when I first heard such a move mooted, but it was definitely long enough ago for my hair to be without a hint of grey and my waistline to have remained effortlessly in check. In addition to the snail's pace attitude and approach of the council/club to the research and planning approval of this particular development, there are strong but complicated rumours that the conditions of the sale negotiated between BSI and Pat Bliss will most likely ensure that nothing happens on the actual relocation to a new stadium front until after December 2007. Exact details are obviously completely sketchy and lack any confirmation in the public domain – and hearsay is notoriously unreliable – but apparently until then, Pat will be contractually due a further payment in addition to the sale sum already paid by BSI. There is also rumour that until that date, John Postlethwaite can't (for reasons not specified and impossibly hard to fathom) get involved to help the council in their search. Whatever the rights and wrongs of these rumours, the Reading Speedway public are stuck with Smallmead for at least a few more seasons and, if these rumours are true, then commercial and common sense will dictate BSI seek deferment at least until then. Though based on past performance, the council will probably ensure the delays continue anyway. However, with a reputation for overcoming obstacles and with man of action JP breathing down their necks, you never know whether the responsiveness of the city council might suddenly markedly improve.

Other commitments meant that I missed the inaugural Elite League meeting at the track and, having missed this milestone, it's now already the start of April and I've yet to pay homage at the home of the Racerdogs. The visit of Ipswich was always one of the encounters I'd always relished when I first started to watch speedway here in the mid 70s but, given the Scottish football like frequency of encounters between Elite League speedway clubs, it no longer holds quite the same excitement. It will be the third fixture at the stadium after last week's meeting with Peterborough was rained off. As I wait patiently in the small queue of cars that try to enter the car park from the roundabout slip road, there's a strong sense of déjà vu all over again though the DDSS feeling is immediately lessened when I realise that this queue has actually been caused by the need to pay for use of the car park. Since I've arrived so early, I thought it was weird that I just couldn't sweep down the slope to have my pick of parking spaces on the potholed wasteland that we call the car park in these parts. I immediately mentally decide that the BSI is clearly to blame for the introduction of these charges and must be profiteering at the fan's expense. Afterwards I learn that this is not the case but, as first impressions count for so much, my aggrieved sense at paying a pound for the privilege of something that had previously been free is compounded by the notice that the attendant hands out that informs you that you 'leave your car here at entirely your own risk'. I'm sure that this was always the reality of the situation but this message needlessly adds insult to injury, no doubt brought about by the information obligations regularly necessitated almost everywhere as a consequence of our increasingly litigious society. I take the chance to debate these charges with the friendly man in charge of the money collection who informs me that payment now guarantees all patrons the additional luxurious service of "patrolling security guards", albeit that theft will be completely the car owners' responsibility. The very shape and lay out of the wasteland ensures that unless there's a good number of diligent security guards, then inevitably there will be many quiet spots where burglars could work undisturbed and rifle through the contents of the cars to their hearts' content. Not that it's likely to be quiet with the regular roar of speedway bikes throughout the evening. Unless these burglars are unlucky, anyone with the audacity to break into the cars is pretty safe in the knowledge that the concentration of the owners will be fully occupied with events on the track rather than unduly concerned about the contents of their cars in the car park. That said any petty criminal that specifically chooses the cars of the typical speedway audience to target is likely to end up regularly disappointed with their pickings. A much better choice would be the Reading Football Club crowd who also use this car park on match day (for £5!), particularly as their resurgence in the past few years has attracted the wealthy glory hunters with their smarter, much more *arriviste* cars drawn here by the chance to share the lustre of recent success. The speedway crowd is much truer to its make do and mend roots, judged by the age and type of car I've often seen here in the past. Still that was the Premier League and now things have gone ELITE!

As I'm so early that, in the manner of an estate agent, I decide to thoroughly explore the stadium and its infrastructure to try to identify the visible changes wrought by the arrival of the new BSI regime at Smallmead.[1] Already the promotion will have had the chance to overcome the teething problems that would inevitably beset any new venture let alone this speedway enterprise; though equally I'm sure that they will have retained the services of many of the long-time race-night volunteers and Reading loyalists at the club.   Last year any estate agents particulars would have said "in need of some modernisation – would suit a DIY enthusiast" and a brief glance at the fabric of the stadium indicates that the same would hold true under the new BSI regime but for the use of a few pots of paint to spruce the place up a bit. However, first impressions can be deceptive and I resolve to investigate as fully as possible. Just getting access is a bit of a palaver in itself since you've barely got a yard or so inside the stadium perimeter when I'm relieved of my entrance ticket by an officious man with a clipboard who brusquely informs me that he's "checking tickets." This was obvious enough, even to me, but he's completely unforthcoming as to the exact reasons for this bizarre behaviour. Maybe the club already can't quite believe the low level of gate receipts for the season so far and have decided to check on the honesty of its gate staff as a possible explanation for the large discrepancy between BSI expectations and reality? One explanation for local reticence to attend could be that prices have dramatically shot up from last year to £15 for adults. This is mitigated if you have children since

---

[1] Though if I were a Reading-based estate agent I would have been kept continuously and fully occupied for the last 20 years on the industrial area that surrounds Smallmead: in fact at everywhere but the stadium itself or its immediate environs. The construction of the Madejski Stadium is well documented and known nationally but right next door there is an example of the latest fashion in business design – the landscaped fenced/gated company headquarters. This one is known as 'Green Park' and it has all the usual accoutrements – ergonomically designed smoked glass eco-friendly building, newly planted trees and newly laid turf as well as wheel-clamping staff and security guards. They also have an entrance sign that almost doubles as a sculpture that is illuminated with bright green lights at night. The juxtaposition of modernity and decay in such close proximity exaggerates Smallmead's position as the poor relation of the area. The clashes are all around. On the other side of the stadium and highly visible from inside are some modernist-looking silver storage tanks used by Courage's brewery to produce industrial quantities of its almost pasteurised liquid that gives their 'beer' its distinctive taste. Even in the far distance there is the ultimate symbol of 21st century environmental responsibility: some large wind turbines. Clearly this is more of a gesture than an alternative power supply source as there is hardly a sufficient number of them – probably only enough to power the bright night-time lighting of a couple of nearby offices. Given their location adjacent to the M4 – in an area of the country known as the 'silicon corridor' because of the rapid rise of conveniently located industrial estates and business parks along the route – and the absence of frequent strong winds, this is at best only a faux concern or maybe even hypocrisy. Whatever the reality, Smallmead has remained an oasis of constancy, albeit of the careworn decline variety, in a rapidly changing light industrial landscape.

great play has been made of the fact that they are admitted free, though by 2007 commercial reality has dictated that they now be charged £5 to enter (except for 'special offers'). Whatever the explanation, it will probably take some time for the new Bulldogs' name and image to bite locally, though the incessant mention of the club on *BBC Radio Berkshire* in recent weeks, at almost noise pollution levels, must surely increase the consciousness that a new brush attempts to sweep clean at Smallmead.[2] After he'd taken my ticket – when I asked him about rain-off arrangements, he immediately confirmed that he wasn't actually a speedway fan, or interested in any form of customer service, by replying "it's not going to rain tonight" – he put a tick on his board and I wandered off to the track shop to buy a programme and survey all the new Bulldogs' merchandise on display.

[2] I can't recall the first time that I saw adverts for the Bulldogs during the commercial breaks between the live *Sky Sports* television coverage of speedway on a Monday night. I remember being initially astonished that I had just seen such a thing and briefly thought that I must have imagined it. Sure enough at the next break, there it was again. Looked at in purely marketing terms these adverts were obviously placed by a blind optimist who is unafraid to appeal to the already converted. I'd previously been informed by the experienced and long-time Reading Racers' Speedway promoter, Pat Bliss, that when the Racers rode in the Premier League she definitely felt that on some nights – when there was an attractive live fixture in the offing on telly (something of a rarity given the blanket coverage) or the threat of rain – then Smallmead definitely lost fans through the turnstiles. Even though the club had run on a Monday night for decades they still suffered in direct competition with the 'free' speedway on the telly. This structural problem hasn't changed and the offer of "the kids go free" type promotions hardly seem enticing enough to lure untold hordes to the track. Another thought soon followed. Even if BSI got a substantial discount from their friends at *Sky Sports* for these adverts, then clearly they must be extravagant enough to have money to burn or have researched some Berkshire/M4 based family demographic that I was completely unaware existed. There's also the issue of the insincerely hammy voiceovers done in a fake enthusiastic American accent that would be more suited to a post Christmas sale at somewhere like MFI and Courts or possibly for some inane apocalyptic encounter on the relentlessly hyped but touchingly ridiculous worldwide wrestling bouts. Whatever this style of voiceover is most suited to, it isn't speedway. Perhaps, this is what to break the mould à la John Postlethwaite means! However, these adverts were like a Sundance-commended or Oscar-winning film for Wim Wenders in comparison to the BSI adverts aired later to advertise the Cardiff round of the Grand Prix series. These unintendedly hilarious adverts ensured that John Postlethwaite wouldn't get invited to appear on *Extras* as even a comic genius like Ricky Gervais wouldn't be able to match the brilliance of the original unintended parody – featured Scott Nicholls, Matej Zagar, Antonio Lindback and Niels Kristian Iverson (I think) camping it up as hip-hopesque 'B' boys from the wrong side of the tracks in what I took to be the famous skateboard park under the A40 near Portobello Market. I imagine the intention was to appear "cool" and "with it" as well as, undoubtedly in capital letters, "DANGEROUS" in an attempt to appeal to that much sought after, but rarely found, demographic of the 'floating' (and flighty) young adult audience by transplanting these riders into a cool "hip-hop, urban rap environment". Every time Scotty or particularly Matty (in either beanie hats or caps dressed in their obligatory hoodies) gurned towards the camera and pulled expressions of faux rebellious intent they only managed to create an effect where they simultaneously looked awkward, nervous, camp and gauche while they appeared as wallies to the sophisticated audience they were intended to impress. It was so badly and woodenly acted that I half expected they were opening scenes from some far-fetched (or spoof) porn film. Giving the lie to the racial stereotype and in a sharp departure from the 'adopted' truism that is invariably inextricably linked to his name in any press coverage he receives, Antonio Lindback confirmed his Swedish background and defied his Brazilian roots by looking the most inept (quite an achievement given the stiff competition he faced for this accolade) of all the riders at adopting insouciant poses or moving gracefully. They say that John Postlethwaite pays such rigorous attention to detail and has such fastidiously comprehensive control of the BSI organisation that he personally vets and approves the many turgid manifestations of its external communications. Even if he's only intermittently informed, you have to imagine that his underlings can't just give free reign to their creative impulses without some sort of approval from the higher echelons of the company hierarchy. On this basis, you have to expect that JP had some part in the authorisation process for both of these adverts. Given the retro, hopelessly passé styling, voiceovers, content and themes – these just cry out "dad dancing" and strongly reek of the involvement of middle-aged WASP males in their formulation and attempt to be "with it" – somebody, somewhere hasn't availed themselves of a wide range of alternative opinions. Maybe this is what future speedway fans will demand, want and expect, but somehow I doubt it. That said, despite enough flesh and booty on display to make you think that the girls had escaped from the latest Mike Skinner video, the presentation of all the riders in this GP advert unexpectedly reaches out in a bold innovative way to a previously untapped potential future speedway audience – the untapped mountain of dosh, known as the 'pink pound', the discretionary spend controlled by the wealthy metropolitan gay demographic. It's a bold gesture and arguably the first genuinely path-breaking piece of marketing by the BSI in many years as these homo-erotic adverts couldn't help but communicate strongly to a new but unexpected demographic. After the initial shock of these astonishingly 'wooden' performances lessened with many frequent viewings (and sometimes were the only highlight of that week's *Sky Sports* televised meeting) but never quite ever deserted me. I subsequently learnt that the '29 Pieces of Gold' theme of this GP advert had been agreed between John Postlethwaite ("he encouraged us to keep it as edgy as we could") and the producer, Nik Merrutia. Laudably and unbelievably at the same time, they deliberately agreed that they would aim to "try something completely different" and "show the riders as young, fresh and urban, with their own street-cred and that would appeal to a slightly different audience as well as existing fans, a new generation if you like." If all hoodies looked like this then they'd always attract the hugs that David Cameron later advocated they should.

Like old Mother Hubbard's cupboard – and in a strange way the layout of the track shop is definitely modelled on this – the shelves of the shop were practically bare. Initially I imagined that the cartoon dog on Prozac that the Bulldogs logo features had seized the previous three weeks' crowds so massively that they'd completely emptied the shop of memorabilia. A cluster of air horns stood forlornly on the glass shelves beneath which was displayed the last three weeks' editions of the *Speedway Star* and Bulldogs' programmes from the last two meetings. There was absolutely zero merchandise on display nor were there a sign to explain when it would arrive. Though this bare shelf policy might be fashionable in the same way as houses no longer have carpets or lino but stripped floorboards, I somehow doubt it. Though then again you never know, with a company like BSI in charge who like to innovate, maybe a Chinese designer had also been expensively hired to improve the feng shui of the track shop by removing the clutter and providing a refreshingly merchandise-free shop! Some things stand the test of time and there were still familiar faces in the shop in the form of the club Press Officer, the diminutive, friendly and preternaturally cheerful Andy Povey, and his mum Win. In the close season, Andy's mood had been up and down like a prostitute's knickers, if his very public resignation on the Reading Speedway website was anything to judge things by. According to the comments in his statement, it was a decision he obviously agonised over for a considerable time before reluctantly concluding that he needed to sever his long-term ties with Smallmead. No sooner had he made up his mind than he exercised a privilege that the dead don't have and gleefully accepted a key position ("Press Officer/Website") within the new Bulldogs speedway organisation. It's a shrewd appointment by BSI as Andy is well liked, well connected, diligent and credible, plus he's Reading through and through so it was ultimately no great surprise that he couldn't drag himself away or bear to be departed from his duties. In fact, I was to see throughout the evening that many old faces remained in situ. In response to my "there's been a few changes then?" Andy deadpans, "just a few."

The most immediately visible of these is the new look programme produced by the *Speedway Star* team. If this doesn't win the 2006 award for the *Speedway Star's* programme of the year I'll eat my yet to be available or purchased Bulldogs cap. Since I have been unconsciously brainwashed – in true NLP fashion – by the creative analyses of club programmes over the years in the *Star*, I know that apparently I should check the page layout and indents but instead I immediately spot that this programme is four-colour throughout and printed on deluxe paper the like of which has never been seen before. It's a very visible sign of the Postlethwaite Corduroy Speedway Revolution made manifest. I am in wonderment – initially at the fact that I've just forked out £2.50 for a speedway programme![3] This is astonishing price inflation. Not that I knew that I needed this product innovation but the lustre and feel of the artefact does communicate that I have something high quality and precious in my hands. On closer inspection, though it's 32 pages long, 11 of these are adverts and the majority of those are very much from the corporate end of the speedway industry (*Sky Sports*, BSI-owned GP, *Speedway Star*) rather than from small businesses with local connections, like the Tadley-based Pet Supplies that had advertised for many years up until 2005. The space advertisement sales team in charge of drumming up custom for the programme have clearly still to find their collective feet as the centrefold race card only has one sponsored heat (number 13 "In memory of RAY CROSHAW lifelong fan") with the remainder of the race card space for hire occupied by repeats: the team Photo (4), website address (4) or the gawping dog logo (6). The lack of paid-for-adverts is further emphasized by the banner at the bottom of the page that reads, "Reading Bulldogs would like to thank all our sponsors for their involvement." Being positive, any prospective advertisers attracted by success on the track will have their choice of prime spaces on the race card. We'll never know what "lifelong fan" Ray would have made of the name change from the Racers to the Bulldogs, but from some of the familiar faces in the crowd that I've spotted already I imagine he'd have made the pragmatic decision to continue to worship at the Smallmead shrine. Those who purchase a programme on a weekly basis will get to read a number of attractively laid out and presented features. The "Promoter's Point of View" from Jim Lynch ("it's another stiff test that we face"); "From the Captain" by Greg Hancock ("we can be Bulldogs or underdogs…we have a young, exciting and ambitious line-up"); "our guest JOURNO" (this week Philip Rising, "what riders actually want and this should not be confused with dirt, is grip"); "Sam says" from "Sporting DIRECTOR Sam Ermolenko" ("it's a rewarding experience working with these

---

[3] In keeping with rumoured mad economics of this whole BSI Reading venture, it's soon claimed that these programmes cost more to actually produce than their cover price. I can't believe that this is the case. Though if regular Monday attendances at Smallmead are as much of a disappointment as John Postlethwaite publicly claimed they were, in the pages of the *Speedway Star* a couple of months later, then more likely than not, the total sales falls short of the print run number and thereby inflates the real unit cost per sale of these luxurious programmes. They are beautiful things and given the size and vibrancy of the speedway memorabilia market as well as the number of avid programme collectors there are around the country, it's a surprise to learn that Reading doesn't make them available for subsequent sale. I've heard many collectors and track shop owners complain that the excess stock is mostly just thrown in the bin?

guys") as well as a number of other features. These include three pages of 'analysis' on the opposition, "British Round Up", Rider Profile (this week Matty Zagar about whom we learn, among other things, has a love of fruit juice, his mum's cooking and has decided never to ride his bike again in his underwear), "Looking Back' (my favourite feature!) and Photo Zone. This double page spread uses the colour of the programme to its fullest effect and utilises images from the last meeting. This week that doyen of speedway photography, Mike Patrick, provides these images but usually the naturally charming Dave Valentine takes the photos for the club. He's hampered in this task though by the bizarre BSI mandate that the centre green has to be cleared of photographers after the fifth heat?! Though BSI do have some previous here since no photographers are allowed on the centre green at all in Grand Prix meetings. Quite what the basis is for this decision is unclear but only optimists or people unfamiliar with speedway would deny themselves the opportunity to capture two-thirds of the action and the excitement as the meeting builds towards its conclusion. Talk that Dave has to pay for the privilege of centre green access only adds insult to this barmy ruling. Despite my caveats and even if the articles are all masterfully written in prime "bland speak", this is a state-of-the-art speedway programme that sheer cost alone will probably prohibit any other British club to attempt to emulate or better. It's a real innovation and something that the BSI should be applauded for as they have "lifted the bar higher", albeit one that was unlikely to figure in the top 20 of any fans' list of future requirements for their club, let alone developing the sport in this country.

In my capacity as an honorary estate agent, the next stage of my examination and reconnaissance takes me up the slope to the back of what the programme describes as "a large bar area" and into the gents' loos. These are still as cramped as ever but they do now actually feature running hot water. There's even soap too (!) and the dryer works but then it always did in this toilet. Sadly though it's still positioned too close to the door to allow prolonged use without frequent close encounters with the wood of its surface and other loo users. There will be many more of these users now, since I've discovered that the first bend loos in the aged blue portacabin type building have finally been closed. This is understandable as they were seriously dilapidated but benefited from a roominess that the grandstand facility doesn't possess and, during the summer, the distinctive bouquet that prolonged heat inevitably creates. Still, it did boast running cold water and extremely pungent soaps, often apparently just used by someone with hands caked in axle grease, and occasional paper towels. If this is another manifestation of the recent corduroy revolution, then as a long-time fan of the club this toilet closure saddens me! It's probably fortunate for BSI Reading that the Bulldogs have so far failed to ignite desire for regular speedway in the burgeoning population of the Berkshire area since I'm sure health and safety, facilities/buildings regulations or some such modern hand-holding risk assessment criteria must surely require more gents' khazis are made available? There has been extensive work on other toilets in the stadium but the general public can't access these because they're in the riders' new changing room facility. The changes here would meet with the approval of the most hard-hearted or fastidiously clean rider and any telly makeover programme host, particularly as the area has been gutted and completely overhauled to bring it in line with the living standards of the 21st century. The differences with the facilities provided by the old regime are night and day. Now home and away personnel alike can luxuriate in these hot showers and change in white-tiled comfort. Sadly, over on our side of the fence, we still remain in the mid 1970s.

Back in the grandstand bar, it's still like being reunited with an old friend fallen on harder times as nothing has apparently changed but then I imagine that this area falls outside the responsibilities of BSI Reading. The décor remains pleasingly unkempt and tatty, the carpet careworn and stained, while the benches continue to provide a glorious view of the track through windows discoloured by the bright but fading sunlight. A casual peer through these shows a stadium that looks spick and span resplendent in fresh coats of paint though the overall fabric of the structure remains mostly the same. Indeed in a world increasingly built on surface appearance, for the first Sky TV transmission from Smallmead BSI had rather bizarrely covered the old unused back-straight stand with blue mesh net to try and blank it out and put green mesh netting on the worn muddy area of the centre green where the tractors turn around on the third turn to make the centre green in some way look complete. A walk outside on the tarmac by the start line and a glance over the fence reveals that during the close season there has been extensive work on the most important component of a speedway stadium – the track itself! The bump or ridge that caught out so many riders on the first bend has completely disappeared to be replaced by a smooth-looking surface contour instead. The shale appears luxuriant and reasonably plentiful, well prepared and lovingly cared for. This is a shocking departure from its more traditional recent slightly rutted appearance that supposedly previously counted as "home advantage." Also in place are the mandatory (cost: £20,000 plus) air fences required by all Elite League teams and a couple of tractors that appear brand new continue to work industriously on the track, even though it's not that long

Fresh paint but no repairs for the stadium wall. © Jeff Scott

The much-loved Bulldogs mascot. © Jeff Scott

Warm inside the grandstand bar. © Jeff Scott

until tapes up. There's an almost spotlessly clean small tractor as well as a big new red one that's presently gouging up impressive quantities of shale in a ten-yard stretch around the start line. So much shale is being aggressively ploughed into large piles by this tractor that you could be forgiven if you thought you'd stumbled upon potato planting season. Maybe this is all part of some elaborate psychology to put off the Ipswich opposition. Standing there gawping, I have a sense that something else is somehow wrong or different and it slowly dawns on me that I can clearly hear the music and announcements. In fact, the volume of these is almost deafening and the culprits – powerful black speakers allegedly borrowed from Terry Russell – are strategically positioned throughout the stadium on the tarpaulin covered dog track.[4] The brightly painted perimeter walls of the stadium are too much of an attraction for me not to also consider closely. Once you stand next to these walls you can see that no attempt at repair to the fabric has been attempted but, in true builder's bodge fashion, thick coats of fresh paint has been applied in an attempt to hide a multitude of evils. Even where some small sections of the prefabricated concrete slabs that form the walls have collapsed, they haven't been repaired or invested in for the future but cosmetically made to look appealing from a distance. Perhaps this is some sort of convoluted metaphor for the reality of the BSI vision for speedway in general and the Grand Prix? Lots of fanfare, bombast and surface glamour and glitz but a haphazard attitude to the long-term fundamentals that inevitably will have to be given attention if difficult future consequences are to be avoided. Not that at Smallmead, there is any real medium- or long-term benefit to be gained for BSI Reading by any serious financial investment in the stadium infrastructure, so a cosmetic surface make over to manage the already considerable decline remains the commercially and architecturally correct decision for them.

This pragmatism is also reflected in their approach to the long-derelict back-straight grandstand. No attempt has been made to regularly open this often-lamented facility to the public, but it has been beautified by a cover in military-style camouflage cladding, albeit in green rather than desert fatigues piebald. Excited talk on the Internet forums did have it that the BSI would have to open this stand to accommodate all the additional fans that they're claimed expertise would encourage to regularly flood through the turnstiles on a weekly basis. But, like much that claims to be authoritative on the forums, this was either wild optimism or misplaced gossip. What this covering does do is look good from a distance and – since the BSI organisation has real expertise in the sale of television rights, packaging and presentation – shows up incredibly well on television. Like the conduct of modern politics and debate so with speedway; if it looks good on the telly and sounds good on the telly

[4] At another meeting the extent of the demand for professionalism in the presentation of a night of speedway was thrown into sharp relief by an apology over the tannoy for those fans who couldn't hear the announcements, times and heat results due to a defective speaker! The apologies were given out so frequently and with such apparent sincerity that I thought it must be a joke or even, like the *Monty Python* sketch with the dirty fork, someone would have to take ultimate responsibility and do the decent thing. Part of the appeal of Smallmead over the years was the chance to strain, but often fail to hear, what was inaudibly being uttered over the tannoy system. This meant that you spoke to a lot more people in case they'd managed to make out what important information was being relayed, plus it had the happy benefit that it considerably increased your concentration levels at the finish of each race. Still it is progress.

then it must be true and becomes the objective reality. I can't help but admire them for this canny presentational awareness and shrewd use of materials.

In the pits there's yet more highly visible signs of the BSI reign since each home rider has a giant blown up photograph of himself as the backdrop to his own particular section of the pits. It has undoubted visual appeal and is distinctive as well as being a departure from the norm within speedway circles. Again this styling will look dramatic and impressive on television as, in fact, it does in real life. Not that I can any longer get a clear photograph of the activity in the pits when I overlook it through the mesh of the fence on the third bend as this aspect of the stadium furniture has been renewed with a fence that features a much finer mesh design. This is a development that will frustrate all amateur photographers among the fans at Reading, like myself, since we've grown used to better visibility of and from our heroes. I've no doubt that this is deliberate and is part of the creeping privatisation of spontaneous public access (and photographic opportunities) except for those carefully manufactured encounters during stage-managed events or 'greet-the-riders' type activities of the traditional parades and laps of honour on the team trailer. Far from being a hive of activity, the Reading side of the pits (the only one you can easily overlook) is filled with languorous riders and quietly efficient mechanics going about their work in a relaxed unhurried manner. John Postlethwaite, dressed in a geezerish yet stylish brown coat beloved of the executive classes when they try to obliquely make a fashion statement but still not stray too far from their humble origins, stands with two children close to the centre of the pits where he greets passers by with a jovial but proprietorial manner. Sadly I've missed the chance to see the ill-fated presentational innovation of the specially purchased Bulldogs team bike covers – to again ape F1 and present the team in a uniformly designed manner – that the riders discarded from their bikes before a race had even been run. Indeed, it was rumoured that BSI spent five figures to get a unique set of mouldings specially made to suit each rider's bike. They were soon discarded after the riders complained they were inflexible and prevented their legs and thighs from gripping into the normal free recesses around the engine and therefore gave them a very unfamiliar ride. Each rider does wear the distinctive team kevlars in the official Bulldogs colours of white, red and blue. Again Internet comment has it that this design did not comply with the BSPA regulations, since these require kevlars/race suit trousers are either completely black or predominantly black. I have no knowledge either way and talk that the Bulldogs have fallen or will fall foul of the authorities and have had to alter their design could be so much hot air or pettily accurate. It would have been sensible for the club management though to study the rules and regulations and thereby avoid snafus with dress codes and the rider averages that so caught them out with Danny Bird's initial inclusion in the team. It's hard to establish whether I'm looking at the original or redesigned team kevlars, nonetheless they're definitely easily spotted and distinctive. As my youth was filled with riders in a rich array of different styled and coloured leathers, I'm not at all comfortable with the will to standardisation that the introduction of team kevlars has thrust upon the sport's participants. As is the way with many recent developments at speedway, it looks good on the telly (and sometimes improves safety) but this comes at a price, which in my view is the loss of individuality and self-expression through each rider's choice of colour and style of clothing. Sure this still exists beyond the track but while everyone looks smarter there has been a loss in the spectacle of the thing. And after all if speedway is about anything then it's about spectacle. Why even the BSPA regulations ban the wearing of bandanas/trailing neckerchiefs (though no one has apparently had the audacity to tell Neil Collins) and the sight of cowboy-esque tassles hanging from the sleeves also seems to have died a death (though again Adam Skornicki and Dan Giffard appear to hoe their own rows here).

After all this estate agency stuff, it's a relief when it's time for the rider parade and introductions. I stand in my favourite spot of recent years – right by the starting gate as I look over the dog track to the speedway circuit. In the heyday of the 70s that has long gone from here and the rest of the sport – never to return despite the ambitions, marketing ideas and brio of *arrivistes* like John Postlethwaite – I would never have been able to stand here. The sheer volume of the crowd would have made this impossible with any level of comfort. Now that we're in the Racerdogs era I can regularly stand here easily in the comfort of a one-deep crowd. I also have my pick of the places throughout the open spaces of the rest of the stadium for this fixture against the Witches. Once this encounter was one of the real highlight of the Smallmead speedway calendar but tonight the only completely full vantage points are some small sections of the home-straight grandstand seating (though even here there's a spectacular amount of choice for stragglers) and inside the grandstand bar, the invariably completely full tables by the windows that run along the length of much of the home straight. From where I'm standing the track looks in pristine condition – the best I can ever recall except for my teenage years of the 70s which you can't always dissociate from your memory probably playing tricks – albeit with hardly any shale on its surface. The excavation of the starting gate has been completed and the shale restored to its uniform flatness so professionally that you wouldn't even guess at the extensive treatment it received unless you'd witnessed it take place.

The loud introductions of all the riders indicates that an expensively assembled 'superstar' home team has really finally arrived after many years of hurt for the supporters at Smallmead.[5] You can't deny that John Postlethwaite has sought to make a huge impression in his first year of promotion as an Elite League club for BSI Reading by investing in order to attempt to gain on track success. He's gone out of his way with expensive innovations in the backroom facilities and staff (Sam Ermolenko, Jim Lynch and Torben Olsen – all these people don't come cheap) as well as the litany of capable riders that now line up for Reading almost amaze – well they impress if they don't quite take the breath away. My immediate thought is "how is he going to pay for all this?" Even if spectator numbers double from what is here tonight, then this level of inflated cost isn't going to be easily covered in either the short, medium or long term. Longevity in speedway promotion depends on a huge number of factors from on track success to relationships with the local community (and local media) or landlords, and a common factor in recent years is that the man at the top has either come from a speedway background or has been steeped in the sport for years in a different capacity. While there have always been a number of new promotions and promoters that have talked the talk and arrived with the bang and glitz of a firework display they've often then not sustained their interest and commitment, petered out or, ultimately, walked the walk to go along with the talk. Other factors often intervene but nonetheless the sport in 2005 has lost clubs with rich traditions, like Hull and Wimbledon, in a fashion that still leaves many unanswered questions about the relationship between their respective landlords and managements. John Postlethwaite and BSI probably have the deep pockets and managerial skills to avoid any number of the snafus that have driven clubs out of business in the last decade but continued, unsustainable losses will ultimately undermine any business irrespective of their products.

Further signs of the changed regime now in operation at Smallmead is the announcements about the "post-meeting press conference" – choreographed by the always energetic front man Jim Lynch – in the bar afterwards and, most visibly of all, the fact that the club now has fully embraced the creeping chauvinism and sexist ethos of other motor sports by employing start-line girls. They're dressed in tight-fitting kevlars coloured to mirror the red, blue, yellow and green helmets worn by the riders. It's a cold night to stand out on the exposed track or sit on the centre green. Close by me, a couple of 10- or 11-year-old boys sum up the emasculated contemporary *Nuts* generation where caricatured images of women, sex and sexuality have seeped into every facet of their lives and coloured their emotional outlook. So much so that they can completely unselfconsciously shout obscenities and lewd suggestions to try to gain the attention of the girl in the green race suit ("the girl in green has the best tits"), albeit without a flicker of recognition from Tamzin all night. Possibly because of their age and the subtlety of their suggestions or perhaps the shrieky pitch of their voices doesn't register in the manner of dog whistles within the human range of audibility. As a team, the start-line girls haven't quite yet got used to the tempo and timings that intermittently alter the smooth rhythm of a speedway meeting. Even when the referee has allowed extra time between the races they still promptly line back up by their respective gates with their umbrellas and stand there expectantly to wait for the riders to fail to arrive. Though with experience and practice this will change as the season progresses.

When it comes to the races themselves, things have got so professional at Smallmead nowadays that the Racerdogs manage to win comfortably without looking really impressive on the one hand or under threat on the other. The ability not to pull so far ahead that the opposition can use the tactical ride and substitute facilities could be the essential black art of strategic speedway management. Though tonight, I suspect that it's just that many of the home riders only have to go through the motions fully confident that a victory will ultimately be easily assured. News that Chris Louis won't take to the track tonight and that the Witches will operate rider replacement in his place instead certainly immediately gives me that strong impression. In fact it's a script of inevitable defeat that Piotr Protasiewicz and, in particular, Mark Loram don't appear to have been informed of beforehand. The third heat has Protasiewicz race excitingly and aggressively shoulder to shoulder with local hero and birthday boy Zagar (at 23 probably still of an age in speedway where he can almost be described as

[5] Though personally I think the turn-of-the-century years of struggle endured by the Racers produced a far better spectacle and more entertainment on a regular basis through a combination of tighter, more compelling races and riders that appeared loyal to the team and part of the community rather than hired hands just here for the night.

youthful and still full of potential, though compared to some of his erstwhile GP rivals this is still perhaps on the cusp of a bit long in the tooth) before he eventually struggles past at the start of the fourth lap. The delay of their tussle is enough of a factor to ensure that Robert Miskowiak wins the heat to tie the scores at nine each. Zagar returns to normal service and easily wins heat 5 from a much more forlorn Protasiewicz by what the announcer notes is "the proverbial country mile." This establishes a lead that the Racerdogs never concede, though the gap between the two sides ebbs and flows at a level where the appearance that Ipswich remain in contention just about persists. The Witches reserve Daniel King doesn't shine like the Racerdogs Janusz Kolodziej, who rides exuberantly to a seven ride 15 (paid 17) points.

Something that hasn't changed – and even the marketing guru bods at BSI Reading can't legislate for or slant the reality of in their press releases – is the olfactory delight that is always any trip to Smallmead (or any speedway meeting). Since they stopped using Castrol R the smell from the bikes has changed its distinctive aroma but still remains fantastically sweet. However, this particular stadium is much better known among regular attendees for the pungent aromas from the sewage works or the Courage Brewery. At the height of the summer these bouquets can positively overpower and drown out the subtler notes of the bikes but tonight, by the start line, the pungent stink of drains pervades throughout. The BSI makeover, obviously, hasn't extended to the investment in a call to the Dyno-Rod people and this smell is enough to curl your hair though it's not quite enough to lessen the nearby mammary obsession of the pre-pubescent boys who hang expectantly off the wires of the fence. One of their fathers – an impressively short man with a moustache – is stood close by but he prefers to stand there impassively without comment or admonishment, though at least he doesn't join in!

Heat 11 is enlivened with a last-gasp third place on the line from the perennially wild Kim Jansson to snatch a point from the oblivious but coasting Charlie Gjedde. These are the kind of thoughtlessly lost points that are irrelevant tonight (though it does narrow the scores to a surprisingly close 34-32) but is an attitude of mind that will have to be vigilantly guarded against if the Racerdogs are to succeed against more dynamic opposition during the season. Before the meeting, promoter Jim Lynch presciently noted: "once the whole team are firing on all cylinders we will be a force to be reckoned with." A couple of 5-1s from the Hancock-Kolodziej combination (with the youngster the 'senior' partner in both races) in the last four heats massages the scoreline to a much more comfortable margin of 50-40 but indicates that the home team has yet to gel, fully find form and race as the finished article that all the expenditure by BSI Reading will ultimately require to justify them.

3rd April Reading v Ipswich (Elite League A) 50-40

A speedway-loving driver. © Jeff Scott

Queues gather at Arlington. © Jeff Scott

Tablets for the Heart
8th April

If there's one team that you definitely always look forward to visiting Arlington it's Wolverhampton. Not only because of the added piquancy of the presence of their ex-rider cum cartoon hate figure Nicki Pedersen – who always raises his already high level of performance for them – but because their team manager the shrewd Peter Adams ensures that no stone is ever left unturned when it comes to the pursuit of victory for his side. Whether it's rider motivation, tactical cunning and chutzpah or sheer effort of will you know that each encounter is not just another day at the office for him. He must look forward to the visits as well since it was only at the end of last season that the Eagles finally broke what had started to be quite a worrying home losing streak against their Wolverine competitors. The reputed general similarity of the Arlington and Monmore Green tracks adds to the closeness of each encounter and, though there are allegedly more 'glamorous' teams, it's a fixture I look for straightaway when the fixture list finally breaks free at a different time each year from the clutches at BSPA Towers.[1]

In his column in the programme, Jon Cook looks forward with relish to the "always close-fought encounters" with Wolverhampton but he mostly concentrates on other matters at the club. The most notable of these is the unveiling of "new sponsors' Meridian Marquees" who, as ever in the tight-knit world of speedway sponsorship, inevitably have fanatical fans in their midst with a prior sponsorship record of support in the same way the murderer always has a hidden link with the victim in television detective dramas. In this instance (among other members of his family) it's Dennis Isaac, a key player at the company who "in particular has been a keen follower of the club for years". However, the ongoing search for "advertising and sponsorship" is a never-ending quest for any speedway promotion and, at Arlington, the last wrinkle to be resolved is the continued campaign to promote the facilities of the "use of the hospitality box on the pits end of the main grandstand". Though apparently this has already received "bookings for company nights out

[1] You'd think that if the authorities were concerned, as is their stated aim, to increase speedway attendances that they'd publish these soon after the BSPA Annual meeting in November. While I'm sure they have many more important things to discuss – with vital leadership decisions to be made, particularly if these can cut costs on the sly but be presented and spun as revolutionary leaps forward, alongside endless tinkering with the regulations in true 'paint the Forth Bridge' style – the chance to agree the next season's fixtures isn't taken then. With everyone in one location and the next year's FIM schedules already set (never mind the fact that they race on a set night in Poland and Sweden that have both miraculously released their following season's fixtures before the end of the year), you'd have thought that some basic horse-trading at that juncture would sort out this essential information at the earliest opportunity. The fans could plan their trips ahead in the full knowledge that this is after all speedway and "the management reserves the right to make alterations without explanation or notice". More importantly, it might reduce the real or imagined 'fixture clashes' that bedevil the composition of British Speedway teams each season when their invariably 'foreign' riders go intermittently AWOL after they discover some 'prior', more important engagement. Though to look at it from a foreign prospective, where do the British speedway leagues get this presumption that they can ride on any night of the week, whilst Sweden and Poland generally plan and control their league fixtures to Tuesdays and Sundays? Then again, something so simple but essential as an agreed fixture list would be difficult to achieve and, probably, require prior agreement of the points limit that is apparently the centrepiece of each year's decision-making process and so hampers any discussions with riders to construct teams before the BSPA conference every season. But that's another aspect of forward planning and we find ourselves going round in circles to where this digression first started!

[2] Jon is quick to draw some conclusions with a hint of *schadenfreude* for the opposition as well. "It must have been a sobering ride home for the Peterborough promotion who have invested heavily in their team this season and their position as title favourites looks a little off the mark at present."

and birthday parties". In a wide-ranging column, there's also news of the new "bad weather days" phone number that is "NOT a premium rate number" as well as a review of the previous week's encounter with Peterborough. It was a meeting during which the Eagles played their 'get out of jail free' card to win by a point and that, without the usual speedway reflex to indulge in excessive and ecstatic hyperbolic descriptions of a dull but televised mundane Elite League encounter or a turgid GP series round, this was genuinely thrilling to watch. In the *Speedway Star* Jon lavished the praise round with phrases like "that is speedway at its most unimaginable best, you could not script it" and he recalls it as the "most dramatic meeting I can remember here" albeit with the double underlined caveat "we realise that our performance in the preceding 12 heats were not up to the standard expected."[2]

It's another lovely sunny evening that shows off the primroses on the verges in the country lanes that surround the stadium to great effect. The atmosphere is only slightly spoilt by the bitterly cold wind that whips across the car park where I bump into the much-travelled Eagles fan Sid Greatley. He grumbles that he's lost his licence for six months for speeding at 40 in a 30 mph zone in Buxton; an obstacle that will put a real kink in his summer speedway schedule "that's knackered me for this season!" Sid is another long-time Wimbledon fan with strong opinions about the recent ill-fated incarnation of the club in its guise as the country's only PLC at the Conference League level. It's also an outlook on events coloured by a personal dislike that he harbours for the PLC Chairman, Ian Perkin, after talk of his son Stuart possibly becoming involved at the club as an announcer came to nought, "Perkin used to do too many things there and not let others have a turn."

Inside the stadium with my usual crowd, the mood is downbeat and critical after Peter Karlsson recovers from a shockingly poor start to then easily pass David Norris on the last bend of the third lap. John Hazelden offers advice "you've got to shut the freaking door Norris, that's what you've got to do" whereas Dave Rice is more puzzled and philosophical after the race as he ponders the whys and wherefores of a race that the Eagles lost 2-4, "he never used to leave the door open like that?" John remains in a mode where his flabber is easily gasted and makes the Swede sound like he's involved in industrial espionage, "everyone knows Karlsson is an inside man – he must know that he's an inside man so why give him the chance!" The talk among their other halves preaches a gospel of slightly longer patience in order to give Floppy time to get into the groove of his season and finally put last year's stop-start protracted recovery from his head injuries behind him. Local gossip has it that Floppy has already been to see one of his sponsors to request further financial help with "his engines" so that also might indicate that he yet possesses remnants of last season's psychological outlook as he still physically sits astride last year's equipment. Whatever the reasons, he's clearly not quite back to the performance and psychological heights he achieved in 2004, so I'd imagine patience, nurture and support will probably be the best course.

The Eagles hit back in the next race to level the scores when the rider that Rye House and Peterborough announcer Craig Saul has nicknamed "The American Express", Brent Werner, wins – one of his two for the club in the three matches he rode before injuries he sustained quickly curtailed his outings for Eastbourne – while Lewis Bridger finishes third. Wolves have Christian Hefenbrock at reserve and although he has a surname that sounds redolent of a lager some multinational brewing giant invents the name of in order to try to foist their awful stuff on the British drinking public, he finishes second in a stylish manner that belies the fact it's the first time that he's ever rode at Arlington. The other Wolves reserve, the locally based guest Dan Giffard, also belies his extensive experience at the stadium when he finishes comprehensively at the rear of the field though this hardly surprises since he only ever really makes up the numbers at the Elite League level. This season he's made the step back up to the Premier League from Conference League Weymouth at another Chris van Straaten track, the newly opened Redcar. Yet another stage in his campaign to resurrect a speedway career hampered by the serious injuries he sustained after a crash at Loomer Road in Stoke. A drawn heat is then followed by the first appearance of Nicki Pedersen who races to a pro-forma and predictable win over Billy Hamill. Heat 6 stirs the interest of those around me sufficiently for John to shout words of encouragement to Andrew Moore, who temporarily rides the outside dirt line in a manner that befits Nicki Pedersen, during his chase to catch the fast gating Hamill: "if he's [Norris] not gonna do it, you do it, son!" A last ditch attempt to pass the American on the fourth bend narrowly fails at the stripe of the finish line and Kevin 'KC' Coombes sings his praises with the possibly fictional claim, "he loves that fourth corner." Albeit this is a love of the last corner that dare not speak its name because a litany of exciting races that involve Andrew in a starring role fails to strongly feature in the pantheon of memorable 2006 Arlington moments. We're then treated to one of those cameo interviews that is a vital part of the Coombes armoury – the brief rider interview between races. This is the ideal length of interview for Adam Shields who prefers to keep his thoughts to himself and only really talks on a need-

'Sports Argus' - on sale here. © Jeff Scott

Nicki reveals all. © Jeff Scott

The Board 51 posse – Judy receives her instructions.
© Jeff Scott

to-know basis in public. Nonetheless, we obliquely learn a lot about the mindset of a speedway rider in this particular interview when Adam gives the game away that the interest shown by the average speedway rider in the scores or match position (except for their own points performance since it directly relates to their pay) is practically nil. It's the diametric opposite of the fastidiousness placed on the scores, averages and obsessively filling out the race card that afflicts speedway fans everywhere. In response to KC's enthusiastic but supremely closed starter-for-ten question about last week's Peterborough meeting, "were you following the scores and knew how far we were down at point before the fight back?" after a brief pause we learn in drawling strine, "naahhh, I knew we were down though!"

There's acrobatics and pain for Brent Werner in heat 7 on the fourth bend when his chain snaps on the second lap of the race as he chases the diminutive Ronnie Correy. This unfortunately catapults him head over heels still in some close but painful form of unity with his machine. Inevitably with the bike in tow the severity of the incident is increased and Brent takes the full force of this fall on his neck. The sheer velocity of the incident takes the bike off on a wild trajectory before it flies to a final standstill over the safety fence. While others collect his bike, Brent sensibly withdraws and takes no further part in the meeting. In almost the same spot during the rerun, Freddie Lindgren has the temerity or foolhardiness, dependent on your point of view, to massively shove Nicki wide only for this not to really impede the speed of his progress round the outside line as he comfortably races away for an easy victory to retain the Eagles narrow two point lead at 22-20. The drama of flying equipment continues in the next race when Lewis comes to grief on the apex of the last bend, parts company from his machine and is thrown over the safety fence albeit without his bike in this instance. This happened only seconds after Andrew Moore has been excluded for a fall that resulted from a failed wall-of-death type manoeuvre round the air fence. The good fortune and resilience of the young is illustrated by the speed with which Lewis vaults rather gymnastically back over the air fence and proceeds to sprint down the pit lane in front of the appreciative main grandstand. This unexpected recovery and dash back catches Jon Cook in no man's land on the track itself where he had rushed out to inspect the damage and offer words of encouragement to his possibly injured rider. Rarely nonplussed or lost for words, Kevin 'KC' Coombes wittily awards Lewis "four faults!" By now Lewis has developed some kind of unconscious attraction for that section of the air fence as evidenced by his collision with it on the third lap of the rerun when he somehow manages to slap it with his back. Though he immediately remounts, the Wolverhampton pair have long since fled the scene.

This is the signal for our not-so-secret-weapon Bob Dugard to weave his magic on the track surface with a lengthy regrade of the surface. It's an activity that gives all visitors to the track the chance to ponder the exact meaning of the SCB regulation that the surface should be 100% consistent as they are often suspicious that certain riders (Martin Dugard, Nicki Pedersen) might receive favourable treatment to the extent their starting gate and dirt line requirements are 110% catered to. Not only does he indulge in an almost dizzying sequence of pirouettes on the tractor – with the grader attached – but he also carefully douses the surface with copious quantities of water. Like many times before, after Bob has given the circuit his attention it will ride completely differently and, hopefully, to the advantage of the Eagles. While these curatorial endeavours proceed in fascinating fashion, Kevin interviews Dan Giffard just prior to heat 9 when he completes his unwanted three ride maximum of successive last places. He's in confident form and has his career plan mapped out in his mind, "the Elite League isn't where I want to be right now, I want to earn a living in the Premier League first."

The next race after the regrade is a superb four-lap contest that could reasonably be dubbed 'the battle of the bionic OAPs' as it features an exciting duel between Deano and Billy Hamill. In age terms, they're both now in their mid-30s and at the far right side of the typical speedway age distribution bell curve. Based on this performance, they're both still some way from the career twilight that you could infer from their ages. Both have bravely fought back from severe career threatening injuries that would have terminated the livelihoods of lesser men and they're similar in that they still retain an enthusiasm for riding bikes without brakes professionally for a living. As an ex-World Champion Billy clearly scaled greater heights than Deano but time is a great leveller and we're treated to four laps of shoulder-to-shoulder combat of the highest order with no quarter asked or given. Deano even temporarily departs the security of the white line in order to battle for the second place that relegates Hamill to third. Adam Shields raced ahead oblivious to win and strung out at the rear is Daniel Giffard *en route* to another zero on the race card that Shieldsy isn't keeping. Very much a poor pay day but mitigated by the low transport costs he'll have since he lives in the general locale of Eastbourne at nearby Stone Cross. The close nature of the contest means that the most enthralling battles occur for the minor places and this continues when Correy and Moore have a ding-dong encounter over third place in heat 10. I have to say that Andrew looks supremely confident tonight out close to the fence on the dirt line and resists strenuous attempts to disconcert by close escort or feigned manoeuvres to pass. It's a useful point gained by the Lincoln-born Englishman as this drawn heat retains the Eagles slender two-point advantage, which the Eagles then retained when Nicki raced to his third win of the night by another country mile.

KC then briefly catches up with Martin Dugard and learns that Lewis has had his clutch adjusted by Nicki and Martin during the interval. This is high-quality help to have on hand but Martin is sympathetic about the challenges Lewis faces in the step up from Conference to Elite League racing, "this will be the biggest change of his career." His youth is an advantage but equally, "do any 16 year olds really listen? He accepts that everyone is trying to help him and his listening, whether or not that's working for him I can't say." In the next race, as if to confirm all that's just been said about his undoubted talent, this youthful protégé storms from the back past Correy and Hefenbrock with great style and holds second place for about half a lap before the experienced Correy then sneaks past. The Eagles lead is reduced back to two points when Hamill beats Pedersen and Floppy finishes last. Not that this bothers Kevin Coombes who's been so enthralled by the action on the track that he feels the need to over-explain his own metaphors, "if it carries on like this all season, we're going to have to issue everyone with tablets – for the heart to stop it beating!"

In the penultimate heat Lewis actually makes the start and leads to the first bend before Adam Shields and Freddie Lindgren overhaul him there. Though later he makes an early entry for the 'Most Spectacular Fall and Throw of Your Bike' award when his celebratory wheelie dismounts him and Start Marshal Alan Rolfe has to step aside smartish to avoid an unpleasant encounter with the runaway machine. Billy Hamill repeats this particular medicine for Nicki in heat 15 to demonstrate that not only was it no fluke but that this late career but injury-free version of the ex-World Champion is still a force to be reckoned with on the track, both home and away. Eastbourne have again beaten Wolverhampton at home, albeit narrowly, and hopefully they've put that jinx behind them and started to gain the confidence that will take them on a run that will see them into the Elite League play-offs.

Afterwards I catch up with Jon Cook for a few words. He's tired of the carping about the slow start to the season, "I can't be bothered to reply to the garbage on the Internet" and prefers to look towards a positive future, "Lewis Bridger will be

[3] His significant improvement and the increased confidence Dan found during the 2006 season in the Premier League at Redcar was reflected in his dominance on the track as well as his rise to popularity among the Bears faithful who, ultimately, voted him Supporters 'Rider of the Year'. Every time I saw him ride, he looked a transformed rider from the one that already performed well in the Conference League for Weymouth.

Anorak weather. © Jeff Scott

The steeds await their masters. © Jeff Scott

a star of the future – he's got the team behind him and a team in place – these are the things I look at."

8th April Eastbourne v Wolverhampton (Elite League A) 46-44

Bank Holiday Double Header
14th April 2006

The Good Friday double-header clash between South Coast rivals Eastbourne Eagles and the Poole Pirates is the ideal way to start the Easter holiday weekend. The pre-race favourites for the bonus point, if not all five points, would have to be the Poole team as they have started the season with much greater flair than the Eagles. The decision by the Eagles to run in the 2006 season with 16-year-old Lewis Bridger as he steps up from Conference League racing to that of the Elite League reserve is one part of a carefully formulated plan engineered by Jon Cook. For the plan to work, the more experienced members of the team have at least to consistently perform to their usual standards for the theoretical expectation of the on-track success for the Eagles to be fulfilled. There's often a gap between plans carefully drawn up round a well-crafted theory and the reality of those tactical plans once they've been put into practice. So it's proved so far this season. A conspicuous lack of race wins has hampered the Eagles results and a plague of inconsistency that finds the team stuck in a "morass." Jon Cook unflinchingly identifies the problem to the *Speedway Star*, "we are not racing with anything more than one true heat leader. Adam is on the edge of consistency [and] it is taking David Norris a while to get back and obviously there is a bit of pressure because we are not winning races." Though Dean Barker emerged with some credit in last week's encounter against Wolverhampton, "we need to realise that the season has now started. A couple of lacklustre performances can be expected but by the time Poole come to town we need to be on the pace. There can be no excuses and we need to be a proper unit."

The perils of Bank Holiday traffic on the way to Wimborne Road has caught me out on a number of different occasions so I set off early for this eagerly anticipated (in this part of the world) Elite League A that is optimistically programmed to have an 11 a.m. start. Though the gates are due to open at 9.30 a.m., I'm so early that I have a car park full of empty parking spaces to choose from and face a lengthy wait before I can even gain access to the stadium. It gives me the chance to contemplate the dark but not yet black clouds in the sky over the stadium that the forecasters claim may contain a threat of showers. Minutes later a MG estate car coloured in that contemporary shade of metallic blue draws up alongside and parks so close to my car that it distracts me from my paper to scowl at this errant driver. It's Jon Cook who, like me, with years of experience behind him here has deliberately chosen a spot as close as possible to the exit to allow a quick getaway and avoid the traditional queues of traffic alongside the fire station that speedway meetings invariably create immediately after the meeting has concluded. In person, Jon comes across as slightly more optimistic about prospects than the downbeat assessment that had been reported in the trade press, "it's damage limitation at the moment, we're really not quite on the pace at the moment so I'd definitely settle for the win at ours and the bonus point!" Our talk moves onto the draft chapters for my book *Showered in Shale* that feature Eastbourne that I've passed to him for his comment, corrections, amendments or deletions. "I've read 'em and there's some things in there that I disagree with but it's your book and the way that you saw things so there's no point in making changes just 'cause I don't like something as it would just spoil the flow of the thing for little reason. Though I would get some of your facts right as these are the types of thing that people will definitely pick up on when they read it." He then proceeds to gently correct ("I think you'll find...") a number of elementary errors that includes transposing Eastbourne staff members with famous boxers of a similar name as well as a number of other avoidable mistakes like my claim that David Norris has also ridden for Oxford when in reality it was Reading. It's all helpful advice that's kindly given without qualm or resentment even though his duties dictate that Jon should really already have headed off to the pits to marshal the riders and mechanics for the morning's racing ahead. For Jon, one draft chapter stands out amongst all the others he's received from me, "the best chapter I've read so far is the Wolves one!"[1] When I tell Jon that through friends I have luckily but anonymously received some unpublished photos of the Wolves fight debacle that I couldn't capture myself (my camera battery had suddenly died on me) even though frustratingly the fight had taken place right next to me. He scowls and observes, "I hope that they're more accurate than some as it was amazing the photos that suddenly appeared on the Internet and only really showed one side of what happened that night."

Inside the stadium, I'm one of the first people to arrive in this part of Wimborne Road via the turnstiles located in the rather deluxe and plush-looking main grandstand, very much in time for an encounter that co-promoters Mike and Matt, in true 'Smashy & Nicey' fashion, term 'the first part of our Easter Egg-Stravaganza." Though it overlooks the back straight this building more than any other within British speedway arguably sets the standard for facilities to which other clubs could/might aspire. There are various areas for entertainment from the lavish facilities expected by corporate sponsors based upstairs in this building to a well-stocked Pirates Bar and refreshment area downstairs for those who wish to eat and drink on the hoof. There's also another bar in the vicinity that is located by a large area frequently used for post-meeting discos they hold at the club but that's presently completely deserted. In fact almost the whole grandstand is empty and it offers a wealth of excellent viewing positions from which to watch the action on the track soon to be occupied by the throng of fans that you'd expect to turn up for any such a derby fixture. Upstairs this is even more impressive though, I believe, some kind of membership scheme applies to those permitted to use these areas. The magnitude of the stadium and the size of the crowd that they regularly attract here means that it's one of the few stadiums in the country that allows you to enter by a completely different set of turnstiles at the opposite side of the track. On match day, this entrance often has the biggest queue since it provides easy access to my favoured grandstand within the ground, namely the much more traditional (but still impressive) home straight one that houses the covered seated terraces overlooking the start line. Though it's still not 10 a.m. the prime positions that aren't reserved for season ticket holders have already started to fill with well-prepared people who've brought along blankets, sandwiches and thermos flasks for the cool and lengthy wait they have until the entertainment commences.

With much time to wile away, this week's match programme makes interesting reading, particularly the 'Bare Bones' column written by Poole co-promoter Matt Ford in which he launches an appeal "to every fan in blue and white" to help identify " a couple of alcohol-induced Pirates fans" who attended the recent away fixture at Swindon as "I desperately want to talk to those responsible." Like Matt I'm confident that the close-knit speedway family will be keen to isolate those responsible who made "abusive and distasteful remarks" towards one of their own team riders, Antonio Lindback. He is "such a wonderful human being, an adorable kid who, like you and me, wants to be loved by everyone. Bear in mind the incredibly difficult start Antonio had to his life, abandoned as a baby in Brazil, welcomed into the bosom of a wonderful Swedish couple who have subsequently released their boy into our responsibility in Britain." As Matt has "always believed speedway is different" he proposes to make the punishment fit the crime and will eschew lifetime bans in favour of a face-to-face

---

[1] Though at this point I had yet to finish the *Bonanza* piece which he subsequently identified "as far and away the most enjoyable of the ones I read as it had something new to say and gave people an insight into something that they might not have known anything about before!"

Choice of photos at Wimborne Road. © Jeff Scott

Neil Middleditch plans aheadl. © Jeff Scott

David Norris starts to warm his bike up. © Jeff Scott

meeting for these shameful people with the rider they abused, Antonio himself. You have to admire Matt for his awareness of his responsibilities to the club, his family, the sport and his employees as well as for his forthright stance on racism. His decision to stand up is unusual in a sport where promoters and the governing body of the sport often prefer to take the easy path, and so to speak sweep the sport's potentially dirty washing under its proverbial but rather substantial carpet.

Inside the plush grandstand, I have to introduce myself to Jane Wooler, the Eastbourne Eagles club physiotherapist, who completely fails to recognise me when I say "hello" even though I'm stood almost right by her. She looks blankly at me before the penny finally drops, "oh, Jeff, I didn't recognise you without your glasses on" which is a bit of a shock to me as I still always perceive myself as only an occasional glasses wearer with a pair handy to be put on at those key moments when I'd like to see "something important." Like speedway racing, football matches, cinema screens, other road users when driving, people a few feet away and the like. So only really those rare instances when vision can enhance your enjoyment or awareness of a situation. She's stood with an attractive younger woman who she introduces as "Charlotte – she's Deano's girlfriend" before she introduces me as "Jeff, he's writing a book on speedway – is it published yet?" This perception that I'm an author results in exactly this sort of question and is one that has increasingly plagued me since the season began. Social pressure and the possible embarrassment of not actually completing/publishing the damned book is the only thing to have kept me going through the long winter months of endless revisions and rewrites of basically the same 40 odd meetings I selected from the many more that I researched and attended in 2005. Not that the lot of an "Official Speedway Club Physiotherapist" is necessarily any easier as the BSPA and the majority of the speedway tracks within the country refuse to recognise that such a position does exist, should exist or that there is an ongoing need for it when the majority of riders that you will watch at any meeting throughout the season will invariably be in recovery from some form of injury or another. Since she failed to persuade the BSPA of the necessity and *bona fides* of her own employment situation with the club, Jane is reduced to gaining entry by other slightly less effective means since, "I'm not recognised by the other tracks so I have to come in as Jon's guest everywhere we ride even though I'll get to treat all the Eagles riders at some point during the season." Her husband Ashley is also here but he's already in the pits since he's the mechanic for Eagles rider Andrew Moore who this season has started the year in the main body of the team (in the notorious and "difficult number two position") rather than at reserve. Consequently, Andrew rides in the first heat of every meeting and finds himself alongside the Eagles number one rider, David Norris, and also is also pitted against the opposition's number one rider. In Poole's case this is the gifted Danish rider Bjarne Pedersen of whom the Pirates think highly enough of to have taken the precautionary and less usual step to tie him to the club for the near future with a two-year contract that covers the 2006 and 2007 seasons. It's a decision they've taken despite the fact that Bjarne has only ever managed two full maximums in his 144 outings during his club career at Poole. While Charlotte and Jane continue off to the ladies, I bustle out to stand by the fence that overlooks the Poole side of the pits area. Most of the home riders already appear to have arrived at the Wimborne Road stadium though the majority of them have yet to change into their smart Pirates kevlars with the distinctive skull-and-crossbones club logo. Some of the start-line girls have already changed into their rather tight-fitting gear and I can't help but notice that their uniforms have been redesigned to eliminate the crop tops that they wore very noticeably last year. This year's style is an all-in-one look featuring a predominantly white top with blue and black markings and trousers that are mostly black but patterned in white from the calf downwards to create the effect that the girls wear cowboy boots. Needless to say, they're still tight fitting and wouldn't be able to be worn by anyone with a poor impression of their own body image or an accurate impression of their actual physiognomy. Though this comprehensive redesign suggests otherwise, I decide that maybe the design used last season hasn't been eliminated for the whole season but just for the colder months of the early season where this sort of exceptionally skimpy attire wouldn't be so advisable. That said another of the start-line girls arrives in her civilian clothes and features what I can only describe as an unfeasibly small miniskirt that shows off her attractive but white fleshy legs to their fullest potential. In contrast her sunglasses are unnecessary large given the lack of sunshine, thick cloud cover and the later forecast of showers but they're also sized in inverse proportion to the microscopic amounts of cloth expended in the manufacture of her skirt. Consequently each lens looks almost the size of the screen you'd have had on the portable telly in your student bedroom. It's an effect that, to my mind, makes the wearer look like a cross between a demented insect with 360-degree vision and Paris Hilton (though if this were the case then there would be no need for knickers underneath the mini-skirt).

To get a view of the activity on the Eastbourne side of the pits I have to move round to the pits gate entrance that the riders use when they unload their bikes from their vans. Through the mesh of the fencing, the rider closest to me is David Norris who's still dressed in his civvies but works feverishly on his bike oblivious to those around him inside the perimeter of the pits fence or outside. He's successively interrupted for a few moments by various other members of the Eagles crew in the form of Lewis Bridger's Granddad and, later Deano in a red tracksuit top. Invariably they share some smiles and banter that is inaudible even though they're only a few yards away, before Floppy again resumes his work and involves some deft kicks that he frequently administers to his machine. Something that is clearly audible is the loud conversation of the two teenage girls next to me that are pressed against the fence and rarely take their eyes off the object of their lustful attentions, the Eagles young protégé Lewis Bridger, once they've finally located his exact whereabouts in this thronged side of the pits.
"Where's Lewis?"
"There!"
"Where?"
"There!"
"Oh, I didn't recognise him with different jeans on."
"Maybe he'll change into two different pairs of trainers like usual?"
"Maybe"
"What's he doin'?"
"Dunno, somethin' with the bike."
"I like his hair like that."
"I liked it the other way too, do you reckon it's different gel?"
"Dunno."
The conversation quickly moves on to a graphical description of the activities they have envisaged should they get the chance for a bit of uninterrupted personal time with him on their own in the future. It's hard to tell what exact age these girls are but based on the rule of thumb that they'll be almost certainly younger than they look, I'd place them as extremely knowledgeable but well below the age of consent. I leave them to it as I gather they're going to keep him in sight for as long as possible this morning though they later hope to persuade their dads to make the trip over to Arlington later on so they can again resume their studies in East Sussex.

I make my way back to the home-straight grandstand and stake my claim to a place reasonably high up and just in front of the start line with a slightly obscured view towards the first bend. Gradually the mechanics or helpers wheel the bikes over to the start line where they're lined up to wait for the rider parade and introductions. The flat-bed lorry with the seats

Another day, another parade lorry. © Jeff Scott

Everyone awaits the end of the rider parade. © Jeff Scott

The view towards the third bend. © Jeff Scott

grumbles into life and putters round to the pits where it's loaded up with the riders and the start-line girls attired in this season's kevlar design supplemented with brollies and jackets as a concession to the still cool morning. I believe that Eastbourne was the first club to launch the concept of an away kit in speedway. This tactic works well in football when it comes to the sale of yet more replica shirts with only marginal/cosmetic changes to the loyal fans but I have my doubts as to whether in speedway the idea that you purchase your team's replica shirt to show your allegiance works that well for the fans (who prefer anoraks) even for the regular uniform let alone the away one. Then again, I'm biased as although there's nothing especially objectionable about the predominantly red colour of the Eagles away shirts they don't please the eye as much as the traditional garb and it seems somehow wrong that there's any need for further differentiation between the teams when the helmet colours already very successfully serve that function. The master of ceremonies Clive Fisher introduces the riders to the by now quite swollen crowd that's stood mostly two deep around the bends and has pretty well filled the grandstand I'm sat in. As is the norm at practically every British track he appears at, Nicki Pedersen is roundly booed although he merely responds with a smile and flourishes a polite wave. Also on the parade is the Pirates mascot, 14-year-old Brendan Johnson, who's announced to the crowd as the team's number eight. After the riders have further warmed their bikes with a few practice laps, the announcer then warns us "the good news is there's a five minute delay to allow the people to get in from the car park." This proves to be a hopeless underestimate of the anticipated delay and when the racing finally gets underway, the additional wait appears to have suited Andrew Moore much more than Craig Boyce who he overtakes with a great manoeuvre on the back straight of the last lap to ensure a drawn heat. What's much more noticeable is the amount of dust that has been thrown up and drifts in a light film under the roof of my grandstand. A further delay is immediately announced (you can tell *Sky* aren't here!), this time since it's "dusty" this will be for "a couple of laps of grading." This and later efforts at some TLC for the track fails to quell the thin eddies of dust that coat all in its path for the remainder of this fixture.

Upon resumption, in the reserves race Lewis Bridger gates superbly to lead for around a lap and a half before Joonas Davidsson finds additional drive to exhilaratingly power past Andrew Appleton and Lewis to win the race easily. Never shy in this part of the stadium to over-celebrate the successes of their own riders, the Pirates fans loudly salute the apparent brilliance of the pass we've just seen. Davidsson conducts a lap of celebration wheelies and is bizarrely joined by Lewis who still likes to take every opportunity to show off to the crowd with a few wheelies of his own, despite the fact that he only finished second. After their earlier threat to put on a combative display and to possibly win a race or gain a heat advantage, the Eagles do both in heat 3 when the locally based Adam Shields wins and thereby Antonio Lindback finds himself sandwiched (rather than loved) between the Aussie and Deano in third place. The early 8-10 lead temporarily mutes the home crowd around me and provokes a few lone cheers from the small contingent of the

Eagles faithful on the fourth bend who've crowded there after the journey over to Dorset.

However, the announcer has his mind on other things: "if you fancy something a bit more refined go to the restaurant for 'brunch' – it's a sort of breakfast and lunch combined." (Perhaps to encourage us all further, the announcer could have added that unlike my sandwiches, any meal served safely inside the back-straight grandstand building wouldn't run the risk of contamination with the bonus additive of shale dust.) This word for me still sounds incongruously exotic and conjures the idea of an unusual combination and something slightly American. And I've got to say that this talk of "brunch" sounds quite an appealing prospect before a more thorough description by the announcer about the fare on offer ("there's gammon with all the trimmings") dampens my appetite with the detail and mental image it conjures up. In fact the food on offer was symptomatic of the Eagles performance throughout the morning, since it sounds good and promises much but when you look at it in the cold light of day, it is a pedestrian predictable repast with nothing to distinguish it from the ordinary and is, in fact, the same old boringly dull stuff dressed up with a different name. Perhaps I'm being harsh, and despite some exciting races, maybe it is a lacklustre Eagles performance that is all down to the assertion by the Pirates and their home track advantage in a display of some considerable mastery over their opponents, though it certainly doesn't look or feel like that. With a win for Krzysztof Kasprzak over Nicki Pedersen in the next race that is so comprehensively easy he has time to pull a celebratory wheelie from the apex of the last bend to the finish line, things didn't bode well for the visitors though the scores are now actually still tied at 12 each.

This lasts as long as it takes the next heat to run before heat six sees Craig Boyce lead from the tapes before he kindly conducts his own tactical masterclass when he shrewdly blocked Nicki so effectively by the fence that he has to quickly shut off and thereby allow his namesake Bjarne roar past for a comfortable lead he then conspicuously fails to relinquish. Job done, Boyce is happy to chug along for a third place ahead of an apparently out-of-touch Andrew Appleton. Heat 7 is the last high point of the Eagles visit when Adam Shields leads from the gate in the company of Deano who then finds himself passed by KK on the back straight of lap two as though he is stood still, though he still manages to hold on from reserve Joonas Davidsson to claim third place and narrow the overall score to 23-19. With brother Daniel also in action, there are enough Davidsson's on show for it to seem as though there's going to be one of them in every race we get to watch. A third place for Lewis in heat 8 prompts him to conduct some solo celebration wheelies as the predictability of the win in his eyes has Craig Boyce fail to indulge the three-deep round-the-bends crowd with any visible signs of his delight. Even the regular clouds of dust can't disguise that there is only ever going to be one team in charge of this fixture.

The tedium of a long interval is relieved by a collection organised by Rob Doran for Antonin Svab for injuries he sustained in Argentina that's gladly carried out by the riders of both teams. It reminds me once again that this proximity to the stars of the shale remain one of the enduring appeals of the broad church that is the sport of speedway. With scores after heat 12 apparently done and dusted (no pun intended) at 41-31, Jon Cook finally unleashes the not-so-secret-weapon that is the sight of Nicki Pedersen in a black-and-white helmet colour on a tactical ride. Rather like the time that Manchester United changed out of their new grey away kit at Southampton – never to wear it again after Alex Ferguson, with straight face, cited the acclimatisation difficulties this unusual colour provoked among his outclassed players as a spurious justification for the inept scoreline – so it is with the Eagles this afternoon. When both Pedersen (N.) and Norris (D.) discard their red away kit and instead appear at the line dressed in the traditional yellow and blue Eastbourne race tops. For a lap or so, Jon Cook appeared to have pulled off a tactical and motivational masterstroke since Pedersen leads from the gate and Floppy occupies a scoring position until the second bend when Pedersen (B.) and Krzysztof Kasprzak easily round him. The Pirates pair then set off in hot pursuit of Pedersen (N.) and both proceed to completely boss the Dane aside with some ease that features passes on the third bend by Pedersen and during the next corner by KK. The report by local reporter Phil Chard in the *Speedway Star* the week afterwards claims that this race "was a real thriller, probably the best race at Poole for several years." While it was a good advert for the sport, this claim either smacks of celebratory hyperbole or, though this has not been my personal experience, provides worrying illustration for the promotional team of Matt and Mike that the overall regular standard of the races at Wimborne Road leaves something to be desired, if this is viewed as some kind of recent pinnacle of achievement by their expert local reporter who's very familiar with all that goes on at this track.

With an initial Eagles 7-2 becoming 6-3 before it transmogrifies into the ultimate considerable displeasure of a 5-1 for the Pirates, all that's left for the Eagles riders to race for is pride and a reduced scoreline in this fixture to provide some sort of hope for the return fixture later. To this end, Adam Shields is thrown the black-and-white helmet in the next race in the hope that the form he's shown to drop only one point in his initial three rides will continue. Sadly it doesn't and the combination of Davidsson (J.) and Lindback (A.) race away to a 5-1 scoreline that completely nullifies the benefit of this tactical ride. For once, even Lewis Bridger decides not to conduct any celebratory laps after his last place in this race. Jon Cook still has enough confidence in his combative Aussie (or perhaps a lack of it in his other riders) to name him to ride with Nicki P in the final nominated race. The thought that the win for Nicki in this race dents Bjarne's maximum hopes for this fixture is scant consolation as is the scoreline that reads 54-36 in favour of the Pirates.

Since the majority of the bank holiday traffic heads to all points west and in the direction of the seaside towns of Dorset rather than out of the county, the journey away from Wimborne Road is only temporarily brightened by my schadenfreudic reaction to the sight of an approximately five-mile solid traffic jam that starts well before the M3/M27 intersection and continues unabated westward. When I journey towards Arlington a hour or so later after a brief stop off for refreshment at my home in Brighton, the stunning beauty that is the panoramic view of the landscape and rolling hills as you breast the upwards slopes of the Downs on the A27 whenever you drive past Lewes is interrupted by a huge cloud of sea fog that appears to be roll quickly in from the nearby coast. Maybe the meeting will be curtailed by fog? But then given the undulating contours of this particular part of East Sussex, the area around the Arlington track is subject to a completely different micro climate and weather system from that in the next village never mind miles back down the road around Lewes.

Jon Cook's programme notes introduces Andrew Appleton as "another British rider, our fifth, are you reading PC?, and one who started his career on our junior track to boot." The Eastbourne team under Jon's tutelage should be lauded as a club that bucks the trend of the dominant philosophy employed by almost every other club in the Elite League, namely change your riders as often as you discard socks and always try to employ foreign riders. The Eagles take the opposite approach and have had the same nucleus of regular riders for quite a few seasons now – this is seen as a fault and severe limitation in some quarters of East Sussex, particularly if you acknowledge the lack of trophies won – and are a club renowned for their employment of British riders. Apart from Appleton in tonight's line up, we have Norris, Moore, Barker and Bridger. None of them high in the firmament of all-time speedway superstars but three of them are locally based and often really excel for the club. Another charm of speedway is that if you're feeling aggrieved about someone or something you just right out and say it. Or write it down in this instance, as Jon clearly has some animus with "PC" aka Peter Collins, the opinionated ex-British World Champion and self-confessed patriot. However, if you'd just arrived from Planet Zog you'd have had absolutely no idea whatsoever about what this reference to "PC" meant – political correctness (unlikely at speedway)? personal computer? (again unlikely) – and along with the arcane complex rules, the mysterious but often internecine disputes and the special codified language of speedway used by speedway people are perhaps some of the factors that keeps the sport from ever branching out to a much wider demographic to attract a bigger contemporary audience.[1]

With an 18-point deficit to overcome, the Eagles are going to have to emerge from staggering around in fog of their own creation and adopt a hit them hard and hit them early approach if they are to stand any chance of winning the aggregate bonus point. The usual crowd I stand with at Arlington aren't optimistic but perhaps this will be the meeting when the Eastbourne riders rediscover their collective heat-winning ways. If judged by the first three heats, the pages of this particular script have got lost in translation somewhere along the way as the Pirates provide all the race winners and thereby lead by a score of 7-11, which is a good sign in a convenience store but pretty useless at a speedway meeting. Of even more concern is the fact that there have been absolutely no overtakes of any description, though this isn't for lack of effort put in by Adam Shields who pushes and harries Grzegorz Walasek for three laps without quite ever finding a route past him. Even the Pirates Daniel Davidsson has thrown off the torpor he'd laboured under all meeting at Wimborne Road to record a race win; though this turns out to be a premature dawn as afterwards he trundles round as the model of consistency in

---

[1] Once you have the world according to "PC" in your mind, it must be hard for Jon to rid himself mentally of his cloying strictures as mention of him surfaces again in the end-of-season Eastbourne review in the *Speedway Star.* "I remember there being a piece very early into the year from Peter Collins suggesting we had only put him [Lewis Bridger] in to fit an average and would be throwing him out. I don't think Peter Collins has ever apologised and it shows his total lack of knowledge of our commitment to the rider."

last place in the remainder of his races. A problem at reserve is to be a recurrent theme throughout the season for the Pirates and proves, along with other factors, fatal to their chances of success in the Elite League.

We finally get to see our first pass of the night when Lewis Bridger blasts round Davidsson (D.) on the home straight during the second lap to race away for a well-earned third place and, with Nicki way ahead at the front, the Eagles finally notch up a heat advantage though this provokes little reaction in the crowd but does generate a series of ecstatic wheelies from Lewis. The thrill of the overtake overwhelms Kevin 'KC' Coombes to the extent that his hyperbole chip kicks in and he describes it as a "brilliant pass" since he apparently forgets for a moment that it was the lesser Davidsson brother whom Lewis has just vanquished. But the way things are presently, we have to take our kicks where we can. And these kicks do very much involve Lewis who has started to get onto the Elite League pace more and more as each meeting passes and often it's only elementary errors or just plain trying too hard that costs him the points. Judged by the scorecard, he's still not an overnight success at this level but given his age and inexperience, many among the Eastbourne faithful would be quick to tell you that his points totals haven't truly reflected the effort, entertainment value or application he puts in. Plus he still never knows when he's beaten nor has he yet learnt to throttle off or not to attempt blasts round the outside at every single opportunity. High hopes are definitely held and as the season progresses his regular partnerships with Deano or Nicki should pay dividends and hasten his rise along his own personal learning curve.

As is often the way, one heat advantage follows another, though in this instance this is helped in no small measure by one of the smallest parts on the track, namely Craig Boyce, who kindly manages to fall and earn himself an exclusion. In the rerun, even when in shocking form (which he isn't tonight) Deano can invariably manage a third place in a three-rider race and so it proves while Shieldsy bests Pedersen (B.) with aplomb. With scores tied at 15 each, the Eagles really must kick on if they're to stand any chance to win the bonus point but sadly David Norris is then involved in a bizarre slow motion fall on the second bend in heat 6 that somehow manages to trap him under the weight of the fence to ensure that he now earns an exclusion. They say the air fence is a vital safety feature but when crashed into from a certain angle (or in this case at a shockingly slow speed) it often appears to wish to hold onto the unwary rider. Judged from afar by his reaction and subsequent body language, it's safe to say that Floppy's not that happy with the world but then the language (body and bad) in the crowd around me isn't that clever either. Mark 'The Bark' Hazelden is unofficially the cheerleader for these vitriolic complaints about our form in the season to date so far in our own unscientific small cross-section of the regular mood of the home crowd and after the meeting, takes it upon himself to email Jon Cook to inform him that people in the crowd have complaints, albeit that they're mostly his own that recycles for effect as though they've been overheard said by others. These skills mark him out for a possible career in politics and, predictably enough, Jon kindly replies with a wish that these people would show some faith and get a grip. In the rerun, the only grip taken is firmly on the bonus point by the Pirates when Krzysztof Kasprzak keeps Andrew Moore firmly at the rear of the race, and gives a masterclass in the dying technique of team riding to guide home Davidsson (J.) in first place.

One thing that can immediately dissipate any voices of dissent among the Eagles faithful, or anywhere come to that, is heedless aggression on the track when it's apparently (unfairly) directed towards your own riders. This season because of their grandson Jordan, the people I stand with every week have moved from our previously preferred spot two yards south of the start gate by board 51 to further back along the straight almost to where it joins the exit of the fourth bend. This move has taken some getting used to and I much enjoyed the view from our previous position but then I prefer the company and the banter even more that you get from John, Judy, Jordan, Mark and Karen Hazelden as well as Dave and Margaret Rice along with Jayne SSS. For once our collective move has improved our view of dramatic action on the track, in this instance an attempt on bends three and four of the first lap of heat 7 by Antonio Lindback who eschews love and instead tries to 'spear' Nicki Pedersen (who was on his outside at the split second he attempted this violent manoeuvre). Ever wily and they say it's often much harder to get the biter bit, with great awareness and foresight Nicki eases back a touch to avoid this desperate lunge and, to a triumphant roar from my section of the crowd, Antonio smashes heavily into the fourth bend air fence. With race stopped and Lindback excluded, Nicki journeys round to the fallen Pirate who appears to tense in the expectation of a fight as Pedersen draws close only to find that the Dane has returned to offer him a lift back to the pits. Mark jokes, "he runs him back but he'll definitely have him another time" while his mother, Judy, is impressed with the maturity that Nicki demonstrates, "there was a time when he would have twatted him without a second thought." From the school of thought that recognises Nicki most often feels that revenge is a dish best served scalding hot, John

Hazelden has a different take on events to the rest of his family, "if Antonio had stayed on I wouldn't have fancied his chances on Nicki's favourite [first] bend as he would have kissed the 'Woodside Studios' [sign] all the way round the bend!" Referee Mick Bates has no choice but to exclude Lindback and predictably Nicki easily wins the rerun but the troublesome Walasek relegates the mostly ineffectual Andrew Appleton into third place to leave the Eagles still trailed off at 20-22. Heat 8 then features a race within a race when Mooro lulls Boycie into a false sense of security by allowing him to lead easily for a couple of laps before he stuns him with a blast past on the second bend of the third lap to win the race. Behind this pair, Lewis makes heavy weather but finally gains third place and demonstrates his impetuous wild side as well as his sheer skill on a speedway bike all in one lap. The last lap to be exact, when he somehow manages to stay on after he nearly crashes into the bend two air fence when under no real pressure, but recovers sufficiently to regain third place through grabbing a big handful of throttle to fly round the fourth bend and just about hold on to the finish line with his leg trailed behind him.

With the Eagles in the lead for the first time tonight, the fog does arrive at the track though Bob Dugard is so often on his tractor tending to the track between races that you could be forgiven for thinking that all the exhaust from his activity had created these volumous and billowing clouds. This season Adam Shields has developed the confidence and Brer-Rabbit-like cunning to invent a tactical ruse to exploit other riders reduced expectations of his own likely performance. Heat 9 is a case in point where he (deliberately) trails KK in third for a couple of laps and, in a shrewd psychological manner, appears to be gradually falling further and further behind only to suddenly surprise the Pole when he unexpectedly blasts past him on the back straight of the penultimate lap to easily secure second place. This is all the better since Deano is ahead by some distance and wins easily. This tactic not only has the element of surprise but also of timing as by the time the opposition rider's victim has recovered his speed and composure, there are insufficient laps during which to stage a comeback. It's not the first time that Adam Shields has used this cunning tactic this season and until his gamesmanship is widely acknowledged it should become a rich source of points.[2]

Floppy wins the next race and as he crosses the line he celebrates with a dramatic punch of the air that he executes with considerable venom and continues this as he comes round on a deserved lap of honour. John notes, "tells you a lot, don't it!" Hopefully, it tells us that Floppy has almost fully recovered from his 2005 injuries and the residual psychological anxieties that continued to plague him as a result during his subsequent many 'comebacks'. We'd all enjoy a consistent return of his usual superlative form around Arlington rather than one more in a series of meetings where he's misfired and frankly struggled to maintain consistency while his performances, apparently unpredictably, alternate between peaks and troughs on an almost race-by-race basis. Well aware that he's a rider subject to fragility based on his own hypersensitive psychological state and rapid mood swings (to far greater extent than all speedway riders invariably do when their form dips), the Eastbourne crowd roar their approval. Sadly the advantage the Eagles gain through this well-received win is restricted since it's only a drawn heat because the Walasek and Lindback team ride to ensure that they keep Andrew Moore firmly anchored at the rear of the field.

[2] Three days later on Easter Monday Adam broke his pelvis while he rode in an obscure part of Poland for his club Lublin. So our chances to closely observe the effectiveness of his own rather unique psychological masterclass were restricted until later in the season. In a group of self-employed people – the reality of what all speedway riders become once they reach a certain level and are able to concentrate solely on the sport during the season – who invariably pride themselves on working no matter what problems beset them, Adam soon marked himself out as one of the hardiest of these 'tough' riders. It was a surprise but a tribute to his determination (and commitment to his bank balance) that he even rode again in 2006, never mind managed to comparatively flourish. On a separate note, as fans you rather hope that the riders (and team management) carefully plot how they are going to tactically approach each race that they feature in and research the characteristics and foibles of the riders they will encounter during their programmed rides. They, obviously, also need to take account of the prevailing track conditions and other relevant factors on the night. Such is the treadmill existence of continuous travel and frequent races against the same cadre of faces week in and week out for many contemporary riders that the reality appears to be that tactical considerations and research only really apply to the GPs, if at all. The custom and practice has resulted in a default groupthink that appears to consider that research and contemplation is best applied to equipment preparation rather than psychological evaluation of your opponents. The 'just go out and ride' approach, once you've chatted to your sports psychologist, souped up your bikes and accordingly adjusted them to the track you're to race on that night, plays into the hands of 'thinkers' like Adam. The effectiveness of his gamesmanship would immediately be ended if his opponents had done their homework on him or had researched the recent performances of the Eagles riders prior to a visit to Arlington. Consequently, in the absence of this forward intelligence, Adam outsmarts everyone when he deliberately hangs back to gain advantage through the subtle use of his own personal rather oblique brand of gamesmanship.

Just as soon as Eastbourne regain their momentum, they lose it again in the next race when Pedersen (B.) surprisingly defeats Pedersen (N.) round his own home circuit to avenge the similar treatment his compatriot had meted out at Wimborne Road earlier in the day. Combined with a third place for Boycie this reduces the deficit on the night to two points with a match score of 34-32. Though it's mathematically possible for the Eagles to gain four successive 5-1s at the same time that the Pirates completely fail with any tactical ride opportunities that such free scoring might provide them with, this would still only lead to a run off for the bonus point. Even if I were surrounded by optimists, which I'm not, they would probably struggle to see the bonus point go anywhere other than back to Dorset and, if the siren voices of pessimism were to gain sway, then a home defeat tonight could very much remain a possibility. Deano wins the next race though Lewis refuses to give up the chase to join him at the front for all four laps before he gives it everything and so comes to grief when he crashes on the final bend of the race.

It appears that all the controversial incidents that enliven this meeting cannot take place anywhere other than around the apex of bends three and four where we all have an uninterrupted view of them from our newly found 2006 collective viewing position. The way I saw the next incident of the night was that both Pedersens arrived into the third bend of the first lap roughly parallel with each other with Bjarne on the outside and Nicki slightly ahead. As is his wont and his reputation, Nicki predictably swept wide and close up to the fence which thereby gave Bjarne the sensible choice to shut off or the professional choice to part company from his bike in a suitably dramatic manner that would convince the referee to exclude Nicki as the guilty party. Rather like dives and simulation in football, sometimes you're lucky if you dive and sometimes you're not. While there's no doubt that Nicki would be and was out to avenge his defeat of two races previously and a hint of this determination might slightly influence the referee further, the basic situation was that Nicki was clearly ahead when Bjarne bailed out. Mick Bates saw the incident the way that I did and excluded Bjarne. It would be fair to say that Bjarne wasn't happy and greeted both Nicki and the referee with gestures that indicated an encounter with the shale had yet to fill him with the joys of spring. To add to the torment, his long slow trudge back to the pits saw him warmly greeted with a crescendo of loud jeers for the length of his walk along the back straight. Ever the contrarian, Floppy wins the rerun but greets the win with a lone punch in the air before he rides round on a victory lap and ostentatiously puts his finger to his lips to shush the crowd. I'm not quite sure what he's advising us, other than maybe not to tempt fate or for his critics to become silent from now on. Whatever it is, it's definitely not clear but the 5-1 race result is and while it takes the match score to a positive 42-36 for the Eagles, the aggregate one remains an irretrievable 78-90. The next race has Bridger appear in place of Andrew Appleton in the vain hope that he will add more points to the scoreline than his reserve partner might, though sadly although he entertains, he runs a fast ridden last place. Nicki wins the next battle of the Pedersens and Floppy finishes third to ensure the Eagles secure the two of the league points on offer 49-41 but remain well off the pace when it comes to the possibility of a bonus point. Based on these Good Friday displays, it's going to be a long season in the Elite League for both teams, particularly for Eastbourne.

Looking to the bright side, five of the home riders appear to have heeded Jon Cook's request for more heat wins and in the comparative Elite League 'A' fixture in 2005 the Eagles failed to win any points at all, so this must count as progress. Afterwards Jon Cook comments, "Poole might have got the bonus point but I think we showed true character. We were four down on two occasions and we battled back. We have got a lot of good out of this." Clearly buoyed by the win, he then goes on to judge the riders' feet as more significant than their throttle hands in this victory, "we got stuck in and found our gating shoes" before he adds, "I thought there were some superb performances all around the shop today. I couldn't fault anyone for the efforts they put in." Jon completely fails to mention the Bjarne exclusion but afterwards Nicki is much more forthright on the incident. There had been a heated exchange of opinions between the Danes and they beg to differ on their interpretations of the build up to and actions that caused the incident, "he was trying to force something that was not going to happen – to try and get me excluded. I was a little bit disappointed and I told him." Poole captain, Bjarne remains phlegmatic and confirms what Nicki has also emphasized, namely that there's absolutely no problem with them and that though they remain friends off the track they both like to compete hard against the other once the tapes have risen. "Nicki and me race hard against each other. Every time we fight like that and our races get better and better. I feel it was wrong that I got excluded because I thought there was slight contact. But that is life." Though the Pirates take some consolation from both the manner of their home victory and the comparative closeness of their away defeat nonetheless, on balance, Bjarne felt, "we should have [won] after we had made a good start."

A Tense Encounter at Brough Park
17th April 2006

Easter Monday found me in the North East to witness two Newcastle sports fixtures in the space of a couple of action packed hours – the first involved my beloved Sunderland at the Stadium of Light and the second was at Brough Park for the visit of the Glasgow Tigers in the second leg of their Premier Trophy (North) fixture against the Newcastle Diamonds. The day started well with an early Sunderland goal before capitulation on a massive scale saw them more or less gift three goals in seven disastrous second half minutes to the frequently excoriated black-and-white opposition in a display that was gutless, inept and pitiful. Even the dreaded Alan Shearer scored from the penalty spot to answer in the best possible manner all those extremely vocal Sunderland fans that frequently doubt his sexuality and parentage in chants that feature at every single game. I have always admired his single minded, combative style in an England shirt and whatever SAFC fans claim, we'd have loved someone that passionate and committed to play for our team over these last few years. Sadly, he was to sustain the injury in the game that would end his season and career prematurely before his scheduled retirement at the end of the season.

Thankfully, I would get to watch the speedway at Brough Park as a neutral but interested spectator. I journeyed over to Byker on the excellent Metro system that connects the City of Newcastle with its poorer, more down-at-heel neighbour though in this particular part of the city the housing and life prospects of the residents echo that of many "Mackems". The win for Newcastle in the football would have lifted many spirits (and restored local honour) within the city limits and would be gleefully remembered for years ahead. Sensibly for this trip, I have decided to disguise my allegiances by not leaving my red and white striped replica shirt behind in Sunderland. Even in the turnstile queue the chatter in lilting Geordie glories in the embarrassment of the despised local rivals. Once I'm inside one of the first people I encounter after I've bought my programme from the stall just inside the stadium perimeter fence is one of the real characters of British Speedway, the always friendly mother of the club's co-promoter, Joan English. She's a passionate woman when it comes to all things Newcastle Speedway though her duties during home meetings severely restrict the opportunity she has to watch the racing, let alone offer loud words of encouragement. Joan has no sympathy for any downheartedness I might feel as a result of our loss, "why, we were always going to win!" she says cheerfully with a happy smirk in her broad Geordie accent. I briefly look at the speedway goodies on display in the rather spartan track shop they have at Brough Park before I try to push my way through the two or three deep crowd that's gathered on the terraces by the fence that separates the fans from the action in the pits. The view from here isn't great as the ascending level of the banked steps of the terraces means that you're often effectively viewing the bustle of the pits from below. The view is good if you're keen to watch what's going on in the Newcastle side of the pits but restricts your ability somewhat if you're similarly keen to watch the visitors.

I hope to say hello to George but learn from Joan that he's probably hard to find on race night but is probably either in the speedway office or the pits, both of which are places I'm not permitted to access. A casual glance over the pits wall quickly indicates that he's in the pits but that now wouldn't be a good time for a chat since he rushes about the place and conducts brief, earnest conversations on the hoof with a furrowed brow. The chap who guards the door that provides access to George's office and the passageway that leads to the pits looks sufficiently austere and unwelcoming that I decide not to leave a message.

Stood alone to one side of the home pits lost in study of the comings, goings and preparations is the Tigers presenter at Ashfield Michael Max who cuts an imposing figure with his hands deep in the pockets of his distinctive trademark red Glasgow Tigers anorak. Obviously he must be lost in deep concentration as he fails to hear me repeatedly call "Michael! Michael!" over the pits wall. It completely fails to attract his attention but does manage to get me wary looks from the Newcastle fans that are crushed up against the pits wall with me. Perhaps, Michael has become so inured to his name being called from anonymous crowds of fanatical fans or groupies keen to share their opinions in minute detail all around the country – over pits walls or through the fences – that he easily zones them all out from his consciousness at every speedway meeting he attends. That's certainly the case today even though I don't use any of the colourful epithets or choice words that he might customarily inspire. Eventually, one of the track staff attracts his attention on my behalf and he glides over though his hands remain resolutely in his anorak pockets as though he's the defending world pocket billiards champion. I update him on my plans and get his email addresses so that I can send him the draft chapters that mention Glasgow Speedway from my still incomplete book *Showered in Shale*. I thank him again for his help with an appeal for assistance to the Ashfield faithful last year and again praise the kind generosity of the lift to the airport that I received that day from loyal Tiger fans Ian Maclean and his daughter, Marian. Michael agrees that this example of the kindness of strangers typifies speedway fans in general and Glasgow fans in particular, "we're always a friendly bunch." Though I gather that friendliness is presently at a minimum in the pits tonight between the riders and team management of both teams as a result of a dispute last night about the choice of Derek Sneddon as a guest replacement for the suspended Jamie Robertson of Newcastle. Jamie is still highly visible though, since he helps out all evening in the pits! The bad atmosphere engendered in the first leg has travelled down the road and across the border to Brough Park tonight for the second leg and Michael alludes to it elliptically though it's only when I chat with fans later that I gather what has been going on and the mystery about what on earth he was talking about to me is solved. "We always have competitive meetings here but you could say that there's some things we're not happy about and while that's all part of speedway, we'll be trying our best to make sure that we answer them on the track tonight!"[1]

Whatever the reasons behind the present tensions, I take a few moments to settle down to read the programme in which George English makes an early assault on the 'Ronnie Russell Deliciously Mixed Metaphor Award' with his 'George's Journal (with George English)' column. After he's tortuously name checked the chorus from artist Dinah Washington's "number 5 hit"(!) from 1959 (when he wasn't yet born) as part of his contrived discussion of last week's Edinburgh home fixture, he laments the dramatic mid-meeting loss of form suffered by his heat leaders as roughly equivalent to the same odds as "Lord Lucan riding into the stadium on the back of Shergar!"[2] Before I can read any further, the parade starts and is dealt with very quickly and, only minutes later, the riders promptly come to the line for the first race on a night that to my southern

---

[1] The back story to this dispute is complicated. The Speedway Control Bureau had banned Newcastle 'A grade' reserve Jamie Robertson for six meetings (four of them suspended until the end of 2007) as a punishment as a result of an "incident" in his hometown that involved the Berwick start marshal on April 8th. Accounts of what went on differ but the *Speedway Star* reported "ugly scenes" before the report went on to mention "he beckoned the marshal over to him and after exchanging words was seen to head butt him twice whilst still wearing his helmet." After the incident Jamie became involved in a further scuffle with another member of the Berwick track staff by the pits before he later threw his helmet at this trackman. When the adrenalin pumps and the red mist comes down, speedway riders often subsequently regret their actions. After a 'heavy' fine and ban was announced the Newcastle co-promoter George English was quoted, "no way can we condone what happened at Berwick, apart from saying Jamie was severely provoked... overall, we feel the sentence is harsh bearing in mind penalties imposed on other riders for comparable – if not considerably greater – offences, particularly in our match at Stoke a year ago." The concept of consistency isn't the first one that you most readily associate with the decision-making processes at either the SCB or the BSPA. However, the sports regulations do clearly allow Newcastle to call upon the services of any other available A-list reserve to replace Jamie for his two matches of suspension, where the reasonably local Glasgow Tigers will provide the opposition. The Diamonds chose the combative Edinburgh rider Derek Sneddon, who already enjoys a feisty relationship with the Tigers fans, as their temporary replacement and advised them on the Thursday prior to the Sunday fixture. It's a tradition in speedway circles that promoters often leave any protests that they might have until a few hours before tapes go up in the mostly vain hope that an adjudication from the SCB referee nominated for the meeting in question or an 'ad hoc' last-minute decision from the member of the BSPA management committee might swing things in their favour. Indeed, the 2006 rulebook states that such decisions by an individual committee member – from a group that comprises Neil Machin, Matt Ford, Peter Toogood, Chris van Straaten, and Dave Pavitt – can be made at the last minute and would be binding on all parties. Though made at the last minute, the protest Glasgow lodged with the referee failed – though it was claimed that initially the Management Committee member on duty (Neil Machin) had ruled Sneddon out until George English made his feelings known and referred to the clear wording in the SCB rulebook that would almost certainly have resulted in Newcastle winning any subsequent protest. Afterwards George English comments, "they apparently believed that as Sneddon had a higher average than Jamie, we were breaking the rules." In actual fact, so long as A-list reserve is replaced with another A-listed rider, their averages are irrelevant. Though Sneddon's average is higher he only scores four (paid five) points that is arguably comparable to what you might expect Jamie Robertson would manage, should he have ridden. More significant, in the opinion of the Newcastle promotion and management, was the detrimental psychological impact that this dispute caused for Sneddon and his team-mates in the fixture at Ashfield since, though the best travellers, the Diamonds went down to a larger than expected 54-36 defeat.

Michael Max studies the form in Brough Park pits. © Jeff Scott

Last minute adjustments by Adam McKinna. © Jeff Scott

blood appears suddenly cold now the sun has set. At Newcastle Speedway, you have two basic viewing options as a fan. Watch indoors from the warmth of the home-straight grandstand where you can stand at the back close to the bar and catering outlet or sit at the tables by the windows and overlook the track. Otherwise, your only option is to stand outside on the terrace steps that line almost the whole length of the straight. Though it's 'fresh', I'd always prefer to stand in the open air as I know that behind the glass the atmosphere created by the noise and smell of the bikes is almost completely lost. Since it's early in the season and only still the spring, the skies quickly darken to require the use of floodlights and thereby create the ideal conditions under which to watch speedway. To add further piquancy to this evocative scene, since I've only been to a few meetings, I've yet to completely overcome the deprivation of the close season and so really enjoy drawing deeply to inhale the pungent bouquet that is the almost perfumed smell of a speedway bike exhaust. There's a good-sized crowd so the terrace is reasonably crowded but not unbearably so. I position myself almost parallel with the start gate about mid-way up the steps so that I look down on the action but not from too distorting an angle. In front of me are a number of Glasgow fans who wear their colours and, like at speedway tracks everywhere, can wear them without fear of intimidation, reprisal or interruption. They have an assortment of other garments of varied ages that bear the Tigers logo and one lady appears to have coloured her hair so that its brightly distinctive pinkie red slightly orangey hue vaguely co-ordinates with the colour scheme of her chosen team. They also have bags of sweets – chosen from the pick-and-mix section of the sweetshop or supermarket – they compete with each other to be generous with and frequently bring out to share with each other (and later me) at selected intervals throughout the meeting. As I stand and listen to their conversations, I quickly gather that none of the rancour that afflicts the riders and associated staff in the pits has communicated itself to these fans who, if they discuss anything intently, it's the prospects for the season ahead and their grievances are more of a general nature to do with the inconsistency in decision-making by different referees rather than the use of Derek Sneddon at reserve. It is a well-worn theme that they are to get the chance to warm to and rehearse further as this meeting progresses.

On my previous visits to Brough Park, it's always struck me that the narrow straights at Newcastle speedway place passing at a premium and to increase your percentage chance of victory makes arrival into the first corner even more important than it already is practically everywhere else speedway is raced. But then my eyes and presumptions can easily deceive since this match served up a feast of bad temper, hard riding and

---

[2] With masterly economy and perhaps betraying an aptitude better suited to national politics, George skilfully dismisses the need to talk about the controversy at Berwick that featured Jamie Robertson with the elegant phrase "all was rosy apart from an unfortunate incident, on which we cannot comment about here at the moment." Before he goes on to honestly relate, as many wouldn't if they held his capacity as co-promoter, the many lessons that can be taken from this away performance by individual team members. "George [Stancl] wasn't too happy with his display", "James [Grieves] picked up six points from his first three rides but they were due to solid gating and his track craft as he struggled with his engine" and with masterly *sang froid*, "Jamie [Robertson] got off to a great start winning heat 2 but had a mixed bag of a night that included a seized engine."

frequent passing on the straights and the bends. George Stancl makes no mistakes and leads from start to finish in the first drawn heat sponsored by Slimming World, after Danny Bird and David McAllan pack the minor places. The next few heats are rich in controversy and in the next heat they have Derek Sneddon, James Cockle and Robert Ksiezak execute some combative but decisive manoeuvres at speed. If anyone doubts the commitment of the riders, the fierce no-quarter-given racing in this heat allay them. The Glasgow pair initially lead before Sneddon overhauls Ksiezak only to find his way past Cockle blocked when that rider occupies his favoured outside line and thereby nearly cause him to come to grief in the fence before he resumes his chase. Almost in the same spot a lap later Sneddon again tries the outside to attempt to pass Ksiezak only for the Australian to collide with the fence in his effort to block Sneddon and thereby get excluded from the rerun as the cause of the stoppage. The Glasgow faithful in front of me aren't sure whether to get more irked with the exclusion or the loss of the potential 1-5. Whereas the nearby Newcastle fans leave James Cockle in no doubt that they disapprove of his use of his bike to initially thwart Sneddon's outside run. Personally, I thought it was an aggressive manoeuvre but, when ahead, it's completely within the rules to use your advantage, spatial awareness and predictive skills to alter your position on the track without the need for a hand signal of warning. Never one to shirk a challenge and without any hint that he will ride any less competitively than usual when he appears as a guest, Derek Sneddon rides so close to James Cockle in the rerun that you'd think they were conjoined twins until Sneddon exits the second bend slightly ahead and pulls away to victory. Not that Cockle then endears himself to the Brough Park faithful when, once again, he blocks an outside blast from Adam McKinna that causes the C grade reserve to dramatically shut off and narrowly avoid an enforced encounter with the safety fencing. By this point, the Tigers fans in front of me warm to their theme that Cockle is a "hard but fair rider" and that they have been robbed with the conversion of a prospective 1-5 heat win into a 4-2 loss in the rerun.

I, for one, eagerly await the next Sneddon-Cockle encounter and I don't have long as they are programmed to meet again in heat 4. If he hasn't already been crossed off the Diamonds party invite list, James Cockle ensures that he is after his next outing in heat 4 when he falls at the back of the field in the first corner only to remount his bike but fails to clear the track. I imagine that he does this deliberately for tactical reasons since the Diamonds two have already clearly swept away into the lead after Shane Parker incorrectly anticipates a rerun for first bend bunching and shuts off in the full expectation of that decision. Though he has sensibly allowed the race to 'run' but left with no choice but to stop it now for safety reasons, exclude Cockle and order a rerun, Dale Entwhistle incurs the wrath of some Newcastle fans for his decision to not now award the race. It would take a brave man to explain to the most irate of these home fans that, however unfair it is that Cockle's calculated actions have stopped the race and thereby rubbed out a certain (barring mechanical failures) Newcastle 5-1 that would take the score to a useful 16-8, the referee can't award a race before a lap has been completed by all four riders.[3] During an evening of tension, petulance and anger, it is Cockle's turn to signal his displeasure in readily understandable fashion to the official in his box in the grandstand, albeit this would prove to be an expensive luxury, as the referee then fined him £100 for going to this trouble. The apoplexy among the Tigers fans directly in front of me is measured and stately but nonetheless keenly felt, "I don't think he really knows what he's doing." With a sense of injustice rampant all round, the rerun has further drama when Sneddon flatters to deceive for sufficient time to delay Parker and thereby lets the occasionally pugilistically inclined but this evening very much the model of restraint, James Grieves, escape at the head of the field. However, on the third lap he then has to retire when the back wheel of his second bike (the first having expired on the warm up lap) locks solid. The win for Parker over Sneddon in what by now has become a match race narrows the score to 13-10 and to judge by the groans of the Newcastle faithful behind me signals the likely end to any hope they have of a possible Diamonds fight back or the outside possibility that they might gain an aggregate victory.

The next race then sees a lengthy philosophical discussion between Glasgow's Danny Bird and the start marshal about the allegedly encroaching position taken by Josef 'Pepe' Franc. After many agitated head movements, waggles of his arms and general sizing up of the exact dimensions of his marked out area of the start gate in the manner of a slightly crazed builder calling round for a quotation on your patio extension, Danny finally settles down to concentrate only for Manuel ("don't mind him, he's from Austria") Hauzinger to burst through the tapes in the manner that suggests he's just received an urgent message to return home as his house was on fire. This brings Mr Sneddon back to the tapes for the third time in five races

---

[3] Although later in the season one nameless referee would in fact (incorrectly) do so, which kind of proves the inconsistency argument that the Tigers fans held to one of the most treasonable offences in the speedway kingdom.

only for him to tangle with McAllan on the first bend which, this time, the referee does deem to be an unsatisfactory start. This is a decision greeted with derision and crescendo of loud tuts and gasps of exasperation in my part of the stadium. This heightened sense of victimisation or having badly wronged someone in a previous life continues for the Tigers fans when Sneddon's increased familiarity with the circuit pays great dividends as he follows 'Pepe' home for a comfortable 5-1 score that the announcer struggles to contain his delight about. Another Diamonds 5-1 follows before Kauko Nieminen scores a double points victory in the black-and-white helmet with the ever-popular Cockle third to reduce the deficit to 25-19.

This level of drama and animus would prove difficult to sustain but who needs warm clothing when the heat on the track warms the mood of the crowd as regularly as this? Though heat 8 does have its moments behind the winner Christian Henry when Sneddon and McAllan led by Cockle all simultaneously lock up on the last bend in a movement that appeared strangely choreographed and designed to ensure the result required by a crooked Asian betting syndicate. The next race proves to be a strategic disaster when Danny Bird, in the race as a tactical substitute off 15 metres, cocks up his approach to the bend on the third lap to allow Hauzinger through to finish thoroughly last. It would be fair to say that he has yet to endear himself to the Tigers faithful if the comments on this and some of his other performances in the club's colours are anything to judge by. Although, that said, a saint would probably struggle to replace Shane Parker's rightfully exulted place of high favour among the Glasgow fans. With the score now poised at 33-23 and the aggregate advantage reduced to eight points, George Stancl is keen to make a point against his old club, so convincingly wins his third race of the night in heat 10. It is a race enlivened by an unchallenged fall by Henry in anticipation of a challenge from the ex-Workington rider Nieminen that never comes with 'public enemy number one' Cockle on the track, albeit with a plausible alibi since he is nowhere near him at the time of the incident.

As there has been a race or two without any hint of brutal riding on show, Danny Bird then redresses the balance when he leads on the straight but found time to take the boxing man's speedway rider, James Grieves, wide for a close inspection of the architecture of the fence. Somehow just about able to stay on his machine, Grieves clamours for what Gary Havelock euphemistically terms "a revenge ride." He fights back with some zeal to be almost on level terms only to rear at the last moment, as though mounted on a bucking bronco that has suddenly gone lame, before he then manages to just about tend his stricken bike slowly to the line ahead of McAllan who has handicapped his own quest for points with a fall and remount. Playing dropsy with his bike is to prove addictive for McAllan who falls with some élan when completely unchallenged after which he stays prostrate on the track long enough for the referee to tire of his gamesmanship and put on the stoplights. With one lap completed and the second underway, before McAllan falls like a Chelsea player shot by a sniper in the penalty area, the match official is able to appease the terrace full of backseat Newcastle-supporting referees and award the race. The Glasgow fans react with resigned equanimity by electing to choose the hard-boiled sweets in preference to the previously popular supermarket own-brand 'Quality Street'. Shane Parker arrives out next dressed in a helmet with a black-and-white cover but appears destined to play the role of the filling in the Grieves-Stancl metaphorical sandwich for a 4-4 drawn heat before Grieves takes it upon himself to further challenge the denture fixative of the fans around me when he then falls at the start of the last lap. The resultant 2-7 puts a whole different complexion on things and the mood lightens in front of me just as quickly as it simultaneously takes a severe turn for the worse among the Diamonds faithful now without even mathematical hope of an aggregate victory.

Even the joy of a last place for Cockle in heat 14 can only provide the diminished consolation of the second helping of sickly dessert for the disgruntled home fans. Though only a little man, Josef 'Pepe' Franc further confirmed his reputation as speedway's equivalent of a cuckoo when he is once more embroiled in a dispute at the start gate. The mild-mannered but respected Shane Parker protests about his position, albeit on behalf of his teammate Nieminen. Though it is all as nought since Kauko quickly falls after the tapes rise and Franc streaks to victory. Not that this really occupies the crowd who are enthralled by a four lap handlebar-to-handlebar duel served up by Stancl and Parker as they alternate throughout and finally enable both sets of fans to unite in agreement and warm appreciation of a race superbly well raced! The Czech rider has also managed to finish the meeting without any hint of the engine trouble that I understand to be a mandatory part of the overall Stancl experience according to my nearby Tigers fans.

It is a fitting end to an encounter that fascinates and enthrals. It is a contest between two combative teams of riders that is ridden with a passion that belies what I previously assumed to be the diminished value and status of the Premier Trophy (North) qualification fixtures. If this sort of meeting were served up every week at Brough Park, they'd have to start charging extra for admission.[4]

17th April Newcastle v Glasgow (Premier Trophy North) 53-42

---

[4] In the match report afterwards on the informative Newcastle Diamonds website George English noted, "there was a lot of bad feeling in the pits and we were just glad to get the meeting out of the way."

May 2006

"There is no place for racism in life, let alone in sport or speedway."
Matt Ford

"At present, it's an old bomber car track and we don't want to see anything that will damage the profile of speedway, which is a professionally run sport and properly structured."
Neil Machin visits the site of a proposed track in Rotherham

"This season is different to any other in recent years and this decision bore no resemblance to the Ipswich decision regarding Pepe last year."
Aaron Lanney reassures an irked John Louis after "commonsense prevailed" in the reassessment of Freddie Eriksson's average provided "some assistance to safeguard my business"

"The whole thing stinks, it was completely the wrong decision and at least 90 per cent of fans would agree... how can our sport be taken seriously when one club is treated differently to another? We have been given a kick in the teeth. With the same treatment that Oxford have just received we could have won the league in 2005. And we are meant to quietly accept it! The decision was totally wrong and the bottom line is, would any of the other 10 clubs in the Elite League have been given permission to use Freddie at a reduced average? Of course not. I feel for Oxford's plight, but this should have been put right before a wheel was turned in 2006."
It's déjà vu all over again for Chris Louis

"The rumours are absolutely not true, it's rubbish, Tony is not retiring early."
Olli Tyrvainen on Tony Rickardsson's future

"There was one massive thing they forgot – the track. You cannot have speedway without a racing surface and the one we faced was a disgrace."
Mark Loram on the condition of the Peterborough track

"The board of Wimbledon Speedway continues to search for a new stadium in the south east and we look forward to making sure the Dons will race again before too long... the real reason for closing speedway down may well be related to the fact that the GRA were taken over by a venture capital company last year and they have other plans for the [Plough Lane] stadium, which we will find out about in the not too distant future."
Ian Perkin writes to the letters page of the *Speedway Star*

"If Rob Godfrey believes teams should not use rider replacement in the Conference League, the place to make that point is at a meeting of Conference League chairmen and not take things out on officials and riders of a rival club. As club chairmen, we are in a privileged position of being able to make changes in the regulations, subject to majority consent, and that is the way these things should be done."
Plymouth team manager David Short after the Devils triumph 44-46 in Scunthorpe

"Shaun [Tacey] is a superb role model as a captain, but he just hasn't been able to produce his old heat leader form. I had to take a hard-nosed decision for the overall good of the promotion. From what many people have told me, Andrew Moore will be a magic signing for us."
Mick Horton

"We have enough trouble keeping fans on the terraces these days and it is the responsibility of every promoter, rider, manager, referee, [Uncle Tom Cobbley] and, indeed, all officials to endeavour as far as they can to give the customer value for money. Otherwise, they will simply stop coming and there will be no speedway.... [the] majority of the riders were prepared to keep going. I have to wonder if there was some influence I am unaware of that caused the referee [Craig Ackroyd] to come and inspect the track when he did, instead of simply putting the green lights on and hitting the button. I must also question whether the course of events would have been different had Newcastle been in the lead 24-12 after six heats instead of being one point down, as was the case."

Dave Croucher ponders the abandonment at Brough Park

"I put my hand up in the air. It is obvious that I saw something. I didn't slow up; I stopped. People say Kelvin had a red umbrella. If I had seen it as a red umbrella, obviously I would not have stopped. Kelvin is a good friend of mine and he only ever tries to help... the reason why I stopped is because I saw a red light. If it was an umbrella then, whatever... that's speedway – it's full of ifs and buts."

David Norris on a mysterious 'red light' incident during a televised meeting at Arlington

"[Ermolenko] said Belle Vue is a slick track and that a rider needs no technique to ride it. He said it's just a rev and go track... Ermolenko was never too good at Belle Vue, neither as a home rider or as a visitor, so maybe his comments are just sour grapes."

Ian Thomas

"Blayne is new to the game and has a lot to learn. His claim that the Boston riders were constantly moving at the gate is patently untrue. I stood by the gate for most races, Blayne was nowhere to be seen and is merely repeating comments made by disappointed supporters. I suggest that he needs to get on the green and then he can speak with authority."

Malcolm Vasey on his less experienced Mildenhall Academy counterpart

The dog that did bark

15th May

With the elevation of Reading in their Bulldogs guise to the 2006 Elite League season, this was the Smallmead meeting that I looked out for with the most relish and interest when the fixture list was published. Redin as we should properly call it were my first love in speedway and though you're extremely lucky if your first love is your only love, years away on the South Coast has had me travel to the lovely Arlington to watch my adopted Eagles. There have still been many seasons, despite living in Brighton, when I've been along to practically every Racers meeting, even during the recent successive *anni horribili* – which perversely I enjoyed for the close meetings and late meeting tension about the outcome – despite living in Brighton. Smallmead still remains for me the true home of speedway in this country and is the place where intuitively I feel most comfortable to watch the action unfold on the track. It's like when you wear an old pair of slippers that you love, you know you could do better but why run the risk of a permanent change? However, with the strategic arrival of the club in the Elite League (while I remain pleased at the opportunity to watch high-calibre speedway riders race at the stadium every week) I feel that something has definitely been lost about the club in terms of the racing offered, the atmosphere and even its ethos. I do appreciate the investment and the ambition shown by John Postlethwaite in his BSI Reading guise and the apparent 'vision' of speedway in the future that underpins their plans. Indeed (as documented earlier in the book when I first came back here on April 3rd but worth reiterating) you can't help but notice certain very visible changes from the team to the backroom staff roster, the improved track surface, new changing rooms, better loudspeakers, posters in the pits, even the new programmes and the like. As well as the extensive slap of paint that has given Smallmead a cosmetic retread but not a structural overhaul and, fortunately from my perspective, has left the familiar fundamentals still in place. It's also good to see that many of the loyal and knowledgeable staff have mostly been retained in their regular capacities and, problematically for BSI Reading and their ambitious revenue projections, practically all the fans have also been retained but sadly not really added to on a regular weekly basis. I've certainly not come along as often this season in protest at the name change to the Racerdogs, the change in ethos and the increased propensity for the team to rack up cricket scores at Smallmead rather than any longer be involved in close contests where there remains some element of surprise about the final outcome (and scoreline) for the majority of the meeting.

Politicians are happiest when they talk about their vision for the future but at their most uncomfortable when they have to live in the here and now. In the season to date, Redin have lost home league meetings but have started to throw off the shackles of inconsistency and, in the form of Janusz Kolodziej, they have a match winner in the reserve position to go along with the big guns of Greg Hancock and Matej Zagar, ably backed up by an able quartet of journeymen all more than capable to contribute points and add strength in depth. Tonight's visitors, the Eastbourne Eagles, shouldn't really present much of a threat, despite the presence of the talismanic Nicki Pedersen, particularly since the recent pelvis injury for Adam Shields has deprived them of the one rider really consistently capable of improving their average. They do, of course, have the ongoing emergence of the young talent that is 16-year-old Lewis Bridger and early indications are that he's settled in well and thrown in the odd exceptional performance. Understandably enough, the various columnists in the Bulldogs' glossy programme name-check the precocious youngster. For Jim Lynch he's "one of Britain's biggest talents" and for guest columnist Philip Rising there's much to admire – and he'd welcome a "new dawn" of British speedway talent – but he sounds a realistic note of caution gained from hard bitten experience through his many dog years in speedway. "So the kid can ride, no doubt about it. But in recent years we have been made aware of several young riders who at the age of 16 or so have looked to have what it takes to reach the top. Most, however, have stumbled upon the way."[1] The always helpful and friendly Andy Povey is even blunter when I catch him for a few words close to the track shop, "I hear he's due a big fall, he'll slow down then or pass the test with flying colours." The track shop looks in a much better state than at the time of my last visit when there was so little stock on display that you'd have thought that there had been a burglary, albeit carried out by exceptionally tidy thieves who'd decided to abscond with the stock but leave the place spic and span. Apparently the lack of some items of stock was due to the fact that BSI Reading, rather ridiculously in the manner of using a sledgehammer to crack a hazelnut, has to assess and pre-authorise all merchandise before it can be stocked. This still didn't explain the lack of Bulldogs-branded merchandise – an obvious starting point you'd have imagined for John Postlethwaite

---

[1] Rising goes on to note, "Great Britain in particular is in desperate need of young riders" and therefore has high hopes of the favourable influence Martin Dugard and others will have on Lewis while he remains immersed in the Eagles milieu. "The danger is that ability alone is not enough. How to harness that talent and to learn what speedway is really all about is the difficult part."

or his highly paid BSI staff to have organised given his marketing background, the lustre of his many previous prestigious employers and his previous involvement in the brand/merchandise-led Formula One circus. Just as doctors often have the unhealthiest lifestyles in contrast to their everyday work advising others, perhaps so it is with marketing experts who forget to address the fine details during a major rebranding exercise that (without adequate research or consultation) changed the Reading speedway brand name from the traditional Racers to the 'iconoclastic' Bulldogs. This is all idle speculation on my part and whatever the exact reasons, the shop now looks better stocked with all the usual speedway paraphernalia and even has some Bulldogs gear (though still not that much and more of the pen and badge variety rather than the higher ticket items such as anoraks and fleeces that always seem so popular, visible and proudly worn by the fans at most other speedway clubs). Though the shop is not quite what it was stock-wise compared to last season, it's still very ably run by Andy's friendly mum, Win, plus the chap who sold the programme is still on the staff and Andy is often found there at some point on race night (when his other press officer duties don't call him elsewhere), so the constancy of the people and its location remains in place and still a charm.

I have quite some time before the rider parade so I wander round to the third bend where I can overlook the pits and gaze through the new fine mesh fencing. This is another addition to the stadium furniture that they've put in this season; specifically, I imagine, with the aim to restrict or interfere with the punters ability to take photos of the riders and mechanics in situ there. On the way back as we head in different directions I bump into Mick Hinves, full-time dental technician and itinerant Eastbourne photographer who's here to watch with his family at the closest track to their house near Heathrow. He's very even-handed in his assessment of the impact of the BSI reign at Reading and not only does he have the advantage of his insider's perspective of the situation but also "hears the Benfield side of things as my wife works in the city." He even does some work for BSI as he provides the photograph that they use in the advert for the Cardiff GP – the one that annoyingly has practically killed off the regular rider action shot, that you used to get on the back cover of the *Speedway Star* every week that I so looked forward to as a teenager and still miss now. Though he lives nearby, he wouldn't contemplate taking photos at Smallmead since not only do you have to pay for the privilege but "Postlethwaite only allows photos for the first five heats, he's quite strict about it for some reason."

Back at my traditional favoured spot (well, since the heyday crowds evaporated from Smallmead) by the greyhound perimeter wall that overlooks the start line and provides a perfect view of the first corner, except for one light pole, I study the programme further. It's a shame that the compositor didn't, as last week's Arena Essex team logo occupies pride of place where the Eagles one should rightfully be used on the race card. The programme is rammed full of corporate-type adverts or else BSI Reading uses the space to promote itself or its associated businesses and business partners. Less than 70 per cent of the content is editorial copy and photos though, to be fair, the visual images look very attractive in full colour and use the space they occupy well. The column by Greg Hancock is a lengthy blow-by-blow account of his latest GP experience in Wroclaw and largely irrelevant to the Elite League job that he's paid for here, which only gets a perfunctory mention in the very last paragraph. The visit of Eastbourne fares less well as they finally just about scrape a mention on the very last line. As a long time Racers fan, I enjoy the "looking back" column the most and is a phrase that John Postlethwaite will have discovered to his irritation is the default setting of most British speedway fans and promoters.

The rider parade is notable to any long-time attendees at Smallmead for the fact that you can actually (loudly) hear it on speakers that are reputedly Terry Russell's. Additional razzamatazz is provided by this season's arrival of the grid girls[2] in their helmet-coloured uniforms cum closely fitted boiler suits. The fixture finds the Bulldogs poised in the top four of the league and ready to kick on, whereas the Eagles find themselves closer to the basement and in need of some urgent revitalisation in their away form if they're to mount a vague challenge and arrive in the play-offs at the end of the season. The unlikely chance that this recovery would start to happen at Smallmead tonight for the already weakened Eagles recedes further with the late withdrawal of Dean Barker with "a virus" to be replaced by Edward Kennett. Further bad

---

[2] Apparently known as the "Making Impressions Bond Girls" since Tamzin, Bianca and Toyah Bond are all sisters and Kate Reay is their cousin.

[3] The arcane details that are the rules contained within the SCB rulebook often defy summary in the manner of unsolvable riddle. The explanation provided in the *Speedway Star* afterwards clarifies the situation succinctly. "Reading had read the rulebook correctly but were told on Monday that a sentence had been left out which related to assessed riders, like Kolodziej, and would not get his new average until the rest of the team in June." Hence he could remain at reserve rather than get promoted to number three as the match programme race card correctly but incorrectly stated, if you get my drift.

news for the visitors comes in the form of the information that despite having an eight-point average and being programmed in the race card to ride at number three, a closer consideration of the rulebook means that Janusz Kolodziej can continue to torment the opposition from the Racerdogs reserve position from which slot he'll be eligible for a possible seven rides![3]

Rather presciently, Jim Lynch noted in the *Speedway Star*, "I honestly believe that we are heading for a big win and not necessarily against one of the so-called weaker teams." The writing appeared to be on the pits wall as early as the first race that Redin won 5-1 only to follow it up with another similar score in the reserves race and thereby effectively end the meeting as a contest. A fall for Andy Smith before he can treat the Eagles riders to the benefit of his trademark hard charging, scything race style allows the Eagles to claim the minor places behind Matty Zagar who won by the proverbial mile. Hopes of the first heat winner for the visitors with the appearance of Nicki Pedersen are short lived as Kolodziej emphasizes his skill and worth to the Racerdogs with a win over the ex-World Champion. After the race, it is announced that the first and second bend speakers refuse to work and profuse apologies are offered, albeit only to those fans who could still hear from the speakers that continue to work. This is a further sign of the changed management attitude at Smallmead to the small but essential details that make up modern perceptions of good customer service. In the past, we were content for the floodlights not to illuminate the whole track and the idea that the speakers should be audible throughout the stadium wasn't ever really a contributory factor to our continued enjoyment. I'm sure some are happier now and some were happier then. The Eagles fans who've journeyed along to watch won't be happy at the apparent capitulation without a struggle that they endured the pleasure of witnessing. After heat 5, the score is already 21-9 and even the home crowd appears to have been stunned into a catatonic state by the ease of the race wins. After another appeal for some cheers, I gradually start to suspect that there is a need for all the fully working speakers to play the music loudly in lieu of an atmosphere or to appeal to those present to rouse themselves sufficiently to show a meaningful reaction. We're then treated to the 'I'll-say-it-so-it-must-be-true' school of attendance calculation with a warm welcome to "the big crowd here tonight", when the evidence of my eyes suggests that they either must all be in the bar or else it's pretty much as per normal for any Monday night you ever have chosen to watch the Racers over recent years. The announcer persists optimistically to ask, "give us a big cheer" only to be greeted with rapturous muteness.

Jon Cook surprisingly eschews the early opportunity to hit back with a tactical ride for Nicki Pedersen in heat 6 although he records the first race win of the night for the Eagles in another drawn heat (that's equivalent to a moral victory here tonight) in a green rather than black-and-white helmet colour. Another equipment failure then hits the Bulldogs but sadly for Eastbourne it's only a malfunction for the umbrella operated by Tamzin the green grid girl. Attempts to mend it are made without success and this, along with a race win for Floppy, bewilder the home crowd into an almost monastic vow of silence broken only by the plaintive, "come on keep the noise going for the Reading boys – keep their spirits up!" Heat 8 sees the grid girls venture out to their positions en masse without brollies in a show of solidarity and another maximum Racerdogs race win to progress the score to 32-16.

Nicki finally comes to the line in a black-and-white helmet colour to start off the inside gate with Zagar outside him. It's the sort of head-to-head race that you can't help but anticipate the chance to watch beforehand. In the event Nicki makes the gate and predictably drifts out to the fence to scupper the outside pass traditionally favoured by Zagar only to be completely scuppered when the Slovenian cunningly cuts back up the inside and, after a brief tussle that Pedersen is now positioned wrongly for, the Racerdog goes on to win easily. With Cameron Woodward trailed off at the back, the 4-4 draw signals the disappearance of any last chance the Eagles had to dent the deficit in the scores and damage limitation must become the order of the night, just in case a bonus point can still be snatched from the return fixture at Arlington. The thrill of the news that the speaker on the first bend has been fixed is scant consolation to those who hoped for a close contest. In heat 10 a determined Lewis Bridger snatches a point right on the line but sadly it's from his Eastbourne team-mate Edward Kennett and gives credence to the rumours that their relations off the track are, at best, only cordial.

In a final throw of the dice, Floppy wears black-and-white in the eleventh heat and rides to an inspired win that features a breathtaking overtake on the first lap when he squeezes through the narrowest of illusory gaps on the exit from the second bend to surprise the Redin pair. This was to be the only point that Kolodziej drops all night and the last race won by anyone in an Eagles tabard. The only way to instil any drama into the evening is to assail the crowd with continuous announcements.

We learn that "*BBC Radio Berkshire* on 104.1 FM" cover every meeting live which is a strange thing to actively draw people's attention to when BSI Reading aren't exactly flush with heaving crowds. The chance to listen to easy wins at Smallmead in the comfort of your home can't exactly be a barrel of laughs for listeners at home since speedway doesn't transfer to the airwaves in same resonant manner that cricket does so magnificently. Also, since I've listened to the commentary myself, it's all roaring bike noise, with commentary done in the manner of a 'Speak Your Weight' machine with narcolepsy. Plus the station boorishly rejoices each and every Redin race win in a manner that illustrates that all concept of BBC impartiality has long since disappeared in this neck of the woods and would, I imagine, ultimately even grate on any listener predisposed to favour the "Bulldogs". Then again, perhaps in defiance of the truism that all publicity is good publicity, allowing this broadcast access is perhaps John Postlethwaite's shrewd choice of not-so-secret-or-subtle weapon to drive people back through the Smallmead turnstiles.

Before the massacre continues in heat 12, the announcer thrills the Smallmead faithful with news about the "post-meeting press conference in the bar afterwards" – this is a hugely positive development that I'm only sorry that I can't stay for, though I worry that these things can attract those that like the sound of their own voice to ramble on at length. I'll reserve judgement and not express my suspicions as to whether any (or all) of Jim Lynch, Sam Ermolenko or John Postlethwaite fall into this category of post-meeting conference participant. Hot on the heals of this news are details to enliven the torpor of the most catatonic and inured of the Racerdogs following, namely "just to let you know, there are some items on sale in the track shop now!" It's a masterpiece of an announcement that makes a virtue of a problem and, by now on a roll, we get a run down of what is there, "pens, badges, stickers and the magazines – the *Speedway Star*, *Backtrack* about speedway in the 70s and 80s and *Vintage Speedway* magazine." It's just a shame for the Eagles fans present that the announcer doesn't continue to exactly list all the food, sweets and drinks available in the bar area. Instead the racing continues and Kolodziej is joined by a resurgent Andy Smith, after he's fought his way past Kennett on the second lap, who combines with the Pole up front for another 5-1 that takes the progressive score to a commanding 49-28.

Heat 13 provides a cameo in miniature of how the evening has gone for both teams when Greg Hancock definitely appears to get a complete flier when he definitely moves at the start but isn't called back by referee Paul Carrington. By lap two, David Norris has caught up and really pressures the American until he cocks up badly on the last bend of the third lap before he then pulls up on the back straight of the fourth lap and despondently trundles back through the pits gate without bothering to attempt to complete the race. The Eagles conclude with a drawn penultimate heat after Simota falls and a second for Pedersen in the last is small consolation when the final scoreline reads 61-34 and the Eagles would only perform worse at Peterborough. It would be the biggest home win of the season for the Bulldogs and arguably instils the whole team with the confidence that, when in form, they could get all the way and win the Elite League at the first time of asking. The Redin rider most pleased with his own return to form was Charlie Gjedde who beat fellow countryman Nicki Pedersen twice on his way to eight (paid 11) points tally that silences the rumour mongers on the grapevine who'd identified him as the rider to be cut from the team after a misfiring start to the season. Understandably team manager Jim Lynch pronounced himself "delighted".

15th May Reading v Eastbourne (Elite League A) 61-34

More queues at Arlington. © Jeff Scott

Nicki holds high hopes for the GP. © Jeff Scott

Karen reads about Nicki's operation. © Jeff Scott

Yet more bark from the Bulldogs
27th May

The chance to avenge the pasting handed out by the Bulldogs at Smallmead 12 days previously comes round quickly though both clubs field very much changed teams. The Eagles have seen Andrew Moore attempt to shore up his tattered confidence by dropping down to 'double up' in the Premier League with Mildenhall. Jon Cook hopes that the decision will be "confidence boosting" for the rider and is keen to emphasize, "the door is not closed on Andrew" but it's hard to imagine that it's presently open by any more than the tiniest of cracks. In his place, Edward Kennett joins and thereby takes the English contingent in the team back up to four riders. Ever willing to bang the patriotic drum Jon is excited by the young riders that will turn out for the Eagles, "it's a mouth-watering prospect to see Ed and Lewis in the same team and it must gladden the heart of all British speedway supporters, even the cynics (you can guess who!), that we have the future of the sport in this country riding together at such a young age."[1] If Jon does have any concerns about Lewis they centre around people "trying to jump on his bandwagon", though this will apparently be held in check by the legendary Eagles team banter in the pits "and we will be doing all we can to keep his feet on the ground and continue his rise to stardom at the appropriate rate."

Someone with more grounds for complaint is Reading team manager Jim Lynch who doesn't even have to search for one since tonight they track a vastly changed team without Matty Zagar and Greg Hancock, both of whom are involved in World Team Cup qualifiers for their respective countries. And most significantly, they're without Janusz Kolodziej who's recently broken his collar bone riding for his club Tarnow in Poland, it's really a significant blow since Janusz has regularly scored points for fun and by the bucketful at reserve. The club number eight, Chris Mills, who also rides at reserve for his Premier League team King's Lynn would like to ride and score with the same fluency at this Elite league level. Rather over-egging the psychological pudding, given that they have a 27-point advantage, Jim prefers to talk in terms of desperately hanging on to the bonus point. He rather conveniently or absentmindedly forgets that not only has the recent change in the averages meant that the Eagles use of the rider replacement facility is now weakened, since David Norris is no longer eligible for one of Adam Shields' rides, but (and it's a big but) he has secured the services of presently the most in-form rider in the world, Hans Andersen. The Dane has ridden superlatively in every European league all season and has been spurred onto even greater performances by his controversial omission for the 2006 GP series.[2] Whatever the reasons for his present good form and his determination on the track, Redin have chosen shrewdly and Hans is the sort of guest rider you'd always want to see turn out for your club in the absence of your own star rider. The encounters with Nicki Pedersen in heats 11, 13 and 15

[1] My guess is that this is another reference to Peter Collins and his yearly 'woe is the British Speedway world' tirade in the manner of Fraser from *Dad's Army* ("we're doomed!") about the lack of upcoming future British World Champions. A very real problem but one that he rehearses every year in the manner of the first cuckoo of spring, albeit that it's always a theme that finds its way into print in a winter issue of the *Speedway Star* in his case.

promise serious thrills and should be worth the admission money alone.

Carrying on where they left off, Eastbourne announcer Kevin 'KC' Coombes informs us that, "Reading have won the flip of the toss" before he switches to that safe topic of English conversation, the weather. Huddled with my usual gang by the safety boards of the last bend, we don't need to be told, "It's a summer night for the thermos and the blanket." There was drizzle as I drove over and not only is it cold and windy but low clouds hang over Arlington and around the vicinity in confirmation of the forecast of showers later. This sort of weather makes the track a nightmare to prepare for even someone as skilled and experienced as Bob Dugard, since you dare not lash too much water onto the track surface in case later rain quickly transforms it into an unraceable gloop. It's soon apparent that referee Chris Gay intends to run the meeting in a quick but orderly fashion barring any delay caused by crashes and injuries. The first race starts promisingly for the Eagles when it's apparent that Edward Kennett hasn't read the script and briefly leads Andersen out the second bend. Next to me Jane, ever one to have a religious slant to her exclamations, enquires, "Jesus – what's up with Kennett?!" before she continues with some bellows of encouragement for his race partner, "David! Go on David!" Floppy stalks the Dane for the majority of the race before he gains real speed into the third bend of the last lap and executes a sharp cut back that nearly catches Andersen on the line. Never one to need an excuse to do a wheelie, Lewis wins the reserves race and celebrates with some exuberance. While we all sign a 'Get Well' card, talk among ourselves turns to Dave Rice (and wife Margaret) who'd usually be stood here with us but for his recent operation to remove an aneurism from his brain. Apparently when he came round, he looked at his wife and said "I'm alive then?" before he almost immediately asked, "has Jeff published his book yet?" [No] and "what's been in the *Star*?" What a man!

Another man we can all marvel at news of is Adam Shields; who has apparently thrown aside the sheets on his Polish hospital bed to launch himself into a supremely rapid recovery regime from his broken pelvis and other injuries. Jon Cook notes, "I have to say on a personal note that I have never dealt with a rider who is so keen to explore every avenue possible and has such a single-minded attitude when it comes to getting back fit and racing for his team." We learn that a recent collection among the Arlington crowd raised "a fantastic £1650" and the "prize draw will be done by Adam Shields in the interval." Shortly afterwards KC informs us that they'll be "no interval tonight, only the natural breaks between races."

The next race up is a 'Battle of the Captains' that doesn't go well for the Eagles when the Redin skipper Travis McGowan wins and Andy Smith rides in his trademark extremely 'hard' fashion to relegate Deano to third. Edward doesn't finish the race at all after he falls. Though we're not *Showered in Shale*, throughout that race and the subsequent races we all get covered in a light film of dust that's blown into our faces by the strong wind and coats everything in its path with a dark brown material. It's best to view this as added minerals when it arrives in your drink or sandwiches but it has to be said, rogue flying dust is a rare occurrence from any track surface prepared by Bob Dugard at Arlington. Lewis makes a real hash of his start in the next race. But though he's last out of the gate by the exit from the second bend of the second lap he's already passed Mills to secure third place in a race where, according to Kevin 'KC' Coombes, "Nicki Picky's (?) winning time" is 57 seconds. Never one to miss the chance to obliquely or explicitly name check the fact that he's the master of

---

[2] This is truly a scandal as the flagship tournament in world speedway is apparently run by the BSI more in the manner that befits schoolyard gangs and features the gerrymandering of the field through the selection of favourites or those who come from countries with viewing audiences of significance to advertisers. If it's bad enough that in 2006 there is no mechanism by which a rider can actually qualify for this event – or even that in the future, since in the manner of a band aid on a wooden leg, only a very limited number of places will be subject to rules of fair competition, luck and skill – it seems capricious in the extreme. Especially given that the selection committee appointed to administer the selection of riders – a constituency of informed opinion ultimately chosen for this role by the commercial rights holder of the event, BSI/John Postlethwaite – can exclude with impunity riders who manifestly should be selected. It's widely seen that unwise and critical comments made by Hans Andersen in 2005 to a Danish newspaper were held against him when the 2006 field was chosen. Not only is there no court of appeal or any means by which the oversight can be rectified, but also this effectively deprives Hans of the chance to become World Champion in 2006. It's a year when he's in the best ever form of his career that, hopefully, will be repeated in other years but lady luck or injuries could intervene to ensure that his name is added to the long list of riders who had the skill and talent but never quite became World Champion. Though he's sensibly borne this ignominious decision with good grace, the rules of the GP series ensure that any points he wins in 2006 ultimately aren't eligible to be counted in the award of the GP crown. Still, this type of iniquity is a logical consequence of the competition being effectively privatised, since it's now owned and run for the benefit of a commercial organisation that has its primary responsibilities towards shareholders and board executives rather than one where the revenues generated go towards some 'general good' for the sport of speedway.

Jordan and Dave communicate with the riders. © Jeff Scott

Global ambitions for Nicki. © Jeff Scott

Practice laps bathed in sunshine for the Robins. © Jeff Scott

ceremonies at the Cardiff GP, Kevin fills the brief time between races with a cheery, "I'll look forward to seeing you at Cardiff." One person who unfortunately won't be there is Lewis Bridger. In a debacle that brilliantly captures the ongoing autonomy that the metaphorical right and left hands of the speedway authorities frequently suffers from, Lewis was originally invited to be one of the 'wild cards' at the event.[3] Only to then almost immediately have his invitation pre-emptorily rescinded when it was realised that under FIM regulations riders aged 16 can't actually compete since they're not officially 'old enough' to hold an international licence.[4]

Though in superb form, Hans Andersen isn't averse to stacking the odds further in his own favour, if allowed by the official, through movement at the start. The initial running of the fifth race is finally called back by Chris Gay, just as Hans reaches the third bend, which at least has the benefit that it allows Lewis to practise another start. The Barker-Bridger partnership has enabled the older Deano to put his team-riding skills to the fore and shepherd his younger partner round the Arlington track. They're well suited as Deano prefers to hug the inside line and Lewis has a natural inclination to fully open up the throttle as often as possible to blast round the outside. However, whenever Deano ventures or drifts wide, he undermines his good work as this sometimes inadvertently hampers the perennially fast acceleration of Bridger. Tonight provides a textbook example of this untimely blocking manoeuvre and thereby allows the combative 'Smudger' to sneak past to gain an unexpected third and take the scores to 14-16. Later Deano confesses all to Doctor Coombes, "I've had a virus for two weeks – I've missed two meetings – I can't get my set-ups right and everyone keeps pulling away from me."

In my group, Jane unseasonably dons her sunglasses to protect herself from the regular wafts of dust that are thrown in our direction each time the riders pass to complete another lap. Perhaps, Chris Gay also wears sunglasses since Edward Kennett is unpunished for his movement at the start and, even though he gets a flier and temporarily leads into the first corner, some form of justice is done when he still finishes last. For once, Karen Hazelden appears to have her wish come true ("we want Norris to have one good ride and then he'll be pumped up") in the next race and he's joined up front by Deano on machinery that intermittently stutters but doesn't prevent him relegating Gjedde to third and delivers

[3] Another quirk of the 'system' is that this remains a gift that resides solely within the purview of BSI/John Postlethwaite to bestow and invariably is used to grant admission to often comparatively inferior (in contrast to the general standard of the regular GP field) riders and cunningly chosen to maximise local interest in the media of the country that stages the Grand Prix round in question. And if an 'arbitrary' selection thereby manufactures an instant 'news' story (or to address a snafu like Hans Andersen's shocking omission) and thereby happily bestows additional publicity on the event and its sponsors.

[4] Jon Cook is not amused. "Surely in this day and age rules should be checked before announcements of this type are made and for someone so young I think he handled the disappointment very professionally." It's not really a surprise that BSI could make this error since they have become used to decision-making by fiat or caveat in so many areas of the GP series – since they control it and have *carte blanche* to frequently alter the 'mistaken' rules that they have themselves created/bungled. To run up against the rules of a governing body is an inconvenience that could be easily avoided with a modicum of forward planning (or familiarity with the relevant rulebook) but the earlier close season debacle – when Danny Bird was prematurely announced in and then pronounced out of the Bulldogs team with a speed that wouldn't disgrace Ben Johnson – shows some organisational previous when it comes to a lack of close study of the regulations that apply to the sport that is the supposed focus of their business and expertise.

a 5-1 that restores parity at 27 each. After a brief blare of music, Kevin is ecstatic enough to pretend to be the *Spitting Image* version of John Major, "once again the boys deliver – oh, yes!" before he soon resumes once more as himself "second – the skipper in bucking bronco style – Dean Barker!" Floppy is out again in the tenth race of the night and wins that one as well but chooses to celebrate with a muted but nonetheless regal wave to the home-straight crowd.

The first head-to-head race between the rival Danish superstars has Andersen get his retaliation in first with an aggressive elbow that would require a trip to the sin bin in rugby league or ice hockey, but here enables him to escape from Nicki. In a collector's item of a race, Nicki then hangs back – apparently satisfied with third place – to conduct a rare (but bizarre) exhibition of team riding with Cameron Woodward in an attempt to guide him home in second place. After Nicki has repeatedly nearly clattered his slightly unpredictable Australian partner from behind during the next couple of laps, common sense and self-preservation has Nicki sensibly abandon him to his own devices in order to guarantee he actually finishes the race. And finish he does roughly a quarter of a lap behind Hans who pointedly doesn't glance back or offer a wave of acknowledgement to his Danish compatriot, so keen is his fervent desire to rush back to the pits. Jane isn't happy, "he wasn't team riding him, he didn't have the speed and Woodward did well to let him past without letting Simota through."

While the dust eddies away towards the car park, the ever-professional Kevin uses the "natural" gaps between races to conduct some interviews. Travis is keen to stake his own place up the bottom of the BSI Reading management team, "I couldn't ask for anything better – we're really spoiled" before he adds in response to a probing question from KC, though the scoreline don't really bear out this claim, "we're soldiering on without our big guns." Keen to learn more, KC ploughs on regardless with a repeat of his previous question but in subtly different words, "how does it feel when you see they're not here?" this provokes a rare flash of Frank Worthington style interview humour ("I rose like a young salmon at the far post and headed home") from Travis, "I'm beside myself but we soldier on and, yes, we miss them!"

Aware that tonight appears to herald a temporary return to the rolling starts of the 70s, Deano attempts to join in, edges to the tapes and somehow holds himself back from touching them only for Chris Gay to sneakily outfox his cunning plan by his choice of that particular moment of withdrawal to release the mechanism. The net result is that the Bridger-Barker combination occupies the rear and Jane's optimistic but forlorn plea ('he's got to red light that one, surely?') remains resolutely unheard and unanswered from above us in the referee's box. But it is inadvertently answered by Andy Smith, when he does the decent thing and tantalises the fence by launching himself directly at it with rocket-like speed as he exits the second bend. The chance of a fourth successive drawn heat evaporates when the reverse of telepathy has Nicki Pedersen suddenly slow dramatically, just before the third corner of the last lap; an action that causes Floppy to have to dramatically bail out from his team-riding formation to avoid a collision. The referee awards the race and with two races to go the Eagles suddenly find the chance to get any home points at all also in doubt as the Racerdogs edge back into a 38-40 lead.

In the penultimate race, Deano spooks McGowan enough for him to fall off his bike just as the Londoner bravely battles past him at the start of the third lap. Sadly, it's not enough as Sam Simota races to his second win in as many races. To distract us from the nail biter ahead where the Eagles need a 4-2 to draw and a 5-1 to win, KC interviews a philosophical and positively loquacious (by his standards) Adam Shields, "If I look at it realistically, I was lying on a track in Poland six weeks ago." We get another of those brief anatomy and physiology refreshers that speedway is so famous for that, in this instance, features a glittering array of painfully broken bones that would cramp the style and test the resilience of a lesser man than Adam.

When what is needed is some measure of restoration to the usually telepathic understanding that exists within the Pedersen-Norris partnership, we don't get to witness this and, after the first bend, the race plays out disastrously for the Eagles and their fans. Norris gates superbly while the Redin pair of Andersen and McGowan execute their plan to drive Pedersen (already on gate 4) close to the fence and out of contention in an attempt to ensure the drawn heat they required to win. Unfortunately, Floppy's bike then immediately develops gremlins; he is passed on either side by the Redin riders and so putters round for another lap before he retires. Left forlorn a long way behind at the back, Nicki repeatedly glances down at his machine before he slows massively and just about avoids being lapped by the Redin riders as they

Cameron waves to admirers. © Jeff Scott

Nice shot of Lucy's (from the 'Sports Argus') handbag and leg.
© Jeff Scott

commence their last lap. Hans Andersen celebrates the win – and an unbeaten five-ride maximum that includes three wins against Nicki Pedersen on his own manor – with ecstatic delight and the accompaniment of readily understandable gestures.

Afterwards, Jim Lynch glories in "a fantastic performance" and correctly notes that the "team really upped their game and pulled off a great result." Ever keen to identify scapegoats, the crowd around me grumbles about the two points that Edward Kennett gained ("is he the 'new' Andrew Moore?"). Afterwards, when interviewed by the *Speedway Star* Jon Cook refuses to look for excuses and notes that though many of the team are under the weather, they can't be faulted for effort. "There are no excuses. We are not good enough…tonight it didn't happen. It is very rare you will see anyone come here and score a maximum while Nicki is in our team but it has happened tonight. That just about sums up the evening."

It's still light as the crowd promptly slips away to their dust-covered cars in the car park outside just after nine o'clock. The fact that it has been such a fast run meeting is one of the few consolations that can be taken from the night. As I drive home, a massive bank of fast-moving thick black clouds hang low over the hills by Lewes, almost obscuring them, illuminated by a weirdly lit, pink-tinged sky. After home defeats by Swindon and now Reading, back at Fortress Arlington a metaphorical dark cloud lingers over the possible Elite League winning credentials of the 2006 Eastbourne team.

27th May Eastbourne v Reading (Elite League A) 42-48

---

[1] In his round up about the 2006 season, Somerset team manager Mick Bell notes, "I thought it was one of those where they would get up and it would be four riders back for the restart. Trouble was, Paul didn't get up." When he came back from injury he suffered from inconsistency, "I think we stayed a little too loyal because we go back a long way together". Mick's suggestion that "a change of track will do him good" will hopefully come true in 2007 since he no longer has a place at Somerset under its new management. Or else, if he doesn't get a berth, his 16 meetings for Somerset for an average of 7.20 will be his final swansong and signal the end of an illustrious career.

"I think we are going in the right direction, but we've still got this problem they don't have in Poland or Sweden, particularly Poland. Every town's got a club where they've got a locker full of leathers, workshops full of bikes, kids come home from school, jump on a bike and are trained by a club trainer, paid by the club... During the winter, I've been riding at Sittingbourne Speedway and it's the ideal place to bring kids on. It's nothing flash, it's got a good little track, a junior track, changing rooms and a burger van, what more do you want?"
Mark Loram

"The former Ipswich favourite has gone through a whole range of changes in the last 18 months. A new club, a new mechanic, a new base in the Black Country and a new girlfriend in Kelly... he has also recruited former World Champion Gary Havelock to be with him at all the GP's, so on and off the track everything appears to be in place."
Mike Berry on Scott Nicholls

"I'm sorry to say that everything was taken, but life goes on and we just have to get on with it. Crying won't bring it back."
Colin Horton after theft of club takings for the Coventry meeting

"The SCB rules clearly state that when there is a ban for an assessed average rider such as Burza, the facility allowed is rider replacement. This covers bans by the FIM, ACU and SCB. It seems that the BSPA took it on themselves to inflict the ban and then tell us quite categorically that the only facility allowed to us on the night was the use of a C grade Premier League/Conference League rider to ride at #1 in place of Burza!"
Peter Waite practises his acronyms

"I've gone on record as saying I would wait until the middle of June before making any further decisions on the team, but Monday night just summed up how I'm feeling about things. I'm not going to name names because our supporters aren't stupid, they can see where the problems are."
Aaron Lanney (though it's easier to spot where the problems aren't on the scorecard)

"Lukasz was a troubled young man, but we fully intended to use him again, and he knew that. It is hard to take in what has happened, and we are all stunned by the news."
Ronnie Russell after the sad news that Lucasz Romanek has taken his own life

"It was a real stunner. Andrew only scored four points in a tough match against King's Lynn, but the fans took to his aggressive style. I talked to the lad to try to persuade him to stay with us, but he's built up quite a debt due to speedway apparently and sounded very worried about it."
Mick Horton on Andrew Moore's shock retirement

"Given that planning permission for speedway at this stadium was turned down a few years ago, it would be a big undertaking. In any case, we would need to discuss such a plan at the Wimbledon Speedway AGM to see if it was a viable proposition. Additionally, the BSPA would have to approve such a proposal. So, even if we decided we wanted to go to Sittingbourne, it would be a while before we could confirm anything. Although we hope to take Wimbledon to a new site, at present

we have no agreement to develop or run speedway anywhere. Any suggestion that we have already identified a site is pure speculation."
Ian Perkin comments on Sittingbourne Stadium rumours

"We did everything but win really and of course it's disappointing. I thought we had a plan for the final but obviously they had a plan too – and ours didn't work."
Alun Rossiter after Belle Vue defeat his riders in the EL Pairs final at Blunsdon

"I have been in speedway twice as long as Frank Ebdon and I don't recall seeing two more diabolical decisions. His officiating was poor all the way through the meeting but his decisions in Heat 15 were disgraceful... I believe Frank Ebdon didn't have his FIM status renewed a few years ago and I feel the SCB should look about doing something similar. Had the exclusions been earlier than Heat 15, I would have withdrawn the team from the meeting. We are in the business of racing and when things like this happen, it does the sport no good at all."
Colin Pratt

"Things have got to improve and, although I don't want to name names, there are no hiding places in speedway. People are putting themselves under the microscope. The guys that put themselves on our team sheet are the ones that could end up taking themselves off."
Neil Machin

"What we saw at Glasgow was a track which was sodden, but which did improve and there were dry lines appearing before the referee made the final decision. But there was moaning and whingeing from a section of the riders and the referee pandered to their opinions. Unfortunately if there's a shower at the wrong time, then some riders just want to walk away without any thought for the spectators who travelled the length and breadth of the country to be there – and they are the ones who pay the wages."
Neil Machin saddles up his hobbyhorse after the abandonment of the PL Pairs at Ashfield

"The angels now have nothing to fear as I can see Carlo saying: 'I'll make a special plaster cast for your broken wing and I'll have you flying in no time!'"
Bert Harkins after the memorial service for speedway doctor Carlo Biagi

"The riders in general are not attacking the first bend or chasing the dirt. They need to be much harder in the first turns. It is so desperately disappointing when these riders are banging in points in Sweden and Poland but looking half-hearted here."
Alun Rossiter

"I was absolutely disgusted by Eastbourne's attitude and if promoter Jon Cook had been here I would have told him so. I was especially unhappy with David Norris and Dean Barker, their older riders, who moaned the most. I went out on to the track as soon as the meeting had been called off and hardly got my shoes dirty. There was no doubt it was raceable. We've short changed the paying public and it wasn't fair to them."
Ian Thomas after the meeting with Eastbourne at Kirkmanshulme Lane is abandoned after 12 heats

"After discussing the situation with him, and listening to his point of view, I said that the good name of Belle Vue was at stake and we weren't prepared to have incidents of that nature again... I said that Tony Mole and I were fans of the Mexicans but that we were disappointed at language used by certain of their members."
Ian Thomas admonishes the beer throwers among the 'Manchester Mexicans'

"Numbers are down and I won't pretend otherwise. It's disappointing but there are reasons, but

by the same token I worry that after eight seasons back at Derwent Park the Workington public are taking us for granted, some have gone away and found other things to do. I'm prepared to admit that we cannot afford to lose spectators like we have this season, it's as simple as that."
Tony Mole

"To be honest I wasn't expecting to get the wild card for this weekend after what happened last year... I said what I wanted to say about being left out of the GP last year. There is still some bitterness, because I am young and I want to win the world championship...I still watch the GP's on the television out of curiosity. I don't make a big thing of it, but I do get cheesed off with some of the riders who have come in instead of me. It would have been easier to have accepted the decision of not being asked back had they replaced me with a rider of a similar level."
Hans Andersen on capricious decision making by the BSI on the field for the 2006 SGP series

1st June

I finally get to see a finished copy of the book from my printers in Milton Keynes (the print-on-demand publishers Lightning Source UK Ltd) and I was simultaneously both highly delighted and immediately irked. I was delighted that it looked so lovely and the pride you get from finally having the thing in your hands after so much effort is considerable (though not as much as I anticipated) but I'm definitely not so happy with the quality of the photos in the finished book, especially as they looked so different and clear on the final PDFs sent to the printer. It definitely fails to show Julie Martin's excellent photography in its best light, let alone my own photographs. There's no doubt it's a bargain in terms of breadth of coverage and the number of pages (508) and words (over 331,000) that you get for £20. I rush to B&Q to buy a dustsheet and a rather flimsy pasting table that I belatedly realise are essential equipment for any aspiring author. Problems at my leaflet printer mean that I will have to set off to Cardiff for the launch of my book at the Grand Prix without anything to hand out to people who decide not to purchase my book...grrhh. I spot my first error – Workington appears to have moved on the map from the north-west coast to inland somewhere near Stoke. This was corrected at proof stage by Rachael Adams but sadly somehow still snuck through to appear the final printed version.

First Night Lessons
2nd June

I set off early to the printers in Milton Keynes to pick up the innumerable boxes, load my car beyond its manufacturer's specifications (in the conviction that I'm about to fund my retirement from phenomenal book sales) that form my small part of the bulk stock and rush the copies cross-country for sale at Somerset Speedway where the always helpful Jo Lawson and Peter Toogood have kindly allowed me to sell my book for the first time. The Somerset fans were welcoming when I met them home and away during the 2005 season and continued to stay in touch to enquire about progress throughout the winter whilst I wrote my book. The majority of my advance orders were from these kindly Rebels fans – Margaret Hallett, Tiny Tim the Hat, Speedway Dave, Johnny Sometimes, Mr & Mrs Miles – and they all waited very patiently as every publication date that I set myself was comprehensively missed! On arrival at the printers I discover that there are way too many boxes to fit into my car without probably breaking it or ruining the suspension. Confident of huge success I order a 750 copy reprint while I'm there but hours later when driving slowly laden down with boxes near Cheltenham, I have second thoughts then make my shrewdest financial publishing decision of the year so far – when I stop at a service station to cancel my just booked reprint. It's a boiling evening at Somerset Speedway but the welcome is even warmer

Enticing Rebels poster. © Jeff Scott

Margaret Hallett (aka Supergran) with Karen inside the Somerset programme stall. © Jeff Scott

from the local fans, promotional team of Peter and Jo, along with Nick and Johnny Barber in the track shop as well as from the visiting fans from Berwick who have loyally come along to see their team before the Cardiff Grand Prix the next day. Berwick ride well but stumble to defeat. Ben Barker really impresses me with his combative riding though sadly 43-year-old Paul Fry sustains a bad injury after he receives the attention of Craig Branney's elbow and suffers a confrontation with the fence.[1] The few copies I do sell are well received and the first ever purchaser of my book at a speedway meeting – the fanatical, obsessive but friendly Berwick-supporting speedway nut and taxi driver Jim Brykajlo from Penicuik – even reads three chapters between races and pronounces it "fantastic". His word of mouth generates some more sales among some other Berwick fans in attendance. I make my second sale to Dougie – Jim's fellow partner in crime at many speedway meetings throughout the country – along with the ladies from the turnstiles at Shielfield Park Lacey (whose name I misspell in the book) and Muriel. I leave with a warm glow from the evening only slightly dissipated by some stolen books and what I think are incredibly low sales only to learn in the coming days that this sales number (nine) is in reality a triumph cum outstanding success! I learn some important author lessons – park your car as close as possible to where you expect to display/sell your book; that it's hot work humping boxes about on a summer evening and, most importantly, have eyes in the back of your head and only ever display a few copies on your table so you can just about manage to guard them while multitasking (signing copies, looking for change, answering questions etc.). The slight late evening wind also teaches me that I will need elastic bands to stop the books ceasing to look pristine since the flapping cover and pages leaves them slightly curled at the edges. When you've got a book display, you also stay right until the bitter end as the last of the stragglers among the fans lurk about by the track shop, the toilets or linger by the track fence. Hope springs eternal with my assumption that every remaining person is a potential book purchaser. Sadly this is misplaced optimism. The long walk to the car is repeated in reverse with pretty well the same number of boxes. Later en route to Cardiff, I find myself stuck in a traffic jam at midnight on the M5.

2nd June Somerset v Berwick (Premier League) 53-39

The Importance of Chalk and Vigilance
3rd June

The Rye House track shop owner, Andy Griggs, has kindly invited me to launch my book and enjoy my first author signing at the inaugural *Speedway Fayre* he has organised with promoter Mike Golding from Poole. I'm unable to get my head in the building when I discover that I'm putatively an attraction – if the information on the Pirates website and the small advert stuck in the building window is anything to judge my fame and popularity by. If I was a fan who'd been attracted to this event, I'd be much keener to encounter or meet the riders Antonio Lindback, Bjarne Pedersen and Edward Kennett rather than some bloke you've never heard of who's written a speedway book you know nothing about. And so it proves. My next important author lesson is that possession is nine tenths of the law and, by the time I arrive at the venue and start to unload my books, table etc.. I discover that every other stall holder has already arrived before me. In fact, they've claimed *all* the best spots and I'm relegated to the passageway *en route* to the pungent toilets. Looking to the bright side though, I do have the benefit of a cooling breeze on a scorching day, the perfumed smell of the gents' toilets, the chance to direct so many people there that I would have made more money charging them for directions and the attention of some OAP drunks who aren't speedway fans and are too inebriated to recall what it is.

I completely fail to learn yesterday's important author lesson about book thefts as at some point during the day a whole box (18) of my books goes missing. I only notice this at the very last moment when I'm reloading my car with my large pile of unsold boxes. Most of these have lived for the afternoon out of my sight under a table in the room that the *Speedway Fayre* was held in, so this box could only have been liberated from there or in transit along the hugely crowded street to my car in the late afternoon sunshine. The discovery that thefts far outstrip my sales on a day when I confidently expected that I might need the services of Securicor to help me home with all the cash that I expected my book sales to generate is, to put it mildly, a disappointment. The next day I completely dismiss the confident assertion of others at Swindon that most crimes, like they do on the telly, require the means, motive opportunity and ability to benefit afterwards. According to them, on this basis it's most likely not to be Colonel Mustard in the conservatory with the lead piping but, in fact, it's likely to be another stallholder rather than my preferred explanation that it was a random, opportunist theft of a heavy box in the street. Whatever the answer, and I'm sure mine is correct, I now realise that trust and extra vigilance is always needed.

I should also add chalk to my list of essential accoutrements for any budding author considering going on the road to promote their books. It quickly becomes clear that *Showered in Shale* is not the *Da Vinci Code* – I'd like to think that it's arguably better written but, the language of sales success can never be gainsaid, particularly as my book sells an infinitesimal fraction in comparison to what Dan Brown sells worldwide in any randomly chosen minute. The level of visitors to the *arriviste Speedway Fayre* that I'm stood in the corridor outside of for the afternoon falls far short of the long-standing rival fayre organised by the Barber family over the road in the Millennium Stadium complex (even though you have to pay a pound to enter) that has become part of the fabric of the overall Cardiff day out for speedway fans who attend the GP. It has the additional attraction that a number of other new speedway books are launched there with authors in attendance. In fact, the question I'm asked fourth most often throughout the afternoon is the slightly indignant "where's Simmo?" since fans enquire about the whereabouts of the legendary Malcolm Simmons who's launching his "controversial" (trademark practically every speedway book published by Tony MacDonald under his well-regarded *Retro Speedway* imprint) autobiography today. Almost as many people ask the third question ("where's the *Speedway Fayre*?" or its variant "where's the *proper Speedway Fayre*?") as the second ("where are the riders?" or its variant "when are the riders coming?"). Though the most popular and winning question is "where's the loo?" These people must have no sense of smell and I must either appear like an authority figure or a receptionist.

Apparently the brand new, launched today Simmo book sells like hot cakes – guesstimates vary from a believable 200 to a barmy estimate of 1000 – and Ian Thomas sells 30 of his great read *Wheels & Deals*. Ian later estimates Simmo sold three copies for every one Ian managed to sell in the three hours he was close by to Simmo there, so somewhere around the lower figure of 200 seems a more reasonable estimate. My need for a security escort to take the cash generated by book sales to the bank doesn't materialise though I do set a new sales record for my book of 11 copies sold and also get to answer many questions – mostly about what my favourite track is and, of course, where the (strong-smelling) toilet is. Two yards away round the corner is the answer and I mentally add a tips bowl to my growing list of essential accoutrements. By the time I leave the Fayre the friendly madness that is the Cardiff GP is in full swing in the sunshine. I take a first-time visitor to the magnificent Millennium Stadium – who as a Cardiff resident is shocked by the huge expanse of empty seats inside the arena. The news that it's a "record crowd" isn't quite correct as the official FIM-certified attendance has been higher in the past (42,000 in 2002) and for a number of years now the 'showcase' event of the speedway calendar appears to have always attracted the rather suspiciously exact official attendance of "40,000". Personally I have a lot more faith in

Message on the blackboard. © Jeff Scott

Advert for the new speedway fayre. © Jeff Scott

Blimey, a £7 GP programme! © Jeff Scott

the figure of 35,251 quoted as the official attendance at Cardiff in 2004 as an exact reflection of numbers present. That said, it's common practice for football clubs to count season-ticket holders as attendees whether or not they are actually present. There's no doubt that this is a lot for contemporary speedway and many more people than any other Grand Prix venue ever manages, but it singularly fails to convince my first-time visitor about the popularity of our great sport in comparison to football or rugby[1].

In a rush of blood just after Christmas I'd decided to treat myself to an extortionately expensive ticket on the first bend of the Millennium Stadium at a staggering cost of £55. This would be called "gouging" in *The Sun* if it were at a Rolling Stones or Madonna concert (and all we get are Tony Bennett and Bonnie Tyler as musical entertainment) but the regular or one-off fans who travel to the Cardiff GP appear happy to pay this or similar sums – the cheapest ticket is still £29 – for the honour of the one meeting a season that can be spent in a deluxe facility, albeit only one that is hired for the night. If we assume an average ticket price of £40, the event grosses nearly £1.6 million which should be enough to keep John Postlethwaite in *Minder*-esque, London geezer type coats and provide sufficient funds to try to buy success in the Elite League with his latest toy, the Racerdogs. The great unspoken in all coverage and hoopla that surrounds this highlight of the UK speedway calendar is the consistently awful nature of the temporary track. Luckily, this year it doesn't look so bad to me as eventually I find myself watching from the 'nosebleed' heights of the back-straight grandstand after I'd won a pair of £29 tickets in a competition organised by *Planet Speedway*. My expensive ticket goes to waste since I don't even manage to give it away, despite an afternoon of trying. The whole of our row comprises of lucky winners and I'm sat next to a hugely enthusiastic Oxford-supporting 11-year-old boy and a man I mistake for his grandfather (on account of his florid complexion and uniquely old-fashioned, noticeably disciplinary approach to parenting skills). The boy refuses to wear the obligatory earplugs, so remains completely alive to every nuance of the toy-town races far below us as well as delights in filling out his programme and the 'vibrant' atmosphere of our part of the stand. The lack of passing and excitement in the races – partly due to the shocking condition of the surface of this temporary track – completely fails to enthral and inspire my first time visitor, though the sheer exuberance of the fans does really impress him – both inside and outside the stadium. He informs me that the stadium catering and bar prices remain at authentic rugby international type levels but views it as an affront to his national pride that we singularly fail to fill the Millennium Stadium ("I can't believe how empty it looks or the lack of atmosphere"). He does approvingly notice the total lack of the obligatory match-day heavy police presence. Any boisterous chippie in nearby genteel Canton gets more uniformed officers on any Saturday

---

[1] Clearly the Grand Prix is primarily designed for the television audience and crowd size will vary according to stadium size as well as the sport's relative popularity in the country where it is staged. The second biggest crowd of the 2006 series was 24,892 in Copenhagen closely followed by 24,500 in Wroclaw with Lonigo a meagre 4,500 – though now looked back on as "4,500 + 1" in some speedway circles – but record breaking since it's the lowest official attendance figure for any Grand Prix round since 1999.

night than attend the GP or lurk outside.

3rd June British Grand Prix – Winner: Jason Crump

A Tale of Two Meetings
4th June

I have my own double header of meetings at which to display my book. Tim Stone kindly gives me pride of place near the turnstiles where I manage to get sunburnt in the late morning/early afternoon sunshine. Sales to the public aren't great (3) but a bloke called Arnie, a chap I've never met before – the great thing about these trips and selling so few copies is that I get to meet 'my public' as they say in show business or readers as they're more commonly known in publishing circles – tells me my book is "the Fever Pitch of speedway". He's so chuffed with it so far that he later kindly comments on the British Speedway forum (where he thinks it might become "the best speedway book ever"). I decide not to argue as I've already by then heard from the hard-working ladies who voluntarily administer and organise the fund-raising activities of the SWARM club at Newport speedway, Jayne and Janet. They have unfortunately taken umbrage to the comments I report in the book that they made last August. I think that they've misread what is written in my book and have chosen to forget, misremember or clarify the sense of what they did say. Nonetheless they make it clear that they only have Newport speedway's interests at heart and have not criticised the track. Not that I said that they did. Nonetheless I'm keen to emphasize to everyone that reads that chapter of the book that they are huge supporters of all things Newport Speedway and, though others have, they HAVEN'T in any way criticised the condition of the track at Hayley Stadium. I beat a hasty retreat only to discover that track photographer Hywel Lloyd also really isn't happy with some comments in the book about the standard of his work subsequently introduced as 'corrections' by Tim Stone into the Newport chapter in question. Hywel is incensed and buys a copy of the book, apparently "to send to my lawyer" and is also adamant that, contrary to Tim's equally definite denials, that he stands by his comments that many people have been previously banned from the club by Tim for actual or perceived minor criticisms/misdemeanours. They say discretion is the better part of valour – and since I've only really had good things to say about the club, its many volunteers and hard working owner/promoter – I resolve not to intrude any further on private grief of whether this is an issue for Hywel's lawyer or not.

Before the gates open, I almost meet the perpetually glowering John 'I'm a Freaking Professional' Jones and his charming lady partner, but don't because they remain studiously standoffish. When I casually ask if they can keep an eye on my boxes of books that I place next to their stall, while I get more stuff from my car (since I'm now convinced that my books are meat and drink to all speedway thieves after I suffered thefts on successive days), John grunts non-committally and they both pull a face as if I'd just asked if I could spray their speedway memorabilia with radioactive pig manure. Subsequently, as actions can say more about you than words, by the time I return my boxes have mysteriously moved a few yards away from their stall. I'm sure that I appear as what I am – a Johnny-come-lately first-time speedway author who they don't know and don't wish to know. Plus, I'm obviously not a "professional" judging by my equipment, merchandise and lack of sun cream or faux oleaginous manner. They have a stall of high quality 'me-too' speedway goods on display in the sunshine that also singularly fails to excite the crowd during the time that I'm there. Interestingly, they allegedly almost became speedway promoters but were outbid by Tony Mole when John Perrin sold Belle Vue!

Traditionally there's always a good-sized crowd on the Sunday after the Grand Prix swelled by the sheer number of speedway mad visitors in the Cardiff area but reportedly still not as many as were in attendance to watch the Newport v Glasgow encounter on the Friday night. I imagine the contrast that any first-time visitor would have noticed between a trip to the Cardiff Millennium and Hayley stadiums. In fact, the more casual Newport experience would be much more in keeping with the day-to-day reality that is the contemporary spectating lot of the average speedway fan. For me this is part of the appeal, probably for the recently involved new breed of entrepreneur attracted by the television cameras and the

Trophies await the victors. © Jeff Scott

Elsewhere Jon Cook spills the beans. © Jeff Scott

A pensive Nick Barber with his sister Bev at their crowded track shop. © Jeff Scott

promise of the commercial opportunities – this stadium and the style of presentation would be illustrative of the severe presentational and infrastructure problem they believe speedway has to face and overcome if it is to survive. But survive on whose terms? Co-existence and mutual support would be preferable but, we've already seen where money and fame are involved, the new breed of 'entrepreneur' promoter bursting with allegedly 'innovative' ideas brooks no compromise and invariably pays scant attention to the culture and tradition of the sport, except where these can be used to set the scene or provide the required hint of spurious 'authenticity of tradition' for the cameras.

The breaking news of the Welsh Open meeting is Adam Shields' rapid return from hip injury. In order to justify his premature return from serious injury, it's claimed Adam says that a broken hip isn't "load bearing" when you're on a bike, so apparently it's safe to ride... Adam comfortably wins his first race but looks tentative thereafter before he withdraws from the meeting without completing all his rides. I do too, when I leave the scorching sunshine to dash like a madman to Swindon where it's initially cloudy and then becomes scorching. I learn from Nick Barber that he also sold 11 of my books at his collector's fair in Cardiff (and had none stolen) so that's a boost. Stood around for the next couple of hours without any sales to cover the inflated cost of display (£70 is the most I'm charged all year on my travels though it's collected promptly with some charm by Wayne Russell) isn't much fun but I manage to meet quite a few people I know. I enjoy chatting with the passers by and meet a charming older gentleman from Belle Vue. Dave Pavitt spends the afternoon in the bar reading the Isle of Wight chapters from my book and comes back to pronounce them "excellent – you capture everything so well". Later Dave Croucher says similar ("it's really very good") before he leaves to miss the crowds in the car park afterwards. Tony Steele kindly tells me it brings a smile to his face every time he reads a chapter and is sure that it will be a great success, if I'm patient. A copy of my book I pass onto a helpful man from Arena Essex (for the legendary photographer and speedway track shop owner Alf Weedon) is stolen from the bar when he's not looking – I suppose all these thefts are some form of a compliment, at least that's how I try to teach myself to choose to see them!

The Pairs is spoilt by some late rider withdrawals from the advertised line up – Peter Karlsson is replaced by Ronnie Correy and Mark Loram has Kim Jansson deputise in his place, thereby at a stroke ending the title pretensions of Wolverhampton and Ipswich, though David Norris replaces Deano to add sparkle to the Eagles line up. Combined with the fact that there are two wonkily different sized qualification groups, the racing struggles to rise above lacklustre on a boiling hot afternoon better suited to the desert rather than Wiltshire and never quite dispels the sense that many of the riders are just going through the motions and that this meeting is a 'come-down' after the comparative exertions that is the adrenaline high of the Grand Prix competition the day before in Cardiff. Beforehand there is much talk about the likelihood that Leigh Adams might achieve a unique treble of successive victories since he won in

2004 with Charlie Gjedde and 2005 with Lee Richardson. Before the season started you'd have expected the Adams-Richardson partnership to ride again this year at Blunsdon but Lee's early season fatigue brought on by the "mistake" of additional guest bookings has compounded the pressure of his already hectic travel schedule to reduce his British average. So Leigh will have to try to triumph with the aid of Sebastian Ulamek. Belle Vue win the final by allowing Leigh Adams to make the mistake of racing away for an easy victory in the race but not on overall points scored, since 'team riding' for second and third places is highly rewarded in this championship. As Ian Thomas noted a few days afterwards "our plan to let him go worked a treat – you didn't exactly need to be mastermind to figure it out but apparently they couldn't. We all expected it to be the slowest heat of speedway ever, as everyone tried hard not to win, but Adams just shot off to leave us where we wanted and we won surprisingly easily". At least this year's result should, albeit temporarily, manage to briefly still the perennial internet forum arguments over (inevitable) home track advantage. With many months' travel around the country ahead of me again this year, I realise I'm going to become an expert on service station toilets and risk developing a persecution complex regarding late-night traffic jams or hold ups caused by the perpetual round of midnight road repairs. Tonight bad traffic near Portsmouth causes delays on the A27 home.

4th June Welsh Open – Winner: Chris Holder
4th June Elite League Pairs Championship – Winner: Belle Vue

Small Crowd at Arlington for televised ornithological encounter
5th June

I rush a box of books over to Martin Dadswell in the Eastbourne track shop where they remain unopened and unloved after underwhelming the shockingly meagre crowd that bothers to turn up for the live televised *Sky* meeting. The always helpful and knowledgeable Chris Durno, the SCB Official, advises that I get a large sign to go with my pasting table to draw attention to myself and advertise the availability of my book at track signings. I add this to my list of essential author equipment. I chat to the gifted but modest Eastbourne announcer Kevin 'KC' Coombes in the referee's box and encourage him to push himself forward and apply for a commentary job on *Sky Sports*, since I'm sure he'd be excellent. He seems strangely shy and reluctant to draw attention to his facility with words on the microphone, as demonstrated every meeting at Arlington, the Cardiff Grand Prix and yesterday's Elite League Pairs meeting. Later I amuse myself by signing the books for when demand picks up (these are then known as "damaged" in publishing circles if a bookshop has the temerity to try to return them). Floppy's always cheerful mechanic Chris Geer – aka Geernob – kindly buys a copy as he's already been completely wound up by Deano (Dean Barker) that his off-the-cuff, drunkenly honest comments from the early morning set up of the *Brighton Bonanza* night had appeared in print. As it happens, I'd edited them so that only the sincere or uncontroversial ones had been caught for posterity. Geernob admits to being too drunk to remember what he said (or even meeting me) but recently had had some anxiety about the career implications of what might have been said and subsequently reported when repeatedly reminded of it by Deano.

It's a sparsely attended Arlington Stadium since we've been blessed with the presence of the *Sky Sports* television cameras and the appeal of the fixture hasn't been helped with Eastbourne still hit by absence through injury of the taciturn Adam Shields, after his expected return to the side was "put on hold". With Jon Cook already talking the language of expectation management for the Eagles faithful "tough decisions and a tough season but still plenty to race for yet, we need your support all the way and hope you can understand that while we are not as assured as previous seasons of home wins we are building some very firm and exciting foundations for the future." Indeed the Eagles not only track four Englishmen in the team of six riders (with rider replacement for Shields) but have three talented younger riders on display in the form of Cameron Woodward, Edward Kennett and Lewis Bridger. Meanwhile Swindon promoter, Alun Rossiter, confidently approaches the meeting with some heightened expectation after an earlier season 55-41 win at Arlington and thereby arrives looking for a "good result" and to "win again".

The likelihood of a Robins victory is extinguished before it's begun when Leigh Adams' bike has an engine failure before he's left the start line in the first heat and the fixture has effectively ended as a contest as early as the fourth heat when the Eagles can only manage a 4-2 to go with the three successive 5-1s they opened the meeting with. The few Eagles fans that there are in the stadium can't quite believe it and although the use of the dreaded tactical ride rule realises maximum points for the Robins through double points victories by Adams and Lee Richardson to narrow the scores to 24-18. This is as close as they get to parity on the night. With some support from Sebastian Ulamek, Leigh Adams conducts an ultimately fruitless one-man resistance campaign that also sees him gain some satisfaction when he defeats home handlebar hero Nicki Pedersen twice in their three late meeting encounters. Pleased with the victory, I leave disheartened at the lack of sales but, for once, experience no traffic delays on the way home.

5th June Eastbourne v Swindon (Elite League B) 53-43

Initial Lesson in Professionalism
6th June
I learn that my leaflets have now been inadvertently delivered to the pub in Cardiff where I had my almost toilet-side display at the *Speedway Fayre* last weekend. The print shop will endeavour to retrieve them in time for my next trip to Sheffield on Thursday. On the phone with Ian Thomas, in the manner of fishermen who talk about the enormous size of the one that got away, we compare notes on venues and sales of our respective books. His book is bound to attract attention given his name and the enjoyable stories within, plus it's been relentlessly promoted in the *Speedway Star* so it's hardly a surprise he outsells me roughly 74 to 1. He kindly agrees to help promote my book at Belle Vue, when they ride against Eastbourne later in the month, but suggests, as "a courtesy" I call the rather territorial (understandably so, given he pays rent for his pitch to the stadium owners) and belligerent Belle Vue track shop franchise owner John Jones to seek his permission in advance to sell my book for only one night. Ian noted "I get on really well with him but he can be difficult and he didn't appreciate it that Chris Morton – he IS Mr Belle Vue, after all – sold his book there last year without asking and definitely didn't give him any commission". On my travels, I have always sought permission from every track shop owner in advance of any visit to sell my book and also offered to pay a nominal commission fee, if appropriate. John "I'm a freaking professional and you're just a freaking prick along with all the other freaking pricks" Jones goes ballistic on the phone when I call to suggest that I might be able to display my books for one evening and bluntly refuses permission. After much swearing and abuse, he then abruptly hangs up "to freaking think about it" before he kindly calls back an hour later to tersely, but nonetheless apparently considerately as he doesn't have to, consent to my attendance on June 19th "though it's against my better judgement as it'll only attract more freaking pricks like you who think they can stick their freaking nose into my freaking business with their freaking big ideas, taking the piss when I'm the freaking mug who pays out to be freaking professional". Later I have my first radio interview with Seth Bennett of *BBC Radio Sheffield* in advance of my trip there in two days' time. It goes so well I decide I'm a natural – in reality Seth is so effortlessly capable and gifted as an interviewer that he allows me to delude myself – and hope that I have a face suitable for radio.

Outsold by Simmo again (and he's not even there!)
8th June
I stand just inside the Owlerton entrance gates and try to hand out my flyers to everyone who passes as they rush from the turnstiles to wherever their favoured spot in the stadium happens to be. Reactions to them vary – some are

immediately thrown on the floor, other people stuff them in their pockets or bags while some refuse them as though I've made a deeply improper suggestion. The promoters Neil Machin and Malcolm Wright consistently attract big crowds to watch Sheffield Tigers Speedway, even for the Premier Trophy qualification matches like tonight's against unfashionable, local rivals Stoke, so my supply of promotional leaflets is soon exhausted. As I continue to lurk by my pasting table and small pile of books (deliberately so to maximise my chances of being able to guard against possible thefts) I listen to a variety of comments, made as though I wasn't the author or as if I were invisible. "It's too expensive here, can you buy it in the shops at discount?" "There are too many speedway books." When eventually someone decides to buy a copy when I ask, "shall I sign it?", he responds with a shrug and a "you can if you want but no need to for me."

When the racing starts I move my table and books round to just beside the track shop run by the always cheery lorry-driving, Derby County fan Mick Gregory – where tonight he's helped by the friendly, speedway programme collecting obsessive Bill, who also works at some of the Dave Rattenberry empire track shops dotted at other speedway clubs around the country. It's a great place to watch the racing from as it overlooks the start line and the first bend, plus the lure of these attractive tables of speedway merchandise attracts almost continuous interest amongst the fans. Though my book stall gets little attention, the free juice stall next to me – that either slims you or gives you a fantastic erection, I'm not quite sure – does extremely well and sells out well before the end of the meeting.

After a number of below par performances, it's imperative that the Tigers win by more than six points (following a 48-42 defeat at Loomer Road) in order to ensure they qualify for a revenue boosting semi-final encounter with Rye House. The meeting with Stoke goes the way of all flesh and isn't even close after the home riders record an untroubled 5-1 in the first heat. Many visiting riders struggle to cope with the peculiar shape of a circuit massively exacerbated by the sheer speeds that its size demands it's ridden at, and the Stoke riders are no exception. By the fourth heat the Tigers were ahead on the night and on aggregate and only the experienced Mark Lemon and Robbie Kessler offered token resistance, when they become the only Stoke riders to actually win a race, albeit only once each. The fourth heat did provide some excitement for the crowd as the lingering bad feeling that still apparently exists between Andre Compton and Alan Mogridge briefly flared into life on the track, but resulted in an exclusion for Moggo for what referee Tony Steele deemed to be "dangerous riding".

The entertainment on offer at Owlerton is nothing if not great value for money as not only do you not have to pay for a programme because a unique race card is provided free of charge, but tonight we're also treated to a special second half that features a three team tournament between Sheffield, Scunthorpe and trackless Hull. Though the teams comprise junior or Conference League standard riders, the racing is committed and highly competitive, arguably more entertaining than a main course that only featured one heat advantage for the visitors. The return to the speedway track of a team with the Hull name hopefully represents a first step on a journey back to the future for the club after the debacle of their premature closure before the end of the season in 2005. It also represents the first steps back to widespread public acceptance (to go along with the private respect and support) for their popular Sheffield based team manager, Dave Peet, who saw his savings lost and reputation briefly tarnished during his brief sojourn as the club's co-promoter. Home advantage ultimately wins out as the Sheffield riders dominate proceedings and illustrate the value of their junior training track when it comes to youth rider development.

As we pack up Mick says "I sold six of Simmo tonight, which I was pleased with as it's new, though he was a bit of a lad." I loiter in the speedway office where the issue of the phantom or real flickering red light apparently evident to the riders during the Premier Trophy ("it was the experienced ones saying this, so I believe them and have to take it seriously") vexes modest but expert referee Tony Steele, the trainee official with him and a rather nonplussed Neil Machin. The lack of sales for my book also perplexes a philosophical Neil "I'd have thought you'd have sold twenty not four tonight – just shows there's no predicting it". As Tony Steele nonchalantly changes out of his smart referee's clothes into his more casual driving attire in the car park, he laconically tells me a story about how he once enjoyed the chance to watch The Sport newspaper get printed. They understand their market so well that they apparently make a profit before they even print a copy from all the space advertising they've pre-sold. They then print the first 200,000 for a tenth of a penny before he sets the conundrum "you're intelligent – they pray for rain every night as after that first 200,000 it's free if it rains – can you figure out why?" I retire to the nearby Garrison Hotel disconsolate and puzzled.[1]

8th June Sheffield v Stoke (Premier Trophy) 57-38
8th June Sheffield v Hull v Scunthorpe (Challenge) 24-14-19

The Book on Showers I've Always Wanted
9th June

Upon arrival I make my only sale of the evening – to Keith the friendly security man on the front gate. On a very warm June evening, it's all down hill from there though I'm very appreciative that admirable and experienced Coventry Bees co-promoter, Colin Pratt, has been extremely kind to let me set up my book stall in the stadium in the area that everyone has to pass after they've funnelled in through the turnstiles. The very experienced Peter York volunteers to promote the book over the microphone, which he does so well I feel like I should buy a copy myself but it apparently doesn't grab everyone else the same way. I do get one lady who exclaims "wow – this is the book I've always wanted, how much is it?" After flicking through it enthusiastically, she almost immediately puts it down with the immortal words, "but it's not about showers, it's about speedway." Though I tell her that this is unlikely as we are at a speedway track after all, she's adamant "I definitely only want it if it's about showers". One man is interested until I say "can I tell you anything about my book?" which causes him to look startled, immediately put it back down on my table and stride off muttering, "oh, it's your book is it?" One young boy says, "daddy, daddy, there's a book that was in the *Speedway Star!*" which fails to halt his purposefully striding father who disappears off, while the boy momentarily lingers uncertainly before he runs off to catch up. Some other young lads look inside the books for ages before one says, "it's big, how many words is it?" When I tell him it's 331,000 his eyes bulge and he nonchalantly observes "Cor – my mum nearly says that many on the phone every night."

Joyce Blythe and her husband Malcolm from the track shop are remarkably helpful, very encouraging and are keen to do everything they can to ensure that the evening is a success. They feel that locating me just after the turnstiles, by one of the tunnels that leads to trackside and next to the bar that shows Germany's first fixture in the World Cup should help ensure that I get people's attention. They're friendly, down-to-earth folk and even managed to sell one of the copies they took into stock, which is much more than I can claim! Hurrah!

What little talk there is, in the section of grandstand that overlooks the start line that I choose to watch proceedings from, centres around the performance of Frank Ebdon in the recent factious and controversial away meeting at Arena Essex. Colin Pratt covers the key events in his programme notes but, ultimately, remains characteristically phlegmatic (though a few words from Colin is often equivalent to a ferocious diatribe from others), "it's very frustrating, but it's history now although obviously I have made my feelings known on the subject." He welcomes the visitors and, he playfully alludes to the last encounter the clubs enjoyed (live on *Sky Sports*) where the national television audience witnessed first hand the sometimes fiery reactions and behaviour of Belle Vue promoter, Ian Thomas. "If Ian does get out of hand here tonight unfortunately we don't have a phone box to lock him in. However, we could accommodate him in one of the side-sheds somewhere by locking him in there if required!" At the interval, Coventry have raced to an untroubled and comfortable ten point lead but afterwards, something must have got into their tea since they falter badly. They lose three of the last five heats to enable Belle Vue to post a much closer final scoreline than really should have been the case. By his own high standards, Jason Crump fails to get a maximum but still posts a 'meagre' 13 (paid 14) points after Scott Nicholls beats him once in their three much anticipated but ultimately anticlimactic encounters. Blissfully completely unaware of anything from

[1] I later learn that apparently very few people – even its target readership of testosterone-soaked males of below-average intelligence aged under 40 – are prepared to risk the 'social disgrace' among the neighbours and newsagent staff that a regular subscription to *The Sport* at their local newsagents would create. However, when it rains it restricts the opportunity for manual labour outdoors, (anonymous) sales direct from shops increase its circulation exponentially since the unexpected chance to peruse the complicated philosophical theses and anatomical pictures it contains in the comfort of your van, portacabin or canteen invariably proves much too hard to resist. I'm still not quite sure that I understand since the ready availability of the papers in newsagents around the country implies that they have to print additional copies most nights in the hope of rain the next day.

my vantage point in the main grandstand, after the meeting the internet forums crackle with opinion and speculation about a late meeting beer-throwing incident that involved the feisty travelling sombrero-wearing 'Manchester Mexicans' and a celebrating Martin Smolinski.

However, romance is in the air as early in the meeting there's a marriage proposal over the tannoy. The ever professional Peter York gets the would be romantic couple-in-question together after Heat 15 and instructs the groom-to-be to "do it properly – get down on your hands and knees to propose!" The broadcast of "will you marry me?" into the portable microphone held close by to the suitor's mouth, immediately gets an affirmative answer and Peter – ever professional and with an eye to a story that will definitely create some more column inches for the club – suggests that they definitely consider the option of a centre-green wedding. What a romantic he is.

9th June Coventry v Belle Vue (Elite League A) 49-42

Peppered in Shale at the Arlington Launch
10th June

I turn up less than an hour before tapes up at Arlington for the fixture against Belle Vue and Neil Hollebon on admissions duty in the car park surprises me when he says, "where have you been? You're supposed to be signing your book here tonight!" I reply that I was but Jon Cook had cancelled it when he told me on Monday that he'd just remembered that he'd previously promised Ian Thomas that he could sign his book. Martin Dadswell in the track shop tells me that I'm supposed to be launching my book and in the pits Jon Cook says, "it's up to you but I'd do a signing". Jon has been very helpful throughout, so I seize the opportunity to stand next to where the *Argus Sports* newspaper sellers Lucy and Lynn usually stand, though tonight a male colleague has replaced Lynn. As ever the headline on the poster they have concerns something to do with Nicki Pedersen – apparently it's an immutable law since in this respect he's the Lady Diana of Eastbourne Speedway as the use of his name in some tangential statement or other guarantees more sales than linking anyone else's name with exactly the same statement. Tonight's headline is something shouty about last week's GP (or the reintroduction of hanging, I forget which). My table of books immediately attracts attention – an unusual event in itself – from Sid Shine who says, "I'd have definitely bought a copy of your book if only you hadn't spelt my name wrong!" Not the best way to start the night or thing to hear – a treble whammy of a lost sale, another error and sincere but slightly querulous excuse that compares poorly to the traditional "I've forgotten my cheque book, otherwise I would have bought a copy".

When I repeat this to Martin in the track shop, he adds insult to injury when he tells me I've also spelt Lance Wyman's name wrong too. The turnstile operator Dave Prodger has his own query, "why did you have to use that photo of me?" The start marshal, Alan Rolfe, appears delighted to run across me and says "It don't matter what people say, it's a tremendous thing to have done, you must be very proud". He likes his photo at the *Bonanza* where he and Kath, like everyone else but Martin Dugard, were defeated by the complex Mensa-like puzzle of how exactly to stack the pallet of fence stanchions. Rather synchronistically, where I've chosen to stand – parallel with the start line but separated from it by a distance of some yards, the blue and yellow wooden safety fence and the concrete stock car wall and link fence – gets repeatedly *Showered in Shale* throughout the evening. This helps me to remember an earlier important author lesson that I'd temporarily forgotten, namely that in the same way smoke gets in your eyes, shale definitely gets inside the books! More elastic bands are definitely needed, not only to stop the pages flapping in the breeze but also to keep these rogue bits of shale out.

One of the best races ever seen in recent years at Arlington featured a duel between Nicki Pedersen and Jason Crump, so the chance to see them resume combat always sends a frisson through the Eagles crowd. Tonight we're treated to four encounters between them that don't disappoint. Sadly for the ambitions of Eastbourne and most likely Nicki's in the Grand Prix series too, Jason continues the superlative form that he's exhibited everywhere he has ridden this season with an

Packed home-straight grandstand at Brandon. © Jeff Scott

Book display waiting to be showered in shale. © Jeff Scott

New sandals for Lucy as Floppy ponders his career. © Jeff Scott

untroubled maximum and a win in the run-off for the bonus point. It's a rare occurrence that has Nicki beaten four times on any evening, let alone by the same person four times on his home circuit. Though Eastbourne easily win the battle of the reserves and post a good overall team performance, they never pull that far ahead of the Aces and Crump's complete dominance of the favourite Danish national in East Sussex ensures that the chance of a welcome bonus point is lost. Afterwards, Ian Thomas describes it as "a brilliant bonus point to win because we only had a six-point lead and I didn't think it would be enough."

Just before I leave I overhear a conversation that suggests that trackless Wimbledon Speedway plc might re-open at a track in West Wycombe. There are so many false and fanciful rumours about new locations, after the sad demise of the club's tenure at Plough Lane that it's best to wait for yet more news in the pages of the *Speedway Star* that appears to operate as some sort of a public notice board for pronouncements on this subject. By the end of the night I have sold two copies, despite a breathless and enthusiastic announcement by Kevin 'KC' Coombes about the availability of the book and its author at Arlington Stadium. The possibility of early retirement has definitely receded almost as dramatically as my naïve optimism since I left the printer's car park with a vehicle fully laden with boxes.

10th June Eastbourne v Belle Vue (Elite League A) 48-42

Candy Needed
12th June

It just goes to show the accepting and mostly live-and-let-live type of sport that speedway is, since Wolverhampton Speedway promoter Chris van Straaten is more than happy for me to try to promote and sell my book at the club. Despite the fact that the chapter on my visit to Monmore Green didn't necessarily show the club or its security staff in the best light. I do have a slight anxiety about the visit and sincerely hope that I don't encounter the Incredible Hulk aka the security man they had there last time.

I set my table up close by the turnstiles next to the large market style structure that is the Dave Rattenberry track shop. Apparently everyone knows Dave as "the Rat" in speedway circles and whenever I watch him throughout the night, it appears that he knows absolutely everyone in the Wolves crowd by name. He seems chuffed that he's pictured in the book. Tonight, though midsummer's night will soon be upon us, there's quite a wind so John Rich kindly suggests that I borrow some of their many industrial-sized bulldog clips to hold my billowing dustsheet to the table. I note another important author lesson and mentally add these indispensable items to my constantly expanding list of essential equipment that, if it continues at the present rate of discovery, will soon require me to have more commodious transport.

News of my visit has been on *Wolfcry* – the unofficial Wolves Internet forum – and is also mentioned in the local paper, the *Wolverhampton Express & Star*. Later their kindly, knowledgeable and very professional reporter, Tim Hamblin, interviews me. His first speedway meeting after nearly 20 years' absence had been last year's fixture cum fight with Eastbourne that I cover in my book; though his understandable worry on the night that it was going to be like that every week has subsequently proved wildly unfounded.

The people who stop by my stall are knowledgeable, interested in my book and ask many questions in a curious, friendly manner. I don't make many sales though and those that I do are to the more avid, Wolverhampton speedway fans who (to a man) all seem genuinely keen to get back home to start to read the book. Between the chitchat and vigilantly guarding my books in case they go walkies, I take the chance to study the match programme for tonight's fixture. In my opinion – and I've absolutely no idea at all of how the *Speedway Star*'s hypercritical close-season reviewer viewed or scored its content, paragraphing, paginations, photo sizing, use of end caps and the like in 2005 – then Wolverhampton is one of most entertaining in the country. In a sport where there is no happy medium among the promoters it seems when it comes to the choice of the style of their weekly column. It's either relentlessly banal (everything is wonderful in the garden – this week's visitors provide a stern test and by the way wasn't last week's meeting fantastic leavened with a self-interested grumble or two). A minority of promoters/team managers are often prone to some very plain speaking in their own columns in their own club programme and the one that appears every week under the by-line of the club's Speedway Manager, Peter Adams, is clearly written by him and stands out as a classic of the genre (as does George English's at Newcastle). Always thoughtful, this week's version critiques the recent Cardiff Grand Prix, "what a great time we all had in the Welsh capital. Of course, the fans make this the occasion it has developed into, coupled with the variety and quality of the presentation as a whole. With all of that stripped away though, the meeting itself was pretty poor fare I thought, though that's only my personal view." On the subject of Tony Rickardsson, "I still maintain him to be the best rider I have ever seen... personally, I wish now that he'd have retired from the GP as undefeated champion last Winter, and he probably does too in hindsight." There are some other lively columns and in his Tim Hamblin relays a wonderful example of Arena Essex promoter Ronnie Russell's often underappreciated dry wit (though with all those defeats you'd certainly get the chance to practise or otherwise go slightly mad). After a narrow defeat by the Wolves, he deadpanned reflectively, "all this bad luck runs back to my childhood. I had a rocking horse. It died."

Shortly afterwards, I'm delighted to be able to join the Wolves faithful crowded together on the start-line grandstand to watch the meeting. Though known locally as the incredible shrinking stadium – since the space available to spectators has sharply declined over many years – the atmosphere is great and heightened by another visit from the local crowds *bete noire par excellence* Nicki Pedersen. He's roundly booed whenever he appears or his name is announced over the tannoy. Due to the similarity of their respective home circuits, all encounters between these two sides are relished by their respective sets of fans and the opportunity to indulge in some pantomime booing makes the whole thing all the more enjoyable. This meeting at Monmore Green is the first leg of the Elite League 'B' fixture and though the Eagles are weakened by the absence of David Norris, they're bolstered by the knowledge that this was the track where the young Lewis Bridger came of age and demonstrated his undoubted potential with a high score on his first ever visit to the track for the 'A' fixture. He starts well tonight too and he combines strongly with Pedersen for maximum points to break the deadlock of successively drawn heats. The Wolves answer back immediately to again tie the scores with their own 5-1 from Lindgren and a noticeably nippy performance from their diminutive rejuvenated veteran rider, Ronnie Correy. The Heat 6 race between Peter Karlsson (showing no ill effects from the "daft falls from a skateboard and trampoline" that recently precluded his appearance for Wolverhampton in the Elite League Pairs meeting) and Nicki Pedersen is worth the admission money alone and is the best I've so far witnessed this season. They race handlebar-to-handlebar, passing and re-passing each other throughout the four laps in an almost breath-taking spectacle before Pedersen wins to edge the Eagles back into the overall lead. Afterwards, local author Mark Sawbridge remarks that they both demonstrated a welcome maturity, since there was undoubtedly a time a few years ago when both might have attempted to put the other in the fence if given half the chance. It just shows that they're ageing gracefully, albeit dangerously, given their chosen occupation. It's safe to say that while ageing is one of life's immutable laws, youthfulness isn't something that you readily associate with a typical speedway audience.

During the interval I return to my table where I obviously look that I've just come up on a down train since a slightly overweight teenager with close-cropped hair quickly but cryptically informs me that my stock of books might get stolen without the services of his protection for the remainder of the meeting or, indeed, without his help to load them back into my car afterwards. Some exercise in the form of all this lifting would benefit his physique but this isn't discussed since he volunteers to ensure that all manner of inexactly articulated ills don't befall the remainder of my evening "for some candy". A phrase that he says in a clipped conspiratorial manner as he knowingly but ostentatiously rubs his fingers together. He glowers a short distance away with what I take to be a look of menace for some considerable time afterwards when I politely refuse his generous offer. A large group of young boys then gather and queue, since they all want my autograph on the postcards that advertise my book that are handily piled up on the table for this very purpose, that is except when they're not blowing away or attracting point blank refusals by passing Wolves to take them off my hands. These lads just won't listen that I'm nobody famous or a person of any relevance when it comes to the world of speedway, so they queue patiently and appear genuinely chuffed with these autographed adverts. I'd be lying if I didn't admit that I found this rather touching.

The interval was taken during a run of consecutive drawn heats and these continue unabated until the result of the meeting hinges upon a last heat encounter that pits the Karlsson-Hamill partnership against the Pedersen-Barker combination for the Eagles. It's a fitting prospect to contemplate and all looked set fair when Pedersen flew from the gate to then be passed by Karlsson, only to then be aggressively barged out of the way by Hamill all within the first lap. As is his wont, Pedersen can take as well as dish it out so accepted defeat with better grace than the ecstatic Wolves faithful on the grandstand steps who loudly relished the result and the manner of its achievement.

My drive home isn't helped by the closure of part of the M6 closest to the Wolverhampton junction, thereby requiring a massive diversion along narrow residential Birmingham roads and so gives me the chance to duel hopelessly with many huge juggernauts keen to use their size menacingly. Later, I'm astonished by the noise and size of the fountains in use at midnight outside the modern-styled service station they now have fully operational at junction 8 of the M40. Surely there's a water shortage and this just can't be one of the important exempt "essential business uses" you often hear mentioned on the news?

12th June Wolves v Eastbourne (Elite League B) 47-43

Best Speedway Book I've Ever Read
14th June

As I walk through the door at my relatives' house in Lynn, the free weekly local paper has a back page article on my 'author visit' to the Norfolk Arena lying face up on their doormat. In fact, due to the contacts and publicity efforts of the always helpful, energetic and conscientious King's Lynn speedway co-promoter Jonathan Chapman, the vaguely exciting news of my visit has garnered quite a few column inches and actually appears in three local papers that day. I'm incredibly impressed and realise all over again that they must really like their speedway in this part of Norfolk. Jonathan has also kindly put the half-page colour advert he suggested that I offer to supply to every track in the country before my visits in his match programme for the fixture against Sheffield. The team are known as the Stars and he has definitely been a genuine one himself with all his help and freely given welcome advice. I gather from him that he and his father think very highly of the book, even though he keeps it in the toilet for occasional study.

Sadly upon arrival at the stadium I discover that he's away this week on holiday abroad to celebrate his 26th birthday. He's the youngest speedway promoter in the country (the next youngest promoter is twelve years his senior so there's quite some age gap!) and is confident, knowledgeable and iconoclastic but also always keen to experiment with new ideas. The recent success of the club in terms of crowds and the incredible transformation of the stadium into arguably the leading speedway venue in the country is testament to the hard work of all the staff and volunteers concerned but especially the vision of his father Keith 'Buster' Chapman, his wife Cheryl and also, lately, Jonathan. All overnight success is invariably the result of hard work and dedicated effort. Buster and Cheryl have been unstinting in this respect for many years and have consistently just got on with things in their own way to develop their business and the speedway crowds. Jonathan has added something further to the partnership and the club has started to slowly get the recognition it deserves in speedway circles outside Norfolk. It's a way which works and is the envy of many other speedway clubs and promoters. Not that they rest on their laurels and Keith is perched high up a ladder attaching the speakers to the floodlight stanchion when I arrive. Keith is the Howard Hughes of speedway, not because he's a reclusive multimillionaire but rather like HH had an obsessive-compulsive disorder about hygiene, so it is with dust at speedway meetings for Keith. He has declared war on it and apparently won, after considerable thought and capital investment into his ongoing campaign. You really can't say that at any other speedway track in the country. It's especially amazing when you think that dust and speedway usually go together like fish with chips. Like all success, this has been hard won by the Chapmans at this vibrant, much-changed track and stadium.

Everyone at the club is welcoming, which extends to the track shop run here by the knowledgeable and friendly Johnny Barber. Also inside the wooden chalet type shop it's good to bump into exiled Wimbledon fan Mike Moseley again, who is recovering well from his stroke, as well as John's brother Nick. I'm no sooner through the door of the track shop hut than John tells me he's read the whole book and is of the opinion that "it's the best speedway book I've ever read"! The long hours he spends at work surrounded by speedway paraphernalia inevitably lures you into experimenting with all the 'gear' – air horns, badges, programme boards, rider photos, calendars, caps, club logoed pens, magazines and, most perniciously of all, books – consequently he's read practically every speedway book that he's ever sold. This is wonderfully high praise indeed!

I get to display my books on a round table of the type that you might find in a wine bar (that's how upscale the fixtures and fittings have become in general at Lynn as everything at the club is gradually updated and transformed) and, after the turnstiles open, I stand next to the programme ladies, Nanette Parsons and Angie Carter. They typify the family ethos of crowds and staff that you find throughout speedway. They're friendly and curious but not nosy. Nanette is a proud grandmother and mother-in-law to Danish King's Lynn based Belle Vue rider Tom P. Madsen, so she knows almost first hand the trials and tribulations that face speedway riders ("it's very hard work cleaning the bike and kevlars never mind the travel") or faced by those married to one ("my daughter always loved speedway, so I suppose it was inevitable she would marry one"). Stalker-like I watch Tom and Samantha from afar. They seem a really happy couple together, while Nanette takes every opportunity to spoil her grandson.

In the programme there's an update on the work and progress of the innovative, path-breaking (for speedway) Study Centre that the club runs. We learn the "children have taken their work very seriously and compiled some brilliant and, in some cases, extremely funny but pertinent questions to ask the team and their managers."

Sheffield don't exactly put up a huge contest, though in the first few heats they do fly from the gate only to be quickly overhauled by the Lynn riders who romp away to a 15-3 scoreline after three heats and thereby effectively end the contest. Given that these two sides are fancied by most observers to be the favourites in all Premier League competitions the gulf between them doesn't bode well for the Tigers promotion or fans. Though that said, Sheffield has relied for years on being similarly dominant around their own home Owlerton circuit in a comparable manner to how the Stars are ascendant tonight around Saddlebow Road. It takes until Heat 6 before a Sheffield rider wins a race (Andre Compton on a tactical ride) and Kyle Legault is the only other rider to do so with a fast paced and aggressive ride in Heat 12. The scoreline would have been even bigger for the home side but for a slight weakness in the reserve positions (if judged by their usual high standards) occupied by Chris Mill and John Oliver, though they still easily outscored their Sheffield counterparts. Tomas Topinka completed a paid maximum despite a foot injury and Kevin Doolan looked unbeatable as he rode to a full maximum.

Neil Machin was fully involved throughout marshalling his team in the pits while attired in a rather natty smart brown leather jacket (which looks very Judge John Deed) and rang all the tactical changes early in the meeting in an attempt to narrow the final score. For Lynn it's a team effort to wrack up the 62-33 win and, surprisingly since it doesn't look like it, the 29-point margin of this defeat turns out to be the best performance of the season by the Tigers at the Norfolk Arena.

Afterwards in the bar, Keith and Cheryl provide a rather sumptuous-looking buffet of sandwiches, sausage rolls and other nibbles for the large number of fans who linger in the stadium bar to celebrate this night of triumph. While he takes a break from working the room, I enjoy a frank and friendly chat with Keith about the club and the present state of speedway within this country. Overall, all at the club have gone out of their way to help make my evening a success, though sales (five copies) have disappointed, particularly in a part of the world renowned as one of the country's speedway hotbeds. I learn another important author lesson that a large crowd and excellent publicity don't necessarily guarantee or translate into great sales. Hum, in many business textbooks they claim that there is a direct correlation...

14th June King's Lynn v Sheffield (Premier League) 62-33

Early Days at Redcar Speedway
15th June

Every time I leave Lynn, I'm always struck by how imposing the large number of churches and their steeples look in the surrounding countryside. You really can't help but notice them far away on the horizon, definitely strangely emphatic and striking in this part of England, with its flat landscape.

The fact that the Redcar Speedway track has been built and opened so quickly in Middlesbrough is testament to the hard work of the many people involved with the club and is definitely a compliment to the vision of Chris van Straaten (Promoter) and Gareth Rogers (Director of Operations), but also the sterling efforts of Glyn Taylor (Track Design/Curator). He's an unassuming, diminutive moustachioed man who's modest but extremely and justifiably proud of all that he's accomplished in such a short time with his track. It's a steeply banked affair that's had a lot of attention lavished upon it and is located in the industrial landscape close by the Tees River that typifies much of the outlook and history of this hard-working town. Glyn tells me that while the last bend appears much higher than its counterpart, this is mostly an optical illusion as in reality it's only nine inches higher. The track is located in a bowl and Glyn would have liked a bit more length but at a compact 266 metres it's still impressive. The rest of the facilities are basic – though there is a pits area, a metal grandstand (without roof) on the home straight, entrance turnstiles and various portacabins that presently serve as the speedway office, track shop, toilets, equipment storage shed etc. – but there are plans afoot for further development at the site. All completely new speedway clubs over the past few years – I'm thinking of Scunthorpe and Plymouth – have initially to cut their coat according to their cloth. They tend to invest in the essentials of the business (the track, pits, toilets, floodlights, speedway office and riders) while pursuing a gradualist approach to other 'nice to have' but not 'must have' elements to a speedway stadium like grandstands with roofs, club catering and bars in permanent buildings etc. Even if you're incredibly popular initially, any sensible business will plan for a possible downturn in fortunes and a possible reduction in gate receipts and catering revenues should there be a decline in popularity (or vice versa). Not only is it the nature of the business beast but also that the long-term trend within speedway has mostly been decline, albeit one managed with greater or lesser degrees of success. That said, Scunthorpe have revolutionised their site with impressive speed while retaining momentum and interest both on and off the track. With someone as canny and strategic as Chris van Straaten at the helm, all the signs are that similar promise will be fulfilled at Redcar. The sports' fans in this region are certainly local, enthusiastic and usually turn out in serious numbers.[1]

The local popularity of the venture was demonstrated on the very first night (April 13th) when the sheer number of people who came along overwhelmed expectations and the infrastructure that there was. Since then the club has continued to fire the imagination of speedway fans in the area helped in no small part by the signing of 'local hero' and club number 1, ex-world champion Gary Havelock, and aided by the appointment of his father and ex-club rider Brian as team manager. Obviously the co-promoters Chris and Gareth have both been round the houses before in speedway and other sports, so they've enjoyed fulsome coverage and coverage in the local media – particularly the local paper the *Evening Gazette* – but they've also managed to assemble a team that is now starting to show an impact on the track as well.

I arrive so early and go to the wrong building from where I see a retro formula 2 car go impressively through its paces on the cut-down version of the racetrack they have there. It's comparatively a motor-sports paradise here and there are even plans to build a speedway training track to develop the talents of young erstwhile riders. After helping a lady unload some things from her car to the bar, the barman very kindly immediately buys a copy of my book. I see this as a great sign for the sales potential of the evening ahead but, in fact, not one Redcar fan buys a copy all night. Though to be fair to them, their club wasn't open in 2005 so I could hardly visit them on my tour and, no matter how many times I utter the reassurance "you would definitely have been featured if you'd been in existence then", it fails to convince the sceptical Bears fans who pass by my table to enter the track shop. Later three Glasgow fans kindly do buy the book with those lovely Scottish bank notes that I'd always welcome seeing a lot more of.

I report to Chris van Straaten in the small, neat speedway office who greets me in the slightly harassed but obligated manner of a vicar at a fete fully aware that he has another parish to rush off to. He's also quick to disabuse me of any thoughts that I might have that I've in any way become an accepted part of the speedway community, when he simply informs me, "you can have your books here but when the turnstiles open I want you to pay your entry like everyone else". Though surprised, I volunteer to pay immediately, "no, I said pay when the gates open."

The meeting will start later tonight because of the earlier England game, a dull match well suited to the radio. Luckily, this gives me the chance to meet Director of Communications Gareth Rogers, as he literally gets his hands dirty while he sets out some of the track equipment on the centre green as well as marks out the various positions for the rider parade for later that evening with Chris van Straaten's tall and industrious teenage son, Mark.[2] Gareth is a talkative and friendly man with considerable speedway experience having been involved in founding or running several tracks – he tells me quite a few unrepeatable stories, particularly about his time at Eastbourne but also elsewhere. He professes to be shocked that Ken Burnett's recent book detailing the History of Eastbourne could appear without an interview with the Dugards, though it was a tradition I continued myself when I published *When Eagles Dared*. He's delighted to be thoroughly involved from the outset at Redcar and, just like everyone I encounter during the evening, he's seized with enthusiasm and gripped with optimism about the future. A crowd of nearly 4000 attended the first meeting and, despite the presently spartan facilities, attendances have remained good. Gareth is also a prolific and engaging author with his book on Wiggy (the late Simon Wigg) – reputedly with direct sales by mail order alone of 1,363 and a further mystery number via the track shops that I can only marvel enviously at – as well as a lavish and unique just published book from Tempus about the Mallory Park road racing circuit. When I see a copy, it's lavishly illustrated and includes oodles of unique archive material.

With all the preparations completed, Gareth almost immediately retires to his car with a copy of my book to read my chapters on the clubs that he knows the best (Eastbourne and the Isle of Wight) and pronounces it a "great read with an unusual approach". Later on the microphone he informs the crowd that "it's a good read" though sadly this fails to ignite any sales interest from Redcar fans. Sadly, I don't get to meet Martin, the *Evening Gazette* reporter who kindly alluded my visit, since he's indisposed and too ill to attend tonight.

The meeting itself isn't much of a contest if solely judged by the final score of 59-36. However, I watch proceedings by the exit of the fourth bend, which is an exhilarating location to stand and one that I enjoy immensely, particularly since it simultaneously allows me to keep an eye on my books on my table outside the track shop (staffed by John Rich and Bill Gimbeth, who should definitely consider working together as a comedy double act). Only Danny Bird provides any resistance for the Glasgow Tigers to the avalanche of race wins for the Bears. Whenever Shane Parker is out of sorts – and it's a rare occurrence – the almost immutable law is that the rest of the Tigers team struggles to make up for these lost

[1] Though Middlesbrough Football Club have arguably tested the level of their fans' loyalty and commitment to the full with some execrable displays and little glory – outside of retaining Premiership status and maintaining a huge wage bill of exotic but underperforming foreigners.

The Redcar track in its newly built full glory. © Jeff Scott

Deserted home straight at Redcar. © Jeff Scott

The newest outpost of the D. Rattenberry track-shop empire.
© Jeff Scott

points. Surprisingly tonight this rarity of an 'off night' kicks in and is too much for them to recover from. Added to this fact is a situation in which the Redcar riders are already clearly and thoroughly "dialled in", as they say, on what will regularly prove to be a testing and uniquely shaped circuit for visiting riders to the North East throughout the season. Much as you'd expect, Havvy is imperious on the track (and off it) at this Premier League level of racing. Tomas Suchanek also looks good when he swoops past the visitors by using his knowledge of the contours of the track to full advantage, but really extremely impressive is the performance of the completely rejuvenated Dan Giffard. He rides with aggression, composure and skill for nine (paid 10) from the reserve position and, based on this display, has effortlessly made the transition from heat leader status at the Conference League level to great capability in the Premier League. I hope that this signals that he's really going to make a real go of it at this level. To show this tenacity and renew his promise is a remarkable achievement that is a testament to his skill, optimism, application and talent after the severe setback of the injury he sustained at Stoke that threatened to curtail his career. One person that I look out for in the pits and its environs is Dan's loyal girlfriend that I met so often last year, Nicola Filmer, but sadly I can't see her to learn her perspective on his progress.

When I leave after the initial rush out from the rough hewn club car park has eventually subsided, the beautiful night sky makes Middlesbrough look magnificent in an industrial but nonetheless powerful way – laid out before me below the dual carriageways flyovers with its many lights glinting attractively – I drive off towards the A19 for a journey that will lead me to the seafront at Roker in Sunderland.

15th June Redcar v Glasgow (Premier League) 59-36

A Mumble on the Centre Green
16th June

It's a marvel how much the A1 has improved as a road but Edinburgh is a town in which I've always found the one-way system a nightmare to negotiate. By the time I arrive at Armadale a couple of hours before the off, the sky is filled with dark clouds and the rain I passed through to get there appears likely to fall imminently but, luckily, doesn't all evening.

The same can be said of the crowd since this Premier Trophy fixture doesn't excite the wavering Monarchs, or many Bandits fans for that matter, to journey in any real numbers to the stadium. Nonetheless, the die-hard fans are reasonably legion and all have to pass my table on the

[2] After a whole season working with him, Gareth thought even more highly of Mark since in his end-of-season-speech and *Speedway Star* 'thank you' advert he was described as "pure speedway genius".

way to their chosen position from a choice of two remarkably different but covered grandstands. I've kindly been helped by Mike Hunter and John Campbell to display my book here. Since I'd honorarily adopted Edinburgh many times during my travels writing the book, I'd hoped for a much better response than the sales of the five copies that I eventually manage – rather synchronistically one for each chapter in *Showered in Shale* that features the Monarchs.

One of the great thrills of researching my book had been the chance to watch the racing from the unique and thrilling vantage point of the centre green. I thought that these days had already gone forever until John Campbell kindly invites me out to be interviewed there by the extremely professional and voluble Monarchs presenter Scott Wilson during the long delay caused by Craig Branney's encounter with the Armadale fencing at the second bend. Craig hit the fence with a real thump that caused it to strongly vibrate after his heavy impact. There's talk of a head injury but Craig clutches his arm when he's driven past my table in his van a short while later. Like many others who do the presenter's job, Scott makes it all appear very easy and, as a fan, you often secretly think that you could very capably step into the breach should they ever be indisposed or get run over by a bus. In fact, even the simplest question causes me to become tongue-tied, (more) inane and repetitive than usual or to just blather with confused incoherence. Mercifully for the sparse crowd, and me, Scott soon realises he has a clunker on his hands and cuts things short without appearing to do so. I definitely won't give up the day job.

Once I get out there onto the hallowed turf of the centre green I don't want to come back. However, even if you ignore how different the racing appears when viewed from this perspective, it also reveals how weirdly contoured the Armadale track actually is compared to how it looks from the other side of the safety fence. This definitely must add to the difficulty its small size and slick surface already present for some visiting riders. It certainly appears to present an insurmountable obstacle to the Berwick riders. Beforehand, John Campbell has claimed that a score of anything less than 70 points for his side will be a disappointment and he definitely expects that the Anderson's Quality Butchers Berwick Bandits will get comprehensively butchered (this wasn't a reference to their main team sponsors). I take this with a pinch of salt as standard promoter's hyperbole. As it is, the Monarchs score a comparatively meagre 61, to Berwick's 34 for whom only Stanislaw Burza (on his first visit) and Michal Makovsky ride with any real vim or tenacity, though Andreas Bergstrom flatters to deceive. I'm always wary of any Stanislaws having years ago made a mistake at work, when I inadvertently had a book printed with the name "Stainslaw" instead of the proper construction of this name. It was a big payday for everyone in the Monarchs team except Sean Stoddart, Derek Sneddon and the Monarch's number 8, Andrew Tully. Matthew Wethers gains an easy 15-point maximum and Theo Pijper (he of the interesting surname in translation), also rides to a paid maximum. Well, I think they do anyway but can't be sure as my interview temporarily throws out my programme entries and hopelessly confuses me thereafter. Until he finishes stone last in the nominated heat, Rusty Harrison appears likely to notch up a paid maximum with some good gating and thereby answers Doc Bridgett's comments about his recent Redcar performance in the match programme, "Rusty didn't have a great night. He does tend to struggle a bit unless the track is so deep no-one else can get round….Rusty needs loads of dirt because he sort of steers round it, but it's hard to get it like that unless it rains a lot. Probably his biggest problem is that he is giving everyone a bike length's start again." And to think that I assumed Rusty was called that because his name is Russell and not because he likes the rain!

Everyone is very friendly albeit reluctant to purchase my book (in my disappointment I forget to ask Margaret in the track shop if she'd like to stock it). Given I love the look of Scottish currency – with all those attractive £10s and £20s – this is a double disappointment. My journey back to the city centre is as confused as my centre green interview, so it involves a tortuous tour of the suburbs and accidentally results in a journey along the bus lanes of Princes Street.

16th June Edinburgh v Berwick (Premier trophy) 61-34

Ponytails and Dreadlocks – A Tonsorial Trip to Berwick
17th June

My arrival at Cara House, one of the country's leading speedway bed and breakfast establishments, nearly coincides with the arrival of Dave Robinson, the trainee SCB referee who'll also be working at Berwick tonight. By day he's a "geographical consultant" (that's a lorry driver to you and me) and apart from the day job, he also puts in long arduous hours on the road going to speedway meetings to learn all there is to know about refereeing in time for his keenly anticipated final examination later in the summer. Dave cuts a distinctive figure and, with his long ponytail, looks like he could immediately step into the ZZ Top line up without difficulty. He spent many years as a mechanic at Reading, where he worked for the great Armando Castagna among others. Consequently, he has lots of stories – my favourite is that he once recommended a number of young promising Swedish riders to Pat Bliss to sign up for the Racers. She eschewed the chance to sign Antonio Lindback but instead preferred Joonas Davidsson. It's a story that thereby sums up the vagaries of the Reading Racers recent history in a nutshell. Dave is very approachable and friendly with a deadpan conversational manner "as I was a mechanic, it'd been 20 years since I filled in a programme so that part of learning to become a ref was hard".

The Cara House landlady Pamela always provides a warm welcome. She also has many stories but, ultimately, is a Berwick fan through and through so her hackles rise at any hint of criticism of the club or its always smiling and affable promoter Peter Waite. She's happy with her mention in my Berwick chapter in the book "though I can't believe I said that about Dick Barrie!" Luckily, we're both positive but the unofficial web forum apparently isn't always so uncritical. I have a lot of time for the unofficial website (and the local paper) since it carries news of my signing at the track tonight. However, all the talk of the internet and on the terraces before this meeting isn't about my book but instead considered the likelihood of another home defeat for the Bandits. It's an opinion given added weight by the run of nine successive defeats, never mind the poor away performance I witnessed at Edinburgh last night as well as the news that a supposedly below-par Craig Branney would ride, despite the arm injury he sustained that caused his subsequent withdrawal from that fixture.

I head off early to the stadium before Dave (who Pamela bizarrely calls "Jeff the Ref") until I take my usual wrong turn, which delays me and I arrive some time after him. The Berwick staff inside the stadium just really can't do enough for me and it's fun to set up my table and just listen to the chatter, gossip and intermittent grumbling, mostly brought on by recent home defeats. I renew my acquaintances with Lacey and Muriel, the lovely ladies from the turnstiles and the friendly Davina Johnston from the programme stall. It's a family affair for the Johnston clan as husband Bob rakes the track and her son David is one of the start marshals. I gather from listening to the conversations that he's the one that Jamie Robertson assaulted on the track during the last Newcastle

Andreas Bergstrom cut out with author. © Jeff Scott

True speedway pub – 'The Grove'. © Jeff Scott

visit.

At Peter Waite's suggestion, my table is ideally positioned between the programme stall and the table where you can buy the raffle tickets to win a mini-quad bike. It's a position with a great view of the track to boot. We all stand close by the giant cut-out figure of Andreas Bergstrom. The raffle and its prize is certainly a popular attraction throughout the evening and it's supposedly something that Peter found inspiration for when he saw a similar competition on the Isle of Wight. My book display attracts considerable interest and enough purchasers that I almost get writer's cramp – well, I exaggerate slightly but by the close of the meeting I've sold 10 copies. I also had the horrible realisation mid-way through the evening that with the excitement and distraction of my book tour I'd missed my sister's birthday. This is an unforgivable oversight I feel guilty for throughout the rest of the night.

I'm also delighted to again get the chance to talk with very knowledgeable and friendly Jim ("hello, it's Jim Brykajlo from Penicuik") the Edinburgh based taxi driver who supports Berwick who was very enthusiastic about my book as soon as he bought it at Somerset, the first night it was on sale. You could call him an uber-fan without fear of inaccuracy. Obsessive, keen and well travelled might be other words that spring to mind, as does genuine. His friend Dougie has read even more of the book than Jim and later kindly comes round to congratulate me on a gripping read which captures so many people, tracks and feelings so well. It's a delight to hear these things and makes all the effort put in writing the thing feel worthwhile.

Where I stand is a great place from which to appreciate the racing from but even better because I get to chat about life and speedway with those who work on or hang out at the raffle stall. Running the stall there's the friendly Amy Pink and her partner Keith Ford. She used to be one of Berwick's start line girls last season, known as the 'Cashmere Girls'. They've split up now for a variety of reasons (including that her friend Jodie is now pregnant with rider Richard Hall's baby) but Amy fondly recalls the height of their popularity last year when on a rare sunny evening the crowd went completely wild when they walked out onto the track. An unusually enthusiastic reaction, compared to the traditional torpor, brought on by their trademark white mini-skirts that turned see-through in the bright light. As true professionals they soldiered on (commando) regardless. Also close by is the mischievous Sarah Ellis along with the very pleasant and talkative Heather McNeilly who supports both Newcastle and Glasgow speedway clubs. She has her own popular website as well! I'll see her again tomorrow at Ashfield Stadium since she's the "green start line girl" there.

From the outset, Berwick race with a determination that definitely catches the Newcastle riders unaware and apparently also surprises the home crowd, albeit that they're much more appreciative of this unexpected turn of events. The Diamonds traditionally don't travel well away from Brough Park and tonight they were further handicapped by the absence of their Shielfield track specialist Josef 'Pepe' Franc who was away riding in a European Championship qualifier. He'll be sorely missed on the track and in the pits as well as in 'The Grove' pub afterwards. The Bandits set the tone with a comfortable win for Burza, now mounted on bikes fitted with engines "from Poland" and collectively they show a desire to win that has them soon establish a sizeable lead of 10 points by the end of Heat 6. In a good overall team performance, everyone contributes but a particularly imperious performance from Stanislaw Burza stands out as the home team highlight, who finally drops a point to an opponent in Heat 15 after the result is already a foregone conclusion. That said, shrewd use of the tactical ride regulations by George English results in six-point rides for both George Stancl and James Grieves, thereby helping to narrow the final scoreline to 51-45. Nonetheless, these are valuable Premier League points for the Bandits and a triumphant Peter Waite appears in even more ebullient mood than usual as he confidently strides about the stadium afterwards.

The most dramatic incident of the meeting is towards the end when Jamie Robertson dramatically bites the dust in mid-celebration wheelie (after a third place!) on the third bend. It's a dramatic crash greeted with some scorn and delight by one of the female Berwick fans close by my table. In the heat of the moment, comments are made which cause Denise Robertson to want to violently protect her brother's honour by attempting to tackle the young woman in question. Speed to anger must run in the family and there's much tutting by the older members of the crowd as an agitated Denise is held apart from the object of her ire by a protective circle of her friends. It's a rarity to see sober women fighting or trying to fight. There's definitely a sense of quiet satisfaction at some form of karmic retribution for Jamie following the assault of his last visit, though this is generally understood but I do hear comments, the polite version of which goes, "chaps like that shouldn't be doing wheelies when they finish half a lap behind the winner, still, what goes around comes around!"

A trip after the meeting to the nearby 'Grove' pub is always a delight – it's old fashioned, welcoming and one of the last true/real speedway pubs frequented by the locals, plus it's supplemented on race nights by many connected with Berwick speedway ranging from the riders and mechanics to the fans. Everyone relaxes in a truly convivial atmosphere and though there's a mix of languages, they rub along with a relaxed manner and an outlook of bonhomie. The Bandits riders appear part of the community here – they may reside many miles away from their native countries but in Berwick, where they live during the season, they're very much part of the community fabric. They blend in so much and, as I'm not from here, it takes me a while to gather that the jovial, always smiling man everywhere about the bar is, in fact, Michal Makovsky. I chat with the keen but polite and diffident Danny Warwick, with the white dreadlock cum Afro hairstyle, who drives a huge distance to ride at Berwick each week from his home on the South Coast near Poole. He's very keen to learn his trade, dedicate himself to his apprenticeship and to try to advance his skills to become a success within the sport. I make further sales to the kindly Grove landlord and to "Jeff the Ref" which takes my total to a new record of 12 copies in one night. It's been the kind of day that makes all the travel worthwhile – friendly people, good racing at a unique track and a convivial evening afterwards. The level of sales gives me renewed optimism for the future.

On the errors front, I have discovered that there are two Scott Smiths – the one I mention in my book is a proud Yorkshireman and not an Australian as I claimed.

17th June Berwick v Newcastle (Premier League) 51-45

Summer Showers at Ashfield
18th June
I finally arrive in heavy drizzle at Ashfield Stadium after quite a struggle to find it or indeed master the local road system. My earlier call to the Tigers switchboard for help when lost was surprisingly answered by the friendly Heather McNeilly, who I'd only just met last night and who helps out as a telephonist on race day before she gets changed (and puts in her hair extensions) for her start line duties. When I finally arrive, I find that the phone constantly rings off the hook with enquiries in the cosy Glasgow back-straight bar cum social club area where it appears everyone who will work here today (except the riders) congregates. Huge numbers of people ring to find out the latest weather forecast and whether the meeting will actually go ahead this afternoon. Heather is very reassuring with all callers. In a rich irony that could only happen in Scotland she gleefully tells me that on the entertainment front there will be some role reversal. All the start line girls will wear trousers but, in the form of a marching band, "the men will wear skirts". Well, kilts – I hope not in the commando fashion of the 'Carry on up the Khyber' film.

In the nearby rather cosy speedway office, Glasgow promoter Alan Dick welcomes me and is keen that I manage to display my table of books successfully. A big crowd is hoped for though numbers may be subdued by the damp start to the day and the later forecast of rain. Alan remains confidant that everything will pass off smoothly and that the meeting will get run. He's anxious that this meeting happens in the light of the logistical complexity that would be involved in gathering these riders all together again for any restaging of the Premier League Pairs. Back outside the office, Joan English (the canny and friendly mother of Newcastle promoter George) delights in overhearing my comment that the Scots speedway tracks (in which I inaccurately, from a geographic point of view, include Berwick) have been the most friendly I've encountered on my travels, except for Somerset. She laughingly corrects me that in fact "the friendliest are the Geordies, but we'll remember you said that when you come!"

Alan Dick kindly gave me permission for my table when I met him at Redcar though, since it was a rather spontaneous last-minute request, available space is at a premium and now extremely limited. Consequently, I find myself next to the track shop in the top far corner of the back-straight grandstand. It's great to have somewhere to shelter from the forecast rain and to display my book but it's a place that couldn't be more off the beaten track as it's away from the natural thoroughfare to the bar and will be tucked away from sight in the corner when only small numbers of fans take their place on terraces. Many people do, in fact, stream past continuously during the meeting within yards to go to the bar but unless they're very observant they all fail to spot me. When friends arrive they say unless they knew I was there they'd never have found me. Nonetheless, the grandstand has a roof so I'll remain dry if it starts to rain again. I'm buoyed up by the popularity of my book at Berwick last night and I'm confident that this will continue in Glasgow both because of the winning combination of knowledgeable Tigers fans and the legendary generosity of the Scots people. My horoscope in the *News of the World* 'Sunday' magazine also bodes well with its promise "destiny sets up a romantic meeting at a racetrack".

As usual, I make a point of enjoying the luxurious privilege of being able to wander about the stadium and its grounds before the turnstiles open. I bump into the referee Paul Carrington who's alive with the thrill of his work the previous night. "It was the best meeting of the season so far, Stoke against King's Lynn, 42 each with a last heat decider win by Stoke 5-1, it was really exciting to watch – never mind referee!"

To my mind, the fact that the riders take to the track at all demonstrates that they are game for a laugh and keen to put on a show for the dedicated audience that has bothered to turn up despite the drizzly weather and the forecast of rain. Quite why we endure a rider parade is a bit of mystery given that a promptly run meeting appears to be the only chance to ensure that all 24 races will complete *tout de suite*. Perhaps, the appeal of the occasion and the faux atmosphere of pageantry stoked up by the men in skirts infect the organisers. Whatever the reason, the riders on this wet and muddy track are going to struggle even if they can get in front and will get absolutely splattered if they don't. Whoever gets to the first corner, assuming they can keep control, will definitely have a huge advantage and have a lot less cleaning of themselves and their equipment to do between the races to boot.

The meeting was a protracted stop-start affair. In fact we had our first stoppage before Heat 1 was even raced, when a shower led to Theo Pijper and Rusty Harrison returning to the pits to join Andre Compton and Ricky Ashworth, who had both sensibly failed to materialise at the tapes. The delay of around half an hour gave us all the chance to ponder the meaning of life and glance at the lavish £3 "Official Souvenir Raceday Magazine", which is what they poshly call the glossy magazine type thing they supply nowadays at these BSPA shared events. It's a change that reeks of management consultants and the ongoing *Sky Sports*/BSI attempt at the 'bourgeoisification' of speedway, where we all have to pretend that it's something that it's not and clap our hands like demented seals whenever we're lucky enough to be thrown the magnificent sprat of the chance to see "top GP riders in action". Inside the "OSR magazine", we could read all the usual rider profiles, albeit on glossier paper and notice that they were high on (colour) photo content but low on original written content, and quietly marvel at what on earth Nigel Pearson's justificatory article about the widely denigrated Premier League play-offs (and giant photo) was doing in the "magazine" in the first place. In the "OSR magazine", we're also treated to some 'Scottish' themed articles that are high on platitudes and stereotypical images but low on detail that border closely on an automatic referral to the commission for racial equality, while they delightfully mix condescension and relentless enthusiasm.

Luckily the racing started after the latest squall of precipitation passed – a weather event that what would either be described as "the rain" or "a shower" dependent on whether you thought the meeting should definitely go ahead or not. Clustered together underneath the shelter of the grandstand roof, we all then saw that Ricky Ashworth was the first to complete four laps and return to the pits with comparatively pristine kevlars. Danny Bird also retained clean kevlars and finished in a quick time in the next race, though behind him it was a mud bath for all concerned and was completed more in the style of a procession than a race. Another shower saw another delay and track inspection, while the grumbles in the crowd grew from a murmur to a droning rumble of complaint. When Heat 3 finally got underway, it could be seen as symbolic of the whole meeting. Chris Neath easily led for three and three-quarter laps in pristine kevlars before he suddenly came to muddy grief on the apex of the last bend. I think a mechanical problem rather than the difficult conditions might have caused his fall. Nonetheless, he found his bike immediately marooned, boglike, in the thick mud of the racing surface. Still on his knees, the other three riders rode past and thoroughly splattered him in more dirt than his tumble as though he were about to star in a commercial for the latest washing powder tablet thing (or, perhaps, slowly enjoy inhaling some pipe smoke for a Condor moment). You didn't need to be an expert in body language to gather that he was not a happy camper before, to much shaking of his head, he hitched a lift back to the pits on the back of Edward Kennett's bike. It had taken an hour to complete three races. In the confusion of repeated track inspections, the always-ebullient Glasgow presenter Michael Max had unfortunately forgotten to mention my attendance to the waiting crowd, though he'd promised that he most assuredly would, which is a crying shame as I had a captive and bored audience. Then again, he must have had a lot of distractions on a tense afternoon of little entertainment and much time to fill because he also forgot to announce the collection for the even more deserving Speedway Riders Benevolent Fund.

An abandonment of the meeting was a foregone conclusion from that point, though there was still the charade of a mass rider inspection to be completed before that was officially announced. In the next day's Scottish edition of *The Sun*, James Grieves (incorrectly spelt as Greaves) in tabloid parlance, lashed out at some rival speedway riders for being "too SOFT" in an article headlined "Greaves mops up". Apparently he rather deludedly believed that with a more realistic and 'can do' attitude among all the riders, the brightening weather would have permitted (processional) racing to continue. However, given his fiery reputation, it was no surprise that James Grieves's famed diplomacy skills did not prevail in the pits at the time. That the meeting should have definitely still taken place irrespective of the "damp" track and conditions would be the default setting of most promoters and this was forcefully expressed privately afterwards and in print by Neil Machin. The need for a scapegoat is always paramount and in this case it was laid at the door of a minority of 'reluctant to ride' participants. It was a decision not suggested or supported by Shane Parker who would still have ridden between the showers, as he was keen to repeatedly state afterwards in the bar to anyone who would listen.

Those in authority and with a vested financial interest in the completion of the meeting specifically named (redacted), shamed and blamed four malcontent riders for influencing the rest to put safety rather than other commercial considerations first. In these situations, the most irked of the promoters usually talk about the wishes of the paying public as paramount (heaven only knows the idea that they would do this is a rare enough occurrence and an indication of how specious these appeals/arguments often are) and the need to satisfy and entertain the public. These often nakedly commercial arguments dressed up as common sense apply even more strongly and are stated much more vociferously – usually after the canard of regard for "rider safety" has been trotted out – if *Sky Sports* are there to televise the meeting.

Nonetheless, despite the protracted delays before the inevitable abandonment, I still have an enjoyable speedway evening in convivial company. The first time I visited Glasgow Speedway last year I was greatly moved by the generosity of Ian Maclean and his daughter Marian who, even though I was a stranger, kindly came to my rescue and gave me a much-needed lift to the airport. This year Ian extends his kind hospitality even further and invites me to stay for the night at his home. So I luckily enjoy the only hot (and scrumptious) meal of my northern tour with his wife Jean and their barrister son and speedway fanatic Alan. Steve Lawson is Ian's all-time favourite rider and he lets me know of another error in my book regarding the great man's highlights video produced for his testimonial in 1988. Of the present generation of Tigers riders, Shane Parker is hugely admired by both father and son as "a giant around Ashfield". They really can't speak highly enough of him for what he does on and off the track, so much so that I imagine beatification can't be far off. Ian reported that he recently mentioned to Anji, Shane's also delightful wife, "we don't have a king and queen in this country [Scotland][!?] but if we did you would be the Queen". A genuine comment that caused her to look simultaneously pleased and bemused.[1]

18th June Premier League Pairs Championship, Glasgow – abandoned after three heats, waterlogged track

---

[1] This meeting had quite a fallout at the BSPA and SCB as rider power was perceived by some as clearly having won the day. The referee Peter Clarke took a lot of flak as there had been far too many on-track discussions with some of the riders showing open dissent against any thought of continuing and this was all done in full view of the fans. To rub salt in the wounds some riders drove out of the stadium before the news of the abandonment had been made to the fans. Subsequently, the referees were told to all toughen up and stand up to the riders instead of "taking the easy way out and taking the money and jumping in the car at the first sign of a rider moaning over a wet track".

Lessons in Professionalism
19th June

I arrive very early at Kirkmanshulme Lane and enjoy a long, pleasant conversation with Belle Vue promoter Ian Thomas. After the initial misstep of our first encounter on a busy televised race night, I've been very touched by Ian's generosity and help on many occasions. This afternoon is no exception since a brief glance in the match programme for this evening's fixture reveals that there is a full-page article on my book in the programme by the esteemed journalist and gifted speedway ghost-writer Richard Frost. He's very complimentary about my book, though he also gently takes the mickey and makes the odd pointed aside. I'm absolutely made up with the coverage and also appreciate his humour.

Like Lear and Cordelia, Ian and I discuss the 'who's in and who's out' nature of speedway book publishing. In a nutshell, I'm still stuck on the sidelines, while Ian has enjoyed some good sales and critical success but, as a fierce competitor, would always judge himself by more exalted standards. As a plain speaker, he also thinks some of the sales figures that I've heard, often apparently authoritatively, for recent rival publications is "b*******". He hopes that my signing goes well, though he has personal reservations as to whether the Belle Vue crowd are the biggest book purchasers in sharp contrast to their number, fervour and history.

Colin Meredith is also in the small speedway office that has been relocated since my last visit. He is an admired trackman whose curatorial skills have done so much recently to improve the reputation and standard of the racing circuit here, after investment in drains and materials by club owner Tony Mole. Despite the threat of rain, he's confident that the significantly improved drainage will allow the meeting to take place.

After I've hung about for a while, the older blokes on the pit gate tell me that John Jones, the Belle Vue track shop franchise holder, has just arrived in his van. Hopefully, the deserted main grandstand building might now be unlocked so that I can unload my boxes of books and set up my display table. For a high commission rate, John has kindly consented, albeit reluctantly, to give me special permission to display my books and sign them on a one-off basis. Demand to do this at Belle Vue is always likely to be high, given the importance and reputation of the club. When I arrive in the bar area where John is clearing his usual space for his track shop tables, he either has poor eyesight that causes him to contort his face or it's a look of withering contempt. We have a brief conversation in the bar.

Me: Hello John, where shall I go?
John: Freak off back to Eastbourne, you freaking prick.
Me: Er, you knew I was coming.
John: I have to put up with freaking pricks all the time, I'm a freaking professional and I'm freaking sick of freaking pricks like you.
Me: But where should I go, so I can keep out of your way?
John: You freaking better, over there by the door (waves his hand in direction of exit from bar to grandstand terraces), freaking do whatever you have to freaking do? What do you freaking do anyway?
Me: When I'm not here, ironically I'm a book publicist.
John: Well freak off back to that. I'm a freaking professional seller of merchandise, who's freaking mug enough to freaking pay rent to freaking sell my freaking stuff here, who's freaking constantly bothered by freaking pricks like you who have freaking big freaking ideas about selling on my pitch without freaking paying for it like I do.
Me: I'll pay you the commission we agreed.
John: Freaking do whatever you have to do.

I beat a retreat back to the pits to collect my car. I bump back into Ian and Colin again by the tractor. Ian says, "I get on well with John though he can be a little bit difficult. Imagine how he would have reacted if I hadn't suggested that you ask his permission first? At least he hasn't said you can't display your book." They both suggest that I position myself by the turnstiles, since it would be the best location to catch people since many fans choose to go upstairs to watch rather than wander through the bar to the grandstand. Ian informs me that as part of Jason Crump's contract – previously agreed with John Perrin – he has the right to exclusively sell his own branded merchandise at the Belle Vue track. "I don't have a problem with that and Jason gives all the profits he makes to a children's charity so it's in a good cause and it's in his contract. When

John found out he went ballistic and demanded we throw Crumpie out; Crumpie wasn't happy either as it was in his contract – it was like World War III down there. John also understandably wasn't happy when Chris Morton signed his book here either – without permission or commission, but he is 'Mr Belle Vue' so he had to put up with it. I've always got on well with John, so you must speak as you find and he does rent the pitch so you can understand it and I did warn you to ask. Just let it go over your head is the best way."

Colin says, "I'd chin anyone who spoke to me like that".

I return to the bar and broach the subject of moving my pitch to the apparently prime position by the turnstiles with John.

Me: Ian says by the programmer seller might be a better place for me to stand.
John: Did he?
Me: Yes.
John: Well you freaking can't.
Me: Why?
John: I'm freaking telling you.
Me: Why?
John: 'Cause of freaking health and freaking safety.
Me: How come the programmer seller can stand there?
John: Freak knows.
Me: Are you in charge of health and safety here?
John: No.
Me: Well I'll wait until they tell me to move then.
John (waves at his space in the bar): Is it freaking alright if I freaking go here then?
Me: I'm not telling you where to go.
John: You freaking seem to think you freaking own the place.
Charming Lady Wife: Let's not even freaking bother to freaking unload, freaking pricks
John: I'm a freaking professional, I pay freaking thousands a year for freaking here, I'm not a freaking prick though people treat me like I freaking am. You stand there and every freaking prick will want to freaking stand there, they'll all get freaking big freaking ideas and it'll attract more freaking pricks like you. (walks towards van) I'm a freaking professional, a freaking seller of freaking merchandise and you're a freaking prick
Charming Lady wife (disembodied voice from inside the van): Let's just not freaking bother, let's go and leave the freaking prick to it.
Me: I'm just trying to display my books, for which you gave me permission last week when I consulted you and we agreed your commission.
John: Freak off and stay out of my way, do whatever you freaking have to freaking do and don't freaking bother me (walks off with box back into the building) you freaking prick.

I wait in my car until the milk of human kindness has possibly started to flow and they have finished unloading. I then, totally predictably, find that the emergency exit doors that they'd been happy to leave unlocked and ajar throughout the lengthy time it took them to unload have now been locked shut to bar this access to the building. Smiling to myself, I drive my car back to the pits and so now I get some additional exercise as I have to walk the length of the home straight to take my boxes to the turnstiles area, where I have permission to do whatever I freaking want to do. I think I might go forth and multiply.

In sharp contrast to John 'I'm a freaking professional you freaking prick' Jones and his charmingly abrasive lady wife, everyone else I encounter at Belle Vue apparently doesn't have a chip on their shoulder and isn't foul-mouthed, abusive, resentful or paranoid. They have all obviously been properly brought up by their parents to treat others in the manner that they'd expect to be treated themselves. Out by the still-closed turnstiles, the talk among the security staff centres on worries that the new owners of the GRA (reputedly a company owned by the serial entrepreneur and businessman Luke Johnson, who has enjoyed success at *Pizza Express* and *Channel 4*) are rumoured to be keen to get rid of all staff aged over 65 before they are subject to the age discrimination legislation that enters the UK statute book later in 2006. Anyhow, that is what the staff understands to be their aim. Many of the people employed here are senior citizens with considerable service and, although they only work part-time, their work as a security man or parking attendant at greyhound and speedway meetings is something that they really value and enjoy. It's both work and provides welcome frequent socialisation with other people – welcome at any age but particularly in older age. Judged by the hours I spend with them, they're very conscientious, naturally people-friendly and can't do enough to help others with directions, banter and assistance. Just the kind of conscientious and friendly employees that any company would ideally want to employ if their business requires that they regularly have to deal with the public and value good customer relations.

My book doesn't prove popular so instead I content myself with trying to give out leaflets that advertise it. Most people are happy to take one though some react as though I've made an improper suggestion and one man mysteriously says as he refuse to take one, "no thank you, I don't have a website". I overhear another lady say to the man she's with, "that's the chappie whose book you're reading". In the end I only sell one copy of the book to a man who loves the book but has left his copy in Tenerife. He's enjoying it so much that he can't wait to be reunited with it. It's strange to hear that one of the few copies that I've sold has already travelled so far! Even on an evening threatened with dark rain clouds, the Aces attract a large number of people through the turnstiles. Lynn Wright, James's mum, busily helps out with ferrying the cash from the turnstiles to locations unknown and Jayne Moss, Buxton co-promoter and Aces fan, works very energetically all evening, despite being noticeably heavy with child.

The meeting itself starts promptly and is almost straightaway under the threat of abandonment due to the light drizzle. This always has an impact on rider safety, not so much for the detrimental impact on the track conditions but because of how it affects the riders' vision. Nonetheless, the referee Dave Dowling runs the heats quickly. The Belle Vue riders' cope better with the drizzle, though they don't really establish a commanding lead until Heat 9 (sponsored by the renowned jokers and notable Aces fans the "Mancunian Mexicans"), a race that is notable for a fine victory on the line for James Wright over Nicki Pedersen (as he slows too early to coast to victory) after a determined last gasp dash up the inside. It's a great scalp for James, who appears understandably delighted with his victory. I stand throughout the later heats with Richard Frost, whom I thank for his kind words in the programme, and John Turner who writes the reports each week for the *Speedway Star*. I learn a lot by just listening to the chitter-chatter of their conversation between races. Earlier, after Kenneth Bjerre has been beaten by Eastbourne's Joel Parsons, Richard remarks with chagrin, "[the result of that race] with Bjerre finishing last behind someone he should beat every time and would in Poland or Sweden, is precisely why we won't win the Elite League this year"

While we wait for the next race, a car owner is summoned to his car over the tannoy. Apparently feral youths from the nearby estates regularly choose to break into cars parked outside the impressive security fence that surrounds the stadium car park (but that requires payment to enter). Since, as I've noted before, speedway provides the ideal distraction for car thieves – since we're all otherwise occupied for 90 minutes with our concentration directed elsewhere as well as the additional advantage that the noise of the bikes provides suitable camouflage.

David Norris has had his sense of humour stolen if his reaction at the end of Heat 11 is anything to gauge things by. Though he finished second (on a tactical ride), he pointedly stops by the start/finish line and picks up the red and black flags, ostentatiously waves them at the referee up in his box and then melodramatically throws them to the floor. This is probably tragedy, comedy, sour grapes or farce depending on your point of view. The meeting ends after the next race without the formality of a track inspection so that, though abridged, the result can still stand.

The crowd flood out through the exits and I wander round to the stand of the club's freaking professional John Jones. After he's finished serving his customer in a butter wouldn't melt in his mouth kind of way, the affected bonhomie immediately fades as he turns to me. I tell him of the limited success of my evening – one copy sold – and proffer his agreed albeit meagre commission. "It don't matter," he barks, though his eyes betray his words. Strangely, for a "freaking professional", he fails to ask about stocking my book. If you judge his merchandise solely by the quality of the badges on sale on his stall, he prefers to stock the modern shoddy-quality identikit versions rather than source the high quality ones that embodied craftsmanship, attention to detail and tradition that previously used to be available at track shops everywhere. Hardly

The lovely 'Scary' Sheila Le-Sage. © Jeff Scott

Alf Weedon in his track shop. © Jeff Scott

A pensive photo of Paul Hurry. © Jeff Scott

surprising, when I think about it afterwards in the car.

I leave after I thank Ian Thomas and outside his office I bump into the always avuncular and cheerful Trevor Geer, Eastbourne co-team manager who's here tonight without Jon Cook because of his knee operation. "Oh hello, how are you? I've read some of the book [borrowed from his son Chris]. It's much better than the usual boring speedway book full of stats or races from long ago – really good, well done". It's genuine people like Trevor, throughout all of speedway really, that washes away the lingering taste that John "I.A.F.P.Y.P" Jones leaves.[1]

The M6 was so awful last week, against all my principles and stupidly in the light of my earnings, I decide to try the toll road that is the Midlands Expressway. Wow – what a great experience. I say this to the tollbooth man along with "it's my first time". He says, in careworn fashion, "yeah, it can be alright at this time of night but in the rush hour it's a different story". An honest reaction, if an off-putting one, which definitely isn't on any pre-prepared script. At 1 a.m. the mystery of the universe in the form of 'why there are such active and noisy ornamental fountains outside the service station building at Junction 8 of the M40 during a drought in Southern England?' still remains unsolved. Creating an improved ambience must be an essential business use after all.

19th June Belle Vue v Eastbourne (ELB) 44-30 (abandoned after 12 heats)

Charmed in Thurrock
21st June
It's a beautiful sunny afternoon when I arrive at the track in Thurrock after a smooth journey on that difficult Dartford Crossing section of the M25. I arrive to disappointing news from Colin, I believe he's called, on the gate who told me that the copy of my book that I had left with him at the Elite League Pairs meeting in Swindon for Alf Weedon had been stolen from the bar there. He just can't understand how it happened, especially as he was one of a large group of around 20 gathered there as the VIP guests of speedway impresario Terry Russell. I know that Terry's brother Ronnie Russell received his copy and I learnt on the phone when I spoke to him earlier in the week that he's pretty pleased with his portrayal in the book. Though it's many hours before the tapes go up, Ronnie is already tearing about the place dealing with numerous last-minute things. We get a brief chance to talk as he wanders back up the hill from the pits to go to get changed into his more debonair promoter's

[1] In all fairness John rightly protects the pitch that he hires each week throughout the season from unnecessary competition. It's also refreshingly honest of him to make absolutely no attempt to dress up or disguise his contempt since I know exactly where I stand with him. Nowhere. I much prefer the honesty of this approach rather than two-facedness.

garb for the evening. At the start of the season the Hammers confounded many critics with a series of comfortable home victories but since then a combination of bad luck, rider injury and absences has played havoc with the team and even the home results. Ronnie has again struggled to find high calibre replacements to ride as guests and is strongly of the opinion that British Speedway at the Elite League level faces some difficult decisions ahead about its future over the winter months of the close season, if it seriously plans to address worrying signs of its continued decline. The demands placed on the gifted speedway riders of this particular modern generation to compete in the Elite League along with the Polish and Swedish leagues as well as the Grand Prix series, never mind the proto-league apparently developing in Russia, inevitably means that something has to give. It appears that thing to give will be the standard of speedway in this country, which is by all accounts has the killer combination of varied tracks and regular racing but remains the most demanding and generally least lucrative for the riders. Often an advocate of unfashionable and unpopular decisions, Ronnie believes that switching to "one race night every week – most likely Wednesdays" should be thoroughly explored as an option. On a lighter note, Ronnie is happy to help the promotion of my book, tells me that I'm "welcome any time" and he remains true to his word (throughout the season).

I carry my table and boxes to outside Alf Weedon's "Speedway and Bangers Souvenir Shop" (well that's what the sign above the shop says), where the fantastically named and gently charming Tom Woolhead has already arrived. He's started to prepare the shop for the evening's activity ahead and for Alf's arrival. Tom notes that Alf remains a canny businessman and jokes that he needs to maximise revenues at the track shop to help smooth the way for his eventual retirement. Since Alf is already 86, quite when this will be is open to question, though equally it's widely held that he's already 'comfortable' financially from years of hard work at speedway tracks throughout the country. Alf isn't as mobile at present following the knee operation that leaves him hobbling about the place.

Tom has been around speedway all his life and has much experience at the track shop. He's extremely welcoming and full of thoughtful advice, which he presents gracefully in a subtle 'maybe you should consider this as we've found it's worked well' kind of manner. He recommends I leave most of my stuff in the car and wait for Alf's arrival to ask for his help rather than just presume it will be okay to have a display just because Ronnie has said so. In the meantime, Tom suggests that I should always display my book in clear plastic bags at every track in order to avoid damage from people looking at them with ketchup covered hands, or the like, and thereby damaging them when they put them down again without having bought them. On the subject of food, the diner at Arena's track is renowned, according to the *Speedway Star* apparently, as "the best place to eat in speedway". It's a sought-after accolade I'm sure and probably subject to stiff competition. All I can say is that it's certainly one of the friendliest, if the welcoming attitude of the girls who regularly serve there is anything to judge it by. The food must be tasty as Tom tucks into his pre-meeting chips and brown sauce with some gusto. Tom is a charming man with a wealth of stories about people, human nature and life, all of which casually slips out during our evening of many snatched conversations.

Alf arrives in mid-snack and immediately, without hesitation, generously tells me to set up my table in prime position right in front of his shop. I will be the first person the fans see as they make their way from the turnstiles to the pits or wherever they stand on the rough-hewn surface of the bowl that overlooks the track at the Arena Essex Raceway. Though, it's sunny there's quite a breeze so I decide to do without my cloth-cum-dustsheet for the table. Adaptability is the key to being a travelling author. Tom insists that I write a sign to advertise some basic information about my book for passers by to notice and become curious about – he suggests that I make a proper one up soonest, to allow people to see a few pages of text, some photos and review quotes. He's sure that people prefer a visual aid since it makes them linger and properly contemplate a possible purchase, maybe next week, if not this. He hands me a black marker pen, some tape and searches out a piece of white board from the storeroom. It's a bit make-do-and-mend, which is an attitude that typifies the presentation and professionalism seen at speedway generally in my limited experience. Offers of help are also the norm at speedway but, nonetheless, I sincerely thank Tom, who says "it's best to help, it only seems like yesterday you were here saying you were doing a book and now it's out – so anything that helps speedway get more people or keeps them has to be supported. Anyway, being nice is what helps the world go round!"

Tonight I'm also extremely lucky that "Scary" Sheila La-Sage of the Arena Essex Supporters Club has kindly agreed to let everyone know about my book as they arrive through the turnstiles or to give them a leaflet. Scary is a unique person –

sincere, genuinely friendly and passionate in her beliefs. She's delighted to be mentioned and pictured in the book and long ago volunteered to help with its promotion at Arena. With someone like Scary on your side, you know that you're always going to do well. Scary dresses in a very distinctive manner at the speedway and she has a whole variety of sashes adorned with self-designated phrases like 'Miss Arena Essex' or 'Miss Behave'. Tonight she also looks particularly glam in a cocktail dress with legendarily short hemline. She has been a committed fan for 14 years and throws herself into fund-raising activities for the supporters club with some zeal, though tonight she'll be pushing my book before she does her usual collection for the raffle.

She's a one-woman whirlwind and, as a consequence, throughout the evening my table attracts a steady stream of fans keen to have a look, if not always buy. Alf insists that I visit the announcer Bob Miller in his box that overlooks the start line to ensure that he mentions my book and signing. He promises that he will and flippantly notes in passing that Arena is a speedway club of many claims to fame "with the biggest car park and the shittiest track". Also inside the rather cosy confines of the box overlooking the start line, is referee Chris Gay who warmly greets me before he congratulates me on the production of the book and enquires about its success so far. I make polite noises. Tonight with his new haircut, tanned face and crisply ironed bright white shirt Chris cuts a very smart figure, rather in the manner of Cabin Services Director on a cruise ship or British Airways plane. During the meeting interval, Chris pops over to the grandstand to buy a copy of my book. I ask about his father Gordon – a lovely retired man with the winning combination of a gentle manner and keen sense of curiosity allied to being a proud Yorkshireman, father and speedway fanatic – who has been in hospital for quite some time since a car crash on his way to watch Chris referee. Chris shocks me when he says matter-of-factly, "he's seriously ill and nearly died on Monday night". I'm lost for words and amazed that Chris still manages to affect an air of equanimity never mind carry out his refereeing duties, as usual, so well.

Just before the tapes rise, Alf has a panic that he's lost his car keys which at a track like Arena would be a nightmare, since the predominantly gravel surface would hamper the ease of any search. I rush to the pits on Alf's instruction to search for a man who might have them, though Alf can't remember his name or what he looks like. I gather that these panics must happen quite often as the news of the loss is treated with studied nonchalance in the pits. They do agree that I have a difficult task to find a man who I can't possibly recognise since I don't know him. I then rush back to the announcer's box to provide details for an all points bulletin for the return of these keys. Later it transpires that fortunately they're in Alf's pocket.

I enjoy my best ever evening of sales (13) with Scary's fantastic help. It's noticeable how friendly and curious everyone who comes to my table is throughout the night. A real pleasure of my travels is the chance to actually meet pretty well everyone who buys a copy of my book in person – it's one of the few advantages of selling so few but travelling so widely to all the tracks. Many people who stop often end up buying one though one man says, "I'm going to speak to my missus and try to get an early birthday present". At one point such a queue of purchasers forms (well two people) that I feel like I'm on some sort of book-signing production line. As a result and because he's out of context away from Sittingbourne where I've always previously seen him – I initially fail to recognise Stuart 'Rat' Lee-Amies. Before the penny drops, the conversation goes
Me: "Why are you buying a copy"
Rat: "I have to get one for my daughter 'cause she's in it"
Me: "Oh, really where? What's her name?"
Rat: "Chelsea"
How embarrassing, it was a delight to meet everyone at Sittingbourne – a genuine grass roots club that represents all that the sport is really about – but particularly Chelsea, who was so proud of her father's involvement in so many different but important tasks at the track. I also admire her because of her ambition to become the first "lady world speedway champion". By all independent accounts she has real talent on a bike and frequently beats her male contemporaries. She was a beguiling combination of a chatterbox and very shy, she was particularly reticent about having her photo taken. I ask Rat to pass on my best wishes to her.

Stood where I am in prime position in front of the 'professionally' run track shop next to my table, I get a superb view of the track, thereby enabling me to watch the meeting throughout without ever leaving my table of books. Arena Essex have secured the exalted services of Scott Nicholls as a guest to ride in the vital number 1 position tonight. In the first race he wins in the fastest time of the season so far – 57.7 seconds. It bodes well for a fighting performance from the home side but, sadly, it turns out to be his only heat win of the night on an evening when the visitors provide the majority of the heat winners. Ipswich are ahead from Heat 2 and never look like relinquishing their lead at any point though, that said, they never quite pull away sufficiently to allow Arena to use the tactical ride regulations (you have to be 9 points in arrears for that). Chris Louis rides like a man possessed throughout the evening in a performance that gains him an impressive 17 points from six rides. It's noticeable at Arena that a large number of fans wear West Ham replica shirts, which further confirms (if the distinctive but melodious accents hadn't already done so) the East End connections of many Arena supporters and the Hammers nickname that links both teams. The connection is further confirmed when I have a lengthy conversation about books, the trials and tribulations of being an author with the convivial West Ham fan, Bill Gardner. His book is due out shortly in paperback and from my many years' experience in publishing I give him a number of useful tips to help sell his brilliantly titled book *Good Afternoon, Gentlemen, the Name's Bill Gardner*. I even volunteer to be his publicist but so far he hasn't got in touch. We both agree that your friends often erroneously presume that you should give them free copies of your work and, the even more important lesson in the life of practically every author – namely, that you're not going to get fabulously rich through your own writing. Indeed, Bill has to share his miniscule royalties with his co-author Cass Pennant. Ignoring that his royalties are split in two, it's a bit of a mystery why they're so low as the book has achieved the sales success (nearly 20,000) and coverage that I can only dream about. It must be the contracts that his publisher John Blake issues to the authors in his publishing stable!

At the shop, I learn a lot more from Tom on how he'd approach selling my book at tracks if he were I. All in all I enjoy a night that restores my faith in speedway people everywhere – after the Tourette's-like outbursts from the vituperative John Jones at the track shop in Belle Vue had temporarily shaken it. There's no doubt that without the enthusiasm and good offices of Scary I would not have achieved the record sales that I have tonight at Arena; though with Alf's generosity regarding my pitch and Tom's sage advice success wouldn't have darkened my door. Whatever Scary has about her and her infectious personality is really quite something – it should definitely be bottled. I resolve to check with her if she can travel to a few forthcoming Arena away meetings at tracks I haven't yet visited with a book display.

Before I leave, I thank Ronnie and agree with him about how knowledgeable his fans are. He inadvertently reveals that he must have read my chapter on him and Arena much more closely than he let on when we spoke on the phone earlier in the week since he casually says "as I said in my interview with you in the book" when reiterating some of his observations on speedway. He immediately invites me to return again and I take his offer in the spirit it was meant – sincerely rather than just as something to say. I've almost become such a regular at the Raceway that Tom kindly explains the back route out of the stadium. This feeling of acceptance or being part of something definitely leaves a warm glow.

As ever, the setting sun adds to the post-industrial charm of this area at twilight with the lights of cars away in the distance as they travel over the impressive Queen Elizabeth Bridge while the banks of the Thames are filled with a myriad of lights from warehouses, offices and factories.

21st June Arena v Ipswich (Elite League B) 42-48

Leaflets quickly find the bin. © Jeff Scott

Panthers and Eagles warm up. © Jeff Scott

Turning Japanese
23rd June

Jon Cook has kindly given me permission to hand out my leaflets to the fans as they enter Arlington Stadium through the cluster of entrance gates. Unusually this fixture is staged on a Friday – solely because of the clash that the Danish Grand Prix on Saturday would cause to the usual Eastbourne race night. As a consequence, the fans will be deprived of watching any of the Grand Prix stars ride –notably Nicki Pedersen and the rider of the moment Hans Andersen – nor will any GP riders be secured as guest replacements. One of the experienced staff voices the opinions of many on the internet forums when he says, "it's another 'rip off the public' meeting this week, just like last week's was against Arena". In fact Eastbourne have secured Mark Loram as a guest and the absence of the so-called GP stars won't make any real difference to the quality of the racing on show, though arguably it will weaken the title-chasing Panthers much more than the Eagles. That said, Peterborough do have Billy Hamill and Todd Wiltshire as guests and now that he no longer rides in the Grand Prix series, they already have Ryan Sullivan on hand. So, on consideration, maybe I'm deluding myself that we're the stronger team on paper.

While I lurk in the car park until the gates are unlocked, Martin Dadswell from the track shop calls through the fence "we still haven't sold a single copy of your book yet!" Not the best news or most auspicious update when you consider that I've already had a signing session, the book has been announced on the tannoy by Kevin 'KC' Coombes and that there has been a mostly praiseworthy article in a recent pink-coloured *Sports Argus*. Martin is lugubrious and taciturn by nature added to which the trials of running the track shop don't always exactly fill him with the joys of life, but my lack of sales appears to summon a glimmer of reaction and prompt a slightly greater spring in his step. Though I couldn't say whether it was joy, *schadenfreude* or sympathy. After I briefly mention my recent track tour, Martin also goes out of his way to tell me that John Jones at the Belle Vue track shop is "alright" and a "good bloke when you get to know him". Though he also apparently "does instantly take against people and once chased old Sid [Greatley], you know him, round the car park trying to hit him". The recollection of this approach to customer care definitely brings a smile to Martin's face, before he wryly observes "I don't suppose you got any Belle Vue programmes for me then?" Martin retreats chuckling, "I really must call him about your visit".

Peterborough had tried to postpone tonight's fixture without success citing the impact of the Grand Prix and premenstrual tension. The combination of the football World Cup, the warm weather, the Friday night staging and the so-called 'weakened' teams do have a detrimental impact on the size of the crowd. This is a shame as I get to hand out fewer leaflets than I'd expect at a usual Saturday night fixture but it has the advantage that I can chat a bit more to anyone, if they are so inclined. I have had quite a bit of experience standing round handing out my leaflets by now. You get handed so many rubbish flyers on any High Street – from pizzas to burgers, to phone companies, credit cards and limited time sales, even about books from Scientologists advertising the Dianetics treatise of L. Ron Hubbard – that some people have a tendency to be reluctant or disdainful. Others remain curious.

Unfortunately, now that I've had the chance to study my leaflet on many occasions, I'd have definitely presented the information more clearly than I have. But then that's hindsight and another lesson to be learnt. I've been so active at giving them away that I have nearly exhausted my initial supply of 5000 copies. Hopefully, it has encouraged the elusive word of mouth that any book requires to be successful. Judged from an actual demonstrable results perspective I have (so far and maybe there's a flood of them waiting) only received one order actually written on this card. In the flesh, people refuse them with varying degrees of politeness but, at least, don't seize the card and immediately rip it into lots of pieces as someone did on Monday night. A simple "no" or "no thank you" would suffice and be more greatly appreciated.

Standing around does give me the opportunity to renew my acquaintance with a friendly lady I met at the Eagles Dinner Dance who remembers me and apologises if she appeared a little tipsy that evening. She wasn't (at that stage), as I recall, though I do remember she was a keen fan, travelled quite a way to watch most meetings from the 'Hailsham Bend' – the third one – and that her sons were already demonstrating some latent talent on a speedway bike at the training track here. In fact, her son glances casually at the postcard flyer and impressively immediately identifies that the photo was taken at Weymouth, that Dave Mason is being thrown in the air in celebratory fashion as well as identifies that riders Dan Giffard and James Purchase are some of those doing this. I'm very impressed with his knowledge and observational skills!

I speak with Kevin 'KC' Coombes as he makes his way into the stadium. He rather worryingly tells me "until I started reading it I had no idea what it was really about". I make a mental note to try to describe it to everyone much better, but especially announcers who have so much power to influence other people over the tannoy or during chance encounters elsewhere in the stadium!

I make my way inside the stadium just before the tapes go up and Martin again calls out from the track shop "no-one's bought one still and there have been loads of leaflets thrown away over there" (he gestures towards the home straight). I had already intended to circle the stadium after the meeting to bin discarded rogue leaflets – partly so as not to devalue people's impression of the book in case they start to view it as litter, but also partly to save the senior citizen who cleans the stadium any additional grief. A brief glance in the nearby litterbins confirms that some people have saved me the trouble. At least they have been tidy.

In his invariably thoughtful programme notes, Jon Cook sympathises with Arena's Ronnie Russell and his ongoing difficulties in his attempt to secure a full team, in this case for last week's meeting. "Ronnie must have tried 20 riders all of whom for various reasons could not or did not want to come to Arlington and it is a situation that has to be addressed over the winter as the dynamics of world speedway have changed to such a degree that rider availability is now probably the biggest problem we face in this country". Given that all riders are self-employed, understandably they will always try to maximise their earnings. For the top stars, the only game in town is the BSI-run GP series, which provides valuable television airtime for their many lucrative sponsors and will, therefore, always remain a priority (and it is best to not even consider how UK club assets can appear without payment in the GP series, never mind that these assets can get injured). The potential level of earnings for riders in Poland (and recently Russia) are reputedly huge and far in excess of that in this country. Added to that, Sweden also represents a more attractive proposition than the UK with a shorter season of fewer meetings on allegedly 'better' prepared tracks. It would appear that we definitely face a problem when it comes to that simple but common denominator of good old 'hard cash' before we even factor in the strenuous demands of our British season and the associated travel. More problems definitely lie ahead for the sport in this country, particularly at the Elite League level, where the *Sky Sports* contract (and its financial and commercial considerations) also exerts a huge and distorting influence upon priorities of the riders and English clubs, and remains a real threat to the future of the sport here should their interest and coverage ever fade away.

This season the group I stand with has undergone a crisis of confidence – well, to be exact, viewing position. Quite how this has happened I don't know. This week we all stand at the exit of the fourth bend. Notable by their absence from our group (and pictured on page 318 of my book), we all still miss Dave and his wife Margaret, away at home while he recovers from an operation to remove an aneurysm. Dave and Margaret are a lovely couple and when Dave woke from his operation he immediately checked that it all hadn't been a vivid dream when he questioned his wife "Am I alive?" He then immediately caught up with that week's news from the latest edition of the *Speedway Star* and specifically asked Margaret to tell me that he liked my advert for my book. What a gent! This week, I notice that on her programme scorecard Karen, who stands by me, has written a note to herself in the margin, "Mum still misses Margaret".

Eastbourne win the meeting easily 55-35 but the fixture is enlivened by a bad rut on bend four (most unusual given Bob Dugard's superb, conscientious and fastidious preparation of the track) and also in Heat 10 when David Norris takes Ryan Sullivan into the fence though the referee bizarrely rules this to be first bend bunching. During the interval, Mark Loram voices what everyone knows, namely that Reading "is not really a World Cup track"[1]. You would like to think that these things were chosen on merit and the facilities offered rather than the ever-tightening circles of influence and commercial complexity. If I were running Poole Speedway Club, I'd feel aggrieved that after last year's great atmosphere and crowd size at the same event – never mind their much better facilities – they were dropped in favour of the new kid on the block, in this case the thrusting John Postlethwaite's presently rather dilapidated Bulldogs home track (but still my favourite) at Smallmead Stadium in Reading.

Much entertainment is always provided by KC, the man on the roving mike with the always unique turn of phrase, choice of question or observations about speedway, life or, another important ongoing reference point, himself. Tonight's gems include:
"Is there anyone here from Ecuador?" [we struggle to get them to come from other parts of Sussex or even other parts of England when their team rides here]
"I've been short listed to appear on the television show *The Weakest Link* – you know the one – I think I'll wear my Eastbourne top."
[On Trevor Geer's birthday the next day] "He's 53 but he looks 70."
After the meeting I duly walk around the stadium picking up stray copies of my discarded leaflets. While I do this I'm reminded of a story from the last (football) World Cup where the Japanese supporters passionately cheered on their team during their matches before they then all stayed for another hour afterwards to completely clean up the grandstand of the minimal mess they'd created. They left it cleaner afterwards than when they arrived. I can't claim to have done the same but maybe the promotional work I'm attempting for my book is causing me to turn Japanese?

23rd June Eastbourne v Peterborough (Elite League B) 55-35

Pirates Ahoy!
28th June

It's another scorching hot afternoon when I arrive at Wimborne Road, home of the Poole Pirates. It always seems to be sunny when I visit this part of the South Coast. The club have gone out of their way to ensure – both beforehand (through the professional offices of the club's knowledgeable, affable and efficient press officer Gordie Day) and on the day itself – that I feel really welcome and the evening goes successfully. I'm to have pride of place by the entrance turnstiles of the modern grandstand. Poole is such a popular team locally that they have two entrances and though it's quite a few hours until the tapes fly up, unbelievably there is already a queue. The club's friendly co-promoter Mike Golding informs me that the other stand has people queuing up from four hours before the start to ensure that they get their favourite place in the old fashioned home-straight grandstand.

The warmth of my welcome ensures that I immediately feel part of the Poole team – a feeling of camaraderie that I gather

[1] Nor is it a venue popular with the fans either as official FIM attendances are given as 2,800 for the Race-Off and 4,500 for the Final!

extends from the staff to the riders themselves. I've just had the great promotional idea, well I think it is, namely to include some shale with review copies of my book as a gimmick when I send them out to national journalists. Mike seems bemused by my request but directs me to the far side of the stadium to where the shale is kept. As luck would have it, they've just had a delivery of the 'new' shale they started to use this season – which is fine and dark red in colour – which they buy from Scotland.

On my way back, I bump into Matt Ford the club's ambitious, successful and young (by speedway standards) co-promoter. He cuts a distinctive figure both for his age and his trademark distinctive blond highlights. He has absolutely no idea about my book but is polite albeit mystified by someone who arrives at his club to collect a carrier bag full of shale.[1] But then, speedway attracts all sorts into its temples. I next make my way to the pits where Gordie informs me "you're most welcome as you're part of the Poole team now." Gordie is extremely busy on race night but somehow creates the time and space to have a timely word with everyone – and I mean everyone! Also in the pits it's a delight to bump into Poole's number 7, Shaun Tacey. He really is the friendliest rider – which is saying something in a sport where riders are renowned for their approachability – and lovely to see him again. He's genuinely curious and apparently excited about my book as well as appreciative when he later sees a copy. The season has started in mixed fashion for Shaun, since a poor start saw him quickly lose his team place at Mildenhall and, as a consequence because of the rules this season, also at Arena Essex immediately afterwards, where he was supposed to be their number eight. He now has another chance to shine at Poole but, given that speedway like many activities is a matter of confidence, a string of performances below his own high expectations has left him struggling for results on the track. Not that you'd guess this from his innate bonhomie or friendly demeanour. One solution to these inevitable crises would be to spend your way out of trouble and invest in new equipment but, without the regular earnings that good scores generate, this isn't possible. Shaun remains hopeful of a sharp improvement in fortunes and so do his back-up team. I also met the outgoing Lynn Hunt, one of the organisers of his testimonial meeting on September 10th at Mildenhall. The idea is to have a real party atmosphere throughout the day itself as well as the night beforehand (!) with an enjoyable and possibly riotous event for all the riders and fans. I donate a signed copy of my book for the raffle and will definitely attend the meeting, though sadly I might have to miss the swinging night before due to a wedding.

Tonight is the first night that I have my own sign – on the advice of Tom Woolhead and Chris Durno – to advertise my book and I position it in pride of place on my table along with the books and my leaflets. Given the club is so well supported, just to stand there handing out leaflets to the constant stream of people that pass is really tiring in the heat. I'm starting to be more sanguine at the often-shocked refusals that the offer of a leaflet can provoke in people. Sales are slow though I do sell a couple to Poole people that I've already met before. In this case in the form of the kindly, smartly dressed gentleman and author, Glynn Shailes, as well as diffident club mascot Brendan Johnson. Glynn has come down from the rather deluxe back-straight grandstand hospitality area, where he tells me that they will be serving a delicious shepherd's pie tonight with a choice of three versions of potato – the mash is apparently quite something – along with some vegetables. Once Brendan has unloaded all the equipment that he needs from his van he buys a copy. As the Poole mascot, his riding and confidence have come on leaps and bounds. He's also an extremely pleasant and modest young man. Definitely a credit to his parents, something I mention to his proud father, Dave, later (they look like two peas in a pod) – a kindly man who affects to be pleased at this news as though he'd somehow missed this considerate attitude in his son.

I view Brendan and his dad as all part of the Weymouth Speedway mafia who are at the track in force tonight. Well they are if you judge it by how many people Julie Martin says "hello" to throughout the evening while we wander round. Jules is the vivacious and gifted official Wildcats photographer who's now even more involved behind the scenes with a few

[1] From his programme notes, I later gather that he's not a happy camper presently on account of a late televised fixture switch that saw the cameras go elsewhere at only 30 hours notice rather than arrive at Wimborne Road as advertised. "WE ARE NOT AMUSED! Take it from us, this is a mild understatement of the way that Poole Speedway and you, the paying public, were treated by Sky Sports just over a week ago." The "Match Sponsor" isn't happy at the loss of "maximum coverage" on the telly either and, overall, it was "a real bombshell that has cost the club many thousands of pounds in lost revenues" due to a "loss of turnstile revenue", some "staging costs" and "lost sponsorship deals." Matt will be "pursuing a compensation claim" against Sky Sports. I gather that all that he achieved was £3,000 which was the normal fee given to a promotion staging a live TV meeting to act as cover for the possible loss of attendance due to the arrival of the cameras.

The glamorous Julie Martin in action. © Jeff Scott

things for when they, hopefully, take to the track once more later in the summer. Jules has specially gone out of her way to come along to catch me in action as I sign my book for a purchaser but, unfortunately, after she arrives absolutely no one buys a copy! We decide that we'll wait in the hope that someone will buy one after the meeting rather than have me stand there disconsolately by my new advert and a pile of books. While we wait for the purchasers that don't arrive the phone on the wall – a freefone line to the local taxi firm – rings by my table. Against Jules's advice I answer it and the cold caller on the other end says "we spoke to you recently about taking up an opportunity to earn extra cash". It is certainly something that's music to my ears presently, what with all the travel and the lack of sales, until it transpires that he would like me to become a cold caller selling "residential improvement products" (that's double glazing to you and me). After a couple of explanations about what speedway is and that he's calling the entranceway of a stadium that stages greyhounds and speedway, he says the immortal words "well I better go as I'm wasting both our times". Well, how often do you hear that from a cold caller?!

With racing just about to commence, Jules points out that my book signing is advertised on the giant electronic scoreboard by the third bend. We watch a few races on the first bend before exploiting the great privilege to be able to watch proceedings from right by the pits. We find a vacant spot right next to Lee Strudwick and his dad, Ian. They're both here tonight, as Lee will ride in the second half Southern Area League fixture between Poole and Rye House. Lee has shown quite a talent on a speedway bike in the last year or two but still remains very approachable and modest. It quickly becomes clear that this was the one vacant spot among the crowd pressed against the fence for good reason – namely that you get completely *Showered in Shale* every time the riders pass. In contrast to the rather fine constituency of the new shale from Scotland that I picked up earlier; the stuff that we're showered in off the track tonight has some very sizeable and painful lumps.

Jules takes a while to unleash her very impressive and professional-looking camera. Because of this unpacking of her equipment, she closely studies but is gutted to be unable to capture any photos of a topless Poole's Antonio Lindback, when he strips off and adjusts his kevlars in mannerly fashion right next to us. It's quite a protracted performance and Jules notes that Antonio is just as much in love with himself as the stream of female admirers he justifiably attracts at tracks everywhere during the meeting and afterwards. Our view back over the pits area allows us to study all the comings and goings – the repairs to the riders' bikes, the last-minute instructions from Neil 'Middlo' Middleditch or Colin Pratt and Peter Oakes and the generally frenetic clamour that is any pits on race night. Jules has definitely clocked the blond-haired Poole number 6, Jonas Davidsson. "Phwoaw" would be a rough translation of her reaction and my impression is that he's definitely noticed her as well, despite the fact that he should be concentrating all his mental energies on the speedway at hand. A short while later, he changes his position between races and stands only a few feet from us, albeit we are separated by an impressive metal fence. Both parties ostentatiously affect ignorance of the other, though later Jules forgets herself and having turned round quickly then giddily notes "oh no, he spotted me looking at him – God it's like I'm 15 again – we're so fickle aren't we? I like him more than Floppy now".

Ignoring the distraction of the eye candy, Jules eventually gets on with the ostensible reason for her visit – capturing the riders in action. I search out the stadium announcer to say a few words about the availability of my book in the bar after the meeting. On my travels I briefly get to speak with the energetic pits marshal Roy Perry and his charming and knowledgeable daughter Louise. She has the enviable privilege to be able to watch her speedway from within the environs of the pits area every week – which is a fantastic treat, a unique perspective and one that she really values. They're both lovely people.

The meeting itself is a peculiar affair. Dependent upon your perspective, either Poole somehow contrive to throw away a 10-point lead after Heat 9 or Coventry have an inspired fight back to reduce the scores to a slender 41-40 after 13 heats. Poole then win the match with a 5-1 before a magnificent ride by Scott Nicholls and Rory Schlein repays the favour to leave the final score at 47-46.

Poole are that professional a club that they even have their own DJ, an array of lights that wouldn't disgrace a nightclub and a small dance floor. The entertainment starts for those that crowd into the bar as soon as the main meeting is over. While I stand around like a lemon with my books on a table at the edge of the dance floor and my sign perched behind me, I attract even less attention and ignore the chance to be brave enough to be the first up to have a dance though the age profile and type of punter that speedway traditionally attracts would always sooner waltz or 'boogie on down' rather than dance frenetically. I decide to cut my losses and take a stock of books round to the friendly Anita in the track shop. She's another very welcoming person who's keen to help me. They have a portacabin overlooking the fourth bend that serves as the Poole track shop and if the crowd of people they always appear to have inside and range of merchandise they stock is anything to go by, they really must do a roaring trade. It's a family affair in the track shop since Anita's capable helper on race night, to cope with the crowd of eager purchasers and browsers inside the cosy confines of this outlet, is her affable daughter Katie.

Later Jules captures a few decent images that further demonstrates her skill behind the lens. Out of the huge number of photos she takes of me standing – completely customerless – with my advertising board and books by the reception area of the stadium. People stop to gawp curiously and do a brief double take, just in case there is a celebrity or rider to hand. When they discover that there isn't, they pass by quickly, still not tempted into an impulse purchase by all the favourable comments prominently glued on my advert.

I would have left at this point but instead have to wait around for Danny Betson to finally move his van since it blocks me in. While searching for Danny I take the chance to snatch a few brief words with the flame-haired Poole and Great Britain Team Manager Neil 'Middlo' Middleditch before he dashes off into the night. I'm impressed that he remembers me and he politely says that he'll look forward to reading my book.
While I sit in my car waiting to leave, Anita from the track shop knocks on my car window and gleefully informs me that she's already sold a copy of my book. Hurrah! I hope that it goes well here, since Poole is the best-supported club in Dorset and, arguably, the country.

28th June Poole v Coventry (Elite League B) 47-46

"Lewis Bridger is amazing to watch and I would just about prefer to watch him than Crumpie at the moment."
Adam Shields

"The rulebook is quite specific and it stops them moving into the main body of the team. They stay where they are, that is what the rulebook says. So, when I appeal, there should be no question we will win the case because the Speedway Control Bureau must rule as their own rulebook says. Frankly I don't think it will come to that as the BSPA will have to back down."
Len Silver after the BSPA committee rule against themselves about PL graded reserves

"Our track is at times the worst in the country. I accept that and I want to make a public apology to both our Premier and Conference League teams."
Mick Horton

"It seems some people are suffering from very short memories as both ourselves and many of our fellow Elite tracks have had to undertake Friday GP trips to the Showground in the past and have done so without the need to complain in public."
Jon Cook after Peterborough grumble about fulfilling a scheduled fixture at Arlington

"Is it correct for an Elite League team manager to be able to use his position as a journalist for a speedway magazine, and national newspapers, to lift stories from another media outlet [*Planet Speedway*] that can be deemed detrimental to another club? In this instance it was Belle Vue who, at the time, were one place above his team, Coventry. Is it right that a team manager should be in that position to unsettle a rival club? And, at the very least, shouldn't Oakes have given me the opportunity to comment?"
Ian Thomas reacts to comment Belle Vue team spirit by Peter Oakes

"Part of the reason I am writing this letter is to reassure everybody that I remain fully committed to my project. In fact I would like to start negotiating with the Big Fella about how I may be able to become more involved in the club for next season."
Stuart Douglas, Arena Essex club sponsor, sends open letter to fans

"The directors also hope to give details about the future of the club. But at the moment I can give no indication of what this might be."
Phatic comment by Ian Perkin prior to the Wimbledon Speedway plc AGM, reportedly to be held "probably in the Chessington area"

"He cited personal problems in Sweden. As a club we could not have done more for him, he had his own mechanic here, his own accommodation and van."
Alun Rossiter after Seb Alden 'walked out" on the club

"I don't know what the referee is thinking about because I didn't touch him. The ref told me I was going too fast on the straight. I can't see anyone going too fast on a speedway track... to be honest I don't think the ref has done a very good job."

Bjarne Pedersen on Chris Durno

"Gordon was very complimentary about the stadium saying it was a very tidy place."
Jonathan Chapman after a visit to the Norfolk Arena by Gordon Ramsay

"This is not meant to sound derogatory, it's not the competition in the UK that you learn so much from, as riding all the different tracks."
Jan Staechmann, Danish team manager

"It is correct that the contract is lodged with the BSPA which clearly states that a payment must be made by Bartlett to White once planning permission is granted. We have looked at the contract in detail in recent days and are happy that this is the case. I can confirm that the BSPA operating licence will therefore not be granted to run speedway at Weymouth until this matter is concluded amicably. The BSPA hopes that common sense prevails in this matter and preferably in the next 48 hours."
Peter Toogood on wrangles over Weymouth Speedway

"It would seem that Poole promoter Matt Ford knew Lindback was going to be injured before it happened. I run an entertainment agency and I've got a job for him as a mind reader anytime he wants it. The fact that Lindback had a fall in Sweden on Tuesday night is quite irrelevant. It was a heavy fall but he walked away from it. I had been told at three o'clock on Tuesday afternoon, at least five hours earlier, that he would be injured for the match at Belle Vue and that [Ryan] Sullivan had been booked in as a guest... I'm sick to death of foreign riders missing matches in this country. The thing is this time it has been sussed. Poole have been caught red handed. I knew 27 hours before the meeting what was going to happen and it is just not right."
Ian Thomas

"We have all explained the rules to Ian and how speedway works, basically that Poole have done nothing wrong, but unfortunately he has taken the usual Ian Thomas stance and failed to listen. Maybe Ian, while doing his detective work, which seemed about as effective as Inspector Clouseau, should have checked with his own rider Simon Stead [witness to incident in Sweden]... if Ian believes riders will slam into a fence at 50 miles per hour on purpose, then perhaps those such riders should be in his circus show."
Matt Ford

"It was crazy to hear that you're not injured, when you are injured and your doctor's told you not to ride. If he wants to talk rubbish, he should talk to me about it, not go in the press like he did."
Antonio Lindback answers speedway's favourite magic man and detective

"It could prove a culture shock for some overseas fans as Smallmead is certainly not the most salubrious of venues for such a prestigious event."
Local reporter Dave Wright sympathises in advance with visitors who will travel to Smallmead for the World Team Cup Final

"One time I was hammering him at table tennis, something like 19-6, and he moved away from the table and said he had trouble with his shoe then came back and beat me 21-19! He just psyched me out, totally psyched me out, and I can see that over the years, when he'd pull up next to you at the gate, he'd half-won the race before he'd even got there. I think he's possibly the hardest, most dominant and most confident person I've ever met. Yet, on the other side, we've had time to relax in each other's company too, along with Neil Middleditch and our other pals, and he can flick the switch and become the ultimate party animal!"

Matt Ford on table tennis with Tony Rickardsson

"I don't know what the future holds, I'll go home, sit down and ponder it, and we'll take it from there really."
GB team manager Neil Middleditch ponders the future after another WTC final defeat

"I was disgusted to see [him], the Team GB manager, wearing not only his Poole manager's shirt, but also his Poole baseball cap, for both the first leg and also in the World Cup Final".
Julie Halliwell writes to the *Speedway Star* about the sartorial style of Neil Middleditch

"The Premier League is better value than it has ever been."
Neil Machin

Vic Harding versus England
1st July

According to Andy Griggs at the track shop, last year's Vic Harding Memorial Trophy event at Rye House attracted a huge crowd and particularly noticeable was the older generation of fans who thronged to Hoddesdon. This year would be a completely different story. Mainly because the afternoon prior to the meeting has the considerable rival attraction of the keenly awaited England versus Portugal encounter in the quarter final of the World Cup and will keep many people elsewhere.

Not that the experienced promoter Len Silver would let something like the most popular television sports event of the year interfere with his plans. Consequently the entrance gates open early and, despite the scorching hot afternoon, quite a reasonable crowd of fans are attracted to the stadium early to sit back, relax and watch the footie on one of the many large screens dotted around the bar or, where it's relatively cooler, on the smaller screens in the shade of the main grandstand. This is also where the eponymous George and Linda Barclay set up their stall to advertise the National Speedway Museum, which today takes the form of a tribute to Vic Harding. Also next to them is a table that the staff of *Retro Speedway* publications use to sell their latest book, the popular and controversial account of his life and career by Malcolm Simmons in his own words but written with the help of Tony McDonald. Simmo is also present to sign his books and chat to the fans so I'm not exactly optimistic that this bodes well for the sales of my book.

I don't have a stall of my own but the Rye House track shop manager, Andy Griggs, has kindly invited me to sell my books from a section of table within his shop that's located every week in this prime position in the stadium. In fact, Andy has been helpful and supportive about my book since we first met and this generous invitation is just another sign of his consideration. He's keen to emphasise that I can come along any Saturday race night evening to sell my books. Not that I'd dare do this without asking the permission of the formidable Hazel Silver beforehand, since (along with Len) she masterminds all operations at the speedway club. Though she doesn't know me from Adam, Hazel kindly gives her permission but points out that there will be a rival attraction in the form of Malcolm 'Simmo' Simmons.

With all my travels for the research on my book, I've got to meet many people throughout the country and at Rye House it's no exception. I'm keen to renew my acquaintance with the young, lively and capable programme sellers that they have here – Danni Smith and Shannon Gutteridge. Sadly, they're just hanging out tonight, though I do eventually get to say "hello". Close to the stall is a very familiar looking silver-haired man whom I know that I know or should know, but just can't quite place. Eventually the penny drops and I embarrassingly realise that it's the author and speedway legend himself, Malcolm Simmons. There is quite a collection of famous ex-riders in attendance here tonight since Michael Lee – the gifted British speedway rider who became World Champion at a remarkably young age – also sits with his family and friends close by.

I'm in august company but sadly my book display doesn't attract a crowd of eager purchasers despite the large advertising sign that I now have. What does attract a large crowd to the grandstand is the penalty shoot out that ends in predictable fashion with England's elimination. I've learnt the double lesson for budding authors that a major rival sporting event on the television will exaggerate speedway's contemporary lack of popularity and, in a sparse crowd, that this effect will always be compounded if a popular ex-rider attends to promote his own book. Nonetheless, I take full advantage of my prime position on Andy's stall to hand out a reasonable number of leaflets and chat to the few people who do show a glimmer of interest.

The book is extremely well promoted throughout the evening over the tannoy by the ebullient and entertaining Craig Saul, the Rye House (and Peterborough) announcer. He speaks often and very favourably about my book – he was one of the first people to ever buy a copy when he picked one up at Cardiff. Craig describes it all evening in glowing terms and coins the excellent phrase "speedway odyssey" to describe it, which I make a mental note to kick myself for having not thought of and to use myself in future. When Craig is on aural entertainment duties at the East of England Showground at Peterborough, I'm reliably informed by the club Chaplain the Reverend Michael Whawell[1], that he also kindly never misses any chance to promote my "odyssey" to the assembled fans.

I eventually only sell four copies of the book and one of these is to my friend Vance King who lives in Hoddesdon and has come along to watch the racing with one of his neighbours. The Memorial Trophy isn't without some exciting moments – particularly the dashing style of Jason Lyons who is in imperious form all night and rides unbeaten to win the trophy. Some further interest is provided by a match race across the generations between Michael Lee, who has to do three laps, and sprightly 74-year-old Len Silver, the Rye House promoter and gifted skier, who has only to complete two circuits. Michael hasn't ridden a machine for years and initially looks slightly tentative when he races into the corners but quickly gains enough confidence to almost but not quite catch Len Silver at the finish line.[2] The meeting suffers a huge delay, and consequently finishes very late, when a bad-looking crash for Jon Armstrong means that he has to leave the circuit in an ambulance for hospital.[3] The crowd, after consultation over the tannoy by Len Silver, elect to wait patiently for the return of the ambulance so that the racing can resume rather than abandon the meeting for lack of sufficient medical cover. During the delay, it's very noticeable that huge numbers of hungry crane flies are attracted from the nearby still water of the canal to dance in the glare of the bright floodlights. As it transpires, the final race of the night is worth the admission money alone and Jason Lyons earns his victory – just desserts for his fast and stylish racing throughout the meeting. As I'm leaving, Hazel suggests that if I want to come back another time I pick a meeting where the crowd will be higher, something I've already made a mental note of myself.

1st July Vic Harding Memorial Trophy (Rye House) –Winner: Jason Lyons

---

[1] Though since he's a bit of a comedian, I think that Michael actually prefers that everyone misspells his calling in the traditional and widely practised fashion – Club Chaplin. Interestingly, visitors to my website use a whole variety of words to try to find my book on search engines like Google and the like. One person conducted a search that led them to my site after typing in "the vicar". That said, others have arrived after typing "girls", though I imagine they were subsequently rather abruptly disappointed at the lack of salacious content.

[2] Len explained the origins of this race to Pete Hill for his review article on the Rye House 2006 season. "It started when Michael and I were skiing in the winter and we ended up challenging each other to a match race. I said to him I'd have to have a handicap, as I'm not in his class, which he agreed. The funny thing was I regarded it as a big joke and the photographs of me on the starting line proved that. I knew I couldn't ride anymore. I hadn't been on a bike for 30 years. But to Michael it was a serious business and he really wanted to beat me. The benefit he gave me was just a bit too big. He had to do three laps to my two and I beat him. It was great fun and we both had a good laugh about it afterwards."

[3] This injury would ruin a season that had started so promisingly for Jon, who had made the step up from Conference League heat leader to Premier League reserve along with Mildenhall. In the five matches prior to the Vic Harding Memorial meeting he'd found a measure of consistency and raced to seven ride paid scores of 17, 14 and 19 points. Afterwards he struggled to even get a point from every race he featured in – though this was compounded by the peculiar BSPA decision to forcibly promote him from reserve into the main body of the Mildenhall team because they'd failed to craft the 2006 regulations thoughtfully – and his highest score was only a paid seven. In 2007 he will ply his trade for Boston in the Conference League, where hopefully he'll regain his form and confidence to appear at the top of their score charts alongside the 'vastly experienced' epithet the mere mention of his name in any report attracts.

The Iwade Colts prepare for action. © Jeff Scott

Camera phone captures the moment. © Jeff Scott

Chelsea, Shannon and Mercedes Lee-Amies with friend.
© Jeff Scott

Scorching Sunday in Sittingbourne
2nd July

It is a scorching hot morning when I arrive at Sittingbourne Speedway club for "Round 3" of their Summer Tournament that will see the Colts pit themselves against Linda's Lancers. The route across the fields to the club appears to have changed and the cars are now parked within the perimeter fence. The happy mix of people on the terraces, in the pits and scattered throughout the site hasn't altered and neither has the emphasis the club places on earnest endeavour and shared experience.

The on-track action has just started. There will be a bountiful afternoon of speedway with numerous races in prospect since there will be an individual tournament followed by some team racing in the junior matches. I immediately make my way up to the referee's box located in the battlements of one of the gun placements (from when the site was used as a military complex) that overlooks the unique staggered start and finish lines at this circuit. The box is crowded and already boiling hot. I ask the announcer for help to let the crowd know about the fact that I'm here and available to sign my book. It soon turns out that he is Derek Barclay, the ex-Wimbledon programme editor.

It's strange how you can get a certain (but incorrect) impression of people before you've ever even met them. Derek and I both suffered from our own misapprehensions as a result of others' actions. I'd first really come across Derek through his various critical and insulting postings about my travels and the book it spawned (though he hadn't actually read it then!) after I belatedly joined the rarefied atmosphere of the Wimbledon Dons Supporters Yahoo forum. I'd been "invited" to join, well I'd practically been obliged to do so really, in order to view what forum members had posted about me after the Wimbledon Speedway plc Club Chairman, Mr Ian Perkin, had taken it upon himself, without my permission, to initiate a "debate" among these die-hard Dons fans on this forum through the selective publication of some extracts of his own choice from the three unpublished chapters I'd sent as a courtesy to him to read/approve/amend prior to publication. His posting was done without prior discussion and, of course, used extracts from my original material for which I own the copyright and which I'm sure any person – let alone a published author like Mr Perkin – would know shouldn't be reproduced without permission. Predictably this particular selection of extracts, taken out of context, had provoked the always contemplative Derek (and others) to comment strongly on what he understood to be the approach of my work and to defend the notionally impugned honour of the club. Suffice it to say, Derek had inferred/implied many things and almost but not quite said I talked out of my "a***" and had, comparatively, quite a natty line in reasonably witty irony and sarcasm. Along with an obsessive concern for the grammatical skills of another poster, albeit a somewhat ironic pedanticism given his own excessive use of exclamation marks. The long and the short of his opinions appeared to be you were either a true believer about pretty everything to do with the club in its Conference League incarnation or, at the first hint of a dissenting personal opinion, you would be deemed an unworthy apostate and cast into eternal damnation.

So it's a pleasure that we can finally get to meet – he seems much younger and less embittered or highly strung than I'd imagined from his 'Mr Angry' style postings. I soon gather he is a staunchly genuine speedway fan of the type I'd met many times previously round the country rather than the thin-skinned, slightly defensive/hectoring one his posts and frenetic emoticon usage on the Dons and British speedway forums might suggest. He also, like many at Sittingbourne and at other clubs throughout the country, voluntarily gives up lots of his own time on a regular basis to further the cause of speedway, younger rider development and all the other unseen but vital tasks without which we'd be deprived of much of our speedway at clubs like Wimbledon (and Sittingbourne). In person, he comes across as a decent bloke – not only because he bought a copy and then announced my book rather positively – but also that he is nothing like his internet persona in the flesh since he is polite and not boorish as well as apparently open to debate and alternative opinions other than his own. He also had a wry, self-deprecating sense of humour, "we're all cowards really on the forum, once we knew that you'd joined we all shut up".

Back outside I bump into the charming George Barclay and we have a brief discussion about the Vic Harding Memorial meeting the evening before at Rye House. George is a lovely man but also is sincerely convinced that we are continually surrounded by the spirits of dead people who are present but invisible to the majority of people, including himself. Unlike the insight his children have into this parallel world, he himself can't sense or see these spirits but his belief in them is, nonetheless, unshakeable and he takes real delight in what he thinks would be Vic's enjoyment of the various celebrations in his name down the years.

The actual racing on the track during the afternoon epitomises all that is good about what the Sittingbourne club really stands for as an institution – namely, full participation for everyone who wants to be involved regardless of their ability levels, gender or age. Viewed from the home straight, I form the impression that the referee must have already put on the red lights to call a halt to some of the races. Often the less-experienced riders on show appear to enter the first turn incredibly slowly before I realise that these particular riders were just being sensibly very tentative![1] Occasionally throughout the afternoon we are treated to the spectacle of Elite League rider and long-time friend of Sittingbourne Speedway Club, Paul Hurry, put his bike through its paces round the circuit. The stylish, confident and capable way that he rides – attacking the corners and aggressively gunning his throttle – makes it appear like a completely different track. It is an exhibition watched closely from the terraces as well as by the riders and mechanics in the pits viewing area.

After the initial rush of four sales, I take the chance to enjoy the racing and the sunshine as well as the opportunity to be photographed with a possible World Champion and female speedway star of the future – the bubbly Chelsea Lee-Amies along with her boisterous younger sisters, Shannon and Mercedes. Chelsea wasn't quite so sure as last year, when I'd first met her, that she'd definitely be a future World Champion. She was proud of her own appearance in my book – in the text and photographs – and she tells me that she's already taken the book to school to show her friends as well as along to show people at Scouts (her mum Helen told me later). Nearby was also the keen as mustard Thomas Naylor who's not only bought a book but also is delighted to make my day when he excitedly takes the chance to pose with the author by my advertising board.

It is definitely these genuine and unselfconscious reactions that make having finally finished and published my book, along with generally meeting people on my travels, the most enjoyable of experiences!

The spectacle that a packed afternoon of racing between riders of varying ages and abilities illustrates how far riders can truly progress with their own differing skill levels through close expert tuition and the opportunity for participation available on the senior/junior tracks at this club. It's a community-based club that exists for the benefit of all and easily lives up to the club motto emblazoned on the cover of the match programme, "Specialising in Amateur Speedway Activities".

2nd July Sittingbourne Summer Tournament (Round 3) – Winner: Speedway

---

[1] I now realise having tried to ride a speedway bike on this circuit myself that they were actually going incredibly quickly!

Run Rabbit Run
14th July

The lure of a chance to watch the Monarchs proves too much on the last day of my holiday in Scotland and, typifying my recent fortune, it coincides with the first day of the recent heat wave after a week of glorious rain and cloud. Edinburgh is a magnificent city at the best of times but bathed in sunshine it looks strangely exotic and foreign. The supporter's club coach organised by Ella MacDonald leaves exactly on time and for the first time in ages, I'm going to a speedway meeting unencumbered (except for the baggage created by my comments) without having any books to sell. Though given how surprisingly few I sold on my last visit to Armadale, I immediately regret this when I see the size of the crowd and the volume of vehicles in the car park.

The very amiable John Campbell stands surveying the last-minute arrivals by the turnstiles and politely asks "have you come to sell your books again tonight?" Though I haven't he's only too happy to suggest that I consider returning another time. With my usual timing it appears that I've arrived a week too late since last week's meeting with Rye House was incident packed and controversial. It featured track inspections following vociferous complaints from some visiting riders, Rusty Harrison's refusal to ride halfway through the meeting and ended in a home defeat. It also featured "a clown of a referee" in the form of SCB Official Daniel Holt who fined John Campbell during the meeting "when I told him what I thought which is my right". John isn't that optimistic of a vital top-eight finish for the Monarchs and thereby book a place in the play-offs but feels "we need to sign someone to give the team that vital spark", particularly as such a move would overcome recent perceptions that the team has an element of staid predictability about it. The search for Rusty Harrison's replacement provides just that opportunity and while the signing of "an Englishman" has fallen through, the club is now in discussions with "a high-profile figure who hasn't ridden in this country before". In a very honest centre-green interview a short while later John thanks everyone in the crowd for turning out in such big numbers and states after a "convivial" board meeting the club "intend to get back to normal as quickly as possible". Since it was an eventful meeting last week, the unusual nature of events meant, "we could have communicated what was happening better and I apologise for that".

John also mentioned that everyone had received a 20% off voucher for the next week's meeting as a token of the club's gratitude. (Strangely I wasn't given this voucher when I entered, though the bloke on the turnstiles did go out of his way to noticeably vet me and specifically ask where I'd come from.) Inside I bump into the warmly friendly Berwick fan "Jim Brykajlo from Penicuik" and his son as well as their friend and Monarchs fan Dougie who owns an impressive collection of "every Monarchs programme ever since 1960 bar five". Dougie is such an avid collector that he even brings his own programme insert to each meeting so that he can retain each meeting programme in pristine condition. Elsewhere I bump into the knowledgeable Edinburgh Speedway author Gary Lough who has just placed a bet "that we win by a 10-point margin, which still means we don't win the bonus point though". It's a comment that sums up many fans attitude to their own team in practically every sport – optimism leavened with suffering, insight and forethought.

In the match programme, Doc Bridgett is scathing of the Rye House riders' attitude the week before towards the track as well as their attitude and approach to racing, "Chris Neath had a lot to say and that reserve Betson was whinging and carrying on". His prescription for all speedway riders is straightforward and to the point. "All you hear these days – 'it's dangerous', 'I'm not sticking my neck out'… well if you're not sticking your neck out, get another job!"

On the track the most entertaining rider of the night in the contest against the Redcar Bears is Henrik Moller. In large part this is due to the endless problems that he has negotiating what I assume is some sort of bump or ridge on the second bend. His first time out in Heat 3, Henrik nearly completely loses control when in the lead before spending the rest of the race fighting his way back through the field brilliantly from last place for second. Two heats later he nearly comes to grief in the same place when he finds the same real or imaginary bump in the track. In Heat 8, he introduces a variation to his struggles when he falls on the first bend in the initial attempt to run this race and in the rerun struggles with his control of his bike in his very own 'Bermuda Triangle' – that is, the second bend to everyone else – before again magnificently carving his way back through the field from last to second. Henrik shocks us all in heat 9 when he safely negotiates what has quickly become known as "Moller Corner" but can still only finish second since he is unable to catch and pass the ex-Monarchs captain, Kevin Little, a man whom the meeting presenter Scott Wilson in all accuracy and without hyperbole can genuinely note "really knows the fastest way around Armadale". Though to be pernickety he actually recorded the fastest time of this meeting in Heat 4 when he won with a time of 57.6 seconds. However, the most impressive rider on show tonight rides for the visitors and is ex-World Champion Gary Havelock who not only lives up to this billing, but also really looks a class apart throughout the evening. Every time he comes onto the track I automatically expect he would win, though tonight he is actually beaten once by an Edinburgh rider, after he's tactically out-thought by a Monarchs reserve. This was in Heat 11 when the often-combative Derek Sneddon pulled off a tactical masterstroke to shoot from gate 4 sufficiently ahead of Havvy and thereby temporarily frustrate his progress and delay him just sufficiently to allow William Lawson to gain enough yards to race away to a comfortable victory.

Since the visitors are Redcar, Scott Wilson takes the chance to interview the club's promoter Chris van Straaten whom he introduces rather grandiosely as "the Vice President of the BSPA". As you'd expect, CVS is experienced as well as practised enough to speak very highly and optimistically of the prospects of contemporary speedway throughout his interview in a 'hear no evil, speak no evil' manner that definitely leaves the impression that all is rosy in the garden. He noticeably answers throughout in a matter of fact but skilful and lawyerly way that wouldn't disgrace a much more highly paid barrister. We learn that there is "a resurgence in speedway" and that the contract with *Sky Sports* is the best thing since sliced bread. The impact of live coverage on *Sky* is identified as "incalculable" (though no one asked the pertinent question – 'so why have crowds not significantly improved then?') – never meaningfully calculated in a recognised mathematical and independently verifiable fashion would be more accurate – and quantified in woolly but incontrovertible fashion as "everybody is more aware of speedway – it's no longer a secret". Tellingly CVS notes that this exposure and coverage "helps with sponsorship" though like the flawed economic model of 'trickle down' these effects have been few and far between outside the chosen few of the Elite League and a limited cadre of superstar riders. Scott returns this analysis to the matter at hand, namely the Premier League – the form of speedway product enjoyed by the Edinburgh fans – and CVS concedes that its prospects are not quite so gloriously bright since it's going through " a transition period" and that "getting those armchair viewers along to the track" has proved intractably difficult.

On a brighter note, the application of his experience and drive has seen CVS fulfil a long-held ambition to "see a rebirth at a venue". The signing of Havvy was "vital for publicity in the Redcar area" and his business plan is "to aim for attendances the same as a third or fourth division football club". As we're in Scotland, this would mean a crowd of around 200 people but CVS is actually talking about the English Division 1 or 2, so this translates into a target of "3000 or so"[1]. If he could wave a magic wand and solve anything, CVS identifies that the "rules are too complex" and need simplifying, particularly since "speedway needs to be a simple sport". Scott is incredulous that a man with his power, position and responsibility can't drive through this revolution but the collegiate nature of decision-making at the annual BSPA promoters' conference apparently prevents change by fiat.

In Heat 13, a rogue piece of shale hits me despite the fact that I'm one row away from the back of the grandstand. Before the start of Heat 14 the crowd are treated to the truly hilarious sight of the less-than-svelte track staff chasing a rabbit that has strayed (again) onto the track. It provides Scott with ample opportunity to try out his awful puns "the staff are haring about after it" and other observations "the track staff are moving quicker than some greyhounds". Though Scott's comment that for entertainment "we have hare coursing as well as speedway here" is perhaps ill advised in the light of the club's innocent entanglement with animal activist vandals earlier in the season! Heat 14 itself features an excellent 5-1 win for the Sneddon-Moller combination, which they celebrate with unrestrained delight as they cross the line, so much so that Sneddon's air punch of joy nearly lands on a surprised Tomas Suchanek as he passes by on the warm-down lap.

The prize draw has reached £149. I don't win but Scott can't resist some playfully suggestive comments with Ella Macdonald throughout the draw process ("keep your bush under cover") and then boosts the possible perceived excitement to be had on the apparently 'racy' weekend supporters club away trip to Rye House and Mildenhall with "keep your batteries in their box as we all know what goes on those trips of yours!"

Afterwards there's time for a couple of second-half races. The first of which, a three-rider affair, only features riders whose

[1] This is rumoured to be the kind of attendance figures that Poole Speedway gets on a regular basis, so CVS definitely sets himself an ambitious target against which to benchmark his Premier League club, particularly as his existing Elite League club, Wolverhampton, doesn't meet this attendance level.

A sun-kissed Derwent Park. © Jeff Scott

Warm shade of the Glasgow area in the pits. © Jeff Scott

Programmes enthral. © Jeff Scott

relations previously also rode in the sport. Most notable of these was Maurice Crang – whose uncle Mark rode for Middlesbrough and Belle Vue – who made a strong entry for the 'weirdest kevlars of the season' award. These had a distinctive pyjama effect design that was set off by the predominant purple colour of his bike! Overall, though I leave without solving the mystery of whether the two copies of my book I left behind last time have sold, I nonetheless really enjoyed the chance to watch an absorbing meeting and have an entertaining night at Armadale among a crowd appreciative of the spectacle on offer and the balmy weather conditions.

14th July Edinburgh v Redcar (Premier League) 53-39

High Drama and Dudgeon at Derwent Park
15th July

A brief stop in Tesco's before the meeting at Derwent Park enables me to pick up a copy of the local paper the *Express & Star*. It's one of a select band of papers in the country that affords proper coverage to the sport. Then again, this is often the case in areas that are traditional hotbeds of speedway. Other places like Poole, Ipswich, Wolverhampton, Eastbourne and King's Lynn spring to mind. There would have been even great coverage of my book but the scheduled review has been delayed since the reporter John Walsh went on holiday, though the kindly Workington programme editor, Tony Jackson, has ensured that news of my visit appears. Tony was the author last year of the stunningly hilarious brochure produced for Carl 'Stoney' Stonehewer's Testimonial meeting[1].

It's boiling when I arrive in the Derwent Park Stadium car park. The Workington co-promoter, Graham Drury, is already there and is removing a large advertising sign from the boot of his car. He has been a generous and enthusiastic supporter of my book from our first meeting but especially since he clapped eyes on it. Unfortunately, Sod's Law has already intervened to slightly scupper his promotion of my book to the Workington faithful. He had intended to mention my book in successive match programmes and include an advert in this week's version. The 6 p.m. postponement of last week's meeting versus Newcastle, expensively and irritatingly for the promotion, means that no Comets fans will have read his wholehearted recommendation of the book in that programme as "an absorbing read". In the pits his wife and co-promoter Denise tells me that Graham has really enjoyed reading it and had his nose avidly stuck in the book for ages "I'll say to him where are you tonight and he'll say Exeter, Hull or the like". To my knowledge, he is the first promoter to have read the book from cover to cover.

For the evening, I'm to camp out by the Comets track shop which is

[1] And in 2007 will progress to become team manager of the club he has followed since childhood.

located in a giant metal sea-freight container adjacent to the pits and the turnstiles, close by some steep steps leading to a gravelled area that overlooks the first bend and the natural bowl of the stadium. It's packed with speedway goodies and memorabilia and very capably run by the bubbly Liz and the extremely knowledgeable Gary. I perch on the end of their outside table as, for once, I don't have my own pasting table since I traditionally don't tend to take it on holiday with me. I only use this after a fruitless search for something suitable for my purpose with the kindly Workington track curator, Tony Swales, among the dumping ground of many years' worth of discarded gear down the side of the stadium where he parks his tractors and other track equipment. It's a veritable treasure trove of rusting goodies – well it would be if you were a scrap-metal merchant – and if I'd wanted a rusting office filing cabinet I'd have been fine. I do find a distressed looking swivel chair but when I pick it up, I'm covered in stinking stagnant water but still take it for something to sit on later. After the sun has dried the water, a strong enough smell remains to discourage me from putting my bum on this particular seat.

Before the turnstiles open, I catch up with the always welcoming and hugely experienced Dave Hoggart, officially designated in the programme as the "Centre Green Announcer" at Derwent Park. We discuss many things but he helpfully tries to suggest some ways that I can improve the sales and profile of my book. "The problem isn't the product quality – it's great – it's more that you haven't got any name and people will always ask 'who the **** is Jeff Scott?'" It's like one of the cars I sell that people have never heard of. Once they get behind the wheel it sells itself, the problem is just getting them there!" Later from the centre green Dave kindly describes the book to the crowd as "the latest and greatest speedway book appreciated by insiders written by a fan for the fans – not the usual drivel from people who jump on the bandwagon."

For the hour before the tapes fly up, I stand patiently by the track shop waiting for some of the crowd to clamour to buy my book. Sadly, many don't even stop to glance in the track shop or enter its baking hot portals, where they'd have to pass by me looking 'hotly authorly'. Once through the turnstiles, most fans either rush off to their favoured spot on the terraces or crowd over to the fence that overlooks the away section of the pits and some even mooch inside the track shop, though the lack of space inside a sea container and the sauna-like temperatures the metal induces soon drives the few that venture inside away again. Quite a few people gather outside to discuss speedway, moan or put the world to rights. The odd person briefly looks at my book but no one buys a copy, although this does give me the ideal opportunity to eavesdrop on many different conversations.

One of the main topics of discussion is the apparently dramatic drop in crowds that attend Derwent Park nowadays compared with the glory days of the recent past. It's a subject that the club's owner Tony Mole has raised in the pages of the *Speedway Star* where he encouraged Workington fans to return to passionately support their local team and not to take its continued existence for granted. I hear many reasons given with confidence and authority for this decline in the crowd size and figures as high as 1500 missing fans are quoted. These explanations range from the plausible to the bizarre. My favourite is the news that the club uses new shale to keep the dust down and allegations that there is now only one really serviceable racing line at the circuit, thereby creating limited passing (I subsequently saw tons). In fact the shale is quite a topic of conversation since it's claimed by one fan that Tony Mole uses his contacts in the aggregates industry to source cheaper shale that has "bigger lumps in it" that sometimes pepper the crowd. Quite how this relates to the price of eggs is unclear but his friend nods sagely and says, "I was hit by a lump the other week and I was standing at the back by the toilets [on the first bend]". Other explanations include what is regarded as the "anonymous" composition of the 2006 team in comparison to the 'glory years' ("these aren't really seen as THE Comets anymore"), the continued absence of the talismanic Stoney on account of the unavailability of a watertight doctor's note from him, home defeats (I couldn't see any in the results so far) and varied moans of disgruntlement with the stewardship of Graham Drury and his wife Denise. Speaking as you find, I don't understand this criticism, particularly if you bear in mind that there is general consensus that crowd sizes at many venues this season have suffered across the country. The current trend downwards is not just because of the soccer World Cup and the regular/saturation coverage of live speedway on *Sky Sports* but, locally and other places elsewhere, also because of economic circumstances and the increased cost of admissions if you take your whole family on a regular basis. The best explanation I hear is, "I think that the kids from 1999-2000 have all grown up – they're 16 or 17 now and want to do other things so it's down to the hard core until the next generation get the bug again."

By the time I get onto the terraces, just in time for the rider announcements and parade, there's already a crowd that would automatically be viewed with pride as sizeable by most other rival Premier League tracks or even the odd Elite one.

Nonetheless, it is noticeably less than my last visit and the main grandstand is particularly empty though the back-straight one has been boosted by an extremely healthy contingent of Glasgow fans.

Despite being bathed in warm sunshine, the first four heats of the meeting doesn't improve the mood of the Comets fans around me since Glasgow roar into a deserved 8-16 lead. The next heat (5) results in a serious injury to (Margaret Hallett's favourite rider) Ritchie Hawkins who hits the fence in front of me with great velocity after an aggressive ride under him by Glasgow's Danny Bird. When taking prompt evasive action that avoids compounding Ritchie's injuries, Tomasz Piszcz also hits the fence but is soon back on his feet after a short delay. Though Ritchie is obscured from view by the fence, it's abundantly clear from the reaction on the faces of the St John and other track staff as well as the riders and the Drury's that Ritchie is seriously hurt. Everyone quickly understands that he is probably unconscious. With calm efficiency, the full range of available medical paraphernalia is utilised on Ritchie's behalf. Syringes are immediately produced (I imagine containing adrenaline) and from the ambulance breathing apparatus and a backboard are produced while Garry Stead holds a drip throughout the lengthy ministrations of the medical team.[2] We'd already heard during the pre-meeting introductions that he was "tired but happy" following the birth of his child earlier in the week and now he diligently finds himself helping as much as he can with Ritchie's recovery. Everyone rallies round though the level of concern (and anger) from the track is palpable.

Rumours spread like wildfire and the reactions on the track give some credence to suggestions that "it's a head injury", "he stopped breathing" and "he swallowed his tongue". No one disputes that there's no give in the safety boards when hit with great velocity. There's also no doubt that speedway is a highly dangerous sport with danger likely to strike randomly without warning. There has been a recent spate of bad injuries to Luke Priest, Ales Dryml and now Ritchie. Fans everywhere immediately react with a mix of horror, genuine concern, sadness and anxiety.

In the heat of the moment, the reaction towards Danny Bird is one of severe condemnation from the crowd and Comets officials alike. By the pits gate, a man in a fluorescent jacket grabs Danny Bird but then thinks better of expressing his feelings further having already gone much too far. Unusually for speedway, there's a short scuffle and altercation on the back straight between a small minority of Comets and Tigers fans, apparently exacerbated by the heat, the strength of divergent feelings about this incident and the heavy prior consumption of alcohol. The referee, Craig Ackroyd, excludes Bird for "unfair riding". It would be fair to say that the crowd and Graham Drury don't welcome this decision as severe enough punishment. A short while later, in response to strongly worded comments shouted at him about Bird from enraged and vociferous Comets fans, exasperatedly yells back: "I asked the ref to ban him from the rest of the meeting!" Anger at Bird's actions and concern for Ritchie's well being understandably clouds most Comets fans' attitudes. Since it took place in front of me – not that it is any justification but perhaps should have been remembered – just before this incident, the roles were almost reversed when on the first bend of the first lap of Heat 5 Hawkins deliberately rode very hard and aggressively underneath Bird to force him very wide and close to the fence. Bird somehow remained on his machine and, as a more experienced rider, retained enough control to remain on his bike and re-engage in his pursuit. On the next lap, in more or less the same place, Bird then immediately returned the equivalent 'hard riding' favour with devastating consequences. Apparently the Workington fans have forgotten or didn't see this prior incident in which rider 'culpability' was completely reversed. But as one rider crashed and the other didn't, impressions and reactions polarise, though it would be safe to say that this event markedly sours the general atmosphere in the crowd around me and there is a noticeable tension as well as continued hostility and strong animosity towards Danny Bird for the remainder of the meeting.[3]

After an inordinately but understandably long delay the meeting resumes and we are treated to a number of exciting races and the quirky mix of incident that makes the sport of speedway so habitual and enthralling. Aidan Collins has to shoulder a lot more responsibility in the absence of Ritchie and, based on this performance, seems a fine prospect when he rides to 12 (paid 16) from seven rides. For Glasgow, Shane Parker looks imperious as he again demonstrates superlatively stylish form all night. He justifiably remains unbeaten with one of many highlights being his daring overtake on the fourth bend during Heat 9. Contrary to the rather vocal naysayers beforehand, not only is there lots of overtaking – no doubt the spectacle was aided by two sets of teams whose riders appeared singly unable to start from the gate at all quickly – but

[2] Workington has by far the most respected doctor in the country attending their meetings, one Andrew Butler.

the fastest time of the season is set by James Wright at 64.4 in Heat 10. This heat is also notable for the fact that though they are massively trailed off at the back, Glasgow's Lee Dicken daringly races past his Tigers team-mate David McAllan on the last bend to seize third place on the finish line. He celebrates this with enthusiasm though it is in fact only a member of his own team that he's beaten for a single point one of them was bound to get![4] The man next to me shouts with quick-witted and wry sarcasm, "well done, Dicken lad!" The new track record lasts exactly one race until Danny Bird lowers the time in the very next heat to 64.3. Afterwards, track curator Tony Swales says when the track is as grippy as this (new shale has been laid during the week) there are often good times set but as a consequence there are often also a lot more accidents.

After the meeting, a sizeable group of Glasgow fans enthusiastically celebrates their victory by the pits, though it has to be said that their riders look very noticeably subdued. The crowd inside the stadium is supplemented at the end of the meeting by a number of interlopers in the form of police officers (one in protective riot clothing!) and outside there is also a police van and car. It's an unusual sight at a speedway meeting though, as it turns out, it is a precautionary measure that is unnecessary. I finally manage to sell some books (two) to departing Tigers fans. Before I leave I look round to thank Graham and Denise for their help and hospitality but they have already quickly left the stadium to go to the hospital to check on Ritchie Hawkins.

15th July Workington v Glasgow (Premier League) 44-46

Boiling in Buxton
16th July

I know that this Conference League derby encounter is keenly anticipated but, on arrival, I'm astonished to find the Dalehead car park completely jammed with vehicles in all directions as far as the eye can see. It looks to be the size of crowd you'd expect to see if Buxton ever staged a round of the Grand Prix series. Sadly, I'm under a misapprehension since this crowd is here to watch the banger racing (or something similar) on the adjacent track that overlooks the speedway facility and was initially the original racetrack when Buxton first opened. It is quite a weekend to visit this part of the Peak District since there is also the attraction of the famous Buxton Festival that apparently features "a feast of opera, music and literature". An afternoon at the speedway holds out similarly enjoyable entertainment prospects as far as I'm concerned and I hope that the clash between the Hitmen and the Spitfires will provide a feast of thrills, spills and enthralling racing. There is also some literature thrown into the entertainment mix at the Dalehead track in the form of a comprehensive selection of speedway books, magazines and other assorted paraphernalia at this particular outpost of the Dave Rattenberry track shop empire. Also over the tannoy there's a good selection of music throughout the afternoon.

There's also tons of sunshine at this exposed but beautiful location and by 12.30 p.m. it's already baking hot. I would have expected much more of a cooling breeze to ripple over the surrounding hills and though there's a wind it only has a hair-dryer quality. Thankfully I'm not heavily pregnant like Buxton co-promoter Jayne Moss, though she makes light of her

---

[3] In a season of successive injuries Graham Drury, in his review of Workington's performance in 2006 in the *Speedway Star*, singles out the incident that caused the head injury to Ritchie Hawkins as the straw that broke their camel's back. "The loss of Ritchie as a consequence of what can only be described as an appalling manoeuvre by Danny Bird was a massive blow to us. Ritchie was absolutely flying at that time, particularly at home, and was riding far better than his average suggests. But because he was only fifth in our averages, the options open to us from rider replacement were very limited. The loss of Ritchie meant we lost that match against Glasgow, which was our first home defeat, and I'm sure that we would have won if he hadn't been injured." In his summary of the season, Glasgow team manager and co-promoter Stewart Dickson saw things differently. He was pleased with the "exciting" win and noted, "Danny Bird was given a very tough time from the home fans when he clashed with Ritchie Hawkins, but it was quite simply a racing incident and thankfully he was able to put that behind him and help the team pick up what was our finest win of the season."

[4] This is often called 'racing for the chip shop money' – when team-mates steal a forlorn third place point of each other.

The only shade for miles. © Jeff Scott

The Buxton and Stoke riders debate conditions. © Jeff Scott

Dave Rattenberry, ICA Crook and John Rich in the Buxton track shop cum sauna. © Jeff Scott

condition, except to say that she has had to cut back on her usual intense travel schedule round the country and into Europe to follow James Wright in the Under-21 Championships to watch the speedway this season. Today she prepares the tickets, programmes and change in the entrance booth to the speedway stadium. There's already a small queue of cars with passengers keen to enjoy the stifling heat in the comfort of their own vehicles. Many of the cars look at an age where they'd be lucky to have had heaters fitted as standard let alone air conditioning, and they park in the best spots inside the perimeter of the stadium, when it officially opens at 1 p.m. The Hitmen have so far won all their home fixtures and, rather even-handedly, have lost all their away ones but Jayne pronounces herself satisfied with the way things have progressed so far. As ever, finances remain tight and careful husbandry of resources continues to be the order of the day.

Inside the metal container that serves as the Buxton track shop, temperatures have already reached sauna-like proportions. Since it's the derby fixture against Stoke, where the avuncular and always helpful Dave Rattenberry also runs the franchise, he's already here and has a cheery word or chat with pretty well everyone who passes. John Rich, who usually runs this shop has brought along his friend who rejoices in the name of ICA (Ian Charles Arthur) Crook. It doesn't seem at all likely that he's involved in any form of criminal activity and his nickname "mushy pea" suggests that he has greater affinity for culinary skills than larceny. The shop is already completely set out in preparation for a flood of eager customers and they've even had an advance order for my book from some kindly soul who'll be in attendance later this afternoon.

Talk turns to those hardy perennial topics of recent speedway injuries – Luke Priest's sounds horrific and something that you wouldn't wish on your worst enemy – and the weather. This very stadium was apparently pretty parky the week before for the visit of Boston. The tradition of sheltering from the cold and viewing proceedings from the comfort of your car that the Buxton fans have is sensible in such weather but is also a hard habit to break if the ring of cars for this afternoon is anything to judge things by. My surmise that the look and generation of these cars wouldn't usually boast air-conditioning as standard proves accurate if judged by how many of them have their car doors open. John rather optimistically reckons that they do this "so they can enjoy the cooling breeze", though I can't feel any in the lee of the track shop and the flags elsewhere hang as limply as a eunuchs' convention in a brothel.

This afternoon's SCB Official is the legendary but still unofficially designated "World's Number 1 Referee" Tony Steele (though I'm sure that he'd modestly dispute this), who sports an extremely clean white shirt with a distinctive "FIM Official" crest-cum-badge on the pocket. Before he inspects the track, he kindly explains the conundrum that he set me at Sheffield – namely why do they pray for rain at the offices of the *Sport* newspaper.

The Buxton team line up as per the programme whereas the Stoke team shift around the programmed order of their riders – to give the sparse crowd something detailed to do between races – and will operate rider replacement for Scott Courtney. The racing is competitive and varied throughout the afternoon, enough to thrill the crowd who stand in the blindingly bright sunshine or seated in the case of those that prefer to watch from their cars. Stoke win the first heat but for the next 13 races Buxton hold the overall lead. We enjoy a couple of races with multiple exclusions that throws up a number of incongruous looking score lines (2-3 and 0-5). Buxton suffer from the withdrawal of their captain Jonathon Bethall after Heat 6, though they still have the very impressive Ben Taylor at reserve and with the Conference League version of John Branney, well off the pace at the Premier League level the night before at Workington, Stoke have the most exciting rider on show. The only way to stop him is to accidentally spear him from behind as Jack Roberts does in Heat 7. This isn't good news for any rider at any time but if you've suffered from serious injuries the previous season and still bear the long-term scars of your operations this is even less good news.

Stoke come back into contention with a tactical ride for John Branney and his double points win helps to pull the score back to 38-35. This clearly delights a tanned-looking Dave Tattum, the Spitfires energetic team manager, who has been a bundle of energy throughout the meeting as he rushes about on the centre green or back and forth to the pits, where he offers a variety of expressive gestures, slaps on the back as well as numerous words of encouragement and advice. Sadly, standing in the heat of the afternoon sunshine has left me feeling most peculiar and severely diminishes my enjoyment of this exciting meeting. By now I have sold three copies of my book and the track shop has also sold a couple. Nonetheless, the thought of a long drive in order to get a lie down means that, for once against all my usual instincts, I decide to leave early. Before I do, I linger by the referee's box to watch the initial running of Heat 13. To great consternation and repeated vociferous objections from a militant group of loud and partisan Stoke fans gathered by the start line, referee Tony Steele excludes Sam Dore. Completely the correct decision in my view but not in the opinion of this hard core of objectors, who express their strong dissatisfaction in what the newspapers used to describe as the 'common language of men'. They fulminate loudly and obscenely as well as categorically doubt his parentage and cast considerable doubt on his widely acknowledged status as the world's leading speedway official. Tony is close by and within earshot but studiously ignores these people and, as they probably teach early in your apprenticeship at the Referee Training School, stares serenely out over the track and pointedly gets on with running the meeting. After I leave, very much against the direction of the racing I witnessed before my premature departure, a last gasp 1-5 in heat 15 ensures that Stoke win this local derby by a single point and thereby triumphantly carries the bragging rights for another season back to Loomer Road.

Take One Wet Track, Just Add Shale and Hey Presto!
22nd July

I arrive early under dark black skies at Loomer Road to find the mood on the entrance gate sunny and welcoming. The friendly Caroline Tattum is already there with her very capable and glamorous team although the turnstiles have yet to open. The team has worked together for some time now and comprises her close friend Gaynor as well as all the lithely attractive start line girls, though a couple of these rest themselves in preparation for the rigours of the evening endeavours ahead. A short while later Caroline's mum arrives and takes her place inside the turnstiles rather than outside with the rest of the ladies, where there is already a queue of mostly ageing vehicles waiting patiently for the gates to open. It's yet another visit to a track where people can watch proceedings throughout from their cars – I still don't understand the appeal of this.

I had particularly enjoyed the banter and the time I spent at the gates on my visit last year when researching my book and it's a shame that I can't hang around again but the lure of later potential commerce calls as I have to set up my book stand. I say 'set up' loosely since I've again arrived without a display table though I do have my trusty handwritten advertising board that now looks somewhat battered from its debut ages ago at Arena Essex. On the way back to the grandstand, I pop into the cluttered office that is the very tanned Dave Tattum's lair and nerve centre of operations. He makes an important sounding phone call while I wait outside the office door keen not to interrupt. He's friendly enough but has lots on his plate at this time every week, though he notes "I'll definitely read your book – but over the winter when I have some time". The Stoke track shop is yet another outpost of the Dave Rattenberry Empire and by the time I arrive everything has already been set up immaculately and Dave, along with the always very helpful John Rich, is already ensconced behind the counter. They apparently know everyone by first name and it's a continual round of greetings as they rest on one of the benches by the large windows of the home-straight grandstand. I enlist the advice of Dave and John about the best location to base myself with my books. This would be right next to the track shop stall but would then block the toilets – probably not popular but one way of getting attention – and most likely, in this increasingly more cautious age, create a fire hazard. The consensus is to go and stand by a big poster situated by the entrance doors closest to the bar. However, it's all settled by Caroline when she arrives who assertively suggests that I go to the far end of the grandstand "where Moggo had his table during his testimonial". Others doubt whether this is exactly an ideal location but I'm happy to be where I'm put, particularly since Caroline has so kindly fitted my visit in. I'm also grateful for the loan of a table from the treasure trove that is the Dave Rattenberry spares cupboard. Not that I'm exactly rushed off my feet with willing purchasers, though I do get to chat with a large number of very affable Stoke fans. I'm also lucky enough to be helped tonight by my extremely thorough proof reader, Caroline Tidmarsh. It's her first visit to Stoke Speedway and just having some help, even though there's not really anyone keen to buy, makes all the difference.

A torrential monsoon-like downpour around an hour before the tapes go up really thoroughly soaks the track and what previously looked like a pretty well prepared surface quickly resembles a bog where puddles of surface water lie on the bends. Some last-minute TLC is administered and the meeting starts just about on time. The first race lasts less than a lap before Christian Henry dramatically slips off on the third bend, gets totally covered in slime and is also excluded for his trouble. In the rerun, the riders look much more tentative and some amusement is caused by Stoke manager Nigel Crabtree's tirade of advice to a fallen Trent Leverington to slither back up from the mud and remount his bike for an uncontested third place. On the gloopy shale surface that the Loomer Road track has suddenly become, Mark Lemon wins the rerun of the first race in a time so slow that the timekeeper uses a sundial.

This is the signal for some extensive attention to the track to commence, while the crowd stands around morosely and loudly contemplates the prospect of an abandonment even though the skies have now brightened considerably. It's looking like just the sort of evening where the riders just go through the motions on what appears to be a treacherous and unraceable track. The cynics close by to me on the grandstand where we overlook the start line claim that tonight's encounter will either flounder to the end of the contest completely held back and ruined as a spectacle by track conditions, or proceed at least until after Heat 6 so that there is no longer any need to offer a refund!

These predictions prove to be completely wide of the mark. The track staff, with the help and extremely active supervision of the energetic Dave Tattum and Nigel Crabtree, quickly place an impressive quantity of fresh shale on the track to soak up and mask the boggy conditions that lie beneath. This is likely to be a much more effective solution than the frequently used heavy dusting of sawdust that you often witness fruitlessly laid on a wet surface elsewhere, but nonetheless crowd sentiment still remains sceptical. Work goes on for so long that the second race doesn't even start until 8.36 p.m. During this protracted interval, I sell a couple of books to fans both called Paul. Before I can launch an appeal over the tannoy for any other Pauls that lurk in the sparse crowd to urgently make their way to my table, a new and yet to be developed target market for the book – an Anthony – arrives to break the sequence. Sadly this is my last sale of the night.

However, during this long break, I take the chance to buy a raffle ticket from his mum in the bar to support the Paul Clews Testimonial – the 'Clewsy Classic' – on September 23rd at Loomer Road and for the chance to win the really fantastic prize offered – a night with referee Chris Durno at any Midlands track of your choice. What a thrill this will be for the lucky winner. I was hugely fortunate last year when writing the book to follow the charming Chris Durno round for the night, while he capably fulfilled his rather complex duties. Speedway referees are a convenient and often handily placed scapegoat well used to intemperate displays of ire from agitated speedway fans at meetings up and down the country. Few fans appreciate how difficult it is to do the job well and make it look so effortless. It is a long night of often intense concentration and remains a labour of love for all those who don the SCB referee's tie and hair shirt. Paul Clews is an exciting and conscientious rider who, though he's only just turned 27, has already been in the sport for sufficient time to qualify for a testimonial. It's hard to juggle a successful speedway career, work full time, have a son who's nearly one (Ryan) and yet still excel on the track as he has again for most of this season. Paul is the type of rider the fans admire for his all-out effort, no matter where he is in the race, and for always having the time and patience for a word with everyone. Though, that said, he is a modest man who prefers to do his talking on the track itself. Earlier in the evening, I thought his mum had turned up to give Caroline Tattum a sick note ("Could Paul please miss this evening's speedway lessons?") to excuse him from his obligation to ride tonight due to his latest painful injury. Though earlier in the week he couldn't even get his boot on, Paul does eventually ride for the Potters. His mum honestly, knowledgeably but proudly admits, "he didn't want to ride and definitely doesn't want to fall off in case it delays his comeback – though now it's drying out, he should be fine now he's out there, except for the vibration".

Once the meeting restarts, it is quickly apparent that we have a racing surface that is surprisingly conducive to close, competitive racing though some sort of bobble on the third bend – that apparently is always there and viewed by many as a 'home advantage' – intermittently causes many of the riders some urgent balance and control issues. It is also clear that tonight's visitors – the Newcastle Diamonds – quickly adapt to the changed conditions with some relish and aplomb. The grumbles of the Potters fans close by me gradually increase to a crescendo as their team falls further and further behind. As early as Heat 4, even though he leads easily, Robbie Kessler does an inadvertent wheelie on the back straight only to be loudly admonished in violent fashion by a disgruntled ferocious-looking lady in front of me "stop freaking showboating and freaking get on with it!" Kessler and Lemon are the only Stoke riders to win in the early heats and by Heat 8 the score is already 19-29 in favour of the visitors, while Stoke riders have so far managed to finish last in every race. Rightly guessing that many people are already taping it, the announcer Derek Turner enlivens proceedings with his announcement "and now the latest results from the World Team Cup Final" only to immediately add, "only winding you up", when the crowd audibly groan louder than usual at the thought that the mystery of this result could be spoiled for them before they get the chance to watch their tape of these proceedings.

The crowd cry out again in frustration only moments later when they learn that the Tattum-Crabtree managerial combination have eschewed the "obvious" chance to immediately use a tactical ride now that they're ten points behind. Instead, in the next race we're treated to a superb 5-1 and exhibition of team riding from the Alan 'Moggo' Mogridge and Paul Clews combination, who finish ahead of Jamie Robertson and the slightly sluggish efforts (by his standards) of the Diamonds captain James Grieves. This great race result for the Potters is achieved despite the best efforts of Robertson, who since the new shale went down has attacked every corner and straight of each race with considerable gusto and élan. (Apparently, without the fear of the conditions manifested by the home team riders, in the previous race he'd treated the crowd to a brave passing manoeuvre before he just about managed not to come to grief with the sheer momentum of his effort on the last bend.) Mark Lemon wins again in Heat 10 with a brave pass on the back straight of the last lap, when he skilfully overtakes the exhilarating visitor Manuel Hauzinger. This delights the crowd – well the ones in their cars at least, who flash their car headlights in praise and intermittently sound their horns during Lemon's celebration lap of honour. It creates a strangely disjointed disco effect in the already gathering gloom of the late evening and further adds to the atmosphere inside the stadium that has already been heightened by the arrival of an unseasonal hanging mist.

The terraces are enlivened with wildfire gossip about a dramatic fight-cum-contretemps between Hans Andersen and Scott Nicholls at the World Team Cup. Most people in the crowd are extremely partisan and patriotic so, even though no one has seen the incident in question, they all confidently claim that the Dane is definitely a "cheating bastard".

The meeting properly slips away from the Diamonds in Heat 11, after initially Barrie Evans aggressively lines up very close to Josef "Pepe" Franc to 'psyche him out', who then, predictably enough and as he was intended to do, complains to the start marshal. After a quick ostentatious check, the marshal (unfairly in my opinion as Evans definitely appears to encroach on the Franc's start gate) shrugs and signals 'get on with it'. It's irrelevant anyway as Franc has an engine failure on the line and Jamie Robertson is unable to finish after his attempt to push home for a consolation point ends because his bike has seized in muddy fashion. The 5-0 heat score that results means that in the space of three races the Potters have speedily overcome a 10-point deficit, without the use of tacticals, and takes the lead on the night by one point. The experience and professionalism of the Potters old guard in the form of Lemon and Mogridge then effectively snuff out any lingering chance of a Diamonds fight back. There is some drama – well more like melodrama crossed with unintentional humour – in Heat 13 when Robbie Kessler falls in theatrical slow motion fashion like a dying swan in order to try to persuade the referee to

Under orders after new shale has been laid. © Jeff Scott

Stoke fans study their programmes and other reading material.
© Jeff Scott

order a restart of the race, after he was noticeably the slowest to the first bend. To the slightly tongue-in-cheek outrage of the crowd, the referee isn't of the view that Kessler was left with 'nowhere to go' and excludes him. For artistic expression, he should have been kept in the race but sadly this criterion doesn't exist in the rulebook. Moggo beats George Stancl in the penultimate heat and though the Diamonds could still snatch victory from the jaws of defeat in the last race with a 5-1, the chances of this immediately disappears with an engine failure for Hauzinger at the start line. It's been a speedway meeting to savour through a combination of excellent racing and dramatic changes of fortune during the course of the evening. Though the World Team Cup Final taking place elsewhere is ostensibly hyped as a blue riband event on the speedway calendar, the quality of the spectacle served up here tonight would regularly attract enthusiastic fans if it were served up all over the country. It is a pleasure to watch and enjoy the action unfold.

Afterwards in the bar, Caroline Tattum suggests that I return in August to have another go at selling my book. Whether it i the overcast skies, the appeal of the opposition or the rival attraction of the World Cup, numbers ar down on normal and she feels "tonight's crowd wasn't that great". Though she puts this slightly differently! The delightful Joan English believes the sharp about-turn in the Diamond's fortunes, from potential triumph to sharp decline after the halfway point, is due to the fact that "with the exception of Manuel, we didn't have any heat leaders tonight". I too would have definitely expected better performances from their experienced riders – particularly James Grieves, George Stancl and Josef Franc. Newcastle promoter George English is, as ever, friendly, courteous and helpful though he won't know I posted this opinion since "I NEVER read the internet, even when we win. I learnt that a long time ago!"

I leave the still crowded and boisterous bar, just as 'the Rat' and John Rich have nearly completely packed away the track shop, while the Potters fans excitedly relive an ultimately easy triumph. It has again been a pleasure to visit the Loomer Road stadium to witness a meeting that I can't imagine will be bettered for racing and entertainment on my travels during 2006.

22nd July Stoke v Newcastle (Premier League) 47-42

August 2006

"They [the shareholders] believe this can herald a new start for the Dons – although obviously there will be no links with the old Wimbledon area name. However, there will be other links with the name made famous at Plough Lane for so many years. We will be known as the Dons – and not necessarily as the Sittingbourne Dons. Of paramount importance, too, is the fact that we will race in the colours used by the old Wimbledon team for so many years... we have the support of the BSPA in making this bid to establish speedway at the Kent track, but this of course subject to us being successful in regard to our planning application."
Ian Perkin with news about Sittingbourne Stadium from the Wimbledon Speedway plc AGM

"Out of the blue last month, we were informed that we had to carry out a summer survey. Finding out in July gave us no chance. And this is bearing in mind that there is already planning permission for a track up there which covers twice the area we have put in for. I think its nonsense."
Allen Trump perseveres in his campaign for Exeter Speedway to race at Haldon Hill

"It is clearly a designated sports area. Much of the heathland in the confines of the racecourse is quality gorse but the area we wish to use is scrub. The racecourse management have offered to replant five acres to replace it.... there is no problem with the horse racing traffic, which includes some 100 horseboxes and thousands of spectators during the day time, so why should the speedway, with 14 riders' vans and a few hundred cars, be a problem in the evening?"
David Short comments on news that Devon Highways want a traffic survey at Haldon Hill

"If crowds don't significantly increase, then Elite League there will be virtually unsustainable. We have been getting crowds of seven to eight hundred[1], which is not much more than what they were getting in the Premier League. Our break even figure is close to 2,000 and we only achieved that on Good Friday when it included 500 free kids... I don't think that people realise how much it costs to run a side containing GP riders like Greg Hancock and Matej Zagar, plus the likes of Charlie Gjedde and Janusz Kolodziej. These riders are expensive especially when they are successful like they are at present. The costs are high and currently unsustainable."
John Postlethwaite

"We are going to start straightaway and I know there is always a risk a planning application will be turned down and I have to be careful what I say for risk of upsetting anyone...speedway might come back to Wimbledon if someone bought the stadium and was prepared to run speedway but I don't think that will happen. This seems to be our best opportunity but I can't guarantee we will get planning permission. We think there's a good chance and the stadium owners think there's a good chance as well."
Ian Perkin talks to Peter Oakes

"It seemed as if we were up against Workington and the referee... I was making official complaints, but eventually the referee refused to speak to me."
Rob Lynn of King's Lynn on referee Rod Smith

"Rod Smith had a lot of whingeing speedway riders around him and he stood his ground. These are the same riders who are getting quite a reputation for themselves in this sport and the referee

was having none of it. A weaker referee might have buckled and just called it off, but the racing was good and there was nothing wrong with the track in terms of the meeting going ahead."
Graham Drury of Workington on the same referee Rod Smith

"I know refereeing is not easy but surely he [Dave Robertson] could see that Stoddart fell for a reason – and that was caused by Mark [Baseby]. A little more thought as to the reasons for the stoppage would get officials back to the actual cause, not the final part of the incident."
Malcolm Vasey offers a masterclass on how to comment on a referee

"I want to stress that we do remain focused on being in a higher league. My comments last week about us not going Premier League as it is now were probably taken out of context. Our focus is to be in a higher league next year if possible. It seems to have caused quite a stir amongst our supporters, and some other promoters for that matter, and I want to stress that we are committed to being in a higher league."
Rob Godfrey, Scunthorpe co-promoter

"Berwick wanted the match abandoned, citing the principle that the safety of their riders was at stake. But, funnily enough, that principle went right out of the window within a few minutes of racing commencing when they got a 4-2 that took them into a one point lead for the bonus instead of being one point down as they were at the end of Heat 11. And, if the track was so dangerous, why was Stanislaw Burza performing donuts on it straight after the final heat? The fact that Burza continued his donuts in the pits, spraying everyone around with wet dirt, simply added to a disgraceful performance from Berwick personnel who showed utter contempt for the Newcastle crowd in their bid to get the meeting called off. Fortunately, Tony Steele was in charge and he was not fooled by Berwick's antics... sure, we are disappointed to miss out on the bonus point, but at least we can hold our heads up high, unlike many people connected with a track about 60 miles north of here."
Newcastle co-promoter George English

"[It] would be in bad taste if [Chris Durno] were to officiate at our meetings in the foreseeable future."
Matt "in eight years of promoting, I have never moaned or complained about a referee"
Ford

"I was disappointed with what happened. I could have ruined Jason's World title hopes because he shut off in front of me. I could have put him out for the season."
Mild-mannered Mark Loram on Jason Crump

"Maybe I shut off a bit harsh over the line but, at the end of the day, Mark had been doing it to Simon [Stead] for the whole of the race... it backfired on Mark, that's probably why he was a bit brassed off. I certainly didn't mean for Mark to crash."
Mild-mannered Jason Crump on Mark Loram

"You don't really need a location link to the club name. That's been proved with the mighty Arsenal, while in rugby union there's names like Harlequins, Saracens and Wasps – none of which specify where they are based. But it doesn't affect their attendances – it's the attraction of what they put on that pulls in the pundits... a new Sittingbourne plc will be floated to promote the team. The Wimbledon plc will go into abeyance but not wound up. Then, if there's any chance of speedway going back into the south London area, we would hold the option on the Wimbledon title."
Ian Perkin outlines his view on the use of 'the Dons' name and some other stuff

"They were all gentlemen... why don't these people study the history of speedway before opening their mouths and casting such a slur on the departed?"
Reg Fearman takes Bob Radford to task about his article on the forthcoming Mike Broadbank testimonial and his comments upon Ted Morse, Ted Nelson and Bert Hearse

"I don't really know or understand why [Reg Fearman] found it necessary to comment. This was not a slur on former Swindon directors who have now passed on, but I am the promoter today and I am only too happy to give a Swindon great, who gave 16 years of service, a little bit of recognition and a financial boost when times are hard for him."
Terry Russell

"We didn't want a history lesson and I don't take back a word of what I said. No slur was intended and the fact that those in charge have passed away was the reason Broady did not say more. We are simply determined to recognise one of the great and most loyal riders in Swindon's history."
Alun Rossiter

"I could not believe what I read in the Letters page – Reg Fearman, no less, waffling on about the history of speedway and injustice. Hello Reg, remember me? I put ten years service into Poole Speedway to be rewarded with a testimonial in 1984 but the Reg Fearman-fronted promotion went into bankruptcy and I received none of the money that people had contributed to what should have been my memorable year in speedway. Not forgetting the numerous riders and businesses that were left high and dry. I still have the paperwork and would be happy to print a list of the creditors who were all taken to the cleaners. How this man has the gall to write and say he takes issue with Terry Russell and Alun Rossiter – who I'm sure he doesn't even know. They are willing to salute Mike Broadbank (who I have known all my life and count as a dear friend). To comment that they should look at the history of speedway is beyond reproach. Unbelievable. People in glass houses springs to mind."
Open letter from Neil Middleditch to Reg Fearman

"You couldn't believe that 60-33 could feel okay, but it does. I should be seriously annoyed about a score like that, but I'm not."
Ronnie Russell after defeat at Smallmead

"If it's raining and you can hardly walk on the track then, to me, it's not a raceable track. It wasn't safe and it was not good for the public because they had paid to see racing, not mud wrestling."
Tomas Topinka on the abandoned meeting at Workington

"First and foremost, I felt sorry for the Chapman's when we went there on Wednesday because it was not their fault that the match was called off after Heat 7. It was unfortunate that the meeting didn't start on time but the abuse they suffered from their own supporters was uncalled for – I've never seen two promoters get so much stick from their own fans. We were disappointed because we felt we could have got the remaining heats in, but I didn't feel it was very professional for Jonathan Chapman to take the microphone and ask the fans what their views were. However, if that's the way he wants to do things, I suppose he'll get on with it, and from me there were no complaints as the best team won on the night."
Graham Drury chooses his words carefully

"I'm not naming names, I don't need to, but the way I felt on Friday I could have sacked five out of the seven riders... we make allowances here and there, but the fans – the ones who pay the wages – see every turn of the wheel. They may not understand the reasons why things go wrong, but they do see the mistakes and there's no hiding place for riders."

Dave 'I'm a teapot' Croucher waters the track. © Jeff Scott

The 'Double Belly Buster Burger' delights Steve Davies and 'the Rat'. © Jeff Scott

Neil Machin after a shock home defeat for Sheffield by Stoke

"I don't think that three riders in a race is acceptable but I also do not think changing the result the next day is acceptable either. Rules are rules. If we do not abide by the rules, we have nothing."
Jon Cook resists speedway anarchy against Arena Essex

"It was a big mess up on my behalf and I'll take it on the chin. I felt that Troy should have been allowed to ride and we'd worry about the result afterwards, but Jon Cook from Eastbourne thought it would be more damaging to change the result afterwards. I tried my best to get a rider there and got it wrong. Any punishment will be minor compared to what we've been through this season. It was not a minor offence, but I made a mistake."
Ronnie Russell explains how we got on the road to potential anarchy

"Staging speedway with The Dons at Central Park is something I am dedicated to."
Ian Perkin

"I didn't get a chance to say farewell to all my friends at Reading Speedway. Following an 18-year involvement at Reading, I resigned on July 20 from being the announcer, as I didn't want to be involved with the present promotion anymore... it was wonderful to be involved at Smallmead and to be the voice of Reading Speedway for over a decade, the fans were all superb and we had some fun."
Dave Stallworthy says goodbye via the *Speedway Star* letters page

"My doctor told me to take two weeks off, but as I needed the points I had to race in the GP. I didn't listen to him, but now I know that I am not fit enough to ride and need to recover my fitness."
Antonio Lindback

"It's got to happen because we've got to give speedway some structure back. Without the structure, it's going to die. Promotion and relegation gives it real credibility to new fans. *Sky* say their viewing figures for speedway have increased but they haven't increased on the terraces. We've got to get people back and that means keeping it simple... maybe take some of these other silly rules out too, like the tactical rides. People don't like them so eradicate them. Make the rules simple so that people can understand."
Rob Godfrey proposes a two tier Premier league with promotion and relegation

"I was disgusted by the attitude and antics of Rye House

and Len Silver and by the abusive language he used to me and the referee Chris Gay."
Mick Horton encounters a swearing OAP

"Too many people have preconceived notions as to what speedway is. They associate the sport with things like Hells Angels and noisy motorcycles."
Ian Perkin prepares to educate Swale Borough Council

"I signed a contract without a fixed number of matches to ride and I have decided to leave the Peterborough team. Recently our relationship has been getting worse. Not all arrangements and agreements were fulfilled, and that's the reason."
Karol Zabik leaves Peterborough

"I wasn't aware that there was anything he wanted that he hadn't got, and we had gone out of our way to help him. He has a right to his opinion but I just wish he would tell us what the problems were."
Trevor Swales comments at the time

"He made a number of excuses that he hadn't been given what he was promised, whereas in fact he had actually been given more, and the whole thing left a very sour taste."
Trevor Swales comments in his end of season review

"Life's what you make it, isn't it?"
1st August

It's always a delight to have to cross the water to the Isle of Wight from Portsmouth Harbour. The car-ferry port is also the ideal place to meet anyone who is anyone connected with speedway on the Island – from the club promoters and staff, riders from both sides, various mechanics and parents as well as the match official. As there is only one way over with a vehicle everyone has to pass through here or hang around on the seats in the ticket office.

When I arrive a slightly harassed but extremely amiable Dave Pavitt is already happily ensconced on the ticket-office seats impressively conducting operations. This involves dealing with a constant stream of people arriving to claim their ferry tickets for the crossing from a huge pile on the table next to his open executive briefcase and a continuous barrage of phone calls on his mobile. Dave deals with everyone with the same friendly manner. He has gone out of his way to be supportive of my book and is definitely of the 'old school' when it comes to his approach to speedway (and new technology!). At one point I overhear him say after a lengthy tale of woe and bad luck, in all sincerity and with a philosophical outlook it's hard to object to, "life's what you make it, isn't it?"

This evening's opponents are the Edinburgh Monarchs and their trip to the Island is part of their brief 'Southern Tour' that also takes them to the wilds of Somerset tomorrow. A large contingent of fans has made the trip on one of the infamous away trips organised by George Taylor (Stadium electrician and Aussie spy" according to Gary Lough) and his wife, Helen ("very nice lady!") – that tradition dictates will involve everyone being based at the Blunsdon Hotel in Swindon. Edinburgh promoter John Campbell has taken the chance for a short holiday with his family down south and pops in to collect his ticket. Dave greets him with the news "your Italian is already here in a blue van" as he waves his hand expansively in the general direction of the car park that constantly alternates between crowded and empty between the regular half-hourly sailings. The bright blue van with Italian number plates in question belongs to Daniele Tessari who'll be making his debut tonight. Relatively unknown in this country, eagle-eyed readers of the *Speedway Star* will have noticed that Daniele finished second overall behind Jason Bunyan in the Ivan Mauger Golden Helmet series in New Zealand over the winter. After a brief but animated discussion about the relative fortunes of their clubs between these experienced promoters and after some passing mention that the Monarch's Matthew Wethers has signed as a number 8 for the Poole Pirates, John departs and Dave returns to the administration of his tickets and his trilling mobile.

Another set of early arrivals for the 4 p.m. is tonight's referee Margaret Vardy, her friendly partner with the dry wit Stephen Davies and the ubiquitous Dave 'The Rat' Rattenberry whom they've given a lift to from Walsall so he can survey the farthest outpost of his track shop empire. There's quite a Walsall theme as Steve and Margaret are both season ticket holders and Steve proudly displays his allegiance by wearing the only Walsall replica shirt I see all evening. The track shop will have a new item of merchandise on sale this evening – Isle of Wight Speedway window stickers – ideal for the car or the bedroom window of any really keen teenager's or obsessive Islanders fans of any age. I have decided not to take my car to the island in case I get lost and Margaret kindly volunteers to take my sign and my box of books over with her while I travel in Dave Croucher's luxurious and giant 7 series BMW. Away from the track he's a car dealer, so he appears to arrive in a different luxurious model of car every week. In this case, we'll travel in a car that he's already sold and is merely transporting to the Island for the buyer. Though it is ten years old, has 180,000 miles on the clock, does 12 mpg and has all the extras like a television (!), plush leather seats etc., I really can't believe that you can pick one up for around £3000. Luckily for the purchaser the car arrives intact after a near miss when we were suddenly confronted with a kerb and fence just as the mobile phone company temporarily distracted Dave from his full attention to the road ahead.

By the time we arrive at the stadium, the jokers in Margaret's car – whom I deduce to be Steve and Dave – have tried to append another quote to my sign filled with praiseworthy comments that reads " the biggest load of fabricated bollocks I have ever read – M. Vardy, Referee". I don't exactly have to be mastermind to figure out that Margaret didn't write this! We're here so early that I'm able to choose my spot to set up my stall, after I've borrowed a small round metal-topped table from the bar. I choose to stand by the turn of the first bend close to the trailer that now forms the track shop and with a great view of the track towards the start line. A glance on page 13 in the programme reveals a review of my book and news of my visit by the experienced and knowledgeable Bryn Williams, who kindly notes that anyone who purchases a copy of my book "won't be disappointed". I make a point of looking him out to thank him and to finally get to meet him properly – Dave Pavitt tells me to look out for a "small, troll of a man". When I eventually find him, Bryn is resting in the riders' and track staff tearoom taking a well-earned rest cum brief respite in advance of his presentational duties. He lives in Kent and has a schedule of work – both writing and presentational duties – that would exhaust a younger man but apparently invigorates him. Everywhere I have heard him present he's always been very wry and witty; in the flesh he's exactly the same albeit continuously swathed in the smoke from his fags.

By the time I leave the tearoom the crowd – whose numbers are traditionally swollen by holidaymakers during the school holiday weeks of the summer season – have begun to arrive through the turnstiles and I rush back to my table just in case I'm losing any book sales. The large contingent of Monarchs fans on their 'Southern Tour' arrive early and make their way to a variety of their previously chosen 'ideal' vantage points within the stadium. Quite a knot of them gather by the railings in front of my table, close by on the grass bank or off to the nearby main grandstand. There are a lot of familiar faces among them including Ella MacDonald and the author from their Championship winning season Gary Lough – as ever slavered in impressive amounts of sun cream to protect against the extremes of sunlight you can experience in England, even despite the markedly overcast conditions. Shortly afterwards the delightful Monarchs fan, Hannah, stops by to sincerely quiz me about the book and the sales success I've enjoyed. Sadly I can't persuade her to buy a copy since she's dyslexic but, nonetheless, she speaks highly of Gary's favourable account of the contents of the book. She travels extensively with her boyfriend, Edinburgh's laid-back Aussie rider Matthew Wethers. As if the journeys required for the Premier League campaign aren't already enough, he has just this week signed to ride for Poole, which will add to the travel burden considerably. Hannah takes this in her stride and seems the sort of optimistic and outgoing person who would relish new situations as an opportunity and experience rather than something to complain about.

For 'The Rat' every speedway meeting is a major social event, like a perpetual Royal Garden Party at Buckingham Palace, without the canapés and except he apparently knows absolutely everyone present. Inevitably he has strong Edinburgh connections, particularly as he ran the track shop there from the late seventies (1978). He helpfully introduces Mike Hunter – slightly unnecessarily as "everyone knows him" – with his familiar sobriquet "Mr. Edinburgh", and the nearby Norrie Tait who Rat notes "is affectionately known as 'Stormin' Norman' – he does the Edinburgh programme shop. I started him off there, he's very good in the programme market and does lots of good things". Norrie nods his confirmation and I get the impression that he's a man of few words in the face of all this unexpected praise, though he does briefly confirm "it's now my 29th season".

Also in this august group by my stall are Dick Jarvis and Les Drury ("the quiet one") who both hail from Kent but are famous for rarely missing an Edinburgh Monarchs' away meeting. They've done this together since the Canterbury Crusaders Speedway Club closed. After the closure, they "couldn't bring" themselves to support either Eastbourne or Arena so the Monarchs were the obvious choice "because they wear the same colours and we were always made welcome!" They both work in the grass roots of the sport at Sittingbourne Speedway where Dick is a pits marshal, and Les works in the official's box. Rat notes, "I'm always pleased to see Les – not just because he's one of the biggest programme collectors in the country". They all chat animatedly about the Monarchs, speedway and express incredulity that Ian Perkin, Chairman of Wimbledon Speedway plc has stated his intention to try relocate this defunct speedway franchise – after they were unwanted by the landlords of Plough Lane – to the dog track in Sittingbourne. The talk is that they await exact details of the proposals and incredulously wonder at how the previously intractable planning obstacles will be overcome. Much more pressing matters are at hand since the meeting has got underway and provides the Edinburgh fans with their first sight on track of their Italian debutant Daniele Tessari. He glides to a well-earned third place in his first ever outing on a British track and Edinburgh surge into an early lead before a 5-1 for the home reserves corrects the situation. Before the meeting when we spoke on the ferry crossing, the Monarchs promoter John Campbell had sensibly dampened expectations about a possible Monarchs triumph – he cited the huge disparity in track size between the teams – and forecast that the 21-point advantage that they already held from their meeting at Armadale would not be sufficient for them to gain the aggregate bonus point this evening.

The most dramatic incident of the night arrives in Heat 3 on the bend in front of us when Henrik Moller and Jason Doyle dramatically collide. Margaret Vardy, the referee errs on the side of caution with her decision to allow "all four" back in the rerun when, to my mind, it was aggressive riding by the young Australian that caused the incident. The crash starts a series of long delays understandably set off by the stoppage to allow the track medical staff and St John Ambulance people attend to both riders. Over the tannoy we learn from Bryn that an ambulance has been called for Moller from the local hospital and is expected shortly. Though he had already promoted my book earlier, Bryn praises the work of the Speedway Riders Benevolent Fund as hugely important, mentions the attendance of the wonderfully named Bernard Crapper who is in charge of the fund and elegantly segues to the fact that I will make a donation for every copy sold to the SRBF to further plug my book. All the while, the riders lie prone on the track though eventually in a show of mind over matter, Doyle struggles to his feet to applause from the crowd. Just prior to that, Mike Hunter had wondered aloud "why did he [Doyle] have to come over so far?" Jason gingerly makes his way back to the pits but his recovery is short lived since a few minutes later his mechanic calls for urgent medical attention for him in the pits. Another ambulance is then required to be despatched to the stadium since while common sense might dictate both riders should go in the same ambulance, Health & Safety rules dictate they cannot!

Taking advantage of the enforced break, Margaret's partner Steve just can't delay any longer going for his treat of the evening from Vanessa's catering outlet in the Clubhouse, the legendary "Double Belly Buster Burger" that they reputedly serve to great acclaim on the Island for a bargain £4.10. He has salivated at the prospect all evening and it's certainly an impressive size. Though he's sung its praises all afternoon, the Rat shows great willpower as he looks on covetously but resists in favour of a refreshing cup of coffee. When the racing eventually resumes, the Monarchs lose the rerun 5-1 and then only manage a couple of drawn heats as the Islanders quickly extend the score to a comfortable 39-21 by Heat 10. The only real resistance to the onslaught of the home riders has been provided by Theo Pijper with a heat win and also, much more excitingly for the touring fans who greet this event rapturously, by Daniele Tessari in Heat 8. Even Mike Hunter allows a smile to play upon his lips, since a rider with some élan, dash and competitive spirit would be warmly welcomed for the rest of the season north of the border and it finally appears that they might have found one. It's a win that wouldn't have been predicted based on three heats earlier when Daniele trailed in forlornly at the back of the race but maybe he was just finding the appropriate line to follow and the correct set up for his bike on the longest track in the country. Later Belle Vue's Phil Morris walked by mysteriously saying "I told you, I told you!" to Mike Hunter who translates this cryptic comment "he'd said earlier that Tessari is a good lad" before he cautions wistfully, "Armadale is totally different but to have someone in the team who can do that [overtake bravely and thrillingly] would be something".

Love it or loathe it, the tactical rider replacement regulations can enliven a meeting since it allows a team to have their riders attempt to double their points when they wear the black and white helmet colour. Two consecutive 1-8 heat results, with wins for Pijper and Wethers, virtually eliminates at a stroke all chance the Islanders have to gain the bonus point they started to expect and these wins provide a real buzz in the crowd among the ostentatiously delighted and exuberantly celebrating Monarchs fans. Even better for the Monarchs faithful, in the first of these 8-1's Tessari beats the highly fancied Chris Holder round his own circuit and so further highlights his promise.

A meeting two weeks previously against Somerset at Smallbrook was mired in controversy when it was abandoned after 14 heats due to the strict enforcement of the 10 p.m. curfew. Tonight this is not the case even though the general consensus among the various watches consulted on our part of the terraces has the time variously between 10.02 and 10.03 p.m. before the final race starts. Steve sagely notes that the only important watch is that owned by the referee that, in this instance, showed something altogether different again, as Margaret later confirms and demonstrates in the bar afterwards. Not that this approach wins her any plaudits with the Isle of Wight Team Manager, Martin 'Mad Dog' Newnham, who's already loudly shared his opinion with her in the referee's box that an earlier "freaking decision had cost us the freaking bonus point". Such is the heat of the moment and the delight of speedway as a sport of contrary opinions. Though the Islanders win on the night, they only do so by 14 points, so the Monarchs thereby confound the gloomy expectations of their own co-promoter and gain their first aggregate bonus point of the season.

The late finish means that we miss the 10 o'clock sailing back to the mainland and the sacrifice of a brief sojourn in the Clubhouse bar for additional refreshments is required. It is heaving with fans, riders, sponsors and luminaries of the sport including former Reading promoter Pat Bliss, who is here to attend her first speedway meeting of the 2006 season. Pat looks like the years have fallen off her now that the stress and cares of the Racers promotion has been lifted from her shoulders. Inevitably the need to make the next ferry sailing causes a mass exodus from the stadium for all those who live on the mainland, so we only catch a brief snatch of the presentation to Chris Johnson for his combative 10 (paid 13) score from six rides.

A trip on the water is always a thrill even for a short distance at night on a car ferry. Because of essential repair work we learn that we're to have a detour to the Inter-Continental area of the mainland port. This provides the opportunity to closely study the variety of Navy vessels mothballed and at anchor in this large port – probably almost all of the fleet given the scale of military cutbacks in our Naval capability – under the watchful gaze and close attention of the harbour police boat that escorts us throughout our trip into port. The change of docking location has left me a huge distance from my car that remains some distance away at the car-ferry port. Since it's well after midnight, this is an inconvenience that's heightened by the repeated public failure of the ferry captain to easily dock his boat. He spends considerable time making small adjustments to the angle of approach of the ferry only feet from the jetty and an inch or two from the harbour wall. The choice language shouted by the Harbour Master and his apoplectic demeanour between barked instructions is a delight to behold. It's a late end to a protracted evening. Referee Margaret Vardy still has to drive back to the Midlands, no doubt to a chorus of snoring from Steve and the Rat, before her 7 a.m. start for work later in the morning.

1st August Isle of Wight v Edinburgh (Premier League) 55-41

52 Years On
4th August
The terrible traffic that the main road to Weymouth suffers from during the summer holiday season again delayed my arrival at Radipole Lane, this time for the inaugural meeting on the 2006 campaign under new promoter Phil Bartlett, who has specially returned to Dorset for the night from his family holiday at Centre Parcs Longleat. After a variety of wrangles and discussions with the adjacent football stadium landlords, the council and the intervention of the BSPA in the dispute with the previous promoter Brian White, the season was finally able to get underway with a challenge match against Carmarthen. It was a historic event for another reason since it was exactly 52 years ago to the day that Weymouth Speedway started in the town back in 1954.

There was slightly more than two hours before the stadium would once more echo to the throaty roar of the bikes and hopefully without undue disturbance to the neighbours as a result of the newly installed noise-mitigation measures. Apparently the recently built impressive-looking tall, cork-coloured fencing along the back straight and partially round the second bend was specially designed to muffle the sound. The place was a hive of activity in the warm sunshine. Most of the riders had already arrived and numerous other vital tasks were still in the process of completion by an army of willing volunteers. The most noticeable aspect of the stadium was the familiarity of the fixtures and fittings, from my visit last season, though the track itself stood out since it had recently been doused in a considerable amount of water. Looked at through untutored eyes, the surface appeared muddy and much more amenable to a pottery class than a speedway meeting. Many of the familiar faces were again already present from last year and I immediately recognised the diminutive Trevor (in charge of admissions for £1 to the home-straight grandstand), the club's historian Ray Collins and, of course, the energetic Julie Martin who has added the role of Press Officer and programme compiler to her roster of responsibilities to go along with her celebrated photographic duties. She arrives clutching a cake that I initially thought was to celebrate the re-birth of the club but, in fact, is a surprise (along with an announcement over the tannoy) for her daughter Leah Cramner who is now five years old. Leah shelters behind her father's legs when I try to speak with her about her birthday presents though I gather from her mum that one of these was an ant farm. Which to my ears sounds a very contemporary eco-friendly gift: I honestly can't recall that many of these were available as presents in my youth!

One of the Press Officer's tasks is the design and layout of the match programme that has kept Julie flustered and busy for quite a few nights recently. I decide not to mention that it's a process that will have to be gone through every week. But, like many things, I'm sure that it gets easier with practice. Later when I checked the proofs I thought it looked really good but on the night, although it bears the signs of its production methods, it appears much more professional than some others I have seen elsewhere. Though the club have yet to embark on any of their away fixtures, this programme doesn't yet include my personal highlight of the season – in my opinion, the most entertaining column in any club programme in the country – the thoughts of Weymouth Wildcats director Jem as outlined in his 'Away Days' feature.

I'm fortunate to be able to be allowed to set up my display table of books just where practically every fan that arrives in the stadium will have to pass at some point during proceedings. It's a strategically chosen spot located close by the grandstand, the toilet cubicles, the burger van, start line and by the pathway that leads to the bar as well as all the other viewing areas round the far side of the track. There's quite a bit of interest in my book table from the crowd that funnels into the stadium early as soon as the entrance gates open. However, not all of this interest is turned into sales but people are well aware of both my book and my visit due to the sterling work of the sports' staff at the *Dorset Echo*. They have kindly mentioned my trip and is additional coverage that follows on from the very kind review some weeks back by Matt Pitman. He even took the trouble to send a clipping of the review to me with a note saying "well done!" which is an unusual but considerate touch that I sincerely appreciated.

I manage to sell four copies of my book before the meeting starts and enjoy some interesting and often lengthy conversations with a variety of people. One topic of debate from a committed Arena fan by the start line was "why doesn't Ronnie Russell consider Dave Mason as a possible number 8 for the club as I'm sure that he'd do a good job for us – I think I'll suggest it!" I also chat briefly to the Strudwicks – Lee (who rides) plus John (who drove) and Niall (who doesn't ride but continues his apprenticeship with some work in the pits and more close observation of the activities there). I also talk at some length to the polite, keen and young Poole-based rider Marc Andrews and his dad. I'd recently seen Marc get shipped off to hospital following a crash at a Southern Area junior meeting at Sittingbourne. One of the hazards of riding speedway is the sometimes regular opportunity it affords to get acquainted with many Accident and Emergency departments up and down the country. Suffice it to say that Marc didn't enjoy his five-hour extended stay in Kent.

While I'm stood by my stall Wimbledon plc Chairman Ian Perkin struts past, with his family in tow, wearing large sunglasses of the type favoured by retired pensioners in Florida. I had gathered from an interview he gave to Peter Oakes in this week's *Speedway Star* that though he is in the area on holiday, he has popped in to study the new sound-proofing measures at the Weymouth club first hand and to gain some tips and ideas for his own future planning applications. It would appear that most Weymouth fans had not been along to watch the brief Conference League incarnation of Wimbledon Speedway at Plough Lane since, while I watched, Ian wandered through the large gathering crowd apparently unrecognised, albeit incognito behind his sunglasses. As an interesting comparison, Weymouth Speedway were involved a serious dispute with the stadium landlords that threatened the future existence of their use of their track, though the consortium headed up by promoter Phil Bartlett managed to successfully smooth over these differences and finally arrive at a mutually satisfactory but amicable resolution.

All thoughts of other tracks are banished from my mind the instant the teams take to the area directly in front of my table for the pre-meeting parade and introductions. With about a 1000 spectators packed around the circuit perimeter, we soon learn that the Wildcats reserve rider George Piper has an extensive fan club if the level of boy-bandesque screams are anything to judge by. He also has impressive quantities of gel on his hair and we're also informed that he celebrated his fifteenth birthday yesterday. The Weymouth club captain, Dave Mason, sports a comparatively sober hairstyle by his usual exotic standards. In the first race, to the untutored eye Carmarthen's Ben Barker appears to negotiate the circuit at extremely high speed and, for once, our eyes don't deceive us as he sets a new track record of 52.8 seconds. I'm sure that the previous record holder Lewis Bridger will feel honour bound to return shortly to try to regain his coveted mantle.

From this race onwards, it's quickly evident that track conditions will be "tricky" throughout the evening. Many of the riders appear to struggle with the bumps on an unpredictable surface. Indeed the inside line automatically favoured by many contemporary riders appears to be particularly treacherous and even the more experienced riders who're already very familiar with the contours of this track, like Dan Giffard and David Mason, visibly struggle to control their machines. Not that anyone minds, as they're only too happy to enjoy the chance to see racing here again on a balmy evening. The first

Weymouth rider to win a race in this latest new era for the club is Jordan Frampton who enjoys more victories than any other Wildcat on the way to only one dropped point from his five rides.

Despite the track conditions, many of the races are extremely compulsive to watch and there are very few grumbles from the assembled crowd around my position by the start line. In contrast, there reportedly are a high level of grumbles, moans and groans from the riders in the pits about track conditions, though thankfully they keep the actual number of predicted falls to a minimum, except for Lee Strudwick who has to withdraw after three races, as a precaution, with a damaged finger. The odd race (Heat 9) is marred by understandable but excessive caution due to worries about the track condition and in the next race David Mason skilfully uses all his experience to manage to control his bike and stay on after he hit a disconcerting bump on bend three. Those riders that venture close to the fence enjoy a comparatively smooth passage round the track. Though falls are at a lower level than you'd traditionally expect for a Conference fixture, some riders are plagued with mechanical problems or sudden retirements and referee Ronnie Allen has to award a number of races. The scores remained reasonably close throughout although at 36-42 after Heat 13 all appeared lost for the home team until an eventful 5-0 in the penultimate race that featured a fall and retirement for an exclusion in an awarded race set up a close finale. In the final race, the excitement of the Weymouth crowd soon subsided after a fast start for a third win for Jordan Frampton soon put the actual result beyond doubt.

The consensus of opinion from the crowd around me is that the evening overall has been a tremendous success and a fillip to the sport within the town. The fact that the Wildcats have lost narrowly by a single point 44-45 is deemed irrelevant. After the meeting finished, and since Ian Perkin was ostensibly here to look and learn, I hoped that he had remained to take good notice of the brevity with which Weymouth promoter Phil Bartlett spoke to the crowd about his plans for the club and the actual condition of the track surface. He acknowledged that the driving force behind his decision to involve himself with the club was, like for many promoters, "pure passion and stupidity". He was also unafraid to be open about his own and the track's shortcomings, "okay I'm not saying it's the best track in the world... it's the one we acquired and with some work it's going to get better" – though he remained optimistic. The evening closed with some additional second half races to the continued accompaniment of the frequent flash of Julie Martin's camera as she documented the action. Afterwards she continued with an endless series of photos as the riders posed with the numerous sponsors in attendance on the centre green.[1]

Weymouth seems to get further and further away each time I drive back after a speedway meeting. It's not so much the distance in actual miles but the concentration levels required to navigate these convoluted roads in the dark countryside. Still, I shouldn't complain as a tired and tiring drive home is the daily lot of most speedway riders though, after I arrive back, I'm fortunate not to have a bike to clean and prepare for my next meeting.

4th August Weymouth v Carmarthen (Challenge) 44-45

A Trip to the Barbers
5th August
My early arrival at Foxhall Heath luckily allows me to avoid the traffic that will flood the roads after the first home game of the Championship season for Ipswich Town versus Crystal Palace match and enables me to watch behind the scenes around the turnstile area on a very hot afternoon in Suffolk. I'm warmly greeted by Nick and Johnny Barber from the track shop and by John Louis who's also just arrived, smartly dressed in his promoter's attire of collared shirt and tie, and who scampers about the place doing important race day tasks and making various last minute adjustments and checks. He

[1] Promoter Phil Bartlett later commented, "the stadium was buzzing. People were shaking my hand, jumping for joy it was a brilliant night. The occasion proved all our patience had paid off. We may have lost the meeting. But we had certainly won the battle of getting back on track."

Noise to a minimum at Foxhall Heath. © Jeff Scott

The St John Ambulance minister to the fallen. © Jeff Scott

warmly welcomes me and it's extremely kind of him to allow me the opportunity to sell my book at his track. When I'd called he'd double-checked who I was: "you're the chap who wrote the book about travelling to all the tracks, aren't you?" The reassurance of the confirmation that I was said author was enough to enlist his help. I like John's approach and enjoy his natural caution with strangers. I like to feel some vague level of increased acceptance here and that I'm less of a stranger to him nowadays.

The Barber family are here in force – John, Nick, their parents (Colin and Mollie) and sister Bev – to set up and work on what are quite an extensive array of tables and a surprising number of nooks and crannies from which to buy various items. Each location has its specialism – for example, one is the main track shop and another booth is solely for the boxes of programmes past and present. The Barbers are the biggest customers for my book, so far, through their chain of track shop franchises, though I remain hopeful that over time Dave Rattenberry will try to run them close. There's quite an animated discussion between the brothers, in an extremely frank brotherly way, about the exact whereabouts of the pens for the stall. These are items that sell extremely well at every track shop in the country and they've recently tried to exhaust the supply they had bearing the GP logo rather than the less time-sensitive stock of Ipswich-branded ones. Their exact whereabouts (not here I gather) is a topic that frequently and fractiously recurs between them as the huge range of merchandise and memorabilia they've unloaded from the van is meticulously set out over the next hour. They appear to know everyone at this track very well. Nick advises that I set up adjacent to the programme stall and next to where they give out the free copies of the *Evening Star*, since these are information magnets that will draw everyone once they set foot through the gates at 6.45 p.m. It's also a location that attracts a lot of wasps.

John was one of the first people to closely read my book and is a big fan as well as advocate of it. He kindly arranged my review by recommending my book to the knowledgeable Mike Bacon of the *Ipswich Evening Star*, who subsequently praised my approach to the topic in print almost as John has continued to repeatedly advocate its purchase to many people at tracks around the country. I'm touched, honoured and grateful, plus it is the kind of thoughtful respect that means so much. Now that *Showered in Shale* has just been so favourably reviewed in the *Speedway Star* both brothers feel vindicated and are convinced that it will sell well as the season draws to a close and in the run up to Christmas. Nick highlights that after a recent glut of speedway books, the volume of them will now subside over the next two months "except for a couple from Tony McDonald – the Tommy Jansson book which will be HUGE, probably unbelievable; oh, and of course the Eric Boocock one though I'm not so sure about that one. So apart from those you should benefit".

While he arranges the piles of programmes in the grotesquely hot booth that the Barbers have at Ipswich dedicated to their sale, John wonders about the fickle outlook of the modern speedway fan. Tonight, rather excitingly in my opinion, will see the return to the Foxhall Heath stadium of the very much in-form Hans Andersen, who at many tracks throughout the country has unfairly become something of a hate figure. He remains venerated by the Witches fans. In contrast, "Scott Nicholls is absolutely hated here now since he moved to Coventry, even though they adored him, worshipped the ground he walked on for years – I just don't understand it". John has also spoken with Ian Thomas about his interview in my book. "I asked him if he'd seen it. He laughed – just like I did when I read it 'cause it caught him so well and you can really just hear him saying all those things – and said he loves it, really loves it!"

While I munch on my food, little Leon whom I met last year on my visit passes by. I'm delighted to see him but he has absolutely no recollection of our meeting or any notion of who I am. Even when I show him his photo in my book, he remains nonchalant and totally unimpressed. After a lengthy lull, only interrupted by the arrival of a phalanx of charity collectors with buckets in aid of the local Air Ambulance, and later the *BBC Radio Suffolk* staff with their rather sleek company car decorated all over in a highly visible manner with logos advertising the station. Once the gates open, it gets completely manic on the programme stall. I hand out leaflets about my book as if they're going out of fashion to an impressive crowd that renews and disperses itself throughout all four corners of the stadium with impressive speed and regularity. I get some kind praise from some Sheffield Speedway fans, a father and son (Paul and Philip Brown) who say they liked the *Brighton Bonanza* chapter so much that they're actually tempted to go this year, if the Sheffield basketball fixtures permit!

I manage to sell a couple of copies before the racing starts, though one of these is because John has sympathetically sent someone over to me rather than make the sale from the stock he already has in the shop. Luckily my stall is ideally located to enable me to watch the races without really having to move, though the sheer volume of people in the way complicates this. I also chat with Dave whom I've previously met at a number of tracks throughout the country and he introduces me to the ex-Mildenhall promoter, Colin Barber. He is just as warm and friendly as his sons and the rest of his family. We have author type discussions about sales, print runs and the unit cost of manufacture of our respective books. I wish for similar success for my book that his (on the history of Ipswich Witches) has enjoyed, though his unit cost remains impressively and unbeatably low. Colin chain smokes as he points out the size of the crowd and notes that Foxhall is one of the few remaining speedway stadiums in the whole country where fans can stand and watch at almost any point around the circumference of the track.

The atmosphere is enthusiastic throughout though tension is kept to a minimum by the fact that Peterborough are effectively a one-man team and even Hans Andersen is unlikely to win this team contest on his own, though his sterling efforts do secure the bonus point for his side. For Ipswich, Mark Loram looks particularly fast and impressive, while Chris Louis also turns back the years to sparkle in a number of his races. On the advice of Nick Barber, I move my table by the track shop for the interval and by the exit after the meeting. Afterwards, it's another long drive home and the roads are remarkably empty. Though it's 1.00 a.m. when I get back home the occasion of the annual 'Gay Pride' celebrations throughout Brighton provides the convenient excuse for screechingly drunken antics to remain noisily in progress outside the happy but unneighbourly pub round the corner from my house.

5th August Ipswich v Peterborough (Elite League B) 51-43

The One and Only Sittingbourne

6th August

The delayed new bridge on the outskirts of Sittingbourne that stood half-completed and forlorn by the A249 has now finally been finished. The continuation of the brand new road up the steep incline of the ramp onto the bridge almost disorients me enough to mistakenly try to cross it. However, no sooner has this bridge opened than it appears that it might have to shut again, due to severe but sincere local doubts about its safety. Not only are there no safety barriers (and it is quite a height over some deep water) or lights at night but there are serious concerns about the flawed construction methods and materials used! Quite an example of British craftsmanship, much more suited to similarly snafus at the Bath Spa complex or the "New Wembley Stadium' than the flatlands of this part of Kent.

Finding my way to the stadium changes slightly each time I travel but always involves a brief drive along a road that will definitely test the suspension of your car. The field just outside the perimeter fence of Sittingbourne Speedway is already impressively crowded with parked vehicles when I arrive a short while before the noon start time. It always seems to be a boiling hot day whenever I come to watch speedway here. I rush to the trackside and I'm just in time for the pre-meeting parade which features the Sittingbourne Crusaders in their first speedway fixture of the season against the Weymouth Wildcats who already field quite a different side from the one they tracked for their inaugural meeting less than 48 hours previously. I buy a programme from the stall outside the track-shop portacabin that this afternoon houses many items of memorabilia as well as a display of information about the Speedway Museum by those wonderfully friendly and indefatigable campaigners on its behalf – George and Linda Barclay.

Pretty well the first person that I bump into at the club is SCB Official Chris Durno who had come along to the meeting with his son Tom. Chris was still smarting from his very public error on live television, when he gave the 'wrong decision' at Oxford against the Poole team that understandably they'd not been too happy with on the night or, for the possibly crucial effect it might yet have on their otherwise rapidly diminishing hopes of reaching the Elite League play-offs. However, like many things in life, everything was not as it seemed. Everyone at home saw frequent replays of the disputed incident many times and from many different camera angles. There was much incredulity and everyone expressed astonishment along the lines that "given that the referee can look at the same replays as us, how could he make this decision?" Chris tells me that he was mortified when he saw the tape AFTERWARDS, but on the night the replays that he could see in the referee's booth were from the angles that made his decision appear sensible rather than the very telling angle that made it look a totally nonsensical decision. It appears *Sky Sports* like to play their own part – whether deliberately or inadvertently for technical reasons beyond their control – to ensure controversy is regularly manufactured for the delight and edification of their armchair audience.

I don't really look at the forums that often, but Chris says that he's heard that a petition has been started against his continuation as a referee. This understandably mortifies him. "I'm prepared to hold my hand up and say I was wrong and live with the consequences of that but I did not see the replay it was claimed that I did at the time otherwise clearly I wouldn't have made that decision!" It sounds outrageous to me that people would start such a thing, speedway people too, who're often so respectful of foibles and the sacrifices that so many people make – including referees – to ensure that we can all watch our speedway. If a rider makes an error or is accused of things from the heinous to the silly, do these self-same people say that they should never ride again? Well, the odd nutter does but it is usually ignored. Everyone makes mistakes and refs, like riders, don't become awful overnight. Maybe these vociferous (armchair) critics could give up all their spare time to do the necessary training, put in the long dedicated hours required of our refs and then, perhaps, show us how it's really done properly under pressure? When he ambles off, Chris appears genuinely crestfallen, though it's now six days later, and personally I believe his explanation of events. Perhaps, *Sky Sports* could take some responsibility and make a statement to clarify whether or not this replay was really available to Chris at the time of his decision? It is the nature of the beast and an inevitable by-product of the "job" of a speedway referee or in fact any sports referee that damnation lurks behind every corner! You have to be incredibly thick skinned and brush off the criticism, but sometimes even the hide of a rhinoceros would not be able to deflect the cynicism of the baying speedway fraternity, plus the losing team always needs a scapegoat and the 'man in the box' is unable to answer back so is ideal to choose to blame.

The cover of my programme proudly advertises the slogan "Specialising in Amateur Speedway Activities". I'm really pleased to discover that the club have included a review of my book inside. I'm touched by this very much unexpected and kindly gesture.

There are quite lengthy introductions during the rider parade on the centre green and lots of alterations to the Weymouth side of the race card. It's safe to say that Conference League speedway is a broad church. The riders that make up any of the Conference Shield teams are little different to that norm and are drawn from a rich variety of sources and the team that Weymouth has assembled for this afternoon is completely indicative of this state of affairs. Interestingly, we learn that the rider at number four this afternoon for Sittingbourne, Dean Garrod, has been ever present in the Conference League since it was founded. Dean undercuts the injected gravitas of this pronouncement when he immediately retorts to the presenter who just outlined this fact, "just shows how old I am!" The riders clearly come in a range of levels of experience as well as all shapes and sizes. The youngest rider on display is the Wildcats 15-year-old George Piper.

I set up my stall and do quite a brisk trade (four books sold) until I sadly run out of stock! Oops. How ridiculous is that? At many tracks I can't sell them for neither love nor money and invariably cart huge boxes of the things around the place, yet this afternoon I have to turn away orders. Though there's a lovely piece in the programme, many people are understandably wary to think of buying a copy without actually getting to see or hold it! One person who is happy to buy a copy on trust is Steve Ribbons, a serial founder/re-energizer of defunct speedway clubs, notably Wimbledon and Rye House. He's a man who's proud of his roots and the fact that he's always risen to positions of responsibility from his place on the terraces. One consequence of this is that he has delightfully strong and forthright opinions on many aspects of contemporary speedway and the characters within the sport, often based on first hand experience. For the next little while I'm fortunate to be able to snatch a few words with him between races.

He quickly lets me know that he's no longer formally involved at Sittingbourne, "I'm taking a year out. Everything that you see here this afternoon is down to Graham Arnold, along with his band of dedicated helpers. It's his football, as it were, and he runs things exactly the way that he wants to. When I was here we put the stands in and I think that there should be more investment in facilities but that is now no longer my decision". Something that exercises Steve much more than developing the infrastructure of the Old Gun Site is the latest suggestion from Ian Perkin that he intends to apply for planning permission to open another speedway club in Sittingbourne. "I know him first hand and when I met him I didn't like him, so I'm not surprised at the arrogance of the man that he now suggests that he'll open a club in Sittingbourne when there's already a club here. I don't think that he'll get planning permission and anyway the BSPA is effectively a private club so, if your face doesn't fit, they don't let you in. Like they didn't want to let me in! And if King's Lynn can object to Swaffham – which is 15 miles away and in a different league – and succeed with their objection, then Perkin should have no chance here. Though that said, it's amazing how the BSPA works if you do happen to get planning permission, as it'll open some closed doors for him. If it doesn't happen, he'll just keep going in ever decreasing circles. He often says he's a lifelong Wimbledon fan, maybe he is. So many people say that they were committed fans. To which I'd say 'where were you the last 11 years [when it was shut/defunct] that it took a knob like me to get it open again?' Anyway, I don't want to talk about him I'm just here to enjoy my Conference speedway here in Sittingbourne – we might even win today the way things are going! What promoters should remember is that wherever you are there are always people cleverer than you, in speedway they're on the terraces and just 'cause you wear a promoter's hat (if there is such a thing!) doesn't make you a genius. So many of them have forgotten that – but I haven't, but then I don't think I'm always the cleverest." All this surmise, anger and theoretical discussion on the Sittingbourne terraces is a delight to get the chance to listen to but strangely irrelevant since the whole of speedway will have to wait for the outcome of the proposed planning application before we can really learn what the next step of this particular campaign will be.

Interestingly, Wimbledon football club are still strongly disliked and sometimes actively hated within football circles, after club chairman Pete Winkleman unilaterally chose to transplant the existing club license to Milton Keynes. The emergence of "franchise" football is still widely despised, as are the football authorities that failed to resist it, so it's ironic that echoes of this process might be repeated with another Wimbledon club, albeit in a completely different sport. Well, except Milton Keynes didn't have a football club already, whereas Sittingbourne do! It was Marx that said: history repeats itself, the first time as tragedy and the second time as farce. Given the repute, fame and history of the Wimbledon name, could this proposed move elsewhere have echoes of Coca-Cola's disastrous attempt at product extension with their disastrously failed introduction of the Desani water brand?

The way things were going on the track made it look highly likely that the Crusaders might race to a home victory this afternoon. By Heat 4, they'd raced into a 10-point lead and by Heat 10 they'd extended this to 12 points. Just before the mid point of the match, I was delighted to bump into Nicola Filmer who'd come over from nearby Ashford in Kent to watch her brother Adam race for Weymouth at reserve. Practically everywhere I went last year, I used to encounter Nicola at tracks all round the country while I researched my book. Though this season I'd looked out for her many times or scoured the pits and the rider's vans area at many meetings that Dan Giffard rode at, she had been absolutely nowhere to be seen. By way of explanation to an unasked question, Nicola immediately says, "we've split up". I make the appropriate noises and say it's a shame and that these things happen. She makes no direct comment but mutters a sort of "um" noise a few times and screws her face up in a manner that says more than money ever could. I excitedly show her my book, which seems to nonplus her, even when I point out photos of her and her brother as well as another of her, her mum and aunt at Rye House. They all came across as genuine and friendly people. Nicola is keener to get an update on her brother so I mention his fall in Heat 2, after which he appeared to get weirdly trapped underneath his machine in a contorted manner; so much so that he was unable to get up and clear the track. I tell her "he did a lot better in his next race when he finished second and looked a lot smoother", before she heads off to the pits to find out more for herself.

Unfortunately, after Nicola's arrival in the pits, Adam runs a couple of lasts in his next two races. The only rider who shows any real resistance for the Wildcats is Dave Mason. He looks pretty well unbeatable every time he comes out onto the track. While we watch him come to the tapes for a tactical ride in Heat 8, I'm briefly joined on the grass banks of the home straight by Graham Arnold, who is dressed in his trademark cap and smart, if dusty, green overalls. One look at these would invariably lead you to immediately mistake him for a paramedic. He is multi-tasking like crazy but remains his usual warm and cheerful self. I think he's a credit to himself, this club and to speedway. Like many hard working artisans though, he's incredibly unassuming and prefers to concentrate on the sacrifices, work and efforts of others or to dismiss his own contribution as expected. You just know that he enjoys the variety of his work at Sittingbourne speedway and, more importantly, its community ethos as well as the sheer variety and volume of people that pass through the club in any month or in any given year. This is a proper club that also runs a team in the Conference Shield and ran in the Conference League last year. Descriptions, by others, of this club as 'amateur' undervalue the thorough professionalism that is closely allied to their tradition and such suggestions are as fatuously inaccurate as they are self-serving. Nonetheless, this contribution to the sport doesn't happen without a huge amount of voluntary effort from a large number of locally based people, including Graham. He started at 3 a.m. this morning and admits, "I've only had a few hours sleep over the past five nights; it's hard, mate, very hard; it's the hardest thing I've ever done but it's worth it!"
I joke, "you might even win this afternoon!" and Graham retorts, "It don't matter to me at all that, I don't look until afterwards. And I don't care, provided that everyone takes part safely, and maybe they improve through the racing – if it's not this afternoon, it'll be another time, just that it's on is the main thing!" For the first and only time this afternoon, a home rider – has finally headed Dave Mason, in this instance, the Crusaders Gary Cottham. Graham matter-of-factly notes, just as he moves off to get on with more of his remaining vital tasks, "get in front of David and he don't want to know!"

Weymouth have brought along a few supporters and they even have their own official photographer in attendance, the gifted and delightful Julie Martin. She has arrived late from Bexhill with her friendly partner John and inquisitive daughter Leah after they'd stayed the night with the Lewis Bridger family. Their journey has been hot and not at all straightforward, just finding Sittingbourne in a strange part of the country where you don't know the routes or roads has proved a trial in the scorching sunshine. Now that they're here, Jules has donned her fluorescent jacket and wasted no time to hot-foot it trackside to get some actions shots.

However, today is a day when the result does matter since Sittingbourne have won the meeting by Heat 13 and eventually run out winners 54-41. It is a historic day and their first home win in 10 years since Sittingbourne last emerged victorious (52-26) versus Ryde on June 30th 1996! It has been a long time in coming and the fans seem pleased but, whether it's victory or defeat, the important thing remains that a club with the aims, ambitions and this track record of success in developing riders of all abilities actually exists in this country! Long may it continue do so.

6th August Sittingbourne v Weymouth (Conference Shield) 54-41

13th August

I had travelled to Sunderland to watch the Black Cats continue their inept start to the 2006-2007 Championship season with a home defeat against Plymouth. I'd travelled by train with a heavy box of my book *Showered in Shale*, since I optimistically hoped to sell them the following evening at Brough Park when the Diamonds raced against the Isle of Wight. Torrential rain saw the abandonment of the fixture early on the Sunday morning without a wheel being turned. It was one of many rain-offs that the Newcastle club suffered throughout the season. I spent the day stuck inside my Roker seafront B&B working on a draft of my book *When Eagles Dared* before I took the long journey home again on the train. If the box of books had seemed heavy on the way up, they felt much heavier on the return journey on a train packed with holidaymakers. Soon these books will be as well travelled as I am. Grrh.

13th August Newcastle v Isle of Wight (Premier League) postponed waterlogged track

Behind the Glass at Sandy Lane
16th August

When I arrive at Sandy Lane under jet black threatening clouds, there's already a small queue of fans prepared to happily wait the two hours until the turnstiles open for the derby encounter with local rivals Swindon. The Cheetahs have been in resurgent form recently after a difficult start to the season under the new promoter Aaron Lanney. When I meet him in his office, he comes across as a practical man who'll take many things in his stride. He has already been on a steep learning curve in the opening months of the season, both on and off the track. There have been many well-documented problems from the early fiasco of the short-term contract for Tony Rickardsson to the life-threatening injuries to Ales Dryml. While Aaron has overcome these difficulties, there's been a procession of guest riders who often flatter to deceive before they don't quite perform as expected in the vital later heats of 13 and 15. Though he still bears some of the psychological scars of this induction to the sport, Aaron remains optimistic and keen to chalk these down to experience.

He has had another shock this week, this time delivered by the BSPA management committee who have decided that Oxford (along with Arena Essex) will play no part in this season's Craven Shield tournament. This hasn't gone down well with Aaron and is a deviation from both the rules of qualification as they were set out at the start of the season or, indeed, what he understood them to be. It's a decision that in some way typifies the often arbitrary decision making of the speedway powers that be and contributes to the widespread opinion outside the sport that, in the final analysis, they're in charge of a sport entertainment where rules can often be altered to suit the current promotional exigencies of the time. Nonetheless, Aaron has tried to proceed in his new position as a promoter in the same manner in which he'd like to be treated himself. He's paid his riders promptly, which they speak of admiringly and as a departure from the norm with some other promotions. Plus he's already paid all of his outstanding loan fees to other promoters at the start of the season rather than, it turns out, at the end of the season, which apparently is the custom and practice among the majority of his contemporaries. Things like this, and the difficulty in attracting large numbers of fans through the turnstiles to watch a team that initially struggled to perform to its potential on a new race night under the auspices of a new promotion, have all had their impact on cash flow. Not that he is at all downcast but just gets on with it and continues to believe that "what goes around comes around".

Outside in the pits I bump into the always friendly and extremely knowledgeable Dave Peet who's here tonight in his new-

View from the grandstand at Cowley Stadium. © Jeff Scott

found capacity of referee's supervisor – a position that has him rove all over the country. He tells me that his good friend who is the Newcastle Start Marshal has asked him, "Have you seen what some twat has written about me in his book?" The object of his ire is my description of his handling of the bonus point run off after last year's controversial Newcastle versus Somerset Premier League encounter. In this instance, the SCB rulebook does corroborate my account and cover the correct procedures that applies to such eventualities. You can only write your impressions and what you see, though I hadn't set out to deliberately irk anyone.

I leave Aaron to dash about the pits and head off to the upstairs grandstand bar to meet with Rob Peasley who has been extremely kind in helpfully ensuring some promotion of my visit. He's got a small piece in the *Oxford Mail*, has placed my advert in the match programme and has already put out a table for me between his programme stall and the track shop. Rob is an extremely dedicated fan of Oxford speedway and is hugely productive on the internet as well as in print. He has plans to publish a book, which I'm not at liberty to go into the details of after being sworn to confidentiality by Rob. Suffice to say it will be of huge interest to more than just Oxford speedway fans and is on a subject that I can't wait to read about myself. Rob is very passionate about this project and it promises to be really quite something when it gets into print next year!

It's quite a family affair at Sandy Lane with the Peasleys as I haven't been there long before I get the chance to buy some (losing) raffle tickets from his mum, Hilary. She's been coming "on and off" since 1968 and she only really missed any meetings when Rob and his brother "were little". Rob's dad has been coming even longer since he's attended since 1957. Rob's brother never really got the bug but Rob most definitely has "I've been a fan since 1980 when I really got into it but I've come since I was born really".

This evening Rob has the latest edition of the magazine he edits, *The Cheetahs Chronicle* hot off the presses and prominently displayed on his stand. Rob is modest and unassuming in person and, though extremely knowledgeable, he wears his expertise lightly. Arguably he has less work to do this year since Oxford no longer run a Conference League side, so the stress of regularly editing the programme no longer exists. He used to design, write and produce this himself. Rob was disappointed that the marks the programme lost for its design (understandable given the means of its production) cost it first place in the *Speedway Star* 'Programme of the Year' awards and subsequently relegated it to fourth by a small margin. His disappointment at that outcome he shrugs off philosophically, which is much more than can be said for the feelings of outrage and disgust created among the fans about the last-minute change in the qualification procedures for this year's Craven Shield. After all, Oxford are the present defending champions and holders of the trophy. There is already a petition and no shortage of people keen to go out of their way to sign it. There's even earnest talk of legal action, which would be even more expensively doomed to failure than any formal appeal to the same management committee of the BSPA who, after all, are the very people who made this recent contentious decision.

Before the turnstiles open, I go to the press box where you get a superb panoramic view of the circuit and its environs to be interviewed by *Planet Speedway*'s diminutive Mark Young for a future broadcast. This radio programme is already essential listening for the speedway community, nationally broadcast and was soon to win an award for its quality. Mark is a big fan of the book but restricts himself to some straightforward questions about things that aren't really covered that much by my book, such as food at speedway tracks. The further publicity is very welcome on such a lively and prestigious programme. One lucky listener will get the chance to win a signed copy of my book as a prize. While the programme is highly regarded, there is a slight tendency to ask key figures in the sport questions of the "how was it for you?" variety. This provides listenable material and doesn't ever offend the natives.

Tonight's edition of the programme is broadcast live from the Sandy Lane press box and is played out over the stadium tannoy system. We all take the opportunity to listen since the programme has quite an Oxford speedway emphasis. From my brief meeting with Mark, I gathered that he not only has many strings to his bow away from his work on the radio but also that he's an articulate and passionate man. Completely forgetting the house style, he instead uses questions that would make an investigative journalist proud and definitely exhibits rottweiler tendencies during his pre-recorded interview with Aaron Lanney. In fact, he monsters him from start to finish with pointed questions along the lines of "as you know there has been a history of uncertainty about the future of Oxford speedway every winter, will you be the promoter next year?" If Aaron has expected an easy ride he doesn't get it and his qualified and slightly shifty answers not only provide the journalistic elixir that is true "breaking news", but have the Oxford fans buzzing as they ponder the implications of his responses!

Initially this is the usual politician's answer of "I'm 100% certain that speedway will be at Oxford next season", before Aaron moves onto rehearse "I've made a lot of friends and put too much into it to walk away", after which he adds the kicker about "outside investment possibilities" in the club and uncertainty as to whether it would be "Elite League or Premier League". The news sends the jungle drums into overdrive within the stadium.

Speedway is a sport founded on gossip with a grapevine that often exceeds the speed of the riders round the track or the modern broadband internet, sometimes with great accuracy but other times firmly off into the realms of fantasy. It has often been repeated that both Terry Russell and Matt Ford, already successful and influential figures within the sport, either already have behind the scenes links with Oxford or have ambitions to do so. Equally tonight, the name of Colin Horton is bandied about with confidence as a possible future owner. However, the more significant news that Oxford might drop down a league adds credence to the swirl of rumours that has it that 2007 might see the Elite League shrink in numbers and the Premier League split into two parts after the arrival of some additional members. These changes, if they happen, would be based on pragmatism forced on some clubs by the logic of economic necessity and the widespread general decline in spectator numbers across all three speedway leagues. Though some clubs buck the trend by having increased and/or healthy crowds, the majority struggle with their cost base on the one hand and a decline in revenues both through the gates and in sponsorship revenues on the other. A revised league structure might provide an elegant solution with, say, the financially more robust clubs forming a top flight Premier League along with, say, Oxford and Arena while the lower tier could admit ambitious Conference League clubs like Scunthorpe. However, this is all surmise and ill-founded rumour. Whatever does or doesn't happen – and you can always guarantee tinkering every year of the negligible or wholesale variety to the rules and structure – as fans, I'm sure that we'll only learn what we're told during the close season after the BSPA Promoter's Annual Conference!

The brief torrential rain shower from the dark threatening sky has further dampened the enthusiasm of the crowd and literally dampened the track. Though as soon as it stops, the track staff are immediately out there to finesse things and we're told "there will be a delay to proceedings until 8 p.m. while we get sawdust down and take the sludge off the bends". By the time the tapes rise, contrary to my expectation after this rain, the crowd on the terraces looks healthy. However, I'm told that these numbers haven't been the norm this season but have been temporarily boosted tonight by the arrival of quite a large contingent of Swindon Robins fans in the keen anticipation of an away victory that will further cement their play off qualification credentials.

Before the meeting starts I bump into the respected speedway author Glynn Shailes who has read my book. He's full of kind praise, "you've really got something there – it's unique – and the way you've done it, it won't date. If people pick it up they'll want to come to speedway". It is really very kind of him to say so but typical of him to be so encouraging. Eventually I sell six copies of my book and one of these is to the very keen and huge Robins fan, Darcia Gingell, whom I met at the Swindon Elite League Pairs meeting. She's fortunate to have a job at the Blunsdon track and travels round the country whenever she can to watch her beloved team, whenever her 'proper' job as a science teacher at a local Swindon comprehensive permits. Tonight, along with many others who've come over from Wiltshire, she's quietly confident of victory.

Sadly for Swindon, it is a meeting that they are never ahead in and the Oxford team continue with their recent good run of form throughout the night. Though, that said, Swindon never really quite get the luck that any challenge for Elite League glory invariably requires. I watch the meeting throughout from the grandstand bar so that I can simultaneously watch the racing through the huge glass-fronted stand and keep an eye out both for potential customers and my table of books. It's definitely different watching from up here – there's the added advantage that you can watch replays on the many television screens that are dotted all around but being behind glass a lot of the natural noise and atmosphere of a speedway meeting is lost. Sadly, once the meeting starts I sell no further copies of my book and after the meeting, the press conference that would have attracted a huge crowd up here actually takes place on the terraces outside. That is where I usually watch from at Sandy Lane, though they say a change is as good as a rest.

If I had been downstairs I would have missed Rob Peasley's many wry comments on the rich variety of incidents that this fixture featured. In Heat 6, the Robins' Mads Korneliussen falls in congested traffic on the second bend of the first lap and proceeds to comprehensively spit his dummy out of his mouth to great derision from the gleeful Oxford fans. To my mind, I rather wittily say to Rob, "He seemed to feel he should have had a second bend bunching call". Ignoring there is no such eventuality in the rulebook (in fact there isn't even one for the "first bend bunching" adjudication that refs use so often!). Rob sees no real grounds for Korneliussen's anger but notes, "Todd did lock up in front of him and maybe that distracted him and he's annoyed with himself?"

Heat 8 is the most eventful of the night. Before it can proceed, the start marshal abandons the race to try to separate Lee Richardson and Davey Watt who are lined up too close together. When he has managed to get them apart enough for his own satisfaction, Lee Richardson, to the considerable glee of the crowd completely up ends himself and is thrown heavily onto the track. Rob notes, "I think him and Davey were trying to go off the same bike! Lee was then so keen to get ahead, he's opened it up and fell off the back". In the re-run, a tradition of my visits to Oxford is upheld – the desire on the riders' part to create bizarre bike sculptures. Last year it was Norris and McGowan, this year it's Tomasz Chrzanowski and Eric Andersson, when Tomasz rears after two bike lengths so that his front wheel lands on Eric's footrest bringing both bikes to an immediate halt in an impressive but sculptural tangle.

Heat 11 is notable for Renat Gafurov riding in a green helmet colour when it should have been yellow. The Oxford fans blame this on the lack of the professionalism of Robins' team manager, the ever-popular Alun Rossiter. Oxford have the meeting wrapped up by Heat 14 though a last heat 5-1 massages the final score line for the Robins to a much closer 48-47. It has been a team effort by the Cheetahs, though Watt and Andersson have starred, while for the Robins the resistance has come from the Leigh-Lee top two combination. As a friendly but downcast Darcia leaves she says, "We really just didn't have the luck tonight, everything that could have gone against us did go against us!"

16th August Oxford v Swindon (Elite League B) 47-46

The Cheetahs Chronicle provides an independent voice on Oxford Speedway. It's published monthly at a cost of £2 and is available from:
Robert Peasley, Editor, *Cheetahs Chronicle*, 21 Brook Hill, Woodstock, Oxon OX20 1JE

Large Crowds Flock Beneath the Lee of the A38 to Watch the Devils
18th August

To arrive at the country's newest speedway is like living inside a modern transport network lesson. This compact circuit is located near to the 'Park & Ride' almost in the lee of the busy lanes of the A38 dual carriageway that pass overhead. The train line also runs parallel so at certain points in the evening you can almost simultaneously see speedway bikes, cars, lorries and trains. The arrival of speedway has proved incredibly popular in the town and regularly attracts crowds of at least 1500 people. Even some of the Plymouth AFC footballers sometimes come along to watch proceedings, such is the level of new-found interest. The reasonable admission charges (£8 for adults) have ensured that people no longer make the first night false economy of stopping their car on the hard shoulder of the northbound side of the A38 to watch the speedway racing for free. Later the programme seller notes, "The police thought it was Christmas, they just couldn't book the people fast enough – they saved £8, got a ticket for £60 and didn't even see all the racing."

That the place is open at all is down to the vision, energy, hard work and commitment of the promoter Mike Bowden and, subsequently, his capable band of volunteers. He's a builder by trade and when you meet him you quickly gather that he's an athletic, down-to-earth and determined man, "You really have to put in the long hours, I arrive at 7 a.m. on match day, and luckily I'm not afraid of hard work". He waves expansively at his pride and joy; "just four months ago this track was a rugby pitch just like the one next to it". Like many promoters Mike has a love of bikes but he also has the advantage of his time as a speedway rider to give insight into the particular outlook of the beast – "I've been on both sides so I know how they really think"– as well as all the healthy network of connections with people throughout speedway that this inevitably provides. Just a few of the names he casually mentions during our brief conversation is a veritable 'Who's Who' of riders, ex-riders and promoters. People like Simmo, Len Silver and Dave Pavitt whom he can always rely on for help and advice. Mike acknowledges that his team are pretty well unbeatable at home, "although all the away riders say they love it here – they soon get used to it and the racing is superb," and probably the strongest in the league. I say "Well, along with Scunthorpe," to which Mike retorts, "We beat them at their place and we beat them here". It's a rivalry that will continue as a quick glance at the fixture list confirms that the teams will meet many more times before the season is through and it's likely that all of these encounters will determine the final whereabouts of most of the trophies. Of special importance in their first season in existence will be the Conference League play-offs where the top two in the league will meet again to determine the champions. Though Mike is quick to point out the error of my presumption that this will most likely will involve a trip to Normanby Road, since the next night's fixture at Hoddesdon between Rye House and Scunthorpe will have a major bearing on final league placings and still holds out the outside possibility of the trophy finally ending up in Hertfordshire, "I'm looking forward to seeing it as they don't have a PL fixture, so Len'll be putting out a strong side".

Mike is only too happy to have me along to sign and sell my book since I will make a donation for every copy sold to the Speedway Riders' Benevolent Fund. He directs me to my pride of place, just where all of the crowd will assuredly have to pass by to make their way to the trackside. The stadium facilities are somewhat spartan in themselves, though all the essentials are in place, yet overall it still shows signs of its recent swift development. But then again Mike is an energetic and determined man as well as a builder so many future development plans are already in hand for further enhancement of the site.

Given the length of my cross-country drive to Plymouth I had been anxious about the weather forecast that promised rain. On the phone before I'd set off Mike had assured me that they'd had two days of sunshine when those in the surrounding area had had rain. So it proved, with a late afternoon of bright sunshine followed by a gloriously warm evening only interrupted by a single but large passing black cloud, even though my journey had been punctuated throughout by torrential downpours. Later, confirming that optimism is a local characteristic, an older gentleman told me, "We have two types of sunshine here – the warm and the liquid variety as it never rains".

The club's announcer and press officer Graham Hambly has kindly highlighted my visit in the local papers and his friendly wife Barbara, with diminutive stature but huge personality, even more kindly volunteers to help me with my bookstall. We work well together and Barbara experiences first hand, as I have many times, what a joy it can be to hand out fliers on my book to often reluctant speedway fans. Mike Bowden forecasts that I would "definitely sell out" of books tonight. While this doesn't happen a steady stream of people come up to chat, pass the time and by the end of the evening ten people have bought a copy. Most impressive, especially when you consider that Plymouth Speedway doesn't even feature as one of the tracks in the book. Maybe this is the key to future successful selling – only go to places that aren't mentioned!

The crowd is huge, even by the so-called august standards of some Elite League clubs, and the programmes quickly sell out which causes some confusion and much muttered disgruntlement. Not half as much disgruntlement as the news that Stoke will track a severely weakened side this evening because we learn that some of their riders have "got stuck in traffic on the way down". The stories of which motorway this alleged black hole of a traffic jam was actually on – the M5 and the M6 are both mentioned during the evening – or the early hour the riders set off brings to mind the *Monty Python* sketch that says, "that's nothing, we used to get up half an hour before we went to bed". There is widespread scepticism in the crowd, particularly as more riders suffer mechanical difficulties with their vans on the day of their scheduled long drive to the Plymouth fixture than practically any other club in the country. To be fair, on the *BBC Radio 5Live* traffic reports I had heard of the horrendous jams on the M6 during my drive down. It has deprived the crowd of the chance to see two very exciting young speedway prospects for the future – John Branney and Ben Barker – and along with rider replacement for Scott Courtney, this ensures the result is definitively a foregone conclusion before a wheel has been turned.

The news over the loudspeakers that the referee Chris Gay has fined the absent riders is no consolation for anybody, these young riders included. Nonetheless, willing replacements have been found and with some swapping around of the teams, along with extensive rewriting of the programme for those lucky enough to have secured one, the fixture is able to go ahead. Many in the large crowd have cannily brought crates, mini-ladders and the like to stand on – a necessity for those of a smaller stature given the sheer numbers of people regularly here and the present lack of grandstands. We're still treated to some excellent racing and the circuit produces some fast times to match the sheer speed with which the riders appear to hammer round it. Under the floodlights in Heat 13, Lee Smart looks really exhilaratingly fast – particularly when he rounds the impressive Adam Allott on the back straight of the final lap – and sets a new track record of 51.8 seconds (0.01 seconds faster than Adam Roynon's set a fortnight previously).

Once the racing starts my book display is understandably ignored. Barbara eats her burger and starts to read my book, "you know, I never thought I'd read a speedway book and I can't believe I'm really enjoying it!" I watch the races or chat with Barbara while my legs get severely bitten.

The other major talking point of the night came in Heat 10, when Sam Dore rides hard under Shane Waldron and is excluded for his troubles. Sam doesn't take too kindly to the news of his punishment, parks his bike by the start gate and enters the referee's box to remonstrate with Chris Gay. After a delay of a few minutes, while the crowd hold their collective breath and peers over for a better view of the expected contretemps, Sam reappears and we hear no news over the speaker system of the large fine we all expect to have been administered. When I catch up with Chris afterwards in the car park he comments, "I said to him as soon as he came in the box 'I hope that you're not going to do anything stupid' – some refs would have fined him heavily on the spot and thrown him out. People usually tell me I'm a 'strong referee' and sometimes that is necessary but I handle all incidents as I think best at the time. Sam wasn't rude or abusive in the box, just het up at what he initially thought was an injustice. I think Sam learnt more from the way I handled it than slapping him a fine and immediately chucking him out of the box without an explanation. His focus became the logic of why he was excluded rather than resentment at any fine or my refusal to explain. Anyway, afterwards we shook hands". While Chris explains the incident to me a lanky young man with longish hair and an Australian accent comes up and speaks to him. Sam Dore – for it is he – has come to thank Chris personally for earlier and to explain himself a little further:
[SD] "Someone did that to me at Newport and I was the one excluded."
[CG] "I can't speak for the ref at Newport, but if you come under someone like that you'll be the one to be excluded unless they're out of control themselves."
[SD] "Thank you for explaining."
[CG] "Look, you shouldn't do what you did today coming to the box – it's your first year, you have the ability so you just have to persevere."
[SD} "Thank you."
[CG] "How are you finding it?"
[SD] "Okay really, I'm getting there."

[CG] "Are you working as well?"

[SD] "Yes, in the mornings, which leaves the afternoons and evenings free for the bike when I'm not racing; it's okay really 'cause I live with my boss. Anyway, thank you."

With a shake of the hand he's off into the night. I've often been impressed by Chris's knowledge, dedication and professionalism — like many of the referees who give so much of their time and energy to the sport — but tonight his consideration along with his basic decency and humanity has shone through very strongly. Effectively, the pastoral care he's offered to Sam has come from his own best judgement of how to handle the situation and, to my mind, is completely spot on. Chris is characteristically modest when I congratulate him about his handling of the situation during the meeting.

As I go to walk away, a wizened, older gentlemen who has hovered nearby throughout these conversations by the armada of riders' vans, calls out, "Thank you Chris, you reffed really good tonight". Smartly attired as ever, Chris pauses momentarily, grins sheepishly and calls back "Thank you".

This sense of community, respect and pride, plus the chance to disagree but not hold grudges, is perhaps what speedway is all about really. Or, at least, it's one example of why it endures and continues to so appeal.

18th August Plymouth v Stoke (Conference League) 64-27

Forecast of Torrential Rain
23rd August

The forecast of torrential rain early evening doesn't make appetising reading for anyone, though that said we're all here and we're all in denial. I think that I got Eve Russell when I called the track before I set off. "What am I supposed to say? I want people to come so I'm going to say that we'll definitely be runnin' but it's all down to Him upstairs, he'll decide and whatever that is we'll put up with!"

The skies appear to bear out the predictions of a likely downpour. Alf Weedon has arrived but his mood is as black as the sky, though it's nothing to do with the weather. Whether it's his age (85) or just general tiredness, today he's lost even the hint of a sunny disposition that I always associate with him. "I freakin' lost my love of speedway a long time ago but now, 'cause of my knee, I've even freakin' lost my love of dancing. I loved my freakin' ballroom dancing but now I can't even do that". Alf fusses around his track shop — arranging the stock, blu-tacking up covers of all the latest magazines that he's just ripped the cover off for this very purpose. He's on his own and his grumpiness makes me wary to enquire where the charming Tom Woolhead, his perennial helper, is tonight. I'd rung Alf yesterday out of courtesy to let him know that I was coming along to this fixture. He sounded very distant, which made me think that he was seriously ill or something. I'd asked, "Are you alright?" but he groggily replied, "Yeah I am, but you just freakin' woke me!" When he'd established that I'm "the speedway book man, I know who YOU are", he kindly commented to me at length about the iniquities of the present state of the speedway book market. In summary, I would say that he wasn't impressed with the calibre of modern day promoters or speedway publishing, nor was he optimistic about future prospects and it's a theme that he returns to with some relish now that I'm closer to hand. "Speedway is a working class sport, always was, always will be — it still is. No one can afford to pay £15 or £20 for a freakin' book. There's too many produced anyway. We need to attract young people along, who we need to get into the sport. They're not interested in expensive books on dead people or people that they haven't even heard of or care about". Alf doesn't hear my assertion that "my book is different" other than to wave his hand dismissively and get on with some further rearrangement of the stock by the odd millimetre here or there so that the displays are all just right in his eyes to attract the meagre discretionary spend that vaguely might float along past the shop on the average speedway race night at Thurrock. I observe all this while I set out my table that Alf, very considerately, again tells me to set up right next to his shop. When I've nearly finished Alf suggests, in a way that you can't say no to, that I also agree to display

Arena speedway office and tyres. © Jeff Scott

Blue and yellow coloured phone box. © Jeff Scott

Referee's Tony Steele and Jim Lawrence make a beeline for the café. © Jeff Scott

some of the other books he's keen to sell from the stock he already holds in his shop. He places copies of three books from the *Retro Speedway* stable of Tony McDonald – Simmo, Booey, Confessions, plus the *Speedway Star* Yearbook (edited by Peter Oakes) – in a prime position at the end of the table. Alf really doesn't miss the slightest sales opportunity.

I leave Alf to it and wander down towards the pits. Most of the riders are already there and I spot that Jason Crump is buying a cup of tea from one of the catering portacabins that are dotted throughout the stadium. The fact that he is buying a cuppa is something that I love about the sport of speedway. It's resolutely normal and unpretentious. Jason is, arguably, one meeting away from his second World Championship crown in the BSI owned GP series. In any other sport, particularly football, there would be a flunky to buy his drinks (assuming tea would be allowed by the obligatory dietician) which, no doubt, would be something fancy and terribly concocted that would have to be called macchiato or end in the word 'chino'. In most other sports, his wealth, fame and status would dictate that he would have had a comprehensive style makeover by now. Not that he lacks the ego you require to ensure that you stand out above your contemporaries in any competitive walk of life, but he has remained resolutely makeover resistant. Though he is much more brushed up than the salad days of his youth and his early days in the sport – particularly when it comes to his keen appreciation of the always-on-show ambassadorial role his success on the track has necessarily thrust upon him – he still wears 'no brand' denim and a thick sweater of the kind Paddington Bear would favour. He is polite to the girl working in the portacabin without being chatty and exists in a zone that retains enough aloofness to thereby protect his privacy. Fortunately the entrance gates haven't yet opened so he doesn't have to put up with the grief that a clutter of adoring fans invariably bring to riders as they casually wander about the public spaces at any track. Later I learn that my praise of the café in the main building in a previous blog had caused some irritation with the people who own these portacabins at Thurrock. They're very friendly when I speak to them and, while I still stand by my praise of the establishment I know, these people can be said to "serve a cuppa fit for a speedway world champion!" I'd definitely use that as a strap line if they had the money or inclination to start an advertising campaign.

On the Arena side of the pits, Ronnie Russell is in full flow. I wait for a while for his entertaining torrent of stories and *bon mots* to temporarily subside before I praise him for the reviews I'd seen of the ITV programme *To Kidnap a Princess*. A primetime programme that dramatically reconstructed the attempt to kidnap Princess Anne in which Ronnie was the real star since he'd more or less single-handedly, and exceptionally bravely, foiled that outrage. Unfortunately for the further elevation of his reputation in the sport, it had clashed on Monday night with the live speedway on *Sky Sports*. I didn't learn about it until my mother told me and I then saw a review in the *Guardian* the next day by Nancy Banks-Smith. She loved "Big Ron" and, from her glowing words of praise, I learnt that Ronnie ran a contract cleaning business at the time. He had intervened as a real-life, true "have a go hero". The type of brave people who act selflessly on instinct usually end up very dead. As is often the way when people judge a book by its cover, the Police had roughly treated Ronnie when they initially mistook him for an accomplice rather than a hero in this audacious plot. Ronnie was the larger than life factor that meticulous planning couldn't have predicted. He is still straightforward and unpredictable now. What you see is what you get. Tonight he needs no second invitation to (modestly) bask in the fame and notoriety that this programme has, once again, re-ignited. RR is keen to stress to all and sundry to downplay any unvoiced complaints of vanity that he hasn't yet found the time to watch it.

As it was a dramatic reconstruction, they had to choose an actor to portray Ronnie. Apparently this actor had confided to others that he saw this role as a dream engagement. "The bloke who played me wants to meet me, he's said 'I love Ron 'cause he does things and gets things done'. They say he really looks like I did in my twenties". Mr Russell is pretty chuffed with all this though he really strains to remain modest, he just about manages to do so with some insouciant aplomb. That said, he struggles to retain his equanimity and stop his pride bursting through a moment later though, "I've been in my grandchildren's history books at school – they've even had to go on the stage 'cause they know granddad!"

On the way back from the pits I bump into Ian Thomas who is mooching by his car and, when he sees me, immediately barks out interrogatively, "what's the freakin' forecast?" It doesn't please him to learn that it's not good, "I hope to freak it's on, it's a freakin' long way to come". Ian and I get on famously nowadays. I find him very good company as well as a mine of information and engaging stories. He insists that I accompany him for his tea in the café – a destination that is already crowded with the great and the good that have dutifully pitched up here in Thurrock tonight. He waves to and briefly greets referees Tony Steele and Jim Lawrence as well as Dave Fairbrother from the *Speedway Star*. His main focus though is to order some food and bolt it down quickly before the rain or the meeting starts. Pleasingly and rather endearingly, to my mind, Ian is very fussy about what EXACTLY he wants for tea. The girl behinds the counter is left in no doubt as to his requirements though the failed battery in his hearing aid doesn't exactly smooth the path to understanding. Ian is unable to locate his spare battery, which frustrates him. He tells me he's deaf in one ear. Stupidly I say, "you'd better get it sorted before the meeting otherwise you'll not hear what's going on in the pits". He retorts as though dealing with a particularly dense child, "I never freakin' wear it in the pits, do I? With the sound of the bikes, I'd get freakin' deafened in the one freakin' good ear I've got left!"

Aside from our all-too-human frailties, we discuss the world from our shared perspective as 'speedway authors' punting round the various tracks of Britain, while Ian concentratedly eats his tea with some gusto – eggs, bacon and unbuttered bread washed down with a cup of tea. He feels the need to explain his fastidiousness unaware how similarly fussy and pernickety I am. His dietary choices have been dictated to him on the advice of his doctor because of his high cholesterol and diabetes. "When the freakin' doctor tells you that you could lose your freakin' eyesight and lose your freakin' legs unless you change, you freakin' take notice!" He pats the slight paunch of his stomach proudly and notes, "I'm now the same freakin' weight as I was in 1998". Ian's book has sold far better than mine but he very courteously pretends that we are equals. I discuss his appearance in my latest book *When Eagles Dared*, which is an account of the Eastbourne Eagles 2005 season but is, also, in many ways a book that could really be any fan's experience of the highs and lows of following their speedway team. Ian features in this book for a meeting at Arlington when he got embroiled live on national television, in a dispute with the Eastbourne Eagles Clerk of the Course (Malcolm Cole) and the SCB Official on the night, Chris Gay. The upshot was that he took umbrage and loudly decided that he had, in effect, been called "a liar". His word had definitely been doubted and things didn't go his way on the night. I assured him that I'd been balanced to all parties in my presentation. "Freak it, say what you want, I don't freakin' care – just make sure that you put in that I called the Vat man, he's a Vat man that one you know, a freakin' liar. It's not often you can get away with calling them anything, let alone a freakin' liar!" I don't recall that he did since I remember that Ian claimed the referee had implicitly called HIM a liar by not accepting his word/version of events. Nonetheless, Ian's delight in being irascible is one of the many genuinely endearing things about him. Being so strong-minded is also a touching and typical attribute. We could have chatted on for ages but I'd just spotted that the gates had opened and my book display called while he had to rush off to the pits for his managerial and promotional duties.

I haven't missed any customers, though I am delighted to see that the energetic and lovely Scary Sheila Le-Sage is close by wearing another of her trademark but distinctive sashes. She looks glamorous but claims that her hair looks like "rats tails". She insists that I come back down to just by the entrance gates, where Joonas Kylmakorpi is perched on his bike and is apparently happy to patiently pose for photographs with any Arena Essex fan who wants to do so or to sign autographs. He has already attracted quite a crowd of old and young admirers. I gather he is one of Scary's real favourites and Ronnie's too, since he also hovers close by to meet and greet, press the flesh and generally be charmingly himself. It is a thoughtful and popular initiative. RR is always unafraid to try new things to ignite the enthusiasm of the regular punters as well as the legions of stay away ones. Scary and her friend Di pose for photos for me with Joonas, who good-naturedly co-operates with everything thrown in his path.

Scary has promoted my book tirelessly at Arena. Without the need to look, she knew exactly the page numbers that the Arena chapter occupies in *Showered in Shale* as well as the page (118) where her own photo appears. She excitedly trills, "I know all the page numbers and some of the text off by heart 'cause I've been asked to read it out so often!" It has started to drizzle and I retreat back to my table of books. For many trips now, all the books have been wrapped in a protective plastic bag to guard them from the elements, flying shale and prying fingers, though I do have one copy for people to thumb through curiously and cover in ketchup or other rogue elements they have on their fingers for this very purpose. I pull the table back under the lee of the roof. Many people come up and chat while we watch the rain. The consensus, realistically enough, is that the meeting won't go ahead tonight. Ronnie comes over the tannoy to update the crowd of his future intentions now that the drizzle has stopped, "the intention is to race tonight – we won't have lengthy inspections of the track but Gerald [Richter] needs to prepare the track fully so that we can race. Now the rain has stopped he can get on with this". No sooner has this news sunk in than the heavens reopen and heavier rain returns. Everyone is resigned to a postponement and typically Ronnie is brutally frank when he comes back to the microphone. "There's lots of surface water and though the top dressing protects the surface of the track, it would take us 30 minutes even if the rain stopped, so reluctantly we'll have to call it off but will restage it on Friday with both teams. And so you're going home disgruntled, I'm sure you are anyway…"

With that news there is a mass exodus to the car park in the rain. At my stall are a small knot of long-time Wimbledon fans – Janet Dixson with her dad Craig Mabey and brother Stephen ("we used to stand by the start gate or with the pit-bend loonies") – who've bought my book but feel disappointed at the complete lack of a chapter on their club. They want to know why, so without going into any detail, I say perhaps Ian Perkin can explain his specific objections to my three unpublished chapters to them personally when they next see him. "We don't like to hear that name – he thinks he's Wimbledon but he's not. He might be good at the financial side but he's hopeless at other things. When he announced he just went on and on, it drives you mad but no one listens or wants to hear it again. In fact, we don't want to stand here in the rain talking about him. Good luck with your book. Goodbye".

23rd August Arena Essex v Belle Vue (Elite League A) – postponed rain

Great Races in the Fens
27th August
Every time I visit West Row, the home of the Mildenhall Fen Tigers, it always seems to be a scorchingly hot day. This afternoon we will be treated to the 'Clash of the Tigers' since both clubs use this nickname and, to my untutored eye, the crowd level just before the start of the meeting with Sheffield looks fairly reasonable. Much more than I'd expected from the frequent complaints of Mick Horton, the club promoter, in the pages of the trade press where, allegedly from the *Field of Dreams* "build it and they shall come" more traditional school of speedway promotion, he often bemoans crowd levels, track quality and beats the drum for ever greater numbers of people to come along on a regular basis to watch the Mildenhall Tigers perform in the Premier League. Later I learn that this afternoon's crowd has been swelled considerably from the norm by a good contingent of Sheffield fans who've made the journey down from South Yorkshire and a

comparatively large number from Ipswich who, without a meeting last Thursday, have come to another part of Suffolk for their weekly fix of speedway. Afterwards the *Speedway Star* reports this as "probably a breakeven attendance".

Sadly I am a week too late at West Row for the controversial and well-attended Premier League encounter with Rye House, where promoters Mick Horton and Len Silver exchanged some full and frank opinions with each other over the attempted inclusion of Ben Powell in the Rye House team. Accounts of 'who said what to whom' chunter on all afternoon, had the internet forums abuzz and made quite a splash in this week's *Speedway Star*. The consensus was that the air turned blue and a frisson of tension remained all afternoon. Great stuff! One question that appears to have been overlooked in the ensuing analysis is 'what has happened to deference in this country when people think nothing of abusing old age pensioners' like Len?

On my travels round the country it has often been hard to attract some attention for my book or signing visit from the local papers. Many of these regional papers give the coverage of speedway lesser priority than other sports and the visit of an unknown speedway author even less. Obviously, this is not the case with the local papers that cover the traditional heartlands of speedway – regional papers like the *Dorset Echo, Eastern Daily Press, Wolverhampton Express & Star, Ipswich Evening Post, Workington News & Star* and so on – but generally coverage is hard to come by. Prior to my trip I contacted 12 different newspapers and radio stations that to varying degrees serve this part of Suffolk with the only interest coming from the conscientious Mike Bacon in Ipswich. So I can definitely sympathise with both promoter Mick Horton and Press Officer David Crane in their attempts to get Mildenhall Speedway to occupy a higher awareness in the consciousness of the local people in this region. David had kindly provided this list of press contacts even though, from the outset, he hasn't exactly been personally enamoured with my book on account of some aspects of my chapter on my visit to Mildenhall last year. Whatever you intend when you write what you see and hear, how people read your work often varies considerably from what you expect. David liked my comments on the late lamented Brian Snowie who I was lucky enough to encounter on my research visit and who, to my mind, still remains notable by his absence this afternoon. Though broadly supportive, David felt I was "long winded", had included too many "irrelevant" sections and was "critical for the sake of it" about the programme and the grid girls. I had hoped to meet him to thank him for his help on my visit but the closest I came to doing so was when his mum came to the track shop on the afternoon of my trip to West Row to find out how my book was selling.

Again I resolved to study the programme and the attractive Mildenhall grid girls closely. My favourite feature from any 2005 speedway programme was the 'Speedway Mastermind Quiz' they had here. Sadly this has been inexplicably dropped but has, unofficially, been replaced in the programme with the amusing game of 'spot the number of spelling and punctuation errors in Mick Horton's Promoters' Piece'. Before the meeting started, one of the girls wandered up to the area where I was based with my bookstall next to the track shop in the shade of the main grandstand. Like many people, they come along to chat at length to the preternaturally cheerful and friendly track shopman, Johnny Barber, who invariably – like all good proponents of the black art of speedway merchandise sales – seems to know everyone personally and to casually find the time to have a cheery word with them. Friendliness runs in the family and it's a pleasure to find that his dad, Colin, has also come along to West Row this afternoon. Hardly a surprise given that he used to be the promoter here but still an education for me, since he knows so much about speedway in general but still manages to wear his knowledge lightly. He also has an even keener interest in philately!

One of the other people drawn to the stand is the Mildenhall (and Ipswich) announcer Kevin Long, who surely must be one of the smartest dressed of this often-unique breed of speedway people anywhere in the country. This afternoon he is resplendent in compere-cum-bank-manager-casual with spotlessly clean white jacket, tie, collared shirt, well pressed trousers and shoes that definitely don't look suited for any walk at all on the rough track surface they've perfected here. If Mildenhall speedway staff had to be based on character types from *Are You Being Served?*, he would play a part that combined the characters of Captain Peacock and John Inman. Working as he does at two tracks, Kevin brings an experience, insight and, most importantly, the gift of enthusiasm and delightfully wrought, but apparently on the spur of the moment, phrases that should really be the *lingua franca* of any announcer's vocabulary. But, sadly, often this isn't the case as it sounds as though the speaking clock acts as a voice model at some (unnamed) locations. Kevin also has a very pronounced tendency to delight in the use of playfully exaggerated double entendres as often as the situation at every speedway track

Another superb array of badges. © Jeff Scott

Sense of anticipation in the Mildenhall pits. © Jeff Scott

he works at theoretically allows. This propensity to "slip one in" occasionally generates a letter of complaint to the Ipswich Speedway Office from fans worried by the effects of his language choices on attending impressionable children. During the warm-up lap, Kevin duly notes after an ambitious and well-executed back straight wheelie that the rider in question was just checking "if he could get it up!" I gather that this is an ongoing but tried and tested part of Kevin's badinage and presentational repertoire.

Crowd numbers are at such a level and the interest in my stand is so slow I decide to wander round the whole circuit, except for the sparsely used start-line grandstand, to hand out leaflets on my book. I continue to be amazed by how many people appear to travel about the country to watch speedway, often they come along when they don't even support the teams involved. If speedway had the professionalism, bravery and transparency to start to actually publish official attendance figures, this conscientious band of speedway zealots, who criss-cross the country as they regularly travel from track to track, would inflate these cumulative overall totals. I begin to wonder if, in fact, I actually fail to sell my book to the very same uninterested but dedicated people everywhere I go? Also here this afternoon are many people from Yorkshire, who congregate on the back straight as it enters the third bend, in a variety of distinctive scarves, caps and t-shirts that have either the Tigers' name or Pirtek sponsors' logo emblazoned prominently on them.

A table in the shade provides an ideal spot from which to view the racing as the riders power from the gate and negotiate the first and second bends. Quite a few other fans are of the same opinion about this vantage point and by the time the fixture commences there's quite a crowd of them including Di Farmer dressed ostentatiously as a mascot in her Tiger outfit. Before a wheel has even been turned there have been many comments about the lady SCB Official Barbara Horley, particularly her recent decision on live television to award a race when it was barely into the second lap.[1] It's the kind of decision that would be remembered about any referee but the fact that Barbara has the continued temerity to be a woman and a female official causes much sexist comment and allows her to be held responsible for whatever ills her critics deem appropriate. All chauvinist males tend to develop an elephant-like memory that is often not backed up with an exact appreciation of the 2006 SCB Handbook of Rules and Regulations. The exclusion of Jordan Frampton in the second heat starts an afternoon of continuous, but often partisan, grumbles about the perceived merits of Barbara's ability to actually referee this fixture in a professional manner. In Heat 3 Jason King is excluded though his bike wins high marks for artistic interpretation and technical merit when it bowls riderless around the length of the bend without the handicap of its usual passenger. Jason himself appears to have badly hurt himself and spends the rest of the afternoon gingerly limping about the pits in a manner that isn't brought on naturally by the use of his steel shoe. In my own attempt at quick-wittedness to a man who

[1] These chauvinistic complaints about her ability are doubly ill judged since the referee in question they complain about was, in fact, Margaret Vardy.

lingers by my table for some considerable time reading sections of my book, before he ultimately decides against purchasing it, when Kevin announces "King has been excluded" I immediately retort "surely that should be abdicated?" After three explanations prompted by a mystified "what?" have not only taken the humour out of the original situation and has me seriously doubting my own view of the world, the re-run of the race provides the only drawn heat of the meeting so far. A win for the other King in the race, the gifted and exciting Daniel leaves the Mildenhall Tigers trailing 6-12 and Kevin has to struggle far more to extract some laughs with his ribald wit than the opportunity to chunter on about a pair of queens would easily provide him with. To pass the time with my reader entranced by my spell-binding prose and in an attempt to break his concentration so that he might actually consider a purchase, I wonder aloud if a reasonably sized group of Tigers, like lions would be, known as a 'Pride of Tigers'.

The question remains unanswered but bad luck befalls Andre Compton when he falls while in the lead of the next race to allow Mildenhall to narrow the gap in the scoreline. On a busy afternoon, Barbara excludes in heat 5 the promising but under-pressure Ben Wilson before he has passed the first bend of the next race – because both of his wheels cross the white line of the bend – which then, eventually, features another comparatively easy win for Daniel King who gains the scalp of the illustrious Ricky Ashworth. In fact, both riders "double up" as they say in speedway parlance and they appear to hold out some promise of future English speedway success since they're both young, hail from these shores and clearly have lots of natural talent along with their undoubted ability. Colin Barber, unlike many of the Mildenhall fans who conspicuously don't boo those refereeing decisions that go 'for them', with cigarette in hand matter of factly notes before the re-run, "Wilson shouldn't have been excluded as he was pushed across the white line by the other riders and should have been allowed back in the re-run under the 30 metre rule". Bizarrely, the real highlight of this three rider re-run race is Jason King's engine failure at the start of his last lap and although he's keen to immediately quit at that moment, some sharp words of encouragement from Mildenhall promoter Mick Horton who shouts from right next to him on the centre green, leaves Jason in absolutely no doubt that his employer expects him to push his bike round the remaining 250 metres of the circuit for a much needed and valuable point for the Mildenhall cause. In order to encourage, cajole and implore him to success within the time he is allowed to do so, despite his age and girth, Mick Horton surprisingly manages to keep up alongside his young rider and defunct bike for the whole of the lap. This is quite an achievement for both men, since Jason really still hadn't recovered from the after effects of his earlier heavy crash (Colin noted acerbically, "poor little bugger is still limping badly") and Mick wouldn't be your first choice if given your pick from amongst the country's promoters for any speedway promotion based relay team. Well, unless you could definitely rely on the post exertion services of an oxygen tent. Nonetheless, rider and mentor combine for a vital point that brings the scores back to level for the only time this afternoon for the expectant and voluble Mildenhall faithful.

Though some of the meting has already passed, King's Lynn Tigger-esque co-promoter Jonathan Chapman has arrived on a reconnaissance trip to study the Sheffield Tigers in advance of their encounter later in the week in the Premier Trophy Final. It's time well spent on last-minute research, though Jonathan is one of the new breed of dynamic young promoters who lay great stress on professionalism in their use of statistics and other 'soft information' about their competitor's riders, crowd numbers and financial status. On this basis, I doubt he will have learnt that much that's new but will have, probably, confirmed his prejudices. One of these opinions – on the tangential but almost related speedway topic of lady SCB officials – he captures rhetorically but succinctly: "They're all freakin' lesbians". When I remind him that, to my limited knowledge, Margaret Vardy definitely doesn't bat for that particular team, he graciously concedes, "well, you know what I mean". It's a point of view that finds a receptive audience among this section of the Mildenhall faithful. Hardly a surprise given their earlier and continuing opinions but it's best not to under-estimate Jonathan in any way, since he chats engagingly with all who wish to in the stadium in a straightforward, easy man-of-the-people manner that belies his shrewd insights and business acumen.

Whatever events transpire on the track, you definitely can't fault the home riders for all out effort, as typified by Jordan Frampton in Heat 8. He falls on the fourth bend to quickly remount and resume the chase only to be dramatically thrown from his rearing bike when he reaches the second bend. It's a fall that catapults him painfully into the fence on his neck. It's a drama that Kevin Long describes in a tabloid manner not fit for the squeamish, "Jason picked up grip coming out of the bend and was thrown like a rag doll at the fence and back down again!"

Sheffield's lead remains untroubled throughout the afternoon. Though their riders have a propensity to ride the outside line repeatedly, the track clearly doesn't have the grip that they'd expect from their own experiences at their home Owlerton circuit. A case in point is exemplified by their Canadian rider Kyle Legault during Heat 12, when he looks stylish (but remains ineffective) during all four laps as he rides the outside line close to the fence but due to the lack of the grip he expects, he completely fails to make any impression on the visibly quicker Daniel King who powers to his fourth consecutive race win.

The West Row circuit is a fair track that arguably often suits the visitors and provides close, compelling racing that is a great advert for the sport, albeit without the requisite high number of fans that the promotion here would prefer and, judged on the evidence of this meeting, merit. People frequently say after races like that witnessed in Heat 13, "it was worth the admission money on its own" and, like all clichés, there is a strong grain of truth in such an assertion. Jason Lyons and Ricky Ashworth indulge themselves in a superb four-lap duel. Afterwards Kevin delightedly and admiringly notes, "no quarter was asked for and none was given, but it was fair throughout". Firm but fair wouldn't cover the exhilaration that this exhibition of skill would provoke in the most hard-hearted critic of these brakeless superstars of the shale (by the way, this race alone gives the lie to the oft repeated but baseless assertion on *Sky Sports* and from certain Elite League promoters that you need to feature "GP superstars" in order to have a high quality race or meeting). Difficult to describe or do justice to in words (or drawing, photos etc.) on the last bend of the third lap Lyons overtakes Ashworth and then menaces him with a close sight of the fence before Ashworth repays the favour when he overtakes Lyons on the next bend at the start of the fourth lap. Phew! What a race. Arguably one of the best I have seen all season, so far.

As if that encounter hasn't provided enough superb racing already, the next race is just as enthralling and exciting, but in a different way. Emiliano Sanchez initially finds himself at the back before he skilfully picks his way past James Brundle with a burst of acceleration from the dirt that for the last third of the meeting has been showered to the outside of the track. He continues to hug close to the fence before he finally picks his way past Jason King with sublime control and careful choice of racing line to win the race. Jason is visibly very upset with himself at allowing the opportunity of victory to slip from his grasp. But given the skill of his opponent's ride on the variable outside line, he should instead see it as a chance to learn another lesson in his ongoing apprenticeship, notably the first rule of track craft – try to use the entire available track to your own advantage. Back in the shady area by the track shop, Colin Barber is mystified as to why the Sheffield riders appear to ride the West Row track better than the home team who should, theoretically, have the advantage of their insider knowledge. "I don't understand these Mildenhall riders – all the dirt is on the outside and they all stick to the inside line!"

Without a chance to salvage anything other than pride from the last race, the Fen Tigers pair of Lyons and King dominate proceedings and Daniel is quite rightly triumphantly welcomed back to the pits after he completes his impressive and stylish five-ride maximum. The final score of 44-46 hints at a close contest but the result was never in doubt practically from the start.

The next day in Scunthorpe I bump into Sheffield promoter, Neil Machin, who correctly observes, "Heats 13 and 14 were what it's all about – it's the sort of racing that you dream of seeing!"

27th August Mildenhall v Sheffield (Premier League) 44-46

How to run the CL Pairs Championship – the Scunny Way
28th August

Anyone who had the misfortune to witness the lengthy, dusty fiasco that was the previous year's CL Pairs event run at Plough Lane under the direction of the Wimbledon Speedway plc management would have questioned whether to attend such a meeting again or, at least, whether – based on that experience – speedway offered any real entertainment or possible enjoyment. Acknowledged on the internet (British Speedway Forum) by some long time Dons fans to have arguably been one of the worst ever meetings staged in many years at Plough Lane, things often resembled a demolition derby in the dust as rider after rider regularly crashed into or through the safety fence. Things could definitely only get better this year, not just because they say lightning doesn't strike twice in the same place, but this year the event will have the ambitious Scunthorpe promotional pair of Norman Beeney and Rob Godfrey in charge of proceedings. They have quickly gained a reputation for adaptability, getting things done professionally and usually very much ahead of schedule at Scunthorpe Speedway.

Just a glance at the huge visible progression of the infrastructure and facilities immediately strikes me as I drive through the gates of the stadium on my first visit to the club for just over a year, and is enough to confirm the determination of the promoters in only their second year in the sport. They also regularly attract a large, passionate and loyal crowd to their home fixtures and continue to have an amicable relationship with their landlords. These are precisely the vital ingredients that a speedway club in any league requires. Away from the track they run a successful car business together and you quickly get the impression that they're prepared to really graft to earn their success and also don't take the speedway world for granted or feel that it automatically owes them a living.

Not that everything goes smoothly all the time at Scunthorpe as the prominently fenced off but clearly half-completed changing rooms and shower block attests to a dispute with the builders. However, it is the only metaphorical cloud on the horizon around the stadium although, overhead, large ominous looking dark clouds appear to bear out the local forecast of heavy showers. In fact, even though we're still in August it feels cold to delicate southerners like myself. I'm so early that the Tesco superstore hasn't long been open when I arrive though there was already quite a crowd of Bank Holiday shoppers. Maybe this is the way many people like to start Bank Holidays nowadays or possibly they were all going home for a bite to eat before deciding if the weather would hold enough to justify a trip to the speedway. The only rider already at the stadium is Seemond Stephens, but then he does live a huge distance away in the South West so an early start just isn't practicable for him. The fact that I've arrived in shorts has Norman remark "God, you're an optimist!" Quite a compliment coming from one half of a promotional duo that have found and overcome the many obstacles placed unnecessarily in their way on the road to fulfilling their dream of building, owning and running a speedway club. The dream has avoided becoming a nightmare and there is still a long list of wishes yet to come to fruition. The dream remains still only half dreamed!

However Norman, like Rob, hasn't forgotten his roots. He also notices that there appears to be different treatment for some clubs and not others. "Why did Redcar get a licence straightaway and initially we didn't?" he asks rhetorically in the full knowledge of the answer to his question. He has other observations and questions but prefers to keep them to himself. Instead he concentrates on the success that is Scunthorpe speedway club, "we've had to stand on our own two feet from the start – some tracks just see money go out of the door every week whereas every penny we've made we have reinvested back into the club". Scunny, along with Plymouth ("they have a track in a field with no base"), are THE big stories in this year's Conference League. His co-promoter Rob has had some of his ideas, ambitions and proposals for the future printed in this week's *Speedway Star*. Many of his suggestions are uncontroversial and others are likely to ruffle feathers, cause contention or resentment in equal measures, if not just ignored. The most significant proposal he puts forward is that there is a need for the existence of a "Premier League 2", or his contention that there should be promotion and relegation between the newly founded Premier League 1 and Premier League 2. Whether these remain just ambitious ideas from a 'junior' promoter or are put into practice by the governing authorities of the sport remains a moot point; personally I imagine that they're unlikely to be saluted even though they have been publicly run up the flagpole. The comparatively closed shop that allegedly exists in 'senior' promotional circles mean that any idea has to overcome real or imagined 'vested interests' or manage to persuade doubting parties with hard financial facts. It's a scenario that is unlikely to succeed all in one fell swoop at the annual BSPA conference in November. No matter what happens, Rob remains convinced that "there

Slight puddle causes concern. © Jeff Scott

Ref's box at Scunthorpe. © Jeff Scott

Rob Godfrey in the Scunthorpe pits (note minimalist bikes in CL). © Jeff Scott

is a need to run speedway professionally as a business" – a situation that by implication he feels doesn't presently exist. It's unlikely that these 'new boys' will garner the responses they'd like this time round, so a patient but attritional approach may be required.

For now they will concentrate on their own business and the matter in hand that is this afternoon's prestigious meeting. They suggest that I base myself with my book table at the far end of the stadium in their newly built clubhouse. It's a portacabin type building with a balcony viewing area in front that overlooks the first and second bends with a great view of the remainder of the track. It has been transplanted here from its original home in Peterborough and is fitted out with a double bar, a pool table and a huge number of framed pictures lining the walls. A bar licence application is outstanding though this didn't stop Tai Woffinden, who held his 16th birthday celebrations here. I am to share the facility this afternoon with the legendary Eric Boocock who will be along later to sign copies of his book. Given that he used to be the Hull promoter and led them to considerable success only a few years ago, you have to expect that he will draw a large crowd. The friendly Bazza Preston, who has a variety of responsibilities at the club that he seems strangely reticent to exactly specify, directs me down to the clubhouse. I don't press him while I carry my boxes, signs and table indoors. He has followed speedway at Scunny since "the old days" in 1976-1977. They were his "first track" and he's chuffed that speedway has successfully returned, "it's good for the town and the community". He is keen to stress to me that rider development must be the cornerstone of any speedway club keen to thrive and survive. Like many commentators he identifies Tai Woffinden and Josh Auty as "great prospects" but also feels "its good to have Tai's dad, Rob Woffinden, back as so many people remember him". There is quite a family connection for the Woffinden family at Scunny – in fact, almost a dynasty since Rob's mum Cynthia looks after rider refreshments in the pits.

No sooner have I set out my books than the heavens open and the track gets very well doused. Despite this "heavy shower", as the promoters later call it, after a brief glance at the BSPA terminology handbook, the strong wind has dried out the surface so much that only one hour later (at 12.30 p.m.) they have to water it! Astonishing really but an indication of how difficult it is to judge these things on a day when rain is forecast. Quite how last year's CL Pairs was allowed to degenerate into the dustbowl conditions we experienced on that day with sunshine forecast is altogether something else and best answered by those in charge then. Scunthorpe have learnt through experience and take what they judge to be the required decisive action. However, they note, "only the third bend is an issue" and, indeed, there is some surface water lying there. Somebody upstairs doesn't want to be kind as it rains again very heavily at 1pm which leaves the track under water in a number of places, particularly the 'problem' third corner. To my untutored eyes a cancellation has started to look a real possibility or we might witness conditions that make good racing unconducive and thereby endure another year of a CL Pairs meeting characterised by one processional race after another. I shouldn't have panicked as the track staff set to work with a 'pleasing to watch' zeal, determination and dedication. It is also something of a truism that riders at the Conference League level will usually take a much more make do and mend approach to conditions than some of their colleagues at other more illustrious levels within the sport. Not that I agree with the knee-jerk comments that you often get from promoters after so-called "rider power" (most apparently feel that this is innately wrong as all power should rest in their hands) leads to the cancellation of meetings when conditions are "dangerous". Given that speedway promoters contract the services of self-employed people who often ride in a different place and country many nights of the week, it's hardly a shock that they have a strict attitude to their own perceived level of safety and a *laissez faire* approach since they know another meeting/day's work will arrive tomorrow or the next day and that meetings will be rearranged. You know when the promoters' arguments are on thin ice since they always throw in the primacy of the needs of the shocked and disappointed "paying fans" to add weight or legitimacy to their arguments. This is often one of the rare occasions that the promoters and speedway authorities grant any credence or status to fan opinions albeit, as is traditional, this remains only lip service since they obviously don't ever really consult them. The ultimate scandal in this respect is the 'independent' official that now adjudicates – apparently solely on behalf of those poor luvvies at *Sky Sports* who wring their hands in agony at the thought of their disappointed advertisers and sponsors (usually a pretty third-rate bunch if judged by the interval adverts during televised Elite League and GP meetings – would you want to buy these products or take their advice seriously?) bleat on with a few canards about the importance of "rider safety" only to always be determined that "the show must go on". Most of the time, when a meeting is forced to proceed in adverse conditions, particularly on the telly, the racing is processional and consistently a shockingly poor advert for the innate attractiveness and exhilaration of the sport.

This is definitely not the case on a hugely entertaining afternoon at Scunny. Rider power asserts itself in the form of a commitment to get on and race, whatever the conditions. In fact, these improve rapidly from the possibly dire and unconducive, mostly due to the hard work of the promoters and their track staff as well as the benefit of a drying wind. There is a delay and since sales are very slow and interest in my book in the clubhouse minimal, I take advantage of this respite to wander round and hand out some more of my leaflets. Again I bump into many people I've met before. One group of fans ask me to sign copies of my leaflet, something that is both touching and bizarre and another fan has brought along his book specially to be signed (as he'd bought it on Amazon). I also take the time to go round to the car park entrance where the club's indefatigable Press Officer, Richard Hollingsworth, supervises arrivals with the friendly club steward Richard Heasman, whom I met last year during my research. He is an entertaining man with a love of speedway along with railways and "big cats". They process the arrivals efficiently but really without sufficient time for a cheery word or bit of banter.

By the time I return to the clubhouse, the plain-spoken Yorkshireman, author and speedway legend Eric Boocock has arrived and is now sat behind his table waiting for an eager queue or crowd of fans. Neil Machin arrives almost immediately with an impressive laminated sign that advertises Booey and has a large blown up image of the cover design of the book. I really must get one of those. Sadly, there really aren't any people really that keen to buy his book or mine. Some have wandered in to look at the merchandise, glance round the building curiously or just spend time closely studying the photos that line the wall. These attract great attention all day. Put a couple of authors into any room anywhere and talk will soon turn to the vexed topic of sales, usually the lack of them. Eric doesn't hold out great hopes of success but, at least, he isn't hundreds of miles from home and has another job to do here this afternoon since he helps and mentors the young English protégé Josh Auty. He tells me that when "Ian Thomas came here, he sat 50 yards from the entrance gates and sold six! And he freaking promoted around here for nine years!" Eric is quite happy to honestly describe the genesis of his book, which I suspect, despite his bluster and studied nonchalance, he really takes great pride in. It is one of those speedway books that you know is well worth reading, just based on the personality and character of the man alone. Furthermore, Eric has experienced speedway from both sides of the fence as a rider and as a promoter – you're left to wonder what stories he left out – and you just know that his straightforward approach to people and life would definitely make compelling reading. Nonetheless, he continues to be modest and self-deprecating, "I can't freaking type and I'm no freaking writer so I recorded 56 hours of tapes and Tony did the rest. It had a few orders when it came out but since then I haven't heard from him".

Eric does attract quite a bit of attention but mostly people just want to chat to him about speedway in general, the good old days, the demise of Hull Speedway (on which he remains very diplomatic) or what the future of the sport holds (Eric has some worries here). He finally sells a book, which makes me envious but seems to dispirit him. He makes a point of lighting a cigarette in the room even though there are blatantly obvious signs everywhere that say "No Smoking". In a loud voice, well beyond a stage whisper, Booey strongly suspects that we won't exactly be able to retire based on sales this afternoon. Though quite a crowd has now built up round the stadium circuit or in pride of place in either of the (new to me) covered grandstands, he is keen to be off and to stop wasting his time. Not that I'm a patient person myself but I remain hopefully optimistic. Before he goes our conversation ranges widely. He praises the Scunny promotion for their hard work and "professionalism" and who are not like some other promoters whom he considers "amateurs" because they treat it as "a hobby" which is invariably "always bad for the sport". He reserves a good deal of ire for the iniquitous warping influence of the *Sky* contract on British speedway, "they just show **** racing on *Sky* most weeks and then claim it's freaking brilliant, no wonder we don't freaking attract more people along, if they're told that's freaking supposed to be great!"

When the meeting eventually gets under way the racing is of a very high calibre from the outset and this continues unabated throughout the afternoon. When presented with a track that they can really race on, and variety of racing lines to choose from, the Conference League riders really know how to entertain and put on a good show. The contrast to last year is huge on the track and, indeed off it, even if you just consider the programme. This year it's 20% cheaper, 20% longer, has fewer adverts and, arguably, the best feature – it has a compact and accurate race card! Another welcome contrast is the fact that it takes until Heat 7 before we have our first crash, after which Benji Compton is excluded. Even then, the riders don't continually hurtle through the first corner safety fence straight from the gate but wait to do so a bit later in the race on lap 2 when they jockey for dominance rather than in constricted space. To be fair, there are crashes and "first bend bunching" incidents at every track and these often remain out of the control of the riders never mind the promoters, though frequently track shape is a contributory factor when combined with a determination to establish a lead. At Scunny, a very small section of fence is repeatedly demolished (five times) right in front of the clubhouse, close to the exit of the second bend, during the course of the afternoon, but this is at varying points in the progression of the races rather than predominantly on the first lap.

Back on the track, irrespective of the number of "incidents", falls, retirements and engine failures throughout the meeting, the racing is of an extremely high calibre and a joy to behold. The chance that there will be something to celebrate locally has been doubled by the fact that Scunthorpe field two teams. When they encounter each other in heat 7, it takes three attempts to complete it. Each race is packed with incident – an exclusion, first bend bunching and a thrilling encounter between the young Josh Auty and the experienced Paul Cooper, who was specially drafted into the Scunthorpe team to replace the injured Wayne Carter – a decision that raised some jealous eyebrows among rival fans but is a completely legal decision under the present rules. Cooper passes Auty on the second bend of the second lap, is then re-passed by Auty who is in turn then re-passed by Cooper. On the third bend of the last lap, Auty makes another run to pass his rival only to try too hard/get a shove – depending on your point of view or where you watch from. Worryingly he lies immobile on the deck for some considerable time until a concerned Cooper draws along side. This is a signal for Josh to immediately leap to his feet and try to lunge at Cooper in an attempt to assault him, though fortunately for him, Josh is restrained by the nearby flag marshal and another man from any further confrontation with the target of his ire. I am placed too far away to judge the relative merits of the legitimacy of the cause of his umbrage. A lady close to me observes, "he's such a nice lad usually". Later Booey wryly notes, "Cooper definitely touched him but the rider on the outside always gets excluded; he should control himself as he's only young and someone will twat him – he's strong mind but they'll be better fighters!"

Throughout the meeting I alternate where I stand between by my table or watching the racing from the balcony. I meet quite a few people who have read my book and think highly of it. There's Holly from Sheffield and her dad as well as Roger Hulbert and Bridget Berryman from Hull. I mistake them for a married couple but they both quickly correct my misapprehension, since they're both just keen fans and often travel to meetings together. Whether related or not, they are warm, friendly and inquisitive people. Roger is also an author and has written a number of books about Hull Speedway, *Craven Park, the First Ten Years* and *Hull Speedway, 1930-1981*. He pays me a high compliment that my description of speedway at Scunthorpe drew his attention to the peculiar way that the noise travels here, something that he hadn't noticed before, despite many visits. Bridget says, "you're much younger than I imagined, I picked you as late 50s or early 60s because of your mature writing style, your observations and because you found the time to do it". Also along for yet more reconnaissance is the indefatigable Jonathan Chapman, who chats to all and sundry to take a well deserved break from his various in depth analyses of speedway. By his reckoning, "it costs £18,000 to run each Elite League meeting". If his calculations are correct, without sponsorship many promoters will struggle to cover their costs through revenues generated via the turnstiles.

Later Roger Westby calls in. This year he attends as a fan since the experienced and entertainingly bombastic Shaun Leigh who adds zest over the tannoy all afternoon has replaced him this season as Scunthorpe's announcer. With the demise of Hull speedway, Roger no longer has a guest speedway slot on *BBC Radio Humberside* but still pens a column for the Scunny programme. He points out to me that Paul Cooper "has never ridden in the Conference League before" and that Benji Compton, his partner in the Scunny 'B' team, also rides for the same Premier League team as Cooper, "so they're both Sheffield riders". They are also the second highest scoring partnership in the qualification rounds and qualify for the final as victors from a bizarre semi-final encounter with Andrew Bargh and Mark Thompson from Mildenhall. First, Thompson wrecks the safety fence and is excluded for his troubles. Then in the re-run, Bargh falls, remounts and then suffers an engine failure that gifts the Scunny 'B' partnership the qualification they would have gained anyway under the 4-3-2 points scoring system by merely finishing the race.

In the final they encounter the Stoke Spitfires partnership of Adam Allott and Ben Barker who, to my mind, were the most exciting riders on display all afternoon. They are both also young men and, for many people, more properly fit the original development methodology of the Conference League. Interestingly, the winning partnership for the last three years has always featured an "old hand" (Mark Burrows twice and now Paul Cooper) as a vital component of the winning partnership. The final fails to reach an appropriate climax when meeting referee, Chris Gay, correctly awards the race to the Cooper/Compton partnership after he has to exclude Barker, despite his sincerely held protests that there should be a re-run. The fact that Scunthorpe 'B' get the title with an awarded race result wouldn't have been their ideal, but a win is a win.

Afterwards I am lucky enough to catch up with referee Mr Gay and he kindly commented on some of the contentious races of the afternoon. "After hearing last year's event took four and a half hours, I wanted to get it through in a reasonable time particularly as many fans and riders had a long journey home. So I awarded races where the result was clear – since the rules are that all have to have completed one lap. I found it a demanding meeting to referee. There were the usual alcohol and drug tests, the flooded track and inevitable incidents with riders giving 100%. It meant a lot to the riders, who are mainly young and genuinely upset if they get excluded. The most difficult decisions were when Richie Dennis packed up just before the finish line in Heat 19 affecting those behind him but not causing a crash. The way I looked on it: it wasn't Dennis's fault he packed up, he stayed on his [racing] line, he was in front of them, no-one crashed, I didn't feel he deserved an exclusion. The only rule he could have possibly been excluded under was unfair riding which I didn't feel it was."

Warming to his theme Chris continued, "then in the Final itself when I knew my decision would decide who won the whole thing. A real big responsibility and not something I welcomed as I'd rather it was decided in the old fashioned way of actually racing to victory. I agreed to speak to Ben Barker on the phone, for his sake really – so he understood the reasons for my decision in the Final to help him come to terms with it. He pleaded with me about including him for an all-four re-run. I didn't show it but found it a bit upsetting particularly from a young man to whom it clearly meant so much. Overall, it's a privilege being a ref but sometimes it takes a lot out of you. Personally I find those genuinely upset rider situations much harder than dealing with the more aggressive or pro-forma complaints."

Overall, the real winner this afternoon is Conference League speedway, and this is due in no small part to the work put in by the Scunthorpe promotion, their professionalism and that of their many dedicated helpers. The racing, organisation and entertainment offered has restored pride and credibility to an event that was poorly served by the lengthy fiasco staged in South London in 2005. The crowd, while not as sizeable as many would have hoped – probably because of the Bank Holiday, the weather and the poor forecast – have been served up an entertaining and quality presentation of a product that will, most likely, encourage them to return again to watch speedway.

28th August Scunthorpe – Conference League Pairs Championship
Winners: Paul Cooper & Benji Compton (Scunthorpe Scorpions 'B')

Amazing what the face painters can do. © Jeff Scott

KING'S LYNN SPEEDWAY STADIUM 1997

Much has changed at the Norfolk Arena. © Jeff Scott

Jonathan Chapman enters into the spirit of the circus theme night. © Jeff Scott

King's Lynn Riders Cap Off Night of Celebration by Sleeping Together!
30th August

When I drive into King's Lynn, they're queuing to leave the place. There's over a two-mile tailback. On the roundabout close by Saddlebow Road, the mobile board display that they use to advertise the speedway by driving round all the coastal holiday camps is parked in a prominent position that can't help but catch the eye. I understand that the sign is accompanied by very loud announcements that I'm sure I wouldn't welcome outside my house but would leave anyone it passes in absolutely no doubt as to the continued existence of their local speedway club. Earlier in the afternoon, the mobile display advert had already been on an extensive local tour and any passing waverers based on its route round the Lynn area will be left in no doubt that there is a meeting being staged in town tonight. It's an important meeting too as it represents the first chance that the club have to gain some silverware this season. They have assembled a very strong side for the 2006 campaign, which finds them unbeaten at home and often victorious on the road. Already nine times this season they have won home fixtures with scores in excess of 60 points and have enjoyed victories by 70 points twice, while their smallest margin of victory in any league fixture is a still convincing 11 points. Usually this would be a sign that the entertainment of the speedway on offer was execrable but, by all accounts, this has not been the case. The recent meeting against the Edinburgh Monarchs was just so – although they won easily by 61-33 the supporters of both teams spoke highly of the quality of the racing. The club started the season as most people's favourites to win every piece of Premier League silverware, provided that the riders steer clear of injury. It's a level of predicted success that should win more plaudits than it does in the press and from their competitors. It would be fair to say that many other promoters view them with envy and grudging respect rather than warmth. Then people will often resent success, particularly as the promotion hoe their own row here and approach the business of speedway in their own unique, straightforward and determined way without the expectation that they will be overwhelmed with support from others or the sports' governing body, the BSPA.

Whatever people think of them, the King's Lynn promotion run a very successful and profitable operation. Like all overnight success stories, they are reaping the fruits of hard work, meticulous planning and their continuous development of their facilities as well as always refining their product proposition based on customer feedback. They definitely value the speedway fans at Saddlebow Road. Jonathan believes that "it's the little things that really count – if you try to save costs by cutting the odd corner here or there, the fans always notice and always remember it". The Chapmans – Keith (Buster) and Cheryl, along with Jonathan – are determined that they will offer and be seen to be offering a quality product, both on and off the track. This manifests itself in many ways. The development and ongoing improvement of the stadium facilities for staff, riders and public alike; and the free entry for children at every meeting – "they're the future generation of fans so why charge them £1 each for the sake of a couple of hundred pounds extra at each meeting? They spend on food and drink anyway, plus they're more likely to come back in the future if they get the speedway bug early," says Jonathan – allied to the free theme events that the club try to stage at many meetings. Tonight's theme is hard to gather exactly but there's clearly a celebration going on and the King's Lynn promotion, like they do often, have again lashed out some money on themed giveaways for the kids. Situated close by the turnstiles, there are elasticated bow ties, foam noses and a couple of face painters. "Phwoaw, I think we have the sexiest face painters in speedway" notes an approving Jonathan who, despite the obligation of his promotional duties, only just about resists having his own face done.

Jonathan and his father are prepared to try many innovations and to search for new ways to organise and run things. They believe that professionalism should extend to all areas of the club and even have rider contracts that stipulate various conditions they consider important that include: all riders to arrive in the pits 90 minutes before the official start time, compulsory smart shirts in the bar afterwards and they also have a system of fines for transgressions at £10 per infringement. They have led the British speedway world through their involvement in educational campaigns to improve literacy, numeracy and the use of information/communications technology. This in turn improves the social cohesion for the local young people who come along to the out-of-school-study-support centre to use the range of facilities on offer at the club. These include a suite of computers and the opportunity to see behind the scenes as well as meet the riders. This level of social responsibility is impressive and precious. Later I watch as Jonathan sweetly, almost paternally, repeatedly takes the time to cajole and encourage these youngsters throughout the evening. The "King's Lynn Speedway Study Centre" – part of the nationwide government initiative called "Playing for Success" – connects the club closely to the local community and establishes a degree of social capital within the local area that is hard to gainsay or better elsewhere. Keith, Cheryl and Jonathan take great pride in this aspect of their business, "our work in the community is hugely respected by the local people and the council". They haven't lost sight of the essential commercial imperatives of their business so have also pitched their stadium facilities on the wider ACU stage and have just landed a "big half million pound ACU event".

I place my book display on my table outside the track shop. Inside Johnny Barber along with Mike Moseley and another man (who works for the police) lay out the stock in preparation for the expected large crowd. It has been a stressful day for a rather hot and flustered Johnny as, at one point, it looked touch and go as to whether he would be able to pick up fresh supplies of King's Lynn branded merchandise from his supplier. Tonight, when passions run high and glory for the club beckons, would be a bad night to have run low on King's Lynn branded paraphernalia. Someone else who has also arrived early is Shaun Tacey, who is here to hand out leaflets that advertise his forthcoming testimonial meeting. He really is a lovely man and greets me with a jovial "I'm doing a 'you', like you did!" Which, roughly translated, means that he has embarked on his own intensive travel schedule to promote his own forthcoming testimonial event, like I had last year when I researched my book and met Shaun seemingly everywhere, This week he will also travel to meetings at Ipswich, Arena and Mildenhall. Shaun is so warm and personable that he's bound to attract attention and I only hope that his hard work is rewarded with a bumper crowd for "the biggest event that West Row has seen for 20 years". Many other riders wouldn't inflict such an intensive schedule upon themselves (or would, more likely, have someone else do it for them) around the tracks, shopping centres, markets and coffee mornings that Shaun proposes to do. It will mean a lot of pressing of the flesh and endless interaction with the public that many riders are often more reticent about and keen to closely control or limit to a bare minimum. When I watch, the manner in which Shaun greets everyone so enthusiastically can only bode well to maximise awareness of his event.

Once the meeting starts, it quickly becomes apparent that this is unlikely to be a close contest. I had actually come to King's Lynn for Sheffield's previous visit in the Premier League when they had lost by a score of 62-33. Given the greater success that the Lynn riders have since enjoyed round the Saddlebow Road circuit and the even higher level of confidence that they now have, it very much looks like another thrashing is on the cards. Though Sheffield traditionally enjoy a considerable home advantage against most teams that visit them, King's Lynn had managed a draw there earlier in the season, so overall prospects appear drastic for the Tigers. The first six heats produce four 5-1's and the visitors appear beaten before they start. It's a state of affairs that they then compound by being very sluggish from the gate. Even when they do manage to roar away from the tapes in the lead, they then appear to mysteriously encounter a severe loss of momentum by the second bend when the Lynn riders easily zoom past them. Maybe there is a boggy area on that bend that only affects the visiting riders? Ricky Ashworth and Benji Compton temporarily lead Heat 5 only for Trevor Harding and Daniel Nermark to easily and effortlessly overtake them both on that bend. In the next heat Jason Lyons makes a lightning start but is then distracted by the "wayward shape" of Troy Batchelor's bike as it pulls alongside him, and is quickly left behind to trail across the line in third place.

When I wander across to stand by the fence that overlooks the pits area, it's noticeable what a hive of activity the Lynn side of the pits is in comparison to the more lacklustre Sheffield side. The Lynn riders and mechanics appear much more buoyant and work in tandem. I retreat to watch the next few races from the raised grandstand that provides a panoramic view of the track and a great vantage point to give me a perspective on the starts and the congested first corner. Lynn continue to ride dominantly and though Tigers guest Jason Lyons actually wins Heat 9, it's not until Heat 12 that Sheffield record a heat advantage. This is helped in no small part by the exclusion of Trevor Harding and, in the re-run, Kyle Legault (or "Leagault" as the race card prefers we know him in this race and also heat 3) wins double points in the black-and-white helmet. This adds a hint of respectability to the scoreline. The meeting is conducted at break-neck pace throughout though things speed up appreciably after the drizzle starts just before Heat 11. As if to signal the end of their prospects of an aggregate victory Ricky Ashworth falls in this race while in the lead. It was a rare sight all night to find anyone in a green or yellow helmet temporarily out in front.

The riders, fans and the Lynn promotion have the good grace to celebrate their eventual 63-32 victory in subdued fashion, though it wouldn't be unreasonable of them to be confident of lifting the trophy almost no matter what happens the next night in the return leg at Owlerton. The traditional end-of-meeting fireworks provide a loud finale to a surprisingly easy victory and in the grandstand there is already confident talk that they might take as many as 500 fans along to watch the Stars lift the Premier Trophy.

My relatives aren't in town tonight and I count myself extremely fortunate that I have been offered use of the well-appointed and comfortable corporate hospitality cabin on the fourth bend that has a shower, sitting room, kitchen and bedroom. "You saw it last year when Tommy Stange was staying there," said Jonathan proprietarily after he'd kindly shown me round the facilities and offered me use of the bunk beds there. Just after I'd made myself comfortable and unpacked my things, Jonathan knocked on my bedroom door and entered to nonchalantly explain that there had been a slight change of plan. "'Cause of the long journey tomorrow and tonight's result, Chris Mills and his dad are going to stay and share the bottom bunk together, so you'll just have to have the top one, if that's alright?" It's more than fine by me since I'll now get the chance to chat to them informally and still avail myself of the Chapmans' kind hospitality. After about an hour writing some material for my forthcoming book *When Eagles Dared*, I finally venture along past the deserted grandstand and into the bar. By now, many of the fans have drifted home and the people that remain all seem to have some strong connection with the club. They're either staff of the bar or track variety, security, riders, start girls, mechanics or members of the Chapman family. Jonathan kindly plays mine host and pours me a blackcurrant and soda water from behind the bar, Buster looks completely chuffed with life and carries Tupperware containers thickly filled with cash under his arm, while his wife Cheryl either chats or busies herself around the room. On my few visits to the track, I'd already noticed that Cheryl has an energy that makes the men in her life look catatonic (and they're very energetic people themselves!). Such is the variety of her responsibilities that it means she often appears to be absolutely everywhere at once. When I query her about this she's effacingly modest, "Keith's always at it and Jonathan never takes any time off".

Jonathan debates in ebullient fashion with Chris Mills and John Oliver whether they can actually have another drink from the bar. They've temporarily broken off from the rather earnest discussions that they've been having with a couple of young women whom I gather work as start girls at the track. Not that you have to be a great detective to figure this out as they both have the words "STARS" picked out in large green capital letters on the bottoms of their black leggings. Chris and John are both keen to drink some more but, the responsible party pooper that he is, Jonathan isn't so sure – "but you've already had two!" – and he repeatedly reminds them about the need for sobriety with another big night ahead. John is 18 and Chris is in his early 20s, so they're understandably reluctant to take on board a message of abstinence, even from their employer who owns a tightly worded contract they've both signed. However, it's a night of celebration and, after a lengthy debate about the relative alcoholic content/strength of the lagers on offer, Jonathan relents at the last minute "alright just one Bud then as it's piss weak anyway" before all the Chapmans depart from the stadium at around midnight after another long but successful day. Their departure signals the pumping electro music to be turned down dramatically by the barmaids ('why does he always turn the music up so bloody loud?") who then start to pack away with a zeal that indicates that they might wish to chase the Chapmans across the car park. John and Chris take this as the signal to pour themselves another tipple each before they return to chat with the enraptured start girls who laugh repeatedly and hang on their every word.

Shortly afterwards, I retire back to my bedroom to do some more writing and wait for Chris Mills and his dad arrive. By 1 a.m. they still haven't so I venture back out into the pouring rain and pick my way down to the bar area in the pitch darkness since the stadium floodlights have now been completely switched off. The bar is locked and deserted without any sign of life. Completely mystified I return and retire to the top bunk. I've been asleep what feels like only seconds when I'm startled awake by the lights coming on in the bedroom. As I'm in the top bunk, it's as though a searchlight has been shone in my face. I'm disoriented and vaguely disgruntled, particularly when I realise that it's nearly 3.30 a.m. When I emerge bleary eyed into the kitchen, John Oliver and Chris Mills are struggling to concoct themselves a supposedly easy-to-prepare late night snack. They're both clearly still wide awake, very cheerful and completely stone cold sober, which immediately indicates that they haven't been out on the lash. When I quiz them they answer suspiciously reticently, "we went clubbing in Lynn but it was completely dead". Not exactly a big surprise on a Wednesday night in Lynn I'd imagine and, call me naïve, but it doesn't strike me as exactly the number one party night in any town, let alone this one. Also, didn't it shut rather late then? I suspect that they have been out with the young ladies I saw them with earlier. Bastards. Apparently Chris Mills' dad had kindly elected to sleep in the van and leave them to get on with an enjoyable night out.

The lads continue to struggle to get their late night meal together. It's my insight into how the influence of continental riders has transformed the attitude and approach of the modern generation of British based speedway riders when it comes to exercise, diet and conditioning. However, late at night, when seized by the munchies or an urgent desire for sustenance, the best laid plans and intentions fly out of the window. This late night meal consists of some spicy chicken flavoured noodles and a tin of Heinz Spaghetti Bolognaise washed down with some cans of Tango. Cooking the damn stuff proves to be quite a challenge for them compared to riding a speedway bike for a living, so I leave them to it. Back on my top bunk, I can hear them talk excitedly about tonight's win and their (colourful) lives in speedway generally. Eventually, well after 4 a.m. they creep into the room in pantomime silent fashion to share the reasonably generously sized bottom double bunk bed. As they struggle with the duvet and lever themselves together into the confines of the bed Chris Mills exclaims, "I know we're friends and we ride together but freaking hell, now we're sleeping together!!" I hear them chat very amiably about tactics, engine set ups, interspersed with a few grumbles about rider X and rider Y, as I finally drift off to sleep.

30th August King's Lynn v Sheffield (Premier Trophy Final, First Leg) 63-32

Problems in t'Pits with Tyres (not Tired)
31st August

What seems like only barely a few moments later I'm woken at around 8 o'clock by the loud sound of tractors already at work. The shale surface of the Saddlebow Road track has to be lifted for the stock car event later that night. It's a busy stadium and, to adopt the parlance of management consultancy, the Chapmans definitely know how to "sweat their assets". After a quick shower, I leave the debris of the night before in the kitchen and head off to the stadium café that is already crowded with workmen and business people as well as Jonathan Chapman and Chris Mills' dad. They've both already enjoyed one of the very reasonably priced breakfasts that I've just ordered as well. I'm told that the café has become increasingly popular with all types of people and during the time I'm there a continuous stream of customers, mostly workmen in their site clothes and muddy boots, fill all the available tables. As this establishment also has free wi-fi access, it's apparently not uncommon for businessmen to get out their laptops to catch up on whatever the electronic equivalent of paperwork is nowadays. Jonathan is reading the report of last night's meeting in the paper very closely, something that strikes me as peculiar as I previously understood that he usually writes it himself.

A few minutes later, Chris and John arrive for breakfast looking sickeningly refreshed while I feel like I completely over-indulged with night on the lash with the start girls, which I most definitely didn't. They too pick up the paper in turns to study the report of last night's fixture. "Freak, there's yet another freaking photo of Tomas [Topinka], do you reckon he has it in his freaking contract that they have to freaking have a photo of him in every report?" They read aloud to each other in turns the exciting relevant bits of the report before the arrival of breakfast distracts them. By then Chris Mills' dad has already left to start to prepare his son's bike for tonight's all-important return meeting against Sheffield. After I joke that I'll have to post on my blog that they slept together it prompts them to wonder aloud about why no speedway riders have ever publicly admitted that they're gay. This in turn prompts a recollection about Daniel Nermark, whose laid-back behaviour and attitude to life could, mistakenly, gain him this reputation. "Doolan rides with Danny in Sweden and he was wearing some pink boxers with a flower motif that Kevin took the piss out of and asked him where he'd got them from. He said 'I stayed over at a friend's house and had to borrow his'. That'd get most people killed with rumours about staying with another bloke, you wouldn't advertise it – but he doesn't care. That's Danny though!" By now, it's so popular and crowded in the café that Jonathan suggests I use the press box for my internet access and to continue with work on my book. You get a panoramic view of the track and the whole stadium from up there in the press box and I can study all the preparation work that continues in the torrential rain to get things set up for the stock car meeting later that night.

Though it's not a long drive to Sheffield, I feel knackered and thank my lucky stars that I don't have to ride! I eventually wander over to the Owlerton stadium car park from the nearby Garrison Hotel, but only after I've fought my way through the perpetual city centre road works that Sheffield delights in all year round while they try to introduce the tram lines that will apparently create the citywide public transport network of the future. I report to Malcolm Wright, the co-promoter at Sheffield Speedway, who slightly gives the lie to P.G. Wodehouse's famous observation that "it is never difficult to distinguish between a Scotsman with a grievance and a ray of sunshine". Perhaps, Malcolm has become an honorary Scotsman – albeit a very tanned, smartly dressed one with a Yorkshire accent – as the news that I'm there to have a book display cum signing doesn't fill him with any more cheer than the prospect of a probably much reduced crowd this evening on account of the comprehensive thrashing that the Tigers received last night in the first leg. I don't take it personally as I'd be disappointed to see me too at just around the same time as the season's first chance of silverware has effectively departed.

A brief trip to the speedway office confirms what I had understood already from Neil Machin that I was expected and welcome tonight. Indeed, a casual glance in the programme would have shown that Neil had praised my book as the one to buy this year, if you could buy only one. Just after I've told him about my fitful night's sleep, Chris Mills arrives to ask if his mum can be added to the guest list on the pits gate.

CM: "My dad's already here but he's my mechanic"
NM: "What's her name?"
CM: "Dawn"
NM: "That's quite appropriate for you, I hear"
CM: "Eh?" [Disconcerted look]
NM: "Dawn – I hear that's an appropriate name for you as you had such a late night last night"
CM: "Oh that [the penny drops, I blush slightly at the broken confidence and Chris glares at me but immediately and quick-wittedly cuttingly retorts], that's quite funny for you Neil"

That's how to handle these promoters! Gratuitously winding Chris up isn't perhaps the wisest action before the meeting.

The hope that Chris and John Oliver both might be very tired, off form, have multiple engine failures and bikes with square wheels is one of the few straws that Neil can delusionally clutch tonight.

There is quite a reasonable crowd gathered outside the stadium. Some of these are prematurely jubilant Lynn fans while others are fans who sensibly mooch by their cars as they wait to see if the dark clouds overhead will, as they threaten, deposit their loads before the tapes rise. Outside and inside the stadium, the Tigers fans search for explanations or crumbs of comfort about the night before or the evening ahead. The consensus is that the King's Lynn management had hatched a dastardly plot that took the form of preparing a clay-based and grippy track surface that would deliberately catch out the

Sheffield riders. Ignoring that the Tigers enjoy their own legendary home track advantage on account of the shape, size, grip and speed of the circuit at Owlerton – talk that Lynn had the "wrong type of surface" sounds far fetched as well as a form of denial that doesn't reflect well on those who utter these claims, and flies in the face of the facts on the night. Basically the Stars riders demonstrated fast gating, greater commitment and a more apparent desire to win than their erstwhile rivals, irrespective of the track conditions. Sophisticated explanations abound with some surprisingly knowledgeable debates that major on the idea that this surface was constructed "out of clay not shale". I must remember to consult the rulebook later or ask the Chapmans if I see them. In the meantime, I stand by my table as the crowds flow past without pause to the grandstand or the pits and don't mention that most literal of speedway truisms, namely that riders ride bikes not tracks.

It soon appears that everyone who is anyone within the speedway world who could make it tonight has come along. After all my sojourns round the country I'm starting to frequently recognise people – even if I don't know their names – from chats with them whilst (hopefully) selling them a copy of my book, seeing them wander past or just noticing them in the crowd. It's these small recognitions that have made me feel much more a part of the speedway community in the last few months. Later I will again see Louise (whom I met on my travels last year at Hull speedway) and whom I've now come realise is a bit of a fixture around certain Northern England speedway tracks. She has now secured work in the pits, I believe, at Scunthorpe speedway so her love of the sport, the bikes, the riders and the whole enchilada still continues. She's come along with her friend Lynn whom I'd not previously met but heard so much about when we spoke last year. They're both here to cheer on the Stars onto victory. They didn't intend to come but the whole lure of the evening and the possible celebrations have proved too difficult to resist.

The night before in King's Lynn, I'd finally met Neil Dyson who'd kindly praised my book months ago on the unofficial Sheffield fans' forum. Tonight he's come along with his mother. He introduces her to me and also buys another copy of my book since it features his quote in the reprinted version. She's already a proud mother and she smiles beatifically when I tell her that her son has shown great consideration towards me. There are a lot of Lynn fans with banners, scarves and air horns all keen to arrive sufficiently early enough to bagsy their traditional fourth-bend section of grandstand, in the vicinity of the pits. In diplomatic fashion, and with a vague hint of what I like to consider as irony, I tell every Sheffield fan that stops for a chat that I reckon they'll "win on aggregate after a run off!" The always cheerful, helpful and well-informed Neil Machin wanders by and *sotto voce* deadpans, "How's it going for you? 'cause I hope it's going well for someone!" It's also good to get a brief chance to catch up with the Tigers enthusiastic and knowledgeable announcer, Dave Hoggart, before he heads off to carefully prepare for his presentational duties. He definitely knows how to wring the maximum excitement out of any crowd and opens his welcome to the visitors with a caustic but witty introduction over the tannoy: "Welcome to our visitors tonight from Norfolk – King's Lynn – a team that Workington promoter Graham Drury recently described as 'a bunch of whingers and prima donnas!'"

Just before the meeting starts, I move my table of books next to the neatly laid out stalls of speedway merchandise that forms the Sheffield track shop so capably run by Mick Gregory. He's a passionate man who has been round the speedway scene for many, many years and appears to know a large number of the crowd who he greets cheerily throughout the night. Away from his work at the track, he makes deliveries all over the country in his lorry. He has an encyclopaedic knowledge of our road network that nearly rivals that of his recall for anything at all to do with his beloved Derby County, where he revels in the discount that his Old Age Pensioner status now allows him on his season ticket. Mick remains gloomy about their immediate prospects of success this (2006-2007) season which is only slightly more hope than he holds for Sheffield's chances tonight of lifting the trophy. Along with his doubts about his football team, Mick apparently has some long held doubts about the strength and ability of the Sheffield reserve pair of Paul Cooper and Benji Compton, who he feels will definitely be no match for the Lynn combination of Chris Mills and John Oliver. In fact, he has quite an antipathy towards Benji Compton, the younger brother of the Tigers captain and Porsche driver, Andre – he of luxuriant eyebrows fame – who is missing once again from the team tonight through injury and is replaced by Australian guest Jason Lyons. Benji fails to score in his opening ride in Heat 2, which gives the Lynn combination of Mills and Oliver a valuable 1-5 that assures their imminent victory even more than it might have been already. Amazing really when you consider that they have had only four hours' sleep at the most last night and yet they win so easily that they make the Tigers pair look half awake, to thereby continue the living nightmare that is the Sheffield supporters' lot this week. Mick isn't ready to forgive and forget when it comes to Benji, who compounds the situation when he manages to fall on the fourth bend of the fourth lap in

Dave Hoggart interviews a triumphant Keith 'Buster' Chapman.

© Jeff Scott

heat 4 after a very determined John Oliver has harried him throughout. It's a vital point gained through application and effort for the Stars and yet another one lost ("completely freakin' thrown away") for the Tigers. Mick throws his hands up in the air in frustration, "Benji will never make a speedway rider as long as he has a hole in his arse. Neil is too loyal to his riders sometimes and the supporters club has just spent £1500 on a new engine for him – as if that's the problem – and then he does that". Mick isn't happy that this considerate gift to his career from the supporters club has just been spectacularly dumped in the dirt.

The next race has the home side assert themselves with a 5-1 although even in this race the third-placed Lynn rider, Troy Batchelor, reveals considerable commitment to the ongoing scrap by the Stars for every point when he nearly snatches third on the line from Kyle Legault. With darkening skies and the first glimmer of momentum from the Tigers, we hear Dave Hoggart appeal for the Machine Examiner (Adrian Lunn) to contact the referee. We're quickly informed by Dave, with a hint of exasperation, or is it nonplussedness, in his voice that "there appears to be a technical query on the tyres". Though the riders attempt to line up for the start of the next race, the two-minute warning is cancelled by the referee, Barbara Horley, who has decided to venture down to the pits to check the actual state of the disputed tyres for herself. In another case of mistaken identity[i], the fans around me gleefully (but completely incorrectly as it was Margaret Vardy) recall Barbara's recent performance on live television with a series of derogatory and witty comments that mark them out as from the widespread speedway bastion of political incorrectness that afflicts even the gentlest man when faced with a female SCB official at their track. Dave Hoggart updates us further with news that "a batch of tyres are faulty" before he adds the word "defective" as if he needed to further clarify it for us all. The delay is all too much for Mick who exclaims, "that stupid woman has gone to the pits!" who correctly notes that she really shouldn't have done so since the licensed SCB Machine Examiner should make the call on all bike matters (otherwise why have them?). In case rumours of dirty tricks have become too rife on these South Yorkshire terraces, Dave assuages anxiety when he tells us on the tannoy, "it's not one team or rider complaining".

Earlier Mick had identified Tomas Topinka as a kind of reverse secret weapon within the King's Lynn ranks, due to his propensity to have a complete mare of a meeting at the first sign of moisture in the track. Tonight the track definitely looks damp and dark rain clouds threaten overhead, though by now they have started to indeterminately mingle with the night sky. No sooner has Mick wondered aloud – at Topinka's apparent conversion to the Owlerton circuit when it has a more aquatic outlook – than he suddenly pulls from the track for no apparent reason in Heat 6, "I knew he'd do nothing here," he cries triumphantly. It's a

[i] Much more than afflicts their male counterparts, it appears that every female SCB official gets blamed for the perceived shortcomings of any female SCB official as though it were they who had exhibited any real (or imagined) shortcoming. Their gender always and necessarily counts against them among many 'traditional' speedway supporters.

retirement that gifts the Tigers a second successive 5-1 and suddenly the situation looks a lot brighter for the home side at 23-13. Throughout the night, there has been a regular trickle of purchasers of my book, not quite a stream of them, but enough to be noticeable and welcome. Demand at Mick's stall is high with the air horns and refill canisters absolutely flying off his shelf until his stock is rapidly depleted. Typically, he has another box at home, but I gather this offers scant consolation. As I'm stood by his stall, many people immediately assume I work there (I have just about perfected my track shop assistant look) and it becomes quite fun to help out. Though, that said, it's amazing the number of people who try to choose to buy something once the riders are under orders at the tapes! I sell a book to a couple called Val and Charlie from Arena Essex who are yet another example of those fans of a certain age who met and found lifelong romance at the speedway (in their case West Ham), the first step in a blossoming relationship that led to marriage, children, grandchildren and wedding anniversaries that require costly but lovingly chosen commemorative gifts in expensive shiny metals or precious stones.

In fact, a 10 point lead is as good as it gets for the Tigers and, with the arrival of Heat 8, the Stars predictably send Troy out in the black-and-white helmet for a tactical replacement ride. Mick isn't happy, "that is the worst rule ever brought into speedway – I don't know a single supporter who likes it!" It takes Batchelor until the second bend of the third lap to hit the front when he overtakes Ben Wilson with some ease to the considerable delight of the large crowd of Lynn fans on the fourth bend. With John Oliver third, the scores narrow to 28-23. The practical implication of this is that the Tigers will now have to win the remainder of this encounter (seven heats) by 5-1s if they are to triumph on aggregate. If there is any air left in the collective balloon that is the Tigers fans' optimism, this result well and truly deflates it. Sadly, it's an indictment of their overall performance to report that the home team then fail to gain a single heat advantage throughout the rest of the meeting. The amazing thing to note, from my point of view, is that I'm completely exhausted after only a few hours sleep and I just have to stand about – not ride a high-powered machine without brakes. Somehow on less rest, Chris Mills and John Oliver play a vital part and contribute to the King's Lynn victory with six (paid eight) and four (paid six) points respectively. Suddenly I feel even more my age!

The older man, who has until now sat silently in his garden chair next to my table, suddenly grins broadly and speaks in a vindicated tone for the first time since his brief mumble before Heat 8, "I'm here to see Sheffield lose, it's good to see someone do a Sheffield to Sheffield". If I understand him correctly, Sheffield often win by a large margin at home – a situation that often enables them to win on aggregate if they keep the scores close when they ride elsewhere on their travels. I understand what he means but if he really wanted to witness Lynn doing a Sheffield to Sheffield he technically should have been at Saddlebow Row last night. I let the matter rest and resume disappointing people who rush up to buy an air horn or replacement canister from the track shop.

Throughout the night a number of readers of my book come up to pass on their feedback. The 'Supreme Salamander' tells me, "I love the style and think it's fantastic the way you put across the points but I hate the footnotes". After the meeting finishes, David from Slaithwaite and his wife make a point of popping by. It's good to see them again and I remember that they bought the book on my last visit to Sheffield (one of the few I sold). David has read the book a chapter at a time in chronological order. He has many perceptive questions that I hadn't ever really formulated a proper answer for. My off-the-cuff answers don't really address the subtlety of his insights or the implied compliments he pays (sorry David). Also I think I was shocked to learn – it's always the way when you look at the world or yourself as others perceive rather than how you see it – that my writing might reveal that I'm still really actually "an outsider", just when I'd started to kid myself I was an "insider". The truth of this perception short-circuits my response at that moment but doesn't, deep down, stop me realising the simultaneously sad and liberating truth of it. He politely doesn't doubt any of my thoughtlessly cryptic answers and explanations to his perceptive analysis of my book. They go to many speedway meetings and rugby league matches ("we like to be outsiders and to observe"), so are attitudinally attuned to the approach I took when writing *Showered in Shale*. "I thought it was very detached – like a Nick Broomfield film – with the supposed naïve outsider asking questions, often pointed questions, that cause people to reveal themselves". They seem genuinely pleased to learn that I have another book in the pipeline.

By now, the celebrations of the King's Lynn riders, mechanics, promoters, staff and fans have reached an epic scale of gleefully joyous proportions, almost as though Lynn had finally gained its independence as a country separate from Norfolk and England after a long campaign. They were definitely all in a mood to celebrate "like it was 19-99" or another similar event. Just in front of where we were standing Buster and Jonathan were being doused in the victory champagne though, this being speedway, I suspected that it was probably some super sweet Cava. The obligatory official photographs for the *Speedway Star* are taken just at that moment. These will capture something that is simultaneously a combination of the scripted and staged but also something joyously spontaneous. Everyone connected with Lynn in any capacity looks ecstatically happy and the Sheffield fans that have hung around for the victory lap and parade of the trophy look on glumly or with dispassionate expressionless faces. So long as they continue to avoid injuries, this could well be the first of many victory celebrations that commentators now confidently predict will be coming the way of the Stars this season. There is absolutely no doubt that they certainly enjoy it to the full and bask in the glory of the moment.

Afterwards the Lynn team manager Rob Lyon dedicates the win to the late Ashley Jones, the popular team member who died during the winter. "We wanted to win something for Ashley and this is perhaps a little bit more emotional than winning the two cups last season".

I call into the speedway office where Neil Machin and Malcolm Wright have already safely ensconced themselves. Apparently the size of the crowd hasn't been as big as they would have liked but, with years of practice as a promoter already behind him, Neil still just about manages to unfurrow his brow, put on his game face and look with studied optimism to Sheffield's future prospects in all other competitions. "There's still a lot to play for and speedway's a funny old game, just when you think you can predict what's going to happen you can't!"

I melt away into the dark night of the half-emptied car park with the idea that there might be some vague but incredibly tangential relationship between my book and the legendary documentaries of Nick Broomfield. Even if it's not true, it's a lovely thought. A consoling thought that makes everything temporarily all worthwhile and all the relentless travel of the last few months (promoting my book) fall into softly backlit but meaningful focus.

31st August Sheffield v King's Lynn (Premier Trophy Final, Second Leg) 48-45 [Aggregate Sheffield 80 King's Lynn 108]

September 2006

"The behaviour of a minority of Coventry fans was nothing short of disgraceful. It is the culmination of two years of frequent attacks on one of the most talented men around on two wheels... at Coventry, the line between acceptable and unacceptable was most definitely crossed. What Hans was subjected to at Brandon was beyond banter and abuse. It was threats and harassment. Hans did absolutely nothing to warrant this treatment and, in my opinion, the perpetrators should be brought to task. I personally felt ashamed to be British and ashamed to be associated with the sport of speedway. To have to smuggle a 25 year old sportsman – whose only crime was doing his job to the best of his ability – out of a stadium is ridiculous."
Mick Bratley

"We were told in 2005 they wouldn't move more than 20 minutes away, that would have been alright. I am a pensioner, how am I supposed to go to Kent?... I know several supporters who will be forced to give up supporting the Dons. Is Ian Perkin going to make arrangements for us to get there?"
Helen Lynn writes to the *Speedway Star* on the proposal to move Wimbledon speedway to Sittingbourne

"Because of the diabolical state the track was allowed to get in during meetings by the speedway promoters. No attempt at all is made to keep the dirt moist and on the track. I'm fed up of hearing promoters complain that they could not water a track, as rain was forecast. Have they not heard of crop sprayers? The final straw for me was the home Premier Trophy match against King's Lynn, when we absolutely threw away the bonus point by leaving the track for the vital Heat 15 more like the M1 than a speedway track."
Long-time Mildenhall fan John Stebbing decides to stop going to West Row

"Maybe they thought I was a terrorist or something! At one stage, they said they were going to deport me. I said, 'Where to? I live in Northampton.'"
Over-zealous immigration officials at Manchester Airport stop Jason Crump

"It was an astonishing decision and one that left everyone at Glasgow and our supporters stunned. Under the rules, when a rider misses a meeting due to a non-speedway injury or illness, BSPA management committee approval is required to re-introduce that rider to the team within seven days. This is standard procedure and permission is normally granted, but for reasons best known to themselves, the management committee declined our request and ruled that Danny had to miss our next two matches. In effect he was banned for being ill."
Alan Dick comments on the suspension of Danny Bird

"I have absolutely no comment to make on that [threat to quit] except to say certain people spit their dummies out when decisions don't go their way. Last year Glasgow said they were dropping down to the Conference League because they were losing money. Did they? No."
BSPA Chairman Peter Toogood replies

"There was something special about him and he was a lovely guy... there are certain things and memories that keep flashing back about Ashley. He made us laugh so often and he will always be a part of King's Lynn speedway."

Buster Chapman dedicates the Premier Trophy win by King's Lynn to the memory of Ashley Jones

"I really feel that if Mr Perkin is successful and promotes it well, Sittingbourne could become a real jewel in speedway's crown, but I also feel the racing would have to be of at least Premier League standard (or preferably Elite) to be viable and that advertising would have to be countrywide."
Chris Watts emails the *Speedway Star*

"My concerns would be the noise again. I would make sure this issue is addressed very seriously on behalf of the local residents."
Manuella Tomes, the Liberal Democrat councillor in whose Sittingbourne ward the Central Park stadium is located

"Last year's argument for the 40-point limit will count against me. I thought it would create rider movement, but I admitted before the season started that it hadn't worked. I'm big enough to put my hands up and say "I got it wrong, this is what I have learnt'."
Ronnie Russell

"What's the point of having a reserve if my points don't count? The fans must have been scratching their heads and wondering what was going on... as far as I'm concerned, most people in the sport know I came second – 12 points is 12 points."
David Mason after his CLRC second place is declared void

"It's always understood that a reserve's points don't count in these events. As a meeting reserve, he just filled in wherever there was a rider missing and would not have raced against all the contestants...the restriction on a meeting reserve has always been there. David has been round long enough to know that... ultimately David was just there to make up the numbers and ensure we had four riders in every race."
Conference League co-ordinator Peter Morrish explains

"I have to say that I think Lindback's attitude is a disgrace. I think he has short-changed British speedway and its fans and Poole fans in particular."
Ian Thomas on news that Antonio Lindback will miss the second-leg encounter of the Knockout Cup semi-final, after he rode in the Grand Prix the previous weekend

"It's still there for us, everyone is fit and I would like us to finish off the bottom and end up on a high note [10th] at the very least."
Ronnie Russell hopes to avoid a hat trick of wooden spoons

Trevor visits Armadale

1st September

After a slow, grunky and tiring drive from Sheffield to Edinburgh, I flop down on the bed of the student halls of residence that I've started to use regularly on my trips to the city. It's just like being a student again albeit without the wild sex, parties, excessive drinking, talking rubbish and the drugs, though because I'm still writing my *When Eagles Dared* book a note of realism has been injected, since it still feels like I'm continually behind with my studies.

The one-way system in the city continues to defeat me though, in my experience, it's a lot easier to get out to the Edinburgh Monarchs track at Armadale than it is to return from it. Even if you ignore how friendly everyone is on the supporters' coach, the chance to let someone else drive you in and out of the city is another reason why I try to use this mode of transport whenever I can. However, tonight I have to get there early to set up my table and put out my books. Inevitably I see more of the city than I intend after my poor sense of direction means that I travel on yet another route there but still somehow manage to arrive in plenty of time before the start time for their Premier League derby fixture with the Glasgow Tigers. I've now been along so many times to visit with my book that I could now officially almost be regarded as a "bad penny". Given the large amount of coverage given to the Monarchs in my book, second only to Eastbourne, I've been disappointed at the low level of sales so far to Monarchs fans. It just shows nothing is ever predictable. Luckily as I arrive the friendly, likeable and always-helpful co-promoter at the club, John Campbell, is there to greet me as he places rubbish in a large black wheelie bin located just outside the entrance gates to the stadium. He's very keen that sales of my book pick up at his track, "I want to be top of your sales league!" I really hope that that is the case too! To help try to boost interest and sales John kindly took a copy of my leaflet on the book to give to Scott Wilson, the ebullient meeting presenter who interviewed me on the centre green earlier in the year, so that he could sing my praises during a break in proceedings at some point in the meeting. Or, if he couldn't go that far, draw attention to my attendance.

The club expect a good crowd tonight to see them race against Glasgow – the "auld enemy". John would like this fixture to be a boost to morale as well as finances after an indifferent season that has so far seen them locked close to the bottom or bottom of the Premier League throughout the campaign. They have endured the deleterious financial impact of a number of rained-off fixtures and, unluckily, have even had repeated problems with animal rights activists/vandalism at the stadium. However, even before a wheel has turned in this fixture, it has already become shrouded in controversy since Glasgow will ride tonight without the services of their heat leader Danny Bird. It took a short while for this news to filter through to me as I'd occupied myself with setting out my table on the grass before I moved it again having trodden in what my dad would rather politely call "dog's muck". As they say, where there's muck there's brass and just like rum goes with coke, where there's greyhounds they'll also be lots of poop. Once I've recovered and cleaned up, news of the BSPA's decision to ban Danny for seven days eventually filters through to me. It's taken with a resigned shrug of the shoulders and a few words of complaint if you are a Monarchs fan or fulminations in almost apocalyptic terms if you followed the Tigers. As far as I could gather the BSPA management committee – comprised of Matt Ford (Poole), Neil Machin (Sheffield), Chris van Straaten (Wolves/Redcar) and Peter Toogood (Somerset) – had applied the rules of the association, after previous infractions, because of a meeting Danny missed as a result of a "non speedway related injury". Quite what the ins and outs of the situation is or was I wouldn't like to comment or speculate upon. Though it would be safe to say that opinions vary and often extend to ridiculous extremes.

The BSPA is often ridiculed and held to be the fount of all evil, or at least any or all of the ills of speedway in this country, on a regular basis. Approximately most nights of the week on the internet forums and slightly less so on the terraces, a common response is to claim, "we definitely don't want this" or "they shouldn't do that". Proposals for how to do things better abound with the intensity of the advocacy usually related in inverse proportion to practicability and/or potential cost of the proposal. Not that the BSPA and SCB aren't often involved in snafus or avoidable ramifications of short-term rule changes and bodged solutions. In Belgium they have a delightful saying, "it was as good as a plaster on a wooden leg" which, in some ways captures, the approach and credibility of some decisions that are made by the speedway governing bodies in Britain. Nonetheless, the job of drawing up the rules, implementing them, never mind the thankless task of running an association of members where everyone's outlook, trading conditions and objectives are radically different and usually in competition with each other, remains an unenviable task. Being elected to or to put yourself up to serve on the BSPA management committee is simultaneously akin to a trip to the dentist; having greatness thrust upon you; to be seen as a form of megalomania and ambition most often associated with politicians; or a means to garner the respect often accorded to estate agents while also simultaneously finding yourself in a coconut shy when you're the coconut. In essence, most right thinking people would avoid any involvement or contamination unless they'd already been fatally drawn into the thing by accident or design. It's invariably a hiding to nothing and, possibly apart from the extremely rare chance to vaguely influence the levers of power so that once in a blue moon your club promotion might just vaguely marginally 'benefit' from decisions made without tangible reward (albeit that you always 'act for the good of the sport' with anything that goes in your favour only ever arriving by accident or without premeditation).

In these circumstances, you're always going to be blamed, and get the dirty end of the stick. That said, this decision doesn't look the brightest when judged against previous precedent or common sense, (though any previous similar behaviour by Danny Bird is studiously not mentioned while it's brushed under a carpet specially loaned from BSPA Towers for this very purpose). If I were the Glasgow promoters I'd view the whole affair darkly and rumours that they could throw their metaphorical toys out the pram to the extent that they might close the club at the end of the season would be hasty but, perhaps, understandable as an initial reaction before wiser more considered counsel prevails. Judged on the atmosphere tonight it is safe to say the next visit to Glasgow by Neil, Chris, Matt or Peter won't see them garlanded with flowers or walking into Ashfield stadium on a laurel and rose petal strewn pathway.

The net result tonight is to deprive Glasgow of a team member who would, most likely, play a vital part in their probable victory with any knock-on consequences that this might then have on their final position in the Premier League. It goes without saying that all the fans here will be deprived of the opportunity to watch a gifted rider and that the spectacle of this contest will be lessened as a consequence.

By the time I have sold only a few books, the fixture is almost under way so I joined the healthy throng of fans standing on the first bend. Given how the Monarchs team have performed so far this season, tonight is as good a chance as they would get to inflict a defeat on their local rivals. It is to be a frustrating meeting for the Monarchs who are never behind at any point but equally, though they often pull into the lead, can't quite escape to win on the night. The rider replacement rides that the Glasgow Tigers use for Danny Bird gain them only six points from his programmed outings, a total that even the most pessimistic of their followers would expect him to usually beat on a trip to Armadale. The most touching incident of this fixture, from my point of view, comes in Heat 2 when Robert Ksiezak and Derek Sneddon clashed on the first bend and thereby cause the Tiger to fall heavily and with due dramatic effect. Derek Sneddon, who I've always viewed as a somewhat rambunctious and aggressive character with an approach that indicates that he's come from the wrong side of the tracks, proves my assumptions completely incorrect when he immediately leaps to his feet and sprints over to solicitously enquire about the health and well being of his fallen rival. It is a crash that will upset Sneddon's machinery for the rest of a chequered night. In the re-run my favourite Premier League reserve, Sean Stoddart, although prone to inconsistency takes advantage of the chance to try again to finish second and with Sneddon in third place the heat is drawn.

In fact, the first four heats are drawn before the Monarchs pair of Matthew Wethers and Henrik Moller combine for a 5-1. The Glasgow fans around me are quick to highlight that this is a race that Danny Bird should have ridden in; as though that were proof enough that the scoreline would have been different. The Monarchs hold onto their lead before extending it in Heat 8 with a win for Stoddart that rather notably features a firm challenge on James Cockle. Without Bird even greater responsibility than normal is to fall to Shane Parker who obliges with a couple of wins, ably supported by Ksiezak in Heat 9 and McAllen in Heat 11, to again level the scores. The fates conspire in Heat 12 to have Sneddon retire when set to combine for a 5-1 with his team-mate Matthew Wethers. The drawn heat features one of the rare points of the evening for Lee Dicken who always gives his all in each race but still often looks well off the pace in practically every race he features in.

Theo Pijper, Edinburgh's most capable and combative rider on the night, then beats Shane Parker in the vital Heat 13 where again the visiting fans loudly remind themselves that they would expect the absent Danny Bird to put up a better showing than his replacement David McAllan. This enables the Monarchs to once again take the lead but an immediate reply by the visitors (helped by Moller's engine failure that leaves him immobilised at the start line) means that for Edinburgh to have any real hope of a win, Pijper will again have to beat Parker in the last race. Both men race hard for victory and pass and re-pass each other in combative but fair fashion before the Dutchman wins to loud acclaim from the home support. Ever the sportsman, Shane Parker makes a point of congratulating Theo Pijper for besting him again in some style.

It is a night of opinions and I take my full chance to bathe in as many of these as possible. Something that many people seem keen to tell me is that the view from the somewhat spartan looking hospitality area is excellent at Armadale and really allows you to see much better over the first bend fence – an obstacle that tends to obscure your appreciation of the finer details of the initial corner from a number of other vantage points on the first and second bends of the stadium. For a good part of the evening I stand next to the kindly, passionate and very well-informed Glasgow fan, Jim Fleming, from Biggar. It's a town name that always sounds exotic to my English ears but having never visited I'm really not sure. He has followed Glasgow for many, many years and still retains a keen enthusiasm for all matters of the shale. Of equal, if not greater appeal to him since the public smoking ban came into force throughout Scotland, is that speedway at Armadale represents one of the last bastions available for those keen to partake in the evil weed. More than once Jim comments, "it's one of the few places in Scotland you can still smoke", usually just before he inhales deeply or lights up yet another evil weed.

Someone who looks well out of sorts tonight but looked something special on his debut on the Isle of Wight is the Monarchs' Italian speedway rider, Daniele Tessari. Maggie at the track shop explains some of the factors behind his loss of form and subsequent travails in Scotland, "he blew his main engine on parade at Somerset and the other one in a heat. It costs over £1,100 for a new engine, which is money that he doesn't have though he has borrowed money off the promotion here for another one. He's homesick and was in tears at King's Lynn as he would like to go home but can't 'cause he's stony broke and can't afford to. He needs some wins but can't see where they're going to come from". It's a situation that probably affects many riders who come to this country in the hope that they will make a decent living from speedway; only to then discover the expense of the sport, self-employment here and the general cost of living all conspire against them to leave them close to destitution and thereby dash their dreams of lucrative speedway success. You would think that they should plan better or have realistic expectations but the very act of getting on a bike indicates an optimism and a reluctance to closely study hard facts (mostly about safety). I was fortunate to witness his debut that night, since it was likely to have been the one swallow that made his summer with the Monarchs.

Another fan takes the chance to give me a lengthy run down on the likely make up of the Monarchs team next season and some thoughts on how to attract more fans to regularly attend fixtures at the club. Basically this strategy involved "getting in a couple of [unnamed] exciting Poles" to thereby fire the imagination, enthusiasm and loyalty of the "24,000 Poles in Edinburgh". Even without the arrival of these Poles, the "team needs rebuilding" and this fan casts his slide rule over the members of the present team – "Sneddon will probably be on a tricky six point average; Tessari will only race six away meetings and five home ones so will have a high assessed average; we should keep Moller and Matthew as well as he always tries hard". I couldn't possibly comment with any authority or insight, so it's best to offer no opinion and not to intrude on something that involves other people's livelihoods and passions.

When the meeting ends I am again by my table but by now it is dark and I am deep in the shadows in the pitch-blackness, but careful not to step on the grass, as people hurry to get away home. Sadly I make no further sales and end the night having sold five copies. However, I do hear voices. They keep calling, "Trevor – how did it go tonight? Trevor –how did it go tonight?" Endlessly every minute or so. After a while I realise that I am in fact "Trevor". I call out "great!" and the voices immediately stop. It is only as I pack up my things that I realise that there had been no announcement to the crowd – by the now long since departed but forgetful Scott Wilson – that I was there or even a mention in the programme to boost interest. Such is life and I'm sure that John Campbell would kindly help in the future. I leave to find yet another complicated route back into Edinburgh, still not sure whether I had been promoted or demoted when called "Trevor".

1st September Edinburgh v Glasgow (Premier League) 45-45

Riders slither away from the start. © Jeff Scott

Scattered shower arrives. © Jeff Scott

The riders thoroughly check out the Ashfield track surface. ©
Jeff Scott

Into the Svelte Mastodon's Lair at Ashfield
3rd September

A piece of spectacularly bad driving was causing huge tailbacks close to Ashfield Stadium when I arrived, many hours before tapes up, for the local derby fixture that would pit the Tigers against the Monarchs. All weekend I had endured another trip to the region messed up by the weather (five postponements in three trips up from the South) when a postponement of the 'Young Guns' fixture at Berwick had left me kicking my heels in Edinburgh. Though on a different side of the country, the heavy morning rain didn't bode at all well for the likelihood of the meeting going ahead as planned. The forecast was for heavy showers in Glasgow.

I got the chance to ponder this on the lengthy diversion in the nearby housing estate to the stadium that comprised uninviting tower blocks, intimidating tenements and residents, plus a magnificent Victorian graveyard. No one I saw was drinking Buckie but the impressively shuttered Off Licence, which looked almost derelict but was actually open if judged by its popularity, doubtless sold the monks' firewater. It was a scene that instantly recalled the comedic rewrite of Queen's popular anthem for the city of Glasgow – the Bowegian Rhapsody.

Though it's not raining when I arrive, nonetheless the sky looks threatening and the car park has many deep puddles. They're always very watchful at the pits gate but also very friendly. There's widespread incredulity at the BSPA decision over Danny Bird and lots of dark mutterings about the underlying causes of it all, let alone the possible ramifications. Concentrating on the matter at hand, no one expects anything other than a resounding home win if the rain holds off, though a big caveat is that from the Tigers only David McAllan and Robert Ksiezak excel in the wet conditions. The star of Ashfield Stadium and a rider that reputedly doesn't relish a wet track, Shane Parker, has already arrived in the pits, unloaded and is now engrossed in the match programme. He cuts a solitary figure since both sides of the pits are deserted of other riders although there is already quite a crowd of mechanics, track staff and assorted other people. Away to our right over by the pit gate, the first of the riders' vans have begun to arrive but have yet to discharge their cargoes. The orange-brown mud of the pits area pathway glistens, splatters the vans and cars as well as cakes everyone's footwear. I'm directed to park my car up the steep slope at the end of the pits that leads to the riders' overflow parking area. I check with the club's presenter and PR man, Michael Max, that I won't be in the way, "don't worry you'll be let know in no uncertain terms if you are!" Perched this high up you get to overlook the general area, consequently you get a fantastic view of the track and the stadium in one direction and the outlying estates in the other. It would be a great and unique place to watch from but I can't, as I'm the grateful guest of the club, here to try to sell my books more successfully than on my previous visit.

Thanks to the charming and urbane Alan Dick, I will have the chance on my visit this time to set up my table in a prominent position in the main grandstand, just where everyone enters/passes and where they stop to buy a programme. Back in the pits, Michael Max chats with Shane Parker in desultory fashion. Michael is irked that he has introduced an unnecessary typo into the programme race card – he spells Tessari as Tesarri (maybe the extra 'R' will make him go quicker?) – "it's the first mistake that I can recall putting in the programme for years". The quiz about present and former riders has caught Michael's attention and they're a bit flummoxed by question number six judge by Shane's furrowed brow and muted reaction. Michael has just read aloud, "Unsuccessful Danish import at Armadale" before he pauses for theatrical effect and adds, "there have been so many bad Danes at Armadale, it's difficult to remember them all" (the answer is Robert Larsen who Gary Lough later notes in exact fashion in a manner that combines objectivity, a look on the bright side and a nod to clutching at straws, "he was our best number four in 1998"). Michael has a sharp and sardonic wit that he flourishes intermittently. He's dressed in his trademark bright red Glasgow speedway anorak that contrasts with his jet-black hair, pale complexion and is his standard attire pretty well everywhere you ever see him working on behalf of the Tigers. Sensible attire rather than fashionable, but a good choice given how often it's rained this year on my visits to Glasgow. It's good to see him, and Michael chats in a manner that mixes curiosity and frequent flashes of waspishness. Unlike my previous visit, I'm keen to ensure that he actually mentions to the crowd that I'm in the stadium this time. Unless you let people know you're there, making a 1000-mile round trip like I will, just isn't as fruitful as it could be. Michael holds all the power metaphorically and, literally, the microphone during each Tigers home fixture. I very much enjoy the banter of his presentations where he effortlessly combines irony and considerable knowledge with flashes of strongly partisan descriptions, while all the while keeping interest levels high. That said he did "forget" to mention anything last time and faithfully promises not to do so again this time. He takes one of the leaflets about my book and stows it away in his pocket. Though interestingly, as we chat, by implication waspishness is a trait he cleverly ascribes to me – a classic example of the conversational passive-aggression I love to practise myself.

[MM] "When I met you, you seemed so polite and innocent yet some of the things you say in the book are quite barbed."
[JS] "I tried to capture what I heard and saw, as you know. Like what though?"
[MM] "What did that woman who runs the B&B where the German rider stayed in Berwick describe Dick Barrie. Oh I remember, 'a pain in the arse'. We always joke about it every time we see each other – I say 'well if it isn't the 'pain in the arse Dick Barrie' and he says 'if it isn't the "lumbering mastodon" Michael Max.'"
[JS] (I laugh but the penny drops as to why Michael accidentally 'forgets') "Oh sorry, she did say that, so it's her opinion but the mastodon thing is just a turn of phrase, well my phrase, that's meant to be descriptive not offensive, plus they're one of my favourite dinosaurs."
[MM] "Oh, don't worry, many people might be offended to be called a "lumbering mastodon" in print but I'm not."
[JS] "Funnily enough I heard the start marshal at Newcastle said to Dave Peet, "Have you seen what some twat has written about me?""
[MM] "It's good that you can repeat that and have the awareness to see yourself as others see you! Don't get me wrong I enjoy it but it's a book for the toilet, not that I want to read everything, but I'm working my way through the Premier League chapters."
[JS] "The toilet?"
[MM] "I did take it outside once, on a sunny day, but it's ideal for the toilet."

Maybe that's the solution to my sales efforts at Ashfield and elsewhere – to get concentrated attention, I should always try to pitch my table in the gent's toilets. On second thoughts, at Ashfield the grandstand ones are delightfully cramped and decidedly old fashioned. The perennial problem of people fiddling with the books they won't ever buy with ketchup-covered fingers would take on a whole new problematic dimension, particularly as there are no washbasins. To avoid this potential issue, I could move my stall to the other end of the stadium where there are excellent toilet facilities in the clubhouse but, arguably less people would pass by there. Like so many speedway clubs round the country, Glasgow are only the tenants of an extremely unfunded football club and so have no opportunity to provide enhanced facilities no matter how much the promoters would like to do so.

This season Michael Max no longer presents at Workington on a Saturday night. "I wanted to concentrate on other things," says Michael in a manner that echoes how senior executives in large corporations always suddenly decide to take on "special projects" but remain at the company content to be apparently powerless. In Michael's case his protestations are true, since he already has a demanding job with Partick Thistle Football Club. Talk of Workington invariably turns to Dave Hoggart whom I incorrectly claimed announced King's Lynn to the Sheffield crowd as "moaning bastards". Michael Max is immediately on his phone to Dave to inform him that he will report him to the BSPA, as "presenters aren't allowed to swear". In fact Dave had cunningly only reported what Graham Drury had said, namely the claim that they were "whingers and prima donnas". I'm not sure what they call it when presenters banter together – or even what the collective noun would be for a group of presenters (a mellifluousness of announcers?). Michael Max flashes a brief triumphant grin since he thinks he has caught out my memory as a misrepresentation or possibly exposed my account of events as misapprehended. He then explains that he was once fined for his comments from the centre green when, as a service to the crowd, he explained the SCB regulations that underpinned the referee's decision. The referee (Margaret Vardy), in Michael's opinion, had a sense of humour by-pass and fined him – a decision that would have caused him to quit speedway altogether since he point-blank refused to pay it on a point of principle. Speedway didn't suffer this needlessly thoughtless loss since the Glasgow management courteously paid this fine, albeit with a similar sense of outrage and burning resentment.[1] Michael has made it a point and a matter of pride to become well schooled in the minutiae and fine detail of the ever-changing SCB rulebook, a knowledge that he gleefully flourishes in almost lawyerly fashion on a frequent basis.

Shortly afterwards, there is a short but intense burst of heavy rain that causes everyone to shelter in the covered parts of the pits or retreat back to the now full car park on the hill and the comfort of their vans. It's over quickly but gives the track a further dousing it didn't need, though you have to hope that the noticeable breeze will help to dry it rather than blow more clouds our way. While I ferry all my things from one side of the stadium to the other, I thank a large very smartly dressed man who passes in the other direction for the hospitality of the Glasgow club. He looks extremely familiar and I assume that he's a Tigers man but, as the words leave my mouth, I realise that it's Alan ' Doc' Bridgett, the artisan of Armadale track curation as well as the Edinburgh club's General and Team Manager. He scowls and snappily retorts, "It's freak all to do with me!" as he ostentatiously hitches his shoulders within his jacket. Oops.

All the volunteer helpers at the Glasgow club appear to temporarily gather close by my table and they're an extremely friendly bunch. Apart from the kindness of the Tigers management allowing me to return, I have been fortunate to enjoy the help of many people to publicise my visit. There's been the Glasgow Tigers Supporters Club, the indefatigable Ian Maclean and the wonderfully named Alun Biggart at the Newsletter. The collective enthusiasm that there is for the club and for speedway generally is a pleasure to behold and be part of. Sadly again, though this time I'm in a much more prominent position, sales remain poor. Ironically, since I was there last time and completely unnoticed, a couple of fans come up and say, "you're tucked away here – you should be by the track shop".[2]

One thing that was a shame was that Michael Max again 'forgot' to breathe a word about my attendance throughout the afternoon. My, what a forgetful chap he is! Though Michael has a lot to remember, rather interestingly Freud had a number of theories and insightful things to say about motivated forgetting and, as so often with Freud, they signal a deep seated neurosis about sex, sexuality or the inability to construct relationships. Maybe the "mastodon" comment has cut more

[1] It's an issue that still has Michael burn with resentment months later as he brings up his brush with the speedway authorities in the form of referee Margaret Vardy again in the 17th February 2007 issue of the *Speedway Star.* "One of the Berwick riders appeared to move on a 15-metre handicap and I quoted the rulebook over the microphone, saying how a starting offence in that situation would result in going back a further 10 yards. Sadly, the referee immediately hit me with a £100 fine which was paid in full, but you can imagine I have my own thoughts on the matter which are probably best kept to myself. Thankfully, I'm still a licensed official for the 2007 season so there have been no further repercussions, but it underlines just how tight the rules have become on presenters." Later Michael goes on to confess, "I'd never liked bikes and I must admit that I still don't understand the technical side of the sport, I just love the racing."

[2] Though speedway everywhere throughout the country is a broad church and attracts people from all walks of life, I'm led to understand by some Tigers speedway fans that among the long-time supporters and season ticket holders, Glasgow boasts an enviable collection of highly qualified fans with multiple degrees, positions of great social responsibility and a wide representation from the professions. You should never judge people by their looks, wealth or job position but not that many British speedway clubs can boast a selection as august as barristers, lawyers, senior policemen, scientists, university lecturers, accountants, computer experts, tonsorial artists and language teachers. This isn't the norm at any other club that I'm aware of, even throughout Scotland with its better education system, let alone England. Should there ever be a version of speedway mastermind played to save my life, I will choose to be represented by the Tigers fans since while most clubs will do well on the speedway specific questions, I'd expect this advantage to show through strongly in the decisive general knowledge rounds.

deeply than I imagined. It's now no longer an apposite description nor remains correct anyway, since Michael cuts a much more noticeably svelte, almost dashing figure nowadays. Perhaps I should have used "forgetful mastodon", it's one to bear in mind for the reprint that doesn't look at all likely based on sales this afternoon.

If sales are poor, the twists and turns of the meeting itself enthrals and I have a fantastic view of the action from the terraced steps of the main grandstand as it overlooks the start gate. Given the slimy, bog-like nature of the track and the cool breeze it's not the ideal day to be a start line girl. Not that they make many concessions to the weather conditions in terms of their outfits though they do have umbrellas. These are useful, for once, after many continuous weeks of uninterrupted sunshine on Sunday afternoons for the club; in fact, ever since my last visit here for the rain swept and abandoned Pairs meeting – perhaps it only rains when I come to the speedway here.

It's Michael's job to explain events, instil enthusiasm in the crowd, pass on information and generally deliver the aural accompaniment to the speedway spectacle we all witness. It's a job he relishes and excels at. Except for my book, he has an astonishing memory with impressive recall for rules and regulations, trivia, great races and riders of the past and, particularly this afternoon, an in-depth knowledge of meteorology. We learn that the Rest of the World team that will visit for the 60th Anniversary celebrations will feature an international and august line up. Among others, there will be Kyle "Lay-Galt" and Adam Shields, "star of possibly the best race ever ridden at Ashfield, with Paul Thorp". See, he can recall this race as though it were five minutes ago and yet fails to recall a book that he's frequently mentioned in!

Despite the evidence of our own eyes, Michael is desperate to reassure us that we have nothing to worry about with all the dark clouds that rapidly sweep by the stadium only to be replaced by yet more of the same. Of much more concern to the Glasgow riders is the treacherous nature of the wet track, which appears to have eliminated any home advantage that they might enjoy only to replace it with lingering doubts about how raceable the surface actually is. Even the equivalent of speedway royalty in Glasgow, Shane Parker, also apparently approaches the conditions tentatively, carefully riding within himself and utilising his years of experience to skilfully, but at moderate speed, pick his way past opposition riders. No such worries or fears appear to bother a gung-ho Monarchs team in the initial five heats – they adapt to the conditions with aplomb and soon race into an 11-19 lead. This silences the home crowd to the extent that you can easily hear the grumbles and almost feel their confidence gradually slip away. Not that Heat 5 has been without some humour brought on by the track conditions. Lee Dicken falls but is then unable to extricate his bike from the mud. He pulls at it with increasing desperation as though he's starring in a silent movie comedy before the imminent arrival of the other riders caused him to panic for his safety and galumph in his steel shoe like a startled heifer to the safety of the centre green accompanied by the appreciative laughter of the crowd.

The general consensus is that in the appropriately named Wethers the Monarchs possess a "wet weather specialist", whereas the only Glasgow riders that allegedly possess an aptitude for the wet are McAllan and Robert Ksiezak, though apparently it's only Ksiezak that remembers this as the team flounder around the track and fail to assert themselves. Given how often it rains up here in my experience, it's quite a failure to not have riders who can adapt to wet conditions and would appear to slightly limit the club's silverware ambitions. Before Heat 6, Michael's presentational approach takes a descriptive turn and he temporarily sounds as though he's on an exotic holiday programme somewhere in monsoon season, "the rain falling lightly with brighter skies behind". These are the words of a supreme optimistic in light drizzle. However, no sooner has he uttered them than magically the sun starts to shine brightly, while he continues and we learn of a " track inspection called for by the Glasgow management". After a short delay while SCB official Mick Bates "consults with both captains", we then learn some technical information, notably that there will be "some grading of the heavy stuff". Anticipating the widespread cynicism that the meeting might continue until after heat 6 has been raced and therefore no refunds would be payable in the event of a postponement, Michael Max is keen to stress the deeply held desire by all involved to ensure that the meeting continues. He explains all this to alleviate concerns and "so as not to con the public". A clincher in this respect is his news, to collective groans from the crowd, that if the meeting were abandoned, then Danny Bird would still be banned for the next fixture – the important Knock-Out Cup fixture with King's Lynn.

During the track grade, I study the programme and find that, very kindly, there is an article that mentions my signing visit. This compensates for the lack of Michael Max's aural reminder and it's good to see that my book is rather uniquely

Under orders. © Jeff Scott

Sunshine breaks through. © Jeff Scott

Unusual speedway dolls. © Jeff Scott

described with an inadvertent neologism as "insightive".

Rather like the before and after adverts for proprietary cleaners, Glasgow clean whiter than white after this thorough track grade of the "heavy stuff". This success is due in no small part to a tactical masterstroke by team manager Stewart Dickson, or blind optimism depending on your point of view, when for Heat 6 he surprisingly brings in Shane Parker for one of Danny Bird's rider replacement rides in the form of a tactical substitute in the black-and-white helmet with a 15-metre handicap. It's a brave move based on Shane's first-race struggle with conditions but then if anyone can excel at Ashfield it's the popular Australian. A move that already had a 'last throw of the dice' feel to it proved to be the crucial race of the match as the 8-1 gained narrowed the scores to 19-20, just at the very moment that the Monarchs threatened to run away with it. The previously notably silent Tigers crowd greets the Parker win with ecstatic cheers and, with their equilibrium restored, they proceed to loudly enjoy the rest of the proceedings. If I were the Monarchs management or supporters, I'd suspect unorthodox practice or further rail against Lady Luck during a season when the sticky end of the stick has always been the handiest for the club.

The Tigers talisman has now got the exact measure of conditions – in fact practically every rider takes the same racing line round the circuit from the track grade onwards – and Shane rides to a successive victory in the re-run of heat 7, after Henrik Moller is excluded when he falls and fails to clear the track promptly. It's an action for which he is loudly booed and derided by the voluble home support. Once they've found the lead they never relinquish it and the crowd find their collective voice to celebrate practically every nuance in the Tigers favour loudly but also to vilify their number 1 Monarchs pantomime hate figure, Derek Sneddon. He rides well and often this afternoon, so it's a relationship that is renewed with some regularity.

Michael has by now abandoned his role as the unofficial weather forecaster for this part of the Glasgow metropolitan area, in order to regale the partisan crowd with the fine detail of the rulebook. The cause of their almost hair-trigger ire is the decision to award a re-run Heat 12 by referee Mick Bates, after an exclusion for the fallen Lee Dicken, that the Tigers faithful definitely felt should have been awarded rather than run again. Also sprawled on the track after a heavy fall, Derek Sneddon spends considerable time on the muddy surface before he is ferried back to the pits via the home-straight grandstands to the accompaniment of loud boos from the crowd which he greets with a broad smile and a wave. Throughout Sneddon's time on the floor Michael, as his wont, hovers attentively close by as though he actually has some supervisory role with the medical and track staff. This stirs my close neighbour on the terraces to observe, "he's not a mastodon – he's much more of a predator, always curious. Look at the way he holds his head to one side, always inquisitive but slightly ghoulish". While Derek Sneddon gathers himself, pats himself down and attends to his bike in the pits, Michael embarks on a lengthy explanation of when a race can be awarded. This further illustrates his own wonderfully selective memory that has an encyclopaedic recall of the clauses, sub-clauses and qualifying criteria that underlies this aspect of the rulebook but, simultaneously, 'forgets' my book-signing announcement.

Rejuvenated and motivated by his jeers, Sneddon wins the re-run and the scores narrow to 38-37 as the wind starts to whip itself up rather strongly. With the addition of persistent drizzle, conditions have deteriorated to the extent that the referee Mick Bates actually abandons the meeting before Heat 14, only a minute or so later, for the riders to rescind this instruction and "say they'll carry on". So often promoters grumble at the deleterious impact of so-called 'rider power' and its fellow cousin, the alleged 'softness' of the modern difficult-to-please speedway rider supposedly always keen not to race at the drop of a helmet or the first sign of moisture. This request to race after an abandonment (such a decision by an official immediately tells you're not present at a televised *Sky* fixture) proves the exact opposite to these claims to be very much more generally the case. The wind and rain provide conditions relished by Sneddon in Heat 14, almost as much as he relishes a slow victory ride past the grandstand to blow exaggerated kisses of celebration at the Tigers faithful. They boo so loudly that they'll soon be invited to start pantomime audience training in city centre theatres. On a one-man campaign to narrow the scores to only one point in heats 12 and 14, Sneddon finally runs out of steam in the last heat. Well, to be accurate, he runs out of time and is excluded under the time allowance to the rapturous delight of the crowd. They're pleased but slightly less ecstatic with the victory which Michael quickly informs us, "we've been unbeaten at home all season in the Premier League which is the first time since the last time in 1995". The man next to me bitterly notes, "and we're unbeaten against the BSPA!"

All the riders are interviewed on the centre green, some much more talkative than others though none are up to Michael's own exemplary standards. Amazing Shane Parker has set a club record for the most points in a meeting – 22 (paid 23) that comprises six wins (one as a tactical substitute) and his initial third. With masterly understatement Shane notes, "It was quite difficult today". As the centre-green discussions close, Michael turns to Alan Dick and says, "good to see you with a smile on your face – at least until you see the size of Shane Parker's pay packet!"

3rd September Glasgow v Edinburgh (Premier League) 49-44

Boom! Boom!
4th September

After I've enjoyed a night of delicious home cooking and the warm hospitality of Ian and Jean Maclean as well as a wistful meander down speedway's memory lane, I set off on the long drive from Kitkintilloch to Smallmead Stadium in Berkshire. I really don't envy any rider or mechanic that has to make this pilgrimage from North to South or vice versa on a regular basis.

The lure of a clash between the Racerdogs and the in-form Bees is hard to resist, particularly so when I can go as the guest of SCB official Chris Gay. I have a huge amount of time for the effort shown by so many dedicated people to make speedway the sport that it is – well – or, at least, the one we enjoy. The referees are another of these unsung heroes who, it's safe to say, no matter whether they make the right decisions or not, are always blamed by somebody. This is all part of the lot of the speedway referee, though you definitely wouldn't hear Chris complain about it. He's a true fan of speedway and relishes his part in proceedings. He's been doing this for quite some time (ten years now) since he first answered an advert in the *Speedway Star* in 1993 and embarked on the two years of laborious travel and training that you have to pass/survive in order to get to travel even more as a qualified SCB referee.

It's a double pleasure for me as not only do I get to watch from the referee's box and walk on the Reading track itself – an exciting first after 31 years coming along to Smallmead – but I also get a unique chance to get to see behind the scenes. There have been many changes at Smallmead since the arrival of the new owners, BSI, during the winter. Many of these changes are dramatic and highly visible, whereas others are purely cosmetic. The basic restriction that the BSI has to work within is that they still have to remain at the careworn (but lovely) Smallmead stadium. A move has been mooted for many years and I'm sure that there is a determination by the BSI Reading (as they call themselves on the company website) management to move to more modern and luxurious facilities somewhere else as yet unspecified in Reading. That would be a shame as the ramshackle nature of the stadium facilities, now well past the glory days of its construction in 1975, is part of the essential appeal for me of watching the speedway here. The area that surrounds the stadium has undergone a huge transformation and Smallmead now provides an oasis of decrepitude in a sea of modern buildings. These surrounding buildings range from the football stadium cum hotel complex that is the Madejski Stadium of Reading Football Club to the adjacent office complex now known, without any sense of irony on an industrial estate surrounded on all sides by busy roads, as "Green Park". There's even an impressive tower that has a sign that illuminates this name in the colour green at night. The club, as ever, maintain that they are just itching to move to wonderful new facilities but are held back by the slow speed of the council search for a suitable location as well as their associated decision making processes. This is, nonetheless, rumoured to be unlikely as the contract conditions that the BSI allegedly negotiated with Pat Bliss, the previous owner of the speedway licence, includes another payment ('tranche' I believe is the word that they use in corporate speak) for her if this move happens before the end of 2007. While the apparently impossible can happen in life and even in the Reading area – the football club playing in the Premier League is illustration enough of how fortunes can change dramatically – 2008 will be the earliest that this move will happen. As a long-time Reading fan I remain sceptical and many supporters still had hair when such a move was first mooted.

Until then the club will just have to make do and mend with Smallmead. One thing that has definitely altered beyond all recognition is the track itself – notably the surface if not necessarily the amount of shale that is to be found on it. The dip into bend 1 has been completely eliminated and the amount of new tractor equipment to maintain and repair it has increased exponentially. As I walk the hallowed damp surface with Chris, I appreciate for the first time, after many decades spectating here, that it has many more contours, slopes and bevels that affect its basic topology. I quickly gather from Chris as we wander round the track that he prefers to do his work as unobtrusively but professionally as possible on race night. While some referees make the point of ostentatiously chatting with the riders, Chris prefers to have a brief polite chat with the promoters and managers, but remain largely detached from the riders[1] and instead devote his time to the many essential preparatory tasks that have to be gone through in the stadium environs generally and much more specifically with the equipment in the referee's box essential to his work later. It's very noticeable that he has a lot of time and affinity with the track staff, the various officials, ground staff and various other personnel that work in the pits from the Clerk of the Course to the Machine Examiner. They are an apparently friendly bunch and he is well received. After a review of the pits, the changing rooms, showers and various other bits of equipment, Chris even ventures out onto the centre green to check that the supervisor of the St John Ambulance staff is experienced in the ways of potential medical requirements at speedway meetings. This mystifies the St John person in question we accost "you know no other referee has ever come out here to see me before and I've been here five years". Nonetheless this is illustrative of Chris's thorough approach to his work. With everyone he's personable and friendly which creates a professional but respectful atmosphere for the work of the evening ahead.

Along with the arrival of the air fences and a PA system that actually works and is audible throughout the stadium, the most visible change brought on by the arrival of BSI at Reading speedway is the giant rider photographs cum signs that adorn each individual rider's station in the pits. The changing rooms and shower areas have also been completely rebuilt to a modern standard and presentationally the stadium has been generally tidied or prettied up. Even the derelict grandstand on the back straight appears more spick and span, albeit cosmetically since it remains out of use for all Reading fixtures. Elsewhere these BSI-instituted developments have only extended to a presentational lick of paint on the stadium wall and the closure of the first-bend toilet block. Inside the main grandstand, the toilet dryers now work every week but the basic infrastructure remains exactly as it was in terms of layout and its careworn, well-used appearance.

Another innovation transplanted from the world of motor racing by John Postlethwaite at Reading this year has been the appointment of Sam Ermolenko to the newly created role within speedway circles of "Sporting Director".[2] He has been

[1] Though I already know that he is always keen to advise and help the younger riders – see my Plymouth and Scunthorpe chapters.

employed to attend to all the backroom activities – bike preparation, set ups, rider psychology and general logistics – while the experienced Jim Lynch gets on with the key tasks of his dual role as promoter and team manager. There is a strong sense that Reading are top heavy on the management side and that this aspect of the club has been over-engineered and incurs premium expenses. Sam's arrival is either a wonderful addition and innovation or else it's as useful as a second bride at a wedding, plus there have been regular mutterings that he should decide which camp he really wants to be in – whether he is the "Director" or still wants to remain one of the lads. Whatever the reality of the situation, there's no doubt that the experience of Jim and Sam costs serious money as does the squad of top-quality riders the Racerdogs have assembled – this is another area of investment authorised by John Postlethwaite. It was a shrewd decision by Postlethwaite to employ a team of gifted, star riders for the vital first season under the new 'Bulldogs' imprimatur and they have fully justified their reportedly high wages with great results on the track that finds the team in prime position to qualify for and succeed in the play-offs. It's the best group of riders that have been on display at Smallmead for many long years – though there have always been superstars, the Reading crowd has taken to the journeymen and triers with equal fervour – and is one that the home crowd can really be proud of should they decide to turn up in the sufficient numbers that the BSI business plan allegedly (rather optimistically) projected before the season started. Only weeks ago, John Postlethwaite took the unusual step of washing the dirty laundry of his disappointing attendance figures in public in the pages of the *Speedway Star*. An astonishing decision by any speedway club owner never mind the most media-savvy one of his generation and one well schooled in public relations, brand management and marketing. It was a piece that mixed moans, observations and comment. The bottom line was that huge costs far exceeded less-than-budgeted-for revenues. Though much of these should come from the sponsorship activities that the BSI have proven expertise with in Grand Prix circles, it's nonetheless a situation compounded by the fickle Reading public's failure to embrace the BSI revolution at Smallmead by consistently ploughing through the turnstiles on a regular basis. Crowd numbers at the meetings I have been to this season have perhaps been slightly higher than last year but not significantly so, and (generous) rumours that attendances average below 1000 paying customers are given visual credence every week I have been. Basic due diligence procedures would surely have quickly thrown up the issue of low average crowd numbers during the purchase process of the previous winter, along with many other important facts crucial to the financial success of the club, if this particular aspect of the speedway licence purchase had followed the traditional business practice you would have expected from a media organisation like the BSI that prides itself on its own contractual savvy and professionalism. Like a marriage in haste, there would be many things for the BSI to repent at leisure. Since his outburst, John Postlethwaite should be happier as crowds have reputedly improved, though I'm sure still not to the levels that he'd like or initially budgeted for in his business plan.

You should always speak as you find and while in the pits I overhear John Postlethwaite speak for the first time in person. I will respect his confidence (and not divulge what sounded like perfectly reasonable complaints about the BSPA and SCB) but I must say that I was thoroughly impressed with his knowledge, passion, and some unexpected flashes of humour as well as his overall enthusiasm. I didn't want or expect to but that was definitely my favourable impression. I wouldn't say that I agreed with some of his perspectives but clearly to see him solely in terms of ego and platitudes is to miss something important about him. Let's hope that his approach and plans for Reading speedway and the Grand Prix series genuinely chimes with other promoters and, more importantly, the general public for the overall benefit of British Speedway. If the impact of his arrival (and others like him) is that the sport can reap benefits for all levels of speedway, we hopefully might avoid his possibly painful prediction for the future that "speedway must change or die". Throughout this chat, because of their respective height differences and proximity, Jim Lynch and John Postlethwaite appear together like a speedway version of Basil Brush and Mr Rodney (or Mr Derek). All that is needed is a quick burst of "Boom! Boom!" for this impression to be completely confirmed.

Back in the referee's box it's very noticeable that you get a superb outlook onto the whole track and wonderful panoramic view of the start/finish line as well as over the outlying area that surrounds the stadium. To get to the box, you have to climb up some steep stairs from the grandstand bar area and then you find yourself thrown back in time to the prefabricated construction style of the 70s in terms of décor and comfort. Spartan would be a word that springs to mind,

---

[2] Interestingly Sam had already had his contract terminated by this point due to a BSI cost-cutting measure. But Sam, keen not to have his "sacking" tarnish his proud career, choose to keep a lid on it and continued to fulfil the role in an unpaid capacity so as to make it appear he had finished the job he set out to do and retain his own personal reputation.

as would shop-soiled, but then so would completely fit-for-purpose. I'd definitely see it as in character with the gradual transformation through extensive wear over the years of all of the stadium furniture and infrastructure. Another very noticeable aspect is the hand-written sign scrawled on the wall above the window of the box that says in large black letters "READING BULLSHITS". I'm not exactly sure why but I suspect that this might have been written by someone disgruntled with recent changes in the management and ethos at Smallmead. It's difficult to point the finger of suspicion at any one disgruntled Reading speedway fan as there have been so many to choose from – though the number of naysayers have now dramatically declined now that the club has continued to enjoy a renaissance on the track. Their vociferousness has subsided but then they haven't really had any forum to complain from, to or in as the *Reading Evening Post* and *BBC Radio Berkshire* both enjoy close links with the club, the club website doesn't deign to stoop to such debate and the *Speedway Star* doesn't provide any sort of outlet other than the letters page. That said, they did recently publish a letter from long-time, loyal club announcer and Reading Racers man through and through, Dave Stallworthy, who excoriated the weakness of this contemporary version of the club's management. It's a view given greater weight by his long service at the club albeit slightly mitigated by the fact of his recent resignation in pique on principle. Allegedly this was after his discovery upon arrival at Smallmead during the World Cup earlier this summer that he had been temporarily relieved of his regular announcer duties on the microphone in favour of the always smooth Kevin Coombes. If not communicated well, this sudden change of responsibilities would understandably peeve many people had it happened to them at their place of employment.

The box itself is cosily crowded. Cosily all within its narrow confines, there's Chris the referee, the man in charge of musical interludes, Tadley-based Paul Hunsdon and the *Evening Post*'s doyen of sports reporting in general and speedway in particular, the avuncular Dave Wright. He watches silently and unobtrusively throughout at the back of the box and is old school enough to eschew a laptop in favour of copious quantities of shorthand.

Both line-ups had a peculiar look with Todd Wiltshire in for Greg Hancock and Mark Loram in for Scott Nicholls along with rider replacement also in operation for the injured Rory Schlein. These choices would then be a factor in the final result but not before we were served a superb exhibition of speedway as well as a tactical masterclass conducted by the experienced Bees team manager, Colin Pratt (on his own tonight with Peter Oakes engaged with his young British rider development duties elsewhere). Beforehand in the pits, Colin kept himself to himself and got on with his job unobtrusively as well as eschewing the larger-than-life approach taken by the 'hail fellow, well met' surfeit of managerial types from his competitors who proprietarily bustle with considerable self-importance about their own section of the pits. A man of few words, he prefers to do his talking on the track. Once Chris Gay has put the riders under orders "Growler" (as Colin is affectionately known) completely comes alive and stays thoroughly engaged in the moment. No sooner do the Bees have an illusory concern about movement at the start line – not the case at all, if judged from my vantage point behind Chris's shoulder – than Growler is standing right by it to ostentatiously stare at the tapes and any wheels that might dare to move under the glare of his additional supervision. Though he doesn't glance up to stare at the referee's box, he doesn't need to as the mere fact that he has walked over from the pits to make the point that he is there to (omnisciently) watch would be more than enough to put most referees on their metaphorical toes. Chris matter-of-factly notes in deadpan fashion, "I see Growler's watching".

A spectacular fall for Travis McGowan in Heat 3 allows the Bees to establish an early lead helped in no same measure by the new version of team riding that the Racerdogs seem keen to hone to perfection throughout the night. Namely, both riders compete for exactly the same spot of the track on the first bend, get massively in each other's way and thereby distract themselves enough to enable their opponents to easily escape. In this instance, such shenanigans also earn an exclusion for the fallen McGowan. In the box, announcer Paul Hunsdon groans before he notes that the McGowan-Gjedde combination notoriously like to clash and fumble together in this manner and their continued use together by Jim Lynch mystifies him. Without the usual support and encouragement that he enjoys from Greg Hancock, the popular Australian endures a shocker of a night that has him only gain a solitary point from four rides. At the start of Heat 4, Billy Janniro had run Zagar wide on the first bend which, from the neutral's point of view, is the ideal start as it makes Matej fight his way through from the back rather than just roar away to victory. The Slovenian tracks Jacek Rempala – who started well only to trail off by the end of the meeting – for two laps inches from his back wheel before he glides past and then shoots away to win easily. Nonetheless, the Bees hold an early lead until the first of an expected stream of Racerdogs 5-1s occurs in Heat 6, but then immediately stops again.

The new form of team riding has become infectious since Zagar and Lemon decide to practise their own version of it on the first bend of Heat 7, which enables the noticeably zippy Chris Harris to escape for his second win of the night. Movement at the tapes causes a restart at the beginning of Heat 8 and a warning for a Racerdogs rider – Janusz Kolodziej – where, from my excellent vantage point I would say that both sets of riders were arguably guilty of this transgression within an almost indistinguishable fraction of a second of each other. Whether the chicken or the egg came first, the Bulldogs mascot chooses the egg to blame and clearly isn't happy but dressed in a giant animal suit doesn't have the grace or communicational subtlety of Growler. The mascot would be excoriated for heinous over-acting if he had behaved like this in a drama improvisation class, let alone as he implores upwards to the box and shakes the yellow flag by the start line vigorously to indicate that Jacek Rempala also moved. Chris Gay remains impassive and just gets on with the various refereeing tasks at hand, including the paperwork bane that afflicts even sports officials nowadays, and by his complete lack of reaction thereby communicates the necessary air of impartiality that an official requires to assert their control of proceedings. Nonetheless, it's a decision that motivates the Racerdogs to power to another 5-1 and find themselves set fair in a comfortable lead at 27-21, a position from which recent history now dictates they will now kick on and stride to the widely expected victory the home faithful have started to become used to. However, the Bees apparently haven't read the script as not only does Smolinski easily lead and win an exciting Heat 9 but Loram uses two laps to size up Gjedde – he harries his back wheel throughout which causes Gjedde to continually glance over his shoulder as he just about manages to hold him off with great aggression, blocking manoeuvres and foresight before he's inevitably passed. It's a pass compounded when McGowan then drifts wide on bend 2 of the last lap to allow Loram past and for the Bees to seize a 5-1. The Bees follow this with a 2-4 in the next heat to tie the scores after another win for the breezy Chris Harris. While the lead alternates from this point, in the form of Loram and Harris, the Bees always seem to have the edge ably supported by a team of riders who have a real desire to win and, apparently, something still in reserve.

It finally all comes down to Heat 15 with the scores level at 42 each and we're to witness the Zagar-Gjedde combination do battle with the Loram-Harris one. Growler is back and hovers at the line to watch the riders at the tapes for possible illegal movement, possibly for its potential psychological effect upon the Racerdogs riders but also the referee. While Harris flies off, Loram is relegated to the back by the apparently immovable force that is the Racerdogs pair of Zagar and Gjedde. Completely engaged in the moment, Growler almost gambols across the centre green to watch from the third bend where his whole body is seized with a varied range of extremely animated tics and gestures, not quite calypso fever but expressive, by his usually reticent standards. Mark Loram, who already knows that he has the psychological hex over him, proceeds to harry Charlie Gjedde enough over the closing two speedy laps to force an inevitable mistake and thereby pass him for a vital third place just as the riders cross the line. Growler ecstatically leaps in the air in celebration and repeatedly thrusts his arms into the air in exultation. Exultant Colin gambols back to the pits gate with his arms aloft in the manner of a champion prize fighter and it's a reaction that betrays the air of studied equanimity that he often tries to project to mask the zealously competitive spirit that invariably burns strongly beneath. His unalloyed joy at a narrow 44-46 win isn't shared where I am in the Reading referee's box where glum faces and a murmured resignation rules since silly thrown away points cost the Racerdogs dear tonight.

The work of the referee doesn't finish with the last race, as there's all the paperwork to complete and yet another trip over to the pits. I leave Chris deep in conversation with the friendly but pragmatic Jim Lynch. While the "Postlethwaite revolution" musters itself to storm force but still blows a good rate throughout speedway and Reading, one irksome 'Spanish custom' that has been retained by the Racerdogs is the re-use of programmes after a rain-off. Tonight's programme costs £2.50 but only has a black and white folded insert for a full-colour programme. This contains the race card, the fixture list and a message from JP that stops short of identifying the need to find a ley line or an instruction to burn joss sticks but nonetheless blathers on in new-age management speak fashion about the necessity to "focus our energies". Thumbing through his well-worked motivational phrase book, he informs us that possible success is "tantalisingly close", though it remains a "tall order" that still requires "heads" to be kept together. JP acknowledges "speculation and comment" about future plans (i.e. will the reportedly below-par revenue performance of BSI Reading mean that there will be no Elite League team here next season?) but teases with the promise of eventual, but as yet unspecified, answers in the future. The ladies who work at the stadium interrupt Jim Lynch in mid-analysis of the night when they call out to him "tonight's programme is a disgrace, it's a rip-off and shouldn't be allowed". Ever professional Jim thanks them for their feedback and wishes them a safe journey home. The crowds have long gone so I decide to leave Jim to identify to Chris how to put the ills of the

Paco in the Arena track shop. © Jeff Scott

Kath Pope brings new bespoke 'Scary Monster' sash for Sheila.
© Jeff Scott

speedway world to possible rights and join them on the road home.

4th September Reading v Coventry (ELB) 44-46

Scary Mk II
6th September

The Arena Essex raceway has been the happiest hunting ground on all my travels for sales of my book. This is due to the tireless promotional efforts of the dynamic and energetic 'Scary' Sheila Le-Sage who I think must, by now, have told every single Arena fan about the book and the fact that she appears in it on page 118. I have always found it a friendly and welcoming place. I've been so often now that it's even more so. However, I can't say that I relish the queues that build up before the Dartford Tunnel. Today's delay starts a mere four miles from the toll barriers and is a comparative not even worth talking about grunky stop-start delay of only 30 minutes. I have even invested in a prepaid 'Dart Tag' that speeds me through the barriers without the need for money and a saving of 6p per journey. They say that if you look after the pennies but produce a speedway book, the pounds just flood out of your bank, well, so I've found. I've arrived so early that the front gates are still locked! Luckily I now know where the less well known other entrance gate is located so enter by the back way and have enough time to park up, relax and listen to a fascinating Radio 4 programme ('Thinking Allowed') on the Swedish Social Model and skateboarding asylum seekers.

When I rouse myself from the car I find Eve Russell busy as ever located in one of the two nerve centres of operations at Arena on race night, in her case the Speedway Office. Ronnie is at the other nerve centre – the pits – or, to be accurate, he presently supervises track preparations. Unlike some of my other recent visits, it's very sunny and the track needs a thorough dousing with water from the bowser. Eve is hopeful that the weather and the chance to see Jason Crump, the newly crowned 2006 World Champion will provoke the legions of wavering or stay away supporters within the Arena fan base to consider a trip along to watch the speedway tonight. I've been so often to the Raceway now that Eve no longer seems surprised to see me or mystified as to who I am. I mention in passing to her that the fans are always friendly and curious here, "nosey more like" she jokes before she resumes the concentrated preparations I've interrupted.

Alf Weedon's track shop remains comprehensively shuttered though outside there is already a large sealed packet of the latest edition of the *Speedway Star*, while just down the arcade of shops that line the grandstand at the Thurrock raceway a neighbouring sweet shop is being restocked from a large van. There's an impressively large display of really bad-for-teeth sweets. I prefer the synthetic really bad-for-you sweets specifically aimed at children with their garish colours, unusual shapes, all loaded with 'E' numbers. These have come from the cash-and-carry or confectionery heaven, as most children would doubtless see it. I think I am safe in saying that Arena Essex boasts the best sweet shop in British Speedway. The deservedly well-renowned café is already open for business and already has a few customers inside who enjoy its filling fare.

Minutes later Alf arrives with his son-in-law Paco who speaks in a manner slightly reminiscent of Harry Enfield's legendary Stavros character. Alf is very particular about the way he'd like the track shop set up and laid out. He barks out often contradictory or unclear instruction to Paco, who is definitely there to help and assist in the same way that Alf is there to continually advise, admonish and correct real or perceived errors. They are clearly very familiar with each other's company and bicker in an absent-minded manner that suggests they're no longer aware that they do this. Paco wants to move the car but Alf is insistent it remains there "until six"; though a short while later he changes his mind and then decides to move it elsewhere.

This gives me the chance to chat to Paco as he enjoys the silence and rests on a stool behind the counter while he flicks through *Reading Evening Post/Backtrack* in a distracted and desultory fashion. He is a matter-of-fact, down-to-earth man who has been around the track shop trade since the golden era of the 1970s. It was a time of huge crowds and similarly huge sales of the *Speedway Star*. Back then Paco had quite an itinerary every week and he remembers it fondly, "the bundles just used to fly out – I would sell them as soon as I could pick them up – you'd sit there and sell". It was a fixed weekly schedule that took in Arena on a Thursday (300 sold), Hackney on a Friday (400 sold), and Canterbury the next day (400 sold) with the highlight of the week at Newport on a Sunday (1300 sold). "They used to get crowds of 4 or 5000 – I made 10p a copy so I got £130 for Newport which was a lot of money then – I used to get paid more than the riders!" These were phenomenal sales and understandably Paco isn't that enamoured or impressed with the decline cum malaise that has affected the crowds and the concomitant purchasing power of contemporary speedway "It's really not the same any more, is it?"

He solves the puzzle of the mystery as to the whereabouts of the charming Tom Woolhead who has been noticeably absent from the track shop on my last few visits. "He didn't want to do the Sundays at the stock car meetings but only the Wednesdays – it's a two-day job and you want to do it or you don't! You can't pick and choose so Alf got rid of him". Paco then claims that Tom "works here on the track or somint" but I find absolutely no sign that this is the case. His claim of Tom's employment elsewhere in the stadium appears to be an urban myth though rumours of great wealth stashed away chez Alf probably isn't if Paco's comments are given credence, "I don't know why he doesn't stop and do somint he wants – he couldn't spend all the money he has in another lifetime, why he keeps comin' here I dunno, he's getting dangerous in that car". When I ask incredulously, "Does he drive on the M25 in rush hour?" Paco snorts, "How the freak else does he get here?" To my untrained eyes the bodywork of the car did look undamaged when I glanced at it earlier. The only thing that really stood out of note on the vehicle was his personalised number plate. Alf's return cuts short our conversation and I retreat back to my own table of books that Alf has again very kindly suggested I place next to his shop. Once more, at Alf's instruction, I also display a selection of other speedway books that are stocked in the shop and Alf is especially keen that I display the 2007 *Speedway Star* calendar. The turnstiles have yet to open but there are a few cars gathered in the giant car park since the main gates have now been unlocked, so the public can gain easy access from the nearby service station roundabout and have their early choice of parking position. This particular service station isn't one of my favourites – and since I did this book and toured round with it I have had the chance to have a close encounter with motorway and A road "rest areas" (as our American friends would style them) throughout the country so I feel I'm becoming quite an expert. I definitely favour the Arena car park every time except, of course, for its lack of toilets and the requisite baby-changing facilities.

When Alf returns he fusses round the shop to check that everything is as it should be and that Paco has presented everything correctly and hasn't altered the presentation of the displays while he's been away to park the car. After all these additional checks are complete, Alf finally settles down for a cup of tea on his chair in the cupboard. I leaf through the huge pile of unsold photographs from previous seasons that are prominently displayed and on sale for a bargain 20p a photo. When I ask Alf why there are so many, he replies, "if they've got no personality the photo's don't sell!" I choose some quirky shots of the apparently personality-less riders; these include Kelvin Tatum, Chalky White, Dean Barker in his brief Hammers incarnation, resplendent with red and blonde hair dye and a rider with impressively prominent ears whose name momentarily escapes Alf.

Ever on the look out for ways to promote the club to its own fans or to make them feel good about themselves or close to the riders, Ronnie Russell has organised another 'Meet the Rider' session before the meeting right by where everyone has to come in through the turnstiles. Quite who the rider on display is tonight I'm not sure as the bike is already there but the rider isn't, sensibly enough since the turnstiles remain resolutely shut and the car park remains defiantly almost completely empty. Ronnie is always friendly and keen to help me, "why don't you go down to the pits and get Jason Crump to autograph one of your books? It's not often you get the chance to have the new World Champion sign one of your books just days after he's won the crown. It should help get interest – for that one at least". Quite how it'll boost sales, I'm not sure, but I'm very appreciative of RR's advice and concern so I hotfoot it down to see Jason. Down in the pits, Jason is happy to sign my book – two, in fact – and you don't have to be a great student of human nature to figure out that he wants to keep our interaction to a minimum and our conversation at the polite level of precisely nil. On my way back to my table by the main grandstand with a couple of signed books I'm proud to have, but not quite sure what to do with, I bump into three generations of the Chappell family, not difficult to do as they're all here together tonight. There's grandmother Joyce, proud mother Janet and young, gifted official Arena Essex photographer Karen. While Alf is still the photographer king around these parts, albeit an ageing less mobile one than previously, a quick glance at the programme reveals that the Hammers have an astonishing SEVEN official photographers. That's one for every rider or, actually, thinking about the injury jinx that has cursed the club these last few years, there will often potentially be more photographers in action than riders! At least, with all the notable action shots during any meeting at Thurrock, hopefully, there's a good chance they will be caught on film or whatever we are now to call this in a digital age. Karen is the youngest of the seven track photographers at Arena and I'd imagine throughout the rest of the country. I have observed her quite a few times now at various tracks, so I know that she's very dedicated, keen as mustard and also a young but skilled practitioner of this art. Like all teenagers, she is incredibly reluctant to have her own photo taken though, except for the one that appears on her business card that proudly announces her as a "Freelance Motorsports Photographer".

Now that I'm back outside the track shop, it doesn't take long for the 'new Tom' to arrive. In fact, the 'new Tom, is the mother and daughter combination of Justine and Zoe. Daughter Zoe is camera shy but her mother is definitely not! In fact I had met them before on my last visit but didn't know that they now worked at the track shop every week. They're both very friendly ladies, personable with the customers and efficient. I still miss Tom though – a very genuine man. The fans understandably seem to be quite enamoured with daughter Zoe and there appears to be a lot more fans who loiter and browse without making a purchase at the shop! The same can also be said for my book display table, which is even less flattered with the custom. While many people say 'hello' and stop to chat they've mostly already got the book or have previously decided against it. 'Scary' has done a wonderful job in raising awareness. This evening she has just taken delivery/charge of her specially commissioned new 'SCARY MONSTER' sash in a fetching black with red letters, which coordinates, nicely with her outfit tonight. She already has on a sash that reads 'SCARY MK 1'. Frighteningly, I learn of the existence of 'Scary MK II', Danielle, though Sheila is keen to reassure me, given the shocked look on my face, "she's just like me though she's only 15!" I imagine that she's wildly enthusiastic too but sadly 'Scary MK I' has to leave as she has to concentrate on attempting to get everyone to part with their £2 for a ticket in the supporters' club lucky draw. Before she departs to persuade the Hammers faithful to put their hands in their pockets for a good cause, I'm persuaded to buy one by the charming Scary and choose "Sittingbourne" as my lucky charm. On the subject of the highly regarded speedway club that already exists in that town without need for another, a very smartly dressed Graham Arnold passes. I don't know why I hadn't heard of him before or noticed him here myself but he is the Clerk of the Course at Arena Essex. It's always a pleasant surprise to bump into Graham or any of the friendly and dedicated volunteers from Sittingbourne. It's not at all clear to me why anyone would presume that such a small and comparatively geographically remote town needs another speedway club in the same place. Still, we shall see what eventually transpires.

I glance in the match programme to read the always honest and entertaining column written by Ronnie that this week features his thoughts on some recent Arena away defeats. After he's noted the caveat that the use of tactical riders heavily contributed to a total of 39 points away at Peterborough, he pronounces this a "respectable" achievement in contrast to the performance at Oxford that "was simply not good enough". Although he notes, "when we got to Oxford the track seemed OK but just prior to the start they roughed it up. That made gating even more important and that was a department we failed in." Though "several top visiting riders" have commented on the fairness of the Arena track and its lack of home advantage, Ronnie still specifically rules out any curatorial gamesmanship, "the only way of altering that [renowned fairness] is for me to have our track roughed up with only the home side knowing where the ruts and holes are." RR concludes with a clarion call to the Hammers faithful, "I now need you all to get behind the team as we go for our fourth consecutive home win against that pack of Aces."

Sadly the visitors hold all the cards, so something that we don't get to see tonight is a close contest although a first heat 4-2 for the Hammers flatter to deceive that this meeting might be closer than it actually turns out to be. Any team with Jason Crump in its ranks is bound to do well and he races to an untroubled five race maximum. It never looks at all likely that he will be beaten. Equally, it didn't look that likely full stop that most of the Belle Vue riders will be beaten. Arena only manage to have four race winners on the night – one of these is Steve Johnston in the black and white helmet in Heat 8 along with Joonas Kylmakorpi who triumphs in Heat 11. That race reduces the deficit to 32-37 which is as good as it gets for the Hammers as the Aces switch back up a gear to record three further 1-5s and another 2-4 to run out comfortable winners by 39 points to 56.

It is a miserable night on the track for the Hammers and a miserable night off it for me in terms of the level of book sales of *Showered in Shale* (two), though some of the other books on display on my table (along with the calendar) sell well. I also haven't bought the winning raffle ticket, so I pack up my things and beat a hasty retreat after I say goodbye to Scary MK I though without laying eyes on the Scary MK II version! I'm looking forward to that another time and, if she's anything like as dynamic as the eponymous Sheila, I'm sure to notice this whirlwind.

6th September Arena v Belle Vue (Elite League B) 39-56

"Back with a Bang" at Shaun Tacey's Testimonial
10th September
As soon as I arrive through the pits gate at Mildenhall Stadium at around 9.30 a.m. I have already gathered from the bleary expressions on everyone's faces that a great night has been had by all the previous evening at the disco cum party preceding Shaun Tacey's big day. There is a school of thought that says you should make sure that you celebrate after your testimonial but, like so many things on the day, the whole event has been organised to be both memorable and fun for all concerned. While many people have helped – and beforehand Shaun has "promoted the event himself" with an extensive travel schedule that took in personal visits to tracks, markets, Tescos, Sainsbury's, car boot sales and other events, including grass tracking, throughout the country in order to try to make it a well-attended success – the person I have dealt with the most since early in the summer is the tireless, cheerful and enthusiastic Lynn Hunt. She has been relentlessly energetic, extremely well organised and completely committed to making the day a success in terms of the complex logistics of the thing as well as, hopefully, financially at the end of the day for Shaun. I imagine it's a thankless, draining and sometimes a nightmarish task but one that she has consistently borne with good humour. Every testimonial needs its own Lynn and, like Alan Partridge, Shaun is lucky to have one like her who'll work so tirelessly and capably on his behalf. Not that she has done anything other than be dismissively modest about her own efforts and instead prefers to (justifiably) praise everyone else's efforts to make the testimonial a roaring triumph every time I speak to her or sympathise about the demands of organising such an event! She has a good sense of humour that verges on the wicked and disrespectful, if the fact that she has already identified me as a bit of a dumbo and so christened me "Blondie" in our regular email exchanges is anything to judge it by.

It's to be applauded that speedway has a testimonial system that enables riders to raise a one-off sum that reflects their service to the sport, though sometimes you have to wonder how some of these riders have exactly been chosen. The fact that Shaun has qualified for such an event raises no such qualms. Unfortunately any testimonial can be hit and miss in terms of the key variables of the weather and size of the crowd that actually turns up. Shaun has gone for a big party the night before the meeting itself and then an auction. The weather gods have looked kindly upon him as it promises to be a hot and sunny day if the strength of the warm morning sunshine is any indication. I'm delighted to have a stall at this event and just to be here as Shaun was one of the loveliest, most genuine of people that I met last year on my travels to research *Showered in Shale*. It's quite an achievement for Shaun to stand out when in fact I met so many delightful speedway people. He is the first person I clap eyes on when I arrive. He's rootling about in his van for something and though he clearly has had a late night, he's his usual ebullient and cheerful self. I nod at the empty car park and a few of the bleary, walking wounded that are slowly emerging from their tents and vans to say "Lynn told me that you wanted all the stallholders here and set up by 10 a.m." He smiles and shakes his head in resigned but nonchalant fashion, "I wish everyone else freakin' had – though it was never going to be a quiet night with Billy Janniro around!" After the night that was, it would be easier to arrive fresh at the West Row stadium from Brighton on the south coast than from the stadium car park or Mildenhall for those who took part in a "great night". The evening had started modestly enough with the Latvian round of the Grand Prix series shown on the telly in the bar. Many had stayed on after the Mildenhall v Somerset fixture at the track last night while other fans and riders had gradually filtered along to the party in the bar to join the celebrations once their meetings had ended in other parts of the country but, most notably, from the Conference League Riders Championship at comparatively nearby Rye House. A boisterous rider who shall remain nameless had, in his cups, started up his bike at 1 a.m. ("it was pretty loud") and these celebrations carried on "until the bar threw everyone out at 3 a.m., though many were still up at 4 a.m." It was clearly going to be a constitutionally demanding day for some riders after their fun of the night before.

Inside the stadium the track was already a hive of activity and for the 28 races that were going to happen this afternoon, Shaun had secured the services of renowned track curator Huggy from nearby King's Lynn. Like many people at the testimonial he showed dedication well beyond the call of duty. He was out on the track as soon as the Saturday afternoon meeting between the Tigers and the Rebels had finished to groom it until 9 p.m. when he then joined the party. Despite the fact that he fully enjoyed himself like everyone else, he was right back to his track curatorial duties first thing this morning to try to prepare an excellent racing surface to withstand the severe pummelling it was about to suffer. Speedway is a sport that usually only has guest riders take to the track rather than guest curators! With his efforts, everyone is very confident the track will be in tiptop condition for a demanding afternoon where it will have to withstand 120 laps of racing. During the season its variable condition hasn't always ensured enjoyable meetings to watch or ride in and consequently it has rarely garnered universally favourable comments. Only last night the Mildenhall Tigers rode to another home defeat, this time at the hands of Somerset, to some further mutterings about conditions. The main grandstand and pits area is still covered in the rubbish and detritus that is inevitably left behind after any meeting. It's still too soon after the night before for anyone to have got round to cleaning up yet, except for Michael – the enthusiastic, friendly and autistic young man who attends every Mildenhall fixture and that I originally met with his parents at Rye House earlier in the year. They told me that he loves speedway and has a keen desire for "order" in almost equal measure. The two go together well with his relentless and engaging curiosity. He is talking to himself and tutting at the sight of the pits area that greeted us both. I take a few trips to ferry my stuff from the car park to the grandstand, while he has taken to frenetically tidying the pits of discarded items. He removes used tyres and neatly stacks them by the stadium wall, and collects abandoned containers, glass and plastic bottles and anything else that offends his sense of proprietary or his keen desire for pristine presentation and symmetrical order throughout this area.

Laurence Rogers is also already at work and is another person who has given considerable time and helps behind the scenes. Just like Lynn, he's also keen to modestly stress the dedicated work of others. For example, he noted that Dingle Brown had yesterday volunteered to pick up the trophies to be awarded this afternoon from the factory in St Ives. He gestures over towards Huggy who is hard at work on the track and though crowd numbers are in the lap of the gods, Laurence takes consolation in the fact, "it's been well promoted, which is more than you can say for many meetings!" This afternoon there will also be guest start-line girls – the so-called "start tarts" from King's Lynn. Laurence is just about to set off to collect them though he's already aware that he will have to travel there by a circuitous route since an accident has blocked the usual main road route there (every road this season leads to Lynn). Such are the trials and tribulations of responsibility, I nonetheless imagine that this is the type of task for which there would be no shortage of willing volunteers keen to share some time with these young women. Even working at the start line is getting competitive nowadays! It's a shame that the Mildenhall Grid Girls aren't displaying their skills this afternoon as I always enjoy seeing them at work (despite the misapprehended impression to the contrary gained by Tigers Press Officer David Crane from his own pre-publication reading of my Mildenhall chapter in *Showered in Shale*). On their website afterwards the Grid Girls congratulate the Lynn ladies on their efforts and overall performance of their duties at the meeting.

Lynn has had very little sleep but, unlike some of the riders and fans, she made a very early start, had a big breakfast to set her up for the day and has been a whirlwind of dynamism (albeit a calm one) about the stadium ever since. Her keenness that the day is a success for Shaun is palpable. To her mind, Shaun has shown "a lot of dedication – he's a real person that's done so much himself to promote it, often you only get a glimpse of the rider and 45 other people do it for you – but not Shaun!" It's difficult to gainsay her comment that Shaun "is a rider of the people – plus he's a lovely bloke, a great father but just not very good with women; don't say I said that, though it's true!" Inevitably there have been some last-minute problems and disappointments. Despite repeated chasing by Lynn in the months beforehand, there have been a number of unforeseen last-minute problems, for example, with the supply of rider goggles that have been advertised as a giveaway to the crowd. Even more irksome – and I'm summarising politely here – has been the unexpected late withdrawal of some recalcitrant riders who have been booked for months, advertised as riding and then have disappointingly dropped out of the event at the very last moment. Some have believable and reasonable excuses whereas other definitely do not! The riders who withdrew so late were Craig Boyce, David Howe, Richard Hall and Glenn Cunningham ("though he definitely has a stomach bug"). However, in speedway as in show business, the show must go on which, in the case of the racing itself, now features welcome replacements in the form of Mark Baseby, Dan Giffard, Andrew Bargh and Gary Cottham. Whatever happens, Lynn isn't going to let anything distract her from the work and tasks at hand or allow anything to take the shine off her day until everything has been completed. She walks off determinedly and remains amazingly cheerful and unfazed. In the programme Shaun gives "a big thank you to Lynn Hunt who has been working at this for me for months and months arranging sponsors, planning this and planning that. It's not been easy and we've had our ups and downs, differences of opinion and the like but on the whole we've been on the same wavelength and today it's all come to fruition".

Back in the shade of the main grandstand, the always friendly Johnny Barber has arrived early as instructed (as he always would anyway) and has already started to unload his van of equipment, stock and memorabilia. Like most weeks at Mildenhall, Michael is already there in close attendance with him to follow his every step and fire a stream of curious but often rhetorical questions at Johnny. He is thoroughly fascinated by and enthralled with the special "£2 bumper lucky dip" cellophane-wrapped gift packs that have been prepared for sale today. After much careful study and lengthy consideration, Michael identifies the two particular packs that he wants and then hides them at the bottom of the lucky dip, "they're my ones, I'll come back and buy them later". For the next few hours, Michael comes back to repeatedly examine that "his" packs still remain though once a crowd gathers by the track shop the worry that they might get sold becomes all too much and he has to buy them to make absolutely sure that he will possess his choice. Like me John has arrived very early, but unlike me, appears to know absolutely everyone who passes. At every track where I see Johnny work, he always appears to talk at length with the most attractive young women. Today is no exception and he chats amiably at great length with Daniel King's attractive young girlfriend Clara Bunting. They clearly get on extremely well and in their topics of conversation range widely from Daniel to track gossip and various in-jokes or people I haven't heard of.

Hard at work all around us as we set up was Carl Harris, the often unfairly maligned (by Tigers fans and Mick Horton) Mildenhall Stadium landlord who was unobtrusively hard at it picking up the rubbish and debris left from Saturday night from off the terraces. All this was after he'd cleared the bar (not an inconsiderable task!), something he started at 9 a.m. though he hadn't left the bar until 5 a.m.! Afterwards Lynn commented that Carl "was totally committed and helpful throughout our dealings with him for the testimonial – he really wanted the day to be perfect".

In the shade at the back of the first-bend grandstand, we have a great location from which to watch the racing and to have a panoramic view of all that is going on at the track. Now that everyone has finally managed to get up and rouse themselves into action, it's amazing how quickly the stadium gets tidied and the track and pits area is readied, in professional fashion, for the arrival of the fans through the turnstiles for the afternoon's racing. In the pits Shaun instructs the stadium announcer about the style of music he'd prefer this afternoon, "the louder the better!" When it's your big event you can demand what you want ("it's my party and I'll cry if I want to") and Shaun is definitely keen to emphasise that the musical accompaniment

Race suits warm in the sunshine. © Jeff Scott

Peggy models Arena doggie jacket. © Jeff Scott

The riders muster. © Jeff Scott

for his testimonial should be "fashionable" and that he'd be happy if the swearword count on the tracks played is upped massively. I don't think that this means Cradle of Filth. However, the announcer pulls a face, "shame we only brought vinyl then." With much more to look into, check or supervise, Shaun strides past purposefully looking slightly hassled and feels that it's going well "so so, so far". Close by, stood by the track fence Dick Swales looks with admiration as Huggy executes yet another perfect pirouette on his tractor as he continues to grade the track to perfection and comments wistfully in a what-might-have-been-manner, "I'm only allowed to water the track". Later it's reported that the riders claim: "It's the best condition that it has been all season".

Back at the track shop the always smartly dressed presenter Kevin Long has arrived and is deep in conversation with Johnny. With his look and demeanour, he wouldn't be out of place on the *Generation Game* and effortlessly combines in one person the attitudinal approach to presentation of Bruce Forsyth and Larry Grayson. When I ask him to describe his approach to his work, he has his tongue firmly in his cheek (and luckily no one else's, though I'm sure he has a few riders in mind should the opportunity present itself), "I'm the cheapest-smartest-most-sarcastic-most-intelligent presenter. I don't have rivals – I'm often imitated, never bettered – I am who I am. A fan with a mike". Clearly Kevin is already on top note and up for a long hard afternoon with his modesty chip disabled. "With my work I'm in the hands of the riders. Like me they're here to put on a show – there are the 'great entertainers': Parker, Pedersen, Dugard, Andersen who the crowd always love to watch or love to hate, usually a mix of both". In fact, Kevin is consistently very articulate throughout his presentations and deservedly prides himself on his own linguistic skills. These are in full flow on race day and also, if we're lucky, in his famous 'poems for riders' that, to echo Ernie Wise, 'what he wrote' for special occasions. Kevin also prides himself on his renowned ability to slip as many double entendres as possible into his work and he allegedly judges the success of these by the volume of outraged letters received by prickly, sweaty-bottomed retired colonel type figures who send paeans of disgust about his obscenities to John Louis at the Ipswich Speedway office. Nonetheless, all this bluster is merely an aid to the entertainment and, in reality, hides a sensitive man who is a keen student of speedway, "every rider knows the 'blind spot' on their own home track. At Foxhall, it's the second bend, if you know where – like all the good riders do – you can get away with blue murder and still make it look like it's the other rider's fault. All the Witches greats could do this, though Jeremy 'Donkey' Doncaster was the best ever!" Kevin has an encyclopaedic recall of the history of his beloved Ipswich speedway and delights to recall, especially for me, the year Ipswich beat Eastbourne eight times (though personally, the arrival of the Witches at Smallmead during my teenage years was always more thrilling). Like all writers, in his case poetry, Kevin has suffered for his art and shudders to recall getting totally soaked by Shane Parker with the centre-green hose ("it's sewage water and I was ill for weeks afterwards"). Sadly, by now duty calls to interrupt our talk, though Kevin expects that every rider will be more than happy to talk with him this afternoon because of the type of event that it is, though often riders are reluctant to speak with any stadium announcer, "as there's nothing in it for them or their sponsors, unlike when they're on *Sky* when it's a different story".

By now the turnstiles have opened and every child that enters is presented with an impressive goody bag of such extreme synthetic sweetness that you suspect that the local dentists are secretly involved in their dissemination. They're definitely my favourite type of sweets – sherbet flying saucers, 'E' number loaded chews, lollies, hula hoops and the like – and I make a point to return many times throughout the day to sample them some more purely in the interests of 'research' though, it has to be said, the children cannily and cunningly ravage the unsupervised 'spare' bags much more often than I manage. We're helped in this by the fact that the event has been catered with enough goody bags for about a thousand hungry children. If it's an embarrassment for an adult like me to show such cravings then the group of Old Age Pensioner fans who brazenly collect numerous bags and remain standing to watch the races shamelessly guarding an impressive pile stacked at their feet, feel no compunction about their greedy selfishness. (Maybe this is their way of boasting that they don't have false teeth or have access to excellent denture fixative?) At the top of the stairs that you have to climb to gain access to anywhere within the stadium you have to pass the helpful Norfolk-based Rye House track shop owner, Andy Griggs. He's volunteered to help run the Shaun Tacey merchandise stall that features the "Lightweight Testimonial Jacket (£30), Polo Shirts (£15) and Embroidered Team Tacey Wallets (£5)" among other specially produced items, all manufactured in the speedway-friendly colour of black. He arrived in good time too despite a late night the night before after the CLRC at Rye House and the traditional midnight peril of road works and road closures on his way home. His stall is positioned in an ideal spot close to the popular raffle ticket stall and both attract a crowd. At work on the raffle stall is the outgoing Arena fan Di Farmer who has also kindly sponsored the riders' tyres, goggle giveaway and the sidecar fuel for this afternoon's meeting.

It's just the sort of sunny day that you would imagine would attract a big crowd to such a well-advertised and promoted testimonial; which appears much bigger than the regular Mildenhall Speedway attendance levels, which have varied in range from around 250 to 700 people on my previous trips to watch speedway at West Row. People estimated the testimonial crowd at "just over a thousand" – a great sign of respect for Shaun – and quite a contrast to usual as we all know how worrying Mildenhall promoter Mick Horton finds his regular crowd size if his frequent public grumbles about them are any indicator. Though the meeting will take place at his track, I gather that he's not in attendance today and there are no comments from him in the testimonial programme, so the weekly 'spot the howler' competition will just have to satisfy itself with another rich source in the form of last night's Somerset programme. Anyone who has shown up to support Shaun is treated to a packed afternoon of racing that features an individual meeting of 16 heats and a 12 lap final, along with five heats of sidecar racing and the only appearance by any team in Wimbledon colours for a challenge match against Sittingbourne. It's a meeting that, if Ian Perkin gets his way with his latest speedway ambitions, would be billed as Sittingbourne Crusaders v Sittingbourne Dons in 2007 should the much trumpeted but mostly vague on important detail plans reported in the *Speedway Star* come to fruition. Sadly, Mr Perkin doesn't turn up to watch the only competitive fixture to feature a team representing Wimbledon speedway unlike so many of the other loyal fans of the club who have done, all bedecked with their distinctively coloured regalia or with clothes festooned with Dons badges or logos. From the plc management team, only the experienced and respected Dingle Brown is in attendance this afternoon when he, as usual, expertly manages the team.

No one I meet has an explanation for Ian Perkin's absence. Maybe just like the New Seekers wanted to "teach the world to sing in perfect harmony", many long hours of work probably still have to be done elsewhere on his much-vaunted suitable stadium search and planning permission campaign we've followed throughout the year in the pages of the speedway trade press and internet forums. The club presently needs to persuade a previously reluctant Kent based local planning authority of the thoughtful strength of its suggestion to run more speedway at a stadium in Sittingbourne. Whatever has the attention of this busy man, he hasn't come along to share in the fun of this testimonial. Not that Ian Perkin is in any way missed by the group of long-time Wimbledon fans – Janet Dixson , her dad Craig Mabey and brother Stephen – who briefly congregate by my table, who're mystified that they failed to see him at Plough Lane in the 1970s "Maybe he was there – you always see lots of faces that you know from then, but no one I know can ever remember him! I've asked everyone and we all can't be going senile, not just yet anyway. That said, the crowds were much bigger than for the Conference League so he would have been harder to spot". Lynn, who has welcomed the help and support that Dingle

Warm up begins. © Jeff Scott

A crowded first bend. © Jeff Scott

Smart casual for Peterborough track curator Mick Coleman.
© Jeff Scott

has unstintingly provided for the event in general, then articulates her own considered opinion, "Dingle is the better ambassador for the club anyway, isn't he?" Sadly for the Dons fans that have turned up to watch, Sittingbourne have recently hit a rich vein of form and have gone comparatively triumph crazy. In recent years the Sittingbourne club have suffered so many defeats on the road and generally, that if these particular knights were to go on a crusade they'd probably have wooden spoons to fight with, not swords. But then at Iwade, Sittingbourne speedway is a proper motorcycling club that has always viewed their primary purpose as the development of young rider talent rather than the arbitrary pursuit of so-called Conference League glory. The Crusaders win this friendly fixture 15-21 with a couple of 1-5s in the last two races of this special six-heat encounter. There was a rather protracted heat 4 that had to be re-re-run and, after it was finally over, presenter Kevin winsomely intoned, "something you always have at speedway meetings, the one that won't go away".

The afternoon passes entertainingly on the track but before it all gets under way we're treated to the sight of Shaun's son Vanns as he proudly circles the track on his bike as the testimonial mascot. Before racing commenced we witness "the awesome Harley Davidson parade", which showcased their throaty engines and paraded each rider individually to introduce them to the crowd with appropriate ceremony. Arguably the race of the afternoon is Heat 8, which was a closely fought, tense race throughout and was just won on the line by a determined Leigh Lanham who came from behind to beat Daniel King. All afternoon, and indeed practically everywhere I've seen him race this season, Daniel was in exhilarating form and excited the crowd with the style, speed and prowess of his racing. When interviewed it's a different story and Daniel clearly reserves his oomph for the shale and not the microphone. Kevin tries to inject a note of excitement and future promise into the interview. His question "Are you looking forward to the final later, if you qualify?" elicits a guarded, "Yeah, I guess so" in response.

Another treat to behold was the sidecar racing we witnessed. If speedway riders are mad, then the sidecar riders are cut from the same bonkers cloth, particularly when they were prepared to aggressively race full out on the narrow confines of the West Row circuit. The shortest straw appears to be held by the passenger who has to clamber all over the equipment at high speed or hangs millimetres from the ground. We learn from Kevin that Andy and Laura Kerrison are the "only father and daughter crew riding in Britain", albeit that they do it on a "Belgian licence" and though they come from Luton they are the "Belgian number ones". My impression is that it's preferable to be a few grains short of a sand pit to actually agree to take part in competitive sidecar racing but apparently the daredevil Laura is "part way through a degree". It must make for some interesting conversations in the Student Union bar, sorry I meant the library, for Laura during term time. It's father Andy's farewell season – he is a former speedway rider from the Isle of Wight and is one of the trainers at Sittingbourne – and like the other pairs, they *really* go for it in every race.

During the interval, the glamorous start line girls from King's Lynn disport themselves on the terraces by the pits for a rest and a bite to eat. They have the confidence and beauty of their youth, though they eat convenience food with a gusto that indicates little time for the adage that "a second on the lips is a lifetime on the hips". They understandably attract admiring glances from hot-blooded and ageing males alike, which is more that can be said for the "new start tart" that totters about in ungainly fashion on 'her' high heels along the back of the grandstand. For dressed without subtlety in the manner of a prostitute with bright lipstick and a five o'clock shadow is Peterborough and Oxford track curator, Mick Coleman. He's certainly thrown himself into the spirit of the day and he joins a rich speedway tradition of cross-dressing, most recently carried on by Peter Oakes at last year's Coventry Dinner Dance event to help celebrate their Elite League Champion's crown. Whether Mick or Peter has the greater panache or closest verisimilitude is hard to gauge as I have only seen Mick. He certainly looks memorable though if he was hoping to supplement his income with occasional street walking it will take a lot of work even to pay for a Wendy House.

Another interval highlight for me is the chance to chat to Michael Lee whom I engage with the immortal words, "You're Michael Lee aren't you?" when he stops by my table of books. This question elicits, as ever on these occasions, an "I am". It's a great honour to briefly talk with him and I stress how I admired his career. Throughout our talk, he's modest and self-effacing "thank you – that was a laugh, wasn't it!" and he makes no mention of the help and advice that he's again started to give to talented young British riders. He's even considerate enough to take a genuine interest in my book.

After he finishes second in Heat 13, Shaun throws his goggles to the crowd. Two young boys immediately fight very determinedly for the sudden chance to own them. The younger and smaller of the two of them resists the bullying violence of the bigger boy, who already has the trophy of a pair of goggles that were thrown into the crowd after an earlier race. The younger boy is incredibly pugnacious but fights a losing battle. No adult intervenes to stop the tussle and whoever the parents of the elder boy are they should be ashamed of his behaviour but much more so of their own parenting skills. Kevin puts on his stern schoolmaster's voice that he reserves for admonishments, or particularly deviant requests, when he appeals "come on, it's supposed to be fun – let's be sensible or at least try to be!" Afterwards I learn from Lynn that she'd ensured that the little boy had been "given goggles and gloves" to compensate for his earlier upset.

The highlight of the afternoon's racing was the eight-rider "12 lapper final". As is often traditional at a testimonial, the rider whose day it is, somehow mysteriously manages to win the day and so it appeared would happen here when Shaun found himself at the front of the pack on an extremely crowded track. Sadly, an engine failure forced his withdrawal and he was replaced at the head of the field by Daniel King who, after he led for what seemed like an eternity (and when I'd totally lost count of the laps completed) also suffered an engine failure. Rather like the Grand National at Aintree, events can become confused (albeit without the added complication of riderless bikes) and where even to finish is some sort of achievement, Billy Janniro won, though Leigh Lanham was then declared the overall winner on total points gained throughout the racing. In reality, whoever rode on the day was a winner and everyone contributed to an enjoyably packed afternoon of racing. Someone I'd never seen race before, Mark Jones from Australia, must surely have put himself into speedway's metaphorical shop window with a 'never say die' display throughout the meeting. Another rider who really impressed was Linus Elkof who not only was an out-and-out racer but also was so keen to take part that Jimmy Jansson kindly drove him over to Mildenhall from Sweden! The blond curls of his hairstyle were also quite a hit with the ladies, particularly Lynn ("the curls on Linus just amazed me, I don't know how he gets his crash helmet on, he is like a white Afro man!").

All that remained was the presentations and victory parades before everyone, with little or no invitation, crowded back into the bar for some refreshment and the auction to raise further monies for Shaun. The crowd of bodies added to the sultry heat of the day but didn't prevent "just about £2000" being raised from the various items of memorabilia and other treasures of some cache from Shaun's racing career going under the hammer. Sadly I had to miss most of this to rush off to join a traffic jam on the M11 that was later capped off in surreal fashion by a one-hour traffic jam just trying to get into the Stansted Airport service station (avoid this at all costs as it's now become my all-time most hated service area, quite an accolade on a road network peppered with execrable rivals). There's even a DVD of the testimonial available to purchase – definitely worth it for the racing but also for the appearance of Mick Coleman as the "new start tart".

The day is a credit to the hard work and dedication of all the organisers, helpers, fans and riders that helped make the event what it was. Afterwards Lynn is bashful to the point of extreme modesty about her own contribution and prefers instead to praise everyone else. She's particularly keen to stress "please give Billy Janniro a boost in your Blog as not only is he the real life and soul of the party but he's got a truly generous spirit that captures the idea of the day but typifies him so much as a person. Billy spent at least twice what he earned over the weekend on fundraising things to help Shaun – what a star!"

10th September "Back with A Bang" Shaun Tacey 10 Year Testimonial, Mildenhall
Winner: Leigh Lanham

"It's just another night for us"
18th September

In my ongoing campaign to closely examine every service station throughout the country in the course of my travel to speedway meetings with my book *Showered in Shale*, I return to another favourite of mine – the Peterborough services just off the north-bound A1 on the A605 at around 4.30 p.m. A trip towards the loo in the modern service stations requires that you have to cross in a semi-circular direction through some open plan piazza-type area cunningly designed by no doubt over-paid architectural-cum-shopping consultants so that you have to pass by every shop and restaurant in the place before you can finally get to spend a penny. A diminutive man that I know I recognise but just can't place passes me on the way out of the gents. Stood in contemplation by the urinals is a great place to ponder the mysteries of life or consider some services you didn't really know that you needed – ranging from car insurance; sat nav that identifies every speed trap in the country (but costs nearly £500 – a price that you have to admire them for asking for but really takes the liquid that's in large supply here); a confidential discussion about erectile dysfunction; a revolutionary diesel engine from Mercedes (that in the copy sounds a contradiction and shit all at the same time); more car insurance; fleet van hire; startlingly effective space adverts at reasonable prices that communicate with one of those lesser known demographics – namely a target captive audience of men with full bladders – or breakdown cover. It then hits me that I had just passed the diminutive Lee Richardson on the way to this small area of advertising heaven.

This is further confirmed when I join the fast-food outlet queue for some of its famous remodified chicken gristle, brown meat and genitalia that they've possibly sand blasted off the carcasses of chickens and remoulded into cute shapes with the additional of the merest hint of flavourings, emulsifiers and lots of other things that just add goodness and taste to the "mouth feel" of the thing. Just in front of me is Chris Geer who tonight will mechanic for Lee and has just ridden up with him in the van from Richardson's home in Hastings – that remote part of East Sussex that doesn't strike me as the ideal location from which to travel internationally or throughout the UK for that matter. As another example of the pragmatism and casual freemasonry of the speedway riding community, David Norris has also travelled up in the van for his duties as co-commentator cum colour man for tonight's live *Sky Sports* television broadcast of this vital clash to determine the "top two" places in the Elite League. Premiership footballers probably still hanker after service station fare but they're forced to try to maximise their performances through a nutritional regime constructed by an army of dieticians, whereas the speedway lads can still just get stuck into the takeaways. Though this is even changing in speedway too, as nowadays we've all become infected by this age of sports psychologists and going to the gym. The nature of the travel involved for speedway people and the late-night finishes to their work, necessarily means that convenience food rather than brown rice is most likely all that will be available and is necessarily going to be high on their culinary agenda. And we all know how addictive this fare is once your body gets the taste for it, never mind the subliminal impact of the relentless adverts. It typifies the accessibility of the sport and the superstars of the speedway world that you can just meet them somewhere so 'normal' as this.

Floppy has already sat down with Lee and their well presented but nonetheless industrially extruded 'chicken' meals but then returns to the counter to ask "can you whip us up some gravy?" It's a request that indicates something about his palate, his optimism as well as the infrequency with which he visits this fast-food outlet brand, as he should know that they don't 'do' gravy to order. They do make the effort to look though, which itself indicates a modicum of success for their staff training programmes. Geernob is his inevitable and usual friendly self with a disposition that is always set to be sunnily optimistic. He explains to Floppy who I am: "You know the bloke that wrote the book that I read bits out to you from!" Floppy furrows his brow, which draws my eye to his rather coolly fashionable spectacles. "Oh right, yeah I loved the fight bit – I'll have to get Chris to read some more to me as if I read too much my head goes funny". Geernob has to wait for his order and, as I munch my chips, we discuss the fact that the Eastbourne season looks like it might finish early in October if the Eagles don't manage to qualify for the Craven Shield Final. Chris shrugs but wistfully adds, "Yeah, if it does, I'll have to go back to a proper job rather than this!"

Inside the massive perimeter East of England Showground fence, the *Sky Sports* outside broadcast equipment is prominently on display with the backroom nerve centre of operations parked directly opposite the track shop. The power of the television contract is such that this fixture had been intended to be run last week but, due to its decisive nature had been rescheduled at the request of *Sky* for live coverage for the apparently never-sated armchair audience. All the regular paraphernalia is here – there's a giant dish, huge container lorries, a coach, their impressively sized mobile canteen as well as enough cables running in all directions on the ground to power a small town. Inside the track shop, John and Nick Barber unpack their merchandise and chat to Swindon Press Officer and successful serial speedway author, Robert Bamford, while outside I set up my table. We're in a prime position to watch the comings and goings of all the *Sky* people. There are many engineers and all the assorted technical and backroom people that you need to organise and run a successful outside broadcast. The technical staff all wear black *Sky* tops whereas the on-screen 'talent' conspicuously wear their own choice of clothes, except for Kelvin Tatum and Jonathan Green who will later change into their smart collared *Sky* shirts. Kelvin appears to know everyone, radiates bonhomie and regales some blokes close to me with a complicated technical explanation about the particular variety of sealant that had caused him problems that weekend on the grass track. Jonathan bounds about energetically making loud, suitably bombastic but important sounding phone calls. However, everyone in the track shop only has eyes for Sophie Blake who glides about the place with insouciant elegance either on the phone, looking wistful or switching her trademark smile on and off as people pass. Nick contemplates the situation and expresses a comment that no-one gainsays, "I think she looks much better in the flesh than she does on telly even – she has a nice chassis, as they say!" Another man in mid-browse through the half-arranged merchandise in the shop retorts, "Yeah, she's been round the block many times already but still has plenty more fuel in the tank".

The conversation in the track shop ranges widely from the current fortunes of Mildenhall Speedway to the fact that the Chapmans at King's Lynn are apparently one of the few clubs to have refused the chance for George and Linda Barclay to conduct a collection for the Speedway Museum Appeal Fund at their stadium, allegedly because of doubts over the detail of the exact arrangements that govern the administration and running of the museum. More people arrive and quite a discussion ensues and many questions are raised with no one there to answer them or allay unfounded fears ('why does the figure of £50,000 have to be raised before it can be built?' "Will you have to pay to enter Paradise Park in order to go to the museum?"). As ever with speedway, a history lesson is never far away and though past experiences provide an interesting context they give no guide or real insight into the present Appeal. I do learn that a speedway museum was apparently set up in 1988 and closed around 1992. After its closure, it's alleged Briggo disposed of all the donated gifts given to the museum – a situation which is only mentioned to raise the theoretical question, "who owns the gifts if it doesn't succeed?" I think it's a great idea and I'm sure it will prosper, particularly given the zealous efforts of so many volunteers and the tireless promotional work put in around the tracks by George and Linda Barclay. Outside at my stall, I overhear a passing *Sky* person on the phone discuss the fare on offer tonight at their canteen, "Yeah, chilli and chickpea curry – my arse later will be minging!"

It's the first time that I have ever met the wry speedway author Robert Bamford. He sympathises about the difficulty of selling a significant number of any book on speedway. I think that he's being modest really given how well his justly praised *Homes of British Speedway* book sells, though he does confess that the books he self-published were more lucrative than those he has had published by Tempus. It's a hardy perennial in book publishing that high unit sales don't necessarily translate into large royalty cheques landing through an author's letterbox. Nonetheless if you total up all the lifetime sales of all his various books and other publications, there is definitely a case to consider that Rob is one of the all-time best-selling speedway authors ever. He wears his knowledge and success with characteristic modesty. Quick to wryly highlight a very possible matter of vexation in my book, Robert asks rhetorically, "has Jason Bunyan caught up with you yet?" That said, he does tell me a story I hadn't heard about when he first came across my book days after publication – when Jon Cook sang its praises and waved it under the nose of the well-connected speedway impresario Terry Russell at Arlington.

Robert had heard that I had offered every promoter the chance to correct and edit each chapter of my book prior to publication. He thought that this was very professional, conscientious and not usual ("I heard from Jo Lawson that she took a few things out"). So did Tim Stone but Robert was surprised to learn of the litigious approach threatened by the Wimbledon plc Chairman, "I always got on well with Ian Perkin but then I never wrote about Wimbledon". Our talk soon turns to news of the power failure that afflicted the recent wedding reception for Terry Russell's daughter. A guest at the event, the Swindon promoter Alun 'Rosco' Rossiter immediately volunteered his practical help and briefly restored the power for about 30 seconds before the event was once again plunged back into darkness. Let's hope it's not an omen or precursor of how the Robins' season will eventually turn out. My eye is caught by the *Guardian* headline, "Man rejects first penis transplant". This causes much hilarity among everyone gathered in the track shop when I draw it to their collective attention, some wince at the thought of such an idea and quite a few suggestions about which promoter was involved in this operation, "it's not XXX [name redacted but as a clue they have quite an ego] is it?" These ribald remarks on male genitalia soon segue into news from Mildenhall speedway where the King brothers broke eggs on the head of presenter Kevin Long to celebrate the end of the season. Johnny recalls that Kevin introduced his centre-green interview with King's Lynn presenter Mike Bennett with "here's the King's Lynn anchor, yes you heard me correctly, the King's Lynn anchor."

Rob mentions that not only is tonight a hugely important meeting for the club, but also "tonight is the first time that Swindon have had all seven riders in the team since June". His hopes remain high after the recent run of form shown by the team. As he goes back to the far corner of the track shop to resume his thorough inspection of the treasure trove of programmes inside, the jovial Peterborough (and Rye House) presenter Craig Saul arrives. He has very kindly praised my book relentlessly and promises to do so tonight. He was the first person to apply the perceptive phrase "odyssey" to describe my marathon trip around the tracks to research my book.

A brief trip to the Peterborough side of the pits finds the invariably affable Trevor Swales in typically laid back and philosophical mood, "we have to win tonight or it's over really!" The possible permutations in the final standings of the Elite League table based on results could make your brain hurt. The popular scenario among Panthers fans has it that "if Peterborough win by eight points and Reading fail to get the bonus point at Belle Vue, then we're top". The pessimists in the crowd note that the 12-point lead the Racerdogs hold over the Aces should be more than sufficient if their present impressive form holds. Another school of more cynical thought has it that the results of these two important matches will be finessed or gerrymandered to ensure final league placings that result in play-off semi-final fixtures that will maximise attendances. This outcome would see Reading v Swindon and Peterborough v Coventry.

On close inspection of the programme I spot a very kind review of my book by Derek Barclay. It's so complimentary that it borders on the oleaginous tone he often reserves for others. Nonetheless it's a delight but represents a sharp departure from Derek's usual subject matter of London speedway meetings, most likely those from long ago at Crayford (I hadn't realised that this Greater London based speedway club was twinned with Peterborough or would be of possible interest to the Panthers fans until I read previous iterations of this column!). In prime position outside the 'professionally' run track shop, my stall intermittently attracts the attention of stragglers throughout the build-up to the meeting, though most people seem keen not to dawdle so instead rush past to secure their favoured place in the grandstand. The Peterborough fan it seems I've met all over the country on my travels, namely Steve, arrives and immediately offers a gloomy prognosis of the Panthers season and its likely *denouement*. "We've got no team spirit, the tactics of team manager are often incomprehensible and he doesn't seem able to motivate them, never mind that most of them are too old and most of the team needs to go. We need to sign young, gifted riders and blood them in the Premier League – if they're successful bring them in, if not get rid. Sounds harsh, but that's life!" I'd hate to hear what he thinks of teams that haven't excelled in the manner Peterborough have all this season in the Elite League – where they've consistently occupied one of the vital top four places that ensures qualification for the play-offs – or his perspective on other less successful teams that he doesn't support.

I only sell two copies all evening – apparently only men with the name "Brian" are allowed to make a purchase. The always modest and friendly Steve Dixon, long-time Belle Vue speedway fan and gifted photographer, has stopped for a chat. We're interrupted by a man who accosts us to inform Steve (who already has a copy), "you must buy this book – it's really good, I'm three-quarters of the way through it". A short while afterwards two men stop by my table. One of them looks at the books on display and says, "what's that?" A question that gets the swift reply from the other, "Oh, it's that *Showered in Shale* thing, I don't think you'll like it". Another lost sale through negative word of mouth! The next two blokes that stop temporarily seem keen to consider a purchase too:

Bloke 1: "Have you got it yet?"

Bloke 2: "Nah."

They hang about and both browse through a copy each for a short while.

Bloke 1: "How much is it?

Me: "£20."

Bloke 1 to friend: "Don't bother then I can get it for £19.99."

With the rider parade already underway, I decide to cut my losses and head for the grandstand. I love to stand at the back of the home-straight grandstand since it is one of those that affords a fantastic panoramic view of the circuit, plus you're at a sufficient height to allow you to gain a better perspective on the manoeuvres and racing lines than when you watch at ground level. It's my favourite time of the year for watching speedway – temperate but sufficiently dark for the floodlights to be used and so add lustre to the drama and significance of the events on the track. The announcer is quite apocalyptic in his pronouncements, "It's winner takes all! Both teams will want to win at all costs this evening!" These sentiments are in marked variance to Alun 'Rosco' Rossiter who manages to simultaneously mix catatonia, over-confidence and arrogance in the same brief sound-bite interview. "It's just another night for us – it's nothing special, we don't do nothing different or flashy to normal. We've had 14 wins on the trot home and away since June, it's quite a run and so we'll just act as normal." Given the benefit (and financial reward) that a home draw in the one-off play-off semi-final eliminator provides, this appears a wilfully lackadaisical approach to take to the most important meeting that the Swindon Robins have had in years or since Rosco became promoter. "That's Rosco for you" and a shake of their heads is the view of the Robins fans that have chosen to stand at the back of this grandstand with me. They also confirm that I'm not going mad since they recall the narrow and unlucky loss Swindon recently suffered at Oxford, that Rosco has temporarily forgotten about, and is a result that appears at variance with his claims that the Robins are on an unbeaten run.

The meeting is dramatic from the outset. Hans Andersen doesn't make the start but he then makes up for it when he aggressively barges between Leigh Adams and Renat Gafurov before his sheer momentum takes him into the second-bend air fence. The velocity of his impact punctures two segments of the air fence and, while these are repaired, I get a further chance to study the great floodlit bowl of the Alwalton Stadium at the East of England Showground. It's particularly impressive when viewed from my position. In the eventual re-run that referee Robbie Perks surprisingly feels should still feature all four riders, Hans Andersen again has no answer for the fast-gating Australian Leigh Adams and the Robins jump into an early 2-4 lead. The tension and anxiety of the fixture then causes Mads Korneliussen to completely burst through the tapes and decimate them. The deadpan Edwin Overland notes with considerable understatement, "The rider in green was a little over-anxious there," before he comes over all wistful for 'days gone by' in the manner of people who regret the passing of the death penalty, "once upon a time the rider would have been excluded but nowadays it's a 15-metre penalty." With yet more time to fill as they tardily repair the tapes, Edwin then additionally notes "he was too keen at the start". It's to be no fairy story for the Robins, as the Panthers romp to a 5-1 and take a lead that will become yet more unassailable as the rest of the evening progresses. Edwin has an infectious style about his presentational work and never hesitates to throw around the hyperbole with great abandon. It's well deserved in Heat 3 when Sullivan and Iversen combine for a successive 5-1 that effectively kills the fixture as a contest. Edwin purrs with pleasure at this spectacle before he, in a rather old-fashioned manner that has been abandoned at tracks elsewhere, painstakingly reads out the work telephone number (01406 330130 in case you need them) of heat sponsor (Mackinder Farmhouse Boarding Kennels of Whapode Road, Spalding – not that it exactly sounds that rural to my metropolitan ears) immediately after he's name-checked their sponsorship of the heat. He does this conscientiously throughout the meeting, so much so that the meeting passes in a constant blur of heat scores, cumulative scores, and race times along with obscure sponsor's names and phone numbers.

The breathless level of his earlier praise leaves Edwin very little room for manoeuvre when some of the subsequent heats prove equally as thrillingly exciting as the heat that he raved about earlier. The natural stop-start nature of a speedway meeting is invariably exaggerated by the presence of *Sky Sports* with the concomitant demands of the advertisers and their need for regular commercial breaks to display their anodyne products and rehearse their marketing messages. Trevor Swales kindly gave me permission to visit the pits and I rush round to watch the meeting from there for a few heats around about the tenth heat. Since the last time I was at the East of England Showground, there has been the addition of a viewing area – well, some metal steps for the riders, guests and mechanics to view proceedings from and the adjacent area has been covered in sand as though more than expected fell off the back of the lorry or that they're going to stage some beach volleyball later. Without these raised steps the level of the nearby air fence significantly occludes a full consideration of the race action on the bends nearest to us. I much prefer to watch from the back of the stand but as the Club Chaplain, The Reverend Michael Whawell, is in the pits the company isn't anywhere near as learned, insightfully ironic or, maybe even, as fanatical since Michael is a true lover of the shale and all who ride on her. The distinctive metal *Sky Sports* booth is close by to us, so we can easily watch Kelvin and Jonathan alternate between languid torpor during the races or frenetic activity of hammily playing up to the camera and the viewers at home. Jonathan Green is so loud that you automatically think that he doesn't really need a microphone to broadcast to the viewers at home. As you'd expect, Kelvin is the most interested in the action on the track throughout the time that I'm there but Jonathan appears totally uninterested when the red-lit gaze of the camera is focused elsewhere. Michael is, as ever, an acute and perspicacious observer of all around him and of life in general. He proudly flourishes his own speedway badge of honour – a credit cum security card style BSPA pass complete with a photo that makes him look severely institutionalised rather than his usual patrician self.

Standing together on the bottom step of the small metal grandstand are Peter Oakes and Tony Steele. They watch and talk about the action in the enthusiastic manner of true fans rather than with the careworn attitude that infects some others who 'professionally' watch so often and whose work means that they are involved in as many speedway meetings a season as they both necessarily are. With the scores poised at 35-31, Peter feels "that it could go either way" before a Panthers 5-1 effectively seals the Robins' fate. Peter still hasn't given up hope of a close contest, "13 could go either way too," he almost shouts to Tony. A rare fall for Leigh Adams has the nearby Reading Bulldogs promoter, Jim Lynch, here to cast his eye over his possible rivals, repeatedly and almost gleefully exclaim, "Now that doesn't happen very often!"

Close by, Sophie Blake interviews a Peterborough rider who intones with the enthusiasm of the speaking clock, "it's great that we're top of the league" which has Jim Lynch retort off-stage as though unofficially part of some double act, "only for two days!" With two heats to go and in the absorbed manner of a committed fan of speedway, Peter still favours the permutations in scores that would maintain the excitement of a close meeting, "if they get an 8-1 and a 5-1 it'll be a run-off for the bonus point". As if Rosco reads Peter Oakes's mind, Lee Richardson comes out for a tactical ride in a black-and-white helmet against Ryan Sullivan and Richard Hall. Not renowned as a great exponent of the psychological side of the sport, Lee tries to 'use his head' with immediately disastrous consequences on the first bend and thereby finds himself completely relegated at the rear of the race without any hope of making up the distance on the lightning quick Alwalton circuit. Jim Lynch can't believe it and delightedly exclaims, "He tried to be clever, Richardson – it's the worst first corner I've seen anyone ride!" As a last throw of the dice in an almost hopeless situation, I think this attempt at tactical sophistry by Lee Richardson was worth a try but when executed this poorly, it's bound to leave you open to derision from all quarters. The last heat has an appearance by Panthers reserve Piotr Swiderski with his last place, good experience for him, and of no consequence to the overall result or the whereabouts of the points on the night.

For the last few heats I've retreated to my table of books outside the track shop. Even though they've just won and ostensibly triumphed in the Elite League (Reading at Belle Vue notwithstanding) the Panthers fans don't hang about to celebrate. They appear much keener to rush off to the car park to join the lengthy queue of rear lights slowly flashing intermittently red in the almost total darkness of the far distance, as they inch their way nearer to home. John and Nick Barber are (like Peter Oakes and Tony Steele) long-time keen spectators of the sport. As though it were some weird scientific experiment in a giant laboratory, each of the final few heats has Johnny Barber endlessly repeat the exact same routine. He casually extricates himself from behind the tables crammed with merchandise, leaves the track shop, trundles down the alleyway that runs alongside the main grandstand that separates it from the bar cum clubhouse building to avidly peer over the crowd and fence to catch the start of each race. These he watches almost to the point of their conclusion, but just as the riders pass the final bend and start to approach the finish line he high-tails it smartish back up the alleyway with considerable speed and agility. He's back once again inside the shop to serve any stray customers in the unlikely event that any of these show a faster turn of speed than he does as he scuttles back along the side passage of the grandstand wall. Otherwise he casually, but watchfully, mentally supervises the young children who invariably fondle the more garish, reasonably priced merchandise and memorabilia that coincides with their Panthers allegiances but which hover on the margins of their acceptable price range. This exercise he repeats endlessly until the meeting concludes. Such is the life of speedway fans everywhere – stuck in the enjoyably delicious rut of their own personal obsessive rituals and behaviours – even those like Johnny fortunate enough to attend the speedway so often because they happen to actually work there. Both Barber brothers look delighted with the turn of events that not only guarantees further excitement and action on the track but is allied to further appearances by potentially high-spending customers off it in their shop for the duration of the play-offs.

18th September Peterborough v Swindon (Elite League B) 53-37

At Owlerton with the Mycenaeans
24th September

I arrive so early for the Premier League Riders' Championship (PLRC) that the ladies from the Sheffield speedway office have still not yet had sufficient cigarettes to think about putting on their coats to venture out for lunch. Not that they will really need their coats – of the smart light rainproof winter variety – since it's an impressively sunny day though it wouldn't be Yorkshire without a real or metaphorical cloud on the horizon. The speedway office is tucked away from the impressive grandstand that inside its portals has dining facilities that are apparently the envy of many other speedway promotions. Sheffield's operation, like many of the other clubs where you could favourably comment on the food provision, only creates profits for the stadium owners rather than the speedway club. The Owlerton office is one of the country's last bastions of committed cigarette smokers. There is always an impressive fug to greet you on arrival through the door and I often wonder if they should get a sign that says "Thank you for smoking". The co-promoter here, Neil Machin, already has a cigarette in his hand but isn't quite as prolific as the ladies.

The meeting will start at 6.30 p.m. and the "engines start" at 6 p.m. according to the £3 'Official Souvenir Raceday Programme' that proudly advertises the sponsorship of the Sheffield Window Centre (among others), who evidently didn't see Neil coming when he approached them for their support for this event. The PLRC is what's, in the parlance of the BSPA, known as "a Shared Event". In plain terms, this means that the profits from the day are divided up between the clubs. In the past when these "Championship" meetings had greater significance for the crowds and the riders, this additional income would be sufficiently noticeable to be welcome. I gather that those days have long gone. In fact as a promoter and a member of the management committee, Neil is in a good position to know what really goes on behind the scenes of contemporary speedway. Though he is much too professional to let on to someone like me, I gather that a number of late rider withdrawals have irked him ("it's only 12.30 p.m. and already I know of three withdrawals"). And, no doubt, will further diminish the status of this event in the eyes of the paying public, or will when they arrive through the gates and the voluble, always enthusiastic tones of Dave Hoggart inform them of the changes they will have to make in their glossy programmes. Neil goes through the rider absences. There's George Stancl ("he's been injured for a while so I know about that"), Garry Stead ("he got injured last night") and Theo Pijper ("he'll probably be heavily fined as he's in France after his grass track meeting was postponed until today"). As members of the public we never learn what, if any, punishment is meted out to these riders. Subsequently I learn that Pijper "broke his wrist on Friday night at Edinburgh" from one fan and that "he has a French licence so he has to ride in these grass track meetings" from another. Whatever the true picture, it's a confusing situation and the bottom line is that not all the advertised riders will appear in this event.

These are the least of the problems that presently assail speedway. When it comes to the riders missing on the night, Neil

A young Gary Havelock fan. © Jeff Scott

Riders on parade for shaven headed fans. © Jeff Scott

Mick Gregory and Bill Gimbeth lay out the Sheffield track shop. © Jeff Scott

is confident "we'll paper over the cracks". Something that is much more difficult to manage, and something that the sport as a whole struggles with, is the complex situation with regards to the multiple clubs that individual riders sign and race for each week in a variety of countries throughout the season. The demands of the Swedish and Polish leagues are well known but stealthily increasing and, even if you ignore the serious impact that the BSI-run Grand Prix series has on the availability of certain 'top' riders, then the issue of the Russian league has now started to rear its soon-to-be ugly but lucrative head. In a nutshell, some British promoters fly riders over (and their family) from, say, Australia, pay for some or all of their accommodation and UK equipment along with a signing on fee and lots of other little things that we can only guess at, only to find that far from inspiring gratitude and loyalty, the rider then signs to race for other teams in other countries. Donning his metaphorical judge's wig, Neil turns all righteously legalistic, "if riders have signed a UK contract they can't sign for overseas clubs – but it's not enforced so they get away with it". The need for promoters to stand up, be collectively counted and address this issue in a unified disinterested fashion urgently presses. It's in the nature of speedway and human nature for the assumption to be that these rules should apply to every business except your own should a good compelling reason for doing otherwise suddenly present itself. In all cases, self-interest ("freak 'em" could be the customer service motto of some promoters, so it's not a surprise that arguments for the 'good of the sport' can also often take a backseat) trumps altruism and so the situation worsens over time and we head to hell in a hand basket. Neil lights another cigarette, drags on it deeply and says, "You can go anywhere you like mate, but I have to get on with things for tonight".

The lack of rider loyalty is a theme that the forthright Mick Gregory in the track shop also warms to later: "The more you pay them – they less loyal they are!" The loss of status of these events among the riders is also bemoaned, "Championships used to be important before the relationship with the riders changed." I have based myself close by to Mick's track shop though I have to leave a large space between my table and Mick's for Eric Boocock ("Booey") who will be along later to sign his book. When he finally arrives with the affable but canny Tony McDonald of *Reading Evening Post*, *Backtrack* and *Retro Speedway* Publishing fame, they choose to base themselves at the other end of Mick's stall so that Booey is the first person fans see when they round the corner. It soon becomes apparent that Booey might develop an industrial strength repetitive strain injury through the sheer volume of books that he will have to sign during the night. As quick as they can open the printer's cartons (20 books per box), it appears that his books sell. At least that is how it appears to me – in the same manner that as a child the desert you like looks so small and is gone in an instant whereas the one you hate appears gigantic and inedible – especially as mine sell much more sedately. To my mind there is a very good-sized crowd compared to the run of the mill speedway meetings. Most notable are the voluble Redcar fans along to support "Havvy" who seem to believe that they are in fact actually at a football match with regards to their boisterousness, chants, singing and general merriment, though this is aided by the easy availability of alcohol. Bill, who works for Dave Rattenberry at Redcar, looks on approvingly in the direction of the noisy Redcar/Havvy faithful. A passing Ella MacDonald confirms the widely held old-school opinion that 'things ain't what they used to be' when it comes to the PLRC. "It used to be a real event, I remember when all the teams used to bring big coaches all decorated and everything – decked out in scarves and their team colours – you used to look forward to seeing what they'd done and how they'd decorated them but that's all gone now. We only brought ten on a mini-bus from Edinburgh and even Workington have only brought a small one". Ella isn't hopeful that an Edinburgh rider will lift the trophy. Theo Pijper has been replaced by William Lawson "and he's only got a small track engine in his bike, so that'll be hopeless here". The few Monarchs fans that there are have gathered in a knot on the third bend where they've been joined by Russell 'Rusty' Harrison who left the club under a cloud earlier in the season. Something that Ella makes a point to remember to highlight to me and, doubtless, will comment upon later to Rusty.

There is also quite a contingent of Glasgow Tigers fans and a lady I recognise from the very helpful Glasgow Tigers Supporters Club seeks me out to offer a few words of complaint about my book.
"I have to complain that we're not in it much!"
"You are."
"You liar we're not – it's all Edinburgh and their coach trip."
"I admit that there could have been more but you can only comment on what happens – I was touched by the help of Ian Maclean and his daughter, Marian."
"Yeah, but it could have been more about us and less about them."
"Well there's lots about the Tigers on my Blog – away at Redcar, Edinburgh and Workington, the Pairs and home against the Monarchs".
"Ach!"

I love the fact that at speedway you usually get to hear exactly what people think and feel about my book, opinions or approach. I like it that there is no hesitation about sharing these thoughts and opinions – it's an honesty that's missing from many other walks of life and speedway is all the more unique and refreshing for it! Throughout the night to the left of my table is Kenneth Brown, an older man with a slight speech impediment, stutter or badly fitted false teeth and a quiet voice – I can't quite decide which. He's definitely quite shy and I can't always catch what he's saying. He's travelled over on public transport from Manchester and, as it's a Sunday, he will have to leave early in order to ensure that he gets home. This will involve a four-mile walk on the last leg of his journey that, judged by his apparent lack of speed and mobility, could take quite some time to accomplish. He is determined though and is clearly a man with great experience of speedway meetings since he has come prepared with an enviable collection of food, drink and useful paraphernalia. His equipment includes the type of large pen with different coloured biros (red, green, blue and black) that I thought they'd stopped making nowadays. The type that you often got as a child for your Spirograph from distant aunties who didn't know that the sheer bulk of the cylinder would definitely preclude its use to create multi-coloured geometric patterns. A quick glance at his programme later reveals that he has his own complicated and multicoloured system of annotation that I can't understand at all. The rider changes present absolutely no difficulty as he has brought his own Tippex for the very purpose of these rider alterations. Impressively practical stuff, albeit slightly messy if you have shaky hands. They say never judge a book by its cover and though his coat and bag are careworn, his speech awkward to easily understand – he easily wins the award for the most obscure and highbrow book I have ever seen at a speedway meeting, well in many places other than a university library for that matter. For his lengthy trip on public transport he has brought along *The Mycenaeans* by Lord William Taylor, published in hardback by Thames & Hudson in 1964 as part of their ethnocentrically named 'Ancient People and Places' series. Kenneth then goes on to explain quite a bit about the Mycenaeans as well as the fascination that they hold for him. I also learn about the interesting life and work of Lord Taylor.

As every Premier League club is represented at the meeting, it's hard to avoid many people that I've met or got to know on my travels. Dave Croucher from the Isle of Wight passes – for once comparatively understated on the bling front by his own ostentatious standards, though even tonight he'd still not be too out of place on a hip hop music video on MTV. Dave professes himself in good form, "I'm as fat as a pig and smoking too much but I'm enjoying myself or trying to". Another group of fans who linger by my stall are outraged that Ronnie Russell chose August 22nd to rearrange the recent Arena v Eastbourne fixture as it clashed with the Matt Read Testimonial at Somerset and thereby forced the withdrawal of many key riders. "Matt nearly lost his life and rode for both Eastbourne and Arena – it's been arranged all season yet this switch of the fixture to Friday freaked it all up and stopped many riders appearing, like Mark Loram". Steve Miles the Peterborough uber-fan[1] and Panthers programme editor calls in. While we chat I notice that he has spiders and ants crawling on his skin – he must have the sort of skin or distinctive smell that's wildly attractive to them – and he casually brushes them off, "I'm turning into Steve Irwin". Luckily we have no rays in Sheffield though a ray of light in terms of his efforts on the track is James Wright who, in Heat 3, looks incredibly fast, stylish and powerful as he chases Shane Parker and nearly catches him on the line. Since I met him and his mum Lynn last year – they're both extremely personable – I have always made a point to look out for his results. He has had an excellent season at Workington and has shown good promise in the Elite League for Belle Vue even though he has often had to ride in the main body of the team in the difficult number two position rather than, more favourably for his earning power, in one of the reserve berths. Sadly, although our paths have crossed many times this season, we've not had the chance to chat. In his next race, Heat 6, he makes the sort of shocking start that really costs you extremely dearly in the Elite League as it does in the highly competitive environment that is the PLRC, where the fast nature of the track only serves to exaggerate the initial split second loss of yardage almost exponentially. Success isn't going to beckon this year for James at the PLRC, though he again shows his mettle with a very hard-fought third place in his next outing gained at the expense of Carl Wilkinson whom he overtakes on the penultimate bend of the last lap.

As always the racing is extremely fast at Sheffield though, given the calibre of the field, gating remains at a premium and restricts the amount of exciting passing manoeuvres after the initial tussle for space and position of the first bend. Beforehand, Havvy rather presciently noted about the Sheffield circuit, "You just lean the bike over and hang on for grim death". An exception to these processional races is the truly exhilarating tenth heat, where the (not fully fit) home favourite with the luxuriant eyebrows, Andre Compton, makes an excellent start only to be passed on the second bend by Magnus Zetterstrom. Though none is needed, Andre illustrates his determination, bravery and knowledge of the Owlerton racetrack, when he pulls back alongside Zetterstrom on the third bend and holds his throttle fully open to re-pass him magnificently by only the merest fraction of an inch from the apparently ineluctable threat of the oh-so-close fence.

At the start of the interval I attract my biggest ever crowd of my travels so far when I have four people waiting to buy a book and have it signed. Well, I have had four people stand there previously at another track but some of them were there to steal rather than buy the books. It's now my turn to almost get repetitive strain injury and I feel elated until I notice that the long line of people by Booey's table stretches back a considerable distance. Immediately after the resumption the large crowd (in the grandstand not standing waiting for Booey to sign his book) is silenced by a dramatic first-bend crash for Andre Compton. He flies over the handlebars in dramatic fashion and lands heavily on the track where he lies prostrate for some considerable time before he finally leaves in an ambulance. The thoughts of the experienced Mick and Bill in the track shop vary. "That's our season over," notes Mick morosely before he continues in an impressively medical vein, "he was only 75 percent fit anyway, it's the ligament on his shoulder [it's his collarbone] and I'm sure that he'll have damaged it again". This pre-existing weakness in Compton's arm contributed to his injury on the night since it appears that he tried but failed to correct the violent movement of his handlebars, just as he left the start only to find that this attempted correction threw him over the top of them. Proud to wear his 2006 Redcar allegiances with distinction, Bill is phlegmatic – and honorarily almost a Yorkshireman (because Cleveland is really only an invention of central government to disguise the fact that it's really Yorkshire) – with his mardy observation, "typical – it's the only time that Havvy has gated all night!" His concern is well placed as Havvy completely fails to repeat the medicine in the re-run – indeed he fails to really gate all night but his speed, experience and skill are fully called upon to make up for this self-imposed additional handicap – which thereby allows Jason Lyons to escape to victory. The perspective of speedway history though, will ultimately dictate that the race itself is more notable for the fact that 16-year-old Tai Woffinden rides (as a reserve replacement for Andre Compton) and acquits himself impressively in this exalted field with a third place. The fact that he's by no means disgraced in the presence of such august company bodes well for his long-term future prospects in the sport.

[1] Voted the 2006 'Fan of the Year' in the poll organised by the *Peterborough Evening Telegraph* for his unstinting support of both the speedway and the often dire football club, where he's a season ticket holder (albeit he's also a not-so-closet Arsenal supporter). It's an accolade he wears modestly after the awards ceremony and he makes light of his narrow triumph over his major rival for the title – a dog!

A long delay ensues as the track has only one ambulance in attendance and it's already otherwise occupied with Andre. This prompts Mick to turn all philosophical and ponder his many years spent at the speedway, "You know, I've only ever seen three riders killed. Amazing when you think how long I've been going and how dangerous it is – especially here. You can never tell by just looking at it. Recently Kyle Legault and Tommy Allen went into the fence and I feared the worst, it looked really bad but they both shot up and started knocking seven bells out of each other so I knew that they must be okay really!"

The Sheffield club photographer, Andy, also drops in,
"I haven't got a decent shot yet!"
"Why – are they all going too fast for you?"
"Nah, it's not that – none of them are together and every race is strung out".

He has a valid point since the starts have been crucial for the riders here all night and so it was to continue to prove throughout. The likely winners, after Andre Compton retired injured from the meeting, always looked likely to come from the experienced trio of Magnus Zetterstrom, Jason Lyons or Gary Havelock. Based solely on the 2006 Premier League averages this should by rights be Zetterstrom but then we all know that statistics are misleading and the enduring beauty of speedway is its unpredictability. Surprises, however, are thin on the ground tonight. There is the usual modern nonsense (not as bad as the play-offs) that the results of the races only determine the qualifiers for another new-fangled contemporary speedway invention I actively dislike – the ubiquitous elimination races of the semi-final and final. According to the PLRC build-up article in the *Speedway Star*, I'm in complete agreement with Havvy on this point. "Maybe I'm 'old school' but I prefer the old 20 heats, everybody meets everybody and the best rider wins. Building up to a final is good for the fans but to get 15 points – a maximum – and then miss out in a one-off final doesn't seem right." Luckily, the slightly more sensible variant operates at Sheffield so the top two scorers from the 20 heats – Zetterstrom and Lyons – are seeded through to the final without the worry or exasperation of sudden elimination in the semis. If the result were determined by the noise of the crowd, then the vociferous support offered to Havvy throughout the meeting would see him win easily. Just like battles aren't won on paper, in the final analysis this isn't a crucial factor. Neither is the advice of three-time PLRC champion, Sean Wilson, part of the Gary Havelock team in his section of the pits. It's Sean's first return to the club since his testimonial in March amid rumours of a terminal fall out with the Sheffield promotion (well, Neil Machin), though his work as Havvy's mechanic for the night or his tuning of a "specialist engine" just for Owlerton doesn't work out as planned beforehand. All this additional help counts for nought when Zetterstrom again gates brilliantly and powers away from Jason Lyons to win the final, become the 37th winner and thereby break the sequence that had seen a Sheffield rider win this championship for the last three seasons. Glimpsed only fleetingly nowadays in comparison to days of yore, Zorro celebrates with his trademark donuts and maniacal almost deranged arm waving. A crowd estimated at over 2000 heads off into the dark Yorkshire night.

Before I head off the short distance from the stadium to the comfortable and well-appointed nearby Garrison Hotel (Sheffield's Premier Speedway Hotel for any visitor wishing to stay the night in South Yorkshire) – uncontroversially enough given its name, housed within the battlements of the old garrison building – I snatch a few words with Booey. To my casual observation, his sales have been fantastic but this is the track that, arguably, you'd expect him to do the best at. Whether sales are high or low, Booey retains his nonchalant equanimity but remains as plainly spoken as ever. "It all depends on the position of the track shop. Here it's great, where they had us at Scunny was good, as we kept dry but freakin' hopeless for sales. Though the racing was much better there [at the CL Pairs], here it was first out of the start and nothing to write home about!"

September 24th Premier League Riders Championship, Sheffield
Winner: Magnus Zetterstrom

Apples Fly at Smallmead during the EL Play-Off Semi-Final
25th September

My journey from Sheffield to Reading goes surprisingly smoothly and as a result I find myself in the vicinity of the stadium horrendously early, so I decide to sample the delights of the nearby M4 service station before heading to the dilapidated car park. I have arranged to arrive early as the friendly and efficient Torben Olsen of BSI Reading has kindly put my name on the gate to celebrate the fact that my book will finally be available from the Reading track shop. It could be nicknamed 'Colditz' as comparative to every other shop in the country nothing gets in and nothing gets out. More accurately, all merchandise and materials stocked there have to have prior approval from the BSI. If the Racerdogs do manage to progress to the EL Play-Off final and that of the Craven Shield, it effectively means that the fans will have a maximum of four meetings to buy the book. This is a shame and disappointment on a number of fronts as Reading feature in four chapters and I have followed them for 31 years since my first inspirational trip to Smallmead in 1975.

It's a situation that hasn't happened through lack of contact with the BSI Press Officer, Nicola Sands, whom I've enjoyed dealing with when I can get hold of her. She immediately got back to me in May when I showed her my usually tangential and brief draft comments on the BSI and/or John Postlethwaite in my book. I was only too happy to make her suggested amendments and I enjoyed her Scots accent that exaggerates her direct, slightly brusque manner. She has a demanding job and my subsequent calls and emails to seek authorisation to get my book stocked met either complete silence or the extremely honest reply to my first attempt at chasing a response after some initial time lapse, "I'm very busy with the GPs now so I won't open this [email] for another week and might not read it then and anyway it's not for me to decide as I'll pass it onto someone else". It's widely rumoured that John Postlethwaite takes a very fastidious and hands-on approach to all communications that emanate from the bowels of the BSI, so the innate difficulty and balancing act that inevitably goes with this demanding position is further magnified. Eventually my request wends its way to the correct BSI 'gatekeeper', Torben, and he responds with, what in comparison, is great alacrity. He's friendly too, welcomes me to Smallmead at the front entrance in confident manner, provides a purple "ReadingBulldogs.com" wristband and then leaves me to it.

While I'm unloading my boxes, I hear a familiar sounding but distinctive Wiltshire accent behind me call "hello" – it belongs to the friendly speedway author and Swindon Press Officer, Robert Bamford. He supports a weird combination of football teams – "Manchester United then Swindon and Chippenham" – but is a dedicated, long-time Robins loyalist. Like many Swindon fans this season he's grown in confidence as results on the track have given the riders, the fans and 'Rosco' belief that they might go all the way this year to championship glory. A huge contingent of Swindon fans are expected for this vital local derby Elite League semi-final play-off fixture. We're so early they have yet to arrive en masse. Robert updates me on the team news. I already knew that with immaculate timing – not at all suspiciously but with "great reluctance but what were we supposed to do?" Rob is at great pains to assure me – the Robins have reported Renat Gafurov for "withholding services". This results in an automatic 28-day ban from the BSPA and enables the Robins to use the rider replacement facility for his absence. Whether this gains them an advantage in the context of his not exactly stellar average is a moot point. Something that does signal that the speedway gods look kindly on the Robins this season is the fact that overnight the Racerdogs captain, Greg Hancock – all-round good fellow as well as inspirational and indefatigable advisor for all his team-mates but particularly of Travis McGowan – will miss this meeting with "reported food poisoning", apparently caught from his wife. If this fixture was so important and it wasn't Greg involved, you'd usually be more suspicious. So while both teams will operate the rider replacement facility, it's definitely a blow that gives the Robins greater cause for confidence.

On the entrance gate is Tadley-based Paul Hunsdon, who tonight has switched from the comfort of the referee's box perched high above the start line in favour of a roving security and facilities management role round the stadium. For this purpose he has donned a sleeveless fluorescent yellow top that, along with his size, height and close-cropped hairstyle, adds authority to his demeanour since it immediately marks him out as an official. Overhead there are some exceptionally dark clouds but in the distance, where the wind blows from tonight and towards the rough direction of Tadley, there are bright, clear skies. The security man on the gate is confident of victory but suspects canny practice by the Robins in their decision to seek a ban for Gafurov, " the Russian's not been here before so would have struggled". My delivery of books to the track shop means that after 31 years I finally get to enter the inner sanctum and see behind the scenes of this outlet. Inside things are very cosy. There is a small stock cupboard area presently packed with excess quantities of recent unsold issues of the *Speedway Star* that all have to have the front cover bar code removed to be sent back to the publisher's offices, Pinegen, as proof of the excess quantity on hand and their subsequent wastage/destruction. As a teenager the shop appeared packed with a treasure trove of speedway goodies that I hankered for but had no money to buy. Nowadays the stringent BSI authorisation procedures means that the limited range of items that are there for sale look somewhat sparse in the spartan surroundings and, I imagine, would only appeal to the keenest of Bulldogs fans. That said, nonetheless it's a massive improvement on the start of the season when Bulldogs memorabilia was almost completely absent and you would have thought that the shop solely existed to display empty shelves and an uncluttered display cabinet. What isn't missing at the shop is a zeal for Reading Speedway as well as a warm welcome from Win [ifred] who runs the shop and is the mother of the Racerdogs diminutive, knowledgeable, friendly but always committed Press officer, Andy Povey. Inside the recently deluxe Racerdogs programme – the most expensive league programme in the country at £2.50, though rumoured to cost more than its cover price to produce – an article by Andy has stirred my nostalgia with a superbly evocative piece on the Reading Racers' 1977 season. In an example of branding gone simultaneously barmily mad and totally unsubtle, this two-page article is bordered with six separate name checks, including the 'child-friendly-look' platitudinous logo, for the new club name which – in case you hadn't gathered or had spent time away on the moon – is now the "Reading Bulldogs".

I wander over to the pits and past the mounted *Sky* camera position that allows the cameraman to film down the length of the back straight as well as cover the third and fourth corners. Also extremely noticeable is the "all expense spared" scoreboard – modelled on the deluxe electronic versions you see at major sports events – that has been transplanted from heaven knows where and erected on the apex of this bend. It's a structure that bears the genesis of its production, since I can still clearly see the outline shape in adhesive of the various country names – used during the recent World Cup meetings staged at Smallmead earlier in the summer – that were originally stuck on the individually coloured (red, blue, green and yellow) boards that it prominently displays. Overall it looks very rickety and more suited to the requirements of a village green cricket team rather than a speedway club. It must have arrived to create a certain impression for the cameras though it will, doubtless, prove useful to those too bemused or rushed between races to fill out their race card or those unable to afford the price of the £2.50 "Reading Bulldogs Speedway Racing Team" programme. While the Swindon side of the pits appears noisy, bustling and full of smiles the Racerdogs side appears subdued or quietly professional depending on your perspective. Steve 'Johno' Johnston arrives wreathed in smiles with a word for everyone he passes. It's widely rumoured that he'd leap at the chance to ride for the Robins and to further that end, he already lives in Rosco's house, while he now resides elsewhere at the pub he runs. Rosco tirelessly promotes the pub at every opportunity. The away trips start from there, meetings about the club are held there and this has led to the witty suggestion that Rosco is better at promoting the pub than the club! Whatever people say, there's no denying the fact that the results on the track have recently justified owner Terry Russell's faith in his abilities. In the pits, microphone in hand, there is a possible fly in the ointment in the form of Richard Crowley from *BBC Radio Wiltshire*. Along with *Sky Sports* television and *BBC Radio Berkshire* (rather impenetrable slogan – "people you know, travel you trust"), this meeting will be covered live on local radio back in Wiltshire. Sadly every time Richard does manage to cover the Robins he's invariably "a jinx" and they stumble to one defeat after another. They're going to have to stop granting him access if this continues to be the case tonight, particularly as it's important to always have someone to blame when things go wrong.

Unsurprisingly, it appears that Robert knows everyone on the Swindon side of the pits and this also holds true for the track staff, mechanics, riders and practically everyone else on the Racerdogs side of the pits too. Even at this exulted and frequently over-praised Elite League level, many of the people who work at the club each week do so voluntarily and for the love of the sport. This contrasts sharply with the approach and attitude of the 'talent' who, in a modern age of a different club in a different country almost every night, are increasingly the most fickle and transient part of the equation. Like every self-employed person, they're understandably keen to maximise their earnings and benefits, but unlike the volunteers they often don't live locally or selflessly exhibit years of loyal service to the club. Rob tuts at the thought of it and shakes his head in a resigned manner, "That's promoters for you; pay the riders silly money and expect everyone else to work for free!"

Throughout the stadium the very visible paraphernalia of a live *Sky* outside broadcast litters the grounds. Along with the raised camera positions constructed from wooden planks and complicated arrangements of scaffolding poles there is, of course, the famous/distinctive interview booth placed right by the pits gate. This choice of location is particularly annoying for me as although I have the rare opportunity of pits access tonight, no matter where I stand in the riders' and guests' viewing area, this construction completely obscures any chance of properly seeing the action along the back straight or the exit from the second corner. Not that I realise this until the racing starts. Nor do the riders; though they have greater permission to wander and so have the option to crowd next to the dog-track catch fence and strain on steel-shoe-clad tiptoe to peer past the booth to get a slightly less restricted but still partially obscured view of the action. This scrum of riders arrives only when the race starts and immediately dissipates as the riders cross the line on the track, which is the signal for them all to retreat back to their own bikes and equipment. A live televised meeting traditionally introduces *longueurs* into proceedings but tonight's will really take the biscuit as the demands of the *Sky* contract, sponsor's advert breaks and the armchair audience will totally destroy the meeting as a spectacle for those that bother to come through the turnstiles. I estimate the crowd at well over a thousand but nothing like the huge numbers that Nigel Pearson explicitly claims have come over from Wiltshire to support the Swindon Robins during his live television commentary on the fixture. The inevitable stop-start pattern of any speedway meeting has always been exaggerated by the presence of the cameras but tonight the reality of this contractual relationship between British speedway, the Elite League and *Sky Sports* will reach its ridiculous but logical conclusion. The reality of the contemporary situation is that the fans who turn up to any televised meeting are merely fodder to provide colour for the cameras rather than valued as paying customers to be feted and, occasionally, taken account of.

All that matters tonight for the television rights' holder and the speedway authorities is the artificial narrative tension that can be eked out from the juxtaposition of each heat from Smallmead when that follows each race from the East of England Showground contest between Peterborough and Coventry. The idea is that the heats will efficiently alternate between the venues, except for commercial breaks, throughout the night and hopefully build up to a thrilling, nail-biting *denouement*. Even though this is likely to be the biggest Elite League crowd that has paid its way through the Smallmead turnstiles since BSI took over Reading, their needs will be secondary to people completely absent from the stadium. A large enough crowd is expected tonight to prompt the club to arrange an overflow car park nearby used on match day by football fans that regularly flood along to see the soccer at the Madejski Stadium. One of the most audible improvements at BSI Reading has been the tannoy system and the club does at least have the good grace (or common sense) to manage the expectations of a potentially restless large crowd through repeated announcements "that the gap between each heat will be longer than normal as the racing alternates with Peterborough for *Sky*". The same would never happen with other sports where *Sky* own the contractual broadcast rights as soccer, cricket, rugby league etc and these respective sports authorities would resist such an imposition, even if they administered a sport as amenable as speedway for such 'thin-slicing'. If anyone is tempted to write a letter of complaint to the speedway authorities, luckily we learn that there's a "BBC reading and writing campaign in the bar"[1]. Letter writers are likely to be thin on the ground, particularly since it's not exactly clear to whom you'd write to on such matters, let alone who would be independent from the contractual negotiation or its associated payments. Even if it was clear, they'll be guaranteed not to react or just to blather on with the usual "necessary exposure for the sport", "improving the profile" platitudes we so often have to listen to uncontested or unsullied with factual information to corroborate the hyperbole of these claims.

The clearest sign of who pays the piper gets the tune they want played is the protracted delay prior to heat 1 which I overlook from the pits viewing area. Leigh Adams and Mads Korneliussen both idle by their bikes to wait for the signal to start their engines and head promptly out to the start gate. Mads calmly sits in completely nonchalant fashion on his bike, content to linger without apparently a care in the world. Leigh Adams appears to live on his nerves and agitates impatiently throughout quite a long delay. Initially he does some further warm-up exercises – arms flailing, knee bending, general stretching – while only a few yards away Jonathan Green and Kelvin Tatum (earlier I overheard one of the mechanics say, "We've drawn the short straw; they've got Sophie and we've got Kelvin") also kick their heels as they wait for the race at Peterborough to be completed. When he does speak Jonathan appears to have his voice modulated at a default setting of loudly bombastic, which suits the relentless larger-than-life bonhomie that he has perfected for the screen. Jonathan also clearly concentrates and tries to remain composed during the delay, while he too awaits his own cue to resume broadcasting. Leigh has by now exhausted his repertoire of exercises and, in an irked manner that defies the normal on-air convention of demarcation between the riders and the broadcast team talent during *Sky*'s live outside broadcasts, loudly

[1] The club is to be applauded for their support of this initiative, though in this respect, the promotion at King's Lynn definitely leads the way when it comes to social responsibility and community action.

demands of Jonathan "how long 'til we race?" Jonathan holds up three fingers and mouths the words "three". This doesn't seem to make Leigh that happy and who can blame him, as the riders are the essential component parts of the drama that is about to unfold on television screens across the country but, like the fans, he momentarily finds himself relegated to secondary consideration in the scheme of things as we wait for the television gods to deign to give their approval for the action to commence. And yet here is Leigh Adams – one of the world's premier exponents of his chosen profession – left to kick his heels close to the Smallmead pits gate. Throughout the night he will also still have to suffer further inordinate delays between races that could fatally disrupt his concentration and that defy the usual swift, repetitive pattern of prepare, race, prepare, race that is the lot of any 'in demand' speedway rider who races in Britain. Just as Leigh is irked by the length of the delay, so too is Jonathan disconcerted by Leigh's pre-emptory interruption and so he spends a great part of the next few minutes before he goes back on air trying to attract – in sign language without being able to leave the interview-cum-presentation booth – the attention of a nearby *Sky* sports gopher so he can mouth to him to look after Leigh Adams and keep him updated on the time before the off. This is very professional of him but the whole scene has the air of a slightly mad, motorcycling version of 'signing' for the deaf. This small incident forcefully hammers home to me that speedway is primarily an 'entertainment' dictated by television much more than it is a 'sport' with the riders much more 'performers' than 'sportsmen'. They're not quite at the circus parping their horns and clapping their flippers, just yet – but this suddenly looks a lot closer to the actual reality of the thing than I'd previously imagined.

Finally the signal is given and the bikes start, Leigh leaps on his bike and sets off for the start line for the first race of the night. The wait clearly hasn't improved either his mood or his concentration and to collective groans from the large contingent of Swindon fans – who have based themselves for the evening en masse on the grass slope that overlooks the third bend in one direction and, with a short walk, the pits in the other – he rather unusually completely misses the start and is comprehensively out-gated by Travis McGowan. Was this lack of reaction or concentration brought on by the inordinate wait? Who can say? It certainly can't have helped his mental preparations. What we can say is that he thunders extremely forcefully under Travis on the third bend directly in front of my position and that of the Swindon fans. In 'real time' without the benefit of replays and at high speed, it looks to me that Leigh has angrily and aggressively completely taken off the leading rider and should be excluded for his actions. We then face another delay, during which Leigh stomps back to the pits in high dudgeon, while the referee Mick Posselwhite contemplates life, the meaning of the universe and numerous television replays. To my astonishment, if no one else's other than the whole stadium of Racerdogs fans, the ref then excludes Travis for reasons that completely escape me. The Reading mechanic next to me puts it very eloquently, "he's going to freaking bottle it – the freaking chicken ref". Maybe it's a new rule for having the temerity to lead a narked Grand Prix rider. In the re-run normal service is resumed when Leigh, after this astonishing reprieve, channels his anger into a superlative start and a tremendously comfortable win to give the Robins an initial 1-5 lead.

Reluctant to immediately give up the brilliant opportunity that a pits pass provides, I wait patiently during the inordinate time taken between heats 1 and 2 – something that characterises the whole night but, at least, gives everyone the chance to study the dilapidated surroundings that still greet you at Smallmead that even BSI haven't sorted but that I personally find greatly adds to the appeal of the place – to see if the view improves. It doesn't and I think even the riders find it frustratingly hard to get a good view round the *Sky Sports* interview booth despite them having the advantage that they can press themselves against the dog track fence to try to see. It's very noticeable that Jonathan Green really doesn't need a microphone to amplify his voice. The Racerdogs have immediately replied with their own 5-1 in that heat and the next sees Lee Richardson recall his time spent at Smallmead in the formative years of his speedway career to win. Albeit if he were really in tune with his formative years spent here, he should have spent time at the back of the race or on the track if he was to provide true authenticity.

A forlorn and dispirited air lingers over the crowd in the stadium during the enforced heat intervals we have to suffer after every single race. The riders take advantage – or, as this is the Elite League, their mechanics do – to thoroughly prepare their bikes for each race. So much so that, unusually, there is no "engine failure" for either side all night and only one retirement by Adrian Miedzinski. Even Jonathan and Kelvin look intermittently bereft and at a bit of loss with what to do with themselves during all the additional time they have. Mostly they content themselves with some earnest study of the television monitor of the races that take place elsewhere at Alwalton Stadium. It's the most post-modern of experiences since we're at a live event but, to really appreciate it, you need to have access to the live television pictures to sense its rhythm and truly understand all the nuances of the meeting.

Someone who does keep very busy is the clamper who operates in the grounds of the modern business park adjacent to the stadium. This development is the ultimate example of the gradual gentrification of the industrial area that has surrounded Smallmead since it opened in 1975. The place is unrecognisable nowadays and the next-door business park has, no doubt, even attracted consultants to find a suitable name to reflect the aspirations of the businesses that chose to locate themselves in these swish contemporary buildings. They have chosen the designation "Green Park" for themselves, which they must be pretty proud of as they have erected a giant illuminated version of this name – lit up in bright green – on a tall column that you can see some considerable distance away. It's not the greatest choice of name as this is hardly a bucolic or verdant area though, that said, the canal is less polluted than it was and they have planted trees and shrubs and generally prettied up the place with turf laid everywhere to enhance the faux countryside effect. The website for this self-important facility boasts, "it's a place where people, as well as businesses – can flourish in beautiful surroundings (!), and with every facility close at hand". It's the nature of modern business to ensconce themselves in gated communities ("private property – keep out") at work and at home, so it's no surprise that they have high fences, security staff and patrols at this site. Rather generously, there are repeated announcements over the tannoy that give recalcitrant drivers one last chance of an amnesty from the clampers if "they report to the nice man at the front of the stadium and move their car immediately from Green Park where they've parked illegally". If they do decide to move their cars – and I would, no matter how bright an idea it seemed at the time to sneak your car onto the nearby driveway when you arrived late at the stadium and found the official Smallmead car park full and couldn't be bothered to drive to the overflow one comparatively nearby – they will save themselves the "£300" clamping fee! Tonight they will even have ample time to move their car between heats and might not even miss a race, should they decide to park their car some distance away at the M4 service station and then illegally walk along the hard shoulder back to Smallmead! The litany of car makes and registrations read out over the loudspeakers gives an unwitting sociological insight into the income levels of traditional (albeit late arriving) speedway fan and their choice of motor. The parking violators all apparently drive cars with ageing number plates and the models chosen include a silver Focus, a purple Corsa, a white Ford, a Seat without a colour and a white Micra among many rainbow-coloured others. This litany of cars contrasts massively with some of the upscale cars that were already parked up at the stadium hours many hours before tapes up – these were all conspicuous by their sheer expense and a distinct lack of speedway related stickers in the windows – a wonderful display of the range of deluxe Mercedes, 4-by-4s, BMWs and other conspicuously consumed cars of that ilk that are traditionally driven by speedway's managerial and owner class.

Back inside the stadium, I move to a better position from which I can easily see all the action and also spend some time on the first bend with a sparse but mixed group of Robins and Racerdogs fans. They're pretty content but not ecstatic as their side hold onto a narrow two-point lead or fail to recover a two-point deficit dependent on their allegiance. Heat 6 has McGowan fall theatrically directly in front of us on the third lap of the race that immediately prompts the fan next to me to derisively jeer, "did you forget your stabilisers?" On the track, there is quite a bit of aggression leavened with determination between both sets of riders. The first running of Heat 7 has Matej Zagar and Adrian Miedzinski smash painfully into the apex of the bend. In the rerun, Zagar aggressively treated Richardson to a close view of the safety fence on the first bend of laps one and two. He did this with almost violent determination but without actually touching him and it was enough of a sign for Richardson to back off and to settle for second place. I also think it signalled the point at which the Racerdogs team psychologically intimidated and defeated their rivals on the night. Zagar definitely has the mental mastery of this Swindon partnership pairing when he next easily defeats them in Heat 10, when he's joined up front by Travis McGowan who scatters the Robins like pigeons frightened by a hungry cat, when he bowls aggressively up inside them.

Worse is to come for the Robins when Leigh Adams appears to be taken off by Zagar in Heat 11 and is then excluded for his troubles by the referee. To my untutored eye this looks a harsh decision. Leigh looks even less happy – as though he's sucking on an angry wasp – than he did earlier while he impatiently waited for the meeting to start. He pointedly waves away Zagar who has come round on his bike to offer him a lift back to the pits. The re-run features a successive 5-1 for the Racerdogs and has their cumulative lead extend to an unassailable ten points. Another long delay allows yet more loud imprecations over the tannoy for the Racerdogs faithful to use the time to rush back to their cars or to the stadium entrance for bargains as "there's 50% off everything at the track shop". I wonder if my books have already been heavily discounted on their first ever night on sale here? It's not until the meeting is nearly at a close that these announcements get the addition of the very important caveat "on Bulldogs merchandise". The club Dinner Dance is also extensively trailed all night but this sounds a hugely expensive and improbably deluxe affair – completely out of keeping with the traditions of speedway or, historically, the club itself – at a swish hotel in Caversham. The ludicrous price sounds way out of the pocket of even most football fans and would never have even been countenanced at such a price or location in the last three decades of the running of this club. It signals the aspirations of the ownership for the future at BSI Reading but sounds to me that something has already got lost or, at least, disconnected between the loyal fans and the new management. The choice of the next musical interlude – a Deep Purple song played loudly on the upgraded speakers the club now owns or borrows – then punctures the pretension and wonderfully illustrates in aural fashion the true roots of the club.

I'm standing behind Swindon owner and speedway impresario Terry Russell in the pits viewing area as he intently studies the race card as if in the vain hope that some applied and intense concentration will alter the desperate look of the scores. He explains to the bloke next to him the failure of the Robins to avail themselves of the tactical substitute rider opportunity they now have the option to use under the present rules to reduce the deficit, "we nearly done it but Leigh said he'd do it in the next one! So three-three here. Please". There's no reason for me to remain here as there's nothing to be gained from either eavesdropping or from the horrendously restricted view the *Sky* booth causes. The general mood on the pits hillock among Swindon riders, mechanics and staff still appears to be one that expects an imminent fight-back rather than the headless blind panic it would inspire in me, if I supported them. Sadly the speedway fairy has deserted the Robins so Terry's wish doesn't come true and the Racerdogs win the heat 4-2 to take the score to a still theoretically and mathematically conquerable 42-30.

I have retreated back amongst the careworn Robins faithful on the third bend and find myself standing next to one of the volunteer track curatorial staff from Blunsdon, the friendly and enthusiastic Graham Cooke, who proudly wears his allegiance on his shirt and on the flag that he's brought along, with his children, for the occasion. He's quick to praise Travis McGowan as a true gentleman when it comes to the frequently neglected skill of saying 'thank you' – "he's a good bloke – Moose always comes out to thank us afterwards". Graham's forecast of the likelihood of success for the Adams-Ulamek combination doesn't bode well for the outside chance of a fight-back by the Robins. "Adams doesn't like riding with Ulamek – he's first out of the gate but often last out of the bend, and he tends to slow as he enters the corners which doesn't help Leigh one bit. This is especially so on away tracks where he gates like lightning but is often slow in mid to late corner on turns 1 and 2. He is then fast down the straight but slows up entering a corner before blasting out of it. This means there is bunching behind on the entry to the corners and that makes it difficult for his partner to make their way through". It's a perceptive analysis that generates a rational concern, which is immediately borne out by events on the track as the black-and-white helmeted Adams can only manage second place behind Zagar. There's clearly no love lost between these two and they conspicuously don't even bother with the post-race charade of pretending to get on or the charade that would usually see one offer the other rider the consolation of a hand of congratulation.

As if this final nail in the coffin isn't enough on its own, the massed ranks of disappointed Robins fans are then goaded beyond all reasonable stoicism by an ill-advised walk on the track by BSI Reading promoter, Jim Lynch, who for reasons best known to himself decides to walk back to the pits on the track directly in front of the third bend. This is supremely misjudged and thoughtlessly incendiary after such a great disappointment that tonight is exacerbated by a much longer time to view proceedings through the bitter optic of alcohol-fuelled chagrin brought on by the lengthy delays caused by *Sky's* transmission needs. The sight of Jim raises gleeful cheers from the Racerdogs fans but immediately causes great disapproval and anger from the fans of his keen local rivals. The courtesy and equanimity of speedway fans is widely acknowledged but this is a test too far. I see an apple thrown close by to Jim (and apparently an air horn was too but I didn't witness that). Though it misses him, in pantomime fashion he affects to be shocked at this lack of 'sportsmanship' and exaggeratedly shakes his head in a schoolmasterly way at the cadre of Robins fans directly in front of him who boo and communicate through some easily understandable gestures. I can't ever recall the sight of anyone other than a rider or member of track staff walking back to the pits via the track during a match (except after an injury), let alone an important one like this when feelings will inevitably run high. Jim has at best been thoughtless and bungling, though I don't excuse throwing objects at him, it's an action that does raise this possibility.

Graham 'Blunsdon Blog' Cooke and son, David. © Jeff Scott

A Sky temple © Jeff Scott

Reading Bulldogs Press Officer Andy Povey © Jeff Scott

In fact it adds a really unpleasant atmosphere to a small group of belligerent and disgruntled Robins fans who then decide to look for a fight. In this case, they light upon the nearest figure of Racerdogs authority in the form of the fluorescent-jacketed Paul Hunsdon. I would say that alcohol gave them 'Dutch courage', except they clearly didn't need that to imagine provocation or to indulge in some fisticuffs. A black-haired stocky, thickset bloke in his early sixties (!) who had a physique clearly well used to manual labour and toned over a lifetime for mindless violence – set off by his 'high mileage' face – tries to manhandle Paul with a view to confrontation. Paul, an imposing figure himself, skilfully defused the situation by his loud demands of, "Don't touch me! Don't touch me!" Without the response he wanted, the would-be assailant glowers at Paul who sensibly has promptly retreated through the pits fence gate to put some much needed fencing between him and the 'still up for it' soon-to-be OAP. This man wore the uniform of chav violence – white trainers, blue casual trousers, tattoos, gold chain, blue track suit top with the cross of St George prominently displayed. He continues to jeer in the hope of a reaction, which never comes. Afterwards Paul tells me, "I'd have been within my rights to have thrown him out then and there with the help of other stewards – but you have to look closely at any situation when you're a steward and do what's best, and that would have made the situation much worse and have set things off in the crowd!" It's a situation he judged to perfection.

I retreat from the glowering male who still shouts and gestures obscenely as he grandstands for his small coterie of dim-witted mates. The vast majority of the Robins fans also shrink away from them as much as they can in a big crowd placed in a confined area. At the top of the slope, like caged animals we all press against the wire fence that overlooks the pits before Heat 15. With the final result a foregone conclusion and with their season's ambitions in tatters, nothing much happens on the Robins side of the pits apart from disconsolate packing away of equipment. Whereas the Racerdogs side is equally becalmed as though they always expected to win and therefore take this important triumph completely in their nonchalant stride. Someone who is evidently completely beside herself with almost orgasmic delight is a rather gamine-looking lady who clasps everyone available in a clinging hug that involves kisses and thrusting her body close to the shale-splattered kevlars of the riders. Each rider gets this treatment in turn – McGowan, Zagar and so on – even if they pretend to half-heartedly suddenly work on their bikes. Even Jim Lynch gets a huge suffocating hug that temporarily dwarfs him. A Robins fan pressed against the wire mesh of the fence remarks sardonically, "Madam – you have no taste!"

Even though the result is a foregone conclusion, we're still treated to a thrilling last heat which has Zagar fight his way back through the field from last place during which time Leigh Adams stalks Charlie Gjedde until he storms past him on the back straight of the fourth lap. This would usually be enough for a hard-fought race victory but as Adams passes Gjedde to enter the final corner, Zagar uses all his track craft and years of hard won knowledge around the varied contours of the Smallmead track – allied to his natural gifts of skill and bravery at high speed – to sweep round the fourth bend and narrowly manage to beat Adams on the line. Needless to say, they again don't shake hands. The meeting closes at around 10.25 p.m. nearly three hours after the scheduled start time. This is not the way to treat the fans that paid to loyally file through the turnstiles.

Wild celebrations ensue among the Racerdogs riders and fans. As the crowd stream away I bump into Darcia, one of the stewards I met at Blunsdon. She's totally disgusted with what she perceives as the vainglorious behaviour of Jim Lynch, "What sort of idiot is he? He really shouldn't do that as a manager – someone should write to the BSPA about it. I'll write – no matter someone chucked it at him, he shouldn't have been there to have it chucked at him!" It definitely sours recollections of what has been a closely contested meeting. For the Robins who stream away into the Berkshire night defeat is just about bearable but lack of grace in victory is not.

25th September Reading v Swindon (Elite League Play-Off Semi-Final) 51-43

Tigers bitten on the Island
26th September

Dave Pavitt is, as usual on a race day, already ensconced on the comfy seats in the Wightlink ticket office. Before he sails to the Island, this is the nerve centre of operations where he calmly deals with a constant stream of riders and mechanics who come in to collect their tickets for the car ferry sailing or as he fields innumerable phone calls on his mobile. If each call heated his phone, it would get red hot as it rings constantly as though his number had somehow got mistaken for that of a busy call centre. This evening's fixture is a huge one for the club since it's the first leg of the Premier League quarter-final play-off against the Glasgow Tigers. Dave is quietly optimistic that his side could provide a shock if they establish a big enough lead from tonight's fixture at Smallbrook. This is reasonably likely since there is a huge contrast in the size and shape of the two tracks though, that said, the Tigers do have the services of ex-Islander Danny Bird. Dave though takes nothing for granted and, when asked as he is repeatedly on the phone or by the stream of people that arrive to collect their ferry tickets, is guardedly cautious about the Islanders' prospects.

Not only does the club have an ownership structure that is unique within British speedway but, because of its location, the club has to maximise its income from attendances in the very narrow time window that is the summer holiday season. During late July and early August, crowd sizes are swelled dramatically by holidaymakers who flock along for something different to entertain themselves with on a Tuesday night. Despite the importance and prestige of tonight's fixture, Dave is very realistic in his expectations, "if we get 300 I'll be pleased".

Already here and waiting patiently for the 4 p.m. crossing is Dave 'The Rat' Rattenberry who shares the driving down from the Midlands in the "Ratmobile" with his good friend John 'Fozzie' Hendley, who works long hours in the Wolverhampton Wanderers Football Club press office. What a wonderful job this must be for any true Wolves fan like Fozzie. It sounds exciting to me and I don't even follow the Wolves. The downside of all this behind the scenes access is that the club invariably expects that you will work very long hours (60 or so a week) without any overtime pay. Though, just like the many people who voluntarily dedicate themselves to help out at speedway clubs round the country, it's also a labour of love for Fozzie. He also likes his speedway and the team often gets space on its achievements (or travails) in the football programme. Tonight is his first ever trip to Smallbrook and he's excited at the prospect ahead.

The Isle of Wight track shop is the furthest flung outpost of the Rat's empire and he's in buoyant mood about the viability of the shop, despite the often small crowd numbers the club attracts through the turnstiles. Any track shop survives on the sheer volume of small, low value "impulse" purchases that people make on pens, boards, air horns and the like. The high number of these low value purchases over the season – providing that you source these incidentals at good prices and with a sensible margin built in – are the cornerstone to a profitable business rather than the 'big ticket' items that sell less frequently. Rat, as you'd expect, keeps meticulous records of sales, stock supplied and weekly takings, "all the little bits add up – people underestimate it but the odds and sods soon mount up. After all, I'm a businessman who's in it for the money like everyone else but you can be nice about it! In this job, I have to deal with some lovely people and some really difficult ones but it doesn't cost you to be friendly". I have found the Rat friendly and helpful in all my dealing with him and, most importantly, as he's keen to point out to me, "I always pay promptly – make sure you mention that!"

It's always a delight to take the ferry over to the Island and Rat kindly offers me a lift with my books and hand-made advertising sign in the Ratmobile along with Fozzie. They're clearly well used to each other's company. The weather is lovely and there's always a real sense of departure and adventure when you leave the quayside at Portsmouth. There's quite a queue of cars and vans. As ever, the most impressive model belongs to the Islanders' away team manager Dave Croucher who this afternoon has arrived in a top of the range Bentley. He's a car dealer by profession and relishes the chance to negotiate at every opportunity. He's on his mobile phone talking loudly and has adopted his confident, matey, professional voice, "which car is it? Oh the silver one – that's a really good choice". Invariably Dave wears a lot of bling and this afternoon he glitters with gold – almost from head to toe – from the rings, bracelets and watch on his wrists to his trademark gold medallion. If there were muggers or car thieves on the ferry over to the Island they'd be sure to target Dave on a weekly basis. Though, that said, his size and confident demeanour reeks of a man who can look after himself and has insouciantly looked after himself many times before. The ferry is crowded with speedway riders and staff. There's Dudley, the ex-track shop manager, whom I haven't seen for some time as a result of his pending divorce, and he's brought along his delightful 19-year-old daughter Sarah. Rather than chat inside, I prefer to take advantage of the sailing so choose the more bracing upper level of the outside deck where Glasgow announcer Michael Max stands by the rail gazing wistfully out to sea. It's a long shared drive down from Glasgow – "most of our riders don't mind the drive here as they live in the South – it's the home meetings that are the long ones for them" – but he's pleased that the fixture hasn't been threatened by the weather. They've had quite enough of that at Ashfield already this season – thank you. Last weekend the club had its sixtieth anniversary meeting; "big crowd, shit meeting" is his blunt verdict. Michael is non-committal about the likely result this evening but, apparently, the team has its game plan for the evening and, even more importantly, a plan of action off the track, "whatever happens tonight, we'll be on that ten o'clock sailing rather than the eleven as that hour makes all the difference on the way back. You get used to it though".

We arrive so early at the stadium that those like myself, Rat, Fozzie, Dudley and Sarah immediately retire to the "5-1 Bar" in the main grandstand for a refreshing cup of tea. We are all served by the warmly friendly Vanessa who, along with many other culinary delights, prepares the notorious Belly Buster burgers in a small kitchen just off the bar area on a race night. While we sit around to pass the time, Rat tells me that Glasgow co-promoter, Alan Dick, is an influential person in football circles; he used to be involved at Partick Thistle but now has left there, yet still maintains an important involvement with this other sporting code, "He was the delegate at the Rangers v Celtic match seeing that everything was just right and reporting back to UEFA". Rat himself is massively keen on football – not only his beloved Wolves that he no doubt discussed at length with Fozzie on the journey – but particularly amateur football. He's an obsessive 'ground hopper' and has travelled throughout the UK and Europe to "2,800 football grounds in 30 years", which even my maths tells me is quite a few each season! After I've liberated a small table from the bar, I set my books up on the banking that overlooks the first bend. The dapper Alan Dick wanders by in his bright red Glasgow Tigers anorak – it's an understated one compared to the more garish varieties favoured by the more committed of their fans – as he carefully studies the track. "It's a lovely place here but they always over-water the track – look at those puddles, it's shocking". I mention that Michael Max comes in for some ribbing on my Blog in my report on the recent derby meeting. In his soft Scots accent, Alan is very definite, "You can say anything you like about Michael – don't feel that you need to stop short in any way!"

My trip to the referee-cum-announcer's box that overlooks a few rows of seats in the grandstand and the start line at Smallbrook finds speedway institution Bryn Williams already in situ for the evening. He draws on his approximately millionth fag of the day as he surveys the programme. Bryn has some illness or disability that you can't help but be aware of – though I'm not sure what but I believe it's rheumatoid arthritis that, when you look closely, causes the fingers in his hand to look both distended and etiolated. Whatever this affliction actually is, he makes absolutely no concession to it in terms of his behaviour and attitude, "Let's face it there's millions of people in the world worse off than me". In fact Bryn handily has quite a few jokes and self-deprecating comments, "The doctor says he could cut off all the arthritic nodules but they'd just grow back even worse. When I say 'what do I do when I meet a beautiful 36 year nymphomaniac?' – he said 'wear long sleeves'!" It's not much of a safe sex message for the medical profession to give out and we both know that the median age among the ladies at speedway meetings is such that it's much more likely to throw up 63 year olds, frisky or otherwise. Bryn had considered having his fingers broken and reset to correct their shape – that would be very 'speedway riderish' of him – but hasn't, "I can't stand pain". Every winter he 'takes in' the sunshine in Australia to help recuperate for the speedway months ahead of him each year.

During each meeting, Bryn's commentary is always a delight to listen to and he has an insider's insight into the machinations and personalities of most people involved in contemporary speedway. His background is in motor claims insurance and he worked 15 years for a Lloyds broker. "I had nine staff and earnt a good whack for those days", until he had a "bad year in 91 when my dad died, my wife had an affair and left me – though annoyingly, given her adultery, she got the council house and the right to buy 'cause we had an eleven year old daughter who I eventually put through university, so her old dad didn't do too bad – and I was made redundant". Rather than buckle under, Bryn got on with life and "looked for work for a few months but at 45 I was already too old". He moved in with his bereaved mother to nurse her through her declining years. Throughout this time speedway has been a constant source of pleasure, interest and release. Sat by the windows, Bryn contently draws on another fag and surveys the tractor that circles the track. More people arrive to fill the narrow but smoky confines of the box, so I beat a retreat as they throw themselves into detailed discussions of the ups and downs, and ins and outs of recent speedway events, gossip and speculation.

The crowd has by now started to funnel into the stadium. I attract some curiosity – people glance over as they pass, some stop to read the review comments stuck on my board and others ponder a purchase but then decide against it. Topics under discussion range widely but, in the light of my extensive travels, I'm invariably asked 'what is your favourite track?' Many tracks have much to recommend them but for different reasons. I like to watch at Smallbrook because of the size of the track, the speeds that they get up to and the banking of the last bend that adds to the thrill of chase and the overtaking here. Everyone is keen to advocate the laudable characteristics of their personal favourite and to persuade me of the validity of their choice. Often these tracks are now defunct and went out of business long ago without my ever visiting. Some Wimbledon fans that gather by my table are still bereft at the recent closure of Plough Lane. One of them, Les O'Keefe, is adamant but vexed, "Though it wasn't anything like it used to be before. It was something really special not like it was recently though that was much better than nothing. For all my life, they say we'd still be there if it wasn't for him, that man, why doesn't he stand aside and let someone like Dingle – a proper speedway man – get on with sorting things back out with the GRA?" Further discussion is cut short by a shout from a passing Dave Pavitt who is on his way to the pits and has by now donned his BSPA promoter's jacket, "don't buy it – it's rubbish!" Grinning at his own mischief he replies to my, "But you said you liked it!" with, "I do and I only say nice things about you; but it's still rubbish!" With this sort of help and advocacy from Dave, it's fortunate that Bryn's dulcet tones soon echo round the stadium with a wholehearted recommendation to any wavering purchasers who lurk in the crowd.

Though it has been a lovely sunny day, I soon get a lesson in what my mum would call "common sense". Notably, that as soon as the sun wanes and starts to dip below the horizon, so does the temperature and light rapidly fades. I soon find myself standing on a hillock in the dark with a sign only the really keen sighted could read and with a table of books that are suddenly sodden with the dew that has quickly started to bend the pages and peel the glued papers from my sign. I make a mental note to myself to remember to bring some clear plastic bags to store all books in for the rest of the season as the levels of damp increase as the nights draw in across the country. Luckily, though hopeless for sales, these are ideal viewing conditions for speedway. The sky round the stadium is darkened and thereby throws the arc of the floodlights on the track into even sharper relief and further emphasizes the spectacle of the contest. Not that the Glasgow riders appear to be at all keen to race and after two heats already trail by 9-3. The score has extended to 23-13 by Heat 6 and so they have to resort to the tactical rules in order to try to stem the flow of points against them. Nieminen wins a close-fought race with Jason Doyle whereas at the back of the race Chris Johnson and Lee Dicken indulge in their own mini-battle for supremacy. Dave Rat isn't impressed with what he sees "It's like an Elite League race this – strung out with two races in one." There's a continued hint of revival for the Tigers in the next race when Robert Ksiezak leads throughout until Jason Bunyan overtakes him in superlative fashion on the last lap. The Glasgow team already appear to have their mind on the earlier ferry sailing home while the Islanders exhibit an overall determination that consistently leaves their opponents in their wake. Even the likely trump cards in the form of renowned heat leaders Danny Bird and Shane Parker isn't the threat anticipated since both appear comparatively out of sorts, with the Australian notably off the pace.

There is quite a bit of entertainment to be had from Bryn's commentary and he indulges in the opportunity to trot out some of his tried and tested stock phrases on the meagre crowd. Before the meeting even starts the arrival on the track of the mascot, Rob Joiner, prompts Bryn to inform us: "He's determined to become the first person born on the Island to ride for the Islanders – but that's in the future and for now he's having his usual spin". In a funny way, in one comment Bryn has summed up both the appeal of speedway – the real chance that with application and ability it is possible to achieve your goals and almost realistic aim to become a star on your local track – as well as the nature of dreams and sincerely held ambitions too. In that these never come true unless you dare to have them in the first place and then decide to act upon them: it's life-affirming stuff! As ever we learn that Ray Morton, "like fine wine matures with age" and when he defeats Shane Parker in Heat 9, Bryn can't help but speak approvingly of his efforts, "Ray Morton winning the battle of the old boys". The sale of the "50/50 draw" raffle tickets allows him to name check "Sexy Sue – the woman with the most distinctive voice in speedway" and he then mentions, as he always does, the interesting fact, "Sue doubles up as the Ryde town crier during the summer months". Summer has passed and so have the crowds. Though autumn is nearly upon us, the Islanders ride with a spring in their attitude and the Tigers ride listlessly without luck. This is typified by an engine failure for Danny Bird at the start line when he has come out for a tactical ride in the black-and-white helmet colour. Nieminen still looks likely to gain some advantage for the Tigers but is superbly overtaken by exciting young Aussie prospect Chris Holder on the second bend of the third lap. Having abandoned all hope of further book sales and with the dew by now thickly coating every book on the table or the box I store the resolutely unsold remainder in, I wander down to the pits where I notice that James Cockle is making a mobile phone call. I did think that this had already been banned since the start of this season in all the leagues to avoid the appearance, if not the reality, of riders responding to outside influences during a meeting. The way that Glasgow have ridden so far, you could almost imagine that James is in touch with an Asian betting syndicate to discuss how much further they should throw this meeting. With only two races to go Glasgow trail 52-29 and look highly likely to be eliminated from the quarter finals, as this level of deficit looks hard to make up at Ashfield in the return leg no matter how well they ride their own home track. Then, as though the betting syndicate have responded to some last-minute large spread bets, Glasgow somehow mange to win the last two heats 2-5 and 1-5 for an overall loss of 55-39. This 16-point deficit looks almost recoverable and the Islanders' management and riders must wonder how on earth a tie that they'd dominated throughout suddenly slipped away in the closing stages. These lost points might come back to haunt them and deny what would have been a well-deserved easy progression to the semi-final stage of the play-offs.

It has barely gone quarter past nine when the fixture ends and the riders can almost pack up in a serenely leisurely fashion and still ensure that they easily catch the earlier ten o'clock sailing. On the ferry home, I overhear talk about the disappointing size of the crowd on the Island tonight. The consensus is that the club only survives through a combination of careful husbandry of the finances, the unique ownership structure, the bumper crowds of the summer, allied to the ownership of the catering and bar facilities at the track but, most importantly, the variety of the other events and activities that they regularly try to stage at the stadium. Thankfully all this in combination allows this wonderful club to survive. Around the country many clubs struggle with crowd numbers and, even more worryingly, with their profitability. The golden age has passed, the licence to print money has long since expired and the heyday could take a long time to return, if it ever does. The list of clubs that are profitable is debated with some heat and contention but the most commonly mentioned clubs that people claim are 'profitable' doesn't provide a very long list. I have redacted the names of the clubs, but if this gossip is accurate, there will be a lot of promoters having to look closely at a balance sheet covered in red ink and having to consider their business plans for the future extremely closely indeed over the winter months, or in the next few years ahead. The oft-repeated saviour that is *Sky Sports* television coverage doesn't seem to translate into increased crowds or sponsorship at the Elite level and definitely has negligible impact outside this rarefied echelon. No matter how you look at, even a serial optimist would struggle to convincingly sketch out a bright future.

26th September Isle of Wight v Glasgow (Premier League Quarter-Final Play-Off 1st Leg) 55-39

October 2006

"The riders were asked to get changed and warm the bikes up, which appeared to be happening. But once they were in the changing rooms they took their own vote and word reached me that all 12 were refusing to ride. I then asked the riders if there was anything else the Newcastle promotion could do to get them to change their mind, but they did not seem interested."
Referee Chris Durno on Newcastle v Redcar abandonment

"We walked the track two or three times and although the referee said the track was fine, we are the ones who ride the bikes and in our opinion the track was not fine. There are plenty of other dates this month to put the meeting on when we can come back and put on a show rather than, at best, watch follow-the-leader racing or, at worst, pick up some injuries."
Gary Havelock

"If it had been me riding, my bikes wouldn't have even come out of the vehicle, it was so bad when I arrived. It was just a mud bath."
Brian Havelock, Redcar team manager and Gary's dad

"The referee said the track was rideable and I agreed with him, so it was purely down to the riders that we had no racing. One minute there was no problem, then the next there were loads."
Darryl Illingworth, Newcastle co-promoter

"There are 101 things I'd like to say on the matter but I'd rather not comment at the moment as it might prejudice any appeal."
Gary Havelock after receiving a two-year suspended ban to go along with the £250 fine on the night

"It's my ambition to see a team made up of British riders here at Oxford. Let's face it, they don't cause you any trouble, they are always here week in and week out and obviously treat British Speedway with the respect it deserves."
Colin Horton looks to the future after buying Oxford

"I was totally disgusted by Rye House's non-appearance. I think it's a disgrace and a slur on Scottish speedway. They should have the book thrown at them for this and, at the end of the day, the buck must stop with Len Silver because he is the promoter. For him to do something like this after more than 40 years in the sport is very sad."
Stewart Dickson after Rye House fail to show for the PL Pairs at Glasgow

"Chris Neath was seriously ill and in hospital. Steve Boxall arrived at Workington with a similar illness to Chris and, additionally conjunctivitis, making vision extremely difficult. The doctor at Workington ruled him out of Glasgow. Stuart Robson, Edward Kennett and Tommy Allen all had injuries aggravated by the heavy conditions of the rain affected Workington track. All three were examined, at my insistence, by the track doctor who ruled each one of them as unfit to race the next day. Each had daily private physiotherapy treatment in an effort to reduce their pain in order to race seven days later. The Rye House reserves, Luke Bowen, Jamie Courtney, Adam Roynon, Ben Powell were all seriously injured. All in all, nine riders were unfit to ride in the Pairs... we informed Glasgow of the situation as soon as the Workington doctor had issued the medical certificates and believed that Glasgow would have called on the services of local riders of some ability to take our place. As it was, the meeting reserves were used. This was not our decision. It is very easy to criticise the fact that we were absent and, of course, that is extremely regrettable. However, nobody has as yet suggested what I personally could have done to solve the problem. Guest riders are not permitted in the Pairs competition so I wasn't even able to go down that road. I apologise to Scottish fans for our non-appearance but, frankly, we had no fit riders and no way of solving the problem."

Len Silver replies and the Workington doctor gets writer's cramp

"I don't mind the banter and the gestures from the terraces but the continuing threats of physical violence and 'in your face' verbal taunts after meetings are another matter, and they are not welcomed by me or my family... I genuinely apologise to those paying public not associated with this group who unavoidably got soaked. My actions were meant to be light-hearted and of a non-violent nature and I obviously regret dousing innocent families who were caught up in my actions of throwing some celebratory water at the Mexican contingent. It wasn't meant to hurt anyone and it was a shame that it was taken the wrong way by some fans who were put in some discomfort. But I will wait with baited breath for a public apology from the minority of the group for their constant physical threats and verbal taunts that I continually receive off the track when not participating as a rider."

Rory Schlein on the 'Manchester Mexicans'

"I want to get Eastbourne back to being run by the fans, for the fans. Jon Cook will remain as co-promoter and day-to-day manager of the team's affairs... I think Jon is the beating heart of the Eastbourne Eagles and I cannot thank him enough for helping me to make this happen. I must also pay tribute to the Dugard family for their help and advice. There is so much expertise around the club that if we all pull together we can show people what a great speedway club really is... [I want] to build on what I think the club stands for: great entertainment, a proud history, a team top riders want to ride for – and a chance for youngsters to have a go, and be nurtured into speedway stars of tomorrow."

Bob Brimson delights in his ownership of Eastbourne speedway

"I know now that it was a bad idea and I am sorry if I have upset people by riding in that meeting. I shouldn't have done it and I know it looks bad; but I didn't do it to spite anyone, I just wanted to see if there was any way that I could race again this season. I am disappointed and a little upset by some of the things that have been said. Ian Thomas seems to have a problem with me, but I don't see what it has to do with him – he's not my boss. He should speak to me about it if he has something to say."

Antonio Lindback attempts to explain his surprise appearance in the Rickardsson farewell meeting

"Sometimes it is too easy to judge. What everyone has to remember is that he is a young kid still. Don't prejudge Anton because he truly wants to ride for Poole. He will play a massive part for this club in the future, so I hope people can forgive and forget."

Matt Ford appeals to those who judge Antonio

"I should stress that the tactical ride rule was implemented by the BSPA. It is a misconception to suggest that it was introduced at the behest of *Sky*."

Richard Clark, editor of the *Speedway Star*

"I get sick and tired of other people within the sport, people who should know better, who turn round and accuse me of using 'chequebook speedway' to win the league title... those people who say that I bought the league are obviously very bitter and twisted and I suggest that they go and

get a life. It's the nature of the sport, I guess, that success is met with jealousy but I would prefer it if we could have a more civilised situation where we congratulate the winners."
Colin Horton answers his critics

"I think Ronnie will have to make some changes."
Leigh Lanham looks ahead to the 2007 season

"I will be staying at Somerset, I am still determined to see the job through and take the club forward, I don't do things by half."
BSPA Chairman, Peter Toogood, scotches sale rumours

"I can remember it very well and particularly David Norris doing this most extraordinary thing. I watched him come back to the pits after a race, sit down, take out this little tin and roll himself a roll up. I remember thinking he's everything in a sportsman I can completely respect... [David] absolutely loves his sport, he's a good friend now and he's very evangelical about the sport, he calls it 'my sport' and I can't imagine football players doing that."
Bob Brimson praises a fellow smoker

"If we are back and racing next year, the whole track will be ripped up and laid properly. The main problem is there is currently no base to this track and we are going to put one in. Without it, the shale can move around and this leaves you with quite a rutty and bumpy surface. You can fill in holes all day long with concrete and shale, but you would just be chasing holes all over the place."
Phil Bartlett promises track changes at Radipole Lane

I don't need to earn money out of speedway but I would like to have some kind of paid directorship at Eastbourne. I'd rather make the club financially sound and I'd like to have a bank balance that means I can view a good year or a bad year as the impostor it is... we only have so many resources and I'm the one who will make the decisions of where we spend the time and the little marketing money we have. I'm quite a demanding person to work for and my brief to Jon is to put out the strongest team you can every meeting within the budget."
Bob Brimson outlines his vision for the future development of Eastbourne

Stabilisers Optional
1st October

It's now many months since the first abortive attempt to run the Elite League Riders Championship in mid-April ended in mutual recriminations and upset between the riders and officialdom in the form of vociferously complaining promoters. Many of those in authority with responsibility for the promotion and/or administration of the sport were keen to deflect attention from their own complicit involvement in the state of affairs that contemporary British speedway finds itself ineluctably locked into with regard to its (death-spiral?) dependence on the availability of superstar riding talent. Some were keen to blame the inexperience and 'weakness' of the referee Daniel Holt as well as to exaggerate the general impact of so-called unfettered rider power rather than conduct any analysis that might responsibly lead to different conclusions. The claim of substantial and reckless 'rider power' is a hardy perennial but often difficult to substantiate when the vast majority of riders are frequently beholden to the capricious whims and commercial imperatives of the British promoters – let alone the frequently changing points limit they tinker with every year at the annual BSPA meeting – for their continued livelihood.

I've arrived early and the always-friendly Poole co-promoter Mike Golding directs me to a table right next to the

Fourth corner action at ELRC. © Jeff Scott

programme stall and the toilets. I'm very early and many of the staff have yet to arrive, let alone report for duty. Those that have stand around or slowly start to prepare for when the turnstiles open an hour or so later. There's a deserted feel to the swish back-straight grandstand they're justifiably proud of at Wimborne Road, which in turn emphasises the end-of-season atmosphere that hangs over the stadium. The weather isn't exactly ideal for speedway racing since the skies are blackly overcast and there's a very strong wind that has the tarpaulins which cover the dog track on the third bend repeatedly billow high in the air in dramatic fashion, having leapt free of the tyres that are usually sufficient to weigh them down. The last meeting at Poole that was held at the track was less than 72 hours ago and that was abandoned. Mike matter-of-factly notes, "You have a problem when it comes to preparing the track if you don't own your own stadium and have to share it with the dogs. That means that once they've prepared the dog track – and they run meetings here on Tuesdays, Fridays and Saturdays – we can't go across it with tractors, though we could do some work on Saturday morning and so we've only really had from this morning to do it properly." Given that this is such a showpiece event in the speedway calendar or, at least, it used to be until the endless rounds of the Grand Prix series inured us all to the thrill of seeing the sport's so-called superstar riders in individual confrontation, each for personal glory on a regular basis. Though the wind might cause the riders problems, Mike remains pretty confident that they have prepared a racing surface that will withstand the demands of 22 heats of racing, though he worries that the weather could still be an issue. "The Met Office forecast says we will get some rain but the heavy stuff is going to miss Poole – we've had no rain here for the last 24 hours at all. Still the sunshine's out, though with this wind they'll need stabilisers going down the straight".

When I wander to the doorway that joins the grandstand to the rest of the outside viewing areas I bump into one of the club's safety stewards. He's proud of the facilities they have at Poole, "We know that we've got it good here when we go to other Elite League tracks, but there's still things that we could do better – like improve the disabled access so anyone in a wheelchair can get all round the stadium if they want. Now we take them in the lift to the first floor to watch but it's like the moon up there as there's no atmosphere and atmosphere is everything at speedway." Despite the years of success and the complacency that one of the best speedway stadiums in the country could engender, it's refreshing that some of the staff at the club aren't prepared to rest on their laurels when it comes to club infrastructure. I know though that all Poole fans would relish some improvement in the results that the club has achieved these past few years to match the quality of their surroundings. We're joined by a couple of other stewards, one of whom is much less positive. They're interested in my travels and enquire about my book. I mention some of the many people I've been fortunate enough to encounter, and get the reply, "if you cover everyone who's here, you'll have lots of the tight bastards in it". Before one steward leaves he nods behind us and says, "I see Lindback is here". When we all spin round to see the superstar in our midst, we discover we've been hoaxed by a gratuitously racist but throwaway comment based on a warped 'humour' brought on by the sight of the African-looking man sat at a nearby table. The friendly steward looks sour and says nothing as he leaves and I immediately wander back to my stall rather than encourage any further inappropriate or uncalled-for comments. There is no doubt that Lindback's stock has recently fallen among the Poole crowd compared to its height in other seasons. The reasons for this are varied. Some people perceive that he has shown a lack of loyalty to the Pirates cause with doubts about his application on behalf of the club in the light of some of the meetings he's chosen to miss; plus there is the overarching factor that the club have failed to secure the expected trophies in recent years and it's human nature to seek at least one scapegoat. The poor form of the reserves has often been raised this season by disgruntled Pirates fans but equally it's a short step among narrow-minded people like this steward to ascribe their perceptions of fecklessness to ethnic difference. Equally, it could just have been a thoughtless 'joke'. There is racism everywhere in Britain, especially among the older generation or in places where the ethnic mix of the population remains predominantly white. Monoculturalism and a comparative lack of ethnic diversity remains the case in many towns in the South East of England outside of London and its conurbations. Poole as a speedway club has already taken a commendable attitude to an earlier season incident with a supporter. The Poole promoter, Matt Ford, rather than take the usual speedway way of sweeping things under the carpet, or attempt to pretend that they don't exist, confronted the issue head on but in a practical manner with an admonishment that mixed condemnation with education. I've met so many lovely people at Poole speedway that this man stands out for all the wrong reasons but really doesn't represent the views of the club or the majority of speedway people who rightly pride themselves on their part in a tolerant and defiantly broad church.

A short while later the turnstiles open and I'm ideally placed by the toilets and the programme stall to hand out leaflets for my new book as the vast majority of the crowd rush past or briefly linger to buy a programme. Though, this being Poole, many of the fans enter on the other side of the stadium so that they can more easily secure their favoured place in the old-fashioned covered grandstand without the glass front that overlooks the start line. Because of the passage of time and changes to the original line up, the Poole promotion have sensibly taken it upon themselves to produce another programme for this meeting priced very reasonably at £2 with a complimentary copy of the original glossy programme thrown in for free to anyone who buys this afternoon's version. This seems both a reasonable and pragmatic decision. Though the programme ladies do a brisk trade they are temporarily interrupted by a 'Mister Angry' figure who demands, in truly unpleasant fashion, that he is "given a free copy of that programme as it's a freaking joke and a freaking rip-off that's typical of speedway nowadays". He warms to his own tirade apparently unaware of how petty-minded and stupid his anger (if not his complaint) makes him appear to everyone else, let alone the child stood patiently by his side. I don't make many sales and a leaflet that advertises my forthcoming book on the Eastbourne Eagles (*When Eagles Dared*) meets blank expressions or outright refusal. To the odd person prepared to stop and listen, I try to explain that it's really an Elite League travelogue that happens to cover the Eagles in depth and that it's a starter primer for those fans that haven't bought my original book *Showered in Shale* because of its size and price. As an explanation it cuts little ice. The kindly speedway author and avid Poole Pirates speedway fan, Glynn Shailes, stops to chat *en route* to the upstairs restaurant and kindly praises my book yet again, "yours is a unique book as it comes at it like no other book has before – it's wonderful, not at all usual and often it's a social history!"

The number of fans coming through the turnstiles has subsided to a trickle well before the rider parade. I retreat to the covered grandstand in search of any spare places that there still might be available. As luck would have it, there's a seat next to Norman 'Nobby' Hall whom I recognise from my visits to Sandy Lane in Oxford where I've seen him at work. He's now 64 and has been going to watch speedway at Oxford since 1950 and proudly recalls an aged photograph from then, "with me sitting on the rail, with the grandstand and me mum behind me". He has many odd jobs around the stadium that he relishes both as an activity and as a way of staying involved with the club, "I pump up the air fence, help the tractor man with the grade, fill the water and do security on the pit gate". He knows about my book, "I hear my grandson is in your book". This turns out to be the photo I have of the mascot there on his small bike, though 'Nobby' didn't know that his picture also appeared in my book. Nobby struggles intermittently to get his words out, "sorry I can't speak – I have Parkinson's". He's come along to the meeting with his friend Lee Morris who has arrived in this country with his 12-year-old son, Nick, so that they can see what racing is actually like here. Back in Australia, Nick already shows signs of great promise and his father beams with pride but also takes a practical approach by helping his son develop and properly serve his motorcycling apprenticeship, since his aim is "to expose my son to the scene over here as we don't have this in

Australia". The size of engine in the bike that you ride is strictly determined by age in Australia (it differs here). Nick presently rides 125cc machines and has won some regional meetings and thereby has qualified to compete for the Queensland State title when he returns home in a few weeks. In the interim he's going to go on an extensive tour throughout Britain and Europe with his dad so that he can get some impression of the sheer variety of the tracks that he'll face when he, hopefully, comes over here to ride in the future. Just listening to the itinerary is exhausting. "We'll go to Coventry, Oxford, Bydgoszcz, Wroclaw, Arena, Eastbourne, Poole ("though it would have been Newport but we diverted here because of the rain-off"), Reading for the first leg of the play-off final, three meetings in Czecho including the 'Golden Helmet' and then back for the second leg of the play-offs at Peterborough". It's a trip I wish that I could go on myself now, though if I'd done so when I was a teenager it would have definitely confirmed any latent obsession I might have harboured to become a speedway rider. They also intend to take in a few junior training tracks during the visit and went to Arlington for this purpose yesterday. Inadvertently, they'd been there when just after mid-day the Craven Shield with Wolves and Ipswich fixture had been abandoned due to the "condition of the track". That was the official explanation anyway. This mystified them as "the track was perfect – slick if anything – though it was more likely all to do with who was guesting for Ipswich. Scotty and Bomber but only Bomber can make it next week".

Any further discussions are interrupted by the action on the track. Rather than just go through the motions as I suspected they might, the majority of the riders appear keen to show great determination and aggression to win their races. Worryingly for the chances of triumph for the rest of the field, Jason Crump wins Heat 3 by a country mile to set the tone for his afternoon. Not that it looked likely from the start when he was forced very wide by Peter Karlsson on the first bend and though Hans Andersen also hadn't made a good gate, he cut back on the inside to take the lead as they all exited the second bend before Crump then effortlessly powered past the field close to the fence and is gone.

Two heats later Greg Hancock tries desperately but doesn't quite catch Leigh Adams on the line. Heat 6 has Simon Stead experience mechanical problems when his chain snaps and very painfully whiplashes his leg. He collapses clutching his limb on the centre green, but only after he has gone to great pains to clear the track and so avoid inconveniencing the other riders with a stoppage of the race. Krzysztof Kasprzak easily wins the award for virtuoso technique on a bike with additional formation dancing when he picks up great speed when second coming into the third bend of the last lap of Heat 9. "Too fast and too tight", notes Nobby matter-of-factly after KK has shot across the apex of the bend at high speed – thereby nearly collecting Nicki Pedersen – before he runs along the edge of the fence only to dramatically depart from his bike and appears to cross the line flying through the air in slow motion on his back without any connection to his equipment that now travels separately from him. In fact, like a riderless horse in the Grand National, the bike explores a route of its own to career across the track (is skilfully avoided by Todd Wiltshire) before it then crosses the line as though ridden by the ghost of speedway past. Even more bizarrely, KK is awarded a third place (though he held second at the exact moment of the fall) by the referee Dan Holt rather than be given the widely expected exclusion, even though he wasn't on his machine, holding it at all or in control of it in any way. The announcer notes, "Krzysztof showed us some entertainment though I'm sure that he won't look on it that way". Nobby says, "I've never seen anything like it" and afterwards Mike Golding is politely mystified, "The ref ruled KK still had one hand on the handlebar when he crossed the line – I don't think he did but that was the way he saw it!" The fall was dramatic and despite the fact, like many speedway riders pumped up on pride and adrenalin, KK eventually gingerly rises to his feet and slowly hobbles back to the pits, while the warm appreciation of the crowd echoes in his ears. Sensibly, he later withdraws from the event without venturing out for another ride.

The meeting has a competitive but old-fashioned air that is increased by the wafts of fine dust that billows across the grandstand every time the riders pass on yet another lap of the track. It's just like old times with the smell of the fuel, the roar of the bikes and a light dusting of shale that coats us all along with any food we've foolishly exposed to the dust plume. In a modern era where this happens less and less and the riders' bikes all have dirt deflectors as standard, it's a welcome return to tradition as far as I'm concerned. Next to me, Nobby shows his Oxford roots every time that Todd Wiltshire takes to the track. He becomes much more animated and not only shouts words of encouragement but also twists his body as though he experiences every movement of the rider and his bike on the track. Later he shouts "go on Todd", while he shakes his fist and his arm in encouragement. After time away from competitive racing, Todd definitely looks well-suited to this company and rides comfortably throughout except for a last place in his second ride. I'm so desperate for sales that when Lee Morris asks how he can buy my book I run back to my car between heats to get him a copy. The things that authors do in the craven pursuit of sales success.

Just in front of our group is another proud father, Garry Hazelden, whose 12-year-old son Shane rides 250cc bikes in second halves, "you won't miss him, he's all in bright red". Garry "spannered for Moggo for seven years" and helpfully explains the complicated rules that apply to engine sizes and your age group as it presently applies in the UK, "from 2006, 14 and over can use a 500cc bike provided that they've passed a proficiency test". Garry appears so well informed about Sittingbourne Speedway that I suspect that he must have some involvement there but I don't confirm this. He is also keen to sing the praises of those involved with young rider development in this country. It's still an uphill struggle and, in the nature of the beast, results take an inordinately long time to arrive (if they do) and the support for young riders isn't at all consistent across the country. Some promoters go out of their way to welcome the youngsters whereas others treat them as an afterthought or an inconvenience. Others are just plain thoughtless, for instance, when the second half races fall victim to the time curfew, though there has been an extended interval during the main meeting that could have been shortened to allow a few more vital minutes of track time for the young riders. "Shane wouldn't be where he is without Peter [Oakes] – the kids really look up to him. The time, determination, dedication and the effort put in by Peter and Graham [Reeve] – you don't get to hear about him behind the scenes, how he helped it get going though it's mostly Peter nowadays – is really something. The under 15s wouldn't be where they are without Peter's vision and application or Graham's help!"

Back on the track, Heat 15 has Greg Hancock aggressively run his most famous speedway race partner, Billy Hamill, very close to the fence right in front of us on the fourth bend of the first lap. The lady in front of me approvingly notes, "Greg has got a lot harder this year". Certain races at the ELRC really stand out as full-blooded and exhilarating. Heat 16 is one of those. Hans Andersen deliberately takes Nicki to the fence in the first and second corner – to slow him down and in the process relegate him to fourth place – before he quickly accelerates to pursue Scott Nicholls down the back straight, who in turn then slows very dramatically to block him, almost as though he'd shut off. There is still no love lost between these two riders. This manoeuvre allows Nicki to pass them both at speed, but apparently oblivious to all around them in their mini-battle for supremacy, Scott and Hans elbow each other on the exit of the fourth bend before Scott then escapes for second place.

Heat 19 also features some brilliant and highly competitive speedway that belies what I still take to be the everyday nature of this event. Leigh Adams purposefully runs Nicki Pedersen right out to the fence on the first bend and it then takes Nicki until the fourth bend of the second lap to find a way past him, only for Leigh to nearly re-pass him in breathtaking fashion on the first corner of the next lap but narrowly just fail to do so. The determined Aussie then just about manages to inch in front of Nicki on the back straight of the last lap before Nicki again asserts his primacy and, typically in this mechanically troubled season, Adams then suffers an engine failure to gain zero points from this race. Both of these races have had the common denominator that they featured Nicki Pedersen. Like him or loathe him (and I like him), it really is never dull when he takes to the track. Rumours that Nicki may be on his way to ply his trade with Poole in the Elite League next year will soon have the Pirates faithful shivering their timbers in approval rather than their usual highly vocal opprobrium. In the final qualifying race of the afternoon, effortlessly confirming that all great riders apparently hit superlative form at just the right time, Greg Hancock looks extremely fast and determined which bodes well for all Racerdogs fans at Wimborne Road who'll be looking for a captain's performance from him against Peterborough in the first leg of the Elite League Play-Off final the next day. The most exhilarating pass of this race is made by Scott Nicholls who blasts confidently round Simon Stead on the last corner of the third lap.

For all the excitement provided by the other riders, the afternoon is completely dominated by one rider, Jason Crump who, based on this performance throughout the whole season, remains streets ahead of his contemporaries and erstwhile rivals in terms of speed, equipment and, most importantly, psychology. His performance is the most notable aspect of the afternoon except for the fact that we've been sprayed with dust throughout. Because I hope to sell some more of my books as people leave the stadium I wander round to the third bend to watch the concluding races. I rather distractingly stand behind a stunning looking woman with a mesmerising figure of Jessica Rabbit proportions. After a few minutes I notice that she's standing with a nondescript bloke who wears a Hells Angel jacket that bears a large crest on the back surrounded with letters that identify his allegiance, in this case to the "Headhunters Motorcycle Club Dorsetshire". I don't often think to call Dorset by its much more traditional name. It's pleasantly old fashioned and his girlfriend confirms the truism that the rebellious, wild blokes invariably get the attention of the attractive members of the opposite sex.

By virtue of their earlier scores, Jason Crump and Nicki Pedersen qualify for the final where they will compete to win a brand new bike. This is enough of a prize to ensure that they vaguely take the race seriously even without the usual key factor of overweening professional pride. In the semi-final, Scott continues to play silly buggers with Hans Andersen when he again deliberately and dramatically slows down on the first bend of the second lap just at the very point when he knows that his opponent will have wound it on to massively accelerate. Hans is really going to have to fully factor this aspect of Scott's nature into his future race plans as his repeated failure to do so again costs him dear when he fails to qualify for the final. Nicki Pedersen is in true wrecking ball form in this race. From gate 2 he takes the rider outside of him, Greg Hancock, straight to the fence on the first bend before he accelerates and repeats the medicine for the race leader Jason Crump on the third and fourth of the first lap. Unlike Greg, Jason fails to be intimidated, keeps his throttle fully open and hangs onto his machine only millimetres from the possibility of a disastrous touch of his handlebars on the fence. Having evaded the predictable manoeuvre and also held his nerve, Jason accelerates to an easy win. Afterwards when interviewed Crumpie notes, "Nicki was very fair, he made it very difficult for me but left me enough room. The last few weeks [since he became World Champion] I've had to think 'do I want to race or just ride the bike round?' – today I just wanted to race!" He really did too, and looked in a class of his own all afternoon. The crowd slowly start to drift away despite the lure of a disco in the grandstand bar until 10 p.m. Afterwards, relaxing in the bar, Mike Golding laconically notes, "if you'd seen the track on Thursday, you wouldn't have predicted we'd have a dust problem. It didn't ride well where it was still soft but overall held up really well".

The talk of the fans as they leave is the superlative performance of Jason Crump. Poole mascot, Brendan Johnson, now recovered from his mid-season injury begs to differ for his own personal reasons, "I don't like Crumpie and didn't want him to win. All the riders I've come across are only too happy to give you some time or advice if they can. I've tried to speak to him a number of times but he just blanks you. He really doesn't support youth which can't be right".

The books on display on my table attract the odd glance from passers by but no sales. As one fan leaves he stops by my table and rather ostentatiously gets out his wallet. After he's rootled about he takes out a coin and walks over to the St John ambulance staff who are stood with their collection buckets close by. I say, "I thought he was just about to buy my book". They laugh and reply, "Why – are they only 10p, then?"

1st October Elite League Riders Championship Poole – Winner: Jason Crump

Is this an apple I see before me?
2nd October

The first leg of the play-offs is just one of those nights that you really can't afford to miss, especially if you have been a devotee of 'Redin' speedway at Smallmead for many years. Given the difficulties that owner John Postlethwaite with all his marketing experience, new ideas, initiatives and television adverts has had in persuading 'new' fans to come along to the stadium to watch the rebranded Bulldogs, you just know that the majority of spectators here tonight will have previously worshipped at this particular shrine. The diehards will all be along. And to be fair to the bloke, it's a shame that success on the track hasn't directly translated into a huge increase in numbers through the turnstiles for BSI Reading, particularly since they have spent so much in an attempt to fulfil their ambitions. Love them, loathe them or even if you've managed to stay indifferent, the sport needs new blood like that provided by John Postlethwaite and his expensively assembled team. Any sport, let alone speedway, always needs people prepared and unafraid to aim for the sky (the heavens that is, not the television company), concoct grandiose plans, put in the effort, carefully craft the press releases, develop rigid hierarchies and authorisation procedures and, then, generally lash the money around. Even Press Officer Nicola Sands who has crossed my name off the guest list – kindly placed there by the Redin through-and-through and always charming Andy Povey – though she will reinstate it if I have "a BSPA pass" (though I'm sure that she well knows that I don't).

Even though it's a while before the turnstiles open there is already a long queue of people not at all put off by the egregious hike in the admission prices to an oligopolistic £17 (weirdly exactly the same figure that Peterborough independently decide to charge the next week), though the Racerdogs management are keen to stress that we receive additional benefits in the form of a live band beforehand and a "free" drink at the bar in compensation for this double figure percentage increase for a meeting that will be shown on live television. No one is apparently put off by the huge puddles in the car park as we're all safe in the knowledge that pretty well no matter what happens the meeting will have to go ahead because the *Sky Sports'* cameras and outside broadcast equipment will be here. Inside, *Sky* have set themselves up in their usual thorough and professional manner, exactly as they were the week before for the visit of Swindon, except that we will also have Sophie Blake in attendance. From the point of view of the expectation of close exciting racing, it's a big disappointment to see that the recent torrential rain has apparently affected the track almost as much as the car park. There are large puddles on all the bends except the second and the track surface looks completely sodden throughout the whole circuit; particularly so on the exit from bend two and along the length of the back straight through bend 3 to its apex. When I arrive, the track staff still vainly try to do some remedial work to improve the condition of the circuit and they spend considerable time in an apparently foolish attempt to scrape the track clear of wet shale. There is even some evidence of flash flooding on the walkway by the start line – most likely a blocked drain – that definitely means that no fans will be able to stand close to the fence there during the meeting unless they've especially worn their wellies to Smallmead. A solitary traffic cone warns of this hazard and confirms the evidence of our eyes though the puddle does appeal enough to attract some children to splash about and play in it. You can't imagine many other major speedway events blithely going ahead with a vital part of the terraces completely flooded and out of commission at arguably the premium spot from which to view proceedings (the start/finish line) on the most important night of the Elite League season. Then, that's speedway and typical of the conditions endured down the years by the long-suffering die-hard fans. With the arrival of the *Sky* monies, the language has changed and the hyperbole increased but the attitude towards the paying public still really hasn't. Everyone reacts in the usual time-honoured speedway fan fashion – we just get on with it uncomplainingly and without reference to the hiked admission prices. It wouldn't surprise me if, after a season when the club has repeatedly boasted of its generosity in granting free entry for children accompanied by an adult, that kids were charged for entry tonight. This should help boost the Racerdogs revenues during a season when they have allegedly spent way beyond their means, failed to consistently attract the people of Reading to Smallmead and generally haemorrhaged cash. Inadvertently, at absolutely no extra expense, they have provided the children with the joyful entertainment of a large puddle to play in.

The Racerdogs promotion has also seen fit to increase tonight's programme price by 20% but, in this respect, they have provided an impressive souvenir in keeping with the importance of the event. Indeed, initial purchasers are further rewarded with a special programme board branded with the 'Sky Sports' logo that is appropriately sized for this larger format programme. As you pass up the walkway from the turnstiles to the edge of the greyhound track fencing, the blokes from the *Reading Evening Post* are keen to hand you a free copy of the paper and stress to everyone that "there's a special feature inside". Which indeed there is, though from the shouty front-page headline ("Hike in Bus Fares") it appears that the local bus company has followed in lock step the premium price leadership exhibited by BSI Reading. Even more interestingly and incomprehensibly, inside this edition there's news from Reading's "bin supremo" that there will be fortnightly recyclable bin collections. The major speedway news of the night from a Racerdogs fans perspective is that the exhilarating Matej Zagar will miss the meeting through an injury he sustained the day before riding in Hungary. Whether this "European Final" was important or meaningless, this is both bad luck but also a further example of how even the most important Elite League club meeting of the season is low down the list of priorities for a self-employed worker (speedway rider) when given the chance to earn a few extra quid rather than to rest or prepare yourself for the most important fixture of your club's season.

BSI is an organisation that vaunts and flaunts its expertise as a media company capable of working with and attracting top-notch advertisers. A casual glance inside the lavish programme reveals that despite the fact that it's the biggest night in Reading Speedway's history in at least the last decade, they still only managed to gain sponsorship for a meagre four of the fifteen heats available for hire. Admittedly, given the rest of the programme is littered with various advertisers this could equally be a shocking oversight; an indictment of the promotional skills of BSI Reading; a sign of the failure of the Bulldogs name to seize the popular imagination of the public or maybe even another sign of the continued unsexiness of the sport of speedway in general because of its older demographic.

The blokes from the *Evening Post* have absolutely no idea about speedway. One asks me, "is it like the Masters or someint like that tonight?" He then thrusts some yellow cards into my hand with a "do you want one of these cards? They're free. We've got a lorry load comin' in a minute – there's instructions in the *Post* as how to use them!" The cards in question have "5-1" printed on one side and "4-2" on the other. The bloke seems well impressed that I know how to use them without need to resort to any consultation of the instructions helpfully printed inside the paper. The growth of big, legible and instructional signs on sandwiches, equipment ("this microwave is not suitable for animals" etc.), street furniture and throughout every aspect of our lives is a bane of modern living and another symbol of an increased will to stupidity in combination with a desire to litigate for compensation wherever possible. On my way to secure a valuable seat in the home-straight grandstand in a prime position that overlooks the start line (an area described on the club website as "undercover seating on the home straight"), I again bump into my companions from the ELRC at Poole yesterday – Nobby, Lee Morris and his son Nick. Like yesterday, we decide to sit together and we're early enough to have our choice of seats while we wait for the 90 minutes to elapse before the tapes rise for the first race of the night.

Far from seeking to innovate when it comes to the choice of music played to the punters at the premium speedway meetings they stage, the BSI as an organisation appears to pride itself to only offer music stuck in a time warp for a certain bygone era of mass entertainment. At Cardiff they at least have the decency to make ironic or slightly fey choices – though I must admit that the 2006 combination of Bonny Tyler and Tony Christie did appeal in a kind of kitsch-cum-retro type way – but tonight at Smallmead as a crowd we appear to have become trapped at speedway's equivalent of Guantanamo Bay. We're definitively a captive audience as we wait for the action to start and BSI Reading appear keen to infantilise us as well as beat us into psychological submission with some loud, garish and atonal music we haven't actually chosen or can turn down. In fact, we have no choice but to sit passively and listen since it drowns almost all conversation. Judged by his coat, maybe a Queen tribute band is in fact John Postlethwaite's favoured choice of music to relax to, though, much more likely, they're somehow related. If none of these explanations apply, they're probably just a rather condescending reasonably priced choice of what they think speedway fans would like to listen to. Whatever the reason, the lead singer greets us with a cheery "Hello Reading!" as though he's mistaken this gig – so strongly redolent of an end-of-the-career booking – for the headline slot at the Reading Festival rather than its reality of the centre green at Smallmead. It must be a nightmare engagement – the chance to play to the older demographic in the form of an audience of uninterested speedway fans who really just can't wait for you to stop. The volume is set at deafening so we're all along for the ride, except for those with adjustable volume on their hearing aids. Sadly the singer affects to persuade himself, if no one else, that we're actually all here to specifically see him and the band. He frequently implores us to rise above our default setting of catatonia throughout the 'gig'. "If you want to boogie feel free!", "Show your hands" and "sing it" are uttered/screeched with apparent sincerity and great regularity, though without any appreciable impact. Apart from a touching lack of awareness, another factor that disrupts the performance is an apparent unfamiliarity with the basic lyrics and mechanics of the Queen oeuvre. "I'm going to sing something – sing it back to me" requests the lead singer before he noisily murders the rather appropriate choice of *Another One Bites The Dust*. Nobby isn't impressed, "I can't hear myself think, let alone speak". With a few more failed imprecations to action or reaction from the stunned captive crowd, the band launch into the most famous Queen song of all which tonight, I think we can call, *Bulldogian Rhapsody*. Nobby shouts above the cacophony approvingly, "They're all out of key now!" When the singer fails to simultaneously hit the high notes and introduces some unusual quavers into "mama, I just killed a man" you really hope that his mum isn't here or, worse still for long-term future embarrassment of the whole family, isn't a Smallmead regular as she'd never live down the horror and the shame of this execrable, almost post-modern performance that unintentionally verges on so-bad-it's-good levels of irony.

Nobby shouts, "They're better on *Stars in their Eyes* than here". A short while later he points out a celebrity a row and few seats away, "that's the dog that was on TV at Peterborough last week". Boy, it is a cutely distracting dog and it sits throughout with its paws on the handrail to apparently follow each race with an intensity that is almost as absorbing as the on-track action. Before we get all the blessed relief of the loud roar of the bike engines rather than the loud violence of the 'music', we endure a final fruitless appeal from the lead singer, "come on Reading – big finish" before they grunkily segue into an atonal unintentionally post punk version of the Queen standard *Radio GaGa*. Nobby shouts wittily, "It's all been GaGa!" At a different volume there might be a career for this band on the chicken-in-the-basket pub and club circuit but based on this display, to paraphrase Alan Partridge, their music would be better suited to the less discerning "spinal cord in bap" crowd.

When they finally mercifully kill the set, the silence is golden though it's broken by the sound of the voluptuous blonde 'green' start girl squealing delightedly with laughter in an unconscious almost childlike manner as she passes deep in conversation with the 'yellow' start line girl. Once this more welcome distraction has passed, talk then turns to injuries. Zagar's possibly disastrous absence from the Racerdogs team is attributed to a "loose nut" that caused his front wheel to unexpectedly come off.[1] While for the Robins, Iversen apparently has "a nasty gash in his arm sustained in Sweden." There are a number of announcements over the tannoy. I suspect that for all new owners of speedway clubs there must be a manual on how not to approach all sorts of things that you can potentially get involved with as a promoter at your own speedway club. In this case the choice of location and price of the annual end-of-season Bulldogs Dinner Dance. If they'd studied the lessons of history, they would know that in his first year at Arlington, Terry Russell chose to relocate the Eastbourne end of season event to the Grand Hotel on the seafront and provide the fans with an expensive repast as well as a confusing canteen of cutlery to choose from. It was an experiment that wasn't repeated. I can't quite be sure but I gather that the Racerdogs event – probably in honour of the avowed mission of the BSI Reading organisation to 'improve' and 'advance' the sport as well as out of a misplaced medium-term desire to bourgeoisify the audience at Smallmead and this shindig – will be held at the Crowne Plaza in Caversham. It's an absolute snip at "£50 for a three-course meal with your choice of some wine". You'll get to "meet the team" and dance the night away at the disco. It's difficult to imagine which of the riders or the die-hard Redin fans will be the most conspicuously out of place. Demand can't be that high as repeated appeals for interest intersperse the race results throughout the night.

It's clear that preparations for the off are well under way. Chris Louis is standing by the start line and waits to record some clip to camera about the sodden track conditions, although the track staff have struggled manfully and have just about succeeded in prettifying the surface sufficiently to impress on camera, if not actually provide the best surface for riders to enjoy during this prestigious and season determining encounter. Given the state of the surface only 90 minutes earlier, it's nonetheless an impressive effort no doubt aided by the traditional lack of shale you can usually expect at Smallmead. Just like freshly baked mince pies are really presented at their best with a last-minute light dusting of icing sugar, then so it is with wet tracks and sawdust. Often miserly on the essential purchases but profligate on the inessentials and keen on anything unnecessarily showy, BSI Reading have apparently only laid in meagre quantities of sawdust to try to soak up the remainder of the surface water and moisture. "They've sprinkled some sawdust out", Nobby notes in passing and at that very moment we're serenaded by the line "since you've been gone" from Aretha Franklin's 'Band of Gold' ("I'm listening to my favourite song – from around 1966-1967 when my first marriage went bust and my missus left me, thank God!"). The exigencies of live television coverage on *Sky Sports* causes the rider parade to start promptly at 7.25 p.m. with the arrival on track of Greg Hancock (with red start-line girl precariously sharing the saddle of his bike), Travis McGowan (with the blue girl), while the vivacious green and yellow girls ride the steeds with a couple of Peterborough riders. The appearance of Hans Andersen in very close proximity to a start-line girl fails to scotch the scurrilous rumours of his proclivities if judged

---

[1] It appears that Zagar's explained or unexplained absence from a team can have equally devastating consequences. Jonas Holmqvist, the *Speedway Star*'s reporter in Sweden explains. "Vargarna have failed in their attempt to prevent Matej Zagar joining newly-promoted Elite League outfit Kaparna. Vargarna, relegated at the end of last season, were in dispute with Zagar after the Slovenian GP star missed the vital away match at Rospiggarna, a defeat that ultimately led to the Wolves surrendering their top-flight status. Zagar was axed and fined 50,000 kronor for not fulfilling his contract. But the money has never been paid and Vargarna refused to allow Zagar to join Kaparna. However SVEMO recently gave Kaparna the green light to use the Slovenian, though Vargarna will keep a bike and an engine they planned to sell cheaply to the rider". I'm not sure what conclusions should be drawn here. Some leap out, most notably that the Swedish speedway authorities appear cut from the same pragmatic cloth as their British counterparts. So the show must go on even if it means you have to look away or hold your nose. It also emphasises that (star) riders can act with impunity, safe in the knowledge that international regulations (if there are any) are unenforceable in the Venn diagram like power triangle that now exists between the major European speedway leagues/countries (Poland, England, Sweden even without the rogue card of Russia or the poor relation of Denmark). Skilled riders know that they can never be held to ransom (only they can do so) and that the limited supply of talent will dictate that there will always be clubs prepared to accommodate them or overlook that they lack loyalty to anyone other than themselves. Still, at least, Vargarna get to keep the bike and the engine.

Flooded concourse by start gate at Smallmead. © Jeff Scott

by the comments of the nearby teenage Racerdogs fans. Then again, they don't exactly mark themselves out as either authoritative or mature, since they've delightfully decorated the free *Evening Post* (5-1/4-2) cards with additional slogans in biro, "FCUK Panthers" and "Panthers Suck". One of the boys is overweight, relentlessly homophobic and wears an Iron Maiden sweatshirt. Throughout the meeting, he dances when Redin wins any race and repeatedly chants "Freak off" with considerable glee. So much so that his blubber wobbles freely and the skin of his skull fights sweatily against his down of close cropped hair. Oblivious to the language, his father eventually scrunches up the defaced sign, just after a demand of "give it here". He then hands over another sign with the instruction "Albert don't ruin it this time". "I didn't – it was Todd that put it on!"

As the riders line up for the first race I think I spot the first visible but really laudable impact of the BSI speedway revolution at Smallmead – two sets of tape mechanisms by the start line. It's a very practical step and a positive innovation that, hopefully, eliminates the possible farce that can ensue whilst people struggle to effect repairs. It also dispenses with the always unsatisfactory spectacle of a hand-held tape start. "They've copied it from Coventry, after they kept having all that trouble with them there", advises Nobby. The first race has Hans Andersen deliver a hefty nudge with his arm that sends Travis McGowan sprawling on the track. Bizarrely, the referee elects to take the easy route and avoid unnecessary controversy, so he instantly calls all four riders back for the re-run. Like many modern speedway meetings, but especially those on wet 'slick' tracks like Smallmead, passing is at an absolute minimum after the first corner, if we witness it at all. In the re-run Swiderski makes the swiftest start and thereby effectively wins this race from the tapes. Not a result that you would have predicted beforehand given the presence of both Hancock and Andersen in the same heat. There is an actual pass in the next race in the form of a cut back by Ostergaard. Heat 3 has Ryan Sullivan powering away from the start, while Kolodziej commits what is effectively the speedway version of a professional foul in the hope of a re-run when, after a shockingly poor departure from the start line, he gives a masterly but ultimately unconvincing impression of a dying swan at the back of the pack on the first bend. To my mind, he appears to fall off in slow motion and 12-year-old Nick accurately remarks, "And no one was even near him!" With his new spectacles still apparently awaiting collection from the opticians, the ref orders another re-run and the immutable law of speedway second chances asserts itself, as what was a Panthers 2-4 now becomes a 3-3 in the rerun to keep the overall scores tied at 9 each.

All of the initial races are influenced by the decision of the ref to hold the tapes for an inordinate amount of time. Though his tactic changes in the fourth race, it doesn't make any difference to the lack of first-bend drama, though the wet conditions do when Jensen locks up and falls. He escapes unscathed when Simota quick thinkingly lays down his machine with considerable alacrity only to have Ostergaard thump into him from behind with some velocity. Only the Poles appear unfazed by the slippery conditions early on and so it is that Swiderski confidently passes Kolodziej on the outside. Anxiety to establish first-bend dominance causes McGowan to weirdly batter Jensen's back in almost rugby fashion, and with considerable force when you consider that he also still had to ride his bike at the same time. This attention doesn't put off Jensen and seems completely pointless since McGowan soon eases past him by the time they reach the third bend. Outside the clampers from Green Park are again working hard this week but generously offer amnesties to anyone prepared to rescue their illegally parked vehicles from the possible horror of a £300 clamping release fee. Over the tannoy we again hear listed another rich mix of more proletarian transport that includes a Ford Explorer, a VW Passat and a Fiat Brava among others that fans have chosen to illegally park. It's a touching courtesy.

Ryan Sullivan is having a variable night so far. He completely fails to gate in Heat 7, then immediately counters by squeezing through an impossible gap on the exit of the second bend to overtake Gjedde. This would temporarily make hope swell in the breast of any Panthers fan watching at Smallmead or on television at home, before Gjedde opens it up on bend three and sails past Sullivan on the outside to secure second place by the exit of bend four and thereby psychologically destroys Sullivan for this race. The Racerdogs have moved into a comfortable 25-17 lead and the next race has Swiderski implement the 'plan B' he'd concocted in the pits beforehand — namely an aggressive broadside on bend one that aims to take McGowan to the fence but instead has the effect of leaving him looking totally silly when Travis cuts back. Though Swiderski then recovers sufficiently to react to the actual race in front of him rather than the theoretical one he initially rode, when he then escapes round the outside. Another lowlight for the Panthers fans is engendered by a fall at the rear by Ostergaard who then, in pantomime fashion, theatrically struggles to raise himself from the cloying muddy surface beneath his suddenly much too heavy to lift machine.

The hike in admission prices for tonight's fixture promised the side benefit of a "free drink" for everyone. In a faint echo of a rich history of other famously ill-conceived marketing disasters, these offers can have unintended consequences and lead to disgruntlement among the punters you had confidently hoped would be grateful. So it has proved all evening in the hugely overcrowded Smallmead bar where queues have been enormous throughout the night as people eagerly queue for their 'free' liquid refreshment. These queues make access to the toilets difficult and, perhaps a function of the potent combination of the original toilet block closure on bend one when the BSI took over at Redin and tonight's drinks policy, the home-straight grandstand toilets attract similarly lengthy queues of disgruntled fans. So, if you want a drink or the loo you have to miss the racing. The bloke close by me complains indignantly at these perceived slights from BSI Reading, "For the second week running they haven't had a student concession admission price and your free drink is only a half of the shittiest drinks — John Smith's or Foster's — not a full pint or much good if you drink cider!" Though they say you can't please the people all the time, he should, at least, count his lucky stars that he wasn't here for the band!

As the track dried or, more likely, as the riders have got used to conditions, the entertainment picks up with a superb last to first pass by Gjedde that by bend four of the first lap of Heat 9 has him find the lead. Back in the pits, apparently unable to countenance any other tactic to stop the Redin onslaught, Trevor Swales again brings out the hapless but combative Ostergaard for yet another rider replacement ride. Even the Reading fan next to me is frustrated with Trevor's approach and it's not even his team, "it just doesn't make any sense as a team tactic". The Elite League title already appears to have slipped away from the Panthers, if judged by the illuminated numbers of the newly erected scoreboard by the pits bend that brightly advertises a 33-21 scoreline. McGowan tries to help what looks to be an increasingly forlorn Panthers cause when he rears massively at the start of Heat 10. It's impressive that he even manages to stay on. Even more significantly, by the time he's reached the home straight for the second time he's managed to pass an apparently asleep Sullivan. The previous four heats have shot by at breakneck speed as though the instruction has come through from *Sky* that schedules and advert breaks dictate the need to finish the meeting tout suite.

The next race finally features the arrival of a Panthers rider in a black-and-white helmet (Hans Andersen) as well as a vociferous complaint from Swiderski in gate 2 that McGowan has encroached on his space by lining up too closely to him. As a psychological tactic it works enough to generate a complaint from the Pole that the start marshal makes great play of ignoring the validity of, before McGowan has sufficient time to add insult to injury when he then massively shoves his rival in the first corner. Swiderski recovers some equanimity and nearly fights back into second place with a spectacular undertake of the Australian on the third bend of the penultimate lap before again nearly catching him on the line.

Craven Shield excitement builds in East Sussex. © Jeff Scott

Afterwards Travis pointedly ignores him, "Travis just didn't want to know," notes Nobby. With the points for Hans Andersen's victory doubled and Swiderski victorious over Lemon, who rode like his name in this race, the deficit has narrowed to 39-30. With the situation desperate, the Panthers again exploit the present rulebook and bring in Sullivan for another tactical ride that again features the often-controversial black-and-white helmet colour. Trevor's decision to surprisingly delay the use of this tactical option suddenly looks truly inspired management when Ryan flies from the gate only to temporarily 'slow' on the back straight before he recovers to zoom away and win. Richard Hall narrowly fails to catch Kolodziej on the line. Whatever the reason, the Panthers have completely awoken from their stupor and retrieved the scoreline to a much more respectable 41-37. What two races previously looked like a certain, comprehensive and easy victory for the Racerdogs, now suddenly looks much more in the balance. However, the recovery is short lived as Hans Andersen and Jesper B Jensen completely fail to team ride in the next race when, on the last bend of the second lap, Hans pointlessly overtakes his partner but then slightly locks up to comprehensively stymie him. This delay is sufficient to allow the alert Hancock to pass Jensen and compound the surprise of the easy Kolodziej victory. In the penultimate race, Gjedde easily passes Sullivan though Hall at least shows some real fight and determination to battle past Lemon on the line.

The last heat is widely expected to allow the Racerdogs to consolidate or extend the 6-point advantage that they hold with the scores poised at 48-42. Tonight, however, the speedway gods clearly frown on the Redin team as the always immaculately prepared Hancock suffers a rare engine failure to gift the Sullivan-Andersen partnership a 1-5 heat win to reduce the final first leg score to 49-47. Rather provocatively Steve, the somewhat excitable and voluble Peterborough fan I'm standing next to triumphantly shouts, "Oh dear, oh dear, an engine failure for Hancock at a most unfortunate time – I really shouldn't gloat at his misfortune!"

It has been a meeting that the Racerdogs never looked remotely like they might ever lose. Only, the invariably unpopular tactical rider replacement facility has kept the scores unfeasibly close and thereby allowed the visitors in with a chance of revenge at the East of England Showground return fixture scheduled for next week.

2nd October Elite League Play-Off Final (1st Leg) 49-47

Jeff Scott's Second Pile of ****

7th October

My latest book arrives by special delivery from the printers in Milton Keynes courtesy of my proofreader Cas Tidmarsh. She's kindly agreed to help to distribute the leaflets that I've had prepared about the book to the fans as they queue outside Arlington stadium. This book is a kind of 'Jeff Scott Starter Kit' to introduce people to my writing for those unwilling or unprepared to pay £20 for *Showered in Shale*. It's called *When Eagles Dared* and is my account of the Eastbourne 2005 speedway season when I attended 34 meetings in addition to the travel that I did for the research on my original book. It's really an Elite League speedway travelogue – since it covers all the teams in the league in reasonable depth – rather than just about the Eagles season. It's written from a fan's point of view – that is without any inside information on the club but based on the evidence of my own eyes, what I gleaned from listening to or questioning others or just by reading the *Speedway Star*, the internet forums and the local newspapers.

It's a delight that it has arrived just in time for possibly the Eagles last meeting of the season or the penultimate one, if they manage to win through on aggregate to the Craven Shield Finals. I have always enjoyed watching the speedway at Arlington. It's a lovely setting in the countryside and features a lovingly well-maintained track set in a compact stadium. The friendly people make you welcome, while the racing is of a consistently high and entertaining standard. The drive to a meeting at any time, but particularly in the summer sunshine, always lifts the spirit and puts a spring in my step. I thought nothing could ever replace the joy that my arrival outside Smallmead stadium could provide and while it remains my first love as a speedway track, Arlington has also been a place where I have relished my speedway in recent years. The club promoter Jon Cook has been unfailingly helpful about all my writing endeavours, even when he had some reservations, and it's thanks to more kind support from him that I'm able to launch my book at the track tonight.

As soon as any new book arrives, I immediately catch myself searching for errors and I don't have to wait long to find them. I like to try to find as many as I can as quickly as I can before someone else points them out to me. Though you always send the book off to the printers completely sure that there are no mistakes, inevitably a form of snow blindness afflicts you whenever you read or proof your own work. I think you unconsciously mentally correct the text to what it should say rather than what it does say. This still happens no matter how many skilled readers you enlist to help find all the mistakes. I'm lucky in that I have had the help of so many kind and diligent friends. The printer has incorrectly given the spine width dimensions to the designer so my name appears on the spine as "Jeff Cott". This is least of the horrors as a quick glance shows that the subtitle features a greengrocer's apostrophe and I've misspelt Wimborne Road in one of the chapter headings (as I did in *Showered in Shale*) but luckily not in the text itself. The gifted *Wolverhampton Express & Star* speedway reporter, Tim Hamblin, at Arlington tonight to report on the Wolves is the first person to point out a true factual (as opposed to a textual one) error since I've transposed Jack Hargreaves for Jon Armstrong in my chapter on the controversial May Bank encounter between the Wolves and the Eagles. I like to think that the chance to spot errors adds to the intensity with which people read the book, plus it allows them to feel much more knowledgeable and diligent than the author.

Whatever the slight faults, it's a pleasure to actually have this book to sell during the dying embers of the Eastbourne season especially as this looked very unlikely at one point. I set my table up in the usual place next to where the ladies regularly sell the *Brighton Argus* in the area just through the turnstiles, below the commentary box and diagonally opposite the track shop run by the always wry, slightly cynical but helpful Martin Dadswell. He delights in his affection that he has a jaundiced view of the speedway world but like so many within the sport, he's really a true fan at heart just one that's seen slightly too much of what goes on behind the scenes. As ever his joy is, in fact, alloyed and his reaction invariably tends towards the sanguine. His first comment is to observe, "I see that you went with that awful title you thought of a while ago rather than the more honest one that I suggested, *Jeff Scott's Second Pile of S*** – more people would buy something called that". With Cas outside to hand most people a leaflet before they even enter the stadium, hopefully there is no danger that any potential interest will not have been slightly stirred. Though she affects to be shy, Cas loves to meet people so this is an ideal task. Before long, fans come up to my table – not to buy a book but to say, "We think that she's doing very well but she says she's cold and thirsty out there – can you take her a coffee?" Afterwards, Cas says, "The people were absolutely lovely – so kind and keen on their team! One older lady said to me that she's already dreading the winter and wonders what she'll do without her speedway every week. I expected lots of people to refuse to take the leaflet but most seemed genuinely interested and stopped to listen. When I walked round inside the stadium, I only found four or five thrown away."

Sadly, a couple of long-time Wimbledon fans refuse a copy of the leaflet after they erroneously claim (based on mis-information) that "he's the bloke slagging off Wimbledon". As Cas notes, "but then they haven't been allowed to read the chapters like I have, so they'd not know that's rubbish – you highlighted the pomposity of that bloke and that poor whatsits Pairs meeting they had – but praised the work and dedication of the volunteers you met and saw at work there. You did take the mickey a bit and repeat what fans said about him but that's what the ones you spoke to thought."

Fortunately, throughout the night, I nearly develop writer's cramp as the fans that have crowded into Arlington show a real taste for the new book and some relish for the kindly praised *Showered in Shale*. Sales are also boosted by the favourable words of resident club MC, Kevin 'KC' Coombes, one of the stars of this latest book and all-round enthusiast for all things Eastbourne speedway. I'm delighted to hear him describe me as, "Eastbourne fan and nutter". Not that everyone is that enamoured with my books:
"Is that the one you want, dad?"
"Nah, it looks hopeless; I want Simmo's one."

I do get to watch some of the initial races of this meeting with my usual crowd of friends by the blue and yellow wooden safety board number 51 (though this season this has now changed to number 57). The impression is quickly formed that the riders of all three teams have a marked reluctance to really try to win or, at least, want to be seen to be trying but only so much as to ensure that the other riders in the race inadvertently triumph. One theory as to why the Craven Shield is often the poor relation at the Elite level of the speedway trophy firmament is that the three team nature of the event means that only the home tie generates income for each club that participates, whereas the obligatory two away fixtures means that they have to incur the additional expenses from, if this were boxing, the 'one purse'. Surely this couldn't be a factor? Especially when qualification for the Final rounds provides an additional and popular home fixture (plus two more away fixtures) as well as the opportunity for a trophy to grace the club's trophy cabinet.

Whatever the intricacies of the finances, a strong impression lingers that perhaps everyone isn't quite trying as hard as they might on this particular night. Many riders also appear to have severe difficulty in negotiating the fourth bend of the track. This is most unusual as the track is invariably groomed within an inch of its life before each fixture by that gifted artisan of the shale, Bob Dugard (and his very capable team), as well as further lovingly tended or altered during the fixture if the need arises. Despite all this preparation, many riders nonetheless struggle in almost the same spot as though there is somehow black ice on that particular part of the fourth bend. The rider that has the most spectacular struggle with this stretch of the track is the often wayward but combative Ipswich rider, Kim Jansson. Experience has yet to mellow his innate wildness and during the third lap of Heat 5 he manages to win a lifetime achievement award for his own unique interpretation of what it means to ride the white line. In this interpretation, he glides over the troublesome area of the fourth bend shale and then attempts to power down the inside of the straight from this bend with a manoeuvre that will have him hug the white line with his tyre. Unfortunately, he makes a bit of a bodge of things. John Hazelden describes this with wonderment, "you know, I've never freaking seen that before! He tried to ride the white line but failed – Jansson locked up, almost did a 360, went up, went down and spun it nearly 360 degrees and left a tyre mark on the centre green. Bob won't like that at all – he goes potty if the stock cars go on it and they get smashed all over the place". Son Mark also has a flabber that is gasted, "it's freaking funny though". As Eastbourne fans, we can appreciate the drama all the better since the race features only Wolverhampton and Ipswich riders.

A sense of intense pride or impending doom at the turn of events on the track is never far away from board 51, since we only deal in extremes. Collectively the Eagles team have yet to grasp the nettle with their talons so far this evening, so opinion has tended towards that perennially favoured by Private Fraser in *Dad's Army*, until Deano and Shieldsy combine for a 5-1 against a rather lacklustre Wolves combination of Karlsson and Correy. John is gleeful, "What a team we are! And even Dave is shouting for Deano." Heat 8 is conducted as though the bend closest to us is a temporary skidpan. Mark Loram, who rides for Ipswich, slips on the 'frost' on the first lap and John notes, "I don't think that Ipswich want to win it either!" Between races there's time to indulge in the wild but inaccurate speculation about the make up of the team next season from unnamed 'sources' deep within the Eagles nest. A 'deep throat' figure seems to delight in passing off flights of fancy as fact. Nonetheless we still lap it up and John has it on great authority that, "Terry Russell's leaving and we're getting a major new sponsor – supposedly Martin Hagon so, therefore, that means Deano's definitely leaving to go Premier next year. Pedersen's off and so is Kennett to Swindon and we're getting Richardson [groan] and Lindback is also to arrive." If correct, these forecasts appear to buck the usual trend at the Elite League level to try to strengthen your team for its polar opposite. Luckily the racing interrupts us and the Eagles continue with their on-track revival that, in the context of the execrable performances of their putative rivals tonight, appears likely to, almost by default, lead them into the finals of the Craven Shield. When Shieldsy slips at said same spot in Heat 12, it's all too much for John, "Nobody's really trying. They're riding round like a load of fairies – I think I'm gonna support Arena next year!" Kevin 'KC' Coombes tries to distract the crowd from the earlier events with a boldly unsubtle plug for the sponsors of this race (with whom I believe he has some connection), "Elite Discos – the number one in mobile entertainment".

I enjoy a night of record sales so I'm distracted from really appreciating the full detail and glory of the Eagles triumph after the interval. I do manage to catch glimpses of the action when I sit for one race with Martin Dadswell perched on the counter of the track shop hut. The view from there is awful so I retreat to watch the rest of the fixture and stand balanced on the metal stanchion of the stock car wall gate within sight of my precious book display table. Eastbourne and fans enjoy the luxury of safety in the knowledge that they have qualified for the final a couple of heats before the end of the meeting. Celebrations almost border on the ecstatic as a result of the two-point margin of aggregate victory over Ipswich who'll probably feel that the result would have been very different if the meeting had been staged as scheduled the week before when they then would have had both Scott Nicholls and Chris 'Bomber' Harris as guests. Life is full of ifs, ands, buts and maybes.

When Jon Cook passes later he smirks before he rather wryly observes, "We fought through to the Final just so as you could have another meeting to sell your book at!"

I can't wait...

7thOctober (Eastbourne v Ipswich v Wolves, Craven Shield Semi-Final, 3rd Leg) 42-33-33 (aggregate 118-116-89)

A Night of Thrills and Talk of Sex at Alwalton
9th October

The biggest crowd of the season for any league fixture in Britain during the 2006 season is expected at the East of England Showground tonight. I'm really early as the traffic on the roads from Brighton to Peterborough has been very light – though anyone who is anyone is keen to get there tonight, if judged by the black Japanese van that proudly advertises "Pebley Beach" and "British Speedway" on its rear as it passes me in the outside lane at over 100 mph on the M11 motorway. One of the great pleasures while promoting my book at speedway tracks throughout the country – apart from meeting all the speedway people and the chance to watch the racing – has been the chance to drive more sedately and listen to the radio during my long daytime and night-time journeys. It must be my age, but the listener selection of golden oldies on *Steve Wright in the Afternoon* is a bit of a must, and today I'd also been lucky enough to catch a fascinating programme on Radio 4 about the increasingly lost tradition of gypsy cooking in this country. The onset of convenience food and the lack of campsites hasn't been a boon to the longevity of these traditions nor to the health and life expectancy of the gypsies, particularly the males. The need to respect your elders is an essential part of the community and they are losing a fight to retain the unique cultural specificity of their way of life, attitude to the world and general outlook. Like many groups they are being swamped by the demands and enticements of consumer culture and ravaged by the relentless will to homogeneity that pervades contemporary life. Often they are not a popular group for many people who live in 'fixed' abodes and resent them when they arrive as neighbours. The traveller community continually has to acknowledge and cope with this hostile attitude towards them as well as overcome the obstacles it creates for their day-to-day existence, never mind the difficulties it causes the long-term existence of their culture. Strange though it may appear on the surface, the loss of cultural sovereignty, quirky specificity and uniqueness is a trait many sub-cultural groups have to face if they are to avoid

Large crowd at East of England Showground. © Jeff Scott

assimilation or extinction. Speedway is no different in this respect and I worry that we're likely to sacrifice our long-term existence in exchange for short-term pragmatism and/or commercial imperatives. You have to ask the question: who exactly guards the speedway flame – whatever we agree it might actually be – for future generations (or even the next decade) and can we trust these guardians to pursue this disinterestedly? If we can't answer these basic questions with any degree of reassurance or certainty – particularly at the national level of our own governing body (ignoring the international level for now) – then all the often-voiced worries about our decline in popularity and ageing demographics of the regular speedway audience will assuredly come resoundingly true. Tinkering with the rules every year, gerrymandering regulations to suit short-term commercial imperatives and clutching the vital but often valorised straw of the "*Sky* contract" doesn't in any way address the structural problems the sport faces. To claim "rude health", or a "steady as she goes" approach is to live in a state of deluded but necessary denial about the future.

Immediately upon arrival tonight at Peterborough, I'm surrounded by visible symbols of the sport's apparent recent success. There's all the very obvious *Sky Sports* outside broadcast equipment; the early queues of people keen to get through the turnstiles promptly to stake their claim for their favoured spot in the stadium – never mind the pits full of many of the gifted superstar riders of this particular speedway generation (with a car park full of their white vans) gathered here in the company of the great and the good of the sport who will also naturally militate to watch this spectacle at Peterborough this evening. I'm sure that there are grounds to sit back and feel a great deal of satisfaction with the present stage that we've reached. But surely the decline in the historic strength of the vibrant Roma tradition, community and cultural practices in this country provides a disturbing counterpoint that should cause all speedway fans to pause for thought. During the radio programme many of the Roma people advanced claims about the innate superiority of their way of life, their sadness and frustration at its loss as well as their ability to "always" be able to spot someone from their community. In the speedway world, we too have many of these consolations but we also don't have the organisation to fight back or resist our slow decline.

These high-minded questions have no place at any time of the year at the majority of places where speedway people congregate. We're all too busy doing or appreciating to philosophise. Tonight is a case in point since the general topic on everyone's mind is sex – isn't it always? – and the specific conversational application of these weighty considerations primarily uses the words "Scott Nicholls" and "Sophie Blake". For thirty years I've purchased *The Sun* and *The Guardian* every day. Because I've been in a rush I haven't had the chance to discover the 'speedway news' contained on page 15 of today's *Sun* newspaper. Hardworking speedway publicist Mark Thursfield alerts me to the controversy when he casually but apparently rhetorically says, "have you seen that speedway has been making the headlines in the *Sun* today, but not in the sports pages?" It would have been hard to miss the headline ("Sleazy Rider: Love rat

speedway star gets TV girl pregnant") or the photos of the pair should I have had the chance to read the paper. Mark outlines the bare bones of the report in genuinely outraged fashion and notes in an aggrieved tone, "it's a complete stitch up, a hatchet job" before he asks in quick fire and practised fashion:
"Are they going to bring up the child in a loving relationship?"
"Yes!"
"Are they keen to be good parents?"
"Yes!"
"Was he living with someone else?"
"No!"
"Are they consenting adults?"
"Yes!"

Mark needed no first invitation to warm to his theme but, sadly, we're interrupted from our discussions by Terry Russell who butts in to brusquely demand of Mark, "where the goodness are all the *Sky* boards? They've been advertised in the local paper as 'free' to the first 500 fans who enter tonight and there's none anywhere around". Terry's face communicates his disgruntlement and he generally gives a good impression of someone who's really unhappy to chew upon this particular metaphorical wasp. Mark doesn't lighten his mood with the factually accurate observation, "*Sky* have cocked up and delivered all one thousand to Reading last week and they were given out before anyone realised what had happened". This sounded a plausible explanation to me and is one that captured and typified in a single instance the kind of marriage enjoyed by *Sky Sports* and speedway. Ever the PR professional, Mark nonetheless promises Terry that he will go off and investigate as well as try to come up with some sort of a solution, unlikely though it is that he will find one.

The consensus in the track shop later on the Nicholls-Blake "GP bonk" focuses, with an attention to detail that typifies speedway fans, on the exact Grand Prix meeting in question and its location. "I wonder if they'll name the baby Lonigo after where it was conceived, just like the Beckhams did?" There's little moral outrage or tutting, though there is a fair degree of envy and self-projection ("who honestly would say no if you were offered the chance?").

I'm left alone with my table of books directly outside the large windows of the already heaving track shop run with great professionalism and much glee tonight, by Nick and Johnny Barber. Nick surveys the crowd and notes approvingly, "we'll just have to raise our game and excel some more", whereas John remains even more practical and commercially savvy, "let's hope for a Peterborough win so the crowd hang about at the end!" When I say alone outside, that's not strictly correct as I've been joined by the bubbly Jo from ReRun Productions whose stall proudly displays the latest and most popular of a huge range of speedway DVDs produced by her husband's company. She attracts quite a crowd to the television monitor that she uses to showcase their handiwork. Jo is a friendly, straightforward lady though I slightly get off on the wrong foot with her when I innocently say, "is it Ken Burnett's company?" I quickly gather that it's not and that there is quite some rivalry and negotiation involved in securing the exclusive film rights to prestigious (or even run of the mill) speedway meetings. The overall commercial imperative appears to be to gain the exclusive rights to film a specific event and to zealously protect your exclusivity, "I wouldn't be surprised to find Ken here filming illegally later, though it's our exclusive". Jo has brought her adorably soppy dog, Dewey (nothing like the character of the Policeman in *Scream* that inspired its name) along for companionship and company, though it's such a softy and so friendly with everyone that it has little use as a guard dog.

Back at my own table, the talk has turned to the topic of sex with newly weds Emma and Alan Morrison. He confides, "I've read your book solidly since I got it," which prompts Emma to complain, "My sex life has gone right downhill for the last two weeks, we only got married four weeks ago and since he got the book it's gone completely fumpf – completely non-existent!" Alan looks sheepish but insists, more to Emma than me, "But it *is* really good though!" Nonetheless, their love still burns strongly enough between them as they leave hand in hand. Moments later someone I'd hoped to bump into all season is standing right there next to my stall – my father's old workmate and dedicated Reading speedway fan, Jesse James (and his son Michael). They both buy copies of my book. Jesse has repeatedly looked in the Reading track shop for it all season without success, completely unaware of the Colditz style ("nothing gets in and nothing gets out") stocking policy unofficially operated by Nicola Sands from BSI as a means of quality control. Jesse also had a fruitless search at all the other rival tracks adjacent to the Thames Valley – Oxford and Swindon. He's pleased to have it now and talk soon turned to matters of Tadley and the Atomic Weapons Establishment at Aldermaston ("Did your Dad ever learn to drive?" "What's he doing with himself?" "How's your mum?"). I told him that my father had often reciprocally asked for information about him and whether I'd seen him. I should have I suppose, given that Jesse hasn't missed a meeting all season, and you'd have definitely thought that he'd be easy to spot among the low attendances that they still attract to Smallmead, despite takeover and rebranding that has seen the advent of the Racerdogs and the glory of Elite League racing return to Bennett Road.

Later, after Jesse departs ("I don't want a book on the Eagles, thank you") another couple arrive but this time they're Peterborough fans and don't bring up the subject of sex. In fact, he's really keen to tell me how much he enjoyed *Showered in Shale*, "it's a fan's book – written honestly that tells it just how it is. I've even fallen behind with my *Speedway Stars*". The lady he's with nods at his confession, "I can't get a word out of him most nights!"

Though not many people stop to buy a book or even look at them, the place is absolutely heaving. I try to pass out my leaflets on my *When Eagles Dared* book but Eastbourne don't exactly seem to be popular among the fans here tonight. Many refuse to even touch the leaflet, "we don't like the budgies or want anything to do with them," is a polite summary of some comments. Others feel that they have to identify some disciplinary concerns they harbour to me, "that Nicki Pedersen should be banned – he'll injure someone soon the way he rides!"

There are rumours that around 6000 people will pass through the turnstiles tonight. The queues of cars that move inexorably slowly bumper to bumper in the distance on the perimeter road towards the overflow car park confirms the innate popularity of this fixture to speedway fans everywhere. This crowd will dwarf the attendance for the first leg at Smallmead and will easily be the country's largest league attendance of the season in 2006. The supply of programmes sells out 30 minutes before the tapes rise. This being speedway, attendance figures will not be published and estimates of crowd numbers will vary dramatically. Takings at the turnstiles will be close to £100,000, more than enough to make a serious dent in Colin Horton's reputed overdraft. Hopefully lightning won't strike twice and the club will avoid a repeat of theft of their takings as happened earlier this season. Just before the off, I manage to squeeze into the back row of the grandstand. We're stood three deep in places along the back walkway of the stand and I can see that the crowd deeply lines the safety fence anywhere you look throughout the stadium. The atmosphere is fantastic and it stirs a nostalgia for what I remember I encountered as a teenager at speedway meetings at Smallmead almost every week at the height of its popularity in my 1970s salad days.

Spotlit under the glow of the floodlights, the bowl of the track is transformed into an amphitheatre and the contest takes on gladiatorial proportions. The Racerdogs are again weakened by the absence of Matej Zagar who has failed to recover from his injuries sustained before the first leg, but as Redin have already won here twice this season their confidence remains understandably high. So does that of the visiting Redin fans who have arrived by the coach load to cheer on their shale heroes. They seem to have congregated en masse on the back straight of the track but initially they don't have much to cheer about as the Panthers gain the only heat advantage of the first three heats. This changes in the fourth when Greg Hancock, in the race on a rider replacement outing for the absent Zagar, and Sam Simota combine for a 1-5 that throws the Racerdogs fans into temporary ecstasy and is the signal for them to give full play to their exuberance on their air horns. Their delight is short lived when at the start of the next race Greg bursts dramatically through the tapes when he tries to out think the referee and anticipate when they will be released. The sight of Hancock bursting through the tapes is unusual in itself, but is more significant since it symptomatically signals the huge importance of the fixture to the riders if someone, as calm and vastly experienced as Greg, is keen enough to entertain the inevitable risk for the fractional advantage that this attempt to predict their release will bring. Despite this setback, the Racerdogs still manage to escape with a drawn heat when Travis McGowan surprisingly out-gates the favoured Iversen/Sullivan home partnership that I would personally have expected to easily press home their supremacy in a three rider race. Interviewed over the tannoy in the pits immediately after this race, Jim Lynch effortlessly combines sour grapes, a unique perspective on the rules of the sport and a mardy outlook, "I'm not going to say anything about the referee but it's silly holding the tapes – let us just get on with the racing as that's what people have come to watch". The presence of the *Sky* cameras and Sophie Blake's[2] roving mike, as opposed

---

[2] Afterwards the consensus was that she acted with "consummate professionalism" throughout the night despite the obvious pressure that the media furore would have placed on her, never mind the prospect that her pregnancy might not be that ideal for her immediate future career terms.

to her roving eyes or hands, in the pits area — sadly deprives the packed crowd of many of the spontaneous al fresco interviews that they could otherwise expect from the riders and team managers as the meeting progresses. Inevitably, the vast majority of these interviews and whatever 'insights' they generate will instead, for sponsorship and publicity reasons, be endlessly lavished on the armchair audience who haven't made the effort to attend the East of England Showground.

The Racerdogs have obviously and sensibly enough identified Hans Andersen as the danger man for the opposition. In the light of this, their tactic in Heat 6 appears to be that Mark Lemon on gate 3 will deliberately disrupt and impede the Dane (who rides off gate 4). The Racerdogs Aussie rider does actually manage to bump him wide on the first corner and although Andersen quickly recovers, enough damage has been done to his progress and Kolodziej has escaped for the win. The intensity of the desire for victory is such among both sets of riders that the first attempt to run Heat 8 has Richard Hall excluded after Travis McGowan in the green helmet colour dramatically hits the back straight fence under considerable but unfair pressure from his opponent. This sudden obstacle is extremely bad news for the following Sam Simota who collides with the fallen bike of his team-mate, and gets immediately caught in a violent jam of man and machine before he repeatedly tumbles down the straight. The speeds that the riders invariably generate around the huge size of the circuit at Alwalton inevitably means that the pain of most falls will be exaggerated. After lengthy treatment on the track, Simota is taken away in an ambulance and the Racerdogs are thereby now reduced to only five fit riders on the night. Despite this further diminution in team strength, in the re-run McGowan and Lemon (now in the race for the withdrawn Simota) win comprehensively and enable the visitors to storm away to a scoreline of 20-28 and an aggregate lead on the night of ten points. The Panthers fans that surround me in the grandstand definitely come from the Private Frazer School of Optimism and even the first Peterborough race advantage since the second heat that a win for Sullivan and a third place for Iversen gives, doesn't exactly console them or halt their loud prognostications of impending doom.

The Racerdogs proceed to maintain their lead with three drawn heats — although they would have pulled further away from the Panthers if Kolodziej hadn't suffered his second puncture of the night in heat 10 — and then really assert themselves further with another 5-1 that features the Lemon-Kolodziej combination. Mark Lemon really rides superbly again and is the surprise ace in the pack for the visitors. With a lead of 31-41 and an aggregate margin of twelve points it appears all done and dusted for the Racerdogs with the only need on the night being to prepare some victory speeches and close out the win over the last three heats. The mood around me in the grandstand is as dark as the night sky and, even if this were a comic book story where you'd expect daring-do, the situation nonetheless looks hopeless for the Panthers.

Still, the much-derided tactical ride regulations can now be used by the home side and, now in last throw of the dice territory, Hans Andersen appears in Heat 13 in the black-and-white helmet colour. The not-so-secret-weapon on the night and the lone Englishman on display here, Richard Hall, also appears in place of the apparently completely out of form/touch Jesper B. Jensen. Little other than three successive maximum heat wins will suffice for the Panthers. Given that the home fans around me feel that Greg Hancock will definitely win a couple of these races — he has, as usual, been in fine form tonight apart from his early tapes exclusion — all the cards and karma appear to run in favour of the Racerdogs. This heat treats us to two races in one with Andersen doing his duty and winning the duel with Hancock, while Hall dices repeatedly at the rear with McGowan. Though he just about manages to pass McGowan on a number of occasions, every time he marginally draws ahead the Aussie rider responds with a burst of speed to pull away again, right until the moment when the extremely determined Hall finally beats him in a close call on the finish line. Never one to shy away from hyperbole, the results summariser Edwin Overland remains reluctant to contemplate the impossible so stays remarkably subdued — "a most enthralling heat 13" is as excited as he gets in contrast to the ecstatic jubilation of the crowd that surrounds me. Subdued, anxious or complaining for so long, the home crowd go absolutely mental and their loud reaction creates an incredible atmosphere that is a reminder of just how much we miss the huge crowds of the sport's heyday at contemporary speedway meetings. Rather than get carried along in the triumph of the moment, some nearby fans still moan that the last gasp point gained by Hall was a tactical disaster since, if he'd finished last, the resultant 6-3 race win for the Panthers would still have allowed Ryan Sullivan to come in as a tactical substitute (because of the eight point deficit on the night) off a 15-metre handicap. Some people are never happy and this perspective mixes pessimism with the blind optimism that an admittedly rejuvenated Sullivan could manage to triumph here tonight with such a handicap.

In fact a huge amount of responsibility still rests on Ryan's shoulders, as the Panthers still require successive 5-1s in the remaining two heats to stage an unlikely aggregate win on the night by a single point. Any other race results will hand the victory to the Racerdogs. In recent years and even this season, Ryan has been plagued with a level of inconsistency that his experience and ability as a rider would lead you not to expect. If it's true that when the going gets tough the tough get going, then Ryan now has an unenviable opportunity to illustrate his true mettle. The tension is palpable as the riders do some extensive gardening of the track by the tapes and this allows me to notice that the start-line girls here all wear perilously high heels – not exactly sensible or ideal for any walk on shale – and appear to have incredibly long legs set off by unfeasibly tight, small shorts in colours that match the regulation helmet colours of red, blue, yellow and green. I make a mental note that I really must get to the opticians as the combination of excitement and poor eyesight stops me from focusing properly on this spectacle. The fans around me loudly hope that the script will have been heroically written along traditional *Boy's Own* lines for the Panthers, though they can't quite believe that they've managed to even get this close, "Reading have had all the bad luck too!"

It's a hugely important race to determine the result of the Elite League season for both sides and, naturally enough, is extremely competitive on the track. Mark Lemon is excluded after he rears on his bike and appears to accidentally or deliberately, depending on your point of view, cut across Richard Hall and thereby clatter him into the home straight fence. The chatter around me is intense, "what do you expect, it is the Elite League final second leg". Another notes that "he can be a bit of a rough rider", although I'm sure that this could apply to both Mark Lemon and Richard Hall as well as numerous other determined riders on display here tonight. There's also the more contentious opinion that, "it's a revenge ride for what Hall did to one of their riders earlier" (though television replays subsequently exonerated Lemon of any premeditation or intent). Richard Hall remains prostrate on the track – apparently until the adrenalin and anger of the incident has dissipated – but instead it appears to have coursed fierily through his veins until it reaches an intensity that forces him to leap to his feet in one bound, almost as though this were an animated cartoon not real life. He is then hugely keen to inflict comic book levels of violence onto Mark Lemon. In order to try to do this, he sets off at great pace towards a fellow rider who has just fallen heavily, at speed, from his machine. Hall's body language effortlessly communicates that he's very, very angry but he's unable to assault Lemon as a group of about seven members of the Peterborough track staff and pits crew strategically gather as a mini-scrum-cum-shield and just about restrain him from violently visiting his anger on the blameless Racerdog. This defensive formation requires some fortitude and they take considerable effort to repel his advances – since he batters his body against the protective human wall that surrounds him as though the life force of species survival, that grips the salmon as it tries to spawn upstream, has suddenly thoroughly gripped him. Eventually calmed, Hall starts to trudge back to the pits until he then dramatically collapses in a heap as though felled by a sniper's bullet – though much more likely, word has reached him from the canny Panthers' team manager, Trevor Swales, that some additional writhing on the centre green in terminally injured footballer fashion will enable his wrecked machinery to receive some further minutes of valuable attention. Out of concern and definitely adding to the effect, members of the St John Ambulance staff gather round to offer what ministration they can to this re-fallen rider. The additional time Hall studiously takes to recover gives the Panthers' fans around me time to contemplate the enormity of the task in hand, "we still need two 5-1s to win, anything less and we lose!" In the re-run, the solitary English rider on display tonight still rides with aggression and tactical savvy that belies the earlier thoughtlessness of his immediate anger, when he blocks the charge of Charlie Gjedde by the fence on the second bend of the second lap. This manoeuvre thereby enables him to slip away to follow home Ryan Sullivan in second place and so ensure that the first of the two essential 5-1 results is in the bag.

The tension remains palpable and none of the Panthers fans around me quite dares to believe that victory is possible. The final heat of the meeting will determine who will wear the Elite League crown and it's amazing to think that the season can come down to one final race, particularly when you realise just how many races there are during the season. The excitement on the night and the fact that the last race determines everything also makes this compulsive viewing for the armchair audience and undoubtedly delights the management of *Sky Sports* as well as their advertisers. The Showground presenters, Craig Saul and Edwin Overland, both appear to read from the same excitable script and accurately note within a minute of each other, "the season comes down to the last heat!" The Racerdogs field the Greg Hancock/Janusz Kolodziej combination against that of the Hans Andersen/Ryan Sullivan pairing for the Panthers. All the Racerdogs need is for either rider to take second place in this race but, bizarrely, Jim Lynch appears to have extreme confidence or presumptuously commits a monumental tactical mistake when, after they win the toss and have the choice of gate positions, he decides to choose gate 3 for Hancock. This was to prove an extremely costly misjudgement as, to the ecstatic delight of the vast majority of the people within the stadium, the Panthers win 5-1 to get the fairytale conclusion to their season that seemed so incredibly unlikely only three races earlier. The Racerdogs team and fans would be justified if they felt that they hadn't had the rub of the green, that injuries and mechanical problems had cost them dearly but, most gallingly, that the widely despised tactical ride regulations had robbed them of the title. Peterborough had taken advantage of the rules as they operated at the time – three times in the course of the two legs and so had been crowned 2006 champions by a solitary point on aggregate. Not that anyone in the crowd was really bothered with the fine detail as they celebrated as though Alwalton had been finally granted independence from a particularly despotic ruler.

I can't stay to watch the full glory of the celebrations as commerce calls and I rush down the steps at the back of the grandstand to my table in front of the track shop. Jo from ReRun is already there with the dog, Dewey, waiting for all the customers we hope will be keen to lash around large quantities of their cash with a wild abandon brought on by the giddiness of this delicious victory. Even more shockingly, the track shop is totally deserted, in Marie Celeste fashion, since neither of the Barber brothers are anywhere to be seen. If this were a horror movie (which it probably was, all things considered, for the Racerdogs fans) then if John and Nick hadn't become diabolically possessed, they'd have been eaten by a hideous monster only leaving a discarded slipper, half-eaten sandwich or partly consumed hot drink and a pipe smoking in the ashtray by their still gently tilting but eerily empty rocking chairs. As it is, the shop is brightly lit and completely deserted. In a manner similar to that of the conveyor belt selection of prizes at the end of the *Generation Game*, I could have had my choice of any item of speedway merchandise from the shop without the need to pay. The most noticeable and prominently displayed items are the large piles of "Peterborough Panthers 2006 Elite League Champions" programme boards! Unbelievable, move over Derren Brown or, to choose a much more appropriate illusionist from speedway's golden era, Romark – it appears the Barbers have the gift to see into the future. Like tricks by either of these illusionists, I'm left to exclaim "how do they do that?" As they're still nowhere to be seen, I ask Jo if she's seen sight or sound of Nick and John, "Yeah, they're going bananas down by the fence – leaping up and down and going mental".

When they finally return flushed with the thrill of victory I quiz them, "I didn't know you were Panthers fans?" "We're not really but it's such an amazing victory and in such wonderful circumstances you just have to celebrate and enjoy the moment as it's unlikely we'll see such a thing happen ever again". Nick is sanguine about the possibility of thefts, "everyone is celebrating and frankly it wouldn't have bothered me if there had been as you had to be there!" The mystery of their predictive powers, as it applies to their stockpile of instant-on-the-night mementos, is revealed as a result of careful planning, product knowledge and plain good business sense since the programme boards they buy allow you to use inserts ("slip in laminates") that can quickly customise any boards. Nick is quietly pleased that his cunning plan has come together, "if they hadn't have won, all it would have cost us is the inserts but now, hopefully, everyone will be mad for them!" When I next see John he confesses, "I don't mind admitting we were shitting ourselves at the thought that they might not win and with three heats to go that did look really unlikely". We can hardly hear ourselves speak for the noise of the huge firework display that has been set-off on the centre green after the lengthy victory parade by the riders and every member of staff involved with the Panthers. The firework display goes on and on, the sky is lit up repeatedly with weird geometric patterns and colours that far exceeds the spectacle of many supposedly intricate bonfire night firework displays that I've been to over recent years. The smell of cordite, or whatever they use, hangs in the air and the smoke drifts all around like a winter fog while a film of incinerated cardboard flutters down from the spent fireworks in the sky. As this finally subsides, while the track shop gets hugely crowded and sadly, before the display has even ended, the light drizzle turns heavier and though I've waited in the expectation of considerable sales – I sell nothing. I keep out some books to get doused just in case the sight of a sodden author and his materials proves a temptation few can resist. In fact, though everyone gallops by exultantly enough, they're only keen to get to the shelter of their cars to swiftly join the huge jam of vehicles that already tries to leave the car park and slowly wend its way along the perimeter road of the Showground.

So the drizzle deprives me of further sales and the jam delays my departure as I face yet another midnight drive home. Nonetheless, it has been a fantastic treat to be present on the night to experience and savour the atmosphere of an old-fashioned sized speedway crowd and to be part of a meeting that built up to such a thrilling climax which will be talked about for years to come.

A Meal Fit for an SCB Official
10th October

As ever, the Isle of Wight's ebullient promoter Dave Pavitt is already ensconced at his usual table in the waiting room area of the Wightlink ferry ticket office. Every week this serves as the temporary nerve centre of operations before he finally boards the 4 p.m. car ferry that will transport him across to the Island and then, via the back roads, into his upstairs office adjacent to the spartan, but rather homely, "5-1 bar" in the clubhouse of the speedway track. Just moments before I arrive, I had to pick my way past an aggressive beggar – a disabled male OAP in a decrepit motorised wheelchair who croaks, "put some coins in there!" and follows it with "freak off then" – as I hobble past fully laden with my heavy boxes and battered advertising sign. Traditionally Dave's default mood is set to 'perennially upbeat' and 'warmly hearty'. This afternoon is no exception though today he appears particularly enervated as a result of the sheer excitement brought on by the spectacle of the thrilling Elite League Play-off final second leg he watched on the telly last night. "Did you see it last night? It was absolutely ace – fantastic telly! What an advert; my phone hasn't stopped ringing with people wanting to talk about it." Dave bats off objections about the warping effect on the scores of the tactical ride regulations, "I don't see any problem with it myself".

Our reminiscences are interrupted by the first of a steady stream of visitors who arrive to collect their ferry tickets from Dave; in this case, Sheffield's young gifted prospect for the future, Ben Wilson. Dave either has the tickets already set out on the table – though he likes to compulsively count them throughout the whole time he waits in the ticket office – or else he fishes them out from his worn but executive looking briefcase where he's temporarily stored them prior to another recount. The home riders often get an envelope, with their names handwritten on them, pressed knowingly into their hands along with their tickets. Dave quizzes Ben in staccato fashion:
"How many in the van?"
"Two"
"Two?"
"Two plus me"
"Two plus you?"
"Yeah"
"That's three!" says Dave in a tone that mixes triumph and patience while he peels another ticket from the wodge that he holds.

The fact that the Isle of Wight have got through to the semi-finals of the Premier League play-offs at all is a surprise, especially since Glasgow specifically choose them (rather than Somerset) to supposedly maximise their chances of success and thereby progress to the semi-finals. The Islanders now remain the only team who finished outside the top four league places who have got this far; though Dave Pavitt, when pressed by others about his thoughts, is very keen not to tempt the speedway gods with talk of further progression, "let's not say nothing until after Thursday". Something that can be spoken about is the need for many more fans to turn up tonight since the crowd for the Glasgow encounter was disappointing if looked at in cash receipt terms, particularly once the factor of the season ticket holders who attended (because they have already paid) is taken out of the financial equation. For every business based on the Island the tourist season is hugely important – including the speedway – and it is a cyclical business, "after the summer it's like switching off the light". Talk of a crowd that exceeded 6000 people at Alwalton puts Dave in reflective mood, "I'd be happy with ten percent of what they had last night".

The journey across on the ferry is always something I relish, and enjoy much more on the way back, if I manage to make the 10 p.m. sailing, though that depends on unpredictable factors like crashes and mechanical failures. Something that can be controlled is the administration of the racing by the referee and tonight's official is the pleasant and efficient Chris Durno who kindly agrees to give me and my boxes of books a lift to the stadium. Chris has been in the trade news quite a bit this season, most recently because of a meeting at Newcastle where all 12 riders took a different view on track conditions to that taken by the Newcastle promotion and the referee. The upshot was an abandoned meeting, but only after the crowd had entered the stadium – with the net result of disgruntlement for everyone, the riders for their £250 fine each, the crowd for the postponement, the promotion for the associated costs of the abandonment (their eighth postponement of the season) and the referee for the opprobrium that has been heaped on his head in a season in which he'd already attracted controversy and headlines. Chris is a very fair-minded chap who, like so many in the sport, attaches primary importance to the safety of the riders, "they'll ride on tracks in much worse conditions before the season is out – it was a typical March or October track, not as good as the summer months but still rideable". Unfortunately on the night, Chris and the promoters had had no indication that the riders had concerns about the conditions or that they would decide to refuse to ride en masse. All in all, it hasn't reflected well on the sport and a cynic might take the view that so long as there was an "agreed restaging date" (which there was – October 22nd), the riders would always view the abandonment as a necessary, regrettable but ultimately remediable evil.

Many people have shared their opinions about this meeting in print, online and in person. On the ferry, a man comes up to Chris and barks, in what I took to be a self-righteous but slightly aggressive and threatening manner: "You should remember that it's the riders who have to ride and without them there's nothing." It's a true enough point and I doubt that there would be many who would disagree. I ask, "Who was that bloke? Was he there or something, as he seems very angry." Chris replies in his laconic and distinctive Midlands accent, "Nah, that's Nick Simmons's dad who always likes to give me a hard time about something every time he sees me – quite how he thinks it benefits him or his son I don't know but it takes all sorts to make a world, particularly in speedway!"

Once you get addicted enough to want to experience it regularly, there is a real glamour and excitement from involvement in the meetings but, despite this, the travel can become a real grind. This appears to be the consensus for everyone involved from riders to authors, mechanics to referees. I've already acquired quite an extensive list of shortcuts to stadiums, favoured service and petrol stations, and gained a good working knowledge of supermarkets adjacent to speedway tracks. Invariably they aren't far away since speedway, for many years now, has been increasingly pushed towards the margins of our social and cultural life in our newspapers and television. This decline in recognition and importance has a physical and geographical dimension as many tracks now find themselves increasingly driven out of city centres (by amenable planning authorities since sceptical ones ensure noise/traffic objections triumph) – a countrywide phenomenon – in favour of locations on the borders of towns, often close by or within ring roads, business parks and industrial estates. Like many fans and riders, referee Chris Durno also has to plan ahead for his long drive home and so he too has developed a comprehensive knowledge as to the whereabouts of many useful facilities. Once we're off the ferry we immediately drive to the Tesco supermarket in Ryde. Like many things on the Island, it's a bit old-fashioned, slightly careworn and on the cusp of past its best, especially since the winds of change, rebranding, and reconfiguration, that has swept like an epidemic through other Tescos on the mainland, has only slightly touched this store but, in the main, has completely passed it by. Inside it's still touchingly cramped and almost has a 'retro' air if that is possible within a modern supermarket chain where one out of every £8 that's spent on groceries in this country is spent at Tesco. Though reputedly they have unrivalled knowledge about what the customers will want in any individual location, so I can only assume the ambience, décor and selections available snugly fit local tastes. On this basis, it would appear that they've managed to resist the urban mores that demands the continentalisation of food choices and everything to be 'organic', in favour of a more "British" and unreconstituted diet. Really unwholesome food by metrosexual standards shouts at you from practically every shelf in this pleasingly cramped and most dimly lit store.

Not only does Chris appear easily able to find his way to the store but also inside he's familiar enough with it to know his way around to find what he wants. I'm delighted to get to shop with him so I can continue my in-depth research into the shopping habits of speedway people when they go to Tesco. In my book *Showered in Shale*, I reviewed and analysed the rather unique shopping basket choices of Greg Hancock and now I get to get some insight into the consumer mindset of the refereeing fraternity. Both of them show good foresight and organisation since they realise that while they're at work at the track they'll not get the chance to sample the culinary fare on offer there. Greg, because he's riding and Chris because he's the meeting official and, therefore, spends his time hunched over the buttons or the paperwork, even if you ignore the

Art arrives in the Bees track shop. © Jeff Scott

Framed commemorative photo only £30. © Jeff Scott

Track shop manager Joyce Blythe shyly models some Bees memorabilia. © Jeff Scott

See Coventry chapter p.257-261

fact that he invariably concentrates so hard and lives on his nerves so much that he doesn't feel hungry or thirsty. They will, however, both want to eat afterwards when the burger van along with any other food outlet in the general vicinity has closed. Chris definitely knows what he wants to eat after the meeting. The contents of his basket quickly accumulates in a practised manner: three "French style" white crusty rolls, salami, a tub of "3 cheese" coleslaw ("much better than the ordinary stuff"), a 'healthy living' prawn mayonnaise sandwich, a six pack of caramel biscuits and a giant but garishly decorated bottle of Diet Kick (a sort of Tesco own-brand Red Bull type drink), "this is the most important thing – it really does keep you awake and it's what I need to get me 'ome". "It really does work" repeats Chris, as though we're both in a commercial and I've doubted claims about its beneficial qualities. I already knew it was the drink of choice for speedway riders before and during a meeting (until they can get to the bar) and now it turns out to be *de rigueur* for the refs as well!

By the time we arrive inside the stadium, the pits' car park is full of riders' vans and we pull alongside Emiliano Sanchez who carefully unloads his bike from his van as though it's precious treasure. He seems a modest, personable, dark-haired man who chats warmly with Chris. Though he's only dressed casually, Emiliano exudes style and dapperness, something that isn't always apparent among the more fashion-challenged speedway riding fraternity, so I immediately ascribe to his Latin American roots. He tells Chris that he isn't going home to Argentina this winter as his girlfriend is English, "it'll be a lot colder than you're used to then!" observes Chris before he remembers global warming, "well, maybe, we don't have such cold winters nowadays".

Because at this time of the season it gets dark so quickly and the spectators don't appear tempted to lurk in the darkness of the first bend, I decide to base myself in front of the track shop. I'll hunt (well lurk hopefully) near the programme stall that everyone has to pass after they enter through the turnstiles. Well, unless they immediately make a beeline for the "5-1 Bar" and ensconce themselves there for the night. There they can avoid the slight chill that pervades the air this evening and watch through the windows of the warmly heated bar or congregate on the outside balcony area that allows you to drink, be merry and enjoy a panoramic view of the speedway. The previous track shop manager, Dudley, has also arrived with his amiable 19-year-old daughter Sarah and he fusses around helping the track shop staff get set up for what we all hope will be an evening of persistent custom. He's an even prouder father than usual this evening. "Have you heard? Sarah has some fantastic news! I'll let her tell you yourself," he exclaims, but he can't help himself and blurts out, "she's passed her driving test, first time, this afternoon!" Sarah appears delighted, nearly as much as Dudley, before she hints aloud about the future availability of her dad's car.

I retreat back to my table by the programme stall. We're all bathed in a very bright floodlight until just about 7 p.m. when a power failure plunges the stadium into darkness, except for the lights in the grandstand building (and bar), the dim bulbs of the perimeter lights, plus the noticeable brightness of the catering hut on the first bend. There's a long and ominous delay during which I hope someone earnestly labours away to ensure that they're quickly fixed so that this prestigious semi-final first leg can proceed. Although, that said, many of the people that funnel past appear to fail to notice that the track is completely plunged into a level of darkness that will preclude any racing tonight if it continues. Rather than aggressively promote my book, I cheerily tell everyone, "can you put 50 pence in the meter now that you're here". Understandably, many people look at me as though I'm demented. If I could hire anyone here tonight to help promote my book by making loud announcements – except Bryn over the tannoy, of course, who despite his really stinking cold and husky voice (though it has a default setting of gravelly, no doubt due to all those cigarettes – a truly impressive number – that he avidly gets through during any fixture) does a sterling job at repeatedly singing the praises of my book – I'd choose "Sexy Sue" from the programme stall. As Bryn never tires of telling us every week, she has "the loudest voice in speedway", something that she hones every Tuesday as she advocates the purchase of raffle tickets or, apparently, throughout the summer months in Ryde working as the town crier. Er, actually, I'm not sure whether this is true or another example of Bryn's wry sense of humour. She loudly advises any waverers who dawdle by her stall that a purchase of the programme would be advisable for such an important fixture. In the lull between arrivals – which rather noticeably there is quite a bit of since people arrive in a trickle except for when the 'speedway special' double-decker buses arrive from the ferry port – she chats to me amiably (albeit loudly). She reminisces, "I still miss Steen [Jensen], I loved little Steen – no one could say 'Sexy Sue' like he could with his accent!" One of the arrivals from the buses is the always friendly and taciturn Poole co-promoter Mike Golding, who not only stops to chat but playfully fingers a copy of my new book *When Eagles Dared* just so he can theatrically reduce his voice to a stage whisper to note in hushed conspiratorial tones, "fancy doing a book on [lengthy pause] Eastbourne!?" he says the 'E' word as though it pains him that it crosses his lips and that he has to deign to acknowledge them. He's a charming man.

Sales are the opposite of brisk though, now that power has been restored to the floodlights, the meeting starts with the rider introductions and parade. Chris Durno, and every member of the Sheffield Tigers team, is keen that this fixture runs smoothly enough to allow everyone to try to make the 10 o'clock ferry sailing back to the mainland. It's the second time in a fortnight that the Islanders have faced opposition with the Tigers club nickname and they'll hope for a repeat of their performances home and away from the recent quarter-final round. Should they win through to the final they will have exhausted all the Tigers that they'll face since Mildenhall completely failed to finish in the top eight places of the Premier League required in order to qualify. You have to ask yourself what sort of bonkers qualification criteria it is that allows more teams from the Premier League to get to the final stages of the season than the number of those that don't? Something is definitely out of kilter with these proportions! If you're going to gerrymander additional meetings into the end of the season, to boost revenues, why not say that everyone qualifies and have done with it. Such a system would only marginally further devalue the present situation where the only 'true' speedway league (i.e. that has a league of sufficient size to ensure that it only has a single home and away fixture against each rival team) fails to crown its eventual rightful champion without the specious but financially lucrative necessity of play-offs?[1] Unlike the fixture with Glasgow in the quarter-final, the home side struggle throughout the night to really establish the dominance that they will need to build up the essential "big lead" from this leg that they will definitely require to take to the return fixture in Sheffield on Thursday night should they retain any outside chance of progression. Though both clubs ride on huge circuits, compared to many of their rivals, they won't therefore expect to so easily disconcert the opposing riders as they regularly do with those who're much more used to tighter, slower confines of smaller tracks. Sheffield assuredly will have their bikes set up and calibrated for lengthy spells of racing with the throttle fully open on the long fast straights of the Smallbrook circuit. Admittedly there is the sharply sloped and cambered final bend at this track, but even that the Sheffield riders exploit much better than many other more tentative opponents.

If there was a script written by the more romantic followers of the sport, then the Tigers haven't read it since they win the first heat and it takes the home side until Heat 6 to even establish any sort of vague lead. By this time Sheffield have

[1] Ironically, there was talk that *Sky Sports* would extend their coverage of speedway during the 2006 season to include the Premier League play-offs. Only after they'd prostituted themselves enough to voluntarily change the method by which the PL champions are identified – we must remember at all times that *Sky* never insist on any changes within the sport since the promoters are happy enough to prostrate themselves for the *Sky* shilling without the need for a formal request – when did the realisation dawn on them that this coverage wasn't going to happen in 2006?

Books for sale with Ray 'Brummie' Billingsley. © Jeff Scott

Jodie Lowry guards the Scott Nicholls merchandise stall.
© Jeff Scott. © Jeff Scott

See Coventry chapter p.257-261

provided half the heat winners in the form of the usual suspects – Ben Wilson, Andre Compton and Ricky Ashworth. As ever we're entertained with Bryn's elegant turn of phrase in his various announcements that he leavens with some of his tried, tested and trusted favourites from his collection of stock phrases. Ray Morton wins the third heat so Bryn takes the early chance to trot out the observation, "like fine wine he matures with age". It's a night when the home side can't ever really pull away from their rivals and although they hold a comfortable lead of six points throughout most of the meeting they never really create a sufficient gap. Admittedly, this has the advantage that it precludes the visitors utilising the tactical ride rules but I'm sure that the riders, like the slightly resigned fans, all know that this type of lead is unlikely to prove enough margin to defend in a few nights' time.

For the Islanders, Jason Doyle is in imperious and exhilarating form. I abandon my books and take the opportunity to wander to the far side of the stadium to watch the action from the raised area of scrubland that overlooks the steep banking of the third and fourth bends. Surprisingly few people watch from here, since they mostly prefer the spectacle granted, along with the comparative warmth and comfort, of the grandstand seats adjacent to the start line. The route by which you approach this unique viewing area isn't clearly marked or easily spotted since it involves skirting past the back of the pits, crossing the rough hewn road, where the tractors park or trundle onto the race track and then up a bumpy slope cum path to an area fenced off with string. Probably for insurance reasons, Bryn exhorts the few fans that there are within the stadium to show some health and safety awareness that, in this instance, translates to 'take extra care on the treacherously slippery slopes that line the majority of the track perimeter in case they slip on the wet, dewy grass'. He doesn't mention this altogether more dangerous viewing area at all, but then only a few hardy souls in the know venture here past the wonderful "Dave Death Motorcycles" sign (undoubtedly the best speedway sign of its kind anywhere throughout the tracks in this country). I'm joined for a while by the charming Sarah, who's still exultant with the triumph of her driving test success though this is sharply coloured and quickly tempered by the sheer cringeworthy embarrassment of an announcement over the tannoy by Bryn, who loudly advertises her news to all and sundry. That's proud fathers for you, since they can unexpectedly make you flush with anger or blush with shyness at the drop of a hat. Afterwards I hear Sarah muttering, "I'll have to have a word with him!" Also close by is the King's Lynn fan on holiday on the Island who, as a treat for himself, if not for his partner, has taken the chance to pay his first visit to speedway on the Island. He's appreciative of the unique view up here now that he's followed my earlier recommendation.

Heat 10 takes place with the additional light provided by the very large two-thirds moon and is enlivened by Jason Bunyan who crashes spectacularly in front of me at the apex of the first corner on the second lap of the race. Now, I've moved back round to rejoin my books, bag, sign and table, in time for the interval, so I see the whole crash in intimate detail. Despite the speed he has generated and the apparent severity of his thumping impact upon the boards of the safety fence, Jason is no sooner down than he immediately rises with great alacrity from the ground, retrieves his bike from where it's slightly wedged between the intersection of the boards and the track and still manages to courteously clear the shale so that the race doesn't have to be stopped. Afterwards when he informs us of the exact details of the result of this race Bryn notes, "the referee Chris Durno congratulates Jason Bunyan for clearing the track so quickly and has awarded him 5.4 for artistic merit!"

I rejoin my stuff to find everything has literally been *Showered in Shale*. To be more exact, it has been caked in thick lumps of shale-like mud and would have suffered much more if Dudley hadn't kindly moved my things to a place of comparative shelter. Now that I study my surrounding much more carefully, I realise that the hollow that I decided to place my table in is overlooked by the part of the safety fence closest to the exit of the second bend. This is just at the point when the maximum quantities of loose material from the track surface will be thrown off the rapidly spinning wheels of the bikes as they transition from a broadside into firing themselves in a straight line at speed down the back straight. In all directions, the floor is a deep brown colour similar to the track surface and is littered with small lumps of shale. To look on the brighter side, my board now has a much more authentic splattered look that neatly echoes the alliterative title of my book *Showered in Shale*. The apposite symmetry of all this fails to impress any fans or persuade them to part with their hard-earned cash. Knowing when I'm beaten, I pack my things into my mud-caked travel bag (one of those with the wheels that I find so annoying when other people ensure that I trip over them) and watch the remainder of the meeting perched on the 'dangerous' slippery grass slope of the first bend that Bryn was so keen to highlight earlier.

The Islanders' luck on the night is summed up by the final race of the fixture and it includes the exhilarating young Aussie pair of Chris Holder and Jason Doyle, who've thrilled the locals all season with their derring-do (and tonight has been no exception). Just when they were ideally placed to record the required 5-1 race result, against the Tigers strange choice of pairing (Compton and Wilson) that would have led to a final score of 52-41 in favour of the Islanders – Chris Holder falls in really spectacular fashion. He remains prostrate on the track surface surrounded by the St John Ambulance staff for a considerable time, long after the race has been award as a 3-3 by referee Chris Durno. This means an actual final score of 50-43 and that the Islanders will only have a meagre lead of seven points to take to Sheffield. The man next to me appears resigned at the likely outcome that this will produce for the Islanders' gallant attempt to upset the season-long formbook, "I don't think that's going to be any good for us". I just about manage to drag my wheelie bag along the stony surface of the path that runs behind the main grandstand, scoring a track in it as I pass, to rejoin referee Chris Durno for a lift back to the ferry port in time for the 10 o'clock sailing. The Sheffield riders and mechanics are working frenetically to load their bikes and tools in the van in a hasty, careless manner that suggests that they have two minutes to evacuate the site before a bomb is exploded rather than still 25 minutes grace before the boat back to the mainland sails. Chris cheerily calls out to Emiliano, "hurry up you're going to miss it". He stares back in bemused fashion as though his considerable facility with the English language has temporarily deserted him or, perhaps, it's just one of the cultural differences over humour that so flummoxes visitors to these shores. Like apparently everyone else with a car in the stadium car park, Chris races through the stadium exit and at breakneck speed along the darkened country and residential roads. I panic for a moment that we will actually miss the ferry as Chris drives the route to the port that the road signs advise rather than the short cut that I'm used to taking with that experienced Isle of Wight track shop franchisee, Dave 'the Rat' Rattenberry. We all easily make the crossing and the restaurant car is again like a 'Who's Who' in miniature of this part of the speedway community. The Islanders' riders and fans that have made this crossing seem somewhat subdued in comparison to their Tigers compatriots. The smartly attired Neil Machin celebrates the victory by holding forth while he painstakingly and carefully cleans the mud off his black dress shoes in the toilets – foot on the toilet with wet tissue in hand. He's confident and satisfied with how the night has turned out. If I were an Islanders fan I think I'd feel like a good shout to overcome my disgruntlement. Back in the 'Pay and Display' car park just outside the ferry port, Dudley ostentatiously fusses around his car while he allows his daughter Sarah to adjust the driver's seat in order to have her first ever legally qualified night drive back to Gosport. Though it takes a while to sort and load my car, they still haven't set off on their momentous journey when I wave as I pull away into the night traffic and road works of Portsmouth city centre.

10th October Isle of Wight v Sheffield (Premier League play-off Semi-Final, First Leg) 50-43

Big Voice in the Black Country
16th October

An uneventful drive to Wolverhampton is enlivened when a convoy of silver Mercedes cars pass me on the M42 that all bear personalised number plates with variants upon the "OK SINGH" theme. At the track, the greyhound meeting is in progress and it's noticeable how few people turn up to watch the dogs' race live though the meeting is shown simultaneously at many betting shops throughout the country. The sight of the dogs in full flight on the sandy track fascinates me, as I've never seen it before. Inside the dog track circuit, a tractor slowly completes many revolutions of the speedway track in preparation for the prestigious and traditional individual handicap meeting (Olympique) that they have held at Monmore Green for many years. Dave Rat is already ensconced behind the counter of his track shop that to my mind has moved, but in a position that he reassures me is "my usual one". Everything is already in place – all the merchandise is laid out attractively and many items have been specially priced at bargain rates to attract the eye and custom of the Wolverhampton faithful – for one of the last speedway meetings that Dave will attend this season. Something that's again not so usual to my casual eye is his assistant tonight, Graham Williams. He's here to help since apparently it's lock up your daughters' time on the other side of the Atlantic as John Rich and Bill Gimbeth are presently on holiday there in Florida. The mind boggles at what they'll get up to out there. Graham seems a plainly spoken man who is keen to let me know that he's definitely his own man and "not freaking John what not". Dave is slightly down in the dumps to have learnt that he has "lost the Birmingham franchise to Nick Barber". Though he pitched for the opportunity to run it and would have brought his local knowledge and Midlands connections with him, he's now kicks himself that he didn't take the time to give Graham Drury a more finely crafted proposal. He confesses that he'd have relished the chance to have done it but notes philosophically, "I could already retire now – getting more money is not why I still do it or want to do it – it's not for myself but more so that I've something to pass on".

As ever, the stall draws a crowd, though the turnstiles are officially not open yet. Nonetheless they have attracted a queue despite a light drizzle that stops as quickly as it has started, enough to signal that it might disrupt my evening with a table of books in the open air. I'm positioned just at the edge of the track shop, right next to the Ratmobile (aka the giant white van that is Dave's chosen mode of transport when he ferries bulk quantities of speedway merchandise to outlets in his track shop empire). Already deep in conversation with Rat is John Baldwin whom he takes the time to introduce to me with the words, "he's one of the first people to arrive at the stadium every week, so he can get a seat in the bar". John has been coming along to speedway since he first went to Wembley with his mum and dad in what he recalls to be 1942, "when I was four or five and me dad used to take me on his shoulders". He was originally a Wembley supporter and recalls regular "crowds of 70 or 80 thousand on a Thursday night". John switched allegiances to Birmingham and then to Wolverhampton when his parents moved so his dad could work at RAF Cosford and he's quick to stress his love of the sport and his huge good fortune, "I've seen the greatest in the world ride here – it's a sport where you can see that, the best, and you don't have to pay the outlandish prices of the Formula 1 Grand Prix or football. In every decade you can name half a dozen superstars, you can't say that the past was better because it's different eras and different riders excel in different decades. There's too many to recall though Jackie Parker was brilliant and one of the most spectacular riders was Hasse Holmquist. He was Swedish and used to put his head under the handlebars 'Craven' style. Of course there was Barry Briggs and Ove Fundin as well as Graham Warren ('he got a plate in his skull'). There are always stars to see here. One thing is you've always got to go with the flow, I didn't think that I'd like the new format of the GPs but now I do! I used to work here at the track for five shillings, which was a lot of money then, for four hours and two free tickets that you could always sell. I used to rake the track as a track grader in the 50s when Bill Bridgett was the promoter and Simcock was the gaffer but age catches up with you and the shale gets really heavy, plus it gets so cold out there".

I think John then became a coach driver but I've slightly lost the thread of the conversation as we've now been joined by another old timer, Brian Ball, who echoes these sentiments or occasionally quietly adds in his own reminiscences, though he's slightly bashful at the idea that I might note down what he has to say ("no one would be interested in that, would they?"). Eventually he relaxes enough to be prepared to recall, "I first came here when it was the 'Wasps', so I reckon it was in the 50s". They both agree that the sport has enthralled, mesmerised and continually drawn them back for more. The exact reason, if they had to put their finger on it, which I insist that they do, escapes them though they think that the reason is partly olfactory, "the smell of the dope – Castrol R – had a smell all of its own". Talk of stimulated senses turns the conversation and John asks rhetorically, "what about Sophie and that dirty bleeder? I said to her the last time she was here that if anyone was going to chat her up it's me! She just laughed and now look at things!" Dave Rat is of the opinion that Scotty gets in the news whether it's something that he's done or not. A case in point is the latest speedway-related *Sun* headline that tries to accentuate his recent "bad boy" persona – this time for an alleged water-throwing incident. "I heard it was Chrissie Harris that threw the water over the Manchester Mexicans – who can be a handful themselves – or a group of them that included Scott. They supposedly took it well at the time but people went on afterwards".

If we look to the matters at hand rather than the world of 'celebrity' speedway gossip, they all agree that the track looks in magnificent condition. "It does all the time here I think, though it's really good tonight, I said to that Kelvin [Tattum] last time he came here 'welcome to a track with shale'. You never see any of the bloody stuff on many of the tracks nowadays". The idea of the race winners being handicapped in their next races really appeals to them as it maximises the need and incentive to pass other riders ("what it's all about really". They hesitate to make predictions "but Peter [Karlsson] always takes some beating round here though Freddie [Lindgren] could be good tonight too". As supporters of their local speedway club they're keen to stress longevity and tradition, "it's the longest running individual tournament around nowadays plus it's got a unique handicap system", they proudly inform me. They're not quite sure of the handicap distances, "it used to be yards but now it's metres and I think it's 30-20-10 metres handicap". [It was 10, 15 or 20 yards.]

After they've left, Dave Rat just about manages to placate a demanding and angry customer who hectors him to find out if Dave will actually finally be able to employ his fabled badge-making and embroidery skills to good effect. In this case to produce the item he has previously commissioned and for which the customer has previously supplied (exacting) specifications. "Just tell me if you can do it for next week or not – it's the last week and the end of the season – and if you can't, don't bother 'cause you've been saying you'd do it for ages now but haven't". Dave tries to be simultaneously non-committal and give some blather in lieu of an exact promise or date that only serves to further provoke the verbal ire of the customer. I leave Dave to resolve this test of his avuncular nature to have a sudden diplomatic fiddle with my own stock.

When I return to beside the stall, a different crowd – this time of track staff – has arrived to discuss the burning issue of the moment, namely censorship and club promoter Chris van Straaten (CVS). Wonderfully trying to singlehandedly defy the impact of technology in the contemporary age, CVS has allegedly taken severe umbrage to critical/"abusive" comments and personal attacks posted on the "Wolf Cry" website forum about the forthcoming Wolverhampton speedway club Dinner Dance. Not the sort of issue that you'd associate with the concept of freedom of expression and human rights in a democratic society, but these are the kind of phrases that this flare up has caused to be bandied about with some abandon. Simply put, as I understood it from eavesdropping, someone has used the "Wolf Cry" forum to post critical comments (the primary use of any speedway forum it seems) about the choice of location – the Wolverhampton Ramada Park Hall Hotel – for this popular event on the club calendar. These critical comments were based on the experiences at the hotel last year by the critical poster in question. Significantly, since this negative experience, the location in question has gained new owners and has undergone a complete makeover of décor, menus and facilities as well as extensive other unnamed improvements. This is something that might lead you to expect that things will have 'improved' compared to the recent past (though to echo, but slightly change, the sentiments of the German Expressionist group *Der Blaue Reiter* – though for them it was "culture" that provoked their ire – 'at the sound of "makeover" the catch comes off my Browning'). Whatever the rights and wrongs of the critique, it has crystallised a number of deeply held reservations that CVS has harboured about this website and the anonymity of the contributors who have often posted critical comments on the site over all sorts of issues at the club in the past. Perhaps it all looks a bit silly and faintly ridiculous that this is the instance (or straw) that has broken the camel's back but there is no doubt that CVS is deadly serious and you kind of sense that once he has issued his edicts that CVS would be totally implacable.

There's no doubt that it's a "huge talking point" and, in an interesting twist, the conscientious founders of the website – the two Marks, Lawton and Rowe – are possessed of degrees of stubbornness that equals that of CVS. They themselves also hold the flame of all things Wolverhampton Speedway close to their hearts. So now we have a situation where both sides of this argument can justifiably claim that they equally conscientiously guard and burnish the Wolves speedway flame. The excellently informative and interesting document that is the club programme for this fixture (which I'll return to shortly) ironically has a club slogan that states, "the strength of the pack is the Wolf, and the strength of the Wolf is the pack". It also implicitly endorses the work of the two Marks' since it has an advert for the "new look *Wolfcry* speedway website" that suggests fans might like to "join our Fans Forum and talk about speedway with Wolves fans from round the country and abroad". The website has traditionally raised additional money, through appeals and donations since its inception, that is used to help individual riders, so there's really no doubt that they're involved in the warp and the woof of speedway here. The consensus by the track shop is that "one intemperate post" (about how "crap" the hotel was last year) has caused a crisis that appears it will result in the closure of the site since rather idealistically CVS insists that to gain his future support all future critical postings will require "that everyone has to use real names to post in future". His suggestion simultaneously defies the netiquette of the use of the technology and the internet generally and, in this context, is Canute-like in its unfeasibility. Nonetheless, that is the condition that CVS requires to be satisfied and this will almost certainly provide a fatal stumbling block. There is widespread scepticism at the feasibility or sense of this request among the track staff gathered by Rat's stall and it's considered risible "that CVS claims none of his staff put critical postings on there". Numerous examples from throughout the stadium staff are given – I have redacted this information but these strongly opinionated posters would appear to be widespread in their job functions at Wolverhampton speedway. It's best not to intrude on private grief and so I leave them to earnestly consider this unique attempt to subvert the protocols and practice of contemporary internet usage. I simultaneously admire CVS for his zealous pursuit of the issue and his intractability when it comes to the protection of what he perceives as the best interests of the club. Equally, it's also real 'cut your nose off to spite your face' territory, since the founders and administrators of the *Wolfcry* forum clearly have gold and black blood coursing through their collective veins!

Personally I have found CVS straightforward and supportive of my book *Showered in Shale* at Wolverhampton and Redcar, despite the fact that the Monmore meeting I attended and wrote about didn't necessarily reflect well on the club's choice of all their staff. The relevant chapter in question also included some critical observations of CVS (though I did put my name to them) so I had expected that he might be less than supportive. In fact, CVS was nothing of the sort and has been pragmatically professional to deal with even though it was always in his power to refuse to help. I admire this commonsense approach and even after the fall out with the *Wolfcry* Marks, he remained happy for them to present their cheques on the centre green with the appropriate fanfare. Equally the people behind the "*Wolfcry*" website were interested and supportive of my book and they helped ensure the success of my first visit. It's a real shame that this independent-minded forum has gone the way of all flesh. Hopefully, it can soon be resurrected.

The programme that you get at Wolves is a true speedway fan's delight. There's a paean to the work of the referee penned by the thorough and conscientious local *Express & Star* reporter, Tim Hamblin. As with his articles in the paper, it's considerate, elegantly expressed, compassionate and well researched. Another gem is the column penned by Wolverhampton manager, Peter Adams. He's a thoughtful and sagacious man anyway, something that comes across strongly in a piece that mixes insight, interest, waspish humour and comment, pointed and otherwise. Anyone would be able to have fun with a retrospective review of the performance of every Elite League's speedway correspondent's predictive abilities about the final composition of the 2006 table, as they suggested them at the start of the season. Some forecasts are woefully inaccurate, wildly optimistic or partisan depending on your point of view. Based on this year's performance, many should be seeking alternative employment or require a crash course to update their speedway knowledge and insights. Peter relishes the chance to conduct his acerbic review and he counts himself part of the school of life of "those with a warped sense of humour like nothing better than to see someone put their foot in it". He notes *en passant*, "as ever, there was an awful lot of wishful thinking last spring, with all bar THREE of the journalists claiming that their team would make the Play-Offs!" Peter praises the *Speedway Star's* Wolves reporter, Nigel Pearson, but then notes, "brickbats must surely go to Ipswich [Elvin King], Belle Vue [Richard Frost] and Arena [Tony Brewer], all of whom were horribly wrong on all fronts". He hasn't forgotten last year either, "last year the Coventry correspondent's [Mike Berry] forecast would have been uncannily accurate had the table been turned upside down".

The programme also includes various other very entertaining features as well as a column by Nigel Pearson in which he writes about some recent "gr8" text messages he's received ("Thanx M8!") that prompts him to provide an eulogy about the brilliance of the Elite League play-off system. He gets so carried away he makes it sound as if it verges on Moses-like miracle status, "the spectacle and drama is truly amazing". Plus, surprise, surprise – Nigel is also a firm advocate of the "tactical ride rule". He clarifies the misperception of that oft-repeated and oh so naughty canard that this "rule" was introduced at the direct behest of *Sky Sports*, "just one final point, those of you who believe the rule was introduced just for *Sky*, remember this – it was one Elite League club at the bottom of the league who demanded the old tac-sub rule be scrapped because they couldn't afford to keep paying their top rider for a gift win in Heat 8! Food for thought going into the winter". It certainly is and provokes a few observations from those around me in the crowd on the terraces before the meeting gets underway:

1. Who was this promoter? Is he by any chance the brother of the person most closely associated with the *Sky Sports* contract and its negotiation?

2. Technically he is, at least, a member of the BSPA so quite rightly should be involved in the decision-making process about rules and regulations. *Sky Sports*, last time anyone looked, were not formally members but are believed to exert some control on decision making despite the fact that television contract payments from the *Sky* deal don't benefit any of the Premier or Conference League clubs.

3. Does the club with the poorest Elite League record and finances dictate the key rule for all speedway clubs and thereby the whole sport and by so doing affect the enjoyment of all fans throughout the country?

4. Can rules be reconsidered in the light of experience or are they set in stone?

5. If *Sky* objected, would this rule be dropped? (Obviously, this is completely unlikely to happen as this rule change totally accidentally dovetails exactly with *Sky*'s understandable desire to maximise entertainment in each and every race, so a little 'structural' help to achieve this never goes amiss).

6. Is this the rule that most holds back the credibility of our sport in the print and broadcast media? Many feel it's indefensible and tortuously difficult to explain, even to people who love and follow the sport.

7. The back issues of the *Speedway Star* that in the Letters pages repeated the methodology and thoughts behind the introduction of this change to the rules as it was related at the time – and quoted the authority figures of Terry Russell and CVS – who explicitly referenced the entertainment needs of *Sky Sports*.[1]

It's always a delight to watch speedway from the packed grandstand terrace at Monmore Green and the night's racing is aided by the end-of-term feel as well as the unique handicap system that places a premium on passing after the initial first four heats have been raced. Heat 3 is enlivened by an inside overtake by Daniel Nermark on the third bend of the first lap and it already appears like it's going to be one of those nights for Ronnie Correy who suffers an engine failure on the last bend when in third place. The meeting also provides the chance to see some promising young continental talent take part in a speedway fixture – some of them for the first time in this country. The riders in question are Claus Vissing and Kenneth Hansen (who had ridden in an individual meeting at Workington a few weeks previously) from Denmark, plus the improbably named teenager, Ricky Kling from Sweden, who sounds like he's a fictional speedway cartoon character. Ricky is initially the most memorable after he only manages to get to the apex of the first bend on his first ever lap in this country before he falls when placed last. For some reason his bike clings to him and manages to completely pin down and immobilise him on the track surface, which thereby causes the race to be stopped by the referee Dale Entwhistle. Normal rules don't quite apply this evening, so a re-run with all four riders is ordered and so promptly gives Ricky yet another chance to try to negotiate the perils of a crowded first bend. The reprieve works well for him until the fourth bend of the first lap, when the experienced Adam Skornicki has to take sudden evasive action brought on by the wayward Kling powering aggressively underneath him on the fourth bend. We're then treated to the sight of the pony-tailed rider being thrown heavily from his machine, after it has bounced off the air fence. All this before Skornicki's bike then still careens on down the track like a riderless horse in the Grand National, until it finally crashes to rest much further down the straight. Despite his earlier generosity, this time the referee has no choice but to exclude Ricky Kling for his actions and so draw to a premature close the first British outing of his ongoing speedway education. It also draws to a close any further participation in the meeting by Adam Skornicki who sadly has been shaken, stirred and concussed by his part in Ricky's apprenticeship. With considerable understatement and in his trademark monotone style Peter Morrish observes that it was,

[1] Kate Hardy wrote in a couple of times to the *Speedway Star* letters page about the relationship between the introduction of the despised tactical ride rule and the *Sky Sports* television cameras. She'd been carefully studying the back issues, "thank you for putting me right over my 'misconception' that the introduction of the tactical rule in the 2004 SkyBet sponsored Elite League had something to with *Sky*". She quotes from interviews that were reported in the *Speedway Star*: "if the cameras are there and it's a bit one sided, well, it would have happened anyway, but we do notice that we get the channel scanners... and at 9 o'clock, if we've got a meeting on and the scores are close, the TV audience increases massively. They're the occasional viewers who flick through and watch it provided it's close. You can increase by 50,000 viewers, which is wonderful" (Terry Russell 15/11/03). Then after the BSPA conference, (Chris van Straaten 29/11/03) "The traditional speedway fan hates change, but we have to think of the new audience, the TV audience....the new tactical rule".

A day in the life of a speedway rider – white van and motorway jam. © Jeff Scott

"a spectacular crash".

From Heat 5 onwards, we soon get into the real meat and potatoes of the championship when the handicap system kicks in for each rider in accordance with where they finished in their previous race. If you won your previous race, you will 'enjoy' the greatest yardage handicap in your next outing. This promises to be an evening when Peter Karlsson spends the rest of his night starting each race an additional 20 yards back from the tapes. Not that this seems to unduly bother him in Heat 5 when he effortlessly picks his way past the majority of the assembled field initially ahead of him to record another heat victory, albeit it did take him until the second bend of the last lap to catch and finally pass Billy Hamill.

Ricky Kling continues his harum scarum approach to his speedway life in Heat 6, though he saves his adventures until the last bend of the final lap on this occasion. Comfortably holding second place under no pressure and with no-one around him, Ricky suddenly loses complete control of his bike and hammers into the air fence at considerable speed, as though he had just decided to retain the element of surprise for a dramatic crash test of the unsuspecting Monmore track safety features.

Another hardy perennial feature of any speedway fixture at Monmore Green is the centre green antics of Ian 'Porky' Jones, who appears to labour under the impression that the fans turn up to watch him and not the riders. I'm told by those around me on the terraces, "he's so awful you get to like him – the other week he said 'Peter Karlsson is the man who put the A back into Super Trouper'[2] and we always say he put the Big **** back into Big Country!" After some biased invective that I believe Ian considers to be due impartiality along with some well-chosen hackneyed *bon mots* beloved of really classy impresarios everywhere, throughout the night Ian proceeds to treat us all to a spectacularly advanced display of "dad dancing" at every available opportunity. With only minor, almost imperceptible variations, he does the same dance time after time, though he holds his body and head in a manner that immediately leads you to think "John Curry" rather than Rudolf Nureyev. In his own mind he probably moves with the grace of Fred Astaire but, to the casual eye of the uninitiated viewer, he lumbers about the place in a series of "dances" and "twirls" much more in a style reminiscent of someone who has unexpectedly trodden on a dangerously exposed live electric wire with wet feet. Each new song provides yet another excuse for Ian to harrumph along the white line of the track in a manner that manages to combine the old-fashioned showmanship of a ringmaster from a provincial circus with the agility of a post-operation physio class at the hospital. There's absolutely no doubt though that Ian not only enjoys himself but throws himself into the thing with gusto. So do the start-line girls whom I prefer to try to watch, and Wolves are definitely a club to be praised for how they buck the trend at many tracks to solely appoint girls based on their perceived physical attributes rather than their

[2] A complicated but ethnocentric local reference to do with the music associated with and played for Peter, as well as his shared Swedish nationality with the performers of the song (Abba).

aptitude and skill at the work. That said, there are a couple of voluptuously shaped girls whose bottoms echo the effects that prolonged exposure to the sponsors of this meeting's popular products (Banks's Beer) will have on the guts of the average middle-aged man. On thing is for sure, the start girls certainly get passionately involved here. None more so than the green start line Christine Goddard, who's affectionately known as "stalker" because of her love of Freddie Lindgren. Despite the loud roar of the engines, I believe I can still pick out her voice bellowing, "go on Frederic" as she implores him to further riding excellence. She comes from a speedway mad family – dad John, mum Joy and brother Dave – who were described to me as, "speedway to the bone – bright, articulate, committed and friendly". Based on Christine's approach, perhaps, the words enthusiastic and loud could be added to this list of their qualities.

Another aspect of the staggered starts that the handicap system ensures during the Olympique, is that the rider who starts from some distance behind those at the tapes invariably arrives into the corner at far greater speeds than the narrow confines of the track traditionally encourages. The effect can be likened to that of a bowling ball flung aggressively at skittles in a ten-pin bowling alley. So it proves in Heat 7, when Adam Shields wallops into a similarly fast starting (though not fast enough to avoid this) Freddie Lindgren with great velocity on the apex of the first corner. This causes Lindgren to fall from his bike in a freestyle fashion that could be seen as a clown's "comedy tumble", but for the unseemly length of time he then subsequently spends in agony on the track surface. In the re-run, after the exclusion of Shields, Lindgren uses his additional speed and local track knowledge to great effect to overtake the race leader Lewis Bridger before he even manages to exit the second bend. Heat 11 is a collector's item by Olympique standards as it pits three riders against each other from the start line! Only Theo Pijper has a handicap (15 yards) and he labours to find any way past the triumvirate of proven losers ahead of him, although he does eventually reel in and pass Kenneth Hansen on the third bend of the last lap. By this point, Ricky Kling has just about clung on to his huge lead to easily win his first race on English soil. The next race features a slow motion fall for Lewis Bridger before the referee again orders all four back for the re-run that Lewis then wins easily from Kerr, Nermark and Vissing.

During the interval, I return to my stall to find that Dave Rat has taken to calling me the "redoubtable Jeff Scott" to lurkers at his stall, though ever-sharp of eye and brain, in honour of how my name appears on the spine of my latest book *When Eagles Dared*, he's written "there's only one Jeff Cott" on my box of books. Sales are non-existent on my stall though Dave trumpets the array of end-of-season bargains on his stall and proclaims news of the "price cuts" as he prefers to call his price reductions. Ian Thomas's excellent book *Wheels and Deals* has fallen in price by nearly a third (from £14.99 to £10) on the express instructions of the *Speedway Star*'s Dave Fairbrother who apparently "wants rid of them". Far be it from me to question this price strategy and even if I ignore that it's been my favourite speedway book of the year so far, surely the end of season and the slow build up to Christmas is precisely the time when you should maintain your prices in hope of pent-up demand? Before the racing re-starts I have time to catch up briefly with the friendly and knowledgeable Mark Sawbridge, author of THE definitive history book on Wolverhampton Speedway, who is fresh from having run the Cardiff marathon the day before. "You run the last bit inside the Millennium Stadium so I took the Tony Rickardsson line – right up close to the fence – round the second bend", though I don't think he quite mounted this fence in the manner Tony famously perfected. He has his commemorative medal with him and makes light of the frighteningly fast time that he recorded in the race. He puts this turn of speed to full advantage a few minutes later when he shoots off to beat the rest of the crowd to queue up for some refreshing cups of tea from the "tea bar" ('the ladies there say they love the speedway fans who are so friendly, whereas the greyhound fans are grumpy, ignorant or both") that are so vital on a cooler late season evening like this. Mark is a bit nonplussed by the apparent imminent demise of the *Wolfcry* website, "It's going to be closed down, I spoke to Mark Rowe and they've decided sod it! They're Wolves fans through and through – just like CVS, who I'm full of admiration for as a promoter and for how much he lives for the club even though he can be a funny bugger sometimes – plus they've raised £3000 for the riders this season though quite how they'll now present it to them in the pits I don't know."

After the interval, barring catastrophe, it appears certain that PK will triumph despite the additional handicap he faces in each of his last four races. In Heat 15 he starts 20 yards back but still expertly manages to pick his way past the other riders using a mix of guile, speed and daring. A note of surrealism is added to the evening by Billy Hamill and the referee when, in Heat 17, the diminutive American is excluded for jumping the 'theoretical' tapes that don't actually exist at his starting point 15 yards back from the physical manifestation of this real obstruction. After some consultation, Billy is eventually allowed back in the re-run from 25 yards back. It's a distance that proves all too much to make an impression from except for his easy pass of Kenneth Hansen, who courtesy of his previous race win in Heat 14, also finds himself with a 20 yards handicap. Daniel "the Nerminator" Nermark wins from the start line though green start-line girl Christine again enthusiastically bellows "Freddie!!!" into second place. Sadly for the spectacle of this passing event *par excellence*, and a real bummer for myself with an open stall of books from which I'd hoped to sell copious quantities to the speedway fans who decide to linger afterwards, it starts to rain. My programme soon becomes a sodden mass and my attempt to record the minutiae of everything as it happens becomes difficult. Though not even the weather can halt the ineluctable progress of PK to the victor's crown, which he ensures with a thrilling ride in the re-run of Heat 20 to complete his maximum (though, in reality, a solitary point would have still earned him the victory). Fortunately for him, the crowd and my blood pressure there is nothing so stupid as further semi-finals and a final to determine the "winner", since the promoters of the event sensibly recognise the traditional view that the point scores gained in the twenty heats of the competition provides the rightful champion. That said three riders are tied on the same score so they have to have a run off in the drizzle to determine who occupies the podium place in third, since "Freddie!!" has already secured a creditable second spot.

We're then treated to trophy presentations and no one can say that the Wolverhampton season is going to finish without a bang since there's a long firework display in the drizzle for those fans still keen enough to watch. Which most are. Then they rush from the terrace (almost as quick as John Cooper Clarke claims "lager turns to piss") to the car park, where Lewis Bridger's van already edges through the hordes for the long journey back to East Sussex without even pausing to have a drink or speak with adoring admirers. I spend quite some time in the crowded bar in search of Tim Hamblin. However, unlike Nigel Pearson whose duties tonight ended almost as soon as they started, he isn't enjoying a drink but elsewhere in the stadium fastidiously conducting a series of very thorough interviews with any rider or member of speedway staff prepared to answer his thoughtful, carefully prepared questions. He won't leave the stadium until around midnight but will still have filed his immaculate, crafted and considered copy ahead of the 7 a.m. deadline that the sports desk of the *Express & Star* requires for his speedway reports. Still searching at the bottom of the stairs from the grandstand bar, I say "hello" to the dapperly dressed Nigel Pearson while he waits outside in the light drizzle for the taxi he's ordered to whisk him away into the West Midlands night. He looks both flummoxed and mystified at my greeting before the penny drops and he punctures any thoughts that my book might vaguely be having an impact in more rarefied and exulted speedway circles, "Oh! Sorry Jeff, I didn't recognise you and had no idea who on earth you were."

16th October Banks's Olympique – A delight to watch the incredibly skilful winner: Peter Karlsson

"Let's be NOISY out there!"
18th October
An often-unsung power behind the throne at King's Lynn speedway club is the friendly, industrious Cheryl Chapman who, every time I'm there, is a ball of energy throughout the stadium. After a huge number of years working together, there is a clear division of responsibility between her and her husband, Keith, "he does his thing and I do mine". And that's before we count in Jonathan. It's a big meeting tonight on the long road of qualification to the play-off final that many Lynn fans consider unnecessary in the light of the fact that the Stars have already finished nine points clear of their nearest rivals in the final Premier League table. However, these additional matches are part of the regulations of the competition they entered and definitely do create the chance to earn some additional significant gate receipts and (if you own them yourselves) additional revenues through the bars and cafes on race night.

The approach of careful husbandry combined with straightforwardness is an example that Cheryl feels isn't always adhered to by all their erstwhile but often more profligate competitors. The Stars haven't always been able to sign the riders that they have researched and targeted for the team because of the lure of the inflated sums that rival promoters are suddenly prepared to offer them to tempt them away elsewhere. There is a world of difference between placing your signature on a contract that offers inflated (above market rate) payments and actually getting paid them, as some riders later learn to their own cost. "We always pay our riders on time as we've agreed and we pay the guests in full at the end of the night, which isn't what everyone does. Lots of riders sign for silly money but then they don't get paid for some of it and when the BSPA get to sort it out at the end of the season they only get paid their minimum – £30 a point I think – rather than the silly money they thought they'd signed for. So they would have always been better off with us." Talk of the governing body of the sport leads onto the shock news of the exorbitant cost of attendance at the obligatory BSPA annual conference, "at some really expensive hotel in Coventry – Jon nearly fell on the floor when he found out it was £900 for the two of them to go – I think they're trying to make it too expensive so that they go back abroad for them in future". These quibbles aside, Cheryl is quick to praise the contribution that the sponsors make to the successful running of the club at King's Lynn, "they really make a difference".

The vexed question of attendances and finances also bothers Jonathan Chapman, who wonders aloud if a continuous diet of success has started to sate the appetite of the fans for speedway at the Norfolk Arena. Even the vital second leg of the semi-final against tonight's opponents – local 'derby' rivals Rye House – doesn't even get the enthusiastic reaction it once did, despite the trademark and relentless local promotion that the club is justifiably proud of creating. Jonathan is slightly morose that interest only hovers around the blasé outside the usual (considerable) hardcore of Lynn fans. "It's weird, last year when we were the underdogs we had huge crowds, this year we've won so much people don't come out in their numbers. Still, it's much better to win the second leg if you're at home as the crowd can enjoy it much more than if you're away".

Back at the track shop, exiled Wimbledon fan Mike Moseley has studied my new book *When Eagles Dared* and decided that a simple flaw that could have been easily rectified at the outset might hold sales back, "you needed a different cover, it's much too similar to the other one". Talk then quickly turns to the likely "further decline in Anglo-Danish relations" – though doubts are expressed that they could actually get any lower – brought on by that weekend's events at the Golden Helmet. Nicki Pedersen allegedly shut off in one race to allow Krzysztof Kasprzak through in the full knowledge that this would thereby deprive Scott Nicholls of a place in the final. The other main talking point is the new speedway television programme written, directed and financed from his own pocket by the regular King's Lynn presenter Mike Bennett. This was shown for the first time on the obscure satellite channel appropriately enough called 'Motors TV' and the programme is to be repeated at many different times throughout the week ("it was much better than the *Bonanza* programme they made last winter, but then *Songs of Praise* would have been too!"). Johnny Barber particularly enjoyed the informative and behind the scenes footage filmed at Mildenhall ("good to see Clara King had one of our air horns in her hand") and the piece they filmed with Len Silver at Rye House. Many felt that Olly Allen ("he shouldn't give up his day job") and Ken Burnett weren't given the most exciting PLRC to cover ("it's no good saying that it's wonderfully exciting if the evidence of your own eyes says otherwise – anyone watching for the first time and being repeatedly told THAT was exciting, just wouldn't bother going to watch a meeting live 'cause it really wasn't"). The difficulty of their task to convey the requisite enthusiasm to the viewers wasn't helped by the apparently random use of the commentary that they'd obviously originally recorded continuously at the event, over the edited version of the racing that they screened. Perhaps an overdub or some post-production would better serve Mike's purpose to attract future sponsors but then these are easy suggestions to make when you don't have to incur these additional expenses in what is, after all, a completely self-financed project. However, Mike pops by to delightedly inform us that, though new ideas in speedway always attract moaners and critics keen to put any new project down, he's been pleased by the overwhelmingly favourable response, "I financed it myself and 95% of people have been positive with only 5% of moans". Until I watched the programme I'd never picked up on the fact that Mike was Scots, "I'm Glaswegian – the accent only comes out when I'm stressed and I was very stressed!"

As usual, Mike is only too happy to mention that I'm at the track to sign my book. Unfortunately, he always does this immediately he sets foot inside the commentary booth and then only the once when it has minimal impact since the stadium barely has any fans in it! Mike never tires to also add his standard quip to his puff, "I told him it would have been a much better book with me in it and he says I will be when he gets to reprint it". Understandably enough, he repeatedly plugs his own work at every opportunity throughout the night – the telly programme and the URL for his website which I fail to note down. When I google the name "Mike Bennett" later I understand that it's not just relentless self-aggrandisement that leads Mike to repeat this information, but the sheer volume of other similarly named people with a strong desire for fame and notoriety who are keen to try to fill up as much space as possible on the web. Mike's column in the programme also allows him the further chance to indulge in some more promotion for the telly programme and the DVDs that his company produces of all of the King's Lynn meetings, "so listen out tonight and I'll tell you what's happening about all of those DVDs". One of Mike's other presentational obsessions is to again and again – in the manner of a harassed geography teacher prematurely tired of life – implore the home crowd to demonstrate their allegiance to all things Lynn with greater, louder and more ecstatic outbursts of noise. His column also reveals his love of the loud sound of adulation and his love of the use of the question mark; particularly it's much rarer three ("???") or six ("??????") variety. Though in person Mike is much more Andy Renko or Mark Belker rather than the suave Captain Frank Furillo he most likely imagines himself to be, he nonetheless adapts Sarge's famous catchphrase from *Hill Street Blues* to his own purposes, "Let's be NOISY out there!"

It's a slow night by my stall though I am kept company by OAP Pete Brannan who chats amiably and combines holding onto his crutches with smoking an endless series of cigarettes. He's proud to tell me that he's come along to watch speedway since he was five (when he went to see Norwich in 1946) and that he rode from 1959 to 1961 for Rye House before he had a crash, the impact of which broke his collarbone as well as broke his "helmet in four and fractured my skull". Since then he's watched King's Lynn from 1965 onwards. However, the lure of the bike proved too much to resist and he rode again two years ago at the age of 63. He benefited from some good advice on the sheer power of the modern bike from King's Lynn star, Tomas Topinka, who sensibly advises that he "watch his right hand" as the throttle can be so unexpectedly powerful. Sadly he's not so likely to get back on a bike (though he'd like too) since he has had some sad medical news, "I've got cancer of the stomach and I've been given until Christmas to live. They've told me I should be in a wheelchair – I have care and strong pills – but I'm keeping as independent as I can". This year he's started to bring his son David to watch the speedway. He hovered close by to us for a while before he got bored and went off to join the queues for food in the hugely crowded Pit Stop café. "I haven't told him it's terminal, he just thinks I'm ill". Rather than dwell on his own misfortune, he's full of praise for Keith, Cheryl and Jonathan, "the Chapmans are fantastic, you really couldn't get any nicer people! I've had a special glass gift engraved with their names made to thank them for what they've done for me – and one for Daniel Nermark but I couldn't afford to get one done for all the riders. I'm going to present them at the Dinner Dance on Monday the 30th – don't tell them or it'll spoil the surprise!" Pete is delighted with how it – what could be his last ever season at the speedway – has turned out. He expects that the Stars will beat the Rye House Rockets, particularly as "they say Edward Kennett don't like it here, just like his uncle Gordon didn't used to like it here and he rode for Lynn for three or four seasons [it was one season in 1983] and then went back to Eastbourne [via Wimbledon]".

There is clearly some rivalry between the clubs if the explanation about the lack of a rider parade by announcer Mike Bennett is anything to judge things by. "If you wondered why we had no bikes on parade as usual, Jonathan asked me to say that we're just extending the same courtesy as we had at Rye House the other night!" Earlier I'd overheard another example of this mysterious antipathy between these sides, "if there's one thing worse than rider injuries and crashes, it's Rye House winning trophies". Generally, as we all know, speedway fans on the whole get on with great equanimity on the terraces. Before the meeting starts, the visitors appear to have brought a strong and competitive side to Saddlebow Road and have boosted their chances of success through the shrewd inclusion of highly fancied and praised young guest reserve riders Josh Auty and Tai Woffinden. All season both have justifiably attracted rave notices for thrilling performances that belie their age and experience for Scunthorpe. The gloomy talk among the Lynn fans in the home-straight grandstand is that they could be a real threat and possible trump card for the Rockets. These dark thoughts are assuaged almost immediately when the excellent powerhouse Lynn reserve pairing of Chris Mills and John Oliver make mincemeat of them in Heat 2, just as they have done with so many other riders this campaign. In fact an opponent in this race has only beaten John Oliver twice all season! The Stars would have pulled ahead even further in the next race if Troy Batchelor, after he'd fought his way from fourth to second, hadn't then chosen to crash heavily into the fourth bend fence on the third lap when tucked in behind Kevin Doolan.

A dramatic fourth heat effectively ends all resistance on the night by the Rockets. First Josh Auty shows his inexperience when he immediately rears at the gate just as the tapes rise and then appears to dramatically throw his bike away from him down the track. Stood nearby on the centre green, Jonathan Chapman helps him retrieve his machine in order to clear the track – so the referee doesn't have to put on the red stop lights – and then offers some words of consolation for the duration of the race. On the third bend of the second lap, Chris Neath powers very aggressively under Tomas Topinka but then drifts wide enough for Topinka to straight away cut back up the inside and easily win.

A break in proceedings for a track grade gives Mike the chance to strut his stuff on the microphone. We get an extensive run down on the various times channel 413 will show his speedway programme. It's like having the obscure satellite section of the *Radio Times* that you didn't think that you intended to watch read out aloud. Before the resumption of the races, we learn the news that Troy is "still shaken but hasn't withdrawn from the meeting yet", but hasn't yet recovered enough to take his place in Heat 5. Jonathan Chapman takes great pride in the extensive range of unique clauses that he inserts in his rider contracts and speaking with Mike Bennett every week is doubtless another one of these. However, the club's star rider Tomas Topinka still isn't prepared to enter into the spirit of the thing or else hasn't yet become inured to Mike's relentlessly jovial but anodyne style of questioning. It's a glorious example of the genre and a wonderful cameo of the lack of rapport they clearly enjoy.

[MB] "Careful, we don't want you to get run down by the tractor! Welcome back!"
[TT] "Thank you"
[MB] "Is it good to be back?
[TT] "Yes"
[MB] "You've fully recovered from your injury?"
[TT] "No"
[MB] "Oh, it's going to be like that – do you remember the Jan Jaros interview?" (I assume that this is a sarcastic reference to another equally uncompelling interview Mike has previously conducted)
[TT] "No"
[MB] "Thank you, it's always a pleasure to interview you!"

A short while later Mike then grabs Olly Allen for a chat in which the interviewee is more forthcoming than Tomas Topinka. Though this masquerades as a supposedly insightful interview about the meeting tonight, the reality is that it is really little more than an extended promotion for the PLRC meeting in Sheffield that finished weeks ago that also happens to be the centrepiece of Mike's television programme and features Olly as one of the wooden co-commentators. Although, to be fair, since he has no part in this meeting to play, except as the brother of Rye House's Tommy Allen, it was always going to be hard for him to add much insight to our enjoyment of the fixture at Saddlebow Road tonight. Olly observes that his co-commentary work was something that, "came easily to me" and Mike takes the chance to praise the manner in which he coped with the interventions of his colleague in the commentary booth, Ken Burnett, "your co-commentator was quite excitable and you kept calming him down".

Thankfully, the racing resumes and Mike again implores the crowd to "make more noise", though the one-sided nature of the contest makes it hard for the neutral spectator, or all but the most dedicated and easily excitable of Stars fans, to get too worked up about the action. More at ease away from the microphone, Tomas Topinka amuses himself by pulling wheelies from the third lap onwards in Heat 7 as he cruises to a shockingly easy victory. Symptomatic of how keenly the Lynn riders still wish to win this contest, despite the enormity of their lead, is illustrated by Chris Mills who determinedly snatches third place on the line from Steve Boxall. By the time announcer Edwin Overland observes after Heat 10, "Daniel Nermark weaves his way through traffic to win" and the score has reached an almost insurmountable 41-21. Mills has been possessed all night by a determination and a burning will to win that has him chase Edward Kennett for the first three laps of Heat 11 before he bravely overtakes on the final bend of the third, only to then immediately power under Sunderland-born Stuart Robson on the home straight for second place behind the far-away Topinka.

During the interval break that will allow Rye House to contemplate the enormity of the disparity in the scores, a man who buys my book is keen to tell me, "I have to buy your book – the humour of your blog persuaded me". It's these little moments that make my travels so enjoyable and he's only the second person (the other was the gifted musician, speedway nut and all-round good bloke Billy Jenkins) I know that has bought a book because of the blog. This was always the intention behind this blog though it has proved to be singularly forlorn in this respect. Something else that is forlorn is the Rye House fight-back in the face of the Lynn onslaught. Only a win while in the black-and-white helmet colour for Steve Boxall during Heat 12 provides any real resistance. The only other Rye House rider to actually win a race on the night is Chris Neath in

Buster grooms the tracks. © Jeff Scott

Kevin Doolan contemplates the track. © Jeff Scott

Keen King's Lynn fan Pete Brannan. © Jeff Scott

the final race when the scores already stood at 57-32, after Lynn manager Rob Lyon had chosen to reward Kevin Doolan and Chris Mills with extra rides. In between these races, Edward Kennett was left in no doubt as to the feelings the crowd harboured towards him, when they took the chance to serenade him back to the pits after an engine failure in front of them. Moments prior to the arrival of these gremlins, the Lynn faithful had lauded Daniel Nermark's battling determination to pass his opponent. The penultimate race started promisingly for Tommy Allen when he made the start only to find that Mills easily passed him at the start of the next lap and Doolan harried him until an elegant manoeuvre saw him past on the last bend of lap three. Even a punctured tyre for Mills during the last lap couldn't stop a victory that he celebrated deliriously and, for once, Mike didn't have to issue an appeal to the crowd for more noise. Though he was keen to emphasize afterwards, "the real Kevin Doolan has returned to the building and how pleased we are to see that!"

I watch the final heats pressed against the broad mesh wire of the high fence that protects members of the public from flying stray bikes but not the occasional shower of shale. Close by is a blonde-haired young woman who bought my book on my first visit to the track and whom I notice is always keenly pressed against the fence every time I come to the stadium. She is in a world of her own, absorbed in the drama of the races and lost in the moment. It's the kind of intensity of concentration and slight mesmerisation that I often see in the faces of devoted fans around the country. Cheryl Chapman walks by with great purpose just before Heat 15 and I call out, "You've won easily". With her mind elsewhere, she barely breaks her determined stride and calls back over her shoulder, "Have we? I've been working in the office. Perhaps next time they won't be so big headed – they didn't even bring the trophy tonight, like they were supposed to, she [Hazel] said, 'there's no point as you won't be winning it!'" Based on tonight, let alone their form this season, it looks likely that this forecast will prove wildly inaccurate.

18th October King's Lynn v Rye House (Premier League Play-off Semi-Final, Second Leg) 60-35

Art Lesson in the Coventry Track Shop
20th October
The shy but gifted and remarkably genuine speedwayman, Colin Pratt, has kindly given me permission to return to Brandon Stadium to try to sell some copies of my books. I hope for greater success than my initial visit on the first night of the football World Cup in Germany, which still represents the nadir of any of my visits if judged in purely sales terms. This time I have been clasped to the metaphorical bosom of the track shop and admitted inside the inner sanctum where I will have my own

table by the door. It's already covered in a beautifully ironed bright yellow tablecloth that has creases of almost military precision. It's the very table from which Ian Thomas completely failed to sell a copy of his enthralling book *Wheels and Deals* and from which, "Booey only sold a few". They have even provided me with some rather handy homemade book display holders fashioned from discarded wire coat hangers.

The array of merchandise inside the shop would gladden the heart of any Bees fan and for the sheer array and inventiveness of branded and appropriately coloured items available it's definitely without parallel on my travels. There's every conceivable item that you could imagine in yellow and black, stamped with the Coventry name or 'Bee' logo (often both) as well as numerous examples of riders who smile at you from all sides of the shop. The products range from the predictable to the inventive. There's all the usual calendars, pens, boards and photographs, plus oodles of commemorative stuff as well as the much more exotic Coventry celebration wine (2005 vintage), doilies, gift vouchers and even an oil painting of Scott Nicholls adds to the veritable cornucopia of articles on display. You just know that if they don't already have it in stock, then it's the sort of shop where they will definitely try to get it. This shrine in celebration to all things Bees is very capably run by the warmly welcoming Joyce Blythe ("me – I'm part of the bleedin' fixtures!"), along with her team of loyal, friendly staff. These include her husband Malcolm, Hazel Billingsley (length of service "too bloody long" but really just four years), Sandra ('been here a long time"), Jonathan ("on videos") and Jodie Lowry ("does riders' merchandise in the separate booth over there behind your table"). It's very noticeable that Joyce simultaneously manages to be in charge but motivate through praise and lead by example. She combines modesty, down to earthiness, commercial opportunism and business savvy in equal measure. Joyce has had to serve her apprenticeship under other managers and it took her a while to get the chance to implement her vision of how the Coventry track shop should look and be run.

First of all she, "did it when Alf [Weedon] was here – I worked for him" and after that she worked for Dave Rattenberry. The arrival of "Mr Sandhu" revolutionised many aspects of the club and the track shop was no exception, "the second year he was here, Mr Sandhu thought he could do a better job here than Dave – it was a speedway track shop as opposed to a Coventry speedway track shop". It was a decision which meant that Joyce "took over in 2004 and running it myself I got the chance to try out a few things". She "transforms the shop for stock cars", but the speedway remains Malcolm and Joyce's first love. She started to open in the off-season in the run up to Christmas, "the first three Saturdays in December in 05 and the same again this year, but slightly different as we start in November". The "Christmas sale", aided by the Bees victory in the Elite League championship final, proved to be a "huge success – oh, tell us about it – we had them queuing from the shop into the car park but they were the best people I've ever known as no one moaned".

Almost as reluctant to accept praise as she is to have her photo taken, Joyce sums up her philosophy as, "if we haven't got it, we'll get it and we'll try to be friendly with it!" Everyone in the shop appears keen to help me to understand the ambience and appeal of this shop as Russell Lowry confirms, "Joyce will try anything once to sell stuff, just so long as it's got a bee on it". These are sentiments that Joyce immediately echoes, "everything has got to have a bee on it" while another customer butts in, "you're a happy go lucky bunch and so helpful". Luckily, my legendary tact surfaces to interrupt these paeans, when I say to the woman stood by Russell, "Are you his partner?" She chokes, glares and is temporarily dumbstruck at the suggestion until she manages to exclaim, "I don't think so! No, don't even go there – he's 46 and I'm 16!" It turns out that this lady is Russell's rather feisty daughter Jodie who works selling riders' merchandise from the stall behind me ("It's my first year here. Some weeks go well and others don't – I sold £500 of Scotty's stuff the week before the GP but tonight I've only sold £58 in total"). She's been coming to Coventry for about 11 years, her favourite rider is Hans Andersen ("I just like him") and she met her boyfriend, Alan, who hovers attentively but wordlessly close by at the shop entrance, via a romance that started on the British Speedway Forum. "We met last year on June 12th 2005. I liked his email address – ihatenickipedersen@hotmail.co.uk – we MSN messengered and got talking. Alan lives in Banbury and supports Oxford, but he comes to every Coventry meeting now. I like Nicki now, though". Alan confirms this but appears extremely reticent (Jodie explains later, "I'm not really talking to him as he's in the doghouse") unlike his girlfriend, "if you have to put anything in your blog, you could tell them how well I do at the shop".

Behind her counter, Joyce painstakingly explains to her staff the wherewithal about the latest line of Coventry Bees merchandise to hit the track shop – in this case the gift vouchers that come in £5/£10/£15 denominations along with a choice of cards, "some for Christmas and others plain." I notice that they all have the requisite Bees logo prominently displayed on them. A delighted customer suddenly interrupts the detailed explanation of the very exact system that Joyce has to record the sales and redemptions of these new vouchers. "This is lovely! These are gorgeous!" they exclaim ecstatically about the framed collage of various photos of the team with a £30 price tag and a decorative surround that says in large letters, "2006 KO Cup Champions". Later I gather Joyce already has plans in hand to catch the impending surge of the Christmas market for yet more framed photographic memorabilia, should the Bees triumph in the 2006 Craven Shield Final. She will work closely with her favoured photographer, whose work she deservedly praises if judged by the rather deluxe presentation of the individual rider photos that completely line one of the walls of the track shop.

An item of merchandise that everyone talks about is the "limited edition" oil painting of Scott Nicholls, priced aggressively at £150, which is perched high above my table. It has been painted by a local artist based on a photograph that, strangely, is also displayed and for sale, albeit at a much more affordable price. Throughout the evening, the painting attracts many studious glances from fans and art lovers alike who can't help but comment: "I didn't know he had a tattoo"; "look how that arm is out of proportion with the rest of him" and "it doesn't look anything like him". Joyce makes no bones about her perspective, "I call a spade a spade as I'm from Yorkshire so I said straightaway – you've done Scotty as a coloured fella! Which she has though it's accurate for the colours of the photo, [points to nearby wall] look how dark it is, but that was wrong as well". In face of such sustained critical analysis, you'd definitely think twice about being an artist in this neck of the woods.

The shop, if not the painting, appears as though it's a magnet for everyone who passes. Solihull based SCB Official Chris Durno often comes to Brandon with his Manchester United supporting son Thomas in tow. He's a well-travelled young man since he frequently accompanies his father on his often-intrepid sojourns to the far-flung frontiers of the speedway firmament. The arrival of Poole co-promoter Mike Golding gives them both the opportunity to ride their respective hobby horses about recent refereeing snafus and to be mutually supportive. Chris alludes to the recent disputatious postponement of the Newcastle versus Redcar encounter and Mike casts his mind back to his own particular bugbear to remember the query raised on live television about the size of Jesper B. Jensen's carburettor last season when Peterborough visited Wimborne Road. Mike is of the opinion that, in some instances, the speedway authorities "don't back the officials", while Chris echoes this and feels that the tools supplied often leave the officials open to ridicule or question, "the [carburettor measurement] tool the ref had been issued with looked stupid and the riders were always going to question something that looked like that".

Shortly afterwards I chat to a very affable bloke in trendy glasses and his mate, whom I'd recently met by my bookstall at Arlington when they stopped by to have a few words. He very kindly praises both of my books and my ears prick up, as he's the first person I've come across to directly praise my latest book, *When Eagles Dared*. I can't quite believe that someone has read it so quickly, "I really enjoyed it – it's great!" From our conversation I quickly gather that he's well informed and a real enthusiast for the sport. I have a brainwave and ask him if he'd consider letting others know about his enjoyment of the book with a post on the Eagles website. I'm surprised when he immediately and bluntly refuses, "Sorry, I'm afraid I can't as the BSPA don't allow it". He must have caught the brief flicker of disappointment and puzzlement that crossed my face:
"You don't know who I am, do you?"
"Er, no!"
"I'm Bob Brimson, the new owner at Eastbourne."
Though I laugh nervously I feel completely stupid that not only had I not put two and two together but also now that he's mentioned it, I finally recognise him from the feature in the *Speedway Star*. Luckily our shared need to watch the racing ends our conversation and soon calls us both away to arguably the most luxurious grandstand in the country.

Though it's reasonably full, the prospect of this three-way Craven Shield encounter (the Final!) hasn't sufficiently enthused the locals to fill the place so there still are some spaces around my favoured spot in the home-straight grandstand that overlooks the start line. Coventry straightaway race to a 5-1 against the Eagles via the potent strike force that is the Scott Nicholls-Billy Janniro partnership. Things continue to look poor for the Eagles when in the clash of the Pedersens, Bjarne bests Nicki in Heat 2. The battle for third place is enthrallingly passionate after the red-haired Tommy Allen scythes aggressively under Lewis Bridger on the fourth bend of the first lap. After he's recovered himself, Lewis typically sets off in full throttle pursuit of his opponent and soon finds himself too close to Allen's back wheel as they enter the last lap. He's also too close for the speed that he generates and so, to my mind, inadvertently clips the wheel ahead just enough to unceremoniously unseat his rival. In his short career, Tommy has already had his fair share of scrapes and contretemps, so his reaction to this unexpected encounter with the air fence and track surface is entirely predictable. He leaps from the floor to stand and confront Lewis by placing his helmet in millimetric proximity to that of his young rival. After some goading and a further helmet/head butt from Allen for good measure, Lewis eventually responds but by then sufficient track staff and officials have gathered to, in Playtex fashion, divide and separate them. Delighted that proceedings have already become so enlivened, the home crowd playfully cheer on the 'fight' in a manner that suggests they had just seen the "baddie" figure take to the stage for the first time at a pantomime or a wrestling match.

After this initial excitement, the Bees fans remain reasonably subdued, partly out of confidence at the likelihood of building a reasonable lead to take on the road to Arlington and then Wimborne Road for the forthcoming two away fixtures that will, hopefully, see the Craven Shield final settled in their favour within six days. But also there is no undue reaction because the result of Heat 3 appears to confirm that everything remains going smoothly to plan when the 'Bomber'/Olly combination gains a 4-2 over Poole's all Polish combination of Kasprzak and Walasek.

Hours earlier on a brief walk to the pits in search of Colin Pratt to thank him for his kind hospitality, I'd stumbled across the bearded Pirates Press Officer and all-round good bloke, Gordie Day, already deep in conversation with the frightening bottle blonde-haired KK. Well as deep as you can be with someone who prefers to converse in Polish – though his English has improved tremendously to the extent that his wry humour now comes across strongly – and, instead of a chat, prefers to conduct a rigorous regime of warm-up exercises. These involve flailing arms in windmill and helicopter fashion, some elaborate stretches and a series of mini-shuttle runs in the still empty pits. A passenger plane flies noisily overhead and Gordie remarks, "that's Middlo". Planes, airports and carefully planned travel schedules are generally close to the heart of any modern, internationally successful rider like KK. "Where does that plane go?" he enquires with an upward nod. East Midlands is my guess and Birmingham Gordie's. "They fly to Poznan?" asks the still curious KK. His nearby bikes look immaculate and his mechanic-cum-mentor sits reading a Polish language magazine. KK appears keen to talk and he's the sort of foreign rider from Poland you can't help but admire (Adam Skornicki is also a credit to his country in my opinion). Not only is he friendly and always professional but his full-on racing style and high level of commitment often leads to exciting racing for the fans yet also means that he's often involved in some quite dramatic incidents and crashes. I have seen a couple of spectacular incidents already this season against Belle Vue and also in the ELRC. KK smiles in recognition and wryly observes, "I fall off the crowd like, but here [gestures] cut hand and here [gestures from the bottom of his legs, via his bum to the top of his back] bad. And £1000 frame – but still crowd like!" His ability to be funny and satirise in English far exceeds that of Gordie and myself in Polish or even some English riders in their own language! The noisy arrival of Craig Boyce interrupts KK's repartee. "Boycie" is another rider that Gordie genuinely admires for his contribution to the Pirates cause, not only his "professionalism" but mostly because "what he has I wish I could bottle; you just don't know how good he is in every department until you work with him closely. You just have to hold your hands up in admiration and we're so lucky we've got him!"

These sentiments are borne out in a duel between Boycie and Deano in Heat 5, somewhat unfairly dubbed the 'Veterans Race'. Both riders have been round the houses and the track numerous times but, arguably, take different approaches to their continuing longevity within the sport away from the track. On the track no quarter is given, though in the 'hardness' stakes Boycie wins out since he's justifiably renowned for his firm approach to erstwhile rivals and a track craft that takes no prisoners, which he implements implacably. Deano cuts inside him on the third bend of the third lap only for Boycie to repost with a full-blooded manoeuvre that has him regain second place as they exit the fourth bend together. This is the second successive 5-1 that the normally reliable Shields/Barker combination has conceded in consecutive races. It promises to be a lengthy night ahead for the Eagles and damage limitation has to be the order of the night for the rest of the fixture if they're to try to protect their chances of overall aggregate success in this competition.

Something that may hold the home side back is the replacement of Martin Smolinski with Paul 'Clewsy' Clews who, although he rides with great heart and gusto, is always likely to struggle to contribute that many points at the Elite League level. This is to prove to be the case since Clewsy rides to an unwanted minimum of zero points from his four rides spent comprehensively at the rear of the field in every race. Riders from all three teams on display have an 'off' night – notably Edward Kennett, Tommy Allen plus the always ambitiously full-throttled and adventurous Lewis Bridger whose collective meagre scores just about approach mediocre. Their scores only rise above the paltry and flatter to deceive as a result of the boost that they receive when they each have a race that features Clewsy. More noticeable and worrying for the assembled Bees fans is the fact that the Pirates appear to 'want it' (whatever this indefinable 'it' really is) much more than the home riders. Maybe because it's late in the season and they have become jaded or that the weight of expectation that rests on their shoulders bears down more heavily on them than on the Pirates, but the Bees never really manage to pull away from the Pirates all evening. Though they remain ahead for much of the meeting, it's never by that much from the Pirates who lurk menacingly while the Eagles mostly flounder (or is it stutter in flight?). Whatever the exact cause, the Pirates run fewer last places than the Bees manage and this determination to take the vital point here or there when they can is a decisive factor to my mind.

My sales at the interval are poor though my conversations are varied. Unfortunately, the excellent presenter they have at Coventry, Peter York, hasn't read out my note advertising my availability to autograph my books (or anything really) that the speedway office promised they'd pass on to him. He comments on events with charm and practised ease. My favourite link was for Rory Schlein, "nicknamed 'poo-boy' by Billy Janniro, rather than the "roo-boy" he has on the side of his van". However, the highlight from the rich but burgeoning pantheon of 'it's a mad, mad world at speedway' occurred in Heat 11, when as Peter elegantly termed it, "the rider in blue [he was actually wearing a yellow helmet colour so it was visually only ever a theoretical "blue" colour!] has been excluded for not being ready to race". Still I find so many speedway conversations informative, bizarre or just plain life affirming that it's invariably a joy to listen while I make no sales. I must admit though that I do have a real pet hate for people who crowd round my table with absolutely no intention of buying a book and who form a defensive shield, and thereby, I suspect, often putting off the prospective casual purchasers who may lurk shyly close by. This is particularly galling when I've travelled a couple of hundred miles and have deliberately waited until after the completion of the meeting, as well as the bitter end of the slow departure of the fans from the stadium, in the hope of a few extra book sales, only to find myself stymied from selling anything by these well-intentioned lurkers. Any slight chance to catch the eye of a possibly wavering potential purchaser passes fruitlessly by in polite chatter. The thought of what has been missed or what might have been doesn't lessen during what the gifted musician and songwriter Terry Callier describes as "midnight miles". When I get this sense of disgruntlement at this thoughtlessness about the true economics of my promotional travel, I consciously try to remain alert to the always available chance to learn or have your life enriched by chance encounters, strange facts and outlooks or insights into "life".

Luckily, I have one such encounter at Brandon with St John Ambulance person Ray, who's come along regularly for 46 years to this track. He's keen to identify for me the changes in the level of medical provision that he has noticed at Brandon over the past five decades, "I supplied the first ambulance they ever had here – they hired it for £10 a meeting and boy we needed it in those days – they have three of them now". Talk of rider comfort and safety quickly brings him onto a lengthy diatribe against the attitude of some *Sky Sports* staff when they televise meetings at Brandon. In fact, though he appeared reticent and shy at the outset of our conversation, the words soon begin to flood out since he has quite a bee in his bonnet about what he perceives to be *Sky's* meddling arrogance and intrusiveness as well as their lack of appreciation of medical matters. "I had Mark [Loram] in the medical room – a genuine bloke, most of them are though the odd one's a bit funny – and he was quite hurt and in pain and the cameraman kept trying to barge in saying he could but I kept shutting the door as he's a patient first and a rider second once he's not right. I let him go to hospital via the back door and they weren't happy when they found out. When Lee Richardson got trapped under the air fence, two of them were hovering there, trying to intrude, poking in their cameras and getting in our way when we're just there to help him. I asked them to go away and they said 'we'll report you' and they did but I was right to want to treat him rather than entertain them. They did report me too but I was told I was right. They've been like it from the start and tried to ban the St John's from the centre green during televised meetings as the fluorescent yellow on the jackets interferes with their cameras or someint. I said 'we wear thems so the riders can see us and recognise us when they need us'. They said 'we don't care everyone has to stand outside the fence'. A bit later I said, 'we've had a chat and we'll stand outside the fence but go home, so without medical cover you can't stage a meeting'. *Sky* said 'you can't do that!' and I said 'we can, we're here voluntarily, so we can do what we like 'cause we do this for love so we can do what we want'. We're still on the centre green as we should be. Not many are at Coventry as they keep it tidy and professional. The best I'd say, as there's never any mess or clutter and just those who have to be there are there!" Before the sound of the engines revving and the distant grumble of inaudible announcements lures Ray back to watch the racing he has one last question, "What is it with *Sky* that they suddenly stop covering speedway after the play-offs? It's like doing the Premiership but not covering the FA Cup Final! Still the way they barge about like they run the place maybe it's better they don't".

The meeting ends with a three-point advantage for the Pirates over the Bees and a 12-point lead over the Eagles. Unless something very dramatic happens at Arlington, this appears to have prematurely ended the need to invest in something with which to clean the silverware with on a regular basis in East Sussex. Only Nicki Pedersen has really shone after he dropped his only point of the night in his first outing against his namesake Bjarne. Much more interestingly, while Lewis Bridger would love to do a celebratory wheelie before every race he's in and usually does one afterwards, if the bike is still in working order, Nicki tends to completely shun them or almost any sign of triumph. Given the number of races he wins a season, this probably reduces the wear and tear on his equipment, avoids repetitive strain injury from frequent waves to the crowd or lends additional credence to the theory that he economises on the methanol in his tank in attempt to gain a fractional advantage through this reduction in the weight of his bike. Tonight, for some reason, Nicki is seized with the joys of end-of-term fever to the extent that he pulls celebratory wheelies on two separate occasions after some easily won races. Given the scores and the torpor of the Eagles performance the man next to me suspects that it's part of a not-so-secret campaign to ingratiate himself with the Coventry fans and promotion, should they do the unthinkable and dump their assumed to be presently in bad odour number one rider, Scott Nicholls.

After a complete absence of any post-meeting sales when my small yellow tablecloth covered spot by the door was comprehensively shielded from prying or speculative eyes for 20 minutes by a phalanx of kindly but eager questioners, the long dark drive home is memorable for extensive lane closures on the M40 and the joy of the complete closure of the M25/M23 exit that I need to get to Brighton. Days later I notice that decorative chevrons have now rather pointlessly sprung up, an event that is probably the modern motorway transport equivalent of spotting a single magpie.

20th October Coventry v Eastbourne v Poole (Craven Shield Final, 1st Leg) 38-29-41

Down Came the Rain
22nd October

When you travel round the country as obsessionally as I do, you soon learn that to frequently check every possible avenue and outlet of immediate, short-term and long-term weather forecasts is the sensible and pleasantly OCD thing to do. All very British though I did find during my time in the Netherlands that the Dutch people do this too (and also see it as one of "their" unique defining national characteristics), even when it's as obvious as the nose on my face that the cold damp of the winters will chill you to the bone before or after the perpetual rain has drenched you. Even if it's true, that objects in the side mirrors of our cars may be nearer than they appear and that the likely colour of the future will gladden the hearts of all Nederlanders – Metcheck, the notoriously unreliable internet weather site I still favour, despite serial inaccuracies in its forecasts for even the next few hours ahead, would indicate that racing in the second leg of the Craven Shield Final isn't that likely to take place at Arlington this afternoon. Rather than sit on the fence, the Metcheck boffins have gone all out with a spectacular forecast of 13.4 millimetres of rain between 15.00 and 18.00 hours. In inches we call that "quite wet". I selfishly really hope that it doesn't rain since this meeting represents the possible *annus memorabilis* (as the gay scene is also known in Brighton) for sales of my latest book *When Eagles Dared*. If it doesn't manage to sell well at Arlington, then comparatively it will remain as popular as a rattlesnake in a lucky dip elsewhere. Plus, by the time next season starts it's hardly likely to set pulses racing even in the Eagles nest as the modern gnat-like attention span will have further dulled the appeal of a book on the 2005 season and consigned it a step closer to the dustbin of history. If said receptacle was located in my Brighton garden, then the rainwater would have already filled it this morning. Even allowing for the warping effects on the numerous microclimates that exist between the BN1 and BN23 postcodes of this part of East Sussex let alone

Instructional signs. © Jeff Scott

A damp pit lane at Arlington. © Jeff Scott

Martin Dadswell and Lucy Cross lurk in the track shop
storeroom. © Jeff Scott

those with anything to do with the Sussex Downs, it's highly unlikely that the weather there will be markedly different enough to permit racing or to find gold at the end of the sales rainbow.

In a fit of pique, I've bravely decided that I might not even to venture over there this afternoon, though just to hedge my bets on the actual weather there I call Martin Dadswell in the track shop hut to check on the situation properly. Though it's almost certainly the wrong type of rain to replenish the parched subterranean aquifers of East Sussex, there's been a lot of it, it's still there and there's promise of more to come. However, the meeting has yet to be formally postponed as Jon Cook has still to arrive in his wellingtons to authenticate the many trackside puddles. He's expected at "around 1.15" to make a "decision", pronounce the last rites or resurrect my hopes of permanently moving some of the boxes of books that clutter my front room. Apart from some morose comment on the weather, Martin also has the bad news that the anticipated re-staging date will be Tuesday October 24th. It will be a collector's item of a meeting as no one can recall a meeting ever having taken place on such a night. It's not possible to run on Wednesday as that is the night already scheduled for the final leg of the Craven Shield final at Poole and Thursday is apparently a no-go because on Saturday a hugely important stock car meeting will take place at Arlington and much more than 48 hours is needed to ensure that everything is in tip-top condition. Such are the perils and obligations of multi-use stadiums. I'm gutted as I've been invited to the SRA Awards Dinner, Dance and Presentations evening as the guest of the *Sky Sports* Press Office which takes place that night too at the Coventry Hilton. My choices appear to be – hope that the rain stops; miss the once-in-a-lifetime opportunity that SRA Awards presents or miss out on the CS Final second leg at Arlington and thereby potentially lumber myself with a mouldering pile of unsold books that might have missed their final chance this season (or possibly ever) to find hordes of eager buyers. Bugger.

When I arrive there are glum faces everywhere. In the car park, in the pits and in the grandstand – though not in the track shop hut, which is crowded to a black hole of Calcutta extent, but where everyone is cheerfully damp. It appears that nobody expects the meeting to actually take place this afternoon. Most admirable are all the fans in the car park who wait with varying degrees of patience. Shortly after I arrive a large coachload of fans turn up from Coventry and sit gloomily looking out of the windows at the rain. Martin splashes out to his van to take delivery of 40 copies of my Eagles book for Tuesday night if, as widely expected, the meeting is restaged then. Not being around will definitely lose me sales but Martin is kind to offer to help by ensuring that bulk quantities are on display at the track shop. He gently takes the mickey as I sign them, "you're damaging them! I had a glance and I much prefer it to your other book – then I s'pose I know many of the people so that makes it more enjoyable. I still reckon you must fancy that Tom [at Arena]!"

I decide to ask the only authority figure from the club who looks vaguely approachable on an afternoon of resigned scowls – Kevin 'C' Coombes–

what he knows about the likelihood of a decision. Like everyone else he's not hopeful but awaits final confirmation from Jon Cook after consultation with the referee. He's not yet had time to read *When Eagles Dared*, "I've glanced at it but my girlfriend has read most of it and she says that I'm in it tons. I did notice that there's lots of words in there that I don't know, so good on you for that! It's not like you've just done a diary – it's a lot of effort that you've put in!" KC is the kind of enthusiastic man who you feel always speaks in exclamation marks.

In the pits it's very noticeable that none of the riders there have yet bothered to unload their bikes or change into their work clothes, in fact everyone shelters from the rain under brollies or the roofed pits. The club physio, Jane Wooler, is there with her daughter, "Is that person you call 'Jayne' in the book supposed to me?" As they arguably live in the closest proximity to the track, they can't believe that this fixture still hasn't been abandoned. This would definitely help them get to the pub while they still serve Sunday lunch. They're also curious as to the whereabouts of the club's youngest rider, "where's Lewis – does he know something that we don't?" Talk then moves onto how exciting it is to watch the-devil-may-care Lewis race on the track but also around the pits. They recall the incident when Deano and Floppy noticed that he foolishly intended to ride his machine though it definitely had a cracked frame, though he was finally persuaded by them to see sense. They put it down to the impetuousness of youth.

I listen as Jane then chats at length with the often reticent conversationalist Adam Shields who's positively voluble by his standards, no doubt because he's in the company of people he's comfortable with being around. He bucks the trend towards warm wet weather clothing by dressing in shorts and trainers.
[AS] "It's a problem if they stage it Tuesday as that's the Speedway Riders Association dinner – it's for all the riders so, hopefully, it won't clash with that"
[JW] "Are you going?"
[AS] "Nah. My mum and sister arrive over [(for his wedding the next weekend] on Wednesday morning at 5 a.m. at the airport so I have to pick them up. That's my excuse!"
[JW] "So you're not going home this winter?"
[AS] "Yeah – but in January."
[JW] "Well think of us stuck here when the weather is shitty."
[AS, in an incredulous tone] "When the weather is shitty?!"
[Me] "It's warm but wet 'n' windy now."
[AS] "Yeh, it's warm for here I s'pose."

Jane's husband, Ashley, sits quietly close by and I quickly learn that he's read the book too, "Did I really say that to you? [at the 2005 Dinner Dance] I must have been pissed".

Back over the far side of the stadium, the odd fan splashes about the car park while the rest sit disconsolately in their cars or on the coach, where all the windows have started to steam up nicely for the long journey home to Coventry. Even more people have crowded into the cramped but dry wooden track shop hut. Martin Dadswell holds court or, at least, is the informal master of ceremonies. He's perched on the bench at the back right next to the attractive Lucy Cross, the always bubbly girl from the *Brighton Argus*, who's "PA & Office Administrator" for the Sales and Marketing department, but is regularly at the stadium on race night to sell copies of the *Sports Argus* and watch Kevin Coombes closely. The general consensus in the track shop hut is that they're all surprised that the meeting hasn't already been abandoned. They take the mickey out of me, particularly my zeal for taking photos of the empty stadium, "Mike Patrick is back!" Outside the friendly Chris 'Geernob' Geer passes *en route* for the steep stairs of the referee's box. In answer to my question about whether Floppy has read my book yet he says, "I don't think so, it's still in the van though I'll check!" As he climbs the stairs the dulcet tones of KC reverberates over the tannoy, "an announcement for all of you waiting in the car park – the referee has postponed this afternoon's meeting which will be re-run on Tuesday when there will be free car parking!"

Afterwards I tell KC I'm shocked at how many people actually turned up in a downpour in the hope that the racing might still be on and he cheerily notes, "they must be real nutters!"

22nd October Eastbourne v Poole v Coventry (Craven Shield Final, 2nd Leg) – postponed waterlogged track

An Evening with Johno at the SRA Dinner
24th October

With great reluctance I decide to forego the brilliant sales opportunity to sell my book *When Eagles Dared* at the re-arranged Craven Shield Final second leg at Arlington, in favour of the invitation of a once-in-a-lifetime opportunity to attend the "SRA End of Season Party and Awards Night" at the plush Coventry Hilton. I was surprised to be invited by the press officer of *Sky Sports*, Jon Sim, and Mark Thursfield of MTA Media (I only met them as a result of Frank Keating's praiseworthy review of my book *Showered in Shale* in *The Guardian*) though I have no hesitation to immediately accept. It's a huge honour and delight since it's an invitation-only industry event for riders and their guests along with promoters, team managers, sponsors, club representatives and selected members of the press. It's a function that has been considerably revamped this year with the support of increased backing from sponsors like *Sky* and Teng Tools. To be invited is brilliant enough but I'm also going to be on the *Sky* table with Jon and Mark along with Sophie Blake! For a moment with this news my mind went blank about the others who are also expected be at the table but these turn out to be Steve Johnston, Chris Louis, Kelvin Tatum, Vic Rigby from the *Sun* and Gary Pinchin from *Motorcycle News*. The dress requirement for the evening is that "gentlemen wear suits", so it promises to be quite posh.

The Coventry Hilton is one of those business hotels that makes great virtue of its convenience to absolutely everywhere from East Midlands airport to Birmingham as well as to numerous towns and attractions throughout the Midlands. This is on account of its incredible convenience to a plethora of motorways – the Ms 40, 42, 69 and 1 but notably the M6. If everyone is mostly expected to go there by car (wonderfully handy though it is for local airports and railway stations) then it's going to have a big car park with tasteful trees, which it assuredly does. Along with too many facilities and services to list or mention that you'd automatically expect from "a top of the range hotel" establishment that it claims to be. It's neither exclusive nor deluxe but the type of upmarket establishment firmly aimed at the expense accounts of middle management executives who invariably have no choice about where their company or customers host the meetings that will require their attendance. The room doors require key cards, you need to be a hotel guest after 11 p.m. to order from the bar and have to use the "room card" they provide at check-in to charge these drinks orders to your room as cash isn't acceptable after this witching hour. The bar area is huge and open plan so has lots of shiny metal with chairs and tables that spray out in all directions and overflow into the adjoining marbled reception area. You don't need to be told that the majority of the "guests" who stay here will be male, middle-aged and will do so alone unless it's one of those rare events where you can bring your wife, girlfriend or hire escort services from one of the many handy conurbations nearby. An unspoken air of sadness and subdued desperation, often combined with thrusting but ultimately frustrated aspirations and ambitions, lurks like an unwanted ghost throughout this conspicuously clean establishment. Like the world over, except for certain parts of the Middle East, America and Asia, the rooms all have pay-on-demand raunchy movies that don't quite verge on the pornographic (but aren't politically correct or gifted with complex storylines) to sate those not drinking themselves to a stupor in the bar. It's definitely not the sort of place that you'd choose to spend your own money or deliberately choose for a "romantic weekend", unless you have a warped view of romance or a fascination with motorways. I don't wish to be too harsh on the Coventry Hilton since it does what it says on the tin and it's a pretty upscale tin at that but, because of my previous work in publishing, I've spent over a thousand nights at such places around the world, so I've grown cynical but also a little tired of their pro-forma atmosphere and pretensions.

Nonetheless it is an extremely posh venue at which to hold what is, to all intents and purposes a speedway event albeit a trade union awards dinner. The Speedway Riders Association is not only a nascent union but also an organisation that wouldn't even hint at being where it is without the work, drive and effort of Shane Parker and his lovely wife Anji. I don't know Shane, but he's one of those types of genuine, altruistic men who, by his attitudes, actions and aura, is a credit to his nation (Australia) as well as his family and upbringing. He's just one of those life-affirming people who play a vital part in their community which, in this case, is the British Speedway community. He has an air of composure and confidence as well as comfort in his own skin that he attractively combines with worldly wisdom and bloody hard work. I don't want to beatify him, nor does his wife Anji, who smiles broadly and jokes, after I compliment Shane on how much the fanatical supporters idolise him at Glasgow Speedway club, "They're lovely people there and really care so much for their club and people do say so many nice things about him but, at the end of the day, I live with him so I know what he's really like!" They're a really dynamic combination together and when I arrive a couple of hours before the big event they both still tear round the place to ensure that all the last-minute tasks are in hand or completed and everything that should or could be done is being done. Predictably enough, they both do this with grace and understated competence. I'm later told by stalwart fan Ian Maclean that if Shane is the King of Glasgow Speedway then Anji is definitely the Queen, "Shane has everything — not only is Anji an extremely pleasant and friendly woman who gives him a lot of support, she can look stunning. The faithful in the Ashfield bar are very fond of her." Shane's commitment, skill, ability, charm and selflessness with everyone in Glasgow (and elsewhere) from fellow riders, to staff and the fans means that he's justifiably often lauded in the same sentence as the hugely admired and many people's all-time Glasgow favourite rider, Steve Lawson.

Still everyone is different and Shane would only ever be modest about his work on behalf of fellow speedway riders and just be very much his "own man." I snatch a few brief words with him inside the large empty auditorium where yet more last-minute preparations still take place before the doors open at 7 p.m. for the guests to be seated. It's a large room that could easily take many more guests than the SRA awards will provide. It has its own bar that, in addition to the main lobby hotel bar, will serve around 20 or so tables with a full service of glasses and cutlery laid out for 12 guests per table. Outside in the hallway by the conference room double doors, there's a seating plan that reads like a 'Who's Who' of contemporary British speedway. All the tables are laid out to face towards the stage with its very impressive awards ceremony presentation stand that looks as though it has been beamed down into the room from an upscale trade exhibition. It has a raised floor, podium with microphone, large reception area and a black marble-topped table supported by three metal futuristic plant holders that are laden with an array of distinctive wooden plaques and glass trophies in a variety of shapes and sizes. There is a large screen that dominates the background of the stand that presently flashes through an absorbing montage of speedway images and clips from races, all topped off with the words "Stars of Shale" in giant letters alongside the usual colourful *Sky Sports* logo. This will form the backdrop to the introductions from the suited and booted Master of Ceremonies Nigel Pearson. Also among the yet-to-be-awarded prizes, is a sheaf of golden envelopes which Sophie Blake will open later when she announces the winners in the time-honoured suspenseful fashion. The overall effect cries out multimedia, slick sleek professionalism and projects an aspirational but modern image that is much more Oscars' night than speedway as it's traditionally lived and known. This, though, is clearly the aim — to distinguish the event and the awards ceremony from long-standing traditional but careworn images and expectations of the sport and, by association, enhance the gravitas and visibility of the Speedway Riders Association. It all looks very impressive and well organised.

The always dapper Nigel Pearson has excelled even by his own dress standards and has, like the true professional that he is, already arrived — to test the microphone, agree the segues and running order while he generally checks through expectations and the plan for the evening — attired in his dinner suit with stiff white collar and bow tie. The smartly uniformed hotel staff also work industriously by the side of the stage and zealously polish huge green cratefuls of glasses for the remainder of the tables. Shane, like Anji who refuses to have her photo taken ("at least wait till I've got my smart dress on later"), is still dressed casually in his trademark combat trousers, T-shirt and zipped sweatshirt and sports a modicum of distinctive face furniture that counts as understated in speedway circles and Brighton but inevitably stands out in the environs of the Coventry Hilton. Shane is very modest about his dynamic role driving the SRA on to its present heights but is equally definite in a quiet forceful way about the need for such an association. He believes that the need for rider representation isn't so much an issue for experienced riders like himself who've been round the block a few times and know the ropes, but is essential for the younger riders as they come into the sport. However, it's an association that doesn't exist solely to boost rider wages, though that is one aspect, but to provide a network of advice and support when it comes to the issues that impact on all riders who try to make a living or take their first steps within the sport. There are a whole raft of practical but unsexy things that should be considered that, particularly for young men new to the sport, are the complete antithesis to the perceived glamour and exhilaration of racing speedway bikes for a living. It is into this gap that the association will attempt to step for the younger riders while it seeks to benefit the riderhood as a whole. To all intents and purposes, the SRA is a kind of trade union (albeit without formal recognition or a statutory right to collect dues from every rider) that seeks to pass on key information and experience and try to avoid the pitfalls when, as explicitly or implicitly throughout the world, the management (in this case the promoters) try to exploit the labour of their staff and seek to negotiate terms and conditions on an individual rather than collective basis. When you're a superstar rider you can command premium level payments and benefits from sponsors, advertisers and promoters alike, but until then your interests are better served by collective action. This could involve health and safety, education, advice on insurance and equipment or even a standard contract or, at the very least, advice on the elements that should be in such an agreement. Many young riders are so keen to ride and get on that they fail to consider or appreciate the benefits of SRA membership (possibly a characteristic trait among teenagers and the early-twenty-year-olds that they know best and don't wish to be 'told' anything), whereas other riders are rather sensibly keen not to appear too knowledgeable or 'militant' when it comes to the negotiation of their benefits in case they're perceived as bolshie or 'difficult'. It's in the promoters' financial interest to portray some aspects of their disagreements with riders individually or collectively as "rider power gone mad", particularly when I'm sure they're aware that most British speedway contracts are uniquely drafted and may not be European employment law compliant. The deliberate conflation or elision by promoters of many different but specific contractual issues or assumptions serves its purpose since it allows any reasonable requests about terms and conditions of employment to be portrayed in the same light as judgement calls, for example, say about the condition of the track and its suitability to racing. These two things are qualitatively different and it's Shane's aim that not only are they treated as such but that the SRA as an association improves the lot of the average rider through greater professionalism of its members when it comes to their duty of care and (contractual and common sense) responsibilities towards the promoters and fans but also that this equally places a legal/contractual obligation on the promoters for this to equally apply to them.

A definite step in the right direction is the decision to try to boost the visibility and significance of the SRA among the riders in general, its members, the promoters and the media by holding an annual event that, over time, becomes a *de facto* significant event on the speedway calendar that's both aspirational and fun! Like many people, Shane is disappointed that the rearrangement of the postponed Craven Shield Final fixture between Eastbourne, Coventry and Poole has, at the last minute, deprived the event of many people ("we're missing Scotty, Nicki and Middlo, for example"). He's hopeful that it will be a BSPA official event from 2007 onwards so that, in future, on the nominated date of the event no other speedway meetings will be able to be run on that night to clash with it. Contractually tonight, all the riders of the Eastbourne, Poole and Coventry teams had to give priority to the fixture at Arlington. Shane is a great believer that everyone with the sport's interests at heart will have to work cooperatively together to protect and develop it in the future. He'd prefer to stress that "there's a need to educate the younger riders in this country" and to progress through mutually beneficial cooperation rather than confrontation, especially when ultimately many of the more onerous/discriminatory rules and regulations, if tested in a court, are poorly drafted and it could well be found that in the final analysis the "SCB rulebook has no status in law." This would have serious complications for relationships and enforceability within the sport but isn't the route that Shane or the SRA seeks to go down. They'd rather boost the image and perceived glamour of the sport to the outside world with an event like this in the hope that it might become the speedway equivalent of the Oscars, plus help achieve a glamour and cache for the sport that would make speedway more attractive to media coverage and prospective sponsors. The stage and auditorium certainly looks the part already but there are many more last-minute things to be checked or done so Shane, like Anji, has to leave to busy himself elsewhere.[1]

I chat with the *Sky Sports* press officer Jon Sim who's confident that the event will go off professionally and create a real splash, particularly compared to last year's SRA meeting and, indeed, any other speedway events. I had dined in this room earlier in the year for the VSRA Dinner Dance and the stage itself as well as the use of multimedia has noticeably improved from then. Though that was an enjoyable event, the use of all these contemporary bells and whistles might not have been so in keeping with the age of the participants, the ethos of the event, or the black-and-white racing footage from that era.

---

[1] Shane, when interviewed in the *Speedway Star* afterwards, explains the SRA mission in greater detail. "I think that, as far as the SRA goes, we've laid the foundations to build on now. There's no reason why this can't become an annual event, and grow bigger and bigger and bigger." The SRA is "trying to achieve something in the sport" and aims for 100 percent membership among the riders, "it's going to be difficult, but we've made 85 percent, if we break the 90 percent, we'll be over the moon." Membership isn't the primary aim of the association, which is, "to work closely with the communities where speedway is held, promote the sport more, elevate the sport as a whole. We want to prove that we can go out and promote the sport, make it better as a whole." Communication between the BSPA and the SRA Shane rather diplomatically calls "good" though he sensibly adds the caveat, "we're in communication, that's a start. To a degree, we're probably taken with a pinch of salt. I think we're listened to, but I don't think a lot of what we say is taken on board. We want a say in our sport, it's our livelihood, we don't want to knock the sport down or work against the BSPA, we want to make the sport better. There's a common goal for everyone." Shane also acknowledged that this year's event fulfilled his aim "to go more upmarket" but because of the frenetic but seemingly endless nature of the work Anji and he put into the night he didn't get the chance to savour and fully appreciate it. "I believe that I'm very fortunate to have a living out of the sport, doing what I love doing. I've ridden professionally for 17 years, I've enjoyed every year, and I wouldn't change it for the world. I go out of my way to help all the young guys coming up in the sport, and if I can make the sport in any way better, then I'll do it. The friends you make in sport, the camaraderie, you can't beat it."

Jon tells me that we'll be without Kelvin on our table due to a knee injury he's sustained at the weekend on a bike. He's definitely the most knowledgeable regular member of the *Sky Sports* speedway outside broadcast team but it's a slight relief for me as I was anxious about this meeting. Particularly as in my book *Showered in Shale*, I'd lampooned his propensity for malapropisms when he commentates live on *Sky* and also highlighted his relentlessly enthusiastic presentational style that he combines with slightly wooden earnestness. However, Chris Louis, Steve 'Johno' Johnson and Sophie Blake will still grace the table. A casual glance at the nametags confirms that I will have Vic Rigby of the *Sun* on one side and Sophie on the other. I've read his speedway columns in the paper but I've yet to meet Vic, though I wonder in which conversational direction I will be naturally drawn to during the evening? It promises to be a memorable night and one that I'll spend in truly glamorous company! By the name tags of the place settings is also a set menu for tonight's meal that, in true speedway fashion, is festooned with almost as many brightly clashing logos as grace the average rider's kevlars. Namely, *Sky Sports*, SRA and the Coventry Hilton. There will be a four-course menu of what I would call a typical 'conference' fare complete with weirdly capitalised but invariably inflated descriptions of what will actually appear on our plates. In this instance, "Cream of Leek and Potato Soup with Tarragon", followed by "Char-Grilled Pork Loin Steaks With Apple, Sage and Brandy Sauce With a Selection of Vegetables and Potatoes", then "Dark Chocolate Torte with Crème Anglaise" plus "Coffee & Mints." Yummy. Though the food is, of course, incidental to the entertainment, the awards ceremony and the company enjoyed at the tables and in the bar afterwards.

It's very crowded back out in the foyer, reception and hotel bar area with large numbers of men in suits and women in evening dresses. There's a very strong contingent of riders with their girlfriends and wives – they all really stand out in their smart attire. Everyone is primped and gelled as they enter in waves through the automatic sliding double doors of the hotel entrance in gaggles or couples and the odd straggler like myself. It has definitely lived up to its billing as a 'Who's Who of Contemporary British Speedway' type gathering. Some guests follow the guidance of Top Cat and "mingle, mingle, mingle"; others like myself hang back and observe the hubbub while some just stick to the group they came with. I stand and gawp while I try to recognise as many people as I can. There's Jim Lynch and his wife, Daniel King in a smart suit and his girlfriend Clara Bunting (mentioned on the seating plan as his wife) in a backless, sideless but not quite revealing black dress that can't help but catch the eye (I make a mental note to tell Johnny Barber about). John Oliver ("I can't afford to do Conference League next year as it's cost me too much money") from King's Lynn really looks the part in a suit but also frighteningly young and healthy. Close by in the bar is his regular reserve partner this season, Chris Mills. As it's the riders' event they have absolute latitude to defy the dress code but most still prefer a suit, which is, if you think about it, the sartorial antithesis of all that the daily life and working conditions of any speedway rider usually stands for. The diminutive Ronnie Correy attends to his hair in the gents' toilet mirror and has dressed as smartly as possible, given he's "come straight from work." A few minutes later I see another rider of a diminutive size, a slightly sheepish looking Andy 'Smudger' Smith who trundles into reception through the glass doors in the company of Gary 'Havvy' Havelock. Both of them conspicuously don't have suits on, though as a concession to the formality of the event they both wear collared shirts (without ties) and Havvy has a nicely groomed and tied-back ponytail. Gary is another rider, like Shane, that I understood to formally be a leading light of the SRA organisation and there's no doubt that his default setting is to strenuously resist 'authority' wherever he finds it, though he definitely retains considerable influence as a spokesman among the rider community. Shortly afterwards I catch sight of a casually dressed Joe Screen with wet or gelled slicked back hair. A general rule of thumb would be to say that the newer a rider is to the sport then the more smartly they have dressed for the occasion, though there are notable exceptions to this rule. Come as you are and be yourself applies throughout the broad church of the speedway community. While many have made the effort to dress in their glad rags, just to be part of this unique event is the main consideration.

In order to get a much better idea of all the people I don't recognise, I decide to review the table-seating plan that's placed prominently by the auditorium doors. Many of the tables have been assigned by speedway club, sponsor or by numerous other names that I don't even vaguely recognise. I notice that Luke Priest's name is on the seating plan, which is good to note after the struggle that he's had to recover from the horrific injuries that he received earlier in the season. To my mind, this is the kind of considerate and motivational invitation that captures the collective community aims and ethos of the SRA organisation. In fact, I'm surprised how many of these names there are that I don't know or even recognise but, before I can ponder this further, I bump into the lovely Neil Street. Inevitably he has on his red jumper and his hair looks a little windswept. It's always a delight to spend any time in Neil's company. He's apparently pleased to see me and I think he finally remembers who I am. We spoke on the phone after Frank Keating quoted him in the *Guardian* article about speedway

Trophies await their winners. © Jeff Scott

The fragrant Sophie Blake. © Jeff Scott

Speedway character Steve 'Johnno' Johnson (I think he likes the book). © Jeff Scott

that also praised my book. I ask him if he finally saw it, "I did. I did. It was good. Jeff Scott called me about it – oh, er, you're Jeff Scott – I bought it actually but I wouldn't buy it again!" We chat about his health and he says that he's in remission from the prostrate cancer he was diagnosed with. He's been to the hospital that day for an implant, "it doesn't take long and it lasts three months, so long enough for my trip to Australia. It reduces your testosterone, which controls the cancer that otherwise, strangely, your testosterone naturally increases. You don't even notice it and I feel really good – though it reduces your libido [laughs], at 75 you can't worry too much about that!" Neil was initially reluctant to make the journey over to Coventry from the West Country but a succession of phone calls about the event in the weeks beforehand persuaded him to come along and show his support, "they all kept calling saying I should come along – Lemo called and then Boycie a few days later and then Jason's wife when he was away. The Aussies always stick together, look out for each other and they said they'd all be here. Things have changed in speedway now – the top riders live in a bubble and they're not part of the community. The connection between the riders and the fans is still there at the Conference League level and some Premier League clubs but mostly it's gone as they're in a different country nearly every night what with the Polish leagues, the Swedish leagues, the GPs and racing here. It's the way of the world. Speedway is still the best motor sport to watch but, as the machines get better and better and the technology improves, it's less and less about skill and control of the bike. Look at Formula 1, when the machines and computers take over it reduces the spectacle!" Throughout our chat, the flow of people towards the auditorium or back from the toilets means that Neil is caught in a perpetual round of waves and "hellos." He's hugely popular and greatly in demand, so it's great that he's decided to be here tonight.

I retreat to the bar and, though it's not yet 7 p.m., they already queue two or three rows deep to get served. The smartly dressed Neil Machin has made it to the bar though language difficulties with the foreign bar staff – not his Yorkshire influenced accent but their total lack of comprehension – appears to hamper the smooth administration of his order so he kindly adds my pint of blackcurrant and soda water to his list of outstanding drinks. In such august company, many promoters, team managers and the like are either too busy or too important to find the time for a chat. This is not the case with the always affable and courteous Workington and Sheffield presenter, Dave Hoggart. We chat about the defunct speedway magazine (5-1) that Peter Oakes used to edit before we move onto the increased demand for Dave's presentational services next season. It could well turn out that he'll be on master of ceremony duty at a different speedway track practically every night of the season. This is entirely understandable since he easily combines the essential qualities of race night presentation – namely, being knowledgeable, bombastic, interesting and informative. Before we can get down to specifics, the bow-tied Nigel Pearson breaks off from his pre-awards dinner 'sharpener' of the lager variety to share with me a few of his thoughts on the recent *Guardian* piece and his views on my book. "You know that if I had a problem with you or your book – I'd say it to your face that's how I am. And I don't have a problem with it or you. It's a different view and well done for having done it! What I did have a problem with, if I'm honest, and I liked some of it and could see where he was coming from with other bits, was where he [Keating] said we only get 500 at a meeting. That's plain wrong and I have a problem with it as we have much more. You might not have told him that and it might be taken out of context, but that's what's been said in a national newspaper – it's wrong, it really puts things back and puts the sport down. I've spent ten years working hard to build the sport up and move away from all that and now you're taking it back to the 70s – when it's nothing like that and it's moved on. I prefer to be honest and it's probably not your fault but that 500 thing sticks and is damaging, really damaging and I'd prefer it hadn't appeared. But it has and I'm not happy about it!"

When we're called through to eat, I find that my place at the table has stayed exactly where it was but some of the nametags have mysteriously moved so that Jon Sim now finds himself next to Sophie Blake. "It's easier for her to get to the stage" claims Jon, almost believably. I'm next to the tieless Steve 'Johno' Johnston on the one side and a friendly *Sky* cameraman who will have to get to work as soon as the formal presentations start. Sophie is sat diagonally opposite in the quiet corner between Jon Sim and Chris Louis. Johno is the life and soul of our table throughout the evening; he enlivens the whole thing and comes across as a genuine, playful man though I suspect that he uses this larger-than-life persona to disguise his serious thoughtfulness. Before the food arrives we've raced to demolish the bread rolls ("strewth, there's even bite marks on the napkins") while Nigel Pearson outlines the prizes in this evening's raffle. Top prize has been donated by Len Silver and is "Seven Days in the French Alps", some books ("there's Ian Thomas's *Wheels and Deals* and Simmo's one the title of which I can't remember") plus there's also an auction for "Jason Crump's 2006 Belle Vue race suit." Johno chirrups in an audibly loud voice, "It wouldn't fit me, he's a fat bastard" as he smiles over at Jason Crump who's sat with his wife on the next table to us. Johno then excitedly tries to persuade a somewhat reluctant table that, "we should all club together" to put in the winning bid for the race suit in the auction, "his GP one went for £800 on eBay, which I'd admit is better but this one will still fetch a good price." It's clear that he's not joking but is, in fact, deadly serious. He even has advice on the bid, "it's got to be a silly figure so that it looks though it's serious, enough to win but not silly money." Talk of the race suit leads to lots of banter with Chris Louis, "When was the last time you paid for a race suit? You're a promoter so you get everyone else to pay for one!" Talk of Ipswich speedway quickly leads Johno to reminisce about the one season he spent racing at Foxhall Heath in 1997, "it was the shittiest bar in the country – only ever half fun on a busy night and with warm beer. When I left it was mathematics, they brought in Tommy Bollox [Tomas Gollob] to replace me, as if he could, you'd have to be a dickhead not to take him on a seven and a half point assessed average. They won the championship the year I left but I had six years at Oxford so it worked out well for me too."

In the face of sustained reluctance Johno eventually puts in a bid of £384.50 which he eventually passes over loudly saying, "That's the bid from this table" though the fact everyone averts their eyes downwards or away in the distance at this precise moment says differently.

The *Sky Sports* triumvirate all clearly get on well together and Johno doesn't hesitate to wade into the topic that everyone's thought about but has been too polite to broach directly to Sophie Blake's face, namely news of her pregnancy and the identity of the baby's father [Scott Nicholls], but only after she greets him with, "Oh, it's Steve 'Big Dick' Johnston, looking smart tonight."

"You scrub up well yourself for a mother!" is the reply followed by a riff that moves onto, "she'll be a fat girl the next time I see her" – though she's very obviously sleek and firm, not at all 'fat' in her tightly fitting evening dress that emphasises her (wildly distracting) décolletage. With expert comic timing, Johno pauses and is rewarded with a fixed smile from Sophie and gets in response an outraged, "I'm not" that he immediately follows with impeccable but warped logic, "you will be when I come back from Aus next year." He's looking forward to his trip back home, "the Danes, the Swedes and the Yanks all get to go back home during the season but it's so far away we can't, so I haven't been home since March." He even enjoys some of the stopovers that you get to experience; he liked the food, people and experience of Hong Kong but is bluntly dismissive about the lack of appeal of some other Asian countries he had stopovers in.

Given how well he's done reporting live on *Sky* and all the extensive practise he's now had, I ask if it's Johno's intention to make a full-time job of his television work after his career ends. "Nah, the work's here – when I finish I'm gonna go back to Aus and as no one knows me work, I can't see what they could get me to do, as they don't do speedway like they do

Prankster Johnno wears my glasses. © Jeff Scott

Stars of the Shale muster. © Jeff Scott

The lovely Anji Parker. © Jeff Scott

here. Don't get me wrong, I enjoy it but I love riding the bike. Always have. My dad had a bike shop and I've always been round bikes all my life so I'll probably do that in some way. I dunno. I enjoy the television work here and laugh me bollocks off every time. I got into it by accident – I find it easy to talk. We're all so diverse away from riding the bike and, not being funny, some of them can't string two sentences together so I got to be involved." When you get Steve to talk speedway he ranges widely and has the zeal of a reformed smoker when it comes to the issue of air fences. "Every track should have an air fence – I used to be not fussed but I've had two big crashes and I was back in the next race. With old fences I wouldn't have been back that season. We pay for dirt deflectors and all the other equipment that we need so the promoters should pay for air fences!" Even with the addition of this safety measure, riders can still get in the wars on a regular basis, as I overhear when later Johno explains his latest crash to the taciturn but friendly *Sun* speedway reporter, Vic Rigby, "The bike went up me arse and then scraped me head – it took the skin off me arse and elbows and back."

There's a warm introductory speech from a slightly nervous Shane ("chairperson of the SRA") Parker, "I would like to give a warm welcome to everyone here on behalf of the SRA, the SRA – so that's twice – we've set out never to be a voice of conflict but one of co-operation. What we have here tonight shows what can happen when everyone works together." He also apologises for the "missing riders" but pointedly notes it's for reasons "outside of our control" and hopes that the event will become a formal part of the speedway calendar so it can avoid such a clash in the future. He thanks the sponsors, *Sky Sports* and Teng Tools, ("who have sponsorship packages for every SRA member") before he thanks "those who have helped make this event possible – Mark Thursfield, Jon Sim, my wife Anji, Mark Lemo and Vee Everson."

We all stand while Nigel Pearson says grace and Johno quips, "that didn't even hurt." I soon realise that I have the best seat in the house – right next to Johno – who, at every opportunity, spends the evening taking the mickey out of everyone on the table or anyone who passes within striking distance. We range widely in our conversation but quickly strike a serious note when Johno says, "I had a friend die of a brain tumour" by way of explanation of his philosophy of life, "I'm on the gas everyday, I've been on the gas every day since then – I'm 35 and single, I'm not saying that's good, but I am – so I can live like this!" Though it's something he's clearly thought carefully about and told numerous times before, Johno definitely pauses for a moment to compose himself at the thought of his dead friend, the speedway rider Simon Wigg. His shaven head has become recognisable as his own distinctive tonsorial style but has only been like that since the day of Simon's brain tumour operation. "We'd been drinking the night before we went to visit him and as he'd had his shaved so we [Joe Screen and Johno] decided to shave all ours off in sympathy and tribute as well as to surprise him. It's a better colour when you look at it now but when you do it your head is as white as sheets – a bright white you can't believe – he didn't know that we'd done it and though he couldn't speak he pissed himself laughing on the pillows, 'you'd have given your left leg for that – you really would!'" Johno trails off momentarily lost in contemplation before he clicks back into his witty, life and soul of the party persona. He's like popcorn, verbally shooting off in all directions, sparing no one, but sharp and affectionate with it in the distinctive strine of his accent. He entertains everyone, even the waiting staff with questions like, "There's so much cutlery here; which end do I start?" "I'll have two glasses", when the wine is poured and to the offer of apple sauce for his lamb, "I just know it tastes better with that apple stuff, I've seen it in the movies."

Johno is even better value once the presentations start and he can heckle to his heart's content in front of a much bigger audience than just our table, namely his peers, employers and contemporaries. They're obviously well used to his uniquely irreverent approach to life and the people around him. The format of the evening follows the fixed format of set-up-visual-reveal-presentation-comment-congratulation-photograph-exit. From behind his lectern as though he's a smartly dressed vicar, Nigel Pearson introduces the award category, outlines the candidates, says a few words and then segues to Sophie on the other side of the stage (sometimes after a short clip of action shots on the screen that dominates the centre of the stand) who then unfastens the relevant gold envelope to announce the winner. They come up for a few words of varying illumination with Nigel and then they pose with Sophie in the centre of the stage as the "official photographer" bustles about industriously and shouts a few instructions as his camera flashes away to capture the presentation for posterity in the pages of the *Speedway Star*.

The first award introduces the latest inductee into the "Speedway Hall of Fame" in the form of Tony Rickardsson. He joins an august list of champion riders that Nigel spells out at length only for Johno to heckle, "What have they ever done for speedway?" There's a statement from Tony that rehearses the usual platitudes and an unconvincing expression of regret about not being able to come along, "To quote a good English expression 'I'm over the moon' but my new job has me spending many hours on it or I would be with you." Speedway is definitely yesterday's toy for Tony. Jason Crump has quickly returned to the scene of the crime of earlier in the year – his 'Guest of Honour' appearance at the VSRA Dinner – and is kept busy all night. Luckily his table is handily positioned close to the stage, though he wins so often maybe it should have been on the stage. He's also inducted into the "Speedway Hall of Fame" and uses his speech for a bit of tub-thumping and oblique shaming on behalf of the SRA, "all you riders out there tonight, you should have been at our meeting this afternoon."

The most well-received award of the night for the most popular and widely respected man in the audience, Neil Street, arrives next in the form of the "Outstanding Contribution to Speedway" award that is announced to loud cheers and spontaneous applause as the whole room stands to congratulate him. Before it's announced Johno heckles Peter Toogood (who he loudly calls "Peter No-Good" throughout the night) as he walks to the stage with, "Why is there a meeting on tonight?" Peter has no answer for a question, I believe, Johno means sincerely, but is rescued by Nigel Pearson's, "Johno shut up for once." Neil is centre of attention and looks sheepish as he negotiates the forest of tables between him and the stage as Johno chirrups, "I hope he's got his hearing aid in!" Presented with his trophy, Neil speaks easily from the heart after a life devoted to the sport, "It just overwhelms me completely! It's wonderful to be here with all these people and it's humbling to receive this award. There's so many people to thank and people like Shane who gives so much."[2]

Whoever had to follow Neil onto the stage for their presentation had, obviously, drawn the short straw as that warm level

---

[2] Afterwards Neil was characteristically modest when he spoke with the *Speedway Star*. "To get it from this group of people, they are the ones who appreciate it more than anyone else. It could have brought tears to my eyes quite easily. I've dealt with riders for so long, I know the sincere ones and the insincere ones, and as I said to Johno, 'Steve I've done something all my life that I have really enjoyed, and if I've helped people, then I'm even more pleased'. As long as I can do that, I'll be happy to stay alive. What I like, and I've been like it all my life, the thing that I thrive on is work seven days a week. I'm never more pleased than when I'm working all the time and generally under pressure. If I'm under pressure, I even feel better about it, for some strange reason. All my life, from a little boy, I was the same. I couldn't help myself. I would have liked to be a World Champion, like my grandson, but it was never there. But I've been fortunate enough to have been able to look into the speedway business, understand people, understand riders... how could you not be enjoying yourself with all these people? We're all friends. I look at the majority of speedway people as a family, like brothers, that's how I refer to them, and I think more of my brothers and sisters than anyone else, and I include all these speedway people in the same category. It's wonderful, and they'll all do anything for you, and I will do anything for them, and not just Australians; it doesn't make any difference. I feel the same with all of them. It's been a wonderful life, and if it continues for some time, I'll be even more pleased."

of love and adulation would always be a hard act to follow. The video montage that was shown to the audience after Nigel had announced the candidates for the "Supporter's Rider of the Year" clearly illustrated that, in their choice of illustrative images of the season, the backroom boys at *Sky Sports* retain a wicked sense of humour. A prominent image was the notorious Sophie Blake interview with Scott Nicholls at what looked suspiciously like the Lonigo Grand Prix. This was shown for much longer than subliminally so we'd all had the opportunity to notice that Sophie's embonpoint indicated that she found herself either excited or cold. To a low level rumble of risqué comment, Sophie tears open the envelope to reveal that Tai Woffinden has triumphed over Tom Brown, Jason Crump and Josh Auty.

Next up is the "Teng Tools Under 18 Rider of the Year", which Pete Toogood collects on behalf of the absent Lewis Bridger who's unable to attend as expected since he's otherwise engaged in the Craven Shield Final second leg at Arlington. Johno again seizes his chance to play to the crowd and hassle the BSPA Chairman about the still unanswered question, "So why are they riding tonight, Pete?" Even Nigel temporarily casts aside his prepared comments in favour of temporarily donning his quite dusty investigative reporters hat to politely ask, "Would you like to respond to that?" More used to being grilled by Nigel on the detail of press releases he has himself previously already approved, a slightly startled PT plays for time with a very husky and waivery voice, "First thing I have to say is that I don't like anyone to hold it [the microphone] for me, I like to do it myself!" Having retrieved the instrument of torture from Nigel's hot tight grasp and settled into an authoritative slightly karaoke posture he feels slightly more comfortable with, Pete fails to give a smoky-voiced rendition of 'My Way' or to even answer the question. "We have had a hiccup, Johno, but I'm not going to answer your question. Though I will say that we need many more Lewis Bridgers in this speedway league."

The award presentations come thick and fast. It develops its own rhythm, Nigel does the official set-ups and Johno adds the ribald comments from the crowd before Sophie does the honours with the envelope and then the winner in question. Each league has a "Rider of the Year" award that Nigel informs the audience is "all decided by the referees who nominate their best three riders on the night at every meeting." This news is greeted with mock groans from the riders in the crowd but, on my travels, I have seen that this 'fun' judgement is part of the statutory paperwork that all SCB officials have to complete at every meeting. Josh Auty is announced as the winner of the Conference League award which provokes a loud cry of "get in there, Josh" from an excitable friend while Johno draws attention to his ostentatious but distinctive hair style as he passes by, "he looks like a skunk!" Steve is man with bags of energy who, I imagine, doesn't like to have to sit still or keep quiet for any length of time. Throughout the awards he repeatedly checks his very modern looking mobile under the table for important text messages. The fervour and regularity with which he checks them leads me to suspect that they might be very salacious or contain news of a subsequent late night assignation. Johno fiddles with his cup and saucer, any remaining cutlery to hand, his name tag, the glasses, he finishes the wine with a slurp and even tries on my glasses, looks around and takes them back off complaining about the strength of the lens, "freak!" Though Nigel informs us "Havvy is in the house tonight" and though he would definitely have scooped the best ponytail award if there had been one, the actual winner of "Premier League Rider of the Year" is Magnus 'Zorro' Zetterstrom. Just like turkeys don't vote for Christmas then unconsciously, if nothing else, Havvy is going to struggle to gain widespread approval from the referees on a regular basis since he's often a tad reticent with authority figures (particularly those he doesn't hold in high esteem) and is often the touchstone for collective rider opinion at meetings. Zorro bounds on stage but can't quite shake the morose outlook that many years of toil as a speedway rider has apparently instilled in his outlook on the world, "It's an easy life being a speedway rider, well everyone says it's an easy life — you get to see motorways and airports and all those sorts of things." There's no ripple of sympathy or agreement but it's a common enough experience in the audience tonight.

Unsurprisingly the winner of the "Elite League Rider of the Year" is Jason Crump even though Johno loudly and repeatedly shouts his own request/advice beforehand, "Don't vote for the ginger kid!" At this rate, Jason is going to need a separate table to store all the trophies he's going to receive at the event. This is only the second time I've seen him speak at a formal function and Jason projects an approach to life that is wry and self-deprecating — an effect emphasised by his deadpan voice — as though his achievement in finally reaching the pinnacle of his chosen sport has instantly mellowed the vim and anger of his youth.[3] Crumpie is relaxed and confident, though Nigel makes it easier when he serves up a predictable question that Jason has been asked a million times before and probably no one in the audience is really at all fussed to hear the answer to, namely how will the defence of his latest World Championship crown go next season. Apparently, "it'll be tough." What's also apparently "tough" is the relentless travel the job requires [I didn't think Coventry was that far or complicated to get to] "as the speedway riders know and like Zorro said, it's all airports, motorways and all that sort of stuff!" Losing his own locks in the good cause of a jape to entertain Simon Wigg has given Johno an obsession with everyone else's hairstyles, "Crumpie you've done really well but can't you sort your hair out or something?" Jason reacts to reveal that he's very familiar with the outbursts and behaviour of Joker Johno, "come up and demonstrate your shoes for us." Johno needs no second invitation to get on the stage and parade his incongruous footwear – shoes that look like they've been recently stolen from a ten-pin bowling alley – and Jason sardonically notes, "they look like they've come from pigeon hole 248." Jason goes out of his way to praise "Anji and Shane Parker who've worked on this for six months [theatrically looks over towards them at the nearby table], if you can stay together through this sort of thing, you're set for life!"

Though there's not an award for the radio programme *Planet Speedway* the organiser's still invite one of the programme's reporters, the diminutive but energetic Mark Young, to say a few words. He sports the haircut of a speedway rider in the 70s and is dressed in the manner of a university lecturer from a fashionable campus around the era of the early 80s, though this is probably an echo of his flamenco guitarist alter-ego Marcos. Mark is fulsome in his praise for the sport, for support that the programme has had from all quarters in the speedway community, the impact it's had and goes out of his way to specifically laud "the fantastic indent we had from Jason Crump!" as the seminal moment that got the *Planet Speedway* snowball rolling onwards to success with the listeners, the BBC and the industry. It's a programme that definitely bucks the national media trend to ignore speedway and has justifiably been lauded as a success, if judged by news of funding for 2007 as well as its recent prestigious industry award. I imagine that this use of the jargon word "indent" left most people in the audience mystified about what exactly Crumpie had done ("I'm Jason Crump and welcome to *Planet Speedway!*"). It's a great weekly radio magazine type format programme on the sport and, as the summer went on, it added a more investigative strand to its approach to complement the more informational 'have a nice day' attitude of some of its earlier programmes and reports. The programme ranges widely, almost as widely as Mark's frequent hand movements that betrayed his nerves as well as semaphored his educational background as a teacher throughout the duration of his time on the stage. Before he bounds back off the stage, Mark promises that, after a winter break, the programme team will return invigorated and keen to once again strip down the metaphorical engine of the speedway world once more.

The next award is the "Best Prepared Track" and Nigel just can't help but play to the audience, "it's voted for by the refs and they're always right! It says here 'many thanks to all the refs for taking the time to vote'." When the Wolverhampton track is selected as the award winner, the ever-gracious Johno shakes his head in disbelief, "that can't have been the freaking night we were there!" Wittily described by Nigel as " a jet set tractor driver", Alan 'Doc' Bridgett, a major figure in the track curation world and in everyday life, ambles to the stage. Of the tracks named as possible candidates for this crown (Wolverhampton, Somerset, Eastbourne and Edinburgh), 'Doc' looks after two of them. His default approach appears to be slightly put upon, no doubt after years of complaints from riders and fans, most of whom on any evening will always feel that they know best what to do when it comes to his work. Nonetheless, the 'Doc' remains phlegmatic in the face of all this thanklessness and sticks doggedly to his own philosophy of track preparation, "you've just got to keep taking no notice." The only cloud on the horizon in his world is, "the dogs are a bit of a pain – they don't finish on race night at Monmore until 6 p.m. – but we work round them."

The trophy for "Promotion of the Year" is judged on a variety of factors – "amenities, innovation and the general promotion of speedway in the community" – and voted on by the membership of the SRA. In a list that includes Reading, Rye House, Peterborough and Redcar, the winner is announced as King's Lynn and an exultant if slightly sozzled Jonathan Chapman leaps to his feet with some hue and cry at the back of the auditorium. Keith 'Buster' Chapman looks delighted but shaken as he follows his son who weaves his way through the tables to the stage. Johno is in his element, simultaneously dispensing brotherly advice to the stage, "watch him Soph, he's slimy" and yelling, "Johnny! Johnny! Johnny! Deaf Freaker!" Rewarded with the finger from Jonathan before he steps on stage, most unusually Johno fails to mention Jonathan's impressively gelled coiffure but instead exclaims with almost paternal pride, "he lived with me when he was 15." Buster is always good value

[3] His grandfather Neil Street put it succinctly later, "Jason now has two world titles to his name, and nobody would discount more joining them in the future. I'm not blowing his bags, but I feel so proud to think that he has ridden so good, and been such a good ambassador to speedway, in the last few years. He may have been a bit fiery early on, but he's more than made up for that. He was desperate to do something and he's proved to be such a good rider. I am always proud when I hear him speak, he appreciates all the things that people have done for him over the years."

and this acceptance speech is no exception, "It's brilliant! This year has been exceptional, last year was brilliant and now this – it really means something – thank you!" Everyone who gets an award gets their photograph taken by Mike Patrick along with the trophy in question and the delectable Sophie Blake. Jonathan flings his arms round the shoulders of his father and Sophie with great abandon and undisguised delight. Already distracted and having checked that no text messages have arrived in the last five minutes, Johno has taken to distractedly looking through the copy of my book *Showered in Shale* that's on the table for Vic Rigby. "I just opened the book and there's Rat, just the sort of person who's worked 30 years in the sport – I like the idea of a book about that!" I show him a few more photos of various characters within speedway that appear in the book including 'Scary' Sheila Le-Sage, "she's mental but a real Sheila, if you know what I mean!"

Mark Young from *Planet Speedway* then returns to the stage to help with the announcement of the "British Radio Listeners Speedway Rider of the Year" award. After we hear of the nominees and joke from Mark about the BBC rather improbably doubling his wages, Sophie tears open the envelope and says the immortal words, "and the winner is…" just then, with immaculate comic timing, Johno interjects with "Bo Selecta." In fact, it's that man Jason Crump yet again who Nigel decides to 'interrogate' with a straightforward loosener of a question, "I presume you've heard the programme yourself?" Jase doesn't hesitate to reply, "Er, no I haven't", despite the earlier fulsome praise for the path-breaking indent he recorded for the programme. If this was a BSPA or SCB enquiry, they'd doubtless brush this under the carpet and Nigel's inclination is also to immediately pretend it never happened and move on as quickly as possible to some other anodyne topics that might get Jason's conversational juices flowing once again.

The ceremony then rushes on to the awards for the "Highest Bonus Point Scorer" from each of the various leagues. Nigel then takes it upon himself to reveal to a room full of riders (the people who get paid for the bonus points) and speedway promoters (the people who pay for the bonus points) that "bonus points are a valuable part of the speedway structure." The announcement that Sam Martin has won the award at the Conference League level has Johno exclaim, "Whey! He's a good kid!" though, just in case the Aussie mafia present at tonight's dinner think he's going soft and becoming all happy-clappy, he loudly calls out, "Well done, Shagger!" Nigel casts aside any residual obsequiousness and employs his conversational upper hand with teenager Sam in the manner of someone speaking to particularly dense deaf elderly relative. Questions include such gems as
[NP] "Lots of bonus points so that must mean you've done lots of team riding?"
[SM] "Well a little bit but I dunno really."
And after a few monosyllabic answers
[NP] "So, what are your aims for next season?"
[SM] "Um, to be World Champion?"

The Premier League winner Craig Branney pronounced himself "really happy" with his award but while reading out the names of the nominees for the Elite League prize, Nigel mistakenly announces "Henning Bager from Ipswich." Only for Johno to helpfully note, "he's from Arena, you dickhead" before Coventry's representative Chris Anderson wandered up to the stage to collect it on behalf of its winner, Billy Janniro. The last of the many presentations over, all the winners are then instructed to come back up to the front so that they can go to the corner of the room and pose for a group photo. Johno calls out, "Soph, Soph, whoever gives you a hard time we'll fight 'em!" This isn't necessary as Sophie's duties have finished for the night and she returns to our table to copy Johno and rap out a few urgent text messages of her own. Johno's boisterous suggestion that it would make a much more memorable photograph for posterity if "all the riders took their dicks out when they take the photo in the corner", is studiously ignored. The ceremony hasn't yet been completed because the raffle prizes have still to be drawn and we await news of the exact amount of the winning bid for Jason's 2006 Belle Vue kevlars to be delivered. On our table, we collectively hold our breaths in case Johno's "bid from the whole table" has been successful. Sophie is lost in her text messages when the raffle prize of a "signed action shot of Scotty Nicholls" comes up. Sat next to Sophie, Chris Louis summons himself from the knife draw to murmur, "that's for you" and Johno consoles her with a stage whisper of "it's not your fault, love." Close by, Ronnie Correy jovially draws himself to his full height to pretend that he has the winning ticket. Shortly afterwards Chris Mills has the great thrill to win a signed photo of Greg Hancock. Finally the draw moves to find the winning ticket for the major prize of the night, "a ski holiday for two in the French Alps leaving January 7th". It's a trip that apparently, for extra company on the slopes, also includes the rest of the Rye House speedway riders on their annual team-building trip in the mountains where Len Silver will shame them all with his superior skiing abilities. Johno, who has his tickets in front of him throughout the night and has groaned as every prize has passed him by, observes, "I've more chance of getting a dry rub off the Pope – that prick – than I have of winning" then leaps to his feet seconds after the words "green ticket numbers 296-300" have sunk in. I'm gutted, as I purchased the strip before he did and own green tickets 291-295 so, unlike everyone else in the room, I know Johno isn't just larking about pretending he's won. Nigel looks startled as a jubilant SJ storms the stage in triumph, "I hope that you can go quicker on skis than on a speedway bike!" SJ launches into his acceptance speech, "thank you mum and dad – I went from a skateboard to a moped and after I could afford a speedway bike I could afford freak all else so I've never had the chance to go on a holiday like this! I need someone for the 'plus one' to go with me and credentials are so long as you're a Sheila and you want the room. Sorry Soph, you've already gone!" the ceremony descends into chaos with Johno on stage and Nigel balefully noting, "Suddenly everybody's Johno's pal now!" SJ can't quite believe it, "That's freaking funny I think".

Around the tables outside the auditorium, people have already retreated into their huddles and close knit groups though many queue at the bar in an attempt to overcome some severe language difficulties with the exact details of their order with the mystified bar staff (should they have been lucky enough to catch the eye of one). An added complication is that unless you are a resident, you won't get served. Not that this bothers non-resident Jonathan Chapman, who arrives at the bar in ebulliently cheerful mood, "I drove up and he [Buster] said he'd drive back and he wouldn't drink but he asked to drink after we won and said 'it's okay, we'll sleep in the car!'" When I'd walked outside only minutes ago a cold dank fog has descended on the car park, so this doesn't sound an inviting prospect to me. Jon Sim from *Sky* says that he might have a spare room available – I mention this possibility to Buster in the toilets before I leave, "what, Jonathan has found a room, you're kidding, God he's a rascal sometimes isn't he!"

24th October SRA End of Season Party and Awards Night – Coventry Hilton

Butterflies, the Five Ps and Big News in the *Sun*
26th October

Another day, another drive and another chance to listen to programmes on the radio I'd otherwise miss. On Radio 4, many theories about the nature of 'love' and also the species survival of the human race are hotly debated. As usual, talk of the 'fight or flight' mechanism is never far away when it comes to love or battle. Butterflies in the stomach or an enervating sense of nervousness are generally common symptoms of 'love sickness' and anxiety before important events. Glenda Jackson noted, "unless you're nervous, you're not going to give a performance that is as good as it could be!" I wonder how nervous the riders are before the third and decisive leg of the 2006 Craven Shield Final at Wimborne Road. They've certainly had long enough to contemplate things since it was postponed yesterday due to bad weather (I was already at Southampton – gnash, gnash before I learnt from the always well-informed Weymouth press officer and photographer Julie Martin).

For the first time on my many trips to this part of Dorset, I notice that nearby to the Wimborne Road stadium there's a slightly run down building that houses the "Poole Conservative Club" on the opposite side of the road to the fire station and the slip road to the match-day car park. The newest building in the vicinity is the glass-fronted grandstand of the greyhound/speedway stadium, while the Tory club echoes the bygone era of the brutalist 1960s and 1970s architectural school of urban design that is typified by many of the buildings close by – the town centre arcade of shops, the car park and even the flyover road. To the sound of announcements from the railway station and the clatter of passing trains, when I wander up to the turnstiles of the new grandstand I'm greeted by the always seriously taciturn and friendly Poole co-promoter Mike Golding, "Oh – I wonder why Gordon [Day] forgot to tell me you were coming tonight?" "Probably because I arranged it with you directly at the Isle of Wight when you said 'just turn up anyway'". With his memory jogged, Mike confirms that it's highly unusual for Gordie to ever miss a Poole speedway meeting before he quickly adds in extenuation, "it's only his second holiday of the year".

Speculation mounts in Dorset about Jason Crump. © Jeff Scott

The friendly and helpful Anita inside the Poole track shop.
© Jeff Scott

Despite the recent heavy rain, Mike is excited about the prospects ahead, "The track looks really good though it's a bit damp on one corner – it should be competitive again tonight," ignoring Scotty had Adam Shields and Nicki off at Arlington. "How's the new book going?" My reply that "I sold so many when I launched it at Arlington that I nearly got writer's cramp," gets the quick as a flash response, "Did you have to write them out for them, then?" Mike kindly allows me to choose where I'd like to have my display so I decide upon what I hope will be the prime position right by the programme stall and toilets. So often this year my book display has been located by the toilets that I'm thinking of calling my next book – an account of my 2006 season – *My Year by the Bogs* or *Everything You Wanted to Know About Speedway & Toilets, But Were Afraid to Ask!* Shortly afterwards the friendly *Dorset Echo* man arrives with the evening papers and also sets up close by, to create what I hope will be a 'golden' rather than a 'Bermuda' triangle of sales. The back page screams with a headline that speculates that present World Champion, Jason Crump, will leave the Belle Vue Aces to become a Poole Pirate next season. "I heard it was Oxford he was going to anyway but isn't this headline just an 'accidental' form of tapping up, that the Poole promotion can deny any association with, as he's still under contract elsewhere?" I innocently ask. The *Echo* man doesn't care how contact is made with Jason just so long as he rides in Dorset since he believes that it would be great for the club and for attendances, plus it would carry on the recent tradition that finds world-class riders (like Tony Rickardsson) racing for the club just when they're at the height of their power.

I'm in an optimistic mood as I hope sales will boom and because my horoscope in the *Sun* claimed, "moonpower in your truth chart makes this the day true love could walk into your life". While this spot doesn't attract sales, many people stop for a brief word as they pass, though none of them appear to be my "true love". The eponymous Eastbourne fan, Sid Greatley, stops by to grumble about his photograph in my latest book, "I wish you hadn't put a photo of me in eating as it makes me look greedy!" Also the news that new Eastbourne owner, Bob Brimson, will bring some fresh thinking from his experiences in the music industry to the club has filled many fans with optimism for the future. They quote Bob favourably since he apparently drew a comparison with the recent history of cinema audiences and the potential of speedway to emulate its success, "15 years ago cinema was dead, old-fashioned and no one went – now it's reinvented itself and has attracted a whole new audience and some of the old one back too". I can't wait for the comfy chairs and the giant buckets of popcorn to arrive at Arlington!

There are also large numbers of Coventry fans that have made their way down to Dorset in anticipation of another possible trophy success for their club. These include Russell Lowry (and his teenage daughter Jodie), who viewed the incident that saw Adam Shields part company with his bike under the close attentions of Scotty differently ("Adam admitted he had laid it down") to many of the Eastbourne fans I've spoken to ("yeah, he only laid it down "cause otherwise he had nowhere to go – it can't be what you'd want or choose to do the week before your wedding!").

Sadly our discussion is cut short by his need to return to the car park to urgently search for a lost bag. Someone who isn't exactly that happy, is the regular *Speedway Star* seller who dashes anxiously about the place still waiting for his delivery of this week's issue, even though the turnstiles have already opened. He expects to sell about 150 copies very quickly on a night like this but can't as, "I'm waiting for a bloke from the Eastbourne track shop to bring them". The great and the good of the speedway world also pass by, particularly from the Isle of Wight speedway club, on their way to points unknown within the stadium. Dave Pavitt passes with a cheery, "You get everywhere – don't you have a bloody job?" and the Islanders very own 'Mr Bling' - adorned with enough jewellery to fit seamlessly, except for his age and ethnic background, into any recent rap, hip-hop and R&B video – Dave Croucher, stops for a few words. He outlines his rather alliterative but pedagogic approach to team talks, "At the start of the season at my team talk, I give each of the riders a 5p coin while I speak to them, though last year I made a point of not giving one to Craig. Then they say 'what's this for?' and I explain it's the five Ps – Perfect Preparation Prevents Poor Performance. Boycie knows this already and anyone who watches him quickly learns that. Doyley [Jason Doyle] has had so much help from Boycie it's unbelievable. All the Aussies have a real sense of community cos they're so far away from home but Boycie has gone out of his way and now Doyley is a real perfectionist too. He never gets a puncture, or grit in his engine, as he knows that hours spent in the workshop mean success on the track. I just wish they'd all learn that!"

Dave really enjoyed the SRA dinner held at the Coventry Hilton the other night and thinks that it's the kind of event that can only be good for the sport. He speaks very highly of another very motivated and hugely community minded Australian rider, Shane Parker, "He's the driving force behind it – the SRA I mean – some promoters see the SRA as 'rider power' which if it happened would tear the sport apart but I think they're just trying to help the young lads, pass on their experiences and point them in the right direction. Just like the Aussies look after their own here but on a wider scale and that has to be good for the sport. The whole event was huge credit to the sport and the SRA. The idea of a 'Speedway Oscars' is a good one and it looked really brilliant – it will continue to grow and grow, so long as *Sky* back it. Personally I don't think that they should have a 'best promotion' or 'best track' – it's different on different nights – as these things only upset people. And anyway, Buster is as crafty as a box of bollocks! He sent all seven of his riders along to the meeting where they voted beforehand, which is just what Len will do next year if he thinks it'll help. They [King's Lynn] deserve it but I still wouldn't have this award in future 'cause of the effect it could have. Overall, it was brilliant though!"

Just as the riders are introduced on the pre-meeting parade, I rush my books and shale-splattered sign back to my car and so have to pass Mike Golding as he watches the last few of the stragglers as they make their way through the turnstiles. "I just heard that Billy Janniro has broken down on his way here and won't be coming – one of ours, Danny Warwick, has rushed home to get his stuff – really bad news for them but, sad to see it that way, excellent for us!" This news definitely appears to signal that the Craven Shield will be going into the Wimborne Road trophy cabinet unless something miraculous happens for the Bees or something equally disastrous happens to the Pirates. To think that a season's quest for honours can come down to whether one of your riders has taken out one of the many AA or RAC policies that they will have been repeatedly offered throughout the season at motorway service stations up and down the country! It's also a shock given how often Billy Janniro has specifically gone out of his way to ride for the Bees when he should have been absent to compete in his US national championships or when his injuries should rightfully have dictated that he didn't venture out onto the track. I arrive on the third bend just in time to see Tommy Allen and Dan Giffard (only in this race because of the absent Janniro) crash dramatically to create a spectacular tumble of bodies and machines that has the ambulance immediately zoom onto the track to attend to them. While they're checked over, I wander into the compact but cosy track shop where you're always guaranteed a warm welcome from Anita (and her daughter Katie) who, as she serves a steady stream of customers, is concerned to hear about the crash, "has anyone gone into the wagon?" Outside the track shop, I bump into the well-travelled and knowledgeable speedway fan, Arnie Gibbons, who is always a mine of information and insight on speedway matters and many other things. He used to be a local councillor and when he was younger he "wanted to be a meteorologist", so he's very familiar with the meaning of all those funny information symbols you get on a weather map. A quick glance at the isobars means that he's able to advise me on the weather I'm likely to encounter over the next few days when I go to display my books at King's Lynn ("it will stay fine") and Rye House ("likelihood of rain"). I also learn that, according to Arnie, the end-of-season interviews with the riders conducted by Kevin Coombes at Arlington that I'd missed last night when I'd been at the SRA Awards dinner "were very revealing – only four are coming back next year or are up for it: Nicki [Pedersen], Lewis [Bridger], Adam [Shields] and David [Norris]". We stand together on the fourth bend to watch the re-run of Heat 1, which takes place without the excluded redhead Tommy Allen and, just after the riders pass, we're coated in a thin film of dust that lightly sprays – well, it gradually wafts towards us like a deadly cloud of poison gas – any fan foolhardy enough to stand on the bends in its gentle path *en route* to the car park. To try to escape the eddies of these fine particles (though without success) I retreat to the home-straight grandstand in time to see the dramatic start to Heat 2 when Lewis Bridger blasts impressively round the outside of the Coventry pair of Chris 'Bomber' Harris and Olly Allen on the second bend of the first lap. The only other drama in this race arrives when Bomber recovers sufficiently from his appalling start to display a unique interpretation of team riding when he aggressively dives under his own partner, Olly Allen, on the fourth bend to secure third place and thereby keep all the valuable third place points money for himself. Inevitably Lewis can't resist the chance to do a few wheelies in celebration, though normal service has been resumed with Nicki who immediately skulks back off to the pits with only the vaguest twirl of his arm in a brief self-congratulatory wave.

It appears that any passes during the night have to mandatorily take place on the second bend of the first lap and Krzysztof Kasprzak executes this with some élan when he appears to fling his bike dramatically past Adam Shields to gain the lead. The real excitement in the race comes from Dean 'Deano' Barker who appears fast, committed and galvanised enough to try to repeatedly force his way past Grzegorz Walasek for the next two and half laps without ever quite managing to find the room (though he had the speed) past the cunning, but experienced Pole who covers the various possible passing lines of the track in the manner of a gifted mind-reader. By now, I've noticed that the Poole start-line girls have taken on the duties and mantle of the start marshal when it comes to the flag-waving duties required to signal the penultimate lap and to signify the end of the race when the riders cross the finish line. On cue, they are passed the requisite yellow or chequered flag to wave, which they each do, in contrasting styles. Some of the girls wave it with incredible gusto whereas some others appear half-hearted, nonchalantly detached or even as though it's something that they definitely don't want to hold for any length of time. They say that you can tell many things about a woman's attitude to the sensual side of life by the gusto with which she eats and maybe roughly the same idea holds true for its speedway equivalent – flag waving? On this basis, judged on tonight's exhibition of flag skills only one of these girls has an unashamedly expressive, abandoned and sensual approach, that almost verges on Latin, towards her life!

Prior to the meeting, the Eagles trailed the Pirates and Bees on aggregate by 12 points and were largely expected to be the makeweight spoilers in a two-way contest between the other two teams. With the non-arrival of Janniro (before Heat 5, the announcer Clive Fisher informed the crowd that "I can tell you that Billy Janniro has been reported to the SCB by the referee for his non-arrival this evening"), the title was effectively gifted to the Pirates. However the Eagles riders rode with a vim, brio and a vigour that indicated that they hadn't been informed of their allotted part in this supposed script. In order to retain the outside chance they have of victory, the Eastbourne riders will consistently have to best their Poole counterparts throughout the night. They achieved this in their first race against the Pirates and they looked likely to continue this dominance in Heat 6 until misfortune struck when Deano fell spectacularly on the second lap and was excluded for his troubles. Unfortunately, the immutable law that surrounds re-runs dictated that while Adam Shields easily led Bjarne Pedersen in the initial attempt to run this race, he wouldn't be able to repeat the surprise or the medicine a second time. The scores move to an ungainly 16-8-12 on the night and 92-84-76 on aggregate with all the teams having ridden four times.

The need for the Bees to urgently seize back the initiative is paramount, and with Harris in the lead, Tommy Allen aggressively muscles between Boyce and Lindgren at everyone's favourite spot to overtake – the exit from the second bend on the first lap. This manoeuvre might be enough to intimidate some of Tommy's nervier erstwhile Premier League rivals but cuts absolutely no ice with the experienced Poole pair. Rather than be psyched out or intimidated, they completely ignore his intervention to confidently pass either side of him, at speed, as they all enter the third bend. By the time they have negotiated the corner, they have effectively extinguished his challenge. The drawn race result suits the purposes of the Pirates campaign for the trophy but not that of the Bees.

Rory Schlein attempts to help the Bees regain some of their customary buzz when a slightly discombobulated rise of the tapes allows the Aussie to escape with a flyer before the consistently impressive on the night, Edward Kennett, blasts superbly round him on – surprise surprise – the second bend of the first lap. Since Giffard trails in far behind David Norris the opportunity to affect a dramatic comeback further recedes from the hands (antennae?) of the Bees. Edward is very familiar with the Wimborne Road circuit from his difficult season at the club in 2005 and in every race he demonstrates, to great effect to the home support, the considerable strides he has made with his confidence and riding style since then. If this improvement and skill is one of the Eagles' secret weapons on the night, then the form of Lewis Bridger round the outside of the circuit is another. The not-so-secret brilliance of Nicki Pedersen provides a role model for Lewis to copy and try to emulate as well as tyre tracks/racing line for him to follow. Pitted against the all-Polish pairing of Kasprzak and Walasek, Lewis rides to a truly exhilarating last place! Prior to the race Lewis warmed up with his very own speedway equivalent of Anthea Redfern's twirl on the *Generation Game* ("Give us a twirl, Lewis", as Brucie would doubtless put it) – in his case a few pre-race warm-up mini-wheelies. Lewis then spends the race almost hugging the safety fence, while sparks repeatedly trail from his steel shoe every time he accelerates along the back straight but simultaneously attempts to 'slow' for the third bend. His never-say-die full throttle approach is hugely compelling to witness and would be difficult to counter but for the ever-wily Walasek's knowledge of the circuit and canny assessment of the psychology of his young opponent. Though markedly slower, Grzegorz repeatedly uses Lewis's own speed to counter his own progress past the Pole with blocking manoeuvres that appear to confound Bridger into slightly shutting off at each and every corner. The rhythm of huge acceleration followed by rapid deceleration mesmerises the crowd and enthrals us, though the Pirates fans enjoyment of these skills is enhanced by another drawn heat that has them now lead the Bees by an almost insurmountable nine points.

The confidence of the home side is such that in the next race against Coventry they only track one rider since Tommy Allen has "officially withdrawn from the meeting because of his injuries". It's a well-founded confidence that a comfortable victory for Bjarne Pedersen, their only representative in the race, capably confirms. Sadly the chance to reorganise the race order of your team between fixtures is a feature of the regulations that govern the Craven Shield competition so the crowd are deprived of the opportunity to watch another epic tussle on the track in the rematch between Scotty and Nicki but, in Heat 11, we do get to see the next best thing with an encounter between Scotty and Shieldsy. The race between them the other night appears to be very much on Adam's mind when he makes the start from gate 2 and immediately moves aggressively towards Nicholls who is outside him. So far so predictable, until Shields picks up some unexpected grip and bullets in a straight line, without the merest hint of a turn, into the air fence on the apex of the bend. Excluded for his troubles, Adam soon hobbles to his feet, but the impact on the air fence leaves it in the same state as the Bees in this competition – completely deflated. During the ensuing 25-minute delay for repairs by a no-doubt dying breed of skilled air fence repairmen, I bump into Julie Martin and her partner John on their way to the "Pirates Bar" in the main grandstand. "Heat 14 is the big one as far as bragging rights go. Dan [Giffard] was better than Lewis when he started at Weymouth last year, then Lewis passed him and now we'll see what the difference is after they've both had another good season in different leagues". In the way that only ladies can, Jules also has the inside scoop on tonsorial matters – namely that the UK's only (white) dreadlocked speedway rider, Danny Warwick, is going bald and hides this with these dramatically different hair extensions (that I've often thought must make things a little cosier than normal underneath his helmet). In the re-run, the Bees extract the necessary but not quite enough 4-2, though Dean Barker again races with some aggression and determination to ensure that he easily secures second place.

During the unexpected interval to repair the air fence, an older lady sat in the seats in front of me asks, "Can I borrow your *Sun*?" When I ask "why?" she says vaguely, as she manically leaves through it, "I dunno, it's someint to do with speedway". Whatever "it" is, is soon drawn to her attention and she reads it with an earnest, enthralled expression for quite some time. I'm pretty curious myself too by now but, before I can retrieve the paper, it has been passed on to someone else who immediately becomes enthralled and cast under its amazing spell. I ponder if there's a particularly juicy letter on the problem page with a speedway theme? Or maybe "Striker" has retired from football to seek pastures new on the shale? Or possibly "Deirdre's Photo Case Book" has some bitingly original and incisive story about sexual politics that features the relationship agonies of dating a speedway rider? Perhaps Mr Perkin has written another missive to the letters page? Or more predictably turgid news has been wrung from the *Sun*'s ongoing fascination with the Scotty and Sophie situation? Whatever it is fascinates everyone who encounters it and they become temporarily frozen in mute concentration before the paper is passed on as though it's in a game of 'pass the parcel'. It certainly wiles away the time and, as this is the ideal moment to try to read your own paper, I cheekily ask for it back from the 74th person it has been passed to. They glare at me as though it's ignorantly rude to make such an impertinent request. I soon find the article in question, which bizarrely appears on the "TV Biz edited by Sara Nathan" page. The first sentence starts, "Bosses of speedway reality show The Race". The full horror of this phrase simultaneously evokes pride, curiosity, anger and repulsion in me. Complicated stuff and it's difficult to concentrate. The essential details are:

1. It will be shown on *Sky* One.
2. Apparently insurance costs have spiralled after Richard Hammond's accident on *Top Gear* and the heightened awareness of possible "danger" among the "celebs".
3. The show will "pit" a men's team against the women's.
4. Celebs already signed up include Jenny Frost, Ingrid Tarrant, Les Ferdinand and Gary Numan.

My mind boggles. I'm simultaneously insulted and fascinated by the post-modern irony of it all. Hasn't Les already done enough with getting his helicopter pilot's licence or by helping to vandalise the Blue Peter garden in his youth? Will Gary race on an electric-powered bike? Can Ingrid phone a friend and will it be Chris? Who from the speedway world will be prepared to prostitute themselves for this base oxygen of increased publicity and national fame? Probably everyone. My mind whirrs and I decide maybe this is the ideal stage for those who love the television limelight to strut their funky stuff? Where will it all take place? Can I go and watch? Will Nigel Pearson commentate? What will Kelvin think? Will Sam be able to read these riders' thoughts as easily as he apparently claims he can in the regular season speedway meetings? Will anyone get injured when, inevitably, they crash? How will the *Speedway Star* report it? Will various posters agree to differ on the British Speedway Forum about the implications of it all in a ping-pong match of bickering and increasingly abusive late-night comments and excessively pointless use of the available emoticons? Why is speedway still only ever really shown on satellite? I really think that we should be told... no wonder I couldn't get the paper back off anyone! I'm interrupted from my reverie by the roar of bikes – albeit without "celebs" astride them – signalling that they're back on the track once more now that the air fence has been re-inflated almost as much as my expectations of this yet to be recorded or televised satellite show.

One faultless display of track craft by Walasek is quickly followed in the next race by another equally impressive example of the genre when Edward Kennett uses all his wiles and hard-earned knowledge of the Wimborne Road track to hold off Freddie Lindgren for three laps. The Eagles thereby gain another welcome 5-1, this time against the Pirates, as the exhilarating 2004 version of David Norris wins the race with some brio, to leave the scoreline much more poised for a possible Bees fight back at a weird looking 26-20-26. Before we can get our collective breath properly back, we're served up another thrillingly competitive race – this time between Harris and Walasek who pass and re-pass each other again and again as they ride handlebar to handlebar for three laps as though it has been rehearsed and carefully choreographed beforehand. Harris eventually masters his opponent though, up front, KK has sailed on oblivious to an untroubled and routine win to extend the Pirates lead on the night and on aggregate to a convincing eight points. The best Eagles combination of the night – Pedersen and Bridger – serves up the killer blow when they race to their second race maximum of the night over the weakened Coventry partnership of Schlein and Giffard. This Eastbourne pairing works very well together, since Nicki can blast off from the tapes in his trademark combative style unencumbered with any vague thoughts about the need to team ride or even the more philosophical need to ponder the exact whereabouts on the track of his team partner. Lewis has his own personal rites-of-passage duel to resolve with Dan Giffard who determinedly manages to pressurise his young erstwhile rival for the first lap. From a Coventry point of view, this has the unfortunate consequence that it severely holds up Schlein in the traffic of their mini-contest. It's an unnecessary delay that Lewis compounds the consequences of when he blasts away from Giffard on the second bend of the second lap. Giffard is left way behind the trademark trail of sparks from Lewis's steel shoe and cuts a forlorn figure off the pace of the race at the back after he's easily passed by his Australian partner.

Bjarne Pedersen, tonight's Poole specialist at race victories in heats where he has no race partner, repeats the medicine against Norris and Kennett in Heat 15, though Edward definitely ensures that he knows that he's been in a race until the latter stages. The Poole announcer, Clive Fisher, has verged on the edge of ecstasy all evening and almost gives full play to his delight when he practically yelps, "we just need a third place in heat 16 and the Craven Shield will be ours!" All that's needed to complete the effect is a flash of lightning, a clap of thunder and a diabolical cackling laugh but instead KK powers to another routine victory. The always keen-to-celebrate Pirates crowd go bonkers, the joy is unalloyed, though the calibre of the trophy is slightly less exalted than it was in the still very recent glory days of treble and double triumphs. Nonetheless, all the riders, mechanics and assorted track staff rush through the second bend pits gate onto the track to administer some full bloodedly energetic bumps to Krzysztof in celebration. Though they're definitely not in a relationship with anything other than Poole Speedway, two Old Age Pensioners in front of me in the grandstand kiss passionately and reactions throughout the stadium border on the continental among the exultant locals.

All that remains is for the formality of the final two races to be run before the trophy can be presented and the laps of honour undertaken with gusto by all connected with the Pirates. Rather than a pedestrian run-of-the-mill affair, Heat 17 has Deano again show his new-found steely determination and huge desire to win or, at least, really assert himself. He does this in a fashion that leads you to wonder why or where this level of controlled aggression has lurked dormant for so long? It's a performance not without a strong end-of-era hint since, if the rumours are to be believed (and heaven knows they're usually completely inaccurate) that this could well be his last ever official ride in Eagles livery. If it is, then there really should have been a cry from the terraces of "Deano — we salute you!", rather than just allow him to slope quietly back off to the pits to pack up his bikes and probably prepare to make the appropriate entrance at the bar by the bright lights of the grandstand disco shortly afterwards. If Eagles fans will look back on Deano's last track manoeuvre with affection then the last heat win for the Pedersen/Bridger combination serves notice about the possible thrills to be experienced at Arlington in the future. Nicki completes his untroubled maximum, though he goes easier on the post-race celebration wheelies than the autumnal madness that briefly infected him at Brandon caused him to do there. Whereas Lewis is so naturally and youthfully exuberant that he would do wheelies until the cows come home, both before and after a race whether or not his actual performance merited the celebration (though it often does). Tonight, his performance does merit acknowledgement (later in the bar, his granddad and mechanic Tony professes to be "really proud of all that he's achieved this season in the Elite League — amazing when you think about it really!"). The Eagles have gained a surprise victory on the night to ensure that they tied on aggregate with the depleted Bees and that, unusually, none of the home teams in any of the home legs of the Craven Shield actually won on their own track.

The Poole celebrations are unalloyed on the track and among the crowd, before they switch inside to continue in the bar and on the dance floor.

26th October Poole v Coventry v Eastbourne (Craven Shield Final, 3rd Leg) 38-29-41 (aggregate 114-105-105)

Ashley was our Number 8 this season
27th October

I'm not sure why it happens so often, but the queue to get out of King's Lynn on the A10 is even longer than usual tonight. Five miles of it, then I suppose it is Friday evening. Obviously they're not speedway fans or they'd stay for the second leg encounter in the Premier League Final play-offs with Sheffield. Not that it exactly looks promising since the Stars conceded four successive 5-1s in the last four heats to turn a comfortable 1-point advantage on the night into an unexpectedly large 15-point deficit. At least, it means that the meeting isn't a foregone conclusion, though given that King's Lynn have scored 60 points or over in 12 consecutive meetings, it's hardly likely to be that close. In fact, it was August 4th when the home side last dipped below 60 points and the smallest margins of victory (8 points) came way back at the start of their season in March. Even more worryingly for those neutrals keen on the spectacle of a close contest, Sheffield have already visited twice this season and gone down to large defeats by 63-33 and 63-32. Sensibly Jonathan Chapman hasn't included the "2006 Fixtures & Results" in tonight's programme though it's still almost a certainty that bookmakers wouldn't give attractive odds on anything but the most unlikely outcome of the fixture (like, for example, Sheffield to again win by 15 points).

The long and winding road that is the A10 is much more enjoyable to drive on in the daylight. As ever in this part of the world, I get to see the kind of farm vehicles that are notable by their absence on the streets of Brighton. Local drivers familiar with the road love to overtake suicidally at speed at the best of times and the appearance of a slow-moving vehicle ahead of them really brings out the devil-may-care attitude in them. Near the end of my journey I'm blessed to see a wide

Photo montage at the Norfolk Arena. © Jeff Scott

Pits gate entrance welcome. © Jeff Scott

Lynn superstar Terry Betts with Pete Brannan. © Jeff Scott

selection of tractor types that include those huge two storey ones that probably do some big and important work on the nearby farms. Quite what I'm not sure, but they're much more awesome and special to look at than the boring array of lorries that usually clog the roads throughout the country. Plus, given the speed they go at, you really get the chance to contemplate them, the countryside and life in general (or possibly the loss of it if judged by the manoeuvres of other road users).

The manner of the defeat and the pressure of all the work to get the stadium ready after a late night doesn't seem to have left anyone on the promotional side of the club feeling that full of beans. Cheryl Chapman didn't go to Sheffield but has heard that the state of the track wasn't exactly stellar. She no longer watches the racing because of the attachment she has towards "her" riders, "I can't watch them – they're my boys, so the thought of something happening to them means I can't watch". Tensions are running high, "I'm stressed and he [Keith] is too – then he's been working here since 5 a.m. – the secret of 27 years is knowing each other, so we definitely avoid each other on a day like today!"

The turnstiles are going to open early tonight; there's already quite a queue and the car-park marshals have to cope with a steady stream of early arrivals. The onset of persistent drizzle isn't good news and when Jonathan Chapman passes, dressed in his trademark blue anorak set off by his hair spiked with industrial quantities of hair gel, he doesn't glance that happily at the sky. "You should have been here for last week's meeting, mate, we had over 4000 and the cars went so far back they jammed the dual carriageway!" I mentally kick myself for spurning the chance to sell my books to the largest crowd of the season at Saddlebow Road. All of the Chapmans have been exceptionally kind to me throughout the season and have really supported my efforts to promote *Showered in Shale*. It's something that you definitely notice and appreciate! As it's raining, Jonathan suggests that I join everyone else under the roof of the outside shelter that's positioned by the thoroughfare from the turnstiles. Nick Barber is already in position there with his tables loaded with huge quantities of air horns advertised at bargain prices and, at the other end, there are the tables for the ladies to sell the programmes and raffle tickets. With a modicum of pursed lips and some jostling of the furniture, my table can just about squeeze into place and I can join everyone out of the drizzle under the roof of the shelter. Minutes later the arrival of two exceptionally rude and frighteningly grumpy women with a large yellow metal newspaper stand on wheels with "*Evening News*" and "*Eastern Daily Press*" on it pre-emptorily barge in, as though it's their god-given right and privilege to immediately disrupt this careful arrangement of tables without care or consideration. Still, in some circles pig ignorance and a complete lack of manners might be a virtue and lead to career advancement. Buster chooses the moment of severest struggle by the permanently tetchy and disgruntled ladies, just as they attempt to manoeuvre their stand into position, to arrive at the scene. He just stands there in silent contemplation with slouched shoulders, a reddening face and a hunched posture that just shouts exasperation without a word being said. Jonathan then arrives which allows some plain words to be spoken. As I'm the obstructive interloper, I immediately volunteer to move (without being asked) though the violent way the ladies had already manhandled my table I thought it best to do so, before they quickly turned it into matchwood. After his dad has left, an irked Jonathan complains, "freaking women, I didn't know they were freaking coming!" The default setting of these ladies remains at stand-offish and superior throughout the time it takes them to quickly sell the meagre stock of papers that they'd brought along. If you were going to try to maximise sales on such a night, I would have thought that you'd be affable with the public as well as bring sufficient quantities to satisfy the demands of a big crowd until the tapes finally rise. That's what the management at the paper would prefer rather than what happened, which was that they ran out of papers early. They then immediately left, which was the only time their expressions changed to approach something that approximated warmth or friendliness.

To start with, the crowd only trickled through the gates after the turnstiles opened, and Jonathan marches past every few minutes to anxiously check. By the time that there's only half an hour until the official start time, the queues have gone completely barmy. The road is filled with a traffic jam and the line of people who patiently wait to enter stretches back at least a hundred yards to the road. Ever keen to be exact, Jonathan notes, "it's not as many as we had for Peterborough last week". There is a school of thought in business that if you keep going back again and again to the same group of customers then their interest and your sales will inevitably decline unless they absolutely must have your products or service. You could argue that this has been the historic trend of the sport where speedway fans have been taken for granted, the promoters (and governing authorities) have preferred to take the money out of the sport when times were good and have failed to adequately invest for the future. So it is with my book at King's Lynn. I have returned to the well too many times and now it's come up dry, even the lure of a new book is a blandishment that they find all too easy to resist. However, as I stand forlornly by my table, I do get to meet the very inquisitive Danish man Svend Elkjaer who, rather amazingly, has been hired by the BSPA "to conduct a Commercial Opportunity Audit". It's a shock to learn that such forward thinking even goes on at BSPA Towers or that they've managed to hire a much higher calibre of consultant than those they employed to conduct the poorly drafted questionnaire of fans in 2005. Svend has an extensive background in sports consultancy and sports marketing research that runs a wide gamut of different sports, though mostly games with balls like hockey, football and rugby. We're able to talk at reasonable length as I'm not exactly encumbered with queues of potential purchasers, particularly as most fans appear keen to secure their ideal spot on the terraces or in the grandstands after they've purchased a programme, some food, an air horn or refill canister and maybe even a paper from the glowering harridans on the stall close by.

Svend has many questions as well as an engaging manner and inquisitive mind but is nonetheless prepared to listen. I point out Tony Steele as an ideal person to talk to as well as Jonathan Chapman whom he has just met. He's very impressed by what he's seen and heard about at Saddlebow Road, since his previous experience has repeatedly shown that 'successful' sports clubs are "always embedded in their communities". This rule applies across the board irrespective of the actual sport and King's Lynn appear to be a good example of a club that understands in order to achieve commercial success you have to be meaningful to the fans in your local area through your activity, both on the pitch/track and off it. In a nutshell, you have to connect with their lives significantly.

"You're always happy to give your money to people you like – to support and help them! If you feel that you mean nothing to them, are being ripped off or you're alienated from the club, its management or players, you'll soon stop going and stay away, often permanently. All the really successful clubs understand that you really have to be part of the community – look at Rugby League, for example, they really know this – and you have to be available. Look, Jonathan stands by the turnstiles and greets the crowd, speaks to people and many people know him, which is how it should be. Everyone tells me that speedway is a well-kept secret but it's going to stay that way unless things start to change dramatically in the way the customers are treated. If it's done properly they come back and stay loyal, if they're undervalued or disrespected they stay away! Whatever people think about John Postlethwaite you have to admire him as he can attract 40,000 to the Cardiff GP when many struggle to get 400". I make the point that they're different types of events and significantly he hasn't so far replicated this apparent facility for 'success with crowds' at Reading. Svend has worked on this speedway consultancy project for a good part of the year and has to report back to the BSPA by December, though the lack of responsiveness from the majority of speedway clubs has rather handicapped his research and will impact on the likely future 'buy-in' to his proposals for the future. He has many interesting and innovative ideas – these include, among many ideas, a loyalty card scheme and an urgent need for the sport to gain credibility with independent outsiders with regard to its governance (which he's heard bad things about on the QT) – but he's been round long enough to be cynical enough to know that change won't happen unless the ideas resonate and the people in authority really have a commitment to seek change. I sincerely hope that such a mood is afoot among the ranks of the promoters but, sadly, I have my doubts about whether they can overcome their individual business needs, outlooks and idiosyncrasies, never mind temporarily casting aside the apparently endemic attitude of 'what's in it for me?' or its twin 'show me the money' – sufficiently to be able to act in concert for the good of the sport. It's much more likely that they will, as usual, go off in numerous different directions in pursuit of their own objectives. Svend believes that good practice with the fans/customers and a meaningful, visible and active role in the community goes hand in hand with the pursuit of the profit motive. The present economic climate where so many tracks operate at a loss or on an uncommercial basis is going to make this a difficult circle to square. In whatever format, the final conclusions of his research and investigations appear, I imagine the grassroots fan will be none the wiser but I soon gather that he is certain to preach his tried and tested off-the-shelf mantra of the importance of the "three Vs: vibrant-visible-viable".

"There are some sports clubs I've been to with Mercs in the car park and cash 'n' carry coffee in the boardroom. It sends the wrong message about priorities. Sometimes speedway comes across as quaint but dirty, there's nothing wrong with being quaint but clean! I know of a sponsor at XXX [name of Elite League club redacted] – so it's not like they don't know, like and support the sport – who went twice with his wife and the food was execrable and the toilets smelt. He took friends along who also thought the food was shit and the toilets smelt. If you don't respect the customers and treat them right they stay away and don't come back!" After Svend goes off for further observation and research about how the King's Lynn promotion efforts "reach out to their customers", I chat with that doyen of speedway referees, Tony Steele, who's come along to get one of the last available fixes of the speedway season. He exceptionally kindly says, "I'd like you to publish my book – I like your writing style and way of looking at the world" (though sadly he won't commit pen to paper until he finally retires in many years' time). Tony then gives me a brief flavour of his own style and outlook when he quotes, in true Charles Schultz/Snoopy fashion (particularly as the opening scene of his book is set at night, albeit not a windy one), the opening paragraph of which he has already planned. It's funny, well observed and intelligent – rather like Tony himself really. He nods in the direction of Nick Barber who is fussing with his air horn display, "look at him with his ripped jeans, you'd never guess how important him and his brother are to the sport if you didn't already know". We agree that they're good people and, along with some others, I stress how kind they have been to help me with my book and the professionalism of their approach to their work. This doesn't surprise Tony who agrees, in his usual wry but thoughtful manner, "they certainly are". Apart from when they're being supportive, they also rip the mickey out of me on a regular basis, often with subtlety but nonetheless with caustic intent as they ensure my will to complacency is kept firmly in check. As a case in point, earlier Nick had greeted me with, "freak me, you're here again [rolls eyes] – you'll be the country's newest promoter soon!" Presently he's gleeful at the prospects of a large crowd, "they're out of their cars and queuing back to the road".

Given that I'm in Norfolk, I've strenuously tried to avoid any mention of the "Alan" word. But then, Norwich is another country compared to King's Lynn so maybe it's safe to utter it after all? The "Alan" in question is that great comic creation Alan Partridge that caused so much upset to the tourist board and the county generally during his fictional *BBC Radio Norfolk* incarnation. In truly cringeworthy fashion, the "AP" character magnificently captures the surface shallow will to feigned enthusiasm and knee jerk resort to cliché that regular live broadcasting invariably places on those who have to earn their living through the use of a live microphone to interact with a real or imagined (listening or not) audience. Nonetheless, to visit Saddlebow Road is to be unintentionally reminded of Alan Partridge once the tannoy cranks up in the form of the voluble speedway version they have here, Mike Bennett, who announces that the rider parade will now take place at 7.35 p.m., and that the start has been delayed until 8 p.m. to allow all the crowd through the turnstiles. This gives Mike much longer than usual to interview any riders prepared to make themselves reluctantly available and also enables him to repeatedly plug his forthcoming DVD of tonight's encounter (which he forecasts will be "thrilling"). It won't be available until December (£20 plus £2 P&P from www.mikebennettspeedway.co.uk). He also implores the crowd to go wild and "make some noise" with a modicum of greater success than usual. Trevor Harding is the first to be interviewed and to laud the significance of the occasion, "we just got into our kevlars in the changing room and our whole season has come down to this!" Mike bangs on a bit with some of his standard stuff about the magnificence of the crowd here tonight and, barely able to constrain his natural will-to-hyperbole, he again soon praises, "the awesome fans who travelled up at Sheffield". Well practised in his answers for one so young, Trevor avers, "it just gets better and better". Which, given that if they win the

League title too, the 2006 King's Lynn team will have then had a magnificent season and have managed to win the treble of team trophies. As the riders come round to the tapes for the first race, Mike builds himself (if not the crowd) up to a crescendo, "we've said it all season, we've meant it all season, we're doing it for Ash [the late Ashley Jones] – let's seal the deal tonight!"

If Sheffield are to stand any outside hope of victory on aggregate then they'll have to perform much better than on their two previous visits. As confirmation of the possible impending struggle to come and sign of their likely luck, the Tigers Ricky Ashworth suffers a puncture on parade. Consequently, he's last to the start line but along with his partner Ben Wilson, he's first away from the tapes. The sight of the green and yellow helmets hitting the front to lead into the first bend temporarily hushes the crowd to an almost eerie silence before Daniel Nermark finally restores (noise and) order by the start of the second lap with a stylish overtake of Ben Wilson. Temporarily caught up in the drama with the rest of the crowd that have again started to find their collective voice, I also exclaim, when Ricky Ashworth aggressively takes off Nermark as he challenges him on the fourth bend. The crowd leave the Sheffield rider in no doubt as to their thoughts on his culpability and parentage. As a neutral you hope for a close contest and/or exciting racing and not only did the initial attempt to run the first heat bode well but I was fortunate enough to see this incident happen right in front of me. However, in many respects this was to be the high point of the Sheffield challenge on the night and the sum of the dramatic tension in the racing. There is definitely a thrill to be gained from the appreciation of the confidence and style with which the King's Lynn riders clinically execute their repeated victories (which understandably has the home crowd in raptures) but, personally, I would have welcomed greater drama or tension throughout the fixture.

In the re-run, Ben Wilson, the sole Sheffield representative, again gates with aplomb to win from Daniel Nermark, who Mike Bennett has inelegantly nicknamed "the Nerminator". As a catchy moniker it tries just a little too hard. Unfortunately it also conjures up memories from my teenage years of the type of nicknames with which pig breeders used to honour their fertile prize boars, during a career in which they impressively sired thousands of piglets with a willing retinue of sows. One of these was alleged to have produced 10,000 progeny and, sadly even though this part of the world is true farming country, at the mention of the "Nerminator" I'm immediately mentally thrown back to the sties of my youth. Mike is philosophical but disdainful about the drawn first heat, "we always like to give the away fans something to cheer about early in the evening," but he moves on to confirm that there are no changes required in the programme except for that caused by a printer's error, "I'm sure that the eagle eyed among you will have seen that Richard Hall isn't riding in heat 6, though I'm sure they'd like him to!" After we've been informed that "Sheffield legend Reg Wilson is the team manager tonight", Mike goes on to glory at length in rapt fascination as to the technology his company has brought along this evening to capture this fixture on DVD for posterity. In his relentless promotion, Mike regularly favours a choice of language ideally suited to dealing with a deaf slightly stupid ageing relative who's not quite paying enough attention, "not one, not two, not three but four cameras on this tonight, you knew we wouldn't miss this – would we?"

Away from Mike who marauds around the pits and centre green, the announcer perched high above the track sagely notes, after a very comfortable 5-1 from the magnificent (all season long) pair of John Oliver and Chris Mills has restored the equilibrium of the crowd "heat two always so so pivotal in any speedway meeting". Elsewhere in the stadium Mike is keen to hear from Jonathan Chapman about his reaction to receiving the award of 'Promoter of the Year' at the SRA Awards Dinner. Claims that Jonathan may have been worse for wear when he went up to accept this trophy with his father, Keith, aren't allowed to rest but then nor are they dispelled:

[JC] "I said it's great being Promoter of the Year but I meant to say you need great riders and a team manager to do that, so I'm saying that now"

[MB] "You are"

[JC] "I am. I was worse for wear, I'd admit, but was looking forward to meeting that Sophie Blake bird!"

[MB] (Interrupts) "I've got the T-shirt"

[JC] (Incredulously) "You have???"

[MB] "Ages ago"

[JC] "Where's the T-shirt?"

[MB] "Under here"

[JC] (Laughs) "It must be a bit old and baggy by now"

The next couple of heats sees the stuffing knocked out of Sheffield's final chance for glory in 2006, when they concede consecutive 5-1s that effectively end the remote chance that this fixture will remain a contest. I'm stood among the ecstatic Lynn fans on the fourth bend who celebrate each resounding heat win with gusto, completely oblivious to the old-fashioned and far-fetched concept that they might enjoy a closer contest much more. Mike is also elated, "another maximum huh huh huh" he chortles as though he's a character in *South Park*. I notice consultant Svend has enthusiastically thrown himself into his research as he wanders past clutching a Styrofoam container of chips from the cafe. He looks a little forlorn in the darkness of his surroundings, isolated in a crowd of happy strangers, as he scuttles around to the back straight. However, on the brightly lit track, the Tigers of Sheffield look completely lost and highly unlikely to manage to approach any sort of performance levels that you could dignify as notionally signalling their determination or defiance. The scores are such and the conclusion already foregone that even Mike struggles to inject faux suspense or excitement into his stream of consciousness, free-association observations. It appears it's quite a task to get any member of the Lynn team to enter into the spirit of the thing or be cogently interviewed. After he has been escorted home by Tomas Topinka in the fourth heat, John Oliver immediately gets on Mike's wavelength and endearingly borrows heavily from a tried, tested and apparently ready drafted bank of centre green interview clichés:

[JO] "I was grinning from ear to ear under me helmet when I saw Tomas lead ahead of me in the corner – you can't ever afford to give an inch, but really not in this meeting – before he went on and won it".

[MB] "What about this great crowd getting behind you?" (It had been silent on my side of the stadium)

[JO] "Um, it's a bit difficult to hear under the helmet, even if there wasn't the noise of the bike".

The Tigers restore some vestige of pride when they manage to hold the Stars to only a 4-2 win in Heat 5 before more bad luck haunts Andre Compton, who suffers an engine failure that is signalled by a plume of smoke that rises from his bike at the start line just as the tapes rise. This further misfortune delights the home crowd who also relish the fact that Paul Cooper of the Tigers has to nurse his bike home for a couple of laps to ensure that they get their solitary point in another 5-1 reverse. That result takes the score on the night to 27-9 and with nine heats to go the Stars already also lead on aggregate. The chance of an interview with Mike appears to bring out everyone's reticence or, at least, to tie their tongues. Team manager Rob Lyon is no different when the microphone is thrust in his face, though to be fair to him he has the distraction of the thought that he still has some management duties to perform. A few easy questions don't tempt him to stray beyond monosyllables and if he were a prisoner of war, "name, rank and serial number" would be as much as we would get. Eventually Mike prises out of him the admission that he wasn't "pleased" with the team's performance at Owlerton before he gnomically adds, "I said plenty of things last night but I can't repeat that and tonight is another night". In fact, he repeats nothing or says anything more for public consumption over the tannoy. Mike is peeved enough to be almost bitter as he pretends to take it in good heart and remarks 'funnily', "thanks for the interview – I really enjoyed it!" With no live interview fodder to hand, Mike contents himself with some ornately descriptive chat about the joy that could be had by the fans in a few months' time when they get to re-live the events of this night on the DVD his company will produce using the full panoply of the amazing technology (well, all four cameras) that they've brought into the stadium for this very purpose.

The pummelling that the Tigers receive is so extreme that the announcer is reduced to endless fascination with the heat times in order to inject a slightly greater air of entertainment into the spectacle served up on track. This is professionalism at its best and there's no denying, "it really is getting faster". In an attempt to stem the tide, Ben Wilson wears the black-and-white helmet colour and finally the Tigers get a stroke of luck when John Oliver falls when leading easily. Gifted a 2-7 win, this brings the aggregate scores level though it's safe to say that the result still isn't in doubt. Sheffield's Paul Cooper then withdraws "as a result of an injury sustained this evening", a decision that will enable him to be replaced in his remaining scheduled rides by Mark Thompson who has struggled so much tonight with the Saddlebow circuit that this is highly unlikely to affect the score materially. The man next to me on the terraces doubts this explanation and shouts, "rubbish" repeatedly, well a word that conveys a similar meaning. The best it seems that the Sheffield fans who have made the journey to Norfolk can hope for is a bit of bump and grind in the first corner from their riders before they succumb to another processional defeat. It's a dull race but it has the 'surprise' that it restores the Stars aggregate but is still enough to get Mike Bennett fantastically excited, "that's the idea – more, more – that's what we need!" In the track shop, the dry and often droll Johnny Barber comments, "it's safe to say that they haven't prepared '2006 Champions' inserts in advance at the Sheffield track shop". If Lynn win tonight it will be a unique Championship double for the extensive Barber speedway track shop franchise empire since the Elite and Premiership crowns will then reside at tracks where they work. It has to be exceptionally good for business but Nick remains cautiously superstitious, "I don't want to say anything in case I fate them – I didn't at Peterborough and I won't here". When I casually glance around the track shop I fail to spot the various 'King's Lynn 2006 Premier League Champions' or 'King's Lynn 2006 Treble Winners' memorabilia that I'm sure they'll have already had produced in advance.

After an even more pedestrian race in Heat 10 Mike Bennett just about shakes himself awake in order to chuckle away but also manage to simultaneously impugn the skill and professionalism of his staff with the four cameras and promote the DVD of the match, "oh, oh…I hope you've got that on video, boys!" His relentless burbling enthusiasm has finally beaten me into submission and I mentally resolve to try not to listen attentively. Just before the interval as I set out my table again in the hope of interval sales that never materialise, I chat with the terminally ill Pete Brannan who appears to have visibly aged in the short time since I saw him last at the semi-finals. He's even unsteadier on his trembling crutches ("I've had some bad news since I met you, they don't like the look of my tests") and confesses that he's left the painkilling medication he needs at home. Not that he's even contemplated the idea of missing this fantastic night of glory for the Stars. Later he galumphs back over to ask if I'll take his photo ("for my boy") with his all-time King's Lynn speedway hero Terry Betts, who has come along to the stadium to present the trophy tonight.[1] He rarely ever visits so his appearance adds to the specialness of the occasion in the manner of a state visit from Royalty. Later Mike Bennett notes, "it's good to see you here, we don't see you often?" which Terry easily parries with, "things change and time flies". Pete is delighted that I've managed to get a photo and appears so emotional that he's close to tears. The theme of my interval is tears, albeit of a different kind, when Sheffield fan Neil Dyson glides by for a brief chat about life, speedway and the unofficial Tigers' website, "we collected £500 through the website and voted to give it to Emiliano – when he saw how much it was I thought he was going to cry!"

With the Premier League long since won and the 'drama' ebbing, the last few heats have the crowd pick on the referee in order to keep themselves amused. Heat 13 takes a few times to get it finally run. In the first attempt Topinka moves, so the race is immediately stopped and referee Chris Gay calls all four riders back. This elicits no comment from the partisan home crowd as it accords with their sense of 'fair play'. In the re-run, Topinka again flies but this time off his bike when all four riders arrive in a bunch at the corner. The decision not to exclude Ashworth causes widespread vitriol and consternation to erupt on the terraces, in the grandstand and along the mesh fencing that lines the straight. Though we couldn't quite see the incident properly through the wires of the fence, the man next to me blithely remarks to his friend, "we've got that **** of a ref, Gay or someint here tonight!" A short while later I'm joined by Arnie Gibbons who was stood in conversation throughout these incidents with his friend Tony Steele. Temporarily donning his anthropologist's gown and exhibiting the close study of human behaviour that Desmond Morris tried to popularise as his own, Arnie says, "it was a rather surprising decision not to award it. I was watching Tony's body language when he did that – he flinched slightly – so I'd say he didn't agree although being Tony he's too diplomatic to say".

In the next race, which Compton started in the black-and-white helmet colour with a 15-metre handicap, Emiliano Sanchez slides off his bike almost in slow motion on the apex of the last bend of the second lap and is then loudly booed for what the crowd perceives as his gamesmanship when he fails to promptly clear the track and therefore causes the race to be stopped with the Lynn pair comfortably in the lead. What the crowd perceived as the theatricality of Emiliano's attempts to free his trapped legs from under the wooden boards of the safety fence is, in fact, another case of when a crash that looks innocuous results in unexpected injury. The ambulance is soon called and a broken foot swiftly diagnosed. His season is well and truly over and his pain is real as opposed to the painful to watch variety that has been inflicted upon the Tigers' loyal travelling fans, despite Neil Machin's defiant talk of a "positive mood" before the contest ("if anyone is capable of beating King's Lynn then it's us" he claimed before he sensibly added the caveat that it "would be a measure of how good we really are"). The correct sensible decision by Chris Gay to order a re-run without the excluded Sanchez isn't popular but makes no difference as Doolan and Mills romp home for yet another 5-1. This was the signal for some barmily ecstatic

---

[1] I'm pleased to say that not only did the photo come out well – Pete has rung up in March 2007 to request further copies for his family – but his cancer is presently in remission. "I'm not well and I'm in a wheelchair but I can't wait for the season to start. I think we're going to do really well again this year. The Chapmans deserve their success to continue, they've been really wonderful with me".

Tony Steele and Arnie Gibbons confer. © Jeff Scott

Happy fans throng the track and centre green. © Jeff Scott

Celebration fireworks. © Jeff Scott

celebrations from the Lynn riders and management, who invade the track in a state of delirium that was widely echoed throughout the stadium. I'm stood behind Mike Moseley and Johnny Barber who have turned out the lights in the track shop and shut it down completely to press against the fence to fully savour these moments. As the true speedway fans that they are, they momentarily break off from their absorbed contemplation of the ecstatic scene before them to earnestly fill out their programmes!

With the final score approaching the stratosphere and victory assured, the Stars can cheekily afford to track the Batchelor-Mills combination against the notional Sheffield powerhouse of Compton and Ashworth – riders that had completely failed to sparkle all night. Chris Gay then confounded his Norfolk critics when he awards the last race before a lap has been completed, but only after Ashworth is excluded for unceremoniously unseating Mills, synchronistically in roughly the same place he took off 'The Nerminator" in the first race of the night.

Buster is overcome but still shouts joyfully over the tannoy, "fantastic team! Fantastic fans! It's awesome!" before he gulps for another breath and continues, "after 41 years King's Lynn are finally champions – it's been lots of heartache, lots of pleasure, my wife has put up with this for 14 years, so I'd just like to thank her". Kevin Doolan immediately dedicates the victory on the night and the performance over the season to the memory of Ashley Jones. He sounds genuinely choked and rawly emotional in his tribute and I'm afraid at that moment that – though I have no connection to King's Lynn – his heartfelt words of loss and dedication choked and overcame me too, so I failed to note what he said.[2]

It doesn't seem possible but afterwards the team and crowd celebrations are even more unalloyed and complemented by a loudly colourful firework display. While the smoke still hangs thick in the air, the majority of the crowd immediately floods through the track gate and onto the shale and centre green to join in the party first hand. The riders slowly parade around the track with the trophy and wave to the few fans that haven't already joined them on their walk or congregate on the centre green. Pride of place isn't given to the trophy but a banner they unfurl to hold in tribute, remembrance and dedication for the absent Ashley Jones. I can't quite read all the words as it's a lengthy memorial dedication but I catch sight of the touching opening phrase "Once a Star, always a Star".

[2] In a press release headlined ASHLEY WAS OUR NUMBER 8 THIS SEASON, afterwards the club officially commented: The King's Lynn 'Money Centre' Stars riders, promotion and management have told how they did a clean sweep of the trophies this year thanks to a big helping hand from Ashley Jones! The young Australian who unfortunately died at the end of last season was always there in the pits with them according to Stars vice team captain, Kevin Doolan, 'Ashley was my best mate and when we all got together at the start of the year I told everyone we would win the league because Ash would be right there with us giving us a helping hand!' In the celebrations that followed Friday night's Grand Final win over the Sheffield Tigers it was no secret that the riders and fans all shed tears knowing that wherever Ashley may be he would be enjoying the moment there with them, Stars boss, Keith Chapman, said 'Ashley only came to us that year but after a few weeks in the team he felt like part of the furniture, he was a real trier and battled for every single point he ever earned, I instantly took a shine to him and bought his contract from Newport so we could keep him, he always had a smile and lots of time for the fans, he was the team's inspiration this year and I'm sure the fans feel the same way!'

Accurately, Mike Bennett shouts, "welcome to the biggest party in speedway" before he interviews a totally incoherent Tomas Topinka who, for once, is happy to have a long conversation but this time his excitable victory chatter is in total gibberish because his fluency in 'English' has temporarily deserted him. In these minutes of collective joy and triumph, absolutely nobody cares!

27th October King's Lynn v Sheffield (Premier League Play-off Final, 2nd Leg) 63-30 (aggregate 100-82)

Season Ends with Fireworks
28th October

I arrive so early at the Rye House speedway stadium that mine is the first vehicle in the car park on an overcast afternoon. When I call out to the man shutting the large metal entrance gates to "hold on", quick to recognise a stranger, he ignores me and carries on but asks, "why?" The organisational glue behind Len Silver's success at Rye House Speedway in Hoddesdon is Hazel Silver. She has given permission for me to be here tonight on Andy Griggs's track shop stall and the mere mention of her name opens many doors or, in this case, gates.

I'm no sooner through these gates when Andy arrives in his heavily laden van. It's a night when a large crowd is expected and sales of merchandise are expected to be brisk. That's what both Hazel and Andy have each separately advised me. Andy has been hugely supportive of my book from the outset ever since he noticed me photograph his track shop in late April 2005. It would be hard to have missed me doing that, but Andy has a keen eye for detail and a keen ear for gossip as well as eyes in the back of his head borne from years of having to ensure that none of his merchandise is stolen by sneaky and light-fingered punters. He even ensured that I could have a place at the *Speedway Fayre* he organised before the Cardiff GP this year with Mike Golding that allowed me to launch my book adjacent to where lots of people would pass by (the Working Men's Club Toilets). Almost straightaway, after we have unloaded the contents of the van, Andy casually disappoints me when he unloads a particularly heavy box and matter-of-factly says, "they're the ones that haven't sold". The maths of the situation baffles me. Another quick mental calculation means that my book has only sold at a rate of around half a copy at meeting at Rye House since June.

While Andy carefully lays out his merchandise on his tables – with the "lucky dip" bags that cost £3-£5 in pride of place – or hangs the huge array of jackets, anoraks and sweatshirts on hangers on the wall behind him, I watch the steady stream of people who search out and speak with Hazel. She appears to be absolutely everywhere, one minute she's in her office and the next she leaves it at speed to attend to something else or, moments later, returns equally determinedly. Evidently Hazel is the vital hub around which everything else revolves in order for any speedway meeting here to run smoothly. Even the vastly experienced Len Silver frequently looks to her for reassurance about the rate of progress on the myriad tasks she's in charge of or for guidance on when he can expect it to have been done by! He's presently pretty bothered about the whereabouts of the bloke to set up the "20 minute" firework display on the centre green that's been widely advertised as the spectacular finale for this evening, after the crowd have enjoyed their last feast of racing for the 2006 season. Hazel isn't at all concerned and is very to the point in her answer, "he didn't turn up 'til five last year".

The young programme sellers from last year, Danni and Shannon, have branched out in their responsibilities at the club on race night. "We don't do programmes now – we do odd jobs!" they proudly tell me later. They're stood in the doorway of the office to receive the riders' tabards from Hazel that, as she leans over and down to their level, she follows up with some painstakingly detailed instructions and a final "get the jackets signed by our riders when they come in, in their vans". The girls nod enthusiastically but must betray some anxiety as Hazel then quizzes them further, "You do know who all our riders are, don't you?" However, a breezy "Yeah" isn't enough reassurance. "Tell me then?" Put on the spot, Danni and Shannon reel off five Christian names of this season's Premier League squad with consummate authority but then they start to stutter and stumble before they accidentally guess a couple more names of riders that are sadly no longer at the club. Hazel slowly and patiently lists one by one all the Rye House riders who have been invited to appear in tonight's championship and then even more carefully stresses those who have subsequently been called up as late replacements for the last-minute drop outs and absentees (Adam Shields, Tommy Allen and John Oliver) – Robert Mear, Harland Cook and Barry Burchatt. The girls smile confidently and scamper off with the tabards. There's an instruction for everybody – some other members of staff are told, "It's £12 for unaccompanied kids as we don't want any yobbos!" Even Len Silver receives a few instructions but then has time for a few words with me. He's pleased with his appearance on Mike Bennett's recently televised speedway programme, "Anything that's good for the sport I'd always like to support, particularly anything that draws attention to speedway in a positive way". He's just about to really get going when he's called away by Hazel.

As soon as the turnstiles open, the track shop attracts quite a crowd and the bargains attract rapacious interest, particularly the discounted items of clothing and the specially priced 'lucky dips'. Andy has kindly given me my own space on the end table closest to the stairs that lead to the bar, toilets and a number of benches with good views of the track that already have "reserved" signs placed on them. My books sell at a rate greater than half a book a meeting and much more at the rate that I'd previously understood that they were here. Not that everyone is enamoured with them as one girl picks up a copy and says to her friend "what are these?" ['Books' we call them] which is a question that causes her friend to pull a face, wince and exclaim "nah" disdainfully. I'm ideally located to listen to the comments of browsers, and help Andy's friendly assistant Doug Boxall when there's a run of customers and Andy's not around. Otherwise I stand about looking what I hope is helpful and welcoming rather than needily expectant. I defend the reputation and stock of the shop to some critical Peterborough fans who say, "it's not as big as I thought it was and there's not much here". They then go on to ponder aloud, "I wonder where Scott will be next season?" before they laugh uproariously at the repetition of their own 'joke' from the Peterborough bar, "they said last week that Hans Andersen can't be here tonight as he's got broken ribs from laughing at Scotty". For a while it seems that only Peterborough fans are allowed to arrive at the stadium, though they're soon gutted when they glance in the programme to discover their current favourite Englishman was never scheduled to ride, "I thought Richard [Hall] was riding – I wouldn't have come if I'd known". An offer of my book or news of the "spectacular" firework display afterwards is scant consolation. Another couple from Peterborough come up to congratulate me on my book, the lady nods to her husband and says, "I've hardly got a word out of him since he started reading your book – he just sits there reading a chapter each night with the dictionary beside him!" Later some Rye House fans remark in a manner that suggests that they were either at a completely different meeting to the one I attended or that they have a predisposition to disliking King's Lynn, "they didn't celebrate very much at King's Lynn last night when you think it's the first championship they have won in 41 years?"

My sales pick up further once Craig Saul arrives and starts to promote every attraction available tonight at the stadium with easy charm and sincere enthusiasm. He ranges widely to mention the delights of the fish bar, the bar itself, my book, the track shop, the racing we can expect and the "spectacular" firework display after the meeting that will require the lights throughout the stadium to be dimmed.[1] There's an end-of-season feel to his announcements especially since it's open season for requests, greetings, birthdays and anniversaries. Craig has the sort of infectious presentational manner that makes even the most anodyne of birthday wishes sound like a wonderfully crafted Shakespearean couplet. He also betrays his roots as a speedway fan through his love of detail and fastidiousness with numbers, "blah blah with three big kisses" or "from Mum and Dad with hugs and two kisses". These announcements counterpoint the factual information that we've all come to expect to hear about the events on the track. Nonetheless it's a virtuoso presentational performance in keeping with some of the close, competitive racing that belies the expectation that many of the riders would just go through the motions this evening. Any thought that this might be the case is dispelled by the hard first corner in the initial race which is won by Steve Boxall. As I listen to Craig talk over the tannoy, it appears that pretty well every rider here tonight has at some point ridden for Rye House or still rides for Rye House. Given that many visitors to Hoddesdon struggle to come to terms with the combination of the slick surface and track shape they have here, this bodes well for future races tonight. The next race features "Stuart Robson – defending champion", who is just back from injury and "2004 Rocket 'Mr Electric' Davey Watt", who goes on to win by the proverbial country mile. The following heat features "2002 winner Leigh Lanham", though he only manages third place behind the newly signed Rocket (for 2007), "16 year old hot prospect Tai Woffinden"

[1] Craig Saul has been the most relentlessly enthusiastic announcer on behalf of my book every week at both Rye House and Peterborough. Indeed, he coined the phrase "speedway odyssey" and has sung its praises repeatedly at every available opportunity. I'm very grateful for all his kind support – thank you Craig!

and one of the favourites for the championship, Edward Kennett. In place of a number on his race tabard, Edward sports a large 'L plate' for reasons that still aren't quite clear, even though in his next race Craig attempts an explanation, "you have noticed that young Edward wears an "L" plate on his race jacket tonight – certainly Edward is doing all the teaching", after he's conducted a lesson in how to win at the line. It was to be an evening of close contests as the previous race had also featured a photo finish, this time between Boxall and Robson that the younger man was adjudged to have won by the width of a tyre tread after an extremely combative race, "no quarter was asked for and certainly none was given".

The heats come thick and fast as referee Barbara Horley runs the meeting as though she's on a promise at the end of the championship or perhaps she's really keen to watch the much-praised fireworks post-haste ("no love shown by this evening's referee as she promptly puts all four riders on two minutes"). I abandon my books until the interval to watch from the comfort of the open terraces on bend three, where space is definitely at a premium. I've joined a couple of families and their kids, most of whom haven't been to a speedway meeting before, except for one bloke in the group who evangelises throughout and explains the complexity of the rules and regulations in a way that makes them unnecessarily complicated. Once the riders have got past the first corner, there has been very little to enliven the quite processional first eight heats, though there has been a number of close finishes on the line that their food distracts them from fully appreciating. At least they've all enjoyed their fish and chips (or sausage and chips) but once these are finished the kids start to get fractious and the lady next to me loudly complains, "bit boring innit?" The comparative lack of entertainment on the track is compensated off it by Craig's chatter and all the aural kisses he continually showers the crowd with between race results when he delightfully reads out assorted rites of passage he's received news of (driving tests, wedding anniversaries etc.). Even the thought-provoking nickname of Chris Neath, apparently known as "Mr Big Stuff" for reasons that aren't clear to me, fails to excite or enthral those around me.

The frequent promise that we'll be soon seeing "under 15 starlets" turns out not to be some scantily clad schoolgirls but instead turns out to be some intermittent demonstration races that feature Poole mascot Brendan Johnson and another young chap called Adam. He is no match for 14 year-old Brendan who wins "in 65.9 which is more than respectable". Luckily for the bored first timers that surround me, Lewis Bridger is his usual full throttle never-say-die self. Heat 10 features an almighty battle between Tai Woffinden and Lewis that Craig inexplicably misses the chance to dub "battle of the non-drinkers and drivers". At the end of the second lap, while in last place, Lewis pulls a huge full-throttle wheelie for the length of the straight that, viewed from our position, appears to have him court imminent disaster at any second as his wheel hovers an inch from the top of the fence. However, it's enough for him to squeeze past Tai, who then bides his time and tracks the Bexhill youngster until he scythes under him on the first bend of the last lap. Unperturbed, Lewis opens it up again and appears to ride the very rim of the fence on the kickboards to win by a yard on the finish line. Though there's still some excitement left to observe even after the race has finished as Tai then crashes spectacularly on the first bend at the start of his fifth lap during a high speed 'warm down' that nearly skittles everyone else off their bikes. Lewis casually avoids calamity with a nonchalant flick of his wheel. In one fell swoop, this one race well and truly lays the ghost that speedway is "boring innit". Craig is delighted to report on "a real ding-dong battle there for third place" before he smoothly segues into promoting the "big teddy bear" that is the somewhat disappointing first prize in the raffle. In order to avoid the possible rush of eager purchasers clamouring for a ticket, he advocates an immediate ticket purchase but warns, "getting it home –that's your problem".

Heat 11 is a collector's item of bizarre events. Josh Auty again demonstrates that he is almost without rival when it comes to throwing his bike down the straight from the start line rather than actually riding it traditionally. It's not the first time I've seen him do this but, whatever his motivation, practice definitely makes perfect though I imagine you feel a bit of a booby stood there bikeless, just as the other riders quickly shoot away off into the distance. Well, all except for the green-helmeted Stuart Robson who has an engine failure on the second bend. Leigh Lanham isn't to be out-done by the youngsters when it comes to spectacular manoeuvres and executes his own marvellous 360 degree turn at the start of the last lap (but still stays on and wheelies home in celebration on a bike with a sick sounding engine) that allows Robert Mear to glide away from him only to come to grief and fall, almost as spectacularly as Tai just did, after the race has finished. Craig takes it all in his stride, though initially it sounds like he's decided to recite his own version of a Spice Girls lyric rather than describe the race, "four very quickly became three became two for effectively a match race!" The people near me have become sufficiently absorbed by the spectacle, though the action is so unpredictable they don't quite know where to look to keep up with things. After Heat 12 we're all treated to what Craig rather formally terms, "while Barry Burchatt comes round on a sudden, unsolicited lap" following his last place.

Sales continue well during the interval, particularly of the discounted merchandise, to the extent that the tables of Andy's track shop soon start to get an almost bare appearance, "it's the biggest crowd we've had all season". The racing is as hot and exciting after the interval as it was before it. Craig notes of Lewis that, "he needs big stuff here" which I take to be a reference to the need for additional points to ensure that he reaches the final rather than anything to do with Chris Neath! The original "Big Stuff" is humbled by unexpected stuff in the form of an engine failure when in the lead during heat 15, after he'd aggressively blasted under a determined Steve Boxall. After the 15 qualifying heats end, two semi-finals and a final will decide the whereabouts of this particular championship. With only 12 riders in the competition in the first place, the semi-finals have a slightly repetitious feel about them, though the determination of the riders to secure the vital top two slots really picks the quality and entertainment of the racing on display up a further notch. The second semi-final showcases yet another thrilling ride from Lewis Bridger who, as the meeting progressed, has ridden the tight circuit wider and wider with greater confidence after each successive outing. Stood on one of the "reserved" tables with many other like-minded fans, I watch Lewis blast round the outside of Leigh Lanham on the second bend of the last lap to win a close-fought victory on the line, despite a last-gasp lunge up the inside towards the finish by his older rival. It's an effort that has Leigh land in a melodramatic heap when he skids out of control across the pits bend and somehow manages to miss Lewis, who goes on to celebrate enthusiastically. But then, that's no indication of anything, since he always does this no matter what his final position in the race was, as that's just how he is (at his age) about his speedway. I've started to mark my programme accordingly before Craig's comment, "one of the very fine prospects for the future except he's here today!" alerts me to the fact that these might be words of commiseration. I tut at my mistake and the addition of some severe crossings out in my programme.

Before the final we're treated to another under-15 exhibition race that Craig terms "the final starlets of the future race" that Brendan again wins albeit in a time of 63.4 seconds. In the final Edward Kennett wins, though not by a great distance, with his "L" plate flapping in the wind. The pass of the race happens when Leigh Lanham and Davey Watt pass either side of Steve Boxall in a thrilling, almost choreographed, manoeuvre on the third bend. My 2006 season ends when the meeting is "pronounced officially closed at 9.22 p.m.", but Craig is keen to look to the positive on behalf of the promising Rye youngster Edward Kennett, "the magic man – what a year it's been for him to reach twelfth in the national averages". Len comes to centre stage on the microphone to round off the season with a few words, "Phew! My heart is still beating quickly – before we congratulate the winners we should have a round of applause for all the riders". Thank you and goodbyes out of the way, Craig returns but having exhausted the supply of messages with kisses, he concentrates instead on safety, "We'll be having 20 minutes of fireworks, so we'll be killing the lights; so don't move around in case you fall and injure yourselves!" I'm not sure that this exactly removes all liability from the speedway club in the case of an accident but it's good advice as the stadium is then plunged into darkness. The fireworks display is a bit like life – slow to get going, vibrant and noisy in the middle and thoroughly captivating before it builds to a crescendo that's low on colour and stops abruptly. By the time bonfire night comes round in the next week or so I'll be an expert on firework displays, having now seen spectacular versions of them at Peterborough, King's Lynn and Rye House.

There's still time for the crowd to besiege Andy's track shop and snap up the collector's item of the "Scott Nicholls T-shirts" that have been reduced to a bargain price of £5, though they're only available in medium with the maternity XXXL version most conspicuous by its absence. My book sales have easily defied the half a book a meeting average but then again, it has also been the best night's business at the track shop all season. Andy, once again, kindly waves away my offer of commission before he becomes deeply engrossed in conversation with Poole co-promoter Mike Golding (and girlfriend Anita). I chat for a while to Danni's mum, Jayne Boxall, who's also the proud mother of Rye House speedway rider, Steve. She's just about learnt to conquer her residual maternal anxiety whenever Steve rides but worries what exactly encouraging him to ride motorbikes from when he was a baby has led him to and, now, where it still might lead in the future. However, she's proudly in on this journey for the long haul and for whatever it might throw up for her son. Jayne just can't praise Len Silver highly or often enough, "we think the world of Len, Steve wouldn't be where he is now without Len and we just can't thank him enough for all that he's done. Hazel too – she pretends to be unapproachable, I suppose she has to with her job, but she's just a big softy underneath. They're marvellous people here, they'd do anything for you and we'd do anything for them". I pack up my worn but trusty book sales paraphernalia of pasting table, signs, leaflets and books for the final time this 2006 speedway season and head out towards the still almost full car park. Things will clearly continue here until long into the night as there are to be speeches and presentations with all the Rye House riders and staff in the bar. Just as I leave, I notice Hazel busily rush towards the crowded room with a clear plastic bag full of trophies of varying sizes and shapes for the end-of-season awards ceremony.

28th October The 2006 Sainsbury's Ace of Herts Championship Winner: Edward Kennett

November 2006

"I can no longer afford to run the club. The Elite League is moving into an era where it's more money-oriented and I have run out of resources. I hope the new regime can sling money at it... it was always my assumption that I would be part of it in the future, but their decision was that the only way they would come in was on the basis of a new broom sweeping clean ... I don't want my knowledge and passion to go down the drain. I'm only going away because this deal from Stuart is on the table. If he had not come forward, I would have found a way to keep the club going and we would have been in action next season. My time at Arena has been difficult and the results have not been what I had desired when I took over. Supporters criticise promoters, but I feel that anyone who does the job deserves a pat on the back as only they know the heartache. Some supporters should thank their lucky stars that they have a team to follow."
With heavy heart Ronnie Russell is lost to the sport and speedway is instantly less colourful

"In speedway terms, I guess it's been a closely guarded secret. Negotiations have been going on for about a month."
Mike Golding buys a majority interest in Somerset

"Regionalising the league makes good economic sense as... northern tracks attract far better crowds than when we have southern opposition."
Newcastle co-promoter Darryl Illingworth looks to the future prior to the BSPA Annual Conference

"It's now public knowledge that Carl has a new job as a postman and that means long hours for sure. It would be great for Workington and for Carl if he were back on track, but only Carl can make that decision before sitting down with the club and discussing terms. It was unfortunate that Carl couldn't be included in the team this year. I met Carl on a couple of occasions and we settled on terms we were both happy with – subject to him getting medical approval. Our own doctor, Dr Butler, who is also the appointed SCB medical officer, couldn't offer any assurances over Stoney's fitness so we had to move on, which is a crying shame. But I can honestly say that if I was staying at Workington in 2007 I would be looking to find a way back for Carl if possible. Right now, the decision appears to be completely in Carl's hands."
Graham Drury

"King's Lynn and ourselves have been the top two drawcards in the league and have been good for business wherever we have been, but now we are both faced with the situation where we will have to devalue those teams. There seems to be a conception that lowering the points limit saves money, but there's no evidence to prove that... I'm sick of developing my own riders, turning them into heat leaders and then having to throw them on the scrapheap."
Neil Machin

"The speedway purists and the vast majority of fans do not believe the rule to be a credible one and, in many ways, it makes a mockery of the sport... we would love to see the rule scrapped but I honestly can't see it happening."
Alan Dick joins the debate

"It has its good points as it helps to keep meetings close and can keep interest going to the end, and who can deny that the play-off final made superb viewing. But, realistically, it does not appear to be right... I think something will be done, and I will be looking for the use of just one double scoring tactical rider outing each meeting."

John Louis sees both sides of the debate

"People don't like change, particularly the traditionalists, but for the new audience it's probably one of the most dramatic and best things we have ever done."

Chris van Straaten defends the tactical ride rule

"We are just the momentary custodians of the sport. Decisions have to be made for the betterment of speedway and we need to make sure we can all have aspirations for success that are realistic."

Jon Cook reminds promoters of their responsibility to history ahead of the BSPA Annual Conference

"The riders know the enthusiasm I have for the job. In fact, it is not just a job – it is a passion, just like my team manager role at Poole. I think the riders appreciate that and, perhaps, that is why they give that little bit extra."

Neil Middleditch is persuaded to remain Team GB manager

"I'm still very upset at the way it was handled, I think it was dealt with very badly. I've said that to members of the management committee. I don't wish to criticise them because they were in a difficult position, but I think it could have been treated differently... the movement of these riders should be exactly the same for every team, that certainly wasn't the case this year. Rye House and Mildenhall were both treated as special cases and they shouldn't have been."

Len Silver remains irked at the way the 2006 regulations were implemented

"We now know the team building regulations and I need to get us off the foot of the table, so some changes will have to take place."

Tim Stone looks to the future

Speedway Proficiency Lessons with the Referees
19th November

Last year I went along to the annual referee s' practice day at Sittingbourne and enjoyed myself greatly as I laughed gently at the exploits of these officials on the big track. I mostly didn't really see the travails of the lady refs on the small 'junior' training track with the reduced 125cc powered bikes. This was probably a mix of sexism and the greater enjoyment that there was to be had elsewhere. Everything was bigger there – the bikes, the track, the size of the middle-aged spreads on display, the talk of success and expertise as well as the egos. What was most marvellous was the gap that clearly existed between what the referees believed to be their skills on the bike (as well as how they clearly mentally visualised the speed, skill and grace of their actual performances), and what was the reality we all witnessed from the sidelines. The enthusiastic way they talked, never mind the thrilled exhilaration they felt, after the completion of each ride upon their return to the pits cum push-off area, was palpable.

The visual image we could all see, except for those in denial (in fact, the majority of the refs), was the far-from-svelte figures clad in tight and ill-fitting kevlars dwarfing their bikes and riding them exceptionally slowly compared to the performance capability of the machine. Or even the inept performance of the most lacklustre second half riders you've ever seen but have often wondered about, either silently or aloud, why on earth do they bother to persevere when they so clearly haven't got 'it'. There was no denying that the refs all enjoyed it hugely and were exceptionally well looked after by the friendly, capable volunteer staff of Sittingbourne Speedway Club. It's a truly genuine speedway club where the ethos isn't placed on a desire to win at all costs but rather upon the safe and enjoyable participation of everyone, irrespective of age or ability.

They're still passionate about their speedway here but in a nonchalant, understated 'let's not make a fuss' kind of way. They're keen to remain the type of club that still offers a forum and a platform for young riders to work towards the fulfilment of their potential on a speedway bike. They have a historic record of success in rider development and a rich vein of contemporary speedway stars have learnt their skills and track craft using the facilities and tutelage willingly still provided (with quiet pride) at the Old Gun Site tracks. In recent years the Conference League, ostensibly founded for the furtherance of the aims of young British rider development, has changed and warped away from its initial, more idealistic aims. This more old-fashioned altruistic ethos has been replaced by a more prevalent 'win at all costs' attitude now coupled with a degree of ambition – manifested in a variety of ways from the use of 'old hands', to the payment of inflated points money or the tracking of exceptionally 'strong' teams – that has restricted the abilities of young riders to gain match racing experience on such a regular basis as in the past or as hoped when the Conference League was formed. Instead the Sittingbourne Speedway Club – along with some other notable exceptions – continues as it always did. It conducts its own meetings and championships and this season (2006) it also entered the Conference Shield competition, where more emphasis was placed on the chance to take part than on the importance of victory. The overall attitude to rider tuition and the care with which they maintain the equipment and facilities makes this one of the ideal places to learn the ropes and try to master the essentials of riding a speedway bike.

A few months ago, I'd been delighted to receive an email invitation from the organiser of the Referees' Practice days, Chris 'Vat Man' Gay (as his own personalised tabard describes him) and with the thought that it would be something really neat to experience and great fun to write about, I'd immediately accepted without a second thought until just after I'd clicked the send button. Since then my mind had been flooded with a mix of practical concerns and wild scenarios of possible and impending disaster. I had wracked my mind to find reasons for a creative but plausible last-minute refusal but by the week before the big day, I really couldn't chicken out without total loss of face. Plus, a number of people had said they'd heard I was "going for a spin at Sittingbourne with the refs" so while I am happy to pretend to be a cowardy custard, being definitely known to be one is altogether a different thing. I'd resisted the thought that I should change my will or make a 'living will' and I managed not to 'Google search' the whereabouts of all the local accident and emergency departments, as I was confident the club would know all about these facilities. So I decided it would be best not to have any preconceived ideas about the facilities or their position in the performance league tables beforehand, should I manage to crush my hip bone or similar like a digestive biscuit after a fall from my bike. Clearly some of the referees also had reservations about the advisability of their attendance as, upon arrival at Sittingbourne, I learnt that Mick Bates had cried off just the night before citing work reasons. This is, at least, a credible explanation; particularly given the huge commitment of time and effort as well as sacrifice that all the SCB referees regularly make during the season. The only other 'no show' was referee Daniel Holt, the wannabe rider who lives the closest to the track who sent his excuses via a text message that didn't arrive so was mistaken, on the day, as absent without an explanation – not even one as weak as Billy Janniro's "my van broke down" effort that fatally scuppered Coventry's chances of Craven Shield glory.

A group of volunteers and referees are already standing together outside the changing rooms ("one shower is now available – [you] no longer have to make do with a hosepipe" according to Chris Gay's cheery email of information and instruction) in a happy but gossipy huddle. The friendly Dick Jarvis is here in his perpetually open but weathered blue anorak with the vertical rainbow effect stripes and his almost matching sweatshirt with the 'Sittingbourne Speedway' logo. He always appears to dress exactly the same no matter what the weather, which today is gloriously sunny with barely a hint of cloud in the sky, plus the forecast chill wind is also presently in abeyance. Dick stands at the centre of the group and shuffles the various coloured bits of paper onto his clipboard that for legal reasons have to be completed by all of today's aspiring speedway riders. Just next to this group, some other men casually but loudly rev up a couple of speedway bikes and thick clouds of exhaust fumes spray into the sky. I'd usually thrill at the sound of revving bikes and breathe in deep draughts of the exhaust fumes as these sounds and smells would invariably signal that the bikes would soon find their way to the track and the racing would soon start. Today, the idea that the bikes would soon be ready for the track fills me with what can only be described as an existential dread. At this point, I should add that not only have I never even sat astride any kind of motorbike in my life, not even a moped or, indeed, the Yamaha FS1E that I hankered after for years but could never afford as a teenager, even if my mum had let me. Also anyone who knows me realises that I am serially clumsy and totally uncoordinated. This isn't too much of a handicap in everyday life if you learn to ignore walking into people in the street, invariably bumping into walls, catching the sharp corners of cupboards or my head on car boots and doors. They're just things you get used to and laugh at if you're friends or family. I learnt long ago to avoid certain sports, never to dance since people either fall about with the mistaken impression that I've deliberately pretended to be someone who dances incredibly badly (I'm not, that's me really trying) or take the mickey. I'm so bad that even the laughable 'dad dancing' and delusional discombobulated shuffles of Ian 'Porky' Jones, Wolverhampton's centre green Fred Astaire manqué, looks totally gainly in comparison. The potential cost in loss of pride or injury through this lack of balance and coordination or commonsense is potentially exponentially increased with the introduction of a high-powered speedway machine into the equation. Reputedly able to accelerate – pound for pound – quicker than a Formula 1 racing car, this definitely appears to me as a recipe for disaster and possible personal injury.

There's desultory talk about changes to the insurance policy, first Dick and then Graham Arnold brandish a piece of paper under referee Jim Lawrence's nose and point to the small print that will increase, as I understand, the cost of insurance for a one-off meeting to £50. Chaos and rebellion are predicted. I'm much more concerned by the half-heard but completely remembered comment from Dick Jarvis as he gets us all to fill out a couple of the required insurance declaration forms as well as a copy of the SCB "One Event Training Registration" form that comes in triplicate like they do everywhere nowadays. Dick is phlegmatic about the level of protection and cover the forms offer, "you have to fill it out but it's not worth the paper it's printed on." I hope this is black humour but, with the anxiety of a trip to the gallows presently upon me, it adds to my burden of worries. After I've certified the rich variety of my conditions, notably that I don't have "any false or missing limbs", "any condition which affects the movement of arms and legs" (apart from nerves or my innate and ungainly lack of coordination) and that I've not suffered from a "nervous breakdown, mental disease or disorder", we're then all sent off for a soothing cup of tea in the clubhouse. None of us will be able to ride until the SCB documentation has been counter-signed by a "SCB Licensed Training Instructor", the search for whom is conducted with the studied nonchalance of a hunt for a recalcitrant odd sock on washday. My hopes that the day will be scuppered by petty legality is dashed when they say that the quietly modest but hard working 'Rat' (Stuart Lee-Amies) will soon arrive to help conduct the training on the "big track" along with the guest tutor for the day, the perpetually hyper-friendly and genuine George Barclay. The referees are chuffed to learn that they will have the honour to learn under the watchful tutelage of the perma-smile of steely silver-haired George, who's just arrived from some sort of road trip with his wife Linda. Their car is impressively full with a variety of boxes but not the suit that George needed to wear the night before at the event he attended, since he absent mindedly set-off without it, even though Linda had hung it up on the cupboard at home in a suit bag. Typically, no obstacle or upset appears to faze George or disturb his calm approach.

The clubhouse affords a great view of the track, which looks particularly smooth and pristine on this lovely sunny Sunday morning. These things don't happen by accident and the condition of all the facilities here are a testament to the hard work and dedication of the volunteers involved behind the scenes at the club. Graham Arnold has slept at the club for the last ten nights so that he can work the long hours required to ensure that everything has been prepared just right. Last Sunday, the club enjoyed a tournament that, by all accounts, featured a fantastic day's racing from the young riders. All of them are presently unable to find a regular team berth at the Conference League level but were given the chance to strut their stuff on the track – an opportunity that they seized with alacrity and skill. When a group of fishermen gather together, the talk invariably turns to the mammoth fish that they've caught, the ones that got away or practical advice on the best 'swims' and similar arcane technical information. When referees gather together they soon get down to some serious discussions of recent eventful meetings or examples of when they've (self-professedly) asserted the iron rod of discipline or gently reminded the excitable riders, team managers and promoters of the actual rules. Phil Griffin officiated at the Craven Shield Final third leg at Wimborne Road that had Billy Janniro fail to arrive for Coventry due to a "broken-down van." It's an excuse right up there with 'the dog ate my homework' in terms of credibility and the consensus among the disbelieving refs is that you'd always set out early for a meeting. So any breakdown within "20 miles of home" would inevitably give you the opportunity to organise a lift with others if you were keen to attend. "I fined him £250. They didn't really protest but Peter Oakes said that he'd broken down but I could see in his eyes that he didn't really believe that. As soon as he didn't show, their chances were ruined though I think Poole would have won anyway. Jon Cook came up and said to me, '"shall we let them run RR to make a contest of it?' Though he knows what the rules are! I said, 'the rules state that there can be no replacements and I know how you like to always stick to the rules'". That quietened him down!" The fact of his non-arrival still surprises me but the refs are much more unshockable and have a simple explanation, "the riders are paid too much so they just don't care if they miss out on meetings they don't fancy, even with the £250 fine."

Jim Lawrence is warmly congratulated on the news of his promotion to the select band of speedway referees who get to officiate at the major FIM events on the speedway calendar, namely in his case the GPs and the World Team Cup. There's much gentle ribbing about the pressure of the television cameras and the chance that the television pundits will have to pick over every single frame of action to second guess or correct his every decision. He's clearly delighted but studiously modest about his selection and proceeds to lay bare the basis of this. It's very good news for him but arguably possibly iniquitous for the wider credibility of the sport, "the FIM and BSI select the refs for the GPs and the WTC – when it comes down to it the FIM aren't really that involved as Ole Olsen and John Postlethwaite have the majority say in it really." While life often involves politics and selection for so many things rests just as much on if your face fits as much as your innate ability, the same holds for speedway. Obviously though there is absolutely no doubt in Jim's case, given his experience and reputation for consistent decision making. Nonetheless, it seems incredible that the owner of the private commercial organisation that profits from their status as the contractual rights holder to the GPs and the WTC can even be involved in the selection process, let alone work in tandem with someone connected to their payroll to determine the meeting officials. Even in football, a sport not renowned for either its transparency or probity, most clubs and all national sides would shy away from the perception of bias and advantage that might arise from such a complex situation. The case of match fixing in Italy has seen Juventus take things further than they clearly have ever been in the speedway world but even the hint of collusion or confusion with commercial needs should be strenuously avoided. As it happens, in some cases the choice of referees has caused great contention – Jason Crump notoriously suffered in 2005 with some peculiar decisions at Cardiff that, along with bad luck elsewhere, effectively undermined his chances of championship success. John Postlethwaite and the BSI have quite a track record of poor decision making as most recently illustrated by their initial decision to exclude Hans Andersen from the original competitor list for the 2006 GP series, which his subsequent results and form as a wild card made look particularly capricious and silly. Allegedly this decision followed hypersensitivity about critical comments made by Hans regarding the administration and organisation of the GPs in the Danish press. Luckily, when it comes to the choice of British referees, no such complaints can be levelled as these appointments are widely seen to have been made based on merit though the selection of officials from some other countries does sometimes leave something to be desired.

The chance of a good sit down and a cup of tea really is hard to tear yourself away from when the alternative prospect is to venture back over to the changing rooms to get kitted out in all the gear required to go racing. I would have had a hearty breakfast or a bacon butty – the smell of the sizzling sausages and bacon would usually have been hard to resist – but nerves and a sick feeling in the pit of my stomach wouldn't even let me force down that many of the "fun size" sweets that had thoughtfully been provided. Reluctantly, with dread in my heart and heavy feet, I'm sent back the short distance to the changing rooms to be reunited with my bag and the "warm undergarments" I brought as an essential part of my wardrobe, at the suggestion of Chris Gay in his helpful email of advice about equipment and preparations for the day. Practically everyone else has already changed and has headed off down to the pits to survey with eager eyes and keen anticipation their choice of steed. You don't have to have been to many speedway meetings to appreciate that riders have to wear quite a lot of protective clothing. The knowledge that this is the case and trying to figure what you actually have to wear yourself is a completely different matter. Everything is superbly and conveniently laid out in a variety of boxes for riders of every size in the anteroom in between the two changing rooms. There are also some volunteers on hand to help with the difficult process of choosing the right size and then attempting to put them on, never mind get this done in the right order. Ignoring my basic but essential anatomical differences, I'm familiar enough with tampons and sanitary towels (or bras) to have a good idea of their purpose, how they might function and might be fitted, but actually doing so I would imagine is a whole different kettle of fish. The choice of implements that I am required to don to ride is something alien and outside my everyday experience. Though dressing up as a child or consenting adult can be great fun, the paraphernalia involved all seems unnecessarily complex and adds to how completely daunted I already feel.

Safe speedway, like safe sex, is always a good idea and a matter of sensible protection, but the range of moulded black plastic I have to choose from simultaneously confuses me and immediately reminds me of all the vulnerable parts of my body that could be potentially damaged. Even if I ignore my deep-seated fear of hospitals and the worry that I won't have the insouciance of Raymond Burr's use of his wheelchair in *Ironside* or the good humour of his portrayal should I find myself similarly incapacitated, all this stuff is just too much of a reminder of my own fragility and mortality. They say your reaction will always be fight or flight. Mine is run for the hills – difficult in the estuary flatlands that characterise this part of Kent – and I would have bolted for the door and the safety of my car, but I'd already been issued with my brand new (and still unopened from their plastic wrappers) blue Wolf Sport kevlars. Anyway, the doorway was blocked by the bloke – kindly Sittingbourne Start Marshal Ian Glover – who patiently helps me choose my things in the correct size and tells me how and in what order to put them all on. On top of everything, my fear of loss of face and social embarrassment are powerful enough forces to keep me at the track so, with fingers shaking as though I'd had a very bad night on the pop, I start to fumble my way towards at least looking the part. My attempt to fit my knee protectors over my long johns went well once I managed to get them the right way up but applying the elbow protectors and the "back board" proved as easily done as trying to conduct your own kidney operation. Instead the patiently helpful Ian kindly suggests, "perhaps you should try the body armour, though it might not fit as it only comes in one size." Confirmation that the passing years have granted you grey hair and additional girth isn't welcome at any time, least of all now when I just about manage to put on and zip myself into said "body armour." In fact, it's rather like a tight black mesh bomber jacket albeit with solid plastic board-like inserts on the chest and back with smaller chicken breast fillet sized lumps of plastic for those delicate and vulnerable shoulder and elbow areas. It's definitely a snug fit but a reassuringly safe one though I do suddenly feel like I've actually been dressed to become a riot policeman. Unlike last year, the club has dispensed with the all-in-one full body suit kevlars (that definitely didn't flatter many of the fuller figured referees on display), in favour of more contemporary styled two-piece kevlars. Well, to be exact, the trousers are made of a substantial material that you imagine won't easily rip when rubbed along a shale surface at great speed, though the matching top is altogether more insubstantial and is effectively like a replica soccer shirt albeit one with the oh-so-useful additional safety feature of the Wolf Sport logo prominently displayed. Helpfully I'm told, "lets hope you can fit into these as 38 inches is the largest waist size they come in!" The billowy shirt hides a multitude of evils and after I've just about managed with the zip, I can't help but notice that the waist of these kevlars appears to have been cut in the low-slung manner beloved of contemporary women's fashionable clothes and the roll of my middle-aged gut delightfully flows over it. I try to set aside the vague worry that I now wear the items intended for the lady riders – though Barbara Horley probably has these anxieties in reverse away in the medical centre where she's 'helped' by Graham Arnold to get togged up. "Funny how it's always Graham that gets to help the women get dressed", I hear the helpers wryly remark. I then have a wide choice of substantial clodhopping boots to choose from a trailer loaded with a huge range of shapes, sizes and fashions outside my changing room. After I've selected the correct size to fit my Cinderella shaped foot, I completely struggle to even get my foot inside one never mind do it up. After much shoving I'm then united for the first time with the steel shoe for my left foot ("if the steel shoe fits, wear it!"). My choice of gloves are the sturdy but malleable fawn leather driving ones that look like they could handle nuclear radiation rather than the more sleek, Alan Partridge rally-car chic-effect ones that are also on offer to me. The goggles are easy to choose and fit but the choice of helmet is not easy. I've never heard it said that my helmet looks small but today I do for the first time after I'm issued with one that looks tight and feels even tighter. I've never had to wear a crash helmet before in my life, so I immediately feel totally constricted and the sheer weight of it makes my head want to loll from side to side. I'm sure that on its own this helmet might produce an instant migraine though not as much as a quick bang to my head from the fence or the floor would immediately induce. Rather than ask, "does my bum look big in this?" I instead worry about the snug-fitting helmet and when I fasten the clasp I nearly suffocate myself, "We'll see how well it's fitted when you hit the fence – if it flies off then it's too loose, if it chokes you to death then it was too tight!" I then put on the final piece of my essential speedway kit – a fluorescent yellow tabard with number "1" on the reverse – for reasons I'm not quite sure of, since the bright blue of the race suit means I'm already highly visible. Maybe I'm going to travel so fantastically quickly that a yellow blur stands out better than a blue blur for the trainers and spectators? Or possibly I've become an honorary St John Ambulance person – though I did earlier overhear simultaneously reassuring and worrying talk that the "qualified" medical staff had arrived – as well as a wannabe speedway rider.

With all my safety gear now in place I hobble down to the pits area in the manner of a lame pantomime pony, but feel like I'm dressed in the manner of someone summoned to a toxic chemical spillage. I move with all the grace and mobility that you'd expect of a deep-sea diver rather than a speedway rider. Even if you allow for the fact of their age and the relatively tailored nature of their own kevlars, it's amazing how svelte, stylish and athletic a figure the average rider manages to cut

Training bikes. © Jeff Scott

Dressed to learn. © Jeff Scott

Don't give up the day job. © Jeff Scott

with all the various layers of these togs on at every meeting. I'm the last to arrive trackside and the group has already moved off to the centre green where we're going to pose for a team photograph by a large sign that says "Sittingbourne Speedway" and a speedway bike. Ever chivalrous, we decide that Barbara Horley, the only lady of our group, can pose on the bike itself. She has the kind of flowing hair that wouldn't disgrace Adam Skornicki, albeit his is blond in a ponytail and hers runs free in more of a salt and pepper hue. Despite being dressed in kevlars, she still manages to effortlessly project the attitude and demeanour of a school art teacher. There was an additional slight delay before we went out to pose since we're all instructed to remove our fluorescent tabards as apparently this is the bizarre contractual condition of the Wolf Sport sponsorship – that results in the provision of our kevlars – to ensure everyone has unfettered sight of their company logo in all team photographs. Still, it's a small price to pay, so we're only too happy to oblige and this fastidiousness provides another welcome delay from the dreaded moment when I will actually have to ride the bike! Our unofficial photographer Christina Turnbull – who's always warmly remembered at Sittingbourne because of her eventful and controversial first ever meeting here (captured in *Showered in Shale*) – afterwards suggests in her lilting Scots accent that I also take the once-in-a-lifetime chance to pose for a photo on the bike. It's obvious that to pose astride the bike for a photograph is infinitely easier than any attempt to ride one. That said, even this proves difficult for me, as my mobility is so restricted that I struggle to even get on a stationary bike. After a few abortive attempts to raise my leg over the machine I mount it from behind. It feels incredibly uncomfortable and supremely basic but, even more worryingly, extremely heavy and it's noticeably difficult to manoeuvre the front wheel. I'm not sure what I imagined but this isn't it! "It's simple but almost prehistoric, not much has changed on it over the years – though its design is ancient, it's there to do the job and go as fast as possible!" Christina matter-of-factly but accurately observes.

Back in the pits, it turns out that Barbara has graduated to ride the big track with the rest of the referees so I will have to get my speedway spurs with adult company on the junior training track. I hobble over to the smaller circuit to discover that unlike the situation if I remained at the big track where we're all in it together, I have been relegated to share my lessons with strangers. This isn't a problem in itself but the crowd of youngsters plus their helpers and parents gathered on the far side 'pits' and 'push out' area promises to compound the embarrassment of my impending travails. The training instructors, Ken Hubble and Paul Heller ("no relation to the rich Heller") already put a young rider through his tentative paces. They have been part of the club since it opened in 1970 and used to ride here. They have a reputation as gifted and patient teachers able to get the best out of all ages and abilities. These are skills that I fully intend to put to the test. I stand there silently in the hope that I'm both anonymous and invisible. Before I can contemplate the full horror of my situation for too long, Tom Naylor summons me onto the track. He supervises all the riders here – this means he manages the riding order (after consulting his clipboard); controls the access of the bikes on and off the track from the pits; operates the rope barrier and offers words of encouragement. He's been involved at Sittingbourne since December 2005 and likes the people and the place, "I'm officially acting as Pits Marshal and ensure everyone gets a fair amount of rides and everyone is kept happy – I think I'm doing a good job at that." Tom lives reasonably locally at Pitsea in Essex and while he's "had a couple of goes on the training school bikes", he's mainly here to generally help out as well as "looking after my son, Rhys." He's keen to stress that he's not a fiercely forceful father living his life vicariously through his son's activities, "I haven't got any ambitions for him, all his ambitions are his own."

The trainer Paul Heller holds the 125cc training bike in position for me to struggle to get onto and I immediately notice that he has a low calming voice and a gentle, reassuring manner when he issues instructions. Stood next to the bike, he has the speedway equivalent of a doctor's bedside manner and shows no reaction to the news that I've never ridden a bike of any sort before now. It wouldn't have been hard to quickly gather given the difficulty and palaver I had to just mount the thing as the constricted tightness of the trousers and the bulk of my safety equipment again hampered my limited coordination and mobility. Though he's given the introductory talk a thousand times before, he nonetheless enthusiastically describes the workings of the bike in comprehensive detail but with great clarity. You just know that no question would be too stupid to ask and that you'll be able to learn the basics of the bike, the track and the essential standard manoeuvres in your own time. His guidance is excellent. Paul suggests a variety of basic but simple things all at once. "Only go as fast as you feel comfortable, you can build up gradually as you gain confidence", though he is particularly insistent about how I approach the corners "throttle off just before you get there, put your leg out firmly and lean the bike so that it glides round and when you reach the apex of the bend you slowly open up the throttle again". He has a soft tone of voice that you imagine would be ideally suited for talking to a group of well-meaning but not especially bright children. He mimes each action, jiggles the bike in illustration of the desired action he describes and succinctly outlines the desired effect. Just as T. S. Eliot so accurately noted, between the idea and the action, or the intention and the deed, "falls the shadow." Years of teaching practice on the training track has taught Paul this too, so he gently but skilfully manages my expectations and his expectations of me as a pupil.

They say that when you train to be a waiter, the key to being able to successfully carry large trays of drinks or food without spillages is never to look at the tray itself but instead focus on a point ahead of you in the distance. I decide that this might be applicable advice in my present situation. Sat on a speedway bike on the narrow confines of the Sittingbourne junior track, the point in the distance comes up on you extremely quickly and is commonly known as a great big wooden safety fence. This looming obstacle is enough to concentrate on in itself without the added complication of my attempt to coordinate the exact degree to which I twist my hand on the throttle. Or, more complicatedly still, even remember to 'throttle off' rather than blithely or absent-mindedly continue when the sight and fear of the suddenly looming fence empties all other thoughts from my mind. My initial difficulties were basic ones – direction, steering in general, throttle control and remembering the simple instructions I'd been given. Most noticeable of all was the sheer speed that I felt I travelled at on the bike. The impression of speed came from the ambient conditions – the feel and noise of the wind as it rushed past – but also the view through my goggles. It's all fine and dandy when the landscape flashes past you in pixel fashion during a video game or even when viewed in comfort through the windscreen of your car, but when tentatively clinging onto a roaring beast of a speedway bike it's a whole different kettle of fish. Initially, I thought that there must have been some equipment mix up and the 125cc machine had been inadvertently switched with its much more highly powered 500cc cousin. The feeling of mortality and vulnerability is inescapably overwhelming. All thought of embarrassment vanished as I clung on for dear life, while I tried to alternate between a seated position or to trap the frame of the bike between my legs, though the frequent arrival of another corner complicated this cunning safety tactic. Somehow I managed to survive five laps of the tiny circuit before I stalled the bike close to Paul. Being the mentor and motivational man that he is, he only had words of praise for me, "you did really well for someone who's never been on a bike before – you can build up at your pace during your next rides, well done!"

I hesitate to meet the eyes of the youngsters, who already patiently wait on their bikes for their next turn on the circuit, or those of their parents and helpers. I think my performance might have tarnished the reputation of the referees further, when I overhear a young lad say, "he's one of the referees" in a tone that mixes pity and contempt (but not awe) and seems to imply that this explains everything. The next young rider is going round the track painfully slowly and has real trouble even negotiating the corners. So I pluck up enough courage to childishly enquire about my comparative performance, "Was

I going as slowly as that when I rode?" I ask Tom, only for him to immediately give a practised reply, "It's not the speed that matters but the confidence." I can't claim to have either but, after a few minutes break, my hands have lost all sign of my *delirium tremens* and safely back on the comfort of terra firma I decide that it wasn't so bad after all. I reckon that I must have approached speeds of around 6 mph and had the additional benefit that I experienced the 125cc machine as though it were really the 500cc variety. There is a brief break for a track grade that involves a white transit van repeatedly circling the track to pack down the shale that my own particular efforts haven't apparently significantly dislodged.

Sat on his bike waiting in line for his next go on the track is 11-year-old Adam Kirby who's come across to Sittingbourne with his mum and dad from Holbeach in Lincolnshire. They've chosen to make the 300 mile round trip, though they have previously practised at his local club, Scunthorpe, but found that, in their experience, the tuition levels are low to non-existent. "They point you at the track, you go out and ride and do it yourself, whereas here, to be honest, they really give you a lot of help." As proud parents they're keen to support Adam in his hobby, "but it's really expensive even though we've done it on the cheap we've spent nigh on a £1000 already. £80 on the kevlars though they should be £300-£500; £50 on the boots; £500 on the bike – it's a 125; £50 on the body armour, plus the trailer for the bike and other odds and sods soon add up." They consult Adam's mum who reminds them of her time and labour, "sewing his name on the back of the kevlars and putting a new zip in the body armour." We would have talked for longer but I'm called back out onto the track and, at least, I've started to put on my helmet, goggles and gloves with greater speed though still without a great deal of dexterity. Nonetheless, the strap still strangles me and the overall effect is that it still makes my head feel like it wants to explode. This time my confidence is sufficient to really open up the throttle much wider – so that I approach speeds that are around 12 mph but feel like something that approaches 100 mph – though this then compounds the difficulty I already have in getting round the corners. It's a situation that's not helped by my ongoing confusion between easing off the throttle and accidentally accelerating just at the point I reach the corner. My clear instructions from Paul are to "put your foot down and straighten your leg" when I reach the bends. This proves an impossible message to communicate to the extremities of my body and, instead, I develop my own unique but bonkers leg trailing style. This involves touching my left foot on the floor before I reach the bend only to immediately lift it again – as though I've just trodden barefoot on volcanic coals – and then trail it uselessly and dangerously behind me as I attempt but fail to raise my bum from the saddle and straighten my right leg on the footrest. Poor throttle control exacerbates my difficulties and a couple of times I scrape the boards of the wooden fence as though I've attempted some slow motion wall of death manoeuvre. The concentration and effort of it all generates huge warmth inside the kevlars and steams my goggles. Paul is full of praise on my return at the improvement I've shown and I hobble back to the pits, still walking as though I'm in deep-sea divers boots albeit with a slightly greater spring in my step and the feeling that I'm no longer so much of an impostor dressed in this manner.

The youngest participant this afternoon is very young and has his own miniature bike that he rides with considerable gusto. In fact, all the other riders appear to ride with greater vim and brio than myself. Some of them even look supremely confident on the bike. They race a good line, execute a smooth slide into and through the bend as well as accelerating comfortably on the straights. They not only have a confidence but also an elegance and grace on their machines, not as polished as the professionals but with notable proficiency. I overhear Paul warn one of the young lads that he should exercise great care on the third and fourth bend, "it's damp there and will stay so 'cause though it's sunny that bit's in the shade so be aware of it, 'cause with the wide line close to the fence that you're riding you could come unstuck." It's humbling stuff to listen to as I've yet to progress to the point where I can control the direction of the bike never mind slide into the corner or start to claim that I have started to 'ride a line' round this small circuit.

Still, the time between my outings on the track gives me the chance to chat to the articulate and friendly teenager, Rhys Naylor, who's very hopeful about a speedway career in the future. He already aims high with his ambitions ("just to make world champion") but realises the need to serve a lengthy and thorough apprenticeship. He's ridden at Reading on a 250cc bike ("the instructor said I was one of the best there 'cause I rode round the boards") and at Arena ("I like that better 'cause I'm the mascot there"). Today he's "back on a 125 to get my confidence back" since he's presently on the slow road to recovery from injury, after he broke his wrist riding at Arena. Not that this has dampened his enthusiasm or blinded him to the good fortune of his situation, "my dad is a very good help to me and the tracks here are good and the instructors are very helpful!" Rhys has already been offered "second halves at Boston" and he's "been offered a place at Arena when I'm 16, though Rye is also a possibility." For now, he's keen to learn and practise as much as possible but can't wait until he's

16 when he "hopes to have a go on a 500cc." Like many of the young men here at Sittingbourne with me, he's proud of and fastidious with his equipment. Close by a couple of other lads chat amiably but authoritatively amongst themselves about various helmet types they hope to persuade their parents to invest in and then compare their goggles to check which of them provide the best protection against the rays of bright sun overhead. Like many of the professional riders, they're knowledgeable about and obsessed with the very latest (most fashionable) piece of equipment in the often-vain hope that it will provide that oh-so-vital fractional advantage.

Feeling increasingly like Jonathan E from *Rollerball*, albeit with clumpy boots instead of roller skates (or a metal ball to chase), I limp back out for my third ride. Paul again issues straightforward sounding instructions in a reassuring soft, low tone. I'm to open the throttle until I reach the corner and then shut off but must bear in mind, "when you shut off the bike straightens up and goes in the direction it's pointed in." This is a subtle reminder that I've a tendency to head directly for the immovable obstruction of the fence rather than glide round the corner. I definitely feel like I've gained in confidence and on the bike the (illusory) sensation of huge speed now rather pleasantly overwhelms me. I still have a definite problem with my co-ordination and an alarming tendency to forget myself and open the throttle rather than throttle off in the corners. After the day finishes, a lady spectator laughingly tells me "we thought you were going to crash through the fence and fly into the tea-room", even though the portacabin with the tea-room inside is 30 or so yards from the track fence! Paul had told me that "when you lose control, self-preservation and natural inclination to panic means you usually shut off", though I tend to find that an accidental and millimetric flick of the wrist has me almost immediately pressed against the fence. Strangely you forget about all the protective clothes you wear and feel incredibly vulnerable – though the body armour constantly reminds you of its presence as it's like having a particularly constricting swimming pool float pressed tightly on your back and chest. In his low friendly voice, Paul remains full of reassurance as well as points to bear in mind. "The difference between that ride and the tentative first outing you had is night and day!" All great teachers challenge you to set higher personal goals but their stewardship also allows you the space to make mistakes and invariably leave you with the impression that you ultimately can do 'nothing wrong' as, no matter what you do, in the grand scheme of things it all wonderfully contributes to your ongoing education.

Almost satisfied with my own improvements, I ponder the vital question of my own nickname. I'm convinced that I've really picked up speed when I ride – in fact, there's already a strong hint of a wild Kim Jansson type recklessness on the track – but I'm sure that those who view from the pits might think otherwise. I decide that the 'Sittingbourne Coelacanth' is pleasantly alliterative and probably captures my true ability and speed on shale. I overhear the parents and helpers talk about the youngest boy, "he just loves being in his kit and forgets about the bike" and a short while later learn a bit of football trivia brought on by Southend's recent historic victory over Manchester United in the cup ("they're the only English team to have a 100% record against Man U").

By the time my fourth ride arrives I've become almost over-confident and Paul's reassuring tone, as he outlines some complex instructions, fools me into the belief that if I nod but only half listen it will enable me to put these instructions into practice. Paul lets me know that he's determined that this will be the ride when I will finally broadside the bike. My 'style' has a number of fundamental flaws not least of which is my weird predilection to trail my inside leg. It's a habit that spells danger should I hit a bump or a rut as I'll have nothing to balance myself with – other than, obviously, my natural 'grace' on the bike – "keep your foot down, that's why it's got a metal shoe on it!" All I have to concentrate on doing is to plant my left foot on the floor as I enter each bend, lean the bike to the left and raise my bum from the seat by straightening my right leg with the application of firm downward pressure on the footrest as I swing out my back wheel. Paul says, "every time you pass me I'm going to stick out my leg to remind you to use yours!" It all sounds so simple. Back on the track I'm simultaneously gripped by a number of fears, all connected with falling off the bike at what appears as 'high' speed to me but a leaden crawl to the small gaggle of spectators. My intentions are all fine and dandy but once I'm back in the saddle again, my whole body refuses to follow my instruction to leave it. Like a particularly complicated dance step or an agonising yoga posture, your mind knows what it wants but your body is damned if it's going to follow. The extra concentration means that I also forget everything that I've learnt so far and my limited throttle control deserts me. Consequently rather than shut off as I approach the first bend, I dramatically accelerate to violently scrape the wooden fence once more in a wall of death fashion and 'badly' crush my throttle hand. At least the pain ensures that I'm in touch with one of the extremities of my body. As promised, Paul repeatedly sticks out his leg in an exaggerated gesture that appears to mark him out as a founder member of the Ministry of Silly Walks. Even this visual reminder doesn't work, it's not that I forget but just that my body refuses to obey and there are so many other things to simultaneously think about. After a few laps of extreme mental effort but absolutely no result when it comes to any vague lean of my bike from the vertical, planting my foot or raising myself from the saddle, I resume my usual pootling round in stop/start fashion without any hint of control. As ever, Paul accents the positive, "you've gone from someone who's never ridden to this – the speed that you've now reached means you have to learn to turn and get that leg solidly down in the corners."

I remain stuck in my own private Idaho on my next ride when my body again resists all instructions from the supposed command centre of the brain. I'm confident enough to try to generate what appears to me as 'huge' speed into the corners in the vain hope that this momentum will somehow force my leg down, bum out of the saddle and straighten my leg sufficiently for my back wheel to vaguely start to hint at a broadside. From many years of spectating speedway races I have a fascination with steel shoes, so you'd think that I would need no second instruction to place mine heavily on the floor in the hope of generating some lovely sparks of my own. No sooner is my foot briefly on the ground than it involuntarily immediately lifts again and trails behind me. If I'm to get any use from this steel shoe, it now seems that it will only be for a bit of 'gardening' of the track before I cruise to the corner. Though even this isn't possible as Paul and Ken push me off each time and, even if they didn't, I'm sure that I'm not yet ready for any extra acceleration into the bend gained through the creation of my own additional trench of shale. Upon my return to his side, Paul identifies some possible future ambitions I might like to countenance if I am to progress, "we've just got to get you to learn to lean the bike, keep your foot down and stand up on the bike – though this does alter the position of your throttle hand so you have to be careful of that!" I joke that if he saw me dance he'd realise how uncoordinated I am. Paul doesn't laugh but suggests that now is the time that I should attempt to ride on the big track, "you'll find it much easier as there's a lot more room on the straights but particularly in the corners, plus you're not turning all the time."

Back over with the grown-ups at the pits, there's a happy and voluble crowd of contented referees. Everyone has had more rides this year because of the reduced number of attendees and under the expert guidance of the calmly helpful George Barclay their general confidence and ability has grown. Barbara Horley has "set her own targets" and advises that I do the same for my one ride on the big track. Chris Gay is ecstatic since he has finally mastered the art of "getting it to slide" which is "a great feeling." He has responded well to his teacher, "George Barclay really wanted me to do that – when I couldn't quite manage it earlier he noticed that my steel shoe was too rough so he went and got his own 'smooth' steel shoe from the car – it's amazing he still travels with it never mind that he wanted to lend it to me so I could succeed!" Chris is transformed, like a refereeing version of Cinderella, since after the steel shoe was fitted, his circumstances dramatically changed. Nearby Christina Turnbull is very impressed with the facilities, and the tuition offered but mostly with the number of young riders on display, "somewhere like here gives you hope for the future – there are huge numbers just champing at the bit with real enthusiasm – they're without fear and they all look really good."

Things have begun to wind down for the day and I get to take the last ride of the afternoon on the 125cc machine that Barbara has ridden here. The difference in track size from the junior to the senior is night and day. After a few extra words of encouragement from George Barclay, I zoom off in search of a corner. These are so far away but wide and gentle in their curve that they appear even roomier than the straights on the junior circuit. Sadly, it seems that I'm even less likely to manage to slide the bike on this track. However, I content myself with the sheer exhilaration of attaining my highest speeds yet on a speedway bike. The sound of the air as it rushes by with a howl as well as the physical sensation of my sheer velocity on the machine thrills me until I hit a bump and nearly lose complete control of the bike. Suddenly, I'm shocked into being a scaredy cat again and all too painfully aware of my own fragility and mortality. It would be just my luck to sustain severe injuries at this late stage in the proceedings! I try for a couple more laps to achieve the merest hint of that elusive slide into the corner without so much as a smidgeon of movement or tilt on the back wheel. It appears that I'm not cut out to even be a bad speedway rider and, quick to admit defeat, I coast to a standstill at George's side, who, being the kindly polite man that he is, tells me, "you did well there – though even getting on a bike I wondered if you'd lost your brains somewhere!"

It has been a unique but strange experience though I need no second invitation to call it a day and retire to the changing room to struggle out of all this kit and head to the tea-room to exaggerate my aptitude and skill levels. Graham Arnold stands on the bank of the pits and looks down onto the crowd of contented referees with proprietorial pride. He says, "I'm just off to undress Barbara – take that anyway you like!" before he calls out to her, "did you enjoy yourself, darling?" Back in the changing rooms, I struggle to unpack myself from my complicated protective kit and clothing, while Chris Gay sits down aglow with contentment at his own achievements and considerable further progress. He doesn't even rush to use the shower that Graham, in the manner of an estate agent, has stopped by to demonstrate and thoroughly sing the praises of "the water's lovely and hot, we leave it on all the time now we've got one."

Showered and changed, the refs gather for tea and sandwiches in the Sittingbourne clubhouse as well as to pick over the events of the day and gossip about speedway in general. They laugh at the recollection of the fact that all day Chris Gay failed to adhere to the sight of the red flag and, despite this warning, invariably proceeded to hone his technique with that crucial extra lap of practice. Apart from fun at everyone else's expense, if fishermen talk about great catches they have known or the one that got away then referees quickly start to compare notes on riders and nightmare meetings. Jim Lawrence holds court in the manner of King Lear's end-of-play chat to Cordelia when he discusses 'who's in and who's out' in the speedway world. All the refs put forward their own particular 2006 story of disaster, intrigue, serendipity or confrontation and there's a rich cast of riders, mechanics, start marshals and promoters that feature. Some come across well and others definitely don't. Christina relates a funny story about her trip with the "master of disaster" Chris Durno and everyone has been exposed to the underbelly of the speedway beast away from the practised pleasantries of the more sanitised version that is presented as verisimilitude to the public gaze on the television or in the pages of the trade press. I will preserve confidentiality but, to my mind, Jim trumped other repeatable stories with chat about his "meeting from Hell" at Mildenhall that featured a "nightmare" of "43 races, two reserve races, 18 re-runs in six and a half hours." Later, Graham Arnold joins in with a spirited defence of what the ideals and philosophy of the Conference League should really be about – the development of youngsters rather than the ambitious pursuit of league success. "Just get the kids involved – Tim Stone is a proper Conference League promoter, just like Buxton and Sittingbourne, rather than someone who runs a PL team in the CL like some clubs do. We've got hundreds of youngsters who all need somewhere to ride and somewhere to learn – they can't get a 125 to do what they want on a big track so we find other ways. And if the kids come the parents come with them." There's much nodding among the referees as they tuck into their sandwiches.

I'm just thankful to have survived the day and to have learnt the valuable but enjoyable lesson that the bravery and skill required to ride a speedway bike marks out the riders as something special. Or mad. It might well be that the bikes appear prehistoric in design and extremely basic in their functions but they are fit for the purpose of thrills and excitement in the hands of someone truly skilled. I now really appreciate how much effort and how many years of practice it must take to be able to perform in any of the speedway leagues, but especially at the highest level. I struggled with only the bike, balance, fear, direction and myself on the track. The very idea that you would ride the machine to its limit, fling yourself and the bike around every track with a mixture of determination and abandon as well as race three other equally possessed and competitive individuals, really does genuinely beggar belief!

The referees start getting ready to leave but Graham Arnold asks them to hang on a few more minutes for the arrival of George Barclay, "he's always the last to leave the track as he just loves teaching, particularly with the kids, we have to drag him away!" As if on cue, a smiling George B arrives to say "thank you to everybody for making it so enjoyable – getting on a bike takes some doing and I'm really surprised to find that the refs are as mad as the riders!" I'm then surprised that he has an Olympic-like presentational medal to hand out to everyone who took part. On one side of the medal it has a crest that says "Sittingbourne Speedway" and on the other it has been engraved with the legend, "SPEEDWAY RIDER FOR A DAY". I think that a day is just about enough for me.

19th November Sittingbourne – Referees' Practice Day

December 2006

"It wasn't an easy decision and it took me a long time to come to this conclusion. I sat down with the whole family and talked about it, looking at every possibility and angle... I didn't want to get into a situation where I carried on riding and slipped from being a heat leader to a second string. Then I'd be remembered as a second string covered in muck!... if I had stayed where I was [Sheffield], I wouldn't have done it, so I owe a lot to Ian Thomas in a way, I owe a lot to a lot of people, the support I had up there, the sponsorship, the friends I made... it's all been fantastic. The first two or three years at Workington, you couldn't wait to go up there. As soon as you got home on the Saturday night, you wanted to go back up there again, the place was buzzing. You'd go to the Isle of Wight and there'd be coachloads of supporters, I'd go to Prague and there'd be coachloads again, it was something else I was very fortunate to have what a lot of riders will never get in a lifetime. I really appreciate the times I have had. The only thing I'd change is I wish I'd taken it more seriously when I was younger."
Carl Stonehewer announces his retirement

"[We have] made no input into plans by the Wimbledon directors to run speedway at Central Park... along with many Wimbledon supporters, the ISTWS believes the world famous Dons name and race colours should lie dormant until such time as the old club may be revived. The ISTWS will never give up hope of Wimbledon Dons racing again. We waited 11 years after the 1991 closure. I'm sure that we can wait another 11 years for the Wimbledon Dons to return, although we would all prefer it was much sooner."
Nick Taylor (Independent Supporters Trust of Wimbledon Speedway)

"Don't worry I hear enough rumours to sink a ship, but I am not going to be drawn on any of them."
Alun Rossiter

"What has happened is part and parcel of trying to bring referees on. It's not as though I have been pushed to one side as I have got a significant number of important fixtures in 2007 and I'm very happy with it."
Tony Steele remains philosophical after it's announced he won't officiate at any 2007 SGP event

"I've heard what some people have been saying, and there's no truth at all in suggestions that I'm pulling out. They may have heard that I have received some offers. I'm pretty laid back about it really. I've no problem with carrying on at West Row next season. But it wouldn't be truthful if I said I'd turn down a good offer."
Mick Horton dismisses idle chatter about his ownership intentions with Mildenhall

"When you are racing a rider who is more experienced than you, you've got to remember that they are very crafty, and they can do things that you're not aware of that can affect you."
A younger Jason Crump quoted by Brian Burford

"Karol [Zabik] declared his future intent to join the Pirates at some stage, but it won't be in 2007, or at least certainly at the start. We accept Karol's position and would like to go on record to acknowledge the professional manner in which he conducted his dealings."

Matt Ford

"The whole Zabik thing has left a very bitter taste in my mouth, and I am not going to let this just slip by. I will be issuing Mr. Zabik with a lovely Christmas present in the form of a solicitor's letter informing him that we intend to proceed with court action against him. Once that is done, Matt Ford can keep him. I cannot go into details as this is now going to go legal. This is not something I wanted to do, but Mr. Zabik's comments have left me with no choice."
Colin Horton

"Even my own riders at Peterborough have been approached by other clubs, do I care, not one bit, if a rider wants to ride for my club then he will, if he wants to go elsewhere then he will, no matter what, it's all part of speedway."
Colin Horton

"I think that [riders] do race too much, especially now with the Grand Prix if you do them. I think it's virtually impossible to do three leagues."
Ryan Sullivan

"It's been a slow process, you can't open a stadium in year one and do things like this straight away, you just can't do it. But we're now getting to where we want to be and by this time next winter, we should have done everything. I read in Jeff Scott's book *Showered in Shale* that Tim Stone of Newport doesn't count us as a club who own their own stadium because we're 'not a stadium but a track in a field'. But Tim's never, ever been here and so if you're reading this, please come and pay us a visit because by next season, it will definitely be a stadium."
Rob Godfrey on what has been achieved so quickly at Scunthorpe

"I wondered how we would fit in and whether the speedway club could find the time for us and help to make it exciting for the kids. But right from the start Buster really has taken us under his wing, and there's been Jonathan and Cheryl and Nathan as well. They have all been brilliant. Buster and Jonathan, I know, really do want this to work, it's been so amazing."
Carol Robertson reviews progress at the innovative King's Lynn Speedway Study Centre

."I don't think that we've made as much progress as I'd hoped. Sometimes I just get worried about how long it takes to do certain things, but we've certainly made some progress... I think it would have been nice to have had some more money coming into the sport. We have increasing numbers watching Elite League speedway on *Sky* Television, and I question whether we've actually used those viewing figures to our best ability.... We are growing old together aren't we, and that concerns me... I'm not saying that the people on the management committee aren't enthusiastic, they all are, but maybe our elastic bands aren't as strong as they used to be!... I can tell you it's the overall consensus of British Speedway to develop British youth. What we don't agree on is the mechanics of how we do it."
New Year message from Peter Toogood, Chairman of the BSPA

A Very Different Set Up for *Bonanza X*
8th December

Despite predictions to the contrary, 2006 will see the *Brighton Bonanza* staged for the tenth time. This year the set up of the event will be made all the easier as the organisers have learnt the lessons from last year's experience and they won't have to cope with the logistical difficulty of staging the *Bonanza* in between concerts, like last year when the concerts by a-ha and the Stereophonics sandwiched either side of the speedway. Apparently the type of bands that can draw a large audience to the Brighton Centre around Christmas only tour and book this venue on an alternate year basis, when they can guarantee that they have a much better chance to fill the place with committed fans. For aficionados of indoor speedway of the shale variety in Britain, Brighton represents the key fixture of the close season when fans can get another fix of their favourite sport during the long winter months of enforced abstinence.

Though in recent years the gap between the end of the season and the start of the next has shortened dramatically, only four months between November 1st and February 28th, the meeting still represents a key event on the speedway social calendar. However, if judged from the coverage given in this week's edition of the *Speedway Star*, you'd be hard pressed to guess the significance and canonical status of the event. Notoriously, the winter months represent the opportunity for more in-depth coverage of the speedway 'rider bites dog' style stories, gossip and team formation news, as well as club-by-club reviews of the previous season. So you would have thought that the occasion of the tenth anniversary of the event would represent an opportunity to review years gone by. And to feature some of the diverse range of riders that make up the field who compete in the afternoon Pairs Trophy and then follow that up with the often more keenly contested individual meeting in the evening, the *Bonanza* Championship. Instead, there's a headline on the fact that Ryan Fisher will compete in the fixture in an attempt to resurrect his chequered Elite League career after his initial foray to establish himself in this country was tarnished by his *enfant terrible* reputation among promoters that he easily gained through some high jinks and some colourful but questionable 'madcap' off-track behaviour. Talk in the *Star* of "one notorious incident" in 2004 at the disco following the Stuart Robson testimonial meeting at Coventry that saw him "escorted off the premises" after "things got out of hand", simultaneously whets my curiosity but isn't the kind of thing that he'd really welcome being reprised for prospective future employers in the trade press. This level of notoriety intrigues, particularly given speedway's propensity to take a vow of *omerta* and 'keep things in the family' when it comes to salacious gossip, unsavoury incidents and questionable behaviour. All this previous history, along with some leg injuries ("breaking both legs in the last two years back in the States") has reduced his UK speedway appearances and a run out at the *Bonanza* has often been the ideal shop window through which riders signal their availability for the season ahead. Any promoter or fan reading the article will have revisited these indiscretions in general terms but equally will have been left in no doubt about his keenness to make amends in the future. The article also reprised the fact that the Buffaloes and Rhino teams would also compete at the event to determine the final whereabouts of the Academy League championship. These Under-15 riders appeared for the first time during the 2005 event and now appear to have become a regular feature of the *Bonanza*. However, apart from coverage of these somewhat tangential angles there's no comment from the *Bonanza* promoters Jon Cook or Martin Dugard and no in-depth discussions of the assembled field of riders, which seems peculiar given that this is the only live speedway event since the season ended. Even the fact that Edward Kennett will defend his individual crown (and attempt to win it for the third year in succession), or even an appearance by Lewis Bridger (the widely commended possible British World Champion of the future) generates no column inches. This contrasts massively with the three whole pages of coverage that the *Speedway Star* dedicated the week before to the release of a DVD boxed set that covered the BSI 2006 GP series, complete with bonus CDs of the World Cup thrown in; despite the fact that the footage featured had mostly been seen before and the behind-the-scenes interviews promised for future years were notable by their absence.[1]

---

[1] But then, it's safe to say that almost anything to do with the GP has recently been granted huge editorial coverage in the magazine during the past few years. When BSI manage to stage championship rounds in European stadiums that require them to construct a "one-off track" (like they do every year at the *Bonanza* albeit with a better racing surface and without the almost obligatory bad ruts) in a stadium not intended for staging speedway, this is treated in breathlessly celebratory prose as though it's an engineering feat equivalent to the construction of the Great Pyramid. The suspense over the announcement of the shadowy decision-making processes that determine who will be the meeting reserves selected by John Postlethwaite and his team of independent advisors for each GP, inevitably garners disproportionate acres of coverage as though this is somehow a newsworthy event roughly on a par with the Resurrection.

Inside the almost completely bare expanse of the Brighton Centre auditorium, Martin Dugard shrugs off the lack of attention in the magazine, "maybe Jon has offended them or someint?" Martin is the last to arrive mid-morning to join our small but perfectly formed team – that also comprises Jon Cook, Martin, Edward Kennett and myself – for this stage of the construction and set up of the track. It still promises to be a long day ahead, although all involved in its construction view the fact that no overnight work is required to set the thing up as a huge mercy. I volunteered quite some time ago to repeat my experience of the previous year that I covered at length in my book *Showered in Shale*. By all accounts that was "an exceptional year", which is a polite way to allude to the unexpected trauma that was the protracted and stressful post-meeting clear up that took just over seven hours and continued until 3 a.m. in the morning (27 hours after our initial arrival in the auditorium).

Our basic problem in 2005 was caused by the plastic sheets that were laid down to protect the expensive and nearly pristine surface of the auditorium floor from the deleterious effects of the 120 tons of shale required to construct this indoor speedway track. Close study only 12 months later illustrates that other users of the Brighton Centre have long since abandoned any pretence at protection of this surface. It has been scored throughout with grooves, indentations and marks of differing length and severity. Enough colours of paint or other indelible material has been spilt across its area to indicate that surely Rolf Harris himself must have painted a large number of his spontaneously constructed artworks here during 2006. Though the lack of other bookings has presented us with the luxury to be able to construct and fit out the auditorium at our own leisurely pace over Friday and Saturday, the size of our team looks pitiful in comparison to the size of the place, which appears to have grown considerably since I was here last year. Given that the auditorium is almost completely empty, I now realise that when I turned up last year the fact that the centre green had been constructed, the white line fully laid, the sheets put down and that the shape of the track marked on its surface, indicated that a huge amount of laborious work had already taken place prior to my arrival. The complete lack of anything other than the basic materials from which we'll construct the track definitely intimidates when you're confronted by the almost total emptiness of this vast space.

Even though I'd helped out until the bitter end of this event last year, I still really have no idea what to expect in terms of what this day's set-up work might involve, the time it would take, the number of helpers there would be or even what I should wear. I know that it is likely to be potentially dirty, dusty work and with the giant doors of the auditorium open, it will most likely be, at best, a cool environment to work in (last year it was absolutely freezing, though that was at night). The question of 'what to wear' is a practical consideration rather than a fashionable one. In the end I elect to take many layers – which I take on and off throughout the day as my temperature oscillates from the wide extremes of cold to completely overheated. Everyone else has dressed in the manner that shows what they deem to be appropriate but reveals that they are much more au fait with this type of work and work environment than I am. They all wear considerably less layers than I do and if they ever feel cold they completely fail to let this register in any visible way that I could spot or appreciate. Edward wears a T-shirt and dark trousers that had already seen good service and some paint in the past. Martin dresses similarly without any concession to anything other than practicality and later very briefly – to my great joy – sports his vital number one *Bonanza* accessory, namely his trademark heavily reinforced black kneepads (he later says to Edward in a tone that mixes boastfulness and conspiratorialness, "you'll regret that you don't have some of these"). Jon is dressed the most nattily of our group in a blue tracksuit, without the slightest hint of shell suit, that is redolent of the lightweight modern material favoured by athletes. The upper part of the garment had a prominent badge cum logo that includes the word "Adur" that I clean forget to read properly. I assume that his outfit came from his continuing football activities as I know that while he dislikes the ethos of modern football and the cosseted, selfish and unreal attitudes of its superstar players he nonetheless still plays very regularly at local club level. Though tall, this probably partly explains his trim athleticism that he studiously masks with his trademark casual, almost languid manner and publicly preternaturally calm exterior. I've seen Martin throw a punch on a speedway track so I know that he can look after himself, and this is also my impression of both Edward and Jon; not that I'm expecting that there will be any need to call upon these skills during the set up. I wear so many layers of clothes in the expectation of cold indoor temperatures that I have the look and gait of a yeti, albeit without its customary mobility. Most vitally of all, I have brought the protective course gloves I bought last year to protect my delicate office-boy's hands. Very conspicuously, none of the others have brought any gloves to wear during the construction.

Much of the equipment that we'll need to use today is either already stacked inside the centre on pallets or outside on the loading bay. Much of it has been borrowed from Arlington or has been stored there since last year ready for the next *Bonanza*. There's a couple of pallets of bright blue-and-yellow painted wooden boards that form the safety fence at Eastbourne speedway during the season along with a couple of pallets of stanchions arranged in the Chinese puzzle fashion that so fascinated (and defeated) me last year. Placed right in the centre of the empty hall, there's another large pallet stacked with randomly sized lengths of wood from which the inner oval of the track is constructed. Some of these are painted white but shale splattered and others are cut in intricate fashion to snugly fit when placed together (though a casual glance indicates that pairing these up will be complicated). In addition there's a couple of pallets of cardboard sheets that the shale will be laid on this year and, most impressively, a pallet of some small but well crafted white boards that will form the curved bend sections of the inner oval of the track. These are made of white-painted wood attached to a larger square of cardboard and have been made to exacting standards as well as stacked and stored incredibly neatly, though they show signs of wear since they're caked in dried shale. Altogether it looks a hell of a lot for four people to unload and put together in the course of one day. It will have to be completed by the time we leave – whenever that will be – as the next morning the first lorry load of shale will arrive from the local quarry of loyal Eagles' sponsors, Robins of Herstmonceux. They employ Edward Kennett and will provide the bulk of the people who import the shale, lay and flatten it for the meeting before they then remove it all again once the racing has been completed. I look forward to seeing them all once more but apart from Edward, they're presently notable by their absence. Outside in the loading bay area is an impressive range of motorised equipment that will be used to lift, dig and transport all the various materials and equipment that the *Bonanza* will require. They have been organised on Noah's Ark lines as there appears to be two of everything – dumper trucks, forklifts, diggers – except there is only one small, military-looking four-wheeled vehicle that, to my eyes, has Martin Dugard written all over it. I confidently expect that he will drive it much more than anyone else since it looks remarkably like the one he drives with some abandon at huge speed round the environs of Arlington every week during the season. When I point this out, "He's never happier than when he's dashing about on that, is he?" Jon shrugs phlegmatically, "Or riding! He only decided last night he was going to again this weekend!"

As an office boy with soft hands, no practical skills to speak of and limited common sense, I'm impressed at the studied nonchalance with which everyone else approaches the task that lies ahead. Jon, Martin and Edward all clearly know each other very well and are comfortable enough in each other's company to continuously josh all day about the alleged deficiencies in the others – whether of character, generosity, fastidiousness, dedication or craftsmanship. They're all from a speedway background so have the immediate advantage of mechanical insight, skill, aptitude and confidence. Despite all this ability throughout the day they kindly don't comment on the speed or accuracy of my work. As a team it's as though the "Three Amigos" have linked up with the mystery character from "Where's Wally?" I quickly decide that I will follow instructions, try to avoid all tasks that require dexterity and volunteer for the grunt work at every opportunity. There is no danger that I will run out of these basic manual tasks, though our small numbers and the fact that many tasks require the combination of knowledge, patience or skill, means that sometimes I have to wait for the others to have completed their more complicated work before I can assist further.

The fact that Martin and Jon have now done this for nine years previously means that they're confident about what needs doing with this level of manpower in the time available, although during the day they both admit that they've again started to suffer from the sleepless nights of worried anticipation that traditionally disrupts their nocturnal patterns prior to the event. At least this year they'll not have to endure the additional stress of the sleep deprivation brought on by the overnight work to fit out the venue. Edward is also very quick and capable, albeit quietly so, as he's helped out with the construction of the *Bonanza* since he was much younger as Martin notes, "one year we did it when Edward was 12 years old with just Chris Geer and us." All day decisions are made collectively after brief discussion and jovial disagreement, though with so many interdependent jobs to be done, everyone is often tempted to switch from one half-done task to another half-completed one. They all reserve the right to take the mickey out of each other for blithely switching from task to task as though they're not guilty of this practice themselves. Before Martin arrived we unloaded some of the cardboard sheets and placed them randomly on the floor – in the rough vicinity of what will form the third bend when the track is built – to allow them to breathe like fine wine and for the kinks in the cardboard to get the chance to straighten out. There are 320 sheets of cardboard and if they're all kinked from the method of their storage on top of each other, then the racing surface will be of the markedly uneven variety favoured by the BSI for the one-off GPs for the duration of the racing. Once

Martin arrives we abandon this barely started task and instead do other chores in the revised order of importance that we've just agreed among ourselves (well, I listened). Namely to lay out the white boards that will form the oval shape of the track before we then place in position on the floor the substantial wooden boards to which we'll affix the stanchions and the safety fence. It all sounds so easy when Martin says, "we'll get the white line in, put boards down and put up the safety fence." There is no additional manpower expected to arrive, apart from a visit by someone else from Robins with a lorry load of "number one", though I do overhear Martin mention that "Deano's called in sick today 'cause he knew there'd be a chance he might be called upon to do some work for once!"

Martin notes with some insouciance to Jon, "There's no blueprint – there was one but I think it got lost last year – so it's lucky that it's all in me head, though if I die you're freaked!" Last year I noticed that the apprenticeship of Martin's years at Arlington working with and the close observation of his artisan father, Bob Dugard, along with his many years' experience at the *Bonanza* had given him a remarkable range of the practical skills you really definitely require to have mastered in order to build a speedway track and successfully use all the associated equipment cum furniture. He does these various tasks with confidence and skill as well as relentless energy, so it's no surprise when he volunteers that he will also construct the starting gate and also be responsible for the installation of their electrics. "I've prepared it already before we came", he says as he nods to yet another impressive pile of stunningly heavy metal boxes that he casually lifted with some ease when he unloaded them quickly from his Dugard company van. Martin's confidence isn't misplaced and clearly he's stored an impressive amount of information in his head that he is able to recall instantly and gnomically as it's required. In the first instance he automatically knows the exact dimensions of the white boards that will form the length of the straight "they should be about 13 metres and 30 centimetres long on the home straight though the back straight is half a metre narrower as it gives more room going into the first bend." Once we've collectively laid out these white wooden planks, Martin assumes control of the tape measure but directs and supervises Jon to ensure that they mark out the exact arc of the bends, "you have to go 7 metres 35 to the centre and hold it there while I mark it out with my red crayon. Where the freak's me red crayon? I get precious about me red crayon, if it's gone we'll just have to go to the kids' shop and get another one." With Jon instructed not to move an inch from a point that's exactly 7.35 metres in from the boards – in case it gets "freaked up" – Martin adroitly draws a perfect arc with the red crayon as he scrabbles on hands and knees with the end of the tape measure in his hand. With the arc finally marked to his satisfaction (after a brief error that he blames on Jon moving), they then transfer to the other end of the auditorium to mark out the other bend. These are the lines that we'll then follow to exactly lay out the smaller white boards with the cardboard square attached ("there should be 32 of those mini-boards at each end unless we've gone completely wrong") before they're then all bolted together once they're in place. As soon as this oval shape has been created we can start to set out the wooden boards that will have stanchions attached to hold the safety fence, while Martin puts in place the concrete bases upon which he will erect the metal poles that forms the starting gate and holds its various mechanisms. Martin remains cheery throughout, "you might have noticed that it's all trial and error" he notes too modestly. Later he also, accurately it transpires, claims, "it's much easier working in a small group as we can really just get on without interruption." This is just as well, since the four of us is all that there is, apart from when members of the Brighton Centre staff or management wander over to confer in jovial fashion with Martin and/or Jon. Inevitably there's a ton of paperwork to be completed to do with the insurance and hire of the Brighton Centre but after so many years here now, they appear to know everyone and manage any administration or anxiety with a joke, a smile, a few well-chosen words and it's a "no problem mate" attitude.

Jon is pretty amazed that he's finally found himself at work on the white lines after nine other years when he's managed to evade this essential task, though his comment, "it's the first time in 10 years I've done the white line" has Martin quickly retort with heavy irony, "what Jon does know about woodwork isn't worth knowing!" Later in the afternoon, we're joined by Gary Robins when he delivers "some Type One from Pyecombe." This turns out not to be shale but the earthy material that they will use to construct a temporary ramp for the dumper truck to gain easy access to the auditorium from the lower level of the road outside the Centre. My overly curious questions about this are answered but greeted with some amusement, "Why do you ask? Are you working for Graham Drury or someint?" Gary knows everyone already and instantly adopts the same casual matter-of-fact attitude of bonhomie that characterises our group.

I'm mostly fully occupied – I place the white line boards in position, hump wooden boards or put the stanchions in their required positions for Edward to fix later with the power screwdriver. Throughout the day, Jon's mobile phone chimes repeatedly as though he also moonlights in a Brighton based call centre. He's brief and to the point with his calls and many of his conversational tropes recur with great regularity, "no problem, mate", "it's no bother, mate" and his main mantra for quite some time during the first few hours of the job, "I'm doing the white line at the moment" or its variant, "as it happens, I'm doing the white line at the moment and talking speedway with Jeff Scott." Elsewhere Edward, whose phone only rings very intermittently, often says, "Yeah, yeah, I'm working on the white line at the moment, yeah, 's goin' alright, yeah." I half feel that I should get my mobile out and talk about this notorious white line just to join in the fun. Jon has to field many calls about the *Bonanza* ("yeah, I'm at the Centre all weekend") and handles calls from various riders including one from Bobby Schwartz. "The riders are dropping out like flies mate, well, Bobby Schwartz is 'cause his mother is really ill but being the bloke that he is he keeps ringing and worrying about letting us down and saying he'll come." Later when he calls again I overhear Jon speak with him really sympathetically, "it's only a speedway meeting mate, you're missing nothing, come in the spring and spend a few more days, hang out in the pits and with the lads, visit old friends and maybe take in a meeting or two at a leisurely pace without the worry of your mother hanging over you which you know is much more important. Nah, really, you'll letting no one down, we'll miss you being here but everyone understands!"

Until lunch I worked mostly with Edward who gets on with things quietly, methodically and efficiently. He clearly works best in his own zone of comparative silence – though both he and Martin protest when Jon repeatedly turns off the radio when the inane chatter of the local station drives him periodically mad. When we're all back together within earshot, Edward casually plays down the chance that he might achieve a hat trick of victories, "let's hope my second bike holds up on Sunday as I'm carrying a bit of weight." This is said as he pats his non-existent paunch for extra effect. They all have quite a laugh together at the notion rumoured on the internet forums that there has been a big falling out with Cookie over the recent news of Edward's move to ride for Poole in 2007. "Did you see on the forums that they offered you £200 a point and I supposedly told you to 'freak off to Poole' when you asked me to match it – these people just have no idea of what went on or that we're friends really!" Jon's offer to go and get everyone a baked potato for lunch has Martin and Edward immediately joke that he's always looks for any excuse he can find not to do his fair share of the work. On his return, Jon notes, "people wouldn't believe that I was still buying you lunch, specially after you've decided to go to Poole but I'll just say to the Eastbourne fans, 'he didn't know what I'd done to it!'" We take a brief break for lunch just around the time the white line is almost completely laid out after about three and half hours of steady work. The chance to sit on the empty seats of the grandstand is a welcome one and I rest my already aching feet.

After the lunch break I work on my own to put out the stanchions and everyone else sets about erecting the first few boards of the safety fence as a team effort. After all the stanchions are out, I work with Jon to put out all the blue/yellow coloured boards that make up the safety fence though he interrupts this to chasten Edward and Martin who've switched to lay out cardboard sheets rather than continue with their work on the fence. "Oi, Jeff just said something good which is 'why are you putting out the freaking sheets?' which is unskilled work that he can do as he's not good at the skilled things when you should be doing the skilled things you're good at that he can't even do?" After some further affectionately critical banter and general incredulity, we all get back to our designated shared tasks and the fact we both need to work together to carry each heavy (to my mind) board gives Jon and me a good chance to chat. He is curious to learn about the success or otherwise of my book, ("Are you pleased you did it?" "Would you do it again?") along with my impressions of the various tracks and people ("Are all the promoters alike or are they completely different?") encountered on my travels as well as what I really got out of doing it ("So, overall, you'd say that you've made some good friends and that it was a life-changing experience!"). We chat briefly about some of the characters in the sport that he knows well from track shop owners, to promoters, referees, and press or publicity people. We share similar dislikes of some people involved in the sport and have a good degree of unanimity on others. We both like Ian Thomas for example, and Jon doesn't disagree with my incredulity or contradict opinion that "John Postlethwaite has voluntarily switched his race night to a Friday, as it's completely against his own commercial interests since he'll experience the same problems with the lack of star riders on that night that everyone else has had to suffer from since the advent of this version of the GPs". It's a fun busman's holiday conversation for me since, although we're in no sense anything like equals, I do still feel that Jon is genuinely curious and keen to learn my impressions, even if sometimes they're critical and don't always accord with his own. He's not surprised that almost universally, with a few notable exceptions he's keen to learn more about, that I've been welcomed and mostly offered great help on my travels or when I researched my book. Though he offers no comment when I say, "many promoters give off a raffish air and can remind you of a rat with a gold tooth." He's remarkably candid about the dramatic fall in attendances at speedway throughout Britain during 2006. This was obviously a prime topic of discussion at the recent BSPA AGM, "we've lost 20% across the sport which is a massive hit!" These sorts of figures are always going to be anecdotal given that the sport very singularly doesn't officially publish actual *bona fide* spectator numbers anywhere. But if you accept the veracity of these claims, it's definitely a worrying development that needs both urgent (believable) explanation and strategic remedy. Not that Jon actually goes into specifics when I quiz him about this decline, but he does reel off some well-rehearsed explanations for the possible reasons behind claims of this apparently dramatic fall through the turnstiles. "The cold March and April we had which stopped people coming at the start – and they never really came back – and then we had the [football] World Cup which kept everyone away in June. It was going to be hard for anyone to recover after that. That said, my experience since being a promoter is that speedway always has a good year in odd-numbered years, as there's not things like the World Cup, Euros or the Olympics to compete against for people's attention. Though it's not just that, but that's a factor but whatever it is, odd years are always best. So hopefully next year, which is an odd numbered year, things will be much better."

The decline in attendances across speedway is also reflected in the reduced numbers of advance bookings that the *Bonanza* has taken for the 2006 version of the event. This is far from a laughing matter and Jon matter-of-factly notes, "We've got to take a good hard look at whether this is the last ever one, as there comes a point where you have to question the effort you have to put in compared to what you get out of it. At the moment we have lower crowds and increased costs – 'cause this year we hired double the equipment to avoid what happened with the clearing up which you saw when you were here last year, which we wouldn't have done if we'd known that the Centre would have no bookings so we could have a few days to work on it rather than overnight as usual. There's a number of other factors as well one of which is that the riders earn too much so the quality of the field falls from what it was and that the crowd got used to, so many of them [the riders] can't be bothered or it's not worth it to them to ride and interrupt their break. Then there's the late finish to the season nowadays – the last two years we've been going right 'til the end of October whereas some other years we've finished in September. So really there's not a big enough gap between the season ending and this to get everyone excited enough to come down in big numbers. And it's not been helped by the only live speedway event of the winter that you can guarantee will be on (apart from Telford which is different anyway 'cause it's on ice) hasn't been properly covered by the *Star*, particularly when you think how much we spent on the advert in there. It's funny, when we used to get it for free they gave us loads of coverage but since we've been paying they just don't want to know. When you add all these things up, we're going to have to take a look at things again in the future to decide what we want to do!" Throughout our conversation, we work hard and well together as a pair. Our only interruption is when all the strain of bending and lifting the safety boards has fatal fashion consequences for me when I irreparably rip the crotch of my favourite waterproof trousers. Edward is the only one to offer any comment when he finds the gaping tear of some amusement.

By now we've finished placing the boards in position, so Jon switches with Martin to assist Edward and I now join Martin in the large space in the middle of the auditorium that will eventually become the centre green. I join his search through the large pile of different sized pieces of wood that should easily form the braces that will hold the oval shaped inside white line in position for the arrival of the track itself tomorrow. This is vital work as without this bracing the track won't be adequately anchored and will slip and slide about in willy-nilly fashion during the racing. This in turn will ripple the shale surface and cause it to rut and break up. Helpfully many of these pieces of wood are numbered, lettered and marked. Less helpfully, there is no apparent coherent plan behind these markings or, if there was, they've become confused and are now all from different years that the event has run in the Brighton Centre. Consequently, our quest is thankless and is like looking for missing pieces in a jigsaw puzzle that is short of a few vital bits and has been mixed with a couple of other incomplete but similar looking puzzles. Nonetheless, Martin is supremely methodical and patient in his search. This mostly involves us both picking up bits of wood to study them for distinguishing marks or an attempt to try to slot them together using the metal brackets that some of them helpfully have for this purpose. Just like the faulty numbering system, there appears to be little rhyme or logic behind the random metal brackets that many pieces have already had attached. My role is to follow Martin in the manner of a faithful spaniel to dutifully echo his own perceptive but unanswerable questions back to him. I can't see that this is really that helpful or useful on my part but he has the good grace to pretend otherwise and remain studiously calm throughout. A practical man to the last, Martin pieces together as much of the structure as he recognisably can before he then elects to do something dramatic. In this case, to saw some of the large pile of surplus bits up and use them to form a bridge to replace the missing pieces in the structure or to firmly anchor and brace the completed sections together. Like the red crayon earlier, he develops quite an obsession with the need for screws but he soon establishes that he'll have to buy these before he returns here tomorrow. Much as he pretends that the practical, conceptual and organisational skills that he has and effortlessly exhibits are nothing out of the ordinary, the fierce pride with which he approached his riding career (and premature retirement) remains and still burns strongly much as he tries to suppress its public manifestations. He delights to prove his father wrong and recalls that before they ever staged the first indoor event, he spoke to Bob who confidently predicted impending doom ("you'll blow your brains out doing that") and wanted no part of the offer to join it. This is a conversation that Martin now brings up every year, "oh, I'm just off out to that thing again where I'll blow my brains out!"

We all entered the quiet and absorbed mental zone that our own particular repetitive tasks encouraged and necessitated. Martin continued to work painstakingly bracing the track on his own and the rest of us worked as a trio. Edward secured each stanchion with four screws that, adhering to modern standards of construction, he used the power drill to screw in. With a wooden safety board leant against each stanchion, Jon then drilled through the two holes (one at the top and one at the bottom of each secured stanchion upright) and the wooden painted safety board. I then re-drilled each hole again from my side of the board before I passed a screw (of varying lengths) back through the board stanchion pole. This screw often took some manoeuvring to get into the exact position for Jon to be able to tighten it firmly in place with a wing nut. This task was then repeated endlessly and ad nauseam for the entire circumference of the track. Edward worked at quite a pace that soon left Jon and I to fumble in his wake. We established a good understanding, pace and rhythm. While some screws or awkwardly placed boards presented difficulties none of them were insurmountable, only a little bit laborious to manage sometimes. Apart from the ringing of his mobile and the need to collect a large batch of complimentary tickets for the meeting on Sunday from the box office, we worked smoothly and efficiently. I'd like to say that the repetitive nature of the task allowed me to enter some Zen-like mental zone during the few hours it took to complete the whole process. This sadly wasn't the case but I gained proficiency with the power drill that I almost marvelled at (indeed, my parents would be gobsmacked that no serious damage to myself, the equipment or boards occurred during my brief reign of handymanship) and with Jon encouragingly patient throughout we were able to systematically work well as a team. I would like to claim that I lost track of the time but the endless inane chatter of the radio DJs, the brief national news headlines and the frequent updates on the local traffic news – of which, really, there was nothing of consequence other than the odd bit of heavy traffic on Brighton seafront or news of the imminent opening of a local swing bridge that was predicted to cause delays but hadn't actually done so yet – kept us all completely in touch with the slow passage of time. With only five boards left to complete, Jon said, "This is getting really boring now," which I correctly took to be the signal that we'd all be able to go home shortly when this particular task was completed. A few minutes later he was also kind enough to add, "I hope that you'll be joining us down Pit Lane on Sunday if you manage to get away from selling your books." Unlike last year when I was asked to vacate the area, this invitation makes me feel completely part of the team.

As we all immediately hurried to leave the building in the manner of schoolchildren about to be released from lessons on the last day of term before the long summer holidays, a quick glance at the auditorium confirmed just how much the four of us had achieved today in the space of eight hours. When we arrived this was all a huge bare expanse that looked nothing remotely like being transformed into something appropriate to stage Britain's premier winter indoor speedway meeting on shale. Lots of work still remained to be done the next day to lay the track and to get things into a presentable and usable state for riders and the public.[2] But, undeniably, the bare bones were now in place and it already had the look if not quite the appearance (as it lacked the essential ingredient – the shale surface of the track) of a facility that strongly resembled a speedway circuit.

I walk home with a personal sense of pride in a job well done (albeit half-completed) by our small team and, to my surprise,

---

[2] This would require the completion of all bracing work, the connection of the electricity to the starting gate and all the lights after they had all been put in place. The completion of the work on the safety fence and it being properly secured in place with the 5-ton-resistant cord (Martin explained to Edward, "it's amazingly strong and can withstand the impact of five Minis crashing into it at once and still not break") we'd carefully left in place for this very purpose. The shale would have to be delivered, unloaded from a stream of lorries, transported into the auditorium, placed in position, rolled flat and watered. As well as a myriad of other tasks, responsibilities, last-minute bodges and all kinds of other snagging work that I have no idea about, experience of or ability to even guess at. The work to stage an event like this is a huge, complex logistical operation that should be admired and marvelled at each time it successfully happens.

done much better by myself than I ever expected. Though I half-expected that the rest of the team had just – by their support, encouragement and by not ripping the mickey out of me when I was slow, cack-handed or dim-witted – kindly enabled me to gain this satisfaction and sense of my own worth to the team. All of them came across as themselves: very capable, hard-working men who are modest about their abilities and artisan skills who just get on with things with the minimum of fuss. These abilities will have come through many years of experience, effort and application but they wear them easily and are illustrative of the fact that the *Brighton Bonanza* hasn't been successful in the past or reached its tenth anniversary by accident or without the good teams put together by Martin Dugard and Jon Cook. Like they say in those credit card adverts (I forget which one) – and apart from irreparably ripping my favourite waterproof trousers – this experience was priceless!

8th December 2006 – Brighton Centre

Another Day in the Life of *Bonanza X*
10th December 2006

I have had a day off from the preparations for the tenth staging of the *Brighton Bonanza X* to watch my beloved Sunderland AFC play Luton at the Stadium of Light before setting off early on a bright, sunny morning to the Brighton Centre. I live just close enough to the seafront to be able to persuade myself that it would be better to carry my box of books and advertising sign down to the Centre rather than lose my parking space by a drive down. It turns out this isn't a good idea as the breeze wants to repeatedly blow the board away and the box becomes really hard work to carry. I'm hopeful that this will be my best ever sales day, particularly as legendarily the fans are so keen to snap up last-minute Christmas presents that the atmosphere gets positively feverish. Many of the main track shop owners in the country – Nick and Johnny Barber as well as Mick Gregory, John "I'm a freaking professional" Jones, and Dave Rattenberry – will have stalls at the *Speedway Fayre* organised by Eastbourne track shop manager Martin Dadswell. Most of them have surplus stock of my books, which they promised to bring along today and that, ever optimistically, I'm hopeful that I'll manage to sell. I have a secret weapon or not-so-secret-weapon as she's so noticeable and outgoing, in the form of my helper 'Scary' Sheila Le Sage from Arena Essex. She's the vivacious self-styled '*Miss Arena Essex*' with a warm, friendly but larger than life personality who's kindly volunteered to hand out leaflets for my *When Eagles Dared* book to fans as they enter the glass swing doors of the Brighton Centre seafront entrance. I'm sure that she'll proudly inform them that she features in both books and that I'd be happy to sign a copy for them at my stall.

The business end of the *Bonanza X* is the back stage entrance that is located down the frequently congested road that leads to the most convenient town centre car parks. The queues of Christmas shoppers in their cars have yet to build up nearby as I totter down the road with my box and sign. Hopefully some of them will think to visit this afternoon after they've shopped, especially as Jon Cook has had adverts placed on eighty billboards throughout the city in an attempt to attract some passing trade from the local population to the event. He seems disappointed that I've completely failed to spot these adverts. This is particularly unobservant of me as a number of these smaller billboards are by my house and I pass them every day. They usually only advertise the frequent stock car meetings they have at Arlington Stadium and, though they register in the sense that I see them, I really couldn't tell you anything about the specifics of these events. I think that we're so bombarded with adverts that cry out for our attention that we fail to notice the subtler, more old-fashioned variety that still remain right under our noses. I did mention to Jon that I had spotted a full-page colour advert for forthcoming events in November and December at the Brighton Centre in the free local *Rocks* monthly listings paper. There weren't that many forthcoming events booked for the Centre, notable or otherwise except for Status Quo in concert the weekend after the *Bonanza X* when the hallways and seats will be filled with even more of the bearded, greying be-denimed older male of the species that is speedway's natural constituency. Though even these no longer attend meetings in such great numbers as in days of yore. I was amused by this advert as it listed in fantastic juxtaposition, 'November 17th The Vagina Monologues' and followed it with 'December 10th Indoor Speedway – the *Brighton Bonanza X*'. Given that this year's

Bonanza X field features a rider with the unfortunate Christian name of Semen it made me chortle but completely failed to raise anything like a smile from Jon when I mention it to him. Instead he just looked at me with total bemusement and in a manner that suggested that I should get out more often.[1]

It's fair to say that, if judged by advance bookings, the field has failed to excite the imagination of the speedway public to the same extent that it has previously. A casual glance at the roll call of riders who have graced this event provides some indication of the absence of the notable names and 'top' riders who choose to no longer appear. Riders such as Mark Loram, Greg Hancock and Peter Karlsson and even the rider who has raced here more than anyone else ever, Brent Werner, aren't included in the field at this year's tournament (though I do spot him watching intently from the crowd later). Neither are the top three riders from the all-time *Bonanza X* averages listed in the programme, the aforementioned Karlsson and Loram as well as the always keenly combative Paul Hurry who thrives on the tight confines of this circuit. Equally, the rider with the all-time lowest average, Charlie Gjedde (who averages an impressive figure of 0.00 from 10 rides) will also not appear this year. It's widely acknowledged that the *Bonanza* field has often showcased new and (possibly) upcoming talent from overseas. I know that the chance to see the so-called 'sensations' for the future like Billy Janniro or last year's Chris Kerr, has historically added to the appeal and anticipation about the event that I've personally felt over the years. At the bottom of the all-time averages for this event are a host of names that have flickered briefly in the British speedway scene and some that haven't even really managed to flicker. These riders appear in an exotic roll call that includes Scott Swain, Jordan Jurezynski, Rafal Szombierski (whose average of 0.89 implies that he might have instantly put the crowd into a deep sleep), Stefan Bachhuber and Artur Pietrzyk. It just goes to show that being cheap to hire and comparatively unknown when you appear at Brighton or to hailing from the admired parts of Eastern Europe is no guarantee of success on the day. Then, ultimately given the nature of the track, this will always be a 'fun' day and should be treated as such by fans and riders alike although, as they often say, as soon as a rider puts on that helmet the desire to compete and to win invariably increases exponentially.

One aspect of the day that I hope remains popular is the Speedway Collector's Fayre. All my favourite track shop owners are there as is that consummate professional John Jones (and his sweetly spoken wife) from Belle Vue who conspicuously doesn't bother to say 'hello' at all during the day. Among the remainder of the stallholders there's a real camaraderie and end-of-term (and retro) feel to the merchandise displayed as well as myriad conversations on rider and promoter gossip, the state of the speedway memorabilia market, the anticipated level of the crowds today, some doom and gloom, bullcrap or ebullient optimism about the turnover of the season just gone and, invariably a hardy perennial topic of intense debate among speedway fans everywhere during the close season (or even during it) – the future of the sport . Particularly as this future applies to the ownership of the track shops since this is a self-interested topic of conversation that excites especial appeal among the majority of stallholders. The 2007 season promises to be one of change, revolution or expansion on the track shop ownership front, well at least for the Barbers and Andy Griggs who attends but doesn't have a stall. The Barbers' association with Peterborough speedway appears to have ended in mysterious circumstances for which Nick has some Machiavellian theories though the poor manner of the communication of this decision by promoter Colin Horton appears to illustrate the increasing use of modern technology in speedway, since it arrived by text message. In romantic relationships, to dump someone by text is the *modus operandi* of the coward, roué or the cad and it's a method that some firms now use to announce redundancies or bankruptcy. Whenever it's used as a means of communication, it doesn't create a warm, fuzzy feeling in the recipient and on this occasion has left Nick nonplussed as to the actual reasons behind the decision, "When Colin [Horton] took over the club from his brother Mick, I thought he was a real breath of fresh air, but now I'm

[1] A snap judgement based on his performance on the tight, tricky indoor circuit of the *Bonanza X*, the wonderfully named Semen Vlasov won't have too much of a British Speedway career. Though, that said, on a proper track who knows how he'll perform? He does have the sort of name that will always attract jokers with (in their own minds) a wit so sharp that they'll cut themselves. The day after the meeting the first funster I spot making such a hilarious play on words on the British Speedway Forums is Derek Barclay who, unusually for him, completely fails to post a snarkily righteous but invariably angry riposte with lots of exclamation marks and emoticons thrown in for good measure but instead wastes his 1004th comment on a tortuous *Bonanza X* themed Semen 'joke'. "Hmm, I was wondering at one point, with Ryan Fisher out and the organisers' needing someone to take his slot in the evening's Individual, whether (as he's 17) they might ask young Matt [Bates]..?? This would have resulted in the intriguing prospect of Master Bates coming up against Semen..??!!" Vaguely in keeping though it is with the relaxed attitude to lifestyles legendarily favoured in Brighton, I'm not sure if I prefer the late-night bombastic, irked more typical Barclay rants to this gentler homoerotic poor man's Jim Davidson variety.

not so sure!" With the arrival of Mike Golding as promoter at Somerset, the Barbers have also lost that shop from their empire though they have replaced it with a new one at Birmingham speedway when it opens in 2007. Later, I forget myself when I chat with Dave 'the Rat' Rattenberry and inadvertently assume, understandably enough without real thought given his location and that the major part of his empire is focused in the Midlands, that his had been the victorious bid for this franchise. After I accidentally congratulate him, he grimaces and says "that's still a sore point with me". There's further chatter about the future of the track shop at Arena Essex as well as the trackshop man (Andy) whose empire has reputedly grown the most for 2007 with the potential addition of Oxford and Peterborough plus some others he will supply but not run. Andy's based in King's Lynn and will now have to travel on successive nights from track to track across a wide geographic area. Not that the travel itself is really any problem to the track shop guys any more than it is to the riders during the season, since for all of them it's the quality and trustworthiness of the backup they receive that matters. This is a key factor in the running and smooth administration of any track shop. Rat has John Rich, Bill Gimbeth and 'mushy pea' (ICA Crook) to regularly call upon to help run his shops and Nick Barber has his family in the form of his brother Johnny and their sister Bev. All these people can set up displays attractively and you can trust them to be friendly, knowledgeable and not to run off with the takings or the stock. Andy, of course, has Doug Boxall to help at Rye House but clearly his choice of help elsewhere is going to be crucial to his ability to offer a successful service and not suffer shrinkage at the till or not wear himself out in the process of doing so himself. That said, the people already at Oxford appeared extremely friendly and trustworthy when I visited.

But that's next season and the *Bonanza X* finds a huge host of stalls that supply everything from books to modern and aged memorabilia to "Speedway Jewellery" as well as a varied selection of bargain 'civilian' clothes (!) that look more suited to a car boot sale but apparently prove popular among the more discerning fans in attendance. Many of these stallholders have been regulars at this event for years and so have witnessed fluctuations in spectator numbers and, consequently, takings. Long-time attendee, Mick Gregory, is strongly of the opinion that, "every year the money goes down and down as the crowds get less and less", while 'the Rat' is even blunter in his assessment, "it's hard here 'cause the event is no longer what it was." Actually he uses another blunter, more descriptive word, but like all the other stallholders, despite the low rumble of complaints, he's still very much here with a large stall in evidence in prime position at the opposite end of the Fayre to me (and the toilets). By a considerable margin the tables most loaded down with merchandise belong to the Barbers who appear to have a surfeit of jackets, T-shirts and hoodies in various team logos but particularly those of Peterborough that they've piled up high and heavily discounted. "I'd be really worried if I had all that stock left at the end of the season as I prefer to clear it all out by now and start each season afresh", notes Mick Gregory sympathetically when he glances quizzically over the mounds of clothing on display on the tables opposite where we are located. We're able to chat on amiably throughout the first hour after the entrance gates have opened at 11 a.m. since we're only intermittently assailed by anything that approaches a group let alone a crowd. We have so much time to chat that after we've covered the topics of speedway and football – Mick is a Derby County season ticket holder at Pride Park but still considers the Baseball Ground to be the true home of the club – talk turns to a topic dear to both our hearts as long-distance drivers: toilets. Well, bladder strength to be exact but they're definitely related. Mick is a mine of information and after we've mostly agreed on the service stations that we like or actively dislike, he hits me with the factual zinger – "you should know this!" – that the longest stretch of motorway without toilet facilities of any description ("and I know 'cause I've looked") is the 81 miles between the last service station on the M1 and the Pease Pottage services at the foot of the M23. It's just the sort of meaningless but unifying campaign issue that could get an ambitious person elected and I'm surprised that David Cameron hasn't yet found a 'green' slant to confirm its importance to a baffled electorate. Mick doesn't know that the shortest motorway in the country is the toiletless 300 yard A635 (M) in Manchester. Ironically throughout our talk and time together at the Speedway Collectors' Fayre, I'm in what I've now realised is my traditional location at any such event, namely right by the toilets. When I met George Best at Stringfellows during the launch of one of his many autobiographies (the brilliantly titled *The Good, the Bad and the Bubbly*) in the late 1980s, he took it upon himself to advise me on how to meet and pick up women at a nightclub ("always stand near to the ladies toilets as they all eventually come to you and you don't have to go looking for them as you can often miss the best ones if you wander round in the dark"). Given that he legendarily didn't have these problems (and didn't the night he gave this advice either), it was kind of him to temporarily put himself in the shoes of lesser swordsmen, cut to the chase and provide practical (but sexist) advice to boot. I'm not quite sure how he'd have viewed being stood next to the gents toilets for all his book signings, let alone to do this at an indoor speedway meeting (with contempt probably) but, at least, my position means that I'll get to see quite a few of the fans as they answer the call of nature. As they bustle past, I struggle to find an elegant way to communicate King's Lynn co-promoter Jonathan Chapman's own unique advocacy for the book, "not being funny, it's the ideal toilet book – that's where I always get to read it!" Given the length of *Showered in Shale*, so much so that reviewers habitually refer to it as a "tome", I ponder whether given the ageing demographic of the sport that I should find some way to promote it today and in the *Speedway Star* as "the ultimate book for the speedway fan with prostrate or constipation issues." Though later we have quite an intense and informative chat about our favoured motorway service station toilets throughout the country (as well as continuing on about prostrates and bladders), Mick Gregory is delighted to have retained his favoured location in this corner of the entrance hall to the Brighton Centre but gutted to now have me as a neighbour, "I'm disappointed the people who were in your spot last year aren't here as they did teas and coffees so they attracted a real crowd throughout the day to their stall and, not being funny or anything, you're not going to do that." Of more concern is the lack of custom, "it was slow last year for the first hour then it picked up but this year [waves his arms expansively at the other stalls] no one is selling owt!"

The second hour before the fans officially depart into the auditorium to take their seats for the rider parade before the afternoon Pairs meeting subsequently was as crowded as he'd hoped and finally brings a proper smile to Mick's perpetually cheery face ("it was really packed in the second hour – I think everyone's done well"). My sales are slow though 'Scary' Sheila has done a excellent job to hand out many leaflets for my *When Eagles Dared* book as these outsell the "tome" quite easily. I know that Sheila has very actively promoted my books when I, rather touchingly, get to sign these leaflets at my stand for some of the keen, younger fans who're under the misapprehension that I'm some sort of notable speedway figure. It makes us all feel good though and I even get to sign the first page of a newly bought "speedway autograph book" (whatever did happen to more old fashioned things like autograph books in this age of instant text messaging and mobile phone cameras?) for a polite, diffident young lady called Emma. In a quirk of business life that's hard to gauge or fathom, Martin Dadswell has sold just as many copies of *Showered in Shale* (two) as I did during the first sales session. He has a simple, down-to-earth explanation, "you're so freaking ugly they're bound to be put off, never mind no one in their right mind really wants your autograph." Martin certainly keeps my feet on the ground in the unlikely event that I ever manage to achieve ideas above my station.

For many, people the *Bonanza X* is just as much about the social side of the day as it is about the meeting itself. I get to say "hello" to many of the people that I've enjoyed meeting on my travels during these past few years. Some people are incredibly familiar (to look at) and I know that I recognise them but I'm blowed if I remember their names and it's now too embarrassing to ask, particularly as I'm not quite sure of the exact context in which I've met them, since these have now blurred into a friendly mass in my mind. I do remember the lovely Julie Martin who rests on the stand for a while, slightly hung over, after a frenetic night spent carousing at the Bridger household, prior to a long day of photography ahead for her. She's crouched by the wooden safety fence, which she wouldn't feel so blithely confident to shelter behind if she knew that I had been involved its erection. As ever, she'll capture copious shots of the thrills and spills as well as closely document every race that Lewis Bridger competes in throughout the event. No doubt, she'll capture some surreptitious photos of Tony Thompson, Lewis's granddad/mechanic, as he lurks in the pits or trackside, though luckily the cold weather at this time of year prevents any of her famous topless shots of him. Another speedway photographer, the knowledgeable and charming Steve Dixon is also here with his lovely and engaging partner Deb – in an 'unofficial' but enthusiastic capacity – to try to capture some high-quality action shots from the event to add to the well-chosen selection already found on his website. Steve is a fans' fan. His even-handed contributions to the British Speedway Forum make a refreshing change from prognostications of doom or wildly impractical suggestions for the future that this site attracts and, in a nutshell, further sums up the thoughtful and fair man that you soon realise he is when you speak to him. He's so thorough in everything that he does that he's even managed to identify that great rarity nowadays – some reasonably priced accommodation in Brighton for the night (the Travel Lodge adjacent to Preston Park for £26) – and helpfully has posted this information on the forum. Some people travel quite some distance to attend this event and some like Arena Essex speedway supporters club even put on a coach to ferry fans to the *Bonanza*. It seems everyone here is a keen collector of some sort or other and everyone has his own speedway memorabilia specialism. Sadly, more often than not, their hobby will involve items such as programmes, badges, bikes, race bibs and the like rather than books. In conversations during the day, I learn that this kleptomaniacal obsessiveness applies in spades to other more obscure things as diverse as Planet of the Apes. Alan Boniface (aka "the scrawny git", according to his co-worker Martin Dadswell) from the Eagles' track shop has this particular predilection and his partner Jan says his collection includes a "creepy looking" over six foot tall life size model of one of the

Apes in full uniform ("you wouldn't believe how much of a struggle it's to get leather boots onto those Ape models!"). She has her own Elvis memorabilia obsession and, I think, there may even be some Daleks in the house. This desire to collect and need for taxonomy all fits in nicely with Dave Rattenberry's own obsession and expertise in the area of European football grounds – over 4000 visited to date – with his latest trip in search of football obscurity to Spain only the previous week. EBay, the increased atomism of modern everyday life and the perils of late capitalism have exacerbated this trend to amass collections. And as there's already been enough talk about toilets, we can ignore Freud's theories about gifts, giving and parental approval. It has to be noted though that with the cast of the speedway mind already predisposed to watch, identify, detail and record discrete events in synchronic and diachronic fashion allied to a widespread need for tabulation and various forms of record keeping, it's hardly a surprise that collections had long ago taken a great stranglehold on the speedway fan's psyche.

One of the joys of having helped with the construction of the *Bonanza X* track is to have been invited along to the "pit lane" by Jon Cook. Sadly my continuing anxiety about stolen books based on my own bitter experience means that, though I've packed them away in the boxes under my table, I still feel a periodic need to pop back and inspect things. In order to get to the "pit lane" you have to elude the security ladies and gingerly pick your way between races down the edge of the safety fence. When you arrive in the pits, there's an understandable tendency for non-participants to feel a bit redundant since the cramped space is filled with people consumed by their purpose – whether riders, mechanics or even family – who crowd together to overlook the safety fence before they rush back outside to the loading bay area of the Centre which serves as the temporary pits for the event. Another perk is that I possess one of the natty grey wristbands issued to 'officials' – with the words "speedway racing" molded into them – that allows access to all areas of the Centre complex though it does look like it has come from the local municipal swimming pool ("would grey armbands please leave the pool immediately!"). It's all very Hollywood to be able to pull back your sleeve and then pass by the friendly security ladies. I have my choice of the empty seats and watch for a while from prime position on the home straight directly opposite the first bend. Though there are more empty spaces in the auditorium than last year, the tickets for the seats in prime position sold out almost immediately months ago to the aficionados of this indoor variety of the sport. It's a delight to be able to queue jump like this and secure prime position in the third of three empty rows that are left vacant for health and safety reasons every year because of the possible danger of errant bikes flying through the air to land painfully on the fans. I already know that the fence isn't quite built to the standards of the Berlin Wall (though the cords that bind it have a breaking strength of "five one-ton Minis" according to Martin Dugard) and in the past I have seen the spectators promptly scatter when a rogue bike flew towards them. I resolve to keep my eyes peeled and affect a macho but studiously insouciant seated posture that I like to feel echoes the look, style and feel of its more prevalent pits lane equivalent among the mechanics albeit without oily hands, boots and jeans or a roll up dangling from my mouth. Sadly this last but essential part of the mechanics potent *lingua franca* is disallowed by the no-smoking policy of the Brighton Centre except by those who rebelliously like to always push the boundaries of acceptable behaviour.

I share my row with another man who has sprawled out in an extremely territorial manner and who bucks the trend of the perpetually friendly speedway crowd by huffing and puffing as he very reluctantly moves aside to let me slide down to the other end of "his" row. All is well until I venture back to check on my stock of books for the first time. As I canter back, keen not have missed any of the drama on the tight confines of the track and particularly the exhilarating first corner, I encounter trouble. If there's one thing that always trumps the power of the 'access all areas' grey wristband it's the megalomania of safety stewards, especially diminutive ones on the cusp of a mid-life crisis. This is further enhanced into an even slightly more objectionable power-mad brew in combination with a uniform (though a small peaked cap would complete this ensemble), small stature and a slight ginger moustache that you'd definitely not be pleased with if you'd just had a Brazilian. Asserting the safety rules with alacrity and relish is fair enough as they are ultimately there to prevent accidents and to try to guarantee that the fans can watch in comfort and safety. However, when regulations are applied inconsistently in a bumptious manner it's a different kettle of fish. The steward decided that I wasn't allowed to return to where I'd just been sitting "for my own safety" ("a bike landed there last year" is his fictitious claim in justification) although to vacate my seat I had to clamber past another man in the same row of seats who he continued to studiously ignore and allowed to continue to sit there afterwards. Maybe he has an invisible force field in the manner of the Ready Brek adverts that repels flying bikes so he doesn't have to move. He's probably related to Mister "Rules are Rules' and though he appears to be much too tall to be family he is miraculously exempt. I begrudgingly remove myself to the spare seats of the East grandstand before I decide to immediately switch to the West side one since the view from these seats involves a large blind spot that covers the area of the first bend where indoors the majority of the thrills and spills occur. In the West stand there is still a blind spot but it's smaller and is on the final bend. In this section of the stand, I join the 'Sittingbourne Massive' in the form of the affable Dick Jarvis, who I sit next to, and his knowledgeable partners in crime/shale – Les Drury, Chris Golding and Ian Glover who take advantage of the available space in this grandstand to spread themselves out.

The races we all watch in the Pairs Trophy are keenly contested throughout and interspersed with heats from the 2006 British Academy League Grand Final – a contest between the young riders in the Rhinos and the Cobras to determine this season's championship victors. As ever, the presentational duties are carried out with great aplomb by the dapperly dressed Kevin 'KC' Coombes and he's joined in the cosy confines of the centre green by some track staff (Roy Prodger and a smartly dressed Bob Dugard in shoes more suited to an early morning church service than the shale), and the perpetually cheerful Alan Rolfe as the start marshal, ably assisted as ever by his equally friendly assistant (and Sittingbourne Speedway Club start marshal) Terry English. The referee in charge of his third *Bonanza* is the prosperously figured Phil Griffin who throughout stands close by to his wood effect referee's box of tricks that houses his control panel and the various coloured light switches. The circuit is so small that Phil spends the entire meeting desperately swiveling on the spot in order to attempt to follow the action, though once the field gets strung out in some races this makes it impossible for him to simultaneously observe all the riders. As this is the *Bonanza*, since 2005 the crowd have been invited to adjudicate on exclusion decisions – they wave one side or the other of the red and yellow coloured pages stapled into the middle of the meeting programme to signal their opinions – and whether a rider takes part in the re-run or is unceremoniously flung out of the race for some transgression or other (most often a crash or a fall of which there are plenty). In keeping with the 'fun' nature of the contest, the crowd can show great leniency, favoritism or cussedness dependent on the incident or rider involved. For the moaning minnies that the British Speedway forum afterwards attracted, this element of intervention by the crowd is another sign of the air of amateurishness that they project onto the event as though all speedway meetings had to adhere to some gold standard of authenticity to truly count as an enjoyable spectacle or contest.[2] Since this interactive aspect of the occasion hasn't always been a feature of the event, it could be argued that the all-time averages of some of the riders present have been distorted by the capriciousness of the crowd's decision-making. Indeed, the reappearance of Oliver Allen in this year's *Bonanza X* recalls the spectacle of his delightful tantrum after he was "excluded" by a show of red cards in 2005. The centre green also has a couple of photographers in situ, the friendly Mick Hinves who's always a fixture at Arlington along with another older man who wears a sleeveless fluorescent top to mark out his 'Official' status. Basic track tools (watering can, rakes and the like) are also scattered about the centre green for any urgent remedial work that's required throughout the day, along with a fire extinguisher, a table of trophies that glint and glisten as they await presentation to the victors and the usual cluster of different coloured flags lined up ready for immediate and dramatic use by Alan Rolfe at the finish line. The white line that marks the actual finish is placed in the centre of the track though the start gate is drawn diagonally across the surface and is set back almost on the fourth corner to ease congestion and thereby maximise the distance on the still short run to the wide but all important first bend.

The fifth race of the pairs Trophy sums up the appeal of the event as well as the difficulty that the holders Edward Kennett and Lewis Bridger might well have to successfully defend their crown as a partnership on the tight confines of the indoor track. Unlike some vocal critical detractors (if that is the right word for posters on the forums who feel able to critique the quality of the event without actually bothering to attend), I enjoy the harum scarum nature of the first corner and the limited opportunities for passing that this small circuit by its size and contours necessarily dictates. Throughout the Pairs event there are so many first bend crashes that for a moment it's almost as if I've been transported down a rip in the space time continuum and I'm back once again at Plough Lane Stadium in the hot summer of 2005 for the tediously lengthy meeting that was the Conference League Pairs Championship. The first corner crush that you get at Brighton totally exaggerates the level of carnage and given the arrival of four bikes together in such a constricted space it's completely to

[2] Interestingly the *Bonanza X* track wore very well throughout the night and completely failed to develop ruts or cut up which, to my mind, indicates the height of professionalism not its obverse. Perhaps this is the required kind of expertise that the BSI might enlist in future to help build their own indoor man-made tracks for the GP series? Though, that said, at Cardiff they already call on the services of that renowned trackman, Colin Meredith, so perhaps the explanation for the excessive wear that often spoils the quality of the racing of this event lies elsewhere in the quality of the materials used or the specifications provided?

be expected. How the riders cope is all part of the fascination, as is the skill to 'baby' the throttle and ride tight to the inside to hug the white line – illustrated to perfection every year by Shawn McConnell whenever he makes the gate or exits the second bend ahead – and thereby maximise your chances to completely dictate the result of almost every race in which they manage to engineer yourself into this position. By occupying this position you effectively limit the opportunities that your opponents behind you have to overtake on the comparatively 'wide' expanse of the first corner, through lunges along the back straight, by last-gasp gallops towards the finish line or the altogether trickier (because it's slightly less roomy) bursts round the outside on the final corner. Another variable is the ever-present danger of rider error since when made these can prove difficult to correct in such a confined space. Engine failures at the *Bonanza X* are almost as rare as admissions of failure from John Postlethwaite in the execution of the grandiose plans he once trumpeted for the international development of the BSI GP series and the worldwide brand sponsorship it would attract.

However, the ostensible need to team-ride during the Pairs Trophy event completely alters the approach, strategy and tactics to races that the riders traditionally employ in the Individual event. Nowadays, it's pretty well held to be an established fact that team riding is a dying tradition but still a much-lamented authentic skill from the pantheon of black arts of speedway that mark out the truly gifted on a machine in the traditional variety of the sport held outdoors on the shale. The need for individual success, the high-powered and easier-to-control bikes as well as huge gulfs in rider abilities between two riders from the same team in the same race, often appear to dictate a 'survival of the fittest' approach to race tactics. Historically it was much more expected and often the norm that the senior partner would use his superior skill for the benefit of the team to mentor and protect his teammate from the attentions of rivals. Dictating the race in this fashion thereby maximised the overall team points score in the race. Like white Christmases in an era of a globally warmed planet, this has mostly disappeared as an experience, though it still remains potent as a concept that's more encountered in the breach than in the observance. Perceptions that many of the itinerant almost journeymen (so called for the miles traveled rather than for their skills) superstar riders of contemporary speedway – that invariably results in a 'it's Sunday it must be Poland; who am I riding for today?' type attitude to their regular and manic commutes around Europe and now even to Russia – leads to a studious 'just look after number one' approach to race tactics rather than one that places any emphasis on the need to look after their partner. At the Elite League level nowadays, it's common to get 'two races in one' which is a bargain in the context of a supermarket but often ultimately a disappointment to witness in a speedway race when a close contest occurs in two separate locations of the track between the 'superstar' pair and the comparative fodder of the 'also rans'. Though that said, this style of race is infinitely preferable to the 'strung out like a line of washing' version that has become an even more prevalent feature of modern speedway racing. Often the only bit of team riding you get to witness is if the riders happen to journey round to the start line together before the race or afterwards on the way back to the pits. There are notable exceptions to this rule among the more old-fashioned collegiate type of rider (Joe Screen springs to mind) but in the superstar class, on the whole, the Hans Andersons and the Nicki Pedersens of this world are purely and simply hired to go out and win a race. The home fans would be irked if they didn't but there's no doubt that we've lost something along the way because of this development. Something that can often be emphasised by the occasional examples of team riding by these premium riders – rare as an orchid on a bowling green – is often then undertaken in a more self-conscious 'look at me team ride' type manner.

Anyway, enough of what we've lost or think we've lost because in the heat 5 race between the much fancied Kennett/Bridger and the Kerr/Giffard partnerships, we're served up with a spectacle that on its own would justify almost any speedway meeting indoors or outdoors and also goes to show that team riding can take place (and have its strategic perils) in even the narrowest of confined spaces. After he ran a third in his first race, Lewis led from the gate and his partner Edward demonstrates complete mastery of his bike and the track to ease his way from third place into second and finally into the lead with quick bursts on his throttle for well-timed elegant passes. Throughout the event, Edward Kennett attempts to dictate each race through his control of the pace of each heat and gradually slows it down as the race progresses. In marked contrast, although he knows that there is little room to race, Lewis just can't resist his natural propensity to race each heat full on and round the outside line closest to the boards. Unfortunately at Brighton, there isn't room for all four riders or even two to really race side by side down the straights so this is an approach that thrills and frustrates in almost equal measure. In fact, it was his patient wait behind his junior partner for the inevitable minor error in angle of trajectory that enabled Edward to easily slip past Lewis. After he'd done so he then attempted to team-ride with his wilder (and by all accounts somewhat fragile after the night before) partner round the remainder of the laps to

Lucy and Alan on Argus stall at Bonanza. © Jeff Scott

Build up for the final. © Jeff Scott

Lightning-quick break-down nearly complete. © Jeff Scott

effectively block out their determined rivals. This worked well for a lap or so until one by one they skillfully manoeuvre past Lewis – Dan Giffard on the second bend of the last lap when he cuts underneath and Chris Kerr when he steals past in true last gasp fashion on the last bend to snatch third place and relegate Lewis to last position. Dan and Lewis have historically enjoyed an intense camaraderie and rivalry over the last couple of years since they rode for Weymouth and hung out together in East Sussex, so it's a race result that Dan greets with some glee when he crosses the finish line despite the fact that he only finished second. Given the ages and nationalities of the riders in this race (Giffard and Kerr are both 22 while Edward and Lewis are 20 and 17 respectively), the skill and tenacity they demonstrate bodes well for the future of the sport in this country since all, except Chris Kerr, are home-grown talents.

The always ebullient and never lost for a word *Bonanza X* aural Master of Ceremonies, Kevin 'KC' Coombes, is ecstatic, "quite simply Brian that is what we are all about!" He then goes onto issue some fulsome but slightly tongue-tied testimony in praise of the second placed rider, "getting stuck in and not being fazed at all and getting stuck in is Danny Giffard." To my mind, and I've advocated this many times before, not only does KC consistently add to the entertainment value of any speedway event where he brings his unique talents to bear – he's equally at home on the Arlington centre green, in the Millenium Stadium for the Cardiff GP or more low key chicken-in-the-basket evenings he hosts in his capacity as a mobile disc jockey. He really should be considered by *Sky Sports* for use at their live speedway meetings as a commentator, primarily because of his quick-witted facility with words, the enthusiasm he communicates and his knowledge of speedway, the riders and fans alike. Not that the fast pace of the afternoon leaves that much time between the races, or the re-runs necessitated by the thrills and spills, for too many *longueurs* to bore the involved *Bonanza X* crowd who enter into the spirit of things with a strong element of theatricality so that it often almost verges on the atmosphere you'd get at a pantomime. This 'behind you' and 'Oh-no-I-didn't-Oh-yes-you-did' outlook is fostered and encouraged by Kevin who's never happier than when playing up the speedway's mini-track indoor version of 'goodies and baddies'.

The exotically named Semen Vlasov manages to get a point when he comes third in heat 6. Though we don't know it at the time, this will be his only point of the afternoon. Since it's his first ever placing on English soil, it's an event that KC can't let pass and so celebrates it extremely enthusiastically. "In third place, looking all wild, but he'll settle down is Semen Vlasov!" This point is really gained as a result of the fact that the fourth placed rider Tommy Allen, who rides as the last-minute reserve replacement for the absent Steve Boxall, struggles even more than him to come to terms with the dynamics of the indoor circuit. This is a surprise since the youngster started his *Bonanza* career with a convincing win in his first ever race in heat 2 but the reality of the different technique required to race in the Brighton Centre really caught up with him. Just because there's a pantomime and school holiday atmosphere doesn't mean that the often low speed but rarely stately tumbles the riders repeatedly endure aren't without cost in terms of either pain inflicted or damage to machinery. In the eighth heat Ryan Fisher falls dramatically on the apex of the first bend in the first lap and thereby immediately ends the supposed mission of his long trip to this country to put himself in the metaphorical shop window. I'm not sure how much his couple of rides impressed prospective promoters (not that I notice that many huddled in the pits lane or seated luxuriously in the grandstand) that his wild days were behind him and advanced his claim that he has a newfound love and dedication for the sport. Initially, KC playfully dismisses the severity of Ryan's plight, though in a nod to his gift for medical descriptions he does note, "concern about the knee and ankle area". These are injuries that could definitely put a kink in any extra-curricular activities he had already planned for his UK trip. By the time of the re-run, we learn that Ryan's condition has worsened, "now the adrenalin has worn off a bit, he's not feeling too clever so he's decided to sit this one out!" In fact he "sits out" the rest of the Pairs Trophy and the individual event in the evening to boot.

A feature of the meeting is that we're treated to an inconsistent choice of headgear when it comes to helmet colours in relation to the spectrum we traditionally witness the riders wear at the track. Charlie Venegas wears a black one for all his rides, some riders wear colours other than the ones they're programmed to wear according to the race card and, in the case of showman Shawn McConnell, we're treated to the sight of an eclectic plumed kind of affair. This is probably appropriate for his age, humour and lack of fashion sense rather than down to any advantage he might gain from its aerodynamic properties. Afterwards on the forums, the range of colours and the failure of the referee Phil Griffin to enforce the rule of law as it applies to the programmed helmet colours is the signal for some wails and much gnashing of teeth. The measures proposed to rectify this failure of the sacrosanct 'rule of law' fall short of the reintroduction of National Service or the birching of serial offenders but leads to bleats, wails and moans about the decline in levels of professionalism at the *Bonanza X* on the internet (BSF slogan: 'Never Knowingly Under Complained'). Personally, it's a change to see a race won with a rider in a black helmet colour, plus with KC at the microphone we get a free pronunciation and phonetics lesson thrown in *gratis*, when he instructs us that Venegas is properly said as "Van-nay-gas." Well, you learn something new every day.

Also keen to learn are the young riders that make up the Rhinos and Cobras teams in the Academy League Grand Final. Sadly, Jake Knight falls heavily on the second bend during the warm up before he's even had a chance to test his mettle against the other riders in the auditorium. In concerned fashion, KC rushes over to the stricken rider to check on his health and while there he leans over the yellow board of the safety fence to politely ask photographer Julie Martin to move to somewhere much safer. Ever keen to find the ideal position from which to get a unique action shot of these daring young men who ply their trade on speedway bikes, Julie has strayed into the no-man's land of the area behind the first bend fence. Given the huge number of crashes by and into the fence at this very point, she really couldn't be more ideally placed to capture the drama – or receive a bike round her head. As KC scuttles back across the track to the comparative calm and sanctuary of the centre green, he's nearly run over by another rider and exclaims, "Blimey Health & Safety – we need a zebra crossing on that bend!" He then confirms the evidence of our own eyes, "There's a problem for Jake, it looks like he's got a twisted knee there." When the riders eventually get to line up at the starting gate, Jake sadly isn't amongst them.

The young riders of the Academy League provide more than enough thrills and gripping entertainment throughout their races in the afternoon and the evening. The third heat takes a few attempts to actually get completed since in the first attempt to run the race, the yellow-helmeted (the young riders all look immaculate, ride gleaming bikes and all wear the correct, designated helmet colours) James Sarjeant falls and the rider in blue behind, Richard Franklin, is unable to do anything other than dramatically smash into him. Though they trail by some yards, the following riders then both struggle to control their bikes enough to pass by the scene of the carnage. Luckily, by a hair's breadth, they just about manage to do so without adding to the pile up. The sight of a disgruntled youngster as he wheels his bike back to the pits after an exclusion as the primary cause of the stoppage (some decisions referee Phil Griffin doesn't interactively allow the crowd to vote on) brings out KC's paternal but slightly patronising side, "James – he's 13 and about four foot one inch – aww!" It is true to say that when the Academy riders walk the track they do completely look the part but they also appear like mini-me versions of the professional riders in their kevlars. It's an effect further emphasised by their track walks and, when team-mates stand together, their disconcertingly earnest tactical discussions accompanied by waves of their arms and confident gestures that concern the conditions, riding lines and the like.

There's an extended break in proceedings before the re-run and KC uses this time to interview Lewis Bridger. It's an exchange that shows that Lewis has come a long way off the track as well as on it during the 2006 season. He's confident and much more articulate when interviewed and almost effortlessly says all the right things, though this skill is always easier to perfect when your comments are sincere rather than trite formulations. He's unstinting in his praise for the man behind the success of the Academy League programme and young rider development in general, "big thanks to Peter Oakes – he got me to the top – I can't thank him enough and he's got everyone to where they are! Without Peter Oakes the boys would just have second halves and not the League which I think is really good."[3] By now Lewis has warmed to his theme, "the breakthrough was a few years ago when we got rides at Cardiff thanks to Peter Oakes" before he shares his praise round and notes, "Eastbourne got me where I am – the second halves getting my time down and down – I wouldn't be where I am, they had the faith in me." Before this paean can continue any further the Academy lads come back out for the re-run. This doesn't last that long before Richard Franklin once again finds himself in the wars. In this instance, his red helmeted team mate Matt Bates smashes into him heavily from behind which dramatically high sides Richard with some velocity over his handlebars for a painful encounter with the shale surface. After news that the race has been awarded and while they recover the bikes and pick up the bodies, KC comes over all Zen in his faux concern, "Richard is certainly getting at one with the track surface tonight [it's the afternoon]" before his natural flippancy in the face of speedway adversity continues, "I think we should have running races as a back-up option just in case!"

Having now worked up a head of steam when it comes to incisive investigative interviews, Kevin tees up his chat with Sergei (or "Sergie" as the programme prefers to christen him) Darkin[4] by recounting the Russian's recovery from the serious injuries that precluded his appearance at the *Bonanza X* in 2005. The programme alludes to these injuries with elliptical understatement in their rider profile of Sergei when they note he "was set to ride in last year's *Brighton Bonanza*, however failed to make his race to be fit in time for the event." It's only a guess but I expect that after his crash in Russia that there were serious concerns about his actual survival during the days he spent in a coma, never mind his broken ribs, collarbone and punctured lung. Jon Cook knows the rider as well as anyone does in this country, especially since Eastbourne own his contract. However, because of language difficulties Sergei very much remains a rider spoken about rather than to, let alone interviewed. Kevin carries on regardless with his build up to an easy loosener of a question "What's it like to be here then, Sergei?" A nonplussed but polite Sergei parries with his prepared answer, "Very good, but sorry I can't understand your question." Interview over straightaway, KC immediately ripostes to blank bemusement, "Since I last saw you I've been practising my Russian, but sadly the crowd won't understand our conversation so we'll have to leave it there!"

---

[3] One of the positive developments to come out of the 2006 BSPA Annual General meeting was the announcement that the activities of the Academy League would be significantly ramped up in the 2007 season. It's a decision that hopefully overcomes the often ignored 'afterthought' status that the Academy League occasionally enjoyed at some tracks in the past, when the track time for the younger riders was sometimes sacrificed at the last minute when the 'main meeting' overran. Hopefully in 2007, with the promoters behind them, these races won't be discarded on the altar of commercial imperatives or, with careful planning, won't regularly fall foul of curfew restraints. Nonetheless, the clarion call of premature congratulatory talk in the press and on the forums of an imminent renaissance that will possibly lead at some point in the future to another British World Champion, should be put aside for concerted effort and action, as the proof of the pudding lies in its eating. Without this necessary but belated remedial action, it is true to concede that we would undoubtedly find British rider development even harder in the future than it is already. There's always the worry that like many new initiatives that are announced after the AGM, they will soon wither on the vine or quietly get discarded a short time hence. However, with a determined and knowledgeable figure like Peter Oakes driving the initiative forward from a position of some influence and considerable experience, if not power, from inside the corridors of the governing authorities of the sport itself, that this surely must lead to an upturn in fortunes in the medium to long term. Equally we must acknowledge that the formal development structure already in place in countries like Sweden and Denmark remains something that must be looked on with envy and concern. Like so many BSPA decisions, the brutal fact is that money invariably has a huge influence and a careful attitude to the control of cost is always a factor. Indeed, this initiative allows the 15 clubs who (in his capacity as Chairman of the BSPA, Peter Toogood notes) have "committed themselves to running matches immediately after senior meetings" to potentially help source talent without the full-on expense of having to run a Conference League team. The promise that riders who progress from the Academy and Conference League systems to eventually ride in the Elite League with an unspecified "discounted average", simultaneously smacks of the huge optimism traditionally associated with politicians' election promises and has the happy benefit that it comes at absolutely no additional cost. Hopefully, there will be a constant stream of riders as gifted as Lewis Bridger but recent past experience hints otherwise.

[4] That's the trouble with foreigners, they have such weird names, no wonder his name is also spelt as "Sergey." In fact Sergei Darkin is a popular Russian name whose British equivalents would be names like John Smith or Dai Davies.

The ninth heat of the Pairs Trophy is packed with incident. Lewis Bridger makes such a shocker of a start because of bike problems that it's not until the last bend of the second lap that he manages to overtake Billy Hiles, the last-minute reserve replacement for Bobby Schwartz. Given his greater ability on the confines of this tight circuit, he passes his erstwhile rival in ungracious fashion when he cuts hard under Hiles only to harshly ride him right out to the perimeter of the track for an unnecessarily close look at the safety fence. This is the kind of overarching will-to-win and keen unblunted competitive edge that's often absent from the psychological make up of British riders when they reach the vital do-or-die races of the GPs or the World Team Cup. So I'd applaud Lewis for zeal but counsel that he picks the riders to bully more carefully. The real drama of the race also happens on this bend in the final lap when, after a few laps where he closely hugged the inside white line, Shawn McConnell tries to ease past the race leader Edward Kennett with a forceful manoeuvre underneath him, just as they enter the corner. There is no space to realistically do so and the net result is that Edward is flung like a rag doll on a bad hair day over his own handlebars. Phil Griffin again eschews any consultation with the crowd and, quicker than anyone could ever raise their red or yellow section of their programmes to adjudicate, he immediately excludes the aggrieved American and awards the race 5-1 to the Kennett/Bridger pair. The pantomime boos for our US visitor, with the distinctive attire, loudly commence but he's belligerent when Kevin grabs him at the scene of the crime for his thoughts on the outcome of his actions. Back on his home soil, they'd definitely say that he's "pumped" and his plume decorated helmet shakes so much in a combination of incredulity and anger that he looks like a demented cockerel. "You can only go slow and I know it's team riding but you've got to RACE and I had to find some way to get past – I'm riding speedway and he's stopping and people expect to see a race!" If Shawn's hope of making the final hadn't already ended before a wheel had been turned with the absence of Bobby Schwartz (and his replacement by Billy Hiles) this race ensured that he now only had the individual event of the *Bonanza X* Championship to look forward to possible success in later that evening.

The completion of the eleventh heat features a comfortable win for the impressive partnership of Oliver "Olly" Allen and Daniel ('Waving Goodbye') King over the unfancied Russians that has KC wistfully allude to the ongoing spate of crashes, accidents and reruns that has characterised the *Bonanza X* so far with a gleeful "it's our first fully completed 5-1 of the afternoon." The next heat has the Dugard/Tomicek pair continue their stately progress towards their likely appearance in the six laps final with an easy but necessary 5-1 against the 'Team Redcar' combination of Dan Giffard and Chris Kerr. Though he finishes last, this race is notable for the way in which Kerr somehow manages to stay on the bike and on the track as his machine violently rears and bucks in a manner that would have lesser skilled riders explode through the safety fencing.

There's a brief interval for the Academy lads to dust themselves down and for the smokers among the riders to snatch a quick fag outside on the Churchill Square car parks slip road adjacent to the Brighton Centre loading bay that is temporarily the pits area for the brief duration of the *Bonanza X*. I rush back to my table at the Collector's Fayre where the majority of the other stallholders have remained to conserve energy, guard their stock and exchange gossip, stealthily compare prices or put the speedway world to rights. I manage to sell a copy of *When Eagles Dared* and 'lose' a copy of *Showered in Shale* that somehow goes walkies despite the fact that I'm stood there gossiping with passers-by on their way to the gents or on their return. The gifted local journalist Paul Watson – Eastbourne contributor and match reporter for the *Speedway Star* as well as Editor of the *Sussex Express* – stops by for a word and shocks me with the news that this *Bonanza X* is his speedway reporting swansong. "This is my last ever speedway meeting, I've been coming since 1965 but it's been brewing for quite a while and I think it's pretty irrevocable – so, perhaps, in five years' time I'll be able to say, like everyone else does who ever went or was once involved, 'Speedway – is that still going?'" Without any success, I try to gently persuade Paul that this is a decision that he'll either regret (apparently he won't) or change his mind about later (ditto). It seems that my verbal skills won't have the Samaritans beat a path to my door just yet as the closest I get to a change of heart is "we will see – I won't say never but that's the way I feel at the moment."

This brief interval is almost over as soon as it started and the racing recommences with a protracted heat that stars the Academy lads. This time it's the turn of George Piper to be involved in the wars with his bike when he crashes on the back straight and finds himself unable to summon the strength or the agility to promptly get from underneath it. Passions run high throughout this cadre of youngsters and George is no exception as evidenced by the manner in which he thumps the fence in frustration. It's not a happy few minutes for him as he then falls on the first bend of the re-run. The Pairs Trophy only has the remaining four heats and a final to run to its conclusion. KC amuses himself by introducing "Mr Slow Edward

Kennett", who confirms his reputation as a track specialist (in all senses of the word since he builds it as well) at the *Bonanza* by effortlessly completing his fourth win in four rides. It's noticeable that in contrast to every other rider on display that he makes no attempt to crouch over his handlebars in the traditional fashion at the start gate but, instead, eschews this posture in favour of sitting rigidly upright on his saddle. It's as though he's a student of the Alexander Technique School of Correct Posture keen to concentrate only on the release of the tapes by the referee. There's probably been some fancy calculation on his behalf that's allowed him to identify that this style and technique pays dividends on the all-too-brief four-rider foray to the vital first bend. Whatever the reason, it works well and leaves the Kennett/Bridger pair poised on 16 points to be one of the two finalists; though possible permutations with the rival Dugard/Tomicek and Allen/King partnerships means that if results go against them, they could still fail to qualify.

Over time every rider develops their own techniques and mannerisms to try to gain that fractional mechanical or psychological advantage over their opponents. In the case of Sunderland born Stuart Robson it's to wear a yellow helmet colour when the programme calls for white and he chooses to do this at the very moment his partner Tommy Allen rides in a green colour when his should actually be coloured yellow. It's enough to give the internet purists conniptions and to bamboozle Kevin who suddenly gets all confused about which rider is really Stuart Robson. The crowd is in no doubt and loudly but good-naturedly lets KC know about his mistake. In the final analysis, the result of this heat is irrelevant to the qualification for the final but is notable for the fact that it's the start of a trend to completely and repeatedly smash to smithereens the safety board at the apex of the first bend. I would say that it's the same board but the velocity generated by the arrival of a speedway bike invariably smashes it into firewood. Initially I worry that this dramatic collapse could be blamed on my handiwork since it's one of those 67 or 68 boards erected by Jon Cook and me. However, the insouciant way in which it's quickly replaced makes me realise that it has, in reality, successfully served its safety purpose under exacting race conditions. The penultimate heat has Semen fall on the first bend and if speedway were popular enough to command regular column inches in the red-top tabloids this would provide sub-editors with some Derek Barclay-esque (arf arf) schoolboyish puns ('Semen was spilt from the Russian's machine'). This race results in a successive 5-1 win for the Dugard/Tomicek partnership, last year's losing finalists, and thereby ties them on 16 points with Edward and Lewis. So both *Bonanza* specialists have possibly steered their team to the final, despite the presence of an inconsistent or underperforming 'weaker' partner.

There's a slight delay before the final heat of the Pairs Trophy that allows me the chance for some banter with the knowledgeable Sittingbourne (Massive) posse who occupy the nearby seats of the East grandstand. We do this in a fug of exhaust fumes. While the bouquet of exhaust you always experience with speedway bikes is evocative of all our youths – and despite the demise of the sickly sweet odour of Castrol R, even the modern equivalent still retains a smell that I'm sure all true speedway fans only need to vaguely sniff to find themselves transported in their minds to trackside – this afternoon it hangs in the roof of the auditorium like the aftermath of an industrial accident. This isn't the pong of our speedway salad days but almost the choking fumes of a stock car meeting in an enclosed stadium or the fog of exhaust that is more reminiscent of the rush hour in central London on a sunny day. Apparently oblivious to this fog, apart from his streaming eyes or runny nose and even though he hasn't bought a programme and appears to record the heat results on a scrap of paper in complicated hieroglyphics, Dick Jarvis corrects my erroneous assumption that the make up of the final is already a foregone conclusion. "A King/Allen 5-1 would give them 17 points and that would eliminate Dugard on race wins as he's dropped a point and Kennett hasn't." Complicated but believable stuff that fits the mathematical complexity that's so beloved of speedway fans everywhere as they fill out their programmes or, more impressively, calculate the latest averages! It's a permutation that's also passed KC by on the centre green as he conspicuously fails to take us through this possible scenario. When the last heat finally gets underway it stops almost immediately again after the destruction and demolition of the safety board that has so offended the riders that they can't help but confront it violently with their equipment. Maybe they have some sort of sweepstake among themselves back in the pits that requires its annihilation? Sadly for Danny and Olly they can only manage a drawn heat against the determinedly combative Giffard/Kerr pair and this thereby denies them their place in the six laps final without the pain of further mathematical enquiry.

Before we're treated to this spectacle, we watch another Academy League race and see another appearance of the 13-year-old rider Shane Hazelton. It's an appearance that causes KC to wax lyrical in a fashion that either touchingly sums up the delightful appeal of speedway or is an apocryphal story embellished and delivered in an exaggerated schmaltzy manner.

"Last year he was watching in the stands here and he turned to his dad and said 'I want to do that' and here he is riding a 500cc[5] bike!" I suspect that the truth is in there somewhere but I can't deny it's a resonant story that briefly entertains and diverts. Before the final, the Sittingbourne Massive stare out through the fug of the fumes and exhaust haze that has billowed upwards to gather close to the ceiling, to ponder the dilemma of the empty seats that litter the raised grandstands of the auditorium. Not that they have any doubt that the event is still profitable. "They say the BSPA staging fee they have to pay is £1500, then there's all the other costs like stadium and equipment hire, the riders' pay and all the insurance but they don't do it for charity so there's still money to be made at it!" Like many fans who later chatter on the forums, they have a variety of suggestions to revitalise the *Bonanza* next year and these range from staging an international team meeting of sorts, paying top dollar for Nicki Pedersen to appear or, something always close to the heart of all those from that part of Kent, develop the talent of young riders by allowing them even more races. They note how enthusiastic and committed they all are, the level of entertainment they offer and, though it's left unsaid, we all know that they'd be cheaper to employ than riders who compete professionally to earn a living.

The outcome of the final promises to be closely fought and appears to hold out the prospect of two close races in one heat with a battle between Dugard and Kennett as well as one behind between Bridger and Tomicek to decide the final outcome. It is a repeat of last year's final with the result in that instance effectively decided by a fall for Tomicek. The 4-3-2 points structure (used only in the final and not the qualifying rounds of this Pairs competition) will ensure that the partnership best able to team ride will most likely triumph. Though this year the auditorium isn't plunged into total darkness for effect just as the riders enter the auditorium in gladiatorial fashion, we're nonetheless still treated to the 'theatre' of a close inspection of the track by all parties by the staggered start gate as they consider their choice of gate positions. However, history does repeat itself though this time the partnership that suffers is reversed, so sadly the final descends into an anti-climax when Lewis is excluded during the first attempt to run the race. It's not a decision he welcomes and consequently he responds with some élan to launch a great display of petulance – or passion – depending on your perspective. He first dramatically throws his bike down in disgust and strumps back to the pits (this is always hard to carry off with real authority as every speedway rider's steel shoe gives them a limping gait that slightly undermines the portrayal of their righteous anger), though not before he further takes out his highly visible annoyance by aggressively smacking the entry gate as he departs the stage. The crowd loudly jeers his petulant departure in a pantomime fashion that definitely wouldn't improve my mood if I already felt piqued at the unfair ways of the world. Afterwards, when I report the incident to stallholder Mick Gregory he sagely notes, "I don't mind that – he showed passion and he wanted to win – that's what's wrong with this country, let alone speedway, there's too many bloody good losers!" Whatever your thoughts there's no doubt about the passion that Lewis shows. Unfortunately as a spectacle, the final is now a foregone conclusion and all that Martin and Lubos have to do to win is to ensure that they finish and don't fall off. Edward Kennett wins his fifth race of the afternoon and is thereby awarded the Dick Bellamy trophy but finds that his individual performance is alone not enough to ensure overall victory, which instead goes to the Dugard/Tomicek partnership.

The interval between the Pairs Trophy and the *Bonanza* Championship would, if I were a spectator, usually be the signal for me to head back home for something to eat. As I'm an exhibitor, the other stallholders have just informed me that this is the key sales period of the day until the racing starts again. Or, hopefully, should be. This is theoretically good news but I'm disappointed to learn that I can't nip out for some food because by now I'm ravenous. Initially a substantial part of the throng of spectators from the Pairs Trophy ebbs away out of the Brighton Centre in search of sustenance and, slightly heretically, somewhere to watch the Chelsea v Arsenal football match on television. Uberfan of Wimbledon Speedway and, recently it sometimes seems if you judge by the critical comments he's recently posted about the supposedly questionable lack of "moral" integrity that my book *Showered in Shale* apparently exhibits, Ian Perkin's honorary amanuensis, Derek 'Del' Barclay drops by. He's with a group of ageing friends who stand a short distance away from my stall to wait for him. They must all be fans of the Dons judged by the array of colourful Wimbledon logos that bedeck their clothing and one of them repeatedly waves to me in the manner of Mr Humphries from *Are You Being Served?* I wave back a few times before I realise that far from being a friendly gesture, the individual in question either has an involuntary affliction or takes the mickey by waving sarcastically. Along with Derek's subsequent comments, it's the only rather fey instance of negativity I personally

---

[5] Er, actually he's really riding a 250cc because of his age and arguably its lower power gives Shane an advantage when it comes to negotiating the narrow confines of the indoor circuit.

encounter all day and ultimately it's hard to be irked by Old Age Pensioner speedway supporters who suffer whatever is the waving equivalent of Tourettes. Judged by his regular contributions to various internet forums, Derek is one of the many righteous 'Mr Angrys' who frequent the twilight of the speedway internet world of forums and so-called debate – particularly when it comes to his pet peeve the iniquitous decision of the GRA to end their relationship with Wimbledon Speedway plc.

It's subsequently a delight to get to chat to some other fanatical speedway fans, in the form of the Sheffield-supporting father and son combination of Paul and Philip Brown, whom I've met before on my travels and who have gathered close by at Mick Gregory's stall. I didn't expect to see them because the lure of the Sheffield Sharks basketball club trumps even their love of speedway. Paul hasn't missed a single game since March 11th 2000 ("I'm not obsessive, I'm just keen!") and has watched the club play more matches than anyone in the actual Sheffield team or on the coaching staff! Though he's probably better placed than the manager to pick the team, Paul isn't so keen at this suggestion, "nah, you can get into trouble for that." They're both keen to tell me that the Sharks are "top of the league" and that a brief respite in fixtures (after their match the night before in Leicester) has enabled them to watch the indoor speedway at Brighton for the first time. It makes a huge contrast with the wide-open spaces and speed of the Owlerton track where they watch speedway during the season. In fact, you couldn't find a greater contrast in track sizes between the dimensions of the Sheffield one and that prepared for the *Bonanza*. The Brown family have known Mick for a long time since his incarnation as the stallholder and purveyor of Sheffield Sharks memorabilia during the club's time at Pond's Forge, "before they moved to the Sheffield Arena in the mid 90s" that signalled the end of his tenure in charge of the club shop. They've continued to stay in touch at the speedway. The elder Brown, Paul, obviously knows his character well since he playfully but rather wickedly notes, "Mick's very photogenic, particularly when you've just given him money!"

After a season spent visiting every track in the country, the questions that people ask when they come up and speak to me about the subject matter of my book still never cease to amaze. For the first time this season I'm asked, "Does it cover the sponsors' outlook as well?" My flippant response that "No-one's really interested in them once the money's in the bank," is ill-advised, as the kindly people in front of me turn out to be Dennis and Jean along with their attractive daughter Cathy from the Eastbourne Eagles main sponsors Meridian Marquees. I quickly correct myself to thank them profusely and to emphasise how important their continued patronage is to the club and its fans. Like many sponsors of speedway clubs and riders throughout the country, they're fans first ("we always stand on the first bend to watch – where do you stand?" Cathy asked curiously in the keen manner of the true fan) and sponsors second, albeit in this instance they're very generous sponsors of the club. They're pleased with the respect and response they receive from their sponsorship and stress how much they appreciate working with Jon Cook. So much so that they have already agreed to renew their sponsorship for next season and express pride in their decision to do so. I also get to chat again with the Peasleys from Oxford, in this instance Rob with his mother Hilary who'd forgotten that she'd previously sold me one of the non-winning raffle tickets at Sandy Lane. They're both very loyal and dedicated Oxford speedway fans who expect a much better season ahead in 2007 although I imagine that they probably think this before the start of every season.

By the end of this session I've finally just about managed to outsell the copies sold by my fellow stallholders Mick Gregory (three) and Martin Dadswell (also three). On Martin's attractively laid out stall there are some distinctive and unique items that, as far as I can see, aren't stocked on any of the stalls of his erstwhile competitors at the *Speedway Fayre*. He displays items such as glass-framed programmes from an array of defunct but resolutely not yet forgotten speedway tracks (Norwich, Southampton, Ashfield, West Ham and Wembley) and some distinctively rendered glass framed drawings of famous speedway stars of previous eras (Bruce Penhall, Michael Lee and other riders of that ilk and era). At the end of his stall is the very corporate looking *Brighton Argus* booth run by the lovely Lucy Cross and her colleague Alan. They still appear to have a big pile of the *Argus* left unsold which is a disappointment for us all as this weekend's paper includes a reasonably long and praiseworthy review by the friendly local sports/speedway reporter Brian Owen of my book *When Eagles Dared*. He much prefers my latest offering to my previous "formidable" book. The *Argus* staff appear to be in much disarray after their Christmas party the night before and sadly they have forgotten to prepare, let alone bring along the usual speedway specific headline to put on display at the front of their booth. They are always shouty, pithy, evocative but often ultimately about frighteningly mundane matters that (away from their speedway news) in the city itself make claims like 'Local Man in Hair Horror', 'Lap Dance Club to Open till 4 a.m.' or 'Councillor Denies Sleaze Allegations'. If Lucy and Alan had been less hung over, they could easily have knocked up an eye-catching headline about the track ('It's Not Big But It Is Clever' says Dugard), the latest Russian visitor to appear at the event ('Semen to Make a Splash at *Bonanza*') or perhaps something more prosaic ('Kennett Defends Crown'). At Arlington these headlines are often composed along the lines of 'Pedersen Lashes Out at Critics', 'Cook Confident of Cup Success', 'Cook Lashes Internet Critics' and, as soon as the Eagles hire a rider with the name Cox, they'll be able to have headlines like 'Cox out for Eagles'. Martin contents himself with mischief and identifies that Lucy from the *Argus* has a long-time unrequited crush on the Arlington's roving DJ and resident MC with the mostest, Kevin 'KC' Coombes. Both Alan and Lucy have tickets for the evening session of the racing though Martin Dadswell claims that her eyes will be glued on Kevin throughout the duration of his centre green duties.

However, with the fans back in the auditorium for the *Bonanza* Championship the lack of *Argus* headlines isn't the key talking point among the many stallholders since this topic is always reserved for a discussion of the takings on the day. John Jones, the self-confessed "freaking professional" from the Belle Vue track shop, doesn't have any time for such namby-pamby discussions about this kind of minutiae and refuses to join in the brief group chatter of track-shop men that convenes in front of the Barbers' large prime position display of stock. He pre-emptorily dismisses talk of failure, "I always make money!" as he bustles back from the loos. The rest of the track-shop men all apparently hold his tempestuous brusqueness in high esteem ("he's a great bloke if you get to know him or, at least, stay on the right side of him") but collectively they don't bat an eyelid at this claim of financial success at the *Bonanza* by Mr Jones.[6] Overall, everyone publicly holds to the bravado that they have "done well despite the reduced crowds" but collectively they haven't had the considerable sales revenue boost that previous years' attendance at the *Bonanza Speedway Fayre* automatically created. The next most significant point of discussion is the decision by the Barbers to pack up their large display of attractive merchandise without even bothering to stay for the last reputed 'rush' of the day at the time of the next interval. The experienced speedway track-shop franchisee, Dave Rattenberry, then also chooses to follow suit – to pack up and vamoose rather than linger to the bitter end. Mick Gregory won't follow suit but is somewhat nonplussed. He treats the sight of all the merchandise from these stalls being methodically but expertly packed away into numerous boxes and stacked up ready to be loaded for a prompt departure with a look of bemusement, as though the world had suddenly been discovered not to be flat after all, "You know, I don't think I've ever seen this in all my years!"

My sales had frankly been very disappointing compared to my own ridiculously inflated expectations, though because various track shop owners had settled up on the monies outstanding from the last month or so's sales during the season I had enough cash in my pocket to worry me that I'd lose it or, given my luck, get mugged when I walked home late at night after I'd helped with the breakdown of the *Bonanza*. Plus, I was by now ravenously hungry and needed to eat before the possible rush of the next interval and my work with the track and equipment breakdown later. For a long-time speedway fan, like myself, to go to a meeting but not watch the speedway is like going to an orgy in order to stand outside with a board that advises people to repent of their sins. It was a definite signal that I'd finally crossed the divide from fan into the world of speedway merchandising (and promotional) circles that I even considered not rushing back to the East Grandstand to watch all the heats. I reasoned that I'd still see the remainder of the races that built up to the hopefully thrilling conclusion of the event and also the Final itself so, for once, I could just about excuse myself missing a few races. Nonetheless I was badly torn and my mood wasn't helped by the weather outside the Brighton Centre as the rain lashed down and the wind blew a considerable gale. So much for the opinions of the global warming deniers but, at least, it was pretty seasonal. I dropped off the cash at home and ordered a burger and chips in what's now insistently known as the North Laine but just used to be called 'the Parallels' in 1980 when I first arrived in the town to study. As it's Brighton this takeaway can confidently charge £9 for a cheeseburger and chips in the knowledge that the tourists and affluent Londoners

[6] And I'm sure that they've all, at some point during the season, after my encounter with this speedway track-shop force of nature told me tales where his legendary stubbornness has flown in the face of his own financial self-interest when the speedway equivalent of a 'gift horse' has presented itself. I dimly recall a story about an offer of an exclusive franchise to sell properties such as Wulfsport or some rider-branded jackets, anoraks or the like being sent away with a strongly worded flea in their ear. Nonetheless, I must say that on balance and in all fairness that I admire and appreciate his 'what you see is what you get' approach towards me, since you know exactly where you stand (total contempt in my case it seems). Though his personal style is always high on the swearword count, there's a refreshing honesty to his disdain that left me in absolutely no doubt as to my lowly position (on the freaking naughty step) and has the virtue that John resolutely hasn't ever tried to be falsely ingratiating towards me, unlike some less honest others during another season of extensive travel.

that now fill the town (er, city) won't bat an eyelid at such ridiculous prices provided that everything is 'organic'. I rush back to the Fayre to eat this, only to discover that Mick Gregory is a fan of organic produce and is more than happy to advocate its consumption as well as pay premium prices for superior quality and taste. He justifies this on the basis that his body is a Temple, albeit one that like mine sometimes appears like it has been ransacked by the Goths. He pronounces the chips "delicious" and fails to quibble at the prices.

I'm keen to learn what I've missed but none of the stallholders have been up to the auditorium to watch so they can only pass on some poor second-hand reports to me third hand. It's no surprise to learn that, while I've been away, apparently there have been a lot of crashes that have caused "exceptional" delays. These were due to a combination of the tight first corner and the fact that this is an individual competition where it's every man for himself and this stimulates, what the *Speedway Star*'s reporter Paul Watson later calls in his report of the event, "a definite desire to win" among the riders. In fact, heat 8 has taken so many attempts to try to complete and the 10-metre penalties have been handed out like confetti that the interval has to be taken early so that men and machines can be given some extra TLC. According to reports afterwards, I have missed the debut race of Jason King (younger brother of hot prospect Daniel King) in heat 6 and before that a "shock winner" in the form of unfancied and pretty well unknown American rider Billy Hiles. The crowd have also redressed the balance when it comes to Oliver Allen, runaway winner of last year's 'Mr Petulant Award' when he received the first ever *Bonanza* red card from the crowd. He who dies by the "red coloured page" also lives by it because in heat 3 he was reprieved by speedway's version of 'Ask the Audience'. As I failed to notice it myself, I also assume that I was absent from the auditorium when Phil Griffin allegedly boogied/danced and sang (or lip-synched) to a Michael Jackson record. This must have been a 'Killer' for anyone who witnessed the unique sight of a referee with rhythm and it was enough to prompt Tina Holmes to email a letter to the *Speedway Star* about this rarity. Although even if you allow for the many empty seats on display, her claim that he did this "when he thought no one was looking" appears hard to substantiate.

During the interval I sell nothing and attract only a couple of glances from passing fans as they rush to or from the toilets. The decision by experienced track shop owners to leave early looks shrewdly prescient. Although the remaining Gregory and Dadswell stalls attract reasonable custom and doubtless John "I'm a freaking professional" Jones saw some more action with the folding ones, everyone soon starts to pack up to leave. I say my goodbyes to various people and the friendly Jo, one half of ReRun Productions, kindly allows me to hide my books under her well-ironed tablecloth. The lovely "Anita from the *Speedway Star*" – though in fact she really only works for them on a freelance basis at events like the *Bonanza* and at the Cardiff GP to look after the press – who I've often seen but never spoken to at Arlington, quickly packs away her calendars and magazines. She's another one of those truly committed Eagles fans you often come across, who have loyally gone along to watch for many years. In her case a surprising 36 years and it's an enthusiasm into which she has now inducted her young son to educate him into the ways of the shale. Afterwards I learn that she also apparently had some details about the new speedway magazine that's rumoured to be due to be launched in Spring 2007 aimed at the nascent, often mentioned but difficult to enthuse teenage reader market. Like the search for the Holy Grail, this might prove an elusive quest though I imagine that the *Speedway Star* has already long ago perfected the breathlessly polite 'hear no evil see no evil' style that could well find itself easily suited to the male under-16 reader. Though that said, it's often claimed that this male teenage demographic now 'grows up so quickly' in cultural and sexual politics terms – with implants for the ladies and similar for the lads where their brains should be – that the salacious reportage perfected by *Nuts* and *Zoo* might more be the editorial attitude required for this magazine to strike circulation gold. In fact, I'm sure much more gossip and information on, say, Sophie Blake or other riders' girlfriends would have general widespread appeal within the sport. However, for the sake of the successful launch of this magazine, let's hope the 'creative brains' behind the laughably awful posturing featured in the 'innovative' BSI 2006 GP adverts or the 'brave' but relentlessly cliché ridden graphics and soundtrack of the Reading Bulldogs television adverts are kept well away from the levers of editorial power. Or, at least, are prevented from any offer of advice on their use, otherwise this magazine's appeal to this important demographic will definitely be stillborn and immediately halt the prospect that these readers might become the future engine of speedway audience growth.

The end of the interval is as long as the majority of the remainder of the stallholders choose to remain. Their experience proves correct. Mick Gregory repeats what Dave Rattenberry had already advised me earlier, namely that if I wait until the end of the *Bonanza* to take down my display, it will be a waste of time and effort. As I live in town, I will stay late to help with the breakdown anyway and as I don't have to drive a long distance home I have the luxury to be able to stay on. I take the chance to move my display away from the toilets to a more prominent position on the recently vacated table at the foot of the main staircase by the exit doors. Into position I quickly transport my leaflets, both specially made *Showered in Shale* posters that have formed the centrepiece of my rather limited display as well as my well-travelled, battered, shale-splattered home-made in board of quotations. I again hide my books under the smart Rerun Productions tablecloth and skedaddle back up to the grandstand to watch the *denouement* of the indoor action unfold.

I rejoin the Sittingbourne Massive in the East grandstand and borrow the exceptionally neatly compiled programme of Ian Glover to catch up on all the results of the races I'd missed earlier. Away to our left a few rows higher in the grandstand it's hard not to miss the speedway equivalent of royalty in this neck of the woods, the boisterous group of mainly men that cluster around Eastbourne's ageing *enfant terrible* Dean Barker. Later KC refers to this group as the "Barker party" and they're definitely an ebullient group that has already indulged in the falling-down water and have a group style of dress that echoes the day wear beloved of the London lad nightclub set that you frequently see arrive in town on a Saturday afternoon to follow their beloved Seagulls, albeit, in this instance, without the blue and white scarves or as many beanie hats. They certainly enjoy their own banter and high jinks, while a few rows further away from them in contrast Brent Werner sits quietly to enjoy the spectacle of an event where he excelled on many occasions. One of the "Barker party" cuts a distinctive figure as he's come in tights and is dressed as Superman. Arguably he's the slightest, shortest and most undernourished-looking superhero that you're ever likely to clap your eyes on and I can only imagine that he's dressed in this fashion as some kind of tribute to Martin Dugard's appearance at last year's event in a similar garb. Whatever the reasons he cuts an eye-catching figure in our grandstand and is soon summoned to a greater stage when KC calls him down to the centre green. Once there, he rides on the mountain bike that is one of the main prizes offered in the raffle that I again don't win. The crowd enter into the spirit of an appearance by an ordinary superhero in their midst (as opposed to the speedway riding versions they admire) with pantomime roars of encouragement as this Superman cycles round in a demented ineffective low gear and attempts some tricks aboard his steed. This mostly involves some attempts at wheelies though the questionable exhibition of his advanced riding technique is quickly cut short when an inadvertent slip causes a painful blow to his groin area from the saddle. The crowd, like Kevin Coombes ("I bet that hurt!"), delights in this misfortune, and this slight but game for a laugh bloke milks it for all he's worth as he grimaces like a trooper and mimes rubbing his groin in a fashion that wouldn't disgrace Marcel Marceau. Like a footballer who plays for time and deliberately runs down the clock after he's been substituted, five minutes later he still agonises for all he's worth as he picks his way slowly along our grandstand walkway and up the stairs back to his seat where his mates afford him a hero's welcome.

It's quite a diversion, but also in my row is arguably the most passionate and hysterical fan in the Brighton Centre. I'd confidently guess that she's a Martin Dugard fan, if only judged by the orgasmic grunts, shouts and claps that greets each and every one of his appearances through the pits gate. Like me she's pleased to see him back racing again and the fact that he does so well on a bike that he's borrowed from Edward Kennett. The merest sight of him back in kevlars sets her off and, in my opinion, it's doubly impressive that he can fit into these without too much difficulty. Sadly I've already missed her reaction to his first two race wins of the afternoon but I'm still treated to a virtuoso display of middle-aged, obsessive fandom throughout the remainder of his rides. She clasps her hands in anxiety or joy throughout, leaps to her feet with strangulated yelps, runs her hands through her hair repeatedly or contorts her body St Vitus fashion. Her verbal range mostly alternates between cries of "Martin!" or more wistful but frequently strangulated advice of "Go on!" It's a display that Martin — my all-time favourite Eastbourne rider — matches on the track with a series of effortless wins in the qualification races, only interrupted with a second place in heat 15 behind "Olly" Allen, that leaves his fan of a lifetime apparently inconsolably bereft and distraught to the extent that she holds her hands up in silent supplication before she buries her face in them in moaning contemplation that leaves only her grey hair on display. Oblivious to this drama played out above him in the stand, Martin just does his thing and ensures his automatic qualification for the final through his finish as one of the overall top two points scorers (predictably the other is Edward Kennett though he too has dropped a point albeit to Martin) with a resounding win over Lewis Bridger who finishes in second place but with a low aggregate points tally of six points. Lewis though, also has admirers — a whole contingent of them — so each time he takes to the circuit, he's greeted with loud, shrill teenybopper type screams that I always thought went out of fashion with the Bay City Rollers. It's an impressive reaction to cause and, before heat 19, KC pauses theatrically in mid-introduction to let the volume of this reaction dissipate before he finishes his patter. After this race, he intones in a slightly stilted manner that leads you to think

Bonanza dynamo Martin Dugard hard at work. © Jeff Scott

Treasured photo of Bill Gimbet. © Jeff Scott

that he might have prepared something to say along these lines as part of his homework beforehand, "The Master of Arlington [M. Dugard] beats the future Master of Arlington [L. Bridger], I have no doubt!" the lady in my row did have her doubts about the likely result of this race and implored Martin to victory almost yard by yard. Kevin also finds time to, very accurately I think, wax philosophical, "Speedway riders across the world, once that helmet goes on, they have to win and that's why we love our speedway!"

The final scores have ended up so tight together that we even have a run-off between the black-helmeted Charlie Venegas and Daniel King that's won from the start line by the American. Not that all-out racing is necessarily the best way to get to the front of the field as the wily campaigner Shawn McConnell illustrates in the highest scorers' run off for the remaining two places in the final. Making a virtue of his invariably slow starts from the gate, he chooses to slightly hang back as all the other riders eagerly charge to the corner only to then pick the ideal line through them all to hit the front and closely ride the inside line to victory. It's the perfect tactic that ensures consecutive victories for the American nation and McConnell's qualification for the six laps final. For this the riders walk out behind their mechanics, theatrically pushing their steeds ahead of them, for some further introductions and faux anticipation that surrounds the choice of gate positions. Offered first choice by dint of his tied points score and victory over Edward Kennett, Martin 'controversially' chooses the outside gate four from which to mount his challenge for individual *Bonanza* glory. Predictably Edward chooses gate one and the last person with a positive choice, Shawn McConnell, deliberates for a moment before he identifies gate three as the best of the remainder. When the tapes rose, it was all over once Martin had made the start and though he pressed hard Edward, as Paul Watson reporting on his last ever speedway race noted in the *Star* afterwards, "could not get in a meaningful challenge in the six laps."

I rush back to my table only to find a complete scene of devastation wrought on the entrance hall by a combination of petty thieves and the moronic approach to customer service and care exhibited by the dimwits of the Brighton Centre security staff who have opened the main doors of the entrance to allow in the elements. And what elements they are tonight as the wind howls with great ferocity inside the building and the rain lashes the seafront outside. It's an ideal wild night for any Brighton resident who loves to watch the awesome power of the sea in full force on the stony beach and it's of such a magnitude as to deceive the occasional tourist who will invariably gets swept to their death when they venture too close (though the tourist board doesn't like to make any great play of this danger in the promotional literature they issue about the appeal of the city seafront). No night in my lifetime will probably ever compare to the great storm of 1987 for power (or devastation) but tonight the wind appears to have reached levels that definitely approach storm force. This gale has scattered my leaflets throughout the place, displaced my board almost to the far wall while some light-fingered tosser(s) have stolen my unguarded posters and a few books. I'm still shocked by petty thefts from speedway people much more than I would be by such actions in everyday life where if you don't exactly expect them you're not exactly surprised either. Though ultimately it's of little significance in the scheme of things and a comparative drop in the bucket to the considerable financial losses I've already wracked up by researching, producing and promoting my books. Nonetheless these actions irk me for their symbolism, way beyond their actual financial cost. In fact, I'd go so far as to say these are not proper speedway people. Sadly all the true speedway people that remain are only too keen to leave the Brighton Centre without so much as a glance as my books. Though this would be hard as the covers flutter vertically and the books struggle to remain on the table in the strong wind that gusts unrelentingly through the doors. An even more foolhardy man stands rather forlornly in the eye of the gale by the exit doors and holds a handwritten sign that advises he's trying to sell *Speedway Star* 2007 calendars at a bargain price of £4. He gets absolutely no takers that I notice, despite the fact that practically everyone has to pass close to him to fight their way out through the gale. The security staff huddles in a group together as waves of speedway fans bustle on their way home or try to shelter inside in the hope that it will subside. The Polish man on the nearby table tells me that the doors opened "10 minutes" and though he's got a poor command of the language he rightly calls this action "silly." Sadly language barriers and his lack of observation skills hampers my attempt to establish if he could provide a description of the thieves. As the covers of my books flutter manically, Derek Barclay stops by again, surveys the emptiness of my area of the hallway and gloats/jokes, "you just don't know when to stop flogging a dead horse, do you?" Shortly afterwards, the friendly and knowledgeable photographer Steve Dixon with his lovely partner Debbie also stop for a few words before they head off to Preston Park. Anyone else who has decided to linger gets short shrift from the security people who pre-emptorily announce in loud instructive voices as they finally shut the doors after all the damage to my display and any chance of additional sales has been well and truly done, "sorry folks I know it's not nice outside but you're all going to have to leave now as we're locking the doors!" This is the kind of customer service that typifies jobsworth Britain. It's just the sort of obstinate and rude 'can't do' attitude – news of which quickly travels beyond our shores to undermine our self-congratulatory misperceptions of our greatness as a nation or island race.

In the time it takes for the crowd to disperse and the security staff to lock down the Brighton Centre as though it contains a horde of items of irreplaceable value as well as for me to take a taxi home with my stuff and then walk back again to the loading bay at the back of the building – the work on the breakdown has already progressed impressively. The logistical arrangements for the breakdown of *Bonanza X* have been conceived completely differently from 2005 by Martin and Jon, with much more emphasis placed upon the breakdown of the actual track rather than the return to storage of the fixtures and fittings that make up the vital furniture of a speedway meeting. Lessons have been learnt so everything has been organised – from conceptualisation of what's expected to be accomplished tonight and what can wait until tomorrow to the amount of mechanical equipment on hand. Everything is geared to maximise the speed and easy convenience of the removal of everything from inside the auditorium to the loading bay outside, from where it can be picked up at comparative leisure tomorrow. We all benefit from the fact (in humour and energy levels) that the more leisurely set-up of the *Bonanza X* over the previous two days hasn't required that we all work for almost 24 hours on the bounce, as was required in other years, before we reach this late stage in the proceedings. Plus, the people here can (and do) stay right until the end rather than drift off as the night lengthens and the shale removal slows to a snail's pace. In fact, this year the whole place is stripped out with a ruthless almost military efficiency as we all work hard as a team in the manner of a ram raid on a well-stocked jewellers. The different philosophy appears to inspire a phenomenal work rate among the people who remain to help with the breakdown. Yet again this year I find it inspiring to be part of this efficient team and also notice how diligently and zealously everyone works with strength, skill and vigour, especially the two one-armed men on the team who swagger about the place and effectively have to contribute almost double the effort to lift the equivalent of their compatriots. The sixteen or so of us were formed from Eastbourne (Jon Cook, Martin Dugard, Kath Rolfe from the Speedway Office, Roy Prodger and his brother Dave, Alan Rolfe, Malcolm Cole, Ashley Wooler, Neil Hollebon) and Robins staff (Edward Kennett, Mick Robins, Gary Robins, John Robins, Norman Robins, Lance Wyman, Dougie Ballard and the industrious Alan Saunders). In the spirit of economics identified by Adam Smith in his various influential theories, but particularly on the *Division of Labour*, and by employing the mass production techniques that made Henry Ford fabulously rich when it came to the motor car, we had all been assigned a specific task or set of tasks to fulfill repetitively. My arrival back at the loading area was greeted with polite surprise but some warmth by Jon Cook who immediately gave me the task he was involved with, namely the separation into different piles of the ruined cardboards sheets – that lined the floor of the auditorium and were covered in shale during the event – from the returnable comparatively undamaged ones. The more pristine examples (though many were far from perfect and the concept of an 'undamaged' board, got more elastic in its definition the longer I did it) were roughly knocked on the floor to clean off the largest lumps of shale still stuck to their surface and then stacked in an orderly pile on a pallet for collection the next day. The battered and broken boards were further smashed down into more convenient, smaller sized pieces and thrown on the rubbish pile that Jon had gradually created close by to the pile of boards that had survived. For a while we shared the work until it became clear that I could manage perfectly well on my own and that Jon should return to the many supervisory duties that running an event of this kind necessarily thrust upon him. Before he left we chatted about the Fayre and the event in general. Though John Berry hadn't sought me out for the brief chat he'd suggested, he had managed to introduce himself to Jon and they'd had a "really good chat about things, mostly what we spoke about the other day." Left to my own devices, this was my task for around the next 90 minutes or so that it took to strip the auditorium of the boards and the compacted shale. These grotty boards arrived with great regularity as the shale was gradually stripped from their surface inside the auditorium. During one lengthy longueur I did venture up to the loading bay to carry the boards down myself only to be admonished by Jon for breaking out from my compartmentalised role in the *Bonanza X* breakdown chain, "Jeff, wait for them to be thrown down as you'll only knacker yourself if you start doing that too!" Alan Rolfe and Kath efficiently carried the majority of these – though others intermittently helped until something more interesting as a task caught their attention or demanded their efforts – and dropped them over the side of the bay for me to collect or manhandle into position with my gloved hands. Again very noticeably I was the only person to wear gloves and, though it was dusty in the bay, the wind provided regular fresh air so we weren't assailed by the choking quantities of shale dust that I'd inhaled so copiously the year before.

My outlook was bounded by my position so I could only guess at what exactly happened inside the auditorium. Positioned where I was, I could see the mounds of shale get gathered in a huge pile on the far side of the loading bay from the dumper trucks driven with considerable skill and control but at great speed in alternation with each other by Edward and Gary. Easily able to identify the office boy in his midst and with half a mind on potential future lawsuits for compensation due to industrial injury, Jon Cook went out of his way to state the obvious as he nods to industrial earth-moving vehicles that bustled about the place at speed: "Be careful you don't get run over by those – as they're dangerous!" Ashley and the one armed man repeatedly climbed up the ever bigger mound of shale to scavenge for rogue lumps of cardboard among the detritus in the manner of destitute and starving children that's sadly played out on rubbish tips around the world. Malcolm Cole passed by many times on a forklift truck that he manoeuvred about the narrow walkways with a precision that was genuinely breathtaking given the confines of the space and the size and weight of the loads he transported. He mesmerised me every time he journeyed past and there were many times throughout that intense period of break down activity that he did so with laden pallets of safety boards, stanchions, tools, electrical equipment and other items of assorted speedway furniture after they had been unassembled and gathered together inside the auditorium. "Malcolm really knows how to drive that thing!" I commented to Jon who nodded agreement, "He does."

By the time I'd finally stacked the last few boards, the sight that greeted me inside the auditorium was still one of great industry but one without hardly any real shale to speak of remaining to be gathered from the floor. There was some loose shale too small to be picked up mechanically yet to be swept up but the auditorium looked almost completely restored to its former empty state, albeit still some way short of pristine. The chance to grab the broom is something that I can't resist as it's definitely a task that I excel at after my years of training as a groundsman at Wimbledon (the famous tennis tournament not the Conference League speedway version that was the reputed home of meetings that regularly featured frequent and thrilling passing). In fact, so many of us have brooms that we soon have to search for anything that resembles a dusting of shale to then sweep it up into something that almost constitutes a pile. Jon Cook interrupts my search for shale dust with "Can I have a quick word?" and we walk a few yards away towards the edge of the empty auditorium for greater privacy. Once there he drops the bombshell, "Just between you and me, I might not be at Eastbourne next season!" It's such unexpected news that I don't quite know what to say but don't have to since Jon matter of factly explains at length the situation and the factors behind his dramatic decision to leave the club. I'm touched that he trusts me enough to take me into his confidence and can only think to garble that I'll miss the chance to work with him. Never one for sentimentality, it's a comment that he brushes off in his usual characteristically phlegmatic manner, "I'll still be around!"

Outside in the loading bay, everything that had been used inside to create the speedway meeting that was *Bonanza X* has already been piled up there ready to be picked up the next morning and transported back to either Herstmonceux or

Arlington. This year's break down process has been conceived, planned and executed with brilliant efficiency at phenomenal pace by the available staff and the extra machinery has aided this task. So much so that by 23.29 we have officially finished! With a job superbly well done, no one needs any second invitation to scarper and the huge sliding metal doors of the stage door cum loading bay entrance are clanged resoundingly shut with some finality by Martin Dugard before he then locks it. In three days the whole event has been constructed, run and broken down again. Martin Dugard and Edward Kennett (along with Jon Cook) were involved from the outset to the end, while in between they competed against each other to the full and raced on the track brilliantly. Martin truly rolled back the years[7] to deservedly garner favourable comments from fans and critics alike. Typical of the man, he shrugged these off with understated grace and considerable modesty, "yeah I'm pleased, but I'm freaking knackered and I could go even better if I [gestures to stomach] was to lose a bit of this!" Edward again effortlessly and modestly managed the transition from speedway star to just another one of the hard-working men from the capable Robins team. This process is helped in no small part by the ribbing he receives from his work-mates. Particularly Lance who, though he sports a more severe hairstyle and more face furniture than last year, hasn't lost his sense of humour and chants "loser" under his breath but audibly enough before he follows it up with a barbed, "He's gonna get the sack 'cause he freaking lost the titles!" In reality, Edward is ultra competitive but has the good grace to roll with the insults and, when I had caught him for a few words on his own earlier, went out of his way to praise Martin's performance, "he probably deserved to win though it was on my bike, wasn't it?"

The privilege that I've been a part of the *Bonanza* team isn't quite as hard won or earned this year given the comparatively early finish but I walk home tired, dusty and elated. The next day Steve Dixon emails and succinctly sums up the appeal of the day, "I can't really understand some of the whinging about it on the British Speedway forum. It's a fun event at the end of the day – with a chance to buy end-of-season cheap goodies! I was never a fan of Dugard and even less so when he decked Andersson at Eastbourne a few years back but give him his due here, he is really class on that tiny circuit."

10th December 2006 *Brighton Bonanza X*
Pairs Trophy winners: Martin Dugard and Lubos Tomicek
Bonanza Championship winner: Martin Dugard

---

[7] If you read the programme, Martin was literally ageless at this event since he was the only rider originally programmed to ride in the main senior events of the day to be to profiled without the specific details of his birthday included.

Afterword

I hope that you enjoyed the journey.

Phew! What a fantastic year I had and what another brilliant experience. I was genuinely overwhelmed with the kindness of strangers and amazed how people went out of their way to help me.

Well, if that was my account of the 2006 season where does the sport now find itself in 2007? There has been the welcome news of the return of speedway to Birmingham in the Premier League and an expansion of the Conference League to include clubs like Sittingbourne and Cleveland. However, as I write these words, there has been the shock closure in mid-season of Oxford speedway — a club with a rich 58-year tradition but beset recently by experience of some of the apparently intractable problems that presently conflict the state of the sport in this country (falling crowds, new ownership, failure to attract top class riders, dearth of British talent etc.). The shockwaves that this will create are, as yet, not fully known but it's clear that there has to be a thorough examination of the governance and strategic direction of the sport as well as due consideration given to its future relationship with its commercial partners, rival speedway associations in other countries and, of course, the elephant in the room of the Speedway Grand Prix, now under the new ownership of IMG. Doubtless, there will be the usual extensive debate and no real action, but the time for the usual fiddling with the deckchairs by the British authorities has arguably now completely passed. More of the same won't cut it any longer and anyone who believes that this kind of tinkering with rules at the margin or similar action in the future will rectify the situation operates under a dangerous delusion. We have to ignore the mumpsimuses, abandon the ineffective elements of the present structure and quickly find radical solutions. Most sensibly this should be the immediate setting up of a completely autonomous and independent body to run the sport headed by someone with the experience, knowledge and power to take difficult decisions. The sport could do a lot worse than appoint the plain-speaking John Berry, who has already suggested his availability, into a position where he could run such a body. The time for this kind of decision is now and collectively with regard to the problems faced — many of them self-inflicted — we now have to piss or get off the pot.

Obviously all mistakes remain my own and I apologise if I have accidentally upset anyone. If you have any comments, of either persuasion, please get in touch via my website on www.methanolpress.com

Every effort has been made to get in touch with all copyright holders and many people featured in the photos but, again, I would be delighted to hear from you to make the appropriate credits or acknowledgements.

I mentioned earlier that I have been overwhelmed with help and kindness. I hesitate to name everyone as, inevitably, I will make a mistake and miss someone I'm extremely grateful to, so, with sincere apologies to those who I do manage to miss out I would like to thank the following people: Peter Adams, Graham Arnold, Simon Astaire, Jonathan Atkins, Mike Bacon, Graeme Bailey, Robert Bamford, Nick, Johnny, Bev and Colin Barber, Derek Barclay, Dick Barrie, Norman Beeney, Seth Bennett, John Berry, Alun Biggart, Annamika Bipat, Pat Bliss, Jo Bloom, Joyce and Malcolm Blythe, Richard Bott, Mike Bowden, Anne Brodrick, Brian Burford, John Campbell, Sarah Chrisp, Kate Clanchy, Jon Cook, Graham Cooke, Kevin Coombes, David Crane, Dave Croucher, Jonathan Chapman, Keith and Cheryl Chapman, Martin Dadswell, Andrew Dalby, Paddy Davitt, Gordie Day, Alan Dick, Chris Durno, Graham and Denise Drury, Steve and Debbie Dixon, Kevin Donovan, Martin Dugard, Neil Dyson, Svend Elkjaer, George and Joan English, Dave Fairbrother, Ben Findon, John Gaisford, Chris Gay, Arnie Gibbons, Bill Gimbeth, Rob Godfrey, Mike and Anita Golding, Mick Gregory, Rob Griffin, George Grant, Andy Griggs, Rumana Haider, Keith Hamblin, Tim Hamblin, Graham and Barbara Hambly, Holly Hodder, Liz Hunt, John Hyam, John, Jordan, Karen, Mark and Judy Hazelden, Ross Heaton, Andy Higgs, Mike Hinves, Richard Hollingsworth, Dave Hoggart, Lynn Hunt, Mike Hunter, John Hyam, Tony Jackson, Sue Jackson-Scott, John James, Adam Jennison, Steve Johnson, Tristan Jones, Juliette Jowitt, Frank Keating, Chris Kinsey, Russell Lanning, Jo Lawson, Mark Lawton, Sheila Le-Sage, Kevin Ling, Hywel Lloyd, Gary Lough, John

Louis, Michael Max, Tony MacDonald, Ian and Jean Maclean, Neil Machin, Julie Martin, Martin Mauger, Dennis McCleary, Allan Melville, Howard Milton, Jayne Moss, Susie Muir, Martin Neal, Bill Norris, Peter Oakes, Torben Olsen, Brian Owen, Gordon Pairman, Shane and Anji Parker, Dave Pavitt, Michael Payne, Nigel Pearson, Rob Peasley, Di Phillips, Matt Pitman, Mark Poulton, Andy Povey, Colin Pratt, Bob Radford, Dave Rattenberry, Andy Renner, Dave and Margaret Rice, John Rich, Gareth Rogers, Jane Rogers, Laurence Rogers, Martin Rogers, Mark Rowe, Ronnie Russell, Graham Reeve, Craig Saul, Pat Sheehan, Len and Hazel Silver, Jonathan Sim, Andrew Skeels, Derek Smith, Tim Stone, Tony Steele, Trevor Swales, Shaun Tacey, Dave Tattum, Caroline Tattum, David Taylor, Mark Thursfield, Peter Toogood, Stuart Towner, Ian Thomas, Dave Valentine, Chris Van Stratton, Peter Waite, Barry Wallace, John Walsh, Nick Ward, Paul Watson, Ros Wesson, The Reverend Michael Whawell, Bryn Williams, Dave Wright and Malcolm Wright.

To pick out anyone in particular would be invidious. However, I owe so many 'thank you's' so I have no choice but to do so. Firstly, thanks to the *Speedway Star* for their permission to reproduce snippets throughout the book from this most esteemed magazine. If you want to read my selections in their original context please look at your own back issues or, if you haven't already, take out a subscription (it's remarkable value). The book wouldn't look as lovely as it does without Rachael Adams's brilliant design and artistic skills, along with her stubborn persistence. When I come back in the next life, I hope that I'm going to be right all the time. There would be many more errors than there are without the diligent proofreading of Caroline Tidmarsh and Vy Shepherd along with speedway fanatic Billy Jenkins who, though I've never met him, has kind of adopted me and kindly advised in so many thoughtful ways. Graham Russel has shown tremendous pedantry and knowledge to wrangle with my words to convert them into some sort of sense. My true friend Sue Young has encouraged me often in so many things and really saved me when I needed that most – for which she has my eternal gratitude. Of course, without the love and guidance of my parents – Mary and Alan – none of this book or so many other things would have been possible. Finally, you can never have too many teachers and I was lucky enough to have been inspired to write my speedway books by a truly great teacher, poet, musician and wit – Michael Donaghy. He is still greatly missed.

Finally, if you go to speedway already why not make a point of taking even more friends this year and if you haven't been for a while or have never been, now is as good a time as any to start!

Yours in speedway!

Thank you for getting this far.

Brighton

6 June 2007

Acknowledgements

Books and magazines

I have quoted with kind permission from the following sources:

Speedway Star (2006)
For subscriptions call 0208 335 1113
Backtrack (2006)
For subscriptions call 01708 734 502
The Voice: The Official Journal of the Friends of Speedway
For subscriptions call 0208 397 6599

Websites

I have consulted and recommend the following websites
<www.speedwayplus.com> Just an excellent site
<www.speedwayworld.com> All the news in detail as it happens
<www.british-speedway.co.uk> The official BSPA website for all the fixture and team information
<www.speedway-forum.co.uk> For strong opinions, argument, rumour and debate, plus too much use of emoticons
<www.speedwayupdates.proboards103.com> For all meetings – as they happen, where you aren't
<www.tattingermarsh.co.uk/blog> Home of the enthralling 'Blunsdon Blog' – a hidden side of speedway

Photographers

Julie Martin <www.juliemartinphotography.co.uk>
Steve Dixon <www.stevedixonphotography.co.uk>

Jazz Musicians

<www.billyjenkins.com> The one and only Billy J – the incomparable speedway/bowls loving Bard of Bromley and progenitor of a distinctively British kitchen-sink jazz sound

Accommodation

All the following warmly welcome speedway fans and have special rates:
Cara House, Berwick-upon-Tweed 01289 302749 <www.carahouse.co.uk>
Waverley Hotel, Workington 01900 603246 <www.waverley-hotel.com>
Garrison Hotel, Sheffield 0114 249 9555 <www.garrisonhotel.co.uk>

Feedback 2006

12th March – Email from Di Phillips, Somerset fan and definitely not a Zorro groupie:
Hope you're ok, just 2 things:
1. Elaine asked to tell you she has been going to Speedway for 35 years not 45 years.
2. Please can you somehow tone down the orgasm bit as the three people I have shown it to say it comes across as I am a Zorro Groupie, and I am definitely not that, just someone who likes to get involved with Speedway and help the riders i.e. doing match reports for Zorro's website.

15th April – Email from the Reverend Michael Whawell, Peterborough Speedway:
Many thanks for the sheets (and sheets, and sheets) of your draft. I'll reply in detail next week – busy day, including a wedding, tomorrow, then off to Sheffield.
Early spot: p.6 in 'Pride of' has me as Club CHAPLIN – I know I'm a bit of a Charlie, but... Chaplain, maybe.

19th April – Email from Rob Godfrey, Scunthorpe co-promoter:
Thanks for the draft copy just a few amendments Gayle is spelt (Gail).
Norm still works with us and it's (Dean and Trish) not Den and Zoe.
Apart from them it is very good and we all enjoyed reading it we are looking forward to seeing the book when it is finished.

20th April – Email from Neil Watson, ex co-promoter Peterborough Speedway:
I guess my Judas comment is going to come back to haunt me – is it libellous or slanderous?!

22nd April – Email from Ian Maclean, generous Glasgow fan:
Have carefully gone over it again and my comments are:
Michael Max has never been 'the announcer' at Glasgow Speedway. He has had to do it on a very few occasions when our long time announcer Jim Coyle has been on holiday and there was no stand-in. He is the 'presenter' of the event.
The late George Hunter was my all time favourite in the 60s during the ten seasons he rode for Edinburgh. I had seen his first appearance on a track at Motherwell in 1958 when he had five seconds and Ian Hoskins correctly realised that he had that magic touch. It was the inclusion of George in the 1971 Glasgow team that lured me back to speedway but George only rode at Hampden Park for not quite two complete seasons – he left I think in August 1972 but I was hooked again and have been a Glasgow fan ever since. George had rightly predicted that the Hampden track was dangerous and unfortunately this was borne out with the instant on-track death of a young Norwegian rider. I think reading your comments might give the impression that George was a Glasgow favourite in the 70s.
The only other thing is that it is Marian not Marion but then only our family would know that.
Apart from the above relatively trivial points I can't see anything that needs changing – it is very good and presents a good impression of speedway fans.
Other general comments on what you have said:
Dust can be a problem on a hot sunny afternoon. As I said Speedway ought to be under lights on a dark night – much easier to prepare a track into the bargain.
You rightly commented on Shane. He is a great ambassador for Speedway and he knows who pays his wages (compare that with the truculent James Grieves).
An example of his personality comes from a recent visit my son made to Stoke. Alan realised that the meeting would be off but went along anyway as he was well up the road from London. He had his 4 year-old with him. The boy has a favourite rider at Rye House but afterwards told his dad that 'the man we were talking to in the bar is now my favourite rider'
Thanks for your generous comments about the lift to the airport. As you know we were going anyway and were only too glad to help.

24th April – Email from Ella Macdonald, Edinburgh Speedway Supporters Club:
I read most of it this weekend on my travels to Stoke and Newport and it was excellent reading.
The only small change I could see was that in the Exeter chapter the fan referred to as John should in fact be Joan. Joan was with us this weekend and she had a good laugh at her 'sex change'.

24th April – Email from George English, Newcastle Promoter:
Well that was interesting, though Newcastle doesn't exactly come out of the two chapters too well does it?
However I will not be threatening you with court proceedings as you have written your perception of events as you saw them. I will be having words with Mick Gregory though! I don't suppose he told you that he has a hidden agenda as far as Newcastle Speedway is concerned.
Just one point, I am very protective of the volunteers who keep Newcastle Speedway going and in the 'Barney in Byker' chapter it looks as though it is my staff who can't find the key. However, that gate is the responsibility of *William Hill* and their staff. I know it's a very small point but it matters to me. Good Luck with the book.

7th May – Email from David Crane, Mildenhall Speedway:
I've had a quick read through and if I'm being honest, I wasn't hugely impressed.
It was good to read your thoughts after meeting Brian Snowie and you summed him up very well which was the highlight for me, as was your thoughts on the comments by a section of supporters on the second bend, that was quite amusing! It felt too long winded and you could have got your observations across in half the space. It also felt you was being critical in certain parts for the sake of it, the grid girls for instance and also the programme. The editor says the mastermind quiz was done by Martyn, not Adam Dudley as referred.
Sections like the following seem irrelevant to include: *'The enthusiastic young boys from in front of me have already beaten to the loos and are in philosophical form when they ask me, "why is everyone's wee yellower than ours?" to which I delight in replying, "you better ask your father". Hopefully, he'll have explained it all to them by the time I return although, maybe, I should rush back myself out of curiosity at his explanation.'* Nevertheless, I look forward to reading your experiences of other tracks, i.e., Ipswich, King's Lynn and Rye House to see how they compare.

17th May – Email from Gordon Day, Poole Press Officer:
Hope I am not too late to point out that the Greyhounds didn't get to Poole until 1960. The track that made way for speedway was a tarmac cycle track – a velodrome if you like, which had been at the Stadium since the thirties.

7th June – Email from Chris Geer, speedway mechanic:
I think it's very good, I've briefly flicked through the book and it's a very honest book and quite funny. Good luck with it and I think you're on to a winner!

12th June – Email- from Pat Bliss, ex-Reading Promoter:
Many thanks for copy of the book *Showered in Shale* – much appreciated. Have not read it all yet although must admit turned straight to the Reading 'bits'. Do agree that Reading has lost its family atmosphere which is a great pity although I do think perhaps I 'got out' at just the right time – time will tell.

26th June – Review by Tim Hamblin, Wolverhampton Speedway programme:
Trouble at the speedway? Just blame author Jeff Scott!

His new book, *Showered in Shale*, is a fan's eye view of the sport compiled as he visited tracks throughout Britain last season. The 500-page softback covers 40 meetings – and quite lively some of them were, too.

Jeff's Monmore chapter concerns a certain Wolves v Eastbourne encounter in which the on-track action was hardly confined to speedway. And while that kind of flare-up is mercifully rare, he did encounter similar incidents elsewhere. *"I think it is a very safe environment,"* he stressed at a Monmore signing session. *"You've got lots of old people here, which is unusual in a lot of sports' environments or any environment in the community."*
"You've got young people who can run around perfectly safely, so I think there's that community thing I was looking at. In all

communities there's disputes, in the nature of the thing. There was an incident here, but equally there was one at Newcastle and there was one at the Isle of Wight. So for a while I thought I was attracting these dramatic contretemps, shall we call them?"

Jeff, though now based in Brighton and a frequent Eastbourne follower, first watched the sport in 1975 at Reading. *"That was the good old days!"* he said. *"You would see all the different nations riding when the Poles used to come, and the Russians, Swedes and Danes. They were like gladiators, they appeared to me like that as a teenager. Particularly under floodlights you've got the drama, the smell — the smell has changed slightly nowadays, obviously, because Castrol R doesn't exist any more."*

"But nonetheless people round the country when I went round doing the book did speak about the smell. The smell and the noise are very evocative of a speedway meeting."

Jeff has a bouncy written style — were there a world market in split infinitives he would be a very rich man — well suited to his subject. Among the vast number of interviews is one with Peter Adams in which the Wolves team manager recounts how the sport got into his blood.

7th July – Email from Mark Poulton, speedway fan:
You won't remember me, but we met late in the afternoon at the Cardiff GP while you were promoting your book, *Showered in Shale*. You asked at the time for me to let you have some feedback on what I thought of the book.
Well, I think it's a simply fascinating and unique observation of speedway in Great Britain in the early 21st century described with a unique and entertaining use of the English language.
I read the Newport entries first as they are my local team, and I must say that considering you hadn't been there before or met the people you interviewed, it is a very astute and accurate observation of speedway at Newport. This for me adds credibility to your observations at all of the other tracks, and very engrossing observations they are. Your descriptions of the various locales and communities in which the tracks reside makes interesting reading. The praise and acknowledgment of the often unseen efforts of the people involved at the tracks is the most endearing for me. These people rarely get the praise they deserve in ensuring the sport survives and their views, along with the supporters views you include, are most interesting. While the riders who risk life and limb providing us with entertainment and the promoters viewpoints are, as always, very interesting.
I feel it is a most noteworthy and colourfully described account of the social infrastructure of speedway in Great Britain in the current age.
I cannot find anything I don't like about your book, it is simply a pleasure to read.
Congratulations, and I hope your efforts get the just reward they deserve.

16th July – Review by Dick Barrie, *Straight Talking* column in Berwick programme:
I'll get into my book-reviewer mode now, and mention that when author Jeff Scott was here a few weeks ago, promoting his newly-published *Showered In Shale* travelogue, he was kind enough to press a review copy, duly autographed to me, into my hands.

Jeff's book is a journal of his personal travels throughout the 2005 season, when he visited a meeting at every track in Great Britain, and I found it absorbing. What makes me appreciate his style of writing is that — while clearly interested in the sport and aware of the general history of speedway — he isn't in any way an "insider" on the scene and definitely not a "sad anorak" of the worst kind, and his conversational way of describing the places he visits and people he meets is candid, well-observed and straightforward.

Yes, there are a few mistakes and errors in the book — but they are honest blunders, not howling clangers. Usually they come from Jeff innocently quoting statements by the people he meets on his travels, who make gaffes which his cheerfully admitted lack of knowledge of the game has prevented him picking up on. However, Jeff has a nice turn of phrase, doesn't pull his punches and isn't scared to offer critical observations when he feels the need!

If you bought the book when Jeff was here, you'll be aware of what it's all about. If you didn't, but fancy a new style of speedway read — or want to provide an unusual gift for someone who would appreciate it etc

25th July – Email from Billy Jenkins, speedway fan:

I'm understanding the slightly confused rhetoric in the speedway press 'self-published by him' states Tony McD tartly in the (self-published) July *Backtrack*.

He comments on the pictures. But the layout is beautiful!!!

Jeff – this is a work of Art. In every way!

I was right to await your signing – as I will drink slowly and deeply.

Coffee and a dip into will proceed AT ONCE!

1st August – Email from Danny Brotherton, speedway fan:

Hi. I loved the book, it reminded me of a Bill Bryson travel book, only with a speedway theme. I have not been in *The Grove* in Berwick since 1980 and it's good to know that it seems to be exactly as I remember it.

11th August – Email from Billy Jenkins, speedway fan:

getting near the end...

don't want it to stop...

find myself taking an even more interest in *Speedway Star* match reports on those you write about...

I picked James Wright for me Fantasy team two years ago... sensed he had potential – and indeed your observations confirm...

Enjoying your blogs a lot...

So what IS it with Wimbledon and Mr Perkins and 'legal mutterings re your copy...!?

I just don't want the book to end...

So I'm reading VERY slowly – and STILL the rhythm is superb

21st August – Email from Arnie Gibbons, speedway fan:

It took about a month in total to finish, and since then I've been reading your blog (dare I visit the Belle Vue track shop?). I think that towards the end it began to feel a bit repetitive (a point I've seen elsewhere about tighter editing). Still overall a fantastic read. The astute point in the *Star* review is its potential to act as a source document of social history.

My one criticism is that it needed some fact checking – there were a number of inaccurate statements largely because people's memory isn't a 100% reliable (particularly when it comes to dates). For example on your blog you refer to Michael Lee as the youngest World Champion – an honour that goes to Ronnie Moore. And Lee isn't even the youngest British Champion, Peter Craven was.

I've just started a new volume of my speedway diaries (I do a match report for every meeting I attend) and recently visited Motala for the Swedish Championships, notching up my first 80cc meeting in the process. (All so that I can hopefully say in six years time "well I saw him when he was 13 and I knew he'd be good then").

Hopefully I'll catch up with you in person soon (although our paths don't look like they will cross in the next few weeks).

29th August – Phone conversation with Jonathan Chapman, co-promoter King's Lynn Speedway

"Yeh I've been enjoying reading it – I've read ours, of course, straightaway and some others but mostly it's just been a few pages at a time. To be honest, and not being funny or nothing, I keep it in the toilet as it's ideal for reading there!"

13th September – Email from Martin Mauger, Hull speedway fan:

You may (and may not) remember me from when we briefly met at Scunthorpe when I bought your book; *Showered In Shale*. Hull fan; Hull Vikings baser and jacket spoke very briefly about Booey's book and Bruce Penhall's?

I just want to say how much I enjoyed it and how very different and refreshing I found it compared with many other publications on the sport. I very much disagree with the guy who said it "should have been (just) a track guide and would therefore date quickly as a result" as all books inevitably date to a varied extent. It is that and much more and will stand as a true and valid account of your travels to every speedway venue in the UK at that time, with a brief account of the history of each town, giving your impressions of finding and entering the stadia as a "regular" punter and also your thoughts on meeting with the people responsible. In many ways I'm surprised at the level of co-operation you experienced as speedway people can be very guarded and reluctant to talk or allow outsiders to even briefly view the inner sanctum, as you discovered at Wimbledon. To call speedway a closed shop would be to call a duck's a*se reasonably watertight. Disappointing to read, though not altogether surprising, was the near future threat by housing developments to various tracks; Glasgow, Edinburgh, Eastbourne, Peterborough, etc.

21st September – Review by speedway obsessive, enthusiast and serial emoticon user Derek Barclay in his *Twenty Twenty* column in Peterborough programme:
Right, back from my hols and time to review the book I've lately been lugging (and it's some lug!) across the beaches of Turkey. Memo to self: pick a lighter book next year and annoy the wife less! But I have to say *Showered In Shale* by Jeff Scott is worth the read even with a touch extra effort: as this is clearly NOT the typical Speedway book and is something close to my heart, a genuine attempt to look at our sport in the wider context of modern Britain.

Some have compared it to Nick Hornby's ground-breaking (and much mimicked) football classic, *Fever Pitch*. I have to say, that only someone who's never read *Fever Pitch* (one of the finest books ever written, in my Gooner-biased opinion!) would make this comparison. Hornby's book is a personal voyage from child to adult and very much in the first person. Scott's Homeric quest is to visit every track in the UK in one season and observe (and he certainly is a comprehensive recorder of the minutiae of these observations); but the 'heroes' of the book and the medium through which the stories are told are third parties: the great, good and mostly spectacularly ordinary folk of British Speedway.

So what IS Scott aiming to do with his book? His thesis is that, *"Speedway is the complete opposite of the contrived experiences of today. The mendacity that is the bane of modern life, the false representations of reality"*. Phew! To Scott, *"the sport represents one of the last true bastions of white working-class culture in the country. Speedway says a lot about people, relationships and community"*. And perhaps most illuminatingly: *"Speedway is an activity that still manages to connect people to a place; their passions to their lives; their dreams to their communities, but without the relentless consumerism and anonymity of so many aspects of contemporary life in our modern society"*.

Yes – Scott isn't going for an easy meander around Britain's 30 or so tracks. And to me, the book is at its strongest when the authorities in his specific observations of a Speedway club with their locale: the sense of place and how the Speedway community there retains a valuable identity which runs contrary to what he observes as the increasingly predictable sameness of the changing British social landscape: as he puts it, *"these pseudo-aspirational zones that frame so much of the modern consumer experience"*.

And Speedway exists (or he seems to argue, subsists...) in a working class environment which as Pete Toogood is quoted as saying, "lacks chimney pots". The struggle of the most taciturn of all his interviewees, the promoters to keep the sport alive in such conditions is a major theme.

As well as a sense of place, Speedway is an appeal to the senses. And Scott at times magnificently captures this. There's sight (*"a race simultaneously appears timeless, caught in the moment and somehow more significant in the overall scheme of things"*); sound and smell (*"they say your smell and hearing are the last senses to go when you die; in which case God must be a Speedway fan as these are the key senses you engage at every meeting. There's the throaty roar of the bikes and the distinctive bouquet and aroma of the methanol"*) and even taste: our sport is compared by someone as like "Marmite – loved by some but inspiring loathing and antipathy in many others".

Hmm. Like the infamous, what is it, vegetable/beef (??!) extract spread, you may like Jeff Scott's book or maybe not: you certainly shouldn't ignore it!

3rd October – Email from George Sheridan, speedway fan:
Thank you for sending me a flyer advising of *When Eagles Dared*. To be honest, I am not hugely interested in the Elite and definitely not in the Grand Prix, so I have to decline your offer. However, I would be interested in the behind the scenes book so please keep me on your mailing list.
Do you know, I still haven't finished *Showered in Shale*, I find it one of those books which you do not want to end, so impressed am I. I totally recognise that other tracks have shambolic meetings (e.g. no water at Reading) and I find your observations to be absolutely spot on.
In short, I am thoroughly enjoying your output and while watching TV recently it all clicked into place.
You are the Michael Palin of speedway literature!

4th October – Email from Bob Radford, speedway notable

I am sorry not to have met you on the night of chapter one when Jason Bunyan scythed down Danny Bird. I was standing in as announcer that night and long delays when a rider is badly hurt in my view required me to be low key and I would not be allowed to say what I thought of that horrendous incident in any case.

As to the music I am afraid that when the old system went to the plastic heaven in the sky, Pat [Bliss] bought (probably on advice) a mini disc player. This left the announcer with a choice of only three discs supplied by the BBC radio station and for the regular guy that meant the whole season! And no, I don't do weddings!

Pat decided to lend me the book, and I must admit I made a slow start. Holidays and other attractions I will use as my excuse. However once I got going I found it compulsive reading and am only sorry Wimbledon decided to be obstructive to your efforts.

You write extremely well and are splendidly observational. Some words I needed to look up in a dictionary but as this will be one of my retirement presents at work when I retire next month, I am currently bereft of one!

In the late seventies/early eighties I ran a column called *Bob Radford's Travels* in *Speedway Star*. Obviously it had a limited time span but in one season in addition to announcing regularly at three tracks I managed to get to all of the others. For the magazine it needed to concentrate more on riders, but I also tried to paint pictures of the venues with words.

In today's heavy traffic world I admire what you have done and the end result is very good. The only private criticism I would have made is that proof reading by a speedway person with a long memory would have resulted in fewer mis-spellings.

In today's vastly overcrowded market of speedway books, yours is refreshingly different. Apart from the reference style books I put it in a class alongside John Berry's *Confessions* and Billy Hamill's *No Bull* both had almost total input from the named author. That does not mean that some others are not good, though many are dire.

Aunty Pat had her book back on Monday when I took her to see *Journey South* in concert at Bristol Colston Hall. She has now promised to read rather than skim!

Well done, hope to meet you someday.

9th October – Email from Geoff Sims, speedway fan:

Thank you for your letter of 30th September. I think it's great the way you signed the first book and the way that you have written thanking me again for buying it. I think it's something that you don't see nowadays and is really welcome.

In regard to *Showered in Shale*, I was quite taken aback at the size of the book and impressed by the obvious effort that you had put into its production. It also seems to have drawn quite a few plaudits, when one looks at the *Speedway Star* letters page, for example.

I have been a speedway supporter for over 40 years on and off and I don't know whether it was partly because I was suffering from the flu when I picked up your book or not, but I didn't find the book that interesting a read (I think that reading the interview with Ian Thomas (?) was the final straw and the book went to the charity shop) and nor was I impressed by the small poor quality photos either.

I don't say this to be negative because your writing style obviously has some appeal, but I would have thought you would have gained from a more lively writing style, less verbiage, fewer but bigger and better quality photos (and better quality paper) and the benefit of some outside advice.

At the end of the day, being a speedway supporter, I still think it's great what you're doing, your manner and all the effort you've gone too, but if you really want to 'set the track alight' I would suggest making changes, otherwise I think future sales may decline.

Maybe you have already with the new book(s) though...

10th October – Email from Di Phillips, Somerset and Zorro fan:

Have finally finished your book, and as requested here are my thoughts:

I loved it, simple as that, I know it took me a while to get through it, but I have been busy through the season at Somerset, coupled with Magnus's website, my cat shows etc, I think you ought to write another one, many thanks for a great ride!

14th October – Email from Rob Bamford, speedway author:

I am trying to read a chapter at a time from 'Showered', although I did start with Swindon! I found it thoroughly amusing how you brought the WH Smith building into a speedway story. Brilliant, never been done before! Your book reminds me of so many characters around the tracks and also the quirky things, unique to each venue. Things that you wouldn't normally think about, but just expect them to be there when you arrive. I'm enjoying the journey, I must say.

Wow, your memory of our meeting at Peterborough [in my blog] is spot on! The only thing that concerns me is the appearance of numbers where speech marks etc should be. Is there any way of avoiding this? Otherwise perfect!

15th October – Email from Geoff Sims, speedway fan and honest book critic:
You may be surprised to hear I've just ordered your second book off your website... partly because I was impressed by your response to my e-mail. I'll let you know my (honest) thoughts on it in due course.

17th October – Unpublished review by Russell Lanning, *Mail on Sunday*
I have often thought of speedway as a huge family that creates a long-winded Christmas between the months of March and October.

As promoters spend months building up to "Christmas" by landing presents on their Santa wish list for their particular clubs, the supporters wake in the spring to find all their friends and family arrive to enjoy the speedway "festive" cheer once again. The truth of the matter is many of the presents break before "Boxing Day" and there are often a few batteries missing in vital other areas.

In a sense *Showered In Shale* – Jeff Scott's Michael Palin-like track trotting around the UK – is my Christmas Yule log fantasy all wrapped up in 503 pages.

It's the simplest idea: man travels around country and gets inside every speedway venue and track, yaks to the rest of the sport's diehards about what really happens at each track domicile. Yet there is a quaint charm about each track Jeff visits as though he were entering a snug café for a cream tea on a quintessential English summer day.

Speedway is one of those strange sports that boasted in the Seventies to have the second largest spectator following to football in the UK; 100,000 avids at Wembley's old Twin Towers in 1972 spending an entire evening jeering legendary Ivan Mauger; speedway enjoyed unbelievable success in 1966 when four-times world champion New Zealander Barry Briggs finished second in BBC's *Sports Personality of the Year* behind English football World Cup winning captain Bobby Moore, but ahead of third placed final hat-trick hero Geoff Hurst. That is the equivalent today of Scott Nicholls taking Wayne Rooney's mantle at the BBC.

But in 40 years of hurt for the sport, speedway is lucky to earn a single mention on December's *Sports Personality of the Year* on the Beeb these days, never mind get an invite for a speedway VIP to sit in the audience. It's almost a case for a Jerry Springer Show with the speedway topic: "I thought my sport had died – but I was wrong." I write this review as a devotee of the old girl – and rather than have the t-shirt, seen the video slogan – I do actually have the anorak to prove it.

After many years of watching my father, Dave, scale the heights, eulogizing on the track greats on terrestrial *ITV* – when the sport had millions rather than hundreds of thousands of viewers via *Sky* – I may be a tad nepotistic but my father's promotional genius knew no bounds.

The facts stack up: as manager and promoter he helped West Ham to the Treble in 1965, won league (1971) and cup (1975) honours while at Eastbourne and added a further league championship medal along with a £50,000 carrot for helping Reading win the top flight title in 1980. And all the time he was holding down a stress-laden showbiz journalistic day to day role at *TV Times*, along with a demanding role for *ITV* covering speedway, darts and ice hockey.

Like a fool, I decided to delve into the promotional speedway quicksand and was for many years, quite rightly, "son of Dave". Yet after managing Eastbourne to two successive Doubles in 1986 and 1987 – and witnessing the racing birth of possibly British speedway's most underachieving rider with such golden natural talent Martin Dugard – I then switched to Wimbledon where I brought over unknown rookie Australian Todd Wiltshire and was present to witness the beginning of another track giant. In that time I helped guide the Dons to a cup final and runners-up in the league before deciding to switch from a career in a toy department into the big wide world of sharks in national newspapers.

Yet despite moving into the national newspaper industry and building up a huge contact base in 15 years, only one present day speedway promoter has had the presence of mind to speak to me regularly and push for speedway – rather than his own club – to get projection in the national press.

That is why Matt Ford, entrepreneurial figure at Poole will always remain the stand-alone promoter of speedway's current new generation. He has the vision to see in the Lanning family – father Dave still working for *Sky TV*, myself at the *Mail on Sunday* and the *Sun* and my younger brother, Phil, deputy motors editor at the *Sun* – that herein lies a family who can spread the speedway gospel and potentially entice a few more to propel his business in Dorset. That is why he will always be successful.

I would like to think, therefore, having digested *Showered in Shale* from cover to cover, my opinion should be viewed as constructive, but honest. First, the bad news. The book contains too many words. A good editor would have cut Jeff's kamikaze keyboard antics by at least a third and yet still retained the wholesome quality of the theme.
We have a sub-editor at the *Mail on Sunday* sports department nicknamed Edward Scissorhands (no prizes for guessing how he has earned his title over the years for his butchering of words) who would have taken to stripping words out at will. I can almost hear his gravel-like tone, peering out from above his bifocals: "Never mind shale, more like showered in overmatter".

Wisened sports hack Tony McDonald is mentioned in the final chapter of Jeff's tome. He speaks a lot of sense. He's been in publishing when I was in short trousers – and he won't thank me for saying that. When he says a 250 page book is long enough... it's long enough, believe me.

End of gripe. The rest is a cornucopian ride through the country on an open-topped bus as Jeff shares the trials and tribulations on speedway's Elite, Premier and Conference three-tier highway. What we discover is that while *Sky Sports* churn out male voiceover men who declare on satellite speedway's Grand Prix "stars", Jeff Scott discovers speedway's real heroes. From the track shop sellers, the wonderful Stoke ladies to the grumpy jumped-up former Wimbledon man now residing at Sittingbourne, they are all the sport's real grafters. They all have a story to tell and they believe they have the key to unlock speedway's safe to a new fan blitz. If only track life were that simple, *BBC2's Dragons Den* opportunists would be forklifting cash at the sport with a *Google*-like business glow.

At a time when sport books are landing on sports editors desks with alarming daily regularity *Showered in Shale* takes a lot of digesting compared to the rest. To read it from cover to cover, the first rule would appear that you must be a died-in-the-wool speedway nut. And there's certainly nothing wrong in that. I was delighted to read journalistic doyen Frank Keating at *The Guardian* deliver such a luminous review to Jeff's work recently. Have no illusions, books like this require huge amounts of personal commitment and dedication to write and underpin. That is why snotty-nosed promoters like Ian Thomas – who Jeff quite rightly names and shames – should know better than to query the author's authenticity.

I sincerely hope Jeff's journey has been worth it. If he has come out of it clutching a few quid on the back of its sales – and in the process earned the Speedway Riders Benevolent Fund a surprise slice too thanks to his generous donation of writing off a percentage per copy – then I will feel contented in the knowledge that it has been a worthwhile adventure.

3rd November – Email from Ian McLeod, speedway fan and proud father:
You may remember my son, Alex, and I met up with you at Poole Stadium on the night of the Craven Shield Final Whilst discussing your wonderful *Showered in Shale*, we mentioned the fact that Alex and I are in the pits photograph in the Weymouth section and you suggested that if I made contact, you could forward a copy of the original or any other shots of that day. I would be very grateful if you could do so and of course I would pay for the cost of the same.
It was a pleasure meeting with you – keep on with your great work.

2nd December – Email from Peter Oakes, speedway man of many hats:
I did spot a few statistical errors and I seem to remember at least one rider changed nationality but it didn't spoil the enjoyment of reading the book.
It certainly kept me interested which is a sure sign that it's worth reading. There are a few other books that are still lying

around waiting for me to finish off but I can genuinely say I read yours from cover to cover.

And I know how difficult it is not to make mistakes, particularly when you are virtually publishing yourself.

Look forward to the next one.

1st January 2007 – Email from John Berry, speedway promoter manqué:

Reached page 200 and stalled!

I'll do you the courtesy of giving my genuine thoughts rather than just the usual patronising stuff. Of course it is far too long. It is also incredibly 'wordy'. A good editor could reduce the thing by a third without effectively reducing any of the content.

That said: I found the concept good and your personal observations most interesting. I also found many of your interviewee's opinions to be excellent. Your own thoughts – not just on speedway but life in general – made for interesting reading.

It was really enlightening to have the genuine considered thoughts and opinions of someone who has watched the majority of his racing from the 'other' side of the fence. All promoters who took the time and trouble to read it would gain an insight into how the people who pay the wages think and feel about the sport and the way it is run.

Even given that I have only read half the book so far, it is clear, and something I would have advised you on, you cannot expect to run a sensible interview with a promoter on the afternoon of a meeting. Too many things are running through his head and it is unfair to expect him to be able to give the kind of time and attention required to produce a sensible conversation.

Having said that, the book does get across just how many minor problems arise and just how easy it is for a promoter to become distracted from the main game.

Bob Radford had warned me it would be difficult to get past the first fifty pages, and it was, but he also said it was worth the effort, and it was. Once familiar with your style, and I suspect as you also began to flow a bit better, the reading became much easier. I could also spot the days when you were 'on form' and the days when nothing seemed to come easily! Been there! Done that!

I shall finish the book, but I have four more on the go at the moment so I shall come back to it but treat it as a series of short essays rather than a page-turner.

Congratulations on what must have been a major project and I hope all the blood, sweat and tears have been worthwhile.

30th January – Email from Michael Stores, speedway fan:

I loved *Showered in Shale* and bought a copy for our library as soon as I could.

It recalled the days when I stood on the terraces at East Boldon to watch the Sunderland Stars/ Gladiators, then to Byker to watch the N*wc*stl* Diamonds when Sunderland closed as well as occasional trips to Teeside to watch the 'Tigers', as they were then.

I moved to Manchester, as a student, in 1982, and revelled in the action at Hyde Road, Kirkmanshulme Lane has never really captured my imagination, but fired up by your book, I'll be making my way there again soon.

Thanks for a fascinating book!

2nd February – Email from John Pharaoh, speedway fan:

We met briefly at the *Brighton Bonanza*, when you kindly signed the 2 books of yours, that I'd just bought from your stall.

I've really enjoyed reading *Showered In Shale*, and was particularly entertained by your descriptions of the Zen-like Nicki P., then having a pee, and of dear old Fast Frank with his ubiquitous document case and 60's fashion sense.

Let's hope you haven't made too many enemies with some of your other asides and footnotes!

I'm looking forward to my next read (*Where Eagles Dared*), which I think I'll start after perusing John Berry's latest addition to the market. By the by, I don't think you'll be getting a Christmas card from Perth, W.A. this year.

Finally, whilst on the subject of taking issue, I must do likewise here and now, on the matter of the shoes on sale at Brighton last Christmas: excellent value, in my opinion at £5.00 a pair, and ideal for my daily trips to nearby Rustington beach to walk the dog!!! So there...

Keep on proving Tony Mac wrong.

speedwaystar

BUY IT... OR WE'LL SHOWER YOU IN SHALE!

SPEEDWAY STAR IS PUBLISHED WEEKLY (£2.50). A ONE YEAR SUBSCRIPTION (52 editions) IN THE UK COSTS £100 (just £1.93 a week). TELEPHONE OUR CREDIT CARD HOTLINE ON (020) 8335 1113 OR WRITE WITH YOUR NAME, ADDRESS, CREDIT CARD NUMBER AND EXPIRY DATE TO: PINEGEN LIMITED, 95 BRIGHTON ROAD, SURBITON, SURREY, KT6 5NF.

Also available from Methanol Press

When Eagles Dared
Jeff Scott

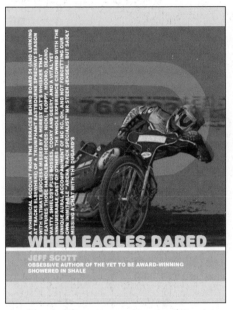

A remarkable read and something completely different to any other books on the overcrowded market. Jeff has a very personal style that you might either love or hate but I found it riveting and enjoyed almost every word.
Peter Oakes, Speedway Star

It's been given the Jeff Scott treatment…he has a quirky style and gives readers something they do not get from the local papers, and the national speedway magazine – a view of the sport from the terraces.
Richard Weston, Sussex Express

172 pages, 158 thumbnail photographs – £10.00

Buy securely online at www.methanolpress.com

Also available from Methanol Press

Shale Britannia
A Sideways Glance at Speedway
Jeff Scott and Rachael Adams

Waves of nostalgia regularly sweep our cultural lives, as we search for a more idyllic time in our recent past that we can affectionately view as somehow untrammelled by the pressures, values and mores of contemporary life. On television, *Life on Mars* superbly captured a hankering for a return to the alleged simpler times of 1970's. In fact the spirit and arguably the values of the 1970's is alive and still well in Britain in 2007 – at speedway tracks round the country!

In its heyday, most British families would have known someone who'd visit the local Speedway track, to inhale the dust and fumes and be thrilled as they watched the boys on bikes without brakes. Sports and events were for local communities, supported passionately without the apparent need for endorsement from television or the outside world.

Time affects even Speedway and Jeff Scott's photographs preserve its contemporary people and places. They are a vivid historical documentary archive. His photographs produce truthful, objective, and candid images from a journey taken round the United Kingdom, as he attended Speedway meetings throughout 2005/6. Unguarded moments are extracted from the swirl of the event.

Picture editor Rachael Adams notes, "sifting through these pictures turned out to be a joy. A nostalgic trip that filled me with sadness, yet also created a tremor of excitement since, once submerged in the drizzle or sunshine of these pictures, they brought back the smell, the noise, the Britishness of the sport. I combed through them: editing, juxtaposing, contrasting, scaling, cropping. And so the narrative emerged. It's a pictorial record of us."

Speedway tracks and their surrounds may lack the sort of crowds that the corporate media values, but they are nonetheless densely peopled with the ghosts of a proud history. With these images, Scott reveals with tender melancholy a community as it struggles to recapture the glories of its past.

256 pages, 245 photographs – £15.00

Buy securely online at www.methanolpress.com

Also available from Methanol Press

Showered in Shale
Jeff Scott

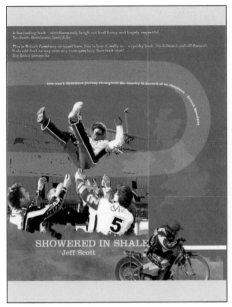

What I regard as one of the most fascinating books I have come across since I saw my first speedway meeting at New Cross in 1946. It doesn't need fact files, historical facts and biographies to make it buzz.
John Hyam, South London Press

A fascinating book that holds up an illuminating mirror to both the sport and the community as a whole... simultaneously laugh out loud funny and hugely respectful. Highly recommended.
Tim Hamblin, Wolverhampton Express & Star

Liberally laced with Scott's dry humour and pithy observations, Showered in Shale is a thoroughly absorbing travelogue that presents a whole new angle on the sport – from a fan's perspective. Never afraid to ask a loaded question and attempt to get to the bottom of everything, Scott seeks out promoters, staff, supporters and a host of characters up and down Britain. The result is an entertaining read... it's unique and refreshingly honest.
Tony McDonald, Backtrack

508 pages, 409 thumbnail photographs - £20.00

Buy securely online at www.methanolpress.com